CW00968616

Studies in Church History

41

SIGNS, WONDERS, MIRACLES
REPRESENTATIONS OF DIVINE POWER IN THE LIFE OF THE CHURCH

SIGNS, WONDERS, MIRACLES
REPRESENTATIONS OF DIVINE POWER IN THE LIFE OF THE CHURCH

PAPERS READ AT
THE 2003 SUMMER MEETING AND
THE 2004 WINTER MEETING OF
THE ECCLESIASTICAL HISTORY SOCIETY

EDITED BY

KATE COOPER

and

JEREMY GREGORY

PUBLISHED FOR
THE ECCLESIASTICAL HISTORY SOCIETY
BY
THE BOYDELL PRESS

2005

© Ecclesiastical History Society 2005

All Rights Reserved. Except as permitted under current legislation no part of this work may be photocopied, stored in a retrieval system, published, performed in public, adapted, broadcast, transmitted, recorded or reproduced in any form or by any means, without the prior permission of the copyright owner

First published 2005

A publication of the Ecclesiastical History Society
in association with The Boydell Press
an imprint of Boydell & Brewer Ltd
PO Box 9, Woodbridge, Suffolk IP12 3DF, UK
and of Boydell & Brewer Inc.
668 Mt Hope Avenue, Rochester, NY 14620, USA
website: www.boydellandbrewer.com

ISBN 0 9546809 1 X

ISSN 0424–2084

A CIP catalogue record for this book is available
from the British Library

Details of previous volumes are available from Boydell & Brewer Ltd

This book is printed on acid-free paper

Printed in Great Britain by
Athenaeum Press Ltd., Gateshead, Tyne & Wear

CONTENTS

PREFACE

'Signs, Wonders, Miracles: Representations of Divine Power in the Life of the Church' was the theme chosen by Brenda Bolton for her Presidency of the Ecclesiastical History Society in 2003–4. The topic was also the subject of the conference organized by the Society as part of the Commission Internationale d'Histoire Ecclésiastique Comparée, which last met in the UK at Durham in 1981. The Society's summer conference and the CIHEC conference were held contiguously at the University of Exeter, and many participants attended both events which meant that they had a week of deliberations. The present volume comprises the seven main papers delivered at the EHS summer conference and the January meeting in 2004, and a selection of the communications offered at the summer meeting, and at the CIHEC conference. We are grateful to the members of the Society who lent their time and expertise to the peer review of submissions, and to the authors for their responses to queries and requests for revision. We would also like to thank the British Academy for awarding us a conference grant which enabled us to meet the expenses of plenary speakers from abroad.

The Society wishes to thank the University of Exeter, and especially the staff at Hope Hall, for their co-operation at the summer conference. In particular, we are indebted to Dr Sarah Hamilton and Dr Alexandra Walsham for managing the local arrangements and organizing the outings. Because the CIHEC and EHS conferences were running in tandem, this was an especially onerous task. Thanks are also due to the Institute of Historical Research in London and its staff for accommodating the January meeting.

As last year, we want to thank Dr Barbara Crostini, who, as Editorial Fellow in Church History, has been responsible for the copy-editing. That she was able to do much of this while in Rome speaks for the miracles of modern technology and for the wonders of her efficiency and dedication to the project. We are again grateful to the Society and to the Department of Religions and Theology at the University of Manchester for providing funding for Barbara's post. We are also indebted to Hannah Williams who has done sterling work in providing administrative support while Barbara was away from Manchester.

Kate Cooper
Jeremy Gregory

CONTRIBUTORS

Brenda BOLTON (*President*)
Formerly Senior Lecturer, Queen Mary and Westfield College, University of London

Kate COOPER
Senior Lecturer in Early Christianity, University of Manchester

Barbara CROSTINI
EHS Editorial Fellow in Church History, University of Manchester

Sally CRUMPLIN
Research Student, University of St Andrews

Françoise DECONINCK-BROSSARD
Professor of English Studies, Université de Paris X

Anna MARIA LUISELLI FADDA
Professor of Germanic Philology, Facoltà di Lettere e Filosofia, Università di Roma Tre

Katherine FINLAY
Research Student, University of Oxford

Thomas S. FREEMAN
Research Officer, The British Academy John Foxe Project, University of Sheffield

W. H. C. FREND
Glasgow and Bye-Fellow of Gonville and Caius College, University of Cambridge

Yvonne FRIEDMAN
Associate Professor in the Department of General History and the Martin (Szuz) Department of Land of Israel Studies, Bar-Ilan University, Israel

Michael GOODICH
Professor of Medieval History, University of Haifa

Laurie GUY
Lecturer in Church History, Carey Baptist College and University of Auckland, Auckland

Bernard HAMILTON
Professor Emeritus of Crusading History, University of Nottingham

Sasha HANDLEY
Research Student, University of Warwick

Katherine L. JANSEN
Associate Professor of History, Catholic University of America

Anthony LAPPIN
Senior Lecturer in Spanish, University of Manchester

Jaime LARA
Associate Professor of Christian Art and Architecture, Yale University

Hartmut LEHMANN
Director, Max-Planck-Institut für Geschichte, Göttingen

G. A. LOUD
Professor of Medieval Italian History, University of Leeds

Iona MCCLEERY
Wellcome Research Fellow, University of Durham

Rosemary MOORE
Honorary Lecturer in Theology, University of Birmingham

Barbara MÜLLER
Oberassistentin, Faculty of Theology, Historical Institute, Universität Bern

Clare PILSWORTH
Wellcome Research Fellow, Centre for the History of Science, Technology and Medicine/Centre for Late Antiquity, University of Manchester

Danna PIROYANSKY
Research Student, University of London

Richard PRICE
Lecturer in Church History, Heythrop College, University of London

William J. PURKIS
Research Student, University of Cambridge

Timothy C. F. STUNT
History Teacher, Wooster School, Danbury, CT

John W. B. TOMLINSON
Research Student, University of Birmingham

Mathilde VAN DIJK
Lecturer in the History of Christianity and Gender Studies, University of Groningen

Grant WACKER
Professor of Church History, Duke University

Tim WALSH
Research Student, University of Manchester

Alexandra WALSHAM
Professor of Reformation History, University of Exeter

Robert WEBSTER
Research Student, University of Oxford

ABBREVIATIONS

ActaSS	*Acta sanctorum*, ed. J. Bolland and G. Henschen (Antwerp, etc., 1643–)
AHR	*American Historical Review* (New York, 1895–)
AnBoll	*Analecta Bollandiana* (Brussels, 1882–)
BAV	Biblioteca Apostolica Vaticana, Città del Vaticano
BHG	*Bibliotheca hagiographica graeca*, Subsidia hagiographica 8a, ed. François Halkin, 3 vols (3rd edn, Brussels, 1957)
BHG Auct.	*Auctarium bibliothecae hagiographicae graecae*, Subsidia Hagiographica 47 (Brussels, 1969)
BHG Nov. Auct.	*Novum auctarium bibliothecae hagiographicae graecae*, Subsidia Hagiographica 64 (Brussels, 1984)
BHL	*Bibliotheca hagiographica latina antiquae et mediae aetatis*, Subsidia hagiographica 6 and 12 (Brussels, 1898–1901)
BHL Novum Suppl.	*Bibliotheca hagiographica latina antiquae et mediae aetatis*, ed. Henri Fros, Subsidia hagiographica 70 (Brussels, 1986)
BL	London, British Library
BN	Paris, Bibliothèque Nationale
CChr.CM	Corpus Christianorum. Continuatio medievalis (Turnhout, 1966–)
CChr.SL	Corpus Christianorum. Series latina (Turnhout, 1953–)
ChH	*Church History* (New York and Chicago, 1932–)
CSEL	Corpus scriptorum ecclesiasticorum latinorum (Vienna, 1866–)
Dsp	*Dictionnaire de Spiritualité ascétique et mystique: doctrine et histoire*, ed. Marcel Viller *et al.*, 17 vols in 21 tomes (Paris, 1932–95)
EETS	Early English Text Society (London/Oxford, 1864–)
Finucane, *Miracles and Pilgrims*	Ronald C. Finucane, *Miracles and Pilgrims: Popular Beliefs in Medieval England* (2nd edn, Basingstoke, 1995)

GCS	Die griechische christlichen Schriftsteller der ersten drei Jahrhunderte (Berlin, 1897–)
HistJ	*Historical Journal* (Cambridge, 1958–) [supersedes *CHJ*]
JBS	*Journal of British Studies* (Hartford, CT, 1961–)
JEH	*Journal of Ecclesiastical History* (Cambridge, 1950–)
JMedH	*Journal of Medieval History* (Amsterdam, 1975–)
JRULM	John Rylands University Library of Manchester
MGH	Monumenta Germaniae Historica inde ab a. c. 500 usque ad a. 1500, ed. G. H. Pertz *et al.* (Hannover, Berlin, etc., 1826–)
ns	new series
OMT	Oxford Medieval Texts (Oxford, 1971–)
os	original series
P&P	*Past and Present: a Journal of Scientific History* (London and Oxford, 1952–)
PS	Parker Society
RHC Occ.	Recueil des Historiens des Croisades, Historiens Occidentaux, ed. Académie des Inscriptions et Belles-Lettres, 5 vols (Paris, 1841–1906)
RS	Rerum Brittanicarum medii aevi scriptores, 99 vols (London, 1858–1911) = Rolls Series
SC	Sources chrétiennes (Paris, 1941–)
Thomas, *Religion and the Decline of Magic*	Keith Thomas, *Religion and the Decline of Magic: Studies in Popular Beliefs in Sixteenth- and Seventeenth-Century England* (London, 1973)
Ward, *Miracles and the Medieval Mind*	Benedicta Ward, *Miracles and the Medieval Mind: Theory, Record and Event 1000–1215* (Aldershot and Philadelphia, PA, 1987)

INTRODUCTION

The great mysteries of the Incarnation, Resurrection, and Ascension reveal to believers that, for God, nothing is impossible. Throughout Christian history, the clearest expression of divine power at work in the world has always been its external manifestation through miracles, those acts of God in which the believer transcends his or her ordinary human capabilities. Preaching in Jerusalem at Pentecost, Peter reminded the men of Israel that God himself had approved those prodigious feats which Christ had performed in their midst (Acts 2, 22). Miraculous activity thus became a crucial part of the witness of the Apostolic Church to the truth of God's word, first directed towards disbelieving Jews, to Gentiles, and later used to implant the first seeds of faith amongst pagans and, even more recently, non-believers. Whilst St Augustine was to perceive the whole of Creation as one great miracle, so that nothing was either exclusively natural or exclusively miraculous, by the twelfth century others were beginning to emphasize that the explanation for such events might well be sought in natural causes rather than in God's will. From the Apostolic Age to the present day then, issues such as the desacralization of nature, comprehending the workings of the universe, apocalyptic events, or scepticism about the intervention of supernatural forces in human affairs inevitably focused serious discussion on how Christians have traditionally regarded signs, wonders and miracles – whether through healing and compassion or through evangelism, revivalism, or mission – and the variety of ways in which these have been used, either to reinforce the faith or sometimes even to exploit it.

In the years on either side of the First Millennium, according to the monk-historian Ralph Glaber (*c.*980–*c.*1046), miracles and *prodigia* were appearing with unusual frequency. Glaber's *Five Books of the Histories* record for posterity that many significant events 'take place in the churches of God and amongst the peoples, especially as the Saviour testifies that, together with the Father and with the aid of the Holy Spirit, He will continue to work wonders in the world until the last hour of the last day'.[1] A thousand years later, two recent events have

[1] *Rodulfus Glaber Opera*, ed. John France, Neithard Bulst and Paul Reynolds, OMT (Oxford, 1989), 2–3.

also given rise to considerable speculation. On 5 September 1998, the first anniversary of the death of Mother Theresa of Calcutta (1910–97), a healing cure in West Bengal was attributed to her intercession. On 11 September 2001 in New York City, St Paul's Church on Wall Street somehow survived the catastrophic attack on the Twin Towers, this small mid-eighteenth-century church remaining almost unscathed on the very edge of Ground Zero. Cure and survival alike are inexplicable, save in terms of the miraculous. While today most churches exercise great caution in claiming the grace of miracles, our secular world is characterized by the hyperbole routinely used to describe unusual events: a premature 'miracle' baby, or some 'miraculous' escape from a disaster, whether natural or man-made.

As the Second Millennium drew to its close, the moment seemed particularly opportune for a reconsideration of the varieties of miraculous phenomena and their impact on Christian history. With precisely this in mind, in 1997, Professor Olivier Fatio, as President of the Commission Internationale d'Histoire Ecclésiastique Comparée (CIHEC), together with members of its organizing Bureau, first suggested marking the new Millennium with an appropriate colloquium. Its theme would be *Reflections and Perceptions of Miracles*, and the location none other than John Calvin's Geneva. As it happened, the Colloquium was held neither in Geneva nor in the year 2000! Instead, acting on behalf of the Bureau and its new President, Professor Walter Brandmüller, the British National Commission of CIHEC shouldered the responsibility of a unique joint meeting with the Ecclesiastical History Society at its annual Summer Conference in July 2003 at Exeter. The remit for these two organizations, whose membership already overlaps, was to combine their respective academic and analytical strengths and, by a slight modification of the theme, so to seek to encourage a wide participation, both geographically and chronologically.

The papers collected here do indeed demonstrate the positive benefits of this collaborative venture by bringing together individual contributors who represent no fewer than eight nationalities and a number of different disciplines. The focus of the volume is neither British nor European but includes topics from the Levant, both Americas, and New Zealand, while ranging chronologically from the Emperor Constantine to Generalissimo Franco, and topically from Gregory the Great and gardening miracles, to angels on the battlefields of World War I. Nor are the contributions exclusively Catholic or Medieval –

although stigmata on the First Crusade, garrulous Italian crucifixes and flying saints in Colonial Latin America might seem to indicate otherwise. Equal weight is given to *prodigia* across the whole spectrum of Protestantism and revivalism, whether Quaker miracles and magic Methodists, Pentecostalism and the early Holy Ghost movement in North America, or speaking in tongues in Sunderland and healing evangelism in Auckland, NZ. The studies included here range from the detailed and local to the broad and interpretative. The centrality of the miraculous to the importance of the Mass, at the heart of which was the transformation of mere bread and wine into the body and blood of Christ, is mentioned only in passing. That papers on snake handling (Mark 16, 18) or the 'Toronto Blessing' were not offered is no surprise although remaining a matter for regret!

That there was a clear vocabulary or a way of speaking about the miraculous provides an undercurrent of continuity for almost any period of Christian history. While certain Late Antique martyrs might be presented as 'divine ventriloquists', miraculously able to speak with two voices – in the simplest of terms for their new converts, and with a greater degree of complexity for catechumens –, Christian missionaries to the recently converted Anglo-Saxons devised significant linguistic procedures in order to convey doctrinal information. This indicated, in the language of revelation, that the most efficacious miracles were manifestations of the direct causality of God. Nor did the vocabulary of the miraculous disappear from the English language at the Reformation, when 'miracle' continued to be used to describe perplexing phenomena. Indeed, the period of the Reformation and Counter-Reformation was precisely the occasion on which the miraculous fell under the closest scrutiny. While English Protestants generally insisted that miracles had ceased with the end of the Apostolic Age, denying that their new religion had any need of them to prove or reinforce its authenticity, they remained attached to a quite surprising number of 'marvels'. The most striking example of linguistic continuity, however, was the 'sign and gift of unknown tongues', given to those who shared the language of Pentecost and the baptism of the Holy Spirit, and which, in the years between 1901 and 1907, helped to encourage adherents in places as far apart as Topeka, Kansas, and Monkwearmouth, Sunderland, to enter the Pentecostal fold.

Above all, however, it was the influence of the healing miracles of Christ, and the teachings accompanying them, which are shown to have every bit as profound an effect on modern revivalist groups as they had on early Christian thought and conversion. That the use of 'miraculous' *per se* – even today – tends to relate to an inexplicable recovery from a serious illness is clearly demonstrable in the parallel drawn between the modernizing of a miracle collection in twelfth-century Durham and the first acknowledged miracle of the Third Millennium, that of Mother Theresa. The 'miraculous' character of newly discovered healing wells, the 'royal touch' to cure scrofula, and the claims of quite ordinary people to heal by the laying on of hands, the public reinstatement of ghosts and ghost stories in the late seventeenth century as at once an outlet for grief, a valid source of spiritual reflection, and as moral exemplars, all helped to show that not only miracles, but signs and wonders too, might serve as a bulwark against a burgeoning atheism and to buttress traditional Christian truth.

Miracles were frequently under attack from Late Antiquity onwards, and provided open targets. Doubt and scepticism – and sometimes invention and fraud too – have always surrounded the miraculous, whilst David Hume's 'corrosive attack' on these phenomena has served to focus recent debate on their interpretation. The ecclesiastical hierarchy saw as its task the need to alert the faithful to the dangers of magicians, healers and miracle-workers in pagan rituals, particularly when such practices were considered to exist side by side with Christian beliefs and customs. The opposition to miracles, couched in terms of Eusebius's charge against the 'magicians' of Simon Magus, became a frequent *topos* in papal letters warning against the activities of demons and evil spirits, which so undermined the Church's teaching on the immortality of the soul and the resurrection of the dead. 'The Christian religion not only was at first attended with miracles', wrote Hume,

> but even at this day cannot be believed by any reasonable person without one. Mere reason is insufficient to convince us of its veracity: and whoever is moved by faith to assent to it, is conscious of a continued miracle in his own person, which subverts all the principles of his understanding, and gives him a determination to believe what is most contrary to custom and experience.[2]

Hume's emphasis on what constituted reliable testimony was also to be linked with supporting indirect evidence.

2 David Hume, *Essays and Treatises on Several Subjects*, 4 vols (Basel, 1793), 3: *An Inquiry concerning Human Understanding*, section X, Of Miracles, Part 2, p. 145.

Another important aspect of the study of miracles, seen most clearly in Central Europe in the seventeenth and eighteenth centuries, was the crucial role of catastrophes – flood, fire, earthquake, plague or famine – and 'prodigies', or warning signs and punishments sent by God, which almost always preceded a catastrophe. Belief in miracles and prodigies had an almost therapeutic effect by creating new hope and by sustaining the will to rebuild what had been destroyed. In England, by the eighteenth century, the vocabulary of signs, wonders and miracles had changed, giving way to the terminology of miraculous providences. Of significance here in the grand providential design was the Lisbon earthquake of 1 November 1755, after which the English and Dutch Protestant chapels were the only ecclesiastical buildings to have remained standing (similarly, the Tsunami of 26 December 2005 where the buildings also included mosques). Yet, this great calamity was now seen by some not as an Act of God but the result of natural causes. The finger of God has given way to the hand of Fate.

Brenda Bolton
St Albans, 16 March 2005

IN HOC SIGNO VINCES: THE ORIGINAL CONTEXT OF THE VISION OF CONSTANTINE

by RICHARD M. PRICE

OF all the signs and wonders, real or imaginary, in the history of Christianity one of the most celebrated is the 'Vision of Constantine' – a vision or dream in which Constantine, meditating an attack on his rival Maxentius in AD 312, was instructed to entrust his fortunes to the Christian God and the sign of the cross, the experience which, supposedly, converted the emperor to the Christian faith.

This story comes in Eusebius' *Life of Constantine*, written in the late 330s, which claims that Eusebius heard it from the emperor's own mouth.[1] A similar story had appeared earlier in Lactantius' *On the Deaths of the Persecutors*, written around 315,[2] which tells how Constantine was inspired in a dream, on the very night before the decisive battle of the Milvian Bridge (28 October 312), to entrust his fortunes to Christ. Historians have generally treated Eusebius' and Lactantius' stories as alternative accounts of the same event.[3] Lactantius' version has generally been considered the more reliable, because of its greater simplicity and earlier date, though Eusebius' narrative has also had its defenders.[4] The purpose of this paper is to argue that no single event lies behind the two accounts, and that neither Lactantius nor

[1] Eusebius, *Life of Constantine* [hereafter: *VC*], transl. with introduction and commentary by Averil Cameron and Stuart G. Hall (Oxford, 1999), contains a discussion of the vision at 38–9 and 204–13. For an extensive bibliography see Rudolf Leeb, *Konstantin und Christus: Die Verchristlichung der imperialen Repräsentation unter Konstantin dem Grossen als Spiegel seiner Kirchenpolitik und seines Selbstverständnisses als christlicher Kaiser* (Berlin, 1992), 129, n. 1. I am grateful to Professor Stuart Hall for helpful comments on an early draft of this paper.

[2] See Lactantius, *De mortibus persecutorum* [hereafter: *DMP*], ed. and transl. by J. L. Creed (Oxford, 1984), xxxiii–iv.

[3] E.g., Robin Lane Fox, *Pagans and Christians* (Harmondsworth, 1986), 613–14, and H. A. Drake, *Constantine and the Bishops: the Politics of Intolerance* (Baltimore, MA, 2000), 180.

[4] Ramsay MacMullen, *Constantine* (London, 1970), 72–7, Manfred Clauss, *Konstantin der Grosse und seine Zeit* (Munich, 1996), 36, and Arnaldo Marcone, *Costantino il Grande* (Rome, 2000), 42, are representative of many in dismissing Eusebius' account as later propaganda. Contrast J. H. W. G. Liebeschuetz, *Continuity and Change in Roman Religion* (Oxford, 1979), 277–8, who is impressed by the distinctiveness of Eusebius' story.

Constantine was telling a story of conversion. I shall suggest that the vision narrated by Constantine and reported by Eusebius took place in 323, more than a decade after both Constantine's conversion and the battle of the Milvian Bridge.

The credit for being the first scholar to have realized that the vision of Constantine as described by the emperor himself had nothing to do with his conversion goes to T. G. Elliott, who first published his theory in the 1980s and developed it fully in a monograph published in 1996.[5] Elliott combined his brilliant re-reading of the account with the claim that Constantine could not have been 'converted' in 312, since he had in fact been a Christian since childhood. I shall examine this additional piece of revisionism, which is less convincing and has distracted the attention of scholars from his reading of the vision.[6] I shall conclude with some reflections on the vision's significance.

* * *

It is important to distinguish between the two main narratives, that of Lactantius and that of Eusebius. Lactantius describes how on the eve of the battle of the Milvian Bridge Constantine was directed in a dream 'to mark the heavenly sign of God on the shields of his soldiers and thus to join battle'. This, Lactantius continues, Constantine proceeded to do, and won his decisive victory over Maxentius on the very next day.[7] It is to be noted that Lactantius does not state that Constantine became a Christian as a result of his experience: his aim is simply to demonstrate that Constantine's success was due to the favour of the Christian God. The dream he attributes to Constantine is closely paralleled by a dream he attributes in the same work to Constantine's ally Licinius on the eve of his victory over the aggressively pagan Maximin Daia in the following year: a monotheistic prayer is dictated to Licinius in a dream and used by his soldiers on the field of battle.[8] The prayer is clearly understood by Lactantius as an expression of faith in the Christian God. He must have been aware that Constantine was committed to Chris-

5 T. G. Elliott, 'Constantine's Conversion: Do We Really Need It?', *Phoenix* 41 (1987), 420–38; idem, *The Christianity of Constantine the Great* (Scranton, PA, 1996), vii: 'This book had its origins in my sudden realization some years ago that Eusebius' story of Constantine's conversion was a fiction or a mistake, based upon the emperor's own story of how God told him to make the *labarum*'.

6 Elliott's separation of the vision from the conversion is not discussed either in Drake or in Averil Cameron and Stuart Hall's edition of the *VC*.

7 *DMP* 44, Creed, 62–4.

8 *DMP* 46, Creed, 66.

tianity in a way Licinius was not, but he avoids any mention of the fact. The close parallel he draws between the Christian Constantine and the pagan Licinius implies that he did not view Constantine's dream as a conversion experience, and the duplication of the dream motif must suggest that both dreams are literary inventions, to reinforce the message that the Christian God is the giver of victory.[9]

The narrative of the vision of Constantine in Eusebius' *Life of Constantine* (I. 27–32)[10] has much to say about the emperor's train of thought. Eusebius narrates how Constantine, meditating on how to embark on a war against Maxentius, observed how pagan worship had led other emperors to disaster while by contrast his father Constantius Chlorus had worshipped the one supreme God and received 'manifest and numerous tokens of his power' (27.3). In consequence Constantine prayed to his father's God to reveal himself. At this point Eusebius says that Constantine himself had told him of 'a most remarkable divine sign' he had once been vouchsafed:

> Since the victorious Emperor himself told the story to the present writer a long while after, when I was privileged with his acquaintance and company, and confirmed it with oaths, who could hesitate to believe the account, especially when the time which followed provided evidence for the truth of what he said? About the time of the midday sun, when day was just turning, he said he saw with his own eyes, up in the sky and resting over the sun, a cross-shaped trophy formed from light, and a text attached to it which said, 'By this conquer'.[11] Amazement at the spectacle seized both him and the whole company of soldiers which was then accompanying him on a campaign he was conducting somewhere, and witnessed the miracle. (28.1–2)

The emperor proceeded to tell how Christ on the following night 'appeared to him with the sign which had appeared in the sky, and urged him to make himself a copy of the sign which had appeared in the sky, and to use this as protection against the attacks of the enemy'

9 For a similar analysis of Lactantius see Joachim Szidat, 'Konstantin 312 n. Chr.', *Gymnasium* 92 (1985), 514–25, esp. 518–19.

10 *Eusebius Werke*, I/I, *Über das Leben des Kaisers Konstantins*, ed. Friedhelm Winkelmann (Berlin, 1991), 28–32 (Cameron and Hall, 79–82; all my quotations are taken from their translation).

11 This is more familiar in the traditional Latin translation, '*In hoc signo vinces*' ('with this sign you will conquer').

(29). When day came, Constantine summoned goldsmiths and instructed them how to make the new standard. Eusebius continues, 'This was something which the emperor himself once saw fit to let me also set eyes on' (30), and proceeds to describe the *labarum* (for this is what it was) in detail, concluding, 'This saving sign was always used by the emperor for protection against every opposing and hostile force, and he commanded replicas of it to lead all his armies' (31.3).

After the description of the *labarum*, Eusebius returns to the vision, offering an account of its aftermath that is centred on his own theme of the revelation of the secret God of Constantine's father, introduced at the beginning of this section (27).

> That was, however, somewhat later. At the time in question, stunned by the amazing vision, and determined to worship no other god than the one who had appeared, he summoned those expert in his words, and enquired who this god was, and what was the explanation of the vision which had appeared of the sign. They said that the god was the Only-begotten Son of the one and only God, and that the sign which appeared was the token of immortality, and was an abiding trophy of the victory over death which he had once won when he was present on earth. (32.1–2)[12]

There is a striking contrast in the interpretation of the vision's significance between the narrative segment before the description of the *labarum* and that after it. But the difference becomes intelligible on the hypothesis that the former segment represents the story Eusebius had heard from Constantine, while the latter expresses his own conviction of what the full fruits of the vision must have been. In Constantine's account the meaning of the vision was a promise of victory over his enemies: in Eusebius' it is Christ's victory over sin and death. In Constantine's story the consequence of the vision was the making of the *labarum*: in Eusebius' it is a consultation with bishops. Constantine's story is indefinite as to place and time, referring vaguely to 'a campaign he was conducting somewhere': Eusebius connects the vision specifically to the attack on Maxentius. Eusebius' additions conflict with the emperor's own story.

What led Constantine to tell Eusebius of the origin of the *labarum* in

12 Cp. I. 42. 1 (Cameron and Hall, 86): 'He took them [bishops] with him whenever he set out on campaign, trusting that in this too the one they worshipped would be present at his right hand'. But at the time of the vision Constantine, according to Eusebius, was not yet a Christian.

the first place? The natural occasion was when he showed Eusebius the standard, as his biographer relates. This was also the occasion on which Constantine is likely to have told him (as mentioned later in the *Life*) of the contribution of the *labarum* to the victory over Licinius in 324.[13] This makes it attractive to date the occasion when Eusebius was shown the standard to the immediate aftermath of this victory – that is, to a meeting between the bishop and the emperor during the council of Nicaea in 325.[14]

How long before this date had the vision taken place? Since Constantine's own story was extremely vague as to location and date, we can redate the vision to a substantially later period than the context provided by Eusebius. Certainly the *labarum* he describes is of later date than the conversion in 312.[15] Because the first direct evidence for the *labarum* links it to the war against Licinius in 324, this makes the campaign against the Sarmatians in 323 an attractive candidate for the campaign on which Constantine saw the vision.[16]

There is no good reason to query Eusebius' claim that Constantine told him of the vision, nor need we doubt Constantine's essential truthfulness, even if his memory may well have embroidered the details. The salient point is a different one – that the connection of the vision to Constantine's conversion is Eusebius' own invention. Constantine's story was uniquely concerned with the origins of the *labarum*. Eusebius' decision to link it to the emperor's conversion was most likely made only when he came to include the story in his *Life of Constantine*. It was a choice that enriched the significance of the vision, and enabled him to make the story of central importance in his account of the emperor's vocation and mission.

* * *

I referred at the beginning of this article to the work of T. G. Elliott, who was the first scholar to realize that the vision as described by Constantine had nothing to do with his conversion. To this he added

13 *VC* II. 8.2, 9.3 (Cameron and Hall, 98).

14 Eusebius met Constantine on only four occasions: in 325 at Nicaea, at 327 at Nicomedia, in 335 at Jerusalem, and in 336 at Constantinople (see Leeb, *Konstantin und Christus*, 138).

15 The reference to 'sons' depicted on it (31.2) implies a date after 317, when Crispus and Constantine II were made Caesars.

16 For the campaign of 323 see Timothy Barnes, *The New Empire of Diocletian and Constantine* (Cambridge, MA, 1982), 75. Leeb, *Konstantin und Christus*, 44–6, similarly dates the creation of the *labarum* to 324.

the claim that Constantine was not 'converted' at all in 312, since he had been brought up by his parents as a Christian and had felt a strong personal commitment to the faith from the start of the Great Persecution in 303. How plausible is this radical piece of revisionism?

Certainly, once we realize that neither the dream narrated by Lactantius nor the vision described by Eusebius were conversion experiences, the question as to when Constantine became a Christian is re-opened. A firm *terminus ad quem* is provided by the letters Constantine wrote to officials and bishops in Africa after his arrival in Rome in 312: these letters express clearly that Constantine considered the Christian cult to be the only one acceptable to the supreme deity.[17] But we are far less well informed about the stages of Constantine's religious development prior to 312. Elliott makes the claim that Constantine had been brought up a Christian by his parents, Constantius and Helena.[18] According to Eusebius it was Constantine who converted Helena; but according to Theodoret Helena brought up Constantine as a Christian.[19] Elliott chooses to believe the latter, but neither account is likely to have been based on solid information.

What should we make of Elliott's claim that Constantius Chlorus was a Christian? Constantine wrote in his letter to the provincials of the east of 324 that 'only my father was engaged in gentle deeds, with wonderful reverence calling upon the Saviour God in all his actions'.[20] By this date Constantine was presenting himself as a member of a Christian dynasty, extending from his father to his sons, as the constant recipient of the favour of the Christian God. But that one of the members of Diocletian's tetrarchy was a Christian is simply not credible. Elliott concedes that Constantius as emperor 'took part, and a leading part, in pagan ceremonies'.[21] But when Constantine and

17 See especially the letter to Anullinus of 313 in Eusebius [*Historia Ecclesiastica*, X. 7. 2: *Die Kirchengeschichte*, ed. Eduard Schwartz and Theodore Mommsen, rev. Friedhelm Winkelmann, GCS ns 6.2, 3 vols (Berlin, 1999), 2: 891] and that of 313/4 to Aelafius in the Appendix to Optatus III, in *S. Optati Milevitani libri VII*, ed. Karl Ziwsa, CSEL 26 (Vienna, 1893), 204–6, transl. P. R. Coleman-Norton, *Roman State and Christian Church*, 3 vols (London, 1966), 1: 54–6.

18 Elliott, *The Christianity of Constantine the Great*, 18, 23.

19 Eusebius, *VC* III. 47.2 (Cameron and Hall, 139). Theodoret, *Historia Ecclesiastica*, I. 18. 1: *Kirchengeschichte*, ed. Léon Parmentier, rev. Felix Scheidweiler, GCS 44.19 (2nd edn, Berlin, 1954), 63; *The Ecclesiastical History, Dialogues, and Letters of Theodoret*, transl. Blomfield Jackson, A Select Library of Nicene and Post-Nicene Fathers of the Christian Church. Second series, 3 (Grand Rapids, MI, 1975), 54 (as I. 17).

20 *VC* II. 49. 1 (Cameron and Hall, 112).

21 Elliott, *The Christianity of Constantine the Great*, 24.

Eusebius claimed that Constantius worshipped the one true God, and contrasted his fortunes to those of the worshippers of idols, it was precisely this that they were denying. The notion of Constantius the worshipper of the Christian God must be dismissed as Constantinian propaganda; the central position of this invention in Eusebius' account of the context and motives of Constantine's conversion undermines the whole account.[22]

If the case for a Christian Constantius is so weak, what should we make of the ascription of Christianity to his son Constantine long before the conventional date for his conversion? Elliott appeals to statements by Constantine in the pro-Christian letters of propaganda that he addressed to the Christians of the eastern provinces in 324: in his letter to the provincials of Palestine the emperor claims that the Christian God 'examined my service and approved it as fit for his own purposes' as early as his assumption of the purple, while in his letter to the provincials of the east he recalls his disgust with the persecution of Christians initiated in 303.[23] But surely the fact that the fully Christian Constantine of 324 interpreted the whole of his previous career as a service to the Christian God is poor evidence of his actual beliefs at a much earlier date.

It has generally been held that a *terminus post quem* for Constantine's conversion is provided by his encouragement of the cult of Apollo, as described in the panegyric of 310.[24] Even though the attendant 'vision' of Apollo is vaguely described and may well be a literary fiction, we have no reason to disbelieve the account of how Constantine visited the shrine and made lavish offerings.[25] This is not compatible with a Constantine already committed to Christianity, since, however imperfect his knowledge of the faith, he will have known from the Great Persecution that Christians firmly rejected the promotion of pagan cult; it is not adequate to dismiss the episode, as Elliott does, as no more than an act of courtesy on the part of an emperor conscious that most of his subjects, and soldiers, were pagans. It is very credible that the process of conversion was a gradual one, and it is possible that

22 For Constantius' religion see further Mark D. Smith, 'The Religion of Constantius I', *Greek, Roman and Byzantine Studies* 38 (1997), 187–208.

23 *VC* II. 28. 2 and II. 49–53 (Cameron and Hall, 105–6, 112–3).

24 *Panegyrici Latini* VII/VI. 21, in *Panégyriques Latins, II: Les panégyriques Constantiniens (VI–IX)*, ed. and transl. É. Galletier (Paris, 1952), 71–2, and *XII Panegyrici Latini*, ed. R. A. B. Mynors (Oxford, 1964), 201–2.

25 For the vision of Apollo see B. Saylor Rogers, 'Constantine's Pagan Vision', *Byzantion* 50 (1980), 259–78.

Constantine may have been sympathetic to Christianity from a very early date;[26] but what evidence there is supports the traditional view that Constantine became a Christian, convinced that only Christian worship was acceptable to the deity, between 310 and his entry into Rome in October 312.[27]

* * *

In all, questions about Constantine's religious development prior to his conversion in (or just before) 312 are too speculative to be profitable; there may, or may not, have been a specific moment when Constantine had what we would call a conversion experience. Eusebius wanted a dramatic conversion story, and concocted one by forcing Constantine's account of a vision into a framework of his own invention. But once we take this account out of the framework that Eusebius invented for it, there emerges the story of a divine inspiration that led an already Christian Constantine to adopt a new standard, as a sacred palladium to assure him of victory. Eusebius interpreted the vision in terms of Christ's victory over sin and death, but the victory that Constantine was concerned with was his own success in war. This concentration on the Christian God of battles was reasonable enough in his particular circumstances, with hostile pagan rivals to deal with; at the time of the vision, at whatever precise date it occurred, it would be absurd to imagine that he would have been attracted by Christian pacifism or interested above all in saving his soul.

We have suggested 323 as a possible date for the vision and the creation of the *labarum*. But in two respects the story relates to long-standing and continuing convictions of Constantine's. First, his adoption of the *labarum* as his standard had been preceded by his use of similar symbols, especially in the period immediately following the victory over Maxentius. Eusebius, writing an expanded edition of his *Ecclesiastical History* in around 314, described a memorial in Rome of the victory over Maxentius in the form of a statue of the emperor with a cross in his right hand.[28] It was at the same time that Lactantius told his story of the dream before the battle of the Milvian Bridge in which

26 That the conversion consisted of several stages over several years is argued by Drake, *Constantine and the Bishops*, 187–91.

27 See Thomas Grünewald, *Constantinus Maximus Augustus: Herrschaftspropaganda in der zeitgenössischen Überlieferung* (Stuttgart, 1990), 78–86, who lists and criticizes other scholars who have tried to make Constantine a Christian virtually from childhood.

28 Eusebius, *Historia Ecclesiastica*, IX. 9. 10–11: *Die Kirchengeschichte*, ed. Schwartz, Mommsen and Winkelmann, 2: 832. This part of the work is dated to *c.*313/4 by T. D.

Constantine was instructed to 'mark the heavenly sign of God on the shields of the soldiers', the sign being a cross incorporating a form of the Chi-Rho (for 'Christos'); we argued above that the dream is a literary invention, but the use of Christian symbols by Constantine's army could still be true. The famous medallion of Constantine minted in Turin in 315 shows both the Chi-Rho monogram in its classic form on the emperor's helmet and a sceptre in the shape of a cross surmounted by a globe.[29] These emblems are not to be conflated into some 'original' form of the *labarum*; they are distinct both from the latter and from each other, but they were certainly antecedents for the creation of the *labarum* some years later.[30]

Secondly, the adoption of the *labarum* was more than simply a further bid for the patronage of the Christian God: it reflected Constantine's conviction, that reached its height on his overthrow of Licinius, that he was the Lord's chosen one. The famous inscription on the Arch of Constantine describes the emperor as moved *instinctu divinitatis* ('by the prompting of the deity'), and this was echoed in the panegyric of 313.[31] A claim to have undertaken his wars 'on the inspiration of God' was made by Constantine himself in his *Oration to the Saints*.[32] Constantine's reception of direct divine guidance became a favourite theme of Eusebius, who in his *Tricennalian Oration* of 336 declared in the emperor's presence, 'You could yourself, emperor, if you wished and had the leisure, tell us of the countless theophanies of your Saviour and his countless appearances in dreams.'[33] Notable in this context is Constantine's own apostrophe to God in his letter to the provincials of the East:

> By your guidance I have undertaken deeds of salvation and achieved them; making your seal my protection everywhere, I have

Barnes, 'The Editions of Eusebius' *Ecclesiastical History*', *Greek, Roman and Byzantine Studies* 21 (1980), 191–201.

29 Leeb, *Konstantin und Christus*, 29–42.

30 The etymology of the word *labarum* is too obscure to reveal anything, as noted by Lane Fox, *Pagans and Christians*, 616 and 766, n. 25. To the discussions he refers to add M. Sulzberger, 'Le Symbole de la Croix et les Monogrammes de Jésus chez les premiers chrétiens', *Byzantion* 2 (1925), 337–448, esp. 419–24.

31 *Panegyricus Latinus* IX/XII. 2. 4, ed. Galletier, 124; ed. Mynors, 272.

32 *Oration to the Saints* 26, in Mark Edwards, *Constantine and Christendom* (Liverpool, 2003), 61. The date of the speech is disputed: Edwards dates it to 313 (ibid., xxix), while Lane Fox had argued for 325 (*Pagans and Christians*, 643).

33 *Tricennalian Oration* 18, in *Eusebius Werke I*, ed. I. A. Heikel (Leipzig, 1902), 259. See too *VC* II.12 (Cameron and Hall, 99–100) for divine guidance in battle.

> led a conquering army. . . . I have consecrated to you my own soul . . ., for I dread your power, which you have revealed by many tokens, confirming the strength of my faith.[34]

The 'seal' is a reference to the sign of the cross and perhaps consciously to the *labarum*; the 'many tokens' are the victories granted to Constantine, which he regarded as public proofs of the truth of the religion he had adopted. His identification of his cause with that of Christ found its final and most extreme expression in the mausoleum he built for himself in Constantinople, where his own remains were to be placed centrally, surrounded by cenotaphs of the twelve apostles, thereby usurping the place where Christ would appropriately have been commemorated.[35]

That Constantine postponed baptism till he was on his deathbed is a familiar fact that no competent historian nowadays would adduce as evidence of a lack of Christian commitment earlier in his reign. It has been suggested that the postponement was because he felt unworthy, or afraid of breaking the Church's moral code.[36] But this does not correspond to the self-confidence expressed in all his surviving utterances. Rather, Constantine felt that during his lifetime he did not need the sacramental route of entry into the Church since he enjoyed his own special relationship with God, as the protector of the people of God, akin to King Cyrus in the Old Testament.[37] The *labarum* expressed the way in which he linked his own cause to that of Christianity. The message of the vision of Constantine was that this standard was not his own invention but had been revealed by Christ himself.

Heythrop College, University of London

34 *VC* II. 55 (Cameron and Hall, 113): see their annotation at 246–7.

35 Gilbert Dagron, *Emperor and Priest: the Imperial Office in Byzantium* (Cambridge, 2003), 139–41. For Constantine as a priest-king representing Christ, see 132–3.

36 Eusebius in his account of the baptism at *VC* IV. 61–4 (Cameron and Hall, 177–9) makes Constantine say, 'I shall now set for myself rules of life that befit God' (IV. 62.3), which implies that he felt a clash between the rule of life incumbent on the baptized and his own role as emperor. But it would be dangerous to build on this pious sentiment of dubious historicity, as is noted by Cameron and Hall, 342.

37 Is. 44, 28–45, 5; Ezra 1, 1–4.

THE PLACE OF MIRACLES IN THE CONVERSION OF THE ANCIENT WORLD TO CHRISTIANITY

by W. H. C. FREND

IN *c.*435 Sozomen, the fifth-century lawyer and continuator of Eusebius of Caesarea's *Ecclesiastical History*, describes how probably near the end of Constantine's reign his grandfather and his family were converted to Christianity. He attributes this to the work of the Palestinian monk, Hilarion. He writes of Alaphion, a friend of the family at that time living in Bethelia near Gaza, a pagan stronghold:

> Alaphion it appears was possessed of a devil; and neither the pagans nor the Jews could by any enchantments deliver him from this affliction, but Hilarion, by simply calling on the name of Christ expelled the demon and Alaphion and his whole family immediately embraced the faith.[1]

Sozomen's grandfather was so amazed at the miracle that he and his family followed suit, and the grandson became the eminent Christian historian in Constantinople in the reign of Theodosius II (*c.*435–40).

Sozomen carried the memory of these events with him in his narrative. He also tells how the Black Sea kingdom of Iberia was converted to Christianity by the work of a Christian woman captive invoking the name of Christ and healing a child of a near-fatal disease.[2] On Rome's northern border, Christian priests who had been taken captive were able to heal tribesmen 'by the name of Christ', and Sozomen tells of the rapid and extraordinary progress of Christianity in his own province of Phoenicia partly as a result of similar events. The age-old pagan priesthoods that had held sway over the population from time immemorial put up scant resistance in face of Constantine's decrees and the influence of holy men.[3]

Disease was the dreaded enemy of the inhabitants of the Ancient World. No one knew how it arose; there were no certain cures. The 'evil eye', often people with blue eyes in a dark-skinned, brown-eyed

1 Sozomen, *Historia Ecclesiastica*, v.15.14–17: *Sozomenus Kirchengeschichte*, ed. Joseph Bidez and Günther Christian Hansen, GCS 50 (Berlin, 1960), 216.

2 Ibid., ii.7.1–12. Also, the case of the advocate Aquilinus, ibid., ii.3.

3 Ibid., ii.6 and ii.5 (pagan surrenders).

environment, was thought to be a potent cause of illness. 'The evil eye owns two thirds of the graveyard' was a proverb quoted among the Berber inhabitants of North Africa as late as the beginning of the last century.[4] Visiting the Roman city of Dougga (Thugga) in western Tunisia during my work as Craven Fellow of Oxford University in 1938, I was struck by the mosaic (probably fourth century) of a large courtyard house. The surface was covered by patterns of vine tendrils surrounding a large eye. This, the evil eye, was the danger. The elaborate vine tendrils were designed to surround it and counteract its effects. The mosaic was not simply for decoration but had been laid down to protect the house and its inhabitants.[5] Elsewhere, one has seen mosaics with similar prophylactic symbols laid at the entrance of houses, while at street corners there would sometimes be phallic symbols aimed, equally, at safeguarding passers-by from harm. The gods of the Graeco- Roman pantheon had the duty of preserving their worshippers from even the slightest sign of harm or illness.

Protection in the provincial world of pagan gods was not only passive. Worshippers expected from them cures, often sudden and apparently miraculous. Celsus in his attack on Christianity in *c.*178 recounts albeit scathingly how 'sorcerers who profess to do wonderful miracles', who 'for a few obols' ply their trade in the market places and 'drive demons out of men, blow away diseases and invoke the souls of heroes'.[6] Origen accepted the reality of magic behind such cures, but adds that no sorcerer combined his tricks with a call to moral reformation, which Christians performing cures did. Celsus also mentions other miracles not of healing, such as those performed by Aristeas the Proconnesian who first of all vanished from human sight and then returned after 'visiting many parts of the world and relating amazing tales'.[7] Origen, writing seventy years later, had to defend Christian miracles, especially those of Jesus, and point out that even if pagan miracles did happen, they did not have the same effect as Jesus's

4 Cited from E. A. Westermarck, *Ritual and Belief in Morocco*, 2 vols (London, 1926), 1: 414; re. fear of the Evil Eye in Syria, see Peter Brown, 'The Rise and Function of the Holy Man in Late Antiquity', *Journal of Roman Studies* 51 (1971), 80–101, repr. in *Society and the Holy in Late Antiquity* (London, 1982), 103–52, 114.

5 Personal observation, summer 1938. I also saw 'evil eyes' painted on the sides of barrows used for selling ice-creams, as well as the Carthaginian 'hand of Fatima'. The laurel was also regarded as a charm against the Evil Eye, see Westermarck, *Ritual*, 1: 108.

6 *Contra Celsum*, i.68, transl. Henry Chadwick (Cambridge, 1953), 62–3.

7 Ibid., iii.26 (trans. Chadwick, 144).

teaching and healing for which individuals were prepared to sacrifice their lives.[8]

In the decades before he wrote, however, the spirit of the age favoured pagan claims. In the second and early third century the Roman empire reached the climax of its achievement, marked by the prosperity of its urban civilization and the political and religious systems that reflected this. The overwhelming majority of the provincials accepted the benevolent providence of the immortal gods of Rome and of the deities that for generations had safeguarded the lives and prosperity of their respective peoples, such as Attis for the Phrygians, Saturn (Baal-Hammon) for the North Africans. In this world Asclepius was the supreme god of healing, accepted as such both by the ordinary provincials as well as the political elite. Celsus is a prime authority, describing how 'a great multitude of men, both Greeks and barbarians, confess that they have often seen and do see, not just a phantom, but Asclepius himself healing men and doing good and predicting the future'.[9] This could be a direct challenge to Christian claims on behalf of Christ, but during the second century Asclepius reigned supreme. Aelius Aristides, rhetorician and philosopher (*c.*165) spent two years at the great shrine at Pergamum dedicated to him, with other worshippers of similar distinction, attending ceremonies in the god's honour. At night he often experienced horrific dreams, both the means of cure and, in Aristides' case, advice to return to his career as a philosopher.[10]

A century later, the important funerary mosaic from Lambiridi in southern Numidia in honour of Cornelia Urbanilla, who died at the age of 28, shows Asclepius as a large prosperous-looking physician apparently taking the pulse of a naked Urbanilla (who has been transformed into a male) and assuring her of salvation 'from the great danger', the period of the Beyond.[11]

8 Ibid., iii.27.

9 Ibid., iii.24 (trans. Chadwick, 142).

10 See Harold Remus, *Pagan-Christian Conflict over Miracle in the Second Century* (Cambridge, MA, 1983), 97–103. Aristides appears also to criticize severely as being shameless, willful and neglectful of the common weal, either Christians, or Cynics (p. 101). Cf. also E. R. Dodds, *Pagan and Christian in an Age of Anxiety: Some Aspects of Religious Experience from Marcus Aurelius to Constantine* (Cambridge, 1965), 40–2, where he describes the terrifying anxiety dreams and megalomaniac fantasies that afflicted Aristides during his stay at Asclepius' shrine.

11 Described, illustrated and discussed in full by Jérôme Carcopino, *Aspects mystiques de la Rome païenne* (Paris, 1942), 208–42.

Against these perceptions the Church in Celsus's time had little defence. In his crafty opening two books of the *Alethes Logos* ('True Doctrine'), Celsus puts in the mouth of a Jew his onslaught against Christianity and above all, its founder. Jesus himself, he asserts, 'was brought up in secret and hired himself out as a workman in Egypt and having tried his hand at certain magical powers he returned from there, and on account of these powers gave himself the title of God'.[12] The apostles were 'eleven infamous men'.[13] Jesus's miracles, such as the feeding of the five thousand were illusions, or the practices of 'wicked men possessed by an evil demon'.[14] Jesus himself was a sorcerer, betrayed by one of his own followers and died in fear and in disgrace.[15] Such a one could not be a 'pure and holy Logos'. Jesus and his supposed miracles were superfluous. As for prophecies concerning his life 'these could be applied to thousands of others far more plausibly than to Jesus'.[16]

Yet all the time Christianity was expanding, Christians, as Origen states, had been able 'to rise above all the people opposing the spread of his teaching – kings, governors, the Roman Senate, rulers everywhere, and the common people',[17] and again he stressed the moral reform of the converts as they heard and accepted the Christian message. By the end of the third century Arnobius, the converted rhetorician from Sicca Veneria in Proconsular Africa (western Tunisia), was able to demonstrate to his pagan audience the superiority of the healing carried out by Christ, without drama and incantations, to that of Asclepius.[18]

The Gospels show how Jesus won the hearts of his hearers in Galilee and Jerusalem by his miracles of healing and the teaching that accompanied them. These miracles continued to have a profound effect on early Christian thought. The healing of Bartimaeus and above all, the raising of Lazarus provided the theme of salvation for generations of Christians who have left their memories in biblical scenes depicted in the Roman Catacombs and, equally effectively, on the elaborately carved sarcophagi commissioned as memorials for the wealthy classes

12 Origen, *Contra Celsum*, i.38 (trans. Chadwick, 37).
13 Ibid., i.62 (trans. Chadwick, 56).
14 Ibid., i.68 (trans. Chadwick, 63).
15 Ibid., ii.31 (trans. Chadwick, 93).
16 Ibid., ii.28 (trans. Chadwick, 91).
17 Ibid., ii.79 (trans. Chadwick, 127).
18 Arnobius, *Adversus nationes libri VII* 1.63–5, ed. Augustus Reifferscheid, CSEL 4 (Vienna, 1875), 43–6.

particularly in Rome and Arles.[19] These were the guarantees of salvation and deliverance from the power of death.

Equally, miracles of healing proved a powerful magnet for the recruitment of believers in the early Church. In Acts 3 and 4, we read of Peter's healing of the lame man, its instant impression on bystanders and attempted action by Caiaphas and his fellow High Priests to silence Peter and the Apostles. The latter were credited to have spread the Gospel as much by preaching, writing and organizing ability as by miracle.[20] In the second century however, as we have seen, Christians were competing, though not always successfully, with their pagan neighbours in healing works ostensibly by miraculous means. Eusebius of Caesarea (*c.*325), recounting the story of the (orthodox) Church's triumph from the Crucifixion to the conversion of Constantine, has this to say about Christian expansion a generation or so after Paul. Following the foundation of new churches by missionaries, these appointed others as shepherds and committed to them the task of tending those who had just been brought in, but they themselves passed on again to other lands and peoples, helped by the grace and co-operation of God, seeing that many strange miracles of the divine spirit were at that time still being wrought by them, so that whole crowds of men at the first hearing eagerly received in their souls the religion of the creator of the universe.[21] These were 'super-preachers' for whom miracles and exorcism were supplements to the power of the word; and Eusebius records memories of their success after two centuries.

The scene was almost certainly Western Asia Minor, where we know that the Church was expanding far beyond the bounds of the Pauline mission by the end of the first century. But there was opposition. Just before, Eusebius's attitude to the work of disciples of Simon Magus in Syria was that they were 'stimulated by demons' and were 'calumniating by magic the great mystery of religion', particularly, the Church's teaching on the immortality of the soul and the resurrection of the dead.[22] The power of miracle could be double-edged.

19 See examples illustrated in Angelo di Berardino, *Encyclopedia of the Early Church*, trans. Adrian Walford, 2 vols (Cambridge, 1991), 2: fig. 152 (Healing of the issue of blood, Milan); fig. 139 (Healing of the Blind Man, Clermont); fig. 259 (Raising of Lazarus, Rome).

20 Origen, *Contra Celsum*, i.62.

21 Eusebius, *Historia Ecclesiastica*, iii.37.3.

22 Ibid., iii.26, transl. Kirsopp Lake, Loeb Classical Library, 2 vols (Cambridge, MA, 1980), 1: 261.

However, the work of the non-orthodox was not always unconstructive. The Gnostic *Acts of John* had a long life, originating traditionally in the second half of the second century in Asia Minor and continuing to circulate until they had become adopted into a Manichean canon two centuries later.[23] The narrator places John in Ephesus. On his arrival in the city he heals Cleopatra, wife of Lycomedes *praetor* of the city, of palsy and revives her husband who had expired from excitement and expectation of the saint's arrival. John continued to perform cures until, in the temple of Artemis itself, he invoked the name of Jesus; the temple collapsed killing the chief priest. The multitude of the Ephesians cry out, 'One is the God of John . . . thou only art God, have mercy on us. [. . .] Now are we turned to thee beholding thy marvelous works'.[24] The city therefore was converted. Whether Christian missions were conducted thus, and whether there were scenes of mass hysteria leading to a wholesale adoption of Christianity by a populace is unknown. The temple of Artemis seems to have been destroyed by the Goths in 263,[25] almost two centuries after the events portrayed in the *Acts of John* were supposed to have taken place. It had not been rebuilt. Even so, in the minds of some early Christian writers miracles played a dramatic part in spreading the Christian message in major cities of Asia Minor.

One other example of crowd psychology may be quoted, and with a better claim to veracity than that cited from the *Acts of John*. Theodoret, Bishop of Cyrrhus in northern Syria *c.*450, witnessed an extraordinary event when staying near the Pillar of Symeon the Stylite at Telnesin forty miles east of Antioch. Symeon was renowned for performing a variety of miracles. Much of his work would now be accounted for as social service. Theodoret himself had been on a rare visit to Telnesin to place a law suit before the holy man as many had done before him and had witnessed his power. In another case the saint had brokered peace between angry neighbours. On another occasion he would be praying

[23] *The Acts of John*, 42, in *The Apocryphal New Testament*, ed. and transl. M. K. James (Oxford, 1926), 228–70, 236–8.

[24] See Ramsay MacMullen, *Christianizing the Roman Empire (AD 100–400)* (New Haven, CT, and London, 1984), 26. For John's cures, see p. 236: 'John by the power of God healed all the diseases'.

[25] See W. H. C. Frend, *The Archaeology of Early Christianity: a History* (London, 1996), 139, giving references to excavations on the temple site by the Austro-Hungarian team before the First World War, with special reference to those by Rupert Heberdey.

for rain to end a drought.[26] Now Theodoret witnessed a memorable scene. 'Beduin', he recounts,

> in many thousands enslaved to the darkness of impiety were enlightened by the station on the pillar.... They arrived in companies, 200 in one, 300 in another, occasionally a thousand. They renounced with their shouts their traditional errors; they broke up their venerated idols in the presence of that great light, and they foreswore the ecstatic rites of Aphrodite.[27]

This was not due to a single specific miracle on the part of Symeon, but his reputation for wisdom, miraculous healings and exorcisms. He was a holy man, and they expected in return for his favour that his God would grant them security and even vengeance on their enemies.

Miracles could be used as a means of converting philosophers overcome by arguments with monks or even to coerce the unwilling.[28] An ascetic of Hermoupolis in Egypt reduced a procession of non-Christian worshippers to frozen immobility in the middle of a road through spells. They were not able to regain the use of their limbs until they 'renounced their error'.[29] If one defied an ascetic, one could even die a horrible death.[30]

In the West dissenters were less harshly treated, but miracles could also be turned to the advantage of the orthodox in conflict with all types of opposition. One such incident took place in Milan in 386 when Augustine himself, recently a catechumen, was in the city and regarded himself still as an onlooker of the miraculous. A dream directed Bishop Ambrose to the site of the burial of two martyrs, Gervasius and Protasius, perhaps martyred under Diocletian in 304, but possibly Palaeolithic skeletons. They were brought in triumph to Ambrose's cathedral. Those 'vexed with unclean spirits' were cured, but the real triumph was the cure of a well-known blind man of his affliction. The effect on the Arian population and the empress Justina was considerable, and cries of 'fake' were raised. Augustine records that while 'not turned to the soundness of believing', the empress 'was turned back

26 Incidents cited from Brown, 'The Rise and Function of the Holy Man', 120–4. Miracles were 'the proof of power'.

27 Theodoret, *Historia religiosa*, 26 (PG 82, 1476A); cited from Macmullen, *Christianizing the Roman Empire*, 1–2.

28 Sozomen, *Historia Ecclesiastica*, i.18.

29 See MacMullen, *Christianizing the Roman Empire*, 62.

30 Ibid., Curse by the Syrian monk Aphraates.

from her fury of persecuting' the Catholics, and the Arians in Milan equally discouraged.[31]

Augustine remembered the incident when he wrote the final, twenty-second, Book of the *De civitate Dei* in 426. At this stage he was engaged in popularizing the cults of foreign martyrs, such as Vincent of Saragossa, to counteract the schismatic Donatist cults of local North African martyrs, especially the victims of the Great Persecution. He had earlier been sceptical about the truth of miracles,[32] but now he realized their value whether or not he took them literally. His masterstroke was to secure for his see at Hippo relics of St Stephen originally brought to North Africa by Paulus Orosius in 416. They had toured numerous sites including Carthage and Calama in Numidia before arriving in Hippo in 424.[33] Augustine enumerates twenty-eight cures associated with the martyr's relics, how gout had been cured of one who had desired baptism, but had been unable to make his way to the font, how a nobleman who hated Christianity had been converted by the influence of the relics and how many who were believers also had been cured of their maladies.[34] Down to the last years of Roman Africa miracles of healing through the agency of the relics of saints and martyrs were, in the hands of Augustine, a powerful means of spreading and consolidating the orthodox Catholic faith.

Miracles, as Origen agrees,[35] have their place in the conversion of the Graeco-Roman world to Christianity and also in strengthening the faith once accepted. Accounts, drawn from varied sources both in East and West, of individual and crowd experiences leave no doubt as to the power of the committed missionary and holy man to sway members of all classes into accepting the truth of Christianity. Miracles, mainly of healing, and dreams, such as Arnobius's,[36] share an important place in the Christianization of the Graeco-Roman world.

But how important were they? Origen, authoritative through both

31 Ambrose, *Ep.* 22; Augustine, *Confessions*, ix.7.16, trans. William Watts, Loeb Classical Library, 2 vols (London and New York, 1912), 2: 32–3; cf. *De civitate Dei*, xxii.8.8.

32 Augustine, *De vera religione,* 25.47 (PL 34, 142) and *Sermo* 99.3 (PL 38, 540) (*c.*400): 'Modo caro caeca non aperit oculos miraculo Domini'.

33 For a discussion and description of the sites identified with the cult of Stephen, see Yvette Duval, *Loca sanctorum Africae: le culte des martyrs en Afrique du IVe au VIIe siècle*, Collection de l'Ecole française de Rome 58, 2 vols (Rome, 1982), 2: 624–32.

34 Recorded by Augustine in sections of his *De civitate Dei*, e.g. xxii.8.

35 Origen, *Contra Celsum*, i.43 and 46.

36 Jerome, Chronicon 313F (ad ann. 327), in *Die Chronik der Hieronymus*, in *Eusebius Werke vol.* 7, ed. Rudolf Helm, GCS 24 and 34, 2 vols (Leipzig, 1913 and 1926) repr. as one volume (Berlin, 1956), 152. Wrongly dated by Jerome to A.D. 327.

his learning and observation of the progress of Christianity in the first half of the third century, indicates that Paul himself placed miracles on a lower level than intellectual gifts as a means of representing the Gospel, and emphasized the moral qualities of those whom he appointed leaders of the churches.[37] Reason and wisdom were to be valued above miraculous workings. Origen himself bears witness to this in his dealings with the young Cappadocian nobleman, Gregory 'the Wonderworker'. Gregory met Origen almost by chance when arriving at Caesarea as an escort for his sister who had married a lawyer on the staff of the governor of Palestine and was due to take up her residence in the provincial capital, Caesarea. Gregory had had some early leanings towards Christianity and willingly gave up a career as a student at the school of Roman law at Berytus (Beirut) to remain with Origen. There he was taken step by step through various philosophical systems until he accepted Christianity as the highest form of philosophy and a rational view of the universe which provided a guide to conduct through the example of Jesus Christ.[38] He was initiated into what he described as 'the great Paradise of God'. For Origen himself Christianity was a movement of spiritual and moral reform which built on current philosophy as well as Scripture. As he describes, some of the most irrational people and those most subject to passions were changed to a more self-controlled life by conversion to Christianity,[39] words used by Justin Martyr nearly a century before.[40]

A sense of belonging to a disciplined 'school' or 'sect' as Tertullian liked to proclaim it in Carthage at the turn of the third century kept Christians together and attracted pagans to them.[41] As early as *c.*170, Lucian of Samosata describing the Christian episode in the life of the exhibitionist and charlatan Proteus Peregrinus, recounts how, when he was imprisoned in Palestine as a 'prophet', 'synogogue leader' and 'lawgiver' of the sect, Christians from far and near descended on the prison

[37] For Paul's downplaying of the apparently miraculous among the Christians of Corinth, 1 Cor. 1, 18–25 (manifestations of human wisdom) cited by Origen, *Contra Celsum*, iii.47–48. For Origen's own view that miracles were secondary to Christian understanding of Christ 'weaving together human and divine nature', see ibid., iii.28. High character was expected of Christian leaders: ibid., iii.28 and 30 (qualities of the leaders of Churches compared with those of city councilors), and miracles secondary.

[38] Described by Gregory himself in his Letter of Thanks to Origen: *Remerciement à Origène*, ed. Henri Crouzel, SC 148 (Paris, 1969), cc. 13–15, 159–73.

[39] *Contra Celsum*, i.68 and ii.50 (moral reformation).

[40] Justin Martyr, *1 Apol.* 14 and *Dialogue with Trypho*, 30.3 and 35.7.

[41] Tertullian, *Apologia*, 38.1 and 39.1.

in the hope that something of advantage would be theirs for participating in Peregrinus's spiritual magic.[42] It was natural for Christians to show solidarity with each other. 'See how they love one another' was a pagan observation;[43] and during his short-lived effort to restore paganism as the religion of the empire, Julian found Christian mutual help and social conscience an immovable obstacle to success.[44]

With mutual solidarity went martyrdom. The Christian willingness to die for his faith became by far the most potent force of attraction to Christianity. The blood of Christians was seed, claimed Tertullian.[45] This, however, was not always the case. In the first two centuries the sight of Christians going willingly to their deaths in the arena converted some prominent individuals such as Justin Martyr[46] and Tertullian himself.[47] But the more usual reaction of beholders was one of amazement tinged with pity. Thus, even those who sympathized watching the end of the martyrs of Lyon in 177 were recorded by the writer, who was himself an eyewitness to their mother-churches in the province of Asia, as saying to themselves: 'Where is their god and what good to them was their worship, which they preferred beyond their lives?'[48] In the Decian persecution in 250 the townsfolk of Smyrna mocked and criticized presbyter Pionius for his desiring martyrdom rather than to follow Bishop Euctemon and sacrifice to the gods. They did everything to persuade him not to forfeit his life.[49] In the Great Persecution, however, the situation was different. Lactantius, an eyewitness of events in Diocletian's capital, Nicomedia in Bithynia, wrote how 'great numbers were driven from the worship of false gods by their hatred of cruelty'. Some suspected that 'the worship of the gods was seen as evil by so many, so that these would rather die than perform sacrifices'.[50] These acts, says Lactantius, 'have great effect' and have been the cause of the increased numbers of Christians.[51]

42 Lucian, *The Passing of Peregrinus,* 11.13, trans. A. M. Harmon, Loeb Classical Library, 8 vols (London and Cambridge, MA, 1913–67), 5 (1936): 12–15.

43 Tertullian, *Apologia*, 39.7; for this writer, Christians were 'brethren' (ibid., 39.10).

44 Julian, *Ep.* 49; see also Sozomen, *Historia Ecclesiastica*, 5.16, 5–15.

45 Tertullian, *Apologia*, 50.13.

46 Justin Martyr, *ii. Apol.* 12.

47 Tertullian, *Apologia*, 50.1.5.

48 Eusebius, *Historia Ecclesiastica*, v.1.60 (trans. Lake, 1: 434–5).

49 'Acta Pionii', ed. H. Musurillo, in *Acts of the Christian Martyrs* (Oxford, 1972), 136–67. The best discussion of these *Acta* is by Robin Lane Fox, *Pagans and Christians* (Harmondsworth, 1986), 460–92.

50 Lactantius, *Divine Institutes*, v.23, ed. Pierre Monat, SC 204 (Paris, 1973), 254.

51 Ibid.

In the Thebaid in Egypt in the final phase of persecution under Maximin in 311–12, Coptic peasants entered on what can only be described as mass suicide in order to affirm their Christianity.[52] It is no wonder the accession of Diocletian in 284 became the beginning of the Coptic Era.

Miracles therefore can be described as one among other factors that drew people to the Christian faith in the first four centuries A.D. This was inevitable. Jesus's first attack on Satan's kingdom recorded in Mark's Gospel had been through the acts of healing. The power of his Name was passed on to his followers. Their powers, however explained, proved stronger than those of their pagan rivals. The story Sozomen tells of the conversion of his grandparents to Christianity did not stand on its own.

University of Cambridge

52 Eusebius, *Historia Ecclesiastica*, vii.9.4–5 (events of 311–12).

VENTRILOQUISM AND THE MIRACULOUS: CONVERSION, PREACHING, AND THE MARTYR EXEMPLUM IN LATE ANTIQUITY

by KATE COOPER*

> Disciples of Christ do not consider how things will proceed in the sight of judges. For thus he forewarned us, saying, '*But when they hand you over, do not worry about how to speak or what to say; what you are to say will be given to you when the time comes; because it is not you who will be speaking; the Spirit of your Father will be speaking in you*'.[1]

THUS defiantly speaks the martyr Tranquillinus to Agrestius Chromatius, Urban Prefect of the city of Rome during the reign of Diocletian, according to the *Passion of Saint Sebastian* written in the fifth or early sixth century in that city. As they considered the interview, sixth-century readers and hearers already knew what we no longer remember, which is that not only Sebastian but the pagan Chromatius too would emerge as heroes of the early Christian story. For according to the *passio* the prefect himself was hesitating on the brink of conversion to Christianity, and would be remembered not as a harsh judge of Christians, but as one of their own number, and the father of the Diocletianic martyr Tiburtius.

With the *Passio Sebastiani* we come face to face with an influential early Christian idea, that the martyr was the quintessential Christian preacher, uniquely able, in his or her complete sacrifice of flesh to the

* I am grateful to the Arts and Humanities Research Board for Research Leave funding in support of this contribution, and to the British Academy for support of the Roman Martyrs Project research on which I have drawn. I am also grateful to Barbara Crostini, Jeremy Gregory, Conrad Leyser, and Joanna Sadgrove for stimulating discussion of earlier versions of this piece, to Brenda Bolton for her kind invitation to address the Society, and to the Williams and Douglas families for memorable hospitality on that occasion. It is dedicated to the memory of Jim Douglas, whose mirth and generosity remain an inspiration to all who knew him.

[1] Matt. 10, 19, cited in *Passio Sebastiani* 45. The *Passio Sebastiani* (*BHL* 7543) appears in the second volume for January of the *ActaSS*, II Ian., 265–78, here, 272. I cite throughout from this version in the footnotes, giving the Latin where relevant, while in the text I have drawn (with some alterations) on the English translation prepared under my supervision by Daniel S. Richter, to be published in a forthcoming collection of Roman *passiones* sponsored by the Roman Martyrs Project of the University of Manchester Centre for Late Antiquity.

Word, to serve as the medium of what might be called divine ventriloquism. The martyr's gift of endurance in the face of death was accompanied by a gift of speech: that of delivering words sent by the Spirit of the Father. This idea had, as we have seen above, a secure biblical basis, but – like so many other ideas borrowed forward from the biblical text to serve later Christian communities – its appearance in the *Passio Sebastiani* was also the culmination of interests and anxieties specific to the *Passio*'s own generation. When we hear Sebastian as he preaches to the pagan officials whose task is to persecute him, we are witnessing a late-Roman understanding – however idealized – of the process of Christian conversion.

Central to the inquiry is the *Passio*'s approach to the relationship between speech and the miraculous. In examining the *Passio*, we will come to understand how at least one group of Christians at the end of antiquity understood the divine intervention that resulted in the attraction of new adherents to the faith. We will see, for example, that, on this understanding, for one of their number to offer a clear and accurate exposition of the faith was an integral part of the mental landscape of the miraculous. How the author of the *Passio Sebastiani* understood the martyr's role as a preacher will hold some surprises. Perhaps most important is the fact that in the *Passio Sebastiani*, as in the other *gesta martyrum*, the 'rational' and 'miraculous' aspects of faith are by no means seen as standing in opposition. Rather, they are seen as working in a kind of divinely inspired synergy. Indeed, the martyr's gift of truthful persuasion – his ability to draw his persecutors toward the faith – was itself nothing short of a miracle.

* * *

I have argued elsewhere that in the period before the conversion of Constantine, Christian writers made imaginative use of the conventions of Roman forensic practice to describe and interpret the seemingly miraculous fortitude of the martyrs as a guarantee of the truth of their belief. The martyr's willingness – and ability – to die an unflinching death for Christian conviction was offered as proof that Christian belief was founded in an incontestable reality.[2] This in turn lent powerful emphasis to the words of faith uttered by the martyrs and recorded in the texts. When the second-century *Martyrdom of Polycarp*

2 Kate Cooper, 'The Voice of the Victim: Gender, Representation, and Early Christian Martyrdom', *Bulletin of the John Rylands Library* 80 (1998), 147–57.

describes, for example, how the bishop of Smyrna was bound at the stake as his executioners prepared to light the fire, the speech serves to record his instruction of the crowd who assembled to watch his execution, but it has a further purpose, to instruct and fortify those who read or hear the account of his death. Polycarp's courage in the face of the flames is a sign of God's seal on his truth, even if his truth was not yet universally acknowledged.

After Constantine's conversion, martyr narratives continued to be produced despite the end of persecution. For post-Constantinian Christians, such as the author of the *Passio Sebastiani*, and the other late martyr romances known as the *gesta martyrum*,[3] the encounter between the Christian martyr and his or her examiners or executioners became a focal point for repeated exploration of the meaning of the change that had taken place. To put it simply, post-Constantinian writers and audiences knew that their world had changed, and they believed that the martyrs were responsible. Somehow, they imagined, the powerful discourse of the martyrs had yielded both earthly and heavenly fruit in the conversion of their persecutors. The point of returning again and again to the martyr and the martyr's preaching was to understand how these words of power had worked upon their hearers, transforming the empire as a result.

* * *

We turn now to approach the problem of the miraculous. In his influential 1981 study, *The Cult of the Saints*, Peter Brown suggested that twentieth-century scholarship on popular religion in Late Antiquity owed a great deal to the eighteenth-century suggestion of David Hume that a persistent opposition holds between the religious ideas of 'the vulgar' and those of learned elites – a view which has since been widely known in Brown's phrase as the 'two-tiered' model. Hume saw 'the vulgar' in Late Antiquity as the manifestation of an ever-present and unchanging force that drags against human society in its struggle toward reason. Its influence on post-Constantinian Christianity was as a kind of inertia influencing the newly Christianized mob to cleave to its own ancient practices and beliefs despite the best efforts of the bishops. Brown in turn saw Hume's *The Natural History of Religion* as having supplied the 'mental furniture' of classic treatments of early

3 On the date and context of the rise of the *gesta martyum*, see Kate Cooper, 'The Martyr, the *Matrona* and the Bishop: Networks of Allegiance in Early Sixth-Century Rome', *Early Medieval Europe* 8 (1999), 297–317.

Christianity and later antiquity, from Gibbon's *Decline and Fall of the Roman Empire* to Dean Milman's *History of Latin Christianity*.[4] Gibbon famously concluded that Christianity was 'corrupted' as a monotheistic religion by 'the vulgar'. The occasion for this corruption was of course the rise of the cult of the saints, 'a popular mythology which tended to restore the reign of polytheism'.[5]

Brown took the 'two-tiered' model as the starting-point for a now-famous critique. To be sure, the charge that cultic activity at the graves of the dead reflected '"pre-Christian" practices' against which bishops must take a stand was linked, in the minds of the bishops themselves, to the idea that Christian belonging itself had been corrupted by the reign of Constantine. An explanation for why the Christian masses were insufficiently Christian, that loomed large in the imagination of both fourth-century bishops and modern historians, Brown argued, was that of 'mass conversion', in which the rabble who gathered around an aristocrat, or around a miracle-worker, would suddenly take up the Christian name – in imitation of the one or in awe of the other – without any process of cultural or ethical instruction.

Brown suspected fourth-century bishops of inventing the phenomenon of 'mass conversion' as a way of accounting for the unsettling perception that a transformation of Christianity was taking place on their watch. The idea of 'the vulgar' was thus not an invention of the Enlightenment, but a reflection of the anxieties of the fourth-century writers themselves.

The 'two-tiered' model has created a landslide that may never have happened; and it has done so because only a landslide of 'the vulgar' into the Christian church could satisfy the demands of its system of explanation when faced with the rise within the Church of new forms of, apparently, 'popular' religious feeling.[6] But Brown thought that the root of the change had little to do with the mysteries of 'popular religion' (a phenomenon which, with Momigliano, he suspected did not exist). Rather, the uncomfortable developments of the fourth century reflected a tension between the biological family and the church as an 'artificial kin group':

4 Peter Brown, *The Cult of the Saints: its Rise and Function in Latin Christianity* (Chicago, 1981), 13–15.

5 Quotation from Gibbon, ibid., 15, n. 55.

6 Ibid., 29–30.

> . . . we must remember that the Christian church had risen to prominence largely because its central ritual practices and increasingly centralized organization and financial administration presented the pagan world with an ideal community that had claimed to modify, to redirect, and even delimit the bonds of kin. The church was an artificial kin group. Its members were expected to project onto the new community a fair measure of the sense of solidarity, of the loyalties, and of the obligations that had previously been directed toward the physical family.[7]

It was the bishop as *impresario* of the cult of the saints who stood as Brown's symbol for the 'public' Christian institutions, in contrast to the 'private' allegiances of the biological family. Though Brown's substitution of concerns around 'public' and 'private' spheres for those around mass conversion is not central to the present study, we will find ourselves returning to texts in which the newly Christianized Roman family looms large. We will see in addition that the scenes of 'mass conversion' in early Christian literature, in which an aristocrat converts with his whole household, have yet adequately to be fully understood.

* * *

I have given so much attention to Brown and Hume in part because despite the great emphasis on 'the vulgar' and on Brown's critique of Hume in recent scholarship, there is still something to learn from Hume himself. It may be that Hume on the miraculous *per se* is rather more edifying than Hume on popular religion in general.[8] Now Hume of course was writing at a historical moment where the ability of institutions to veil relations of power with mystery was beginning to be challenged. This project of demystification, which contributed to the great projection theories of religion of the nineteenth century, has had mixed results for our ability to think analytically about the miraculous. But when the analysis is uncoupled from the reductionism that often accompanied it, it reflects a vivid sense of what is at stake in Christian institutions. Despite his own susceptibility to the charge of 'dogmatic atheism'[9] and his disinclination to credit the miraculous, Hume saw it

7 Ibid., 31.

8 Hume elaborated his view of the miraculous in Section X, 'Of Miracles', of the *Enquiry Concerning the Human Understanding: an Enquiry Concerning the Human Understanding, and an Enquiry Concerning the Principles of Morals*, ed. L. A. Selby-Bigge (Oxford, 1894).

9 Discussed by Mark Sainsbury in his review (*TLS* 15.10.04, 4–5) of Robert J. Fogelin's *A Defense of Hume on Miracles* (Princeton, NJ, 2004).

as a matter of professional competence to account for what would make a sane person wish to credit what he himself rejected.

Where Hume can shed valuable light on early Christian accounts of the miraculous is in his emphasis on the problem of reliable testimony. Hume isolated the problem of indirect evidence – reported experience, hear-say, and other second-hand knowledge – as a specific type of evidence whose properties must be perfectly understood by the philosopher, especially where evidence for and against a suspension of the laws of nature was concerned. 'No testimony is sufficient to establish a miracle, unless the testimony be of such a kind, that its falsehood would be more miraculous, than the fact, which it endeavours to establish'.[10] Unlike the early Christian bishops, Hume took it as given that no philosopher of his day would be presented with compelling direct evidence on this point.

Indeed, for Hume, it was impossible to establish the veracity of a witness to such a compelling degree, since the reporting of a miracle as truth could essentially be taken as proof of a source's weakness. We should not be so naïve, however, as to imagine that early Christian writers were oblivious to the problem of a source's veracity where the miraculous was concerned. Both Pagan and Christian literature abound with advice on how to recognize religious con-artistry, and the presence of claims to the miraculous tended to be a trigger for scrutiny against the criminal profile.[11] This may explain why the *Passio Sebastiani*, like the other *gesta martyrum*, is so deeply concerned to establish the credentials of the martyr as witness early in the narrative, long before he seals his good intentions by dying the martyr's death which confers the title *martyr* derived from the Greek *martyros*, meaning witness.

Surprisingly, the veracity of the Christian 'message' may not actually have been the central concern of the men and women who joined the early Christian community as adult converts. But it was paramount in the re-telling, in the meaning attributed in retrospect to the conversion encounter. It is this tension between historical event and pastoral invention which we must be careful both to notice and to respect. We will see below that great attention is paid to the words of the martyr,

10 Hume, *Enquiry*, X.I.91, ed. Selby-Bigge, 115–16.

11 One might compare, for example, the third-century pagan Lucian of Samosata's *Life of Alexander of Abonuteichos* with the roughly contemporary figure of Simon Magus in the Christian *Pseudo-Clementine Recognitions*, to gain a sense of the ecumenically agreed profile of this kind of individual.

and to the problem of bringing alive for the *Passio*'s audience the force – and truth – of his preaching.

* * *

When we turn to our second theme, that of conversion, we encounter a historiographical landscape perhaps even more thorny than that of the miraculous. In trying to understand the conversion of the ancient world to Christianity, modern historians have generally adhered to one of two broad paradigms. The first, espoused by Arthur Darby Nock in his 1933 study on conversion, suggests essentially that Christianity attracted converts on the basis of its ethical magnetism. Nock understood conversion as a matter between an individual and his conscience. It was

> the reorientation of the soul of an individual, his deliberate turning from indifference or from an earlier form of piety to another, a turning which implies a consciousness that a great change is involved, that the old was wrong and the new is right.[12]

Nock's idea of conversion as 'the reorientation of the soul' owed something, to be sure, to the idea of conversion as a 'watershed experience' described a generation earlier by William James.[13] It goes without saying that this idea was patterned on the sensibilities of the elite male in his capacity as a reasonable individual.

But in an influential study of 1983 Ramsay MacMullen asked what was left of conversion without the elite male at the centre of the process. He suggested that at least two distinct types of conversion could be discerned in the sources for early Christianity. One type applied to the elite man of reason who interested James and Nock, while another involved crowds responding to direct or reported contact with the miraculous and was triggered by performances of divine power. As early as the late second century, MacMullen reminded his

12 Arthur Darby Nock, *Conversion: the Old and the New in Religion from Alexander the Great to Augustine of Hippo* (Oxford, 1933), 7. Danny Praet, 'Explaining the Christianization of the Roman Empire: Older Theories and Recent Developments', *Sacris Erudiri* 33 (1992–3), 5–119, 8–9, situates Nock's views alongside those of his continental contemporaries.

13 In his Gifford Lectures of 1901–02, printed as *The Varieties of Religious Experience: a Study in Human Nature* (London, 1902). Indeed, Nock wrote the introduction to the 1960 reprint of James's volume (Glasgow, 1960); the relationship between the two is discussed by Fausto Parente, 'L'idea di conversione da Nock ad oggi', *Augustinianum* 27 (1987), 7–25, 7–8.

readers, the pagan Celsus had ridiculed Christianity for the tendency of its practitioners to play to the excessive credulity of the 'simple folk'.[14]

MacMullen concluded his argument with the seemingly logical suggestion that a pattern of elite conversion could only account for a fraction of the actual population who must have joined the movement as it gathered force: 'if we are . . . to estimate Christianity as an historical force, that drew in scores of thousands, we must take account (even if we cannot quite enter his thoughts) of Everyman as well'.[15] I have used the phrase 'seemingly logical' because there is a gap in the logic. MacMullen does not consider the possibility that elite and popular conversion were somehow interdependent. Rather, his 'Everyman' is an independent soul, one who may well be swayed by demagoguery but who nonetheless makes his own decisions based on the public record rather than peer pressure or the whim of his patron.

In his attempt to be fair to 'Everyman', MacMullen scrupulously avoids imputing motivations other than the ethical or supernatural. He means to play fair with religious 'belief' as he understands it, and to steer as far from reductionism or a crass consideration of material motivations as his admittedly iconoclastic sensibility will allow. MacMullen puts his starting-point thus:

> excluding consideration of any rewards that awaited new recruits – rewards spiritual, social, emotional, and financial – which came only *after* conversion; for it seems fair to define our topic, conversion, as that experience by which non-believers first became convinced that the Christian God was almighty, and that they must please him.[16]

But the reader's ear should dwell on the phrase 'first became convinced'. For both elites and Everyman, MacMullen clearly has in mind a scenario in which the individual is struck by a bolt of conviction – by a *message* – before he or she knows very much at all about the group attached to it. However ambivalent MacMullen may be toward a model of conversion in response to preaching, his view of conversion is very much centred on belief.

It should have been within the powers of eloquence simply to talk

14 Ramsay MacMullen, 'Two Types of Conversion to Early Christianity', *Vigiliae Christianae* 37 (1983), 174–92, 187. See also his *Christianity and Paganism in the 4th to 8th Century* (New Haven, CT, 1997).

15 MacMullen, 'Two Types of Conversion', 188.

16 MacMullen, 'Two Types of Conversion', 184.

people into belief. Was the job so difficult? But instead, what is ordinarily attested in conversion-scenes are responses to demonstrations of superhuman power: perceived as miracles, in turn they were perceived as proofs of genuine divinity attaching to whatever deity was invoked and credited.[17]

Here as elsewhere, MacMullen has made an invaluable contribution to our understanding of what might be called a late ancient 'theology of divine empowerment', in which figures such as Constantine gave their allegiance to the God who seemed best able to serve as protector and champion. We will see below, however, that once our source base is widened to include the martyr acts and later *gesta martyrum*, we do in fact encounter numerous scenes of preaching. In these texts preaching and the miraculous are represented as working in unison rather than opposition. Why remains an open question. Perhaps the post-Constantinian authors of the *gesta* were aware of the imaginative power of the miraculous, and wished to ensure that it was firmly tethered to an acceptable Christian message. Alternately, they may simply not have perceived the two modes of conversion as standing in opposition. Before we take up this question, however, we must consider the changing scholarly understanding of the social 'rules' by which religious groups achieve the kind of startling demographic expansion that characterizes fourth-century Christianity.

* * *

One of MacMullen's central aims in his work on conversion has been to give a rational account for how Christianity grew as rapidly as it did across the fourth century. The figures for Christian affiliation seem to have mushroomed from something like a tenth of the Empire's population of roughly sixty million at the beginning of the century to something like a half – roughly thirty million – by the century's end if not before.[18] MacMullen understandably questioned whether two to three million people per decade (or perhaps far more if the thirty-million mark was reached by 350 as some scholars believe) were converting to

17 Ramsay MacMullen, 'Christianity Shaped through its Mission', in Alan Kreider, ed., *The Origins of Christendom in the West* (Edinburgh, 2001), 97–117, 98–9.

18 The numbers (six million and thirty million respectively, against an estimated population of sixty million in 'the Mediterranean world', are MacMullen's ('Christianity Shaped through its Mission', 10). Their shape aligns fairly well with those cited by Rodney Stark, *The Rise of Christianity: a Sociologist Reconsiders History* (Princeton, NJ, 1996), 5–11, although Stark believes the fifty per cent mark was reached earlier, by around 350, and, as we will see below, has a very different idea of how the numbers were achieved.

Christianity on the basis of a deeply considered understanding of Christian preaching. To repeatedly access new recruits in the millions, he argued, the Christians would have had to reach far beyond the sliver of the population who made spiritual decisions on the basis of a sophisticated grasp of theological concepts.

But not all means of reaching a wide audience involve crowds or miracles. In his 1996 study, *The Rise of Christianity: a Sociologist Reconsiders History*, Rodney Stark has called attention to the importance for early Christianity of two themes which emerge from demographic and fieldwork-based study of nineteenth- and twentieth-century American groups that achieved explosive religious growth. The first is a matter of arithmetic. If a group is able consistently to sustain a growth rate of circa forty per cent per decade – the rate achieved, for example, by the Mormons – by the third century of growth the numbers involved will tip dramatically into the millions.[19] The point here is that seemingly modest gains – each member of the faith attracts less than one convert every two decades – will begin over time to 'add up', through a process similar to the compounding of interest. Converting a hundred thousand souls does sound like something that should involve large and dramatic events, but if a million evangelically-minded brethren each engage in a quiet chat here and there with friends or relatives, the growth can seem to happen 'by itself'. On Stark's view, a thousand low-key conversations between friends are worth more than one Cecil B. De Mille-style extravaganza.

Stark's second and perhaps more startling point is that an individual's initial reaction to the 'message' of a religious movement does not govern whether or not he or she will eventually convert. To be sure, after the fact both the convert and the agent of conversion perceive the 'message' as having been the crux of the matter, but fieldwork on 'before' and 'after' perceptions shows that among the group of contacts who do eventually join a movement, there is not an unusually high evaluation of a group's message after the first substantial contact, as against the reaction of other individuals who do not eventually convert. Stark characterizes the early American followers of the Reverend Sun Myung Moon who were the focus of his fieldwork with John Lofland in the early 1960s:

19 Stark, *Rise of Christianity*, 5–11, drawing on Rodney Stark, 'The Rise of a New World Faith', *Review of Religious Research* 26 (1984), 18–27.

> Had we not gone out and watched people as they converted, we might have missed the point entirely, because when people retrospectively describe their conversions, they tend to put the stress on theology. When asked why they converted, Moonies invariably noted the irresistible appeal of the Divine Principles. . . . But Lofland and I knew better . . . we could remember when most of them regarded the religious beliefs of their new set of friends as quite odd.[20]

At this first stage, even a future convert is often firm in the conviction that his negative reaction to the 'message' is unshakeable.

What seems to distinguish those who don't convert from those who do is social chemistry with members of the group. Lofland and Stark discovered in their fieldwork with Moon's followers that the successful and lasting conversions tended to parallel networks of family and friendship. Either a Moon follower would strike up a friendship with an 'outsider', or a new convert would begin to have an influence on the other 'outsiders' who were already his or her friends before the conversion. If an 'outsider' family member began to spend more time with a new convert in the hope of drawing him or her away from the group, she or he was as likely to join the group in turn as to succeed in reversing the conversion.

The principle at work here is that people tend to 'rationalize' their religious and other affiliations to reflect and reinforce social attachments such as family and friendship. 'In effect, conversion is not about seeking or embracing an ideology, it is about bringing one's religious behaviour into alignment with that of one's friends and family members'.[21] Stark reinforces his suggestion by reference to a variety of empirical work on other religious traditions, but he seals it with reference to a single evocative statistic, drawn again from his own study of the Mormons. In one Mormon mission, the rate of eventual conversions achieved by unannounced door-to-door visits to strangers was one in a thousand. But if the missionaries made first contact while guests in the home of an individual's own friends or family, the success rate was one in two.[22]

20 Stark, *Rise of Christianity*, 19, drawing on John Lofland and Rodney Stark, 'Becoming a World-Saver: a Theory of Conversion to a Deviant Perspective', *American Sociological Review* 30 (1965), 862–75.

21 Stark, *Rise of Christianity*, 17–18, with discussion of the 'control theory of deviant behavior' underlying the analysis.

22 Ibid., 18; see also Rodney Stark and William Sims Bainbridge, 'Networks of Faith:

If we follow Stark, MacMullen's moment at which the convert 'first became convinced' is the result, rather than the cause, of a strong relationship with group members. Indeed, it may well happen *in spite of* – rather than because of – the message carried by the group. We might in turn ask whether the public preaching to crowds – assuming it happened at all – was in fact a way of 'preaching to the choir', of providing a focal point for the 'networking' being done more invisibly by group members. To be sure, theories derived from twentieth-century fieldwork can offer at best only a heuristic device for exploring ancient evidence. But it is useful to recognize that dramatic demographic growth could have taken place incrementally, through the kind of informal channels that would not necessarily appear in the historical record, rather than through documented occasions involving crowds.

But if bishops were happy with the number of converts the faith was attracting, they may still have wondered whether even the enthusiastic converts actually had a clear idea of the content of the tradition.[23] Whether by displays of miraculous power or by means of lay 'networking', new members were coming into the Christian community through avenues that were beyond the reach of episcopal 'message control'. By the early fifth century, Augustine of Hippo worried that Christians who knew and cared about the Church's ethical traditions could find themselves dismissed as extremists. Alan Kreider puts it this way:

> Augustine thought of the early days of the church, recorded in Acts 2, when people were 'thoroughly and perfectly' converted. Even in his day, he knew some people who sought to follow Christ, to pray for their enemies, and to distribute their goods to the needy. To their behaviour . . . the response of many baptized people was incredulous: 'Why are you acting crazy? You're going to extremes; aren't other people Christians?' [24]

If 'going to extremes' was what the Church had always been about, would it be the same Church if the 'extremists' were increasingly in the

Interpersonal Bonds and Recruitment to Cults and Sects', *American Journal of Sociology* 85 (1980), 1376–95.

23 MacMullen himself has called attention to this fact, in e.g. 'Christianity Shaped through its Mission', 106–9.

24 Alan Kreider, 'Changing Patterns of Conversion in the West', in idem, ed., *The Origins of Christendom*, 3–46 (here, 34), citing Sermons 88.12–13 and 14.4 respectively, in the translation of Edmund Hill (New York, 1990–).

minority? This was the question Augustine and others asked themselves.

In a well-known passage of *De catechizandis rudibus*, his treatise on how to handle enquirers – potential converts – Augustine recognized that an enquirer's motivation might well be less than edifying. It might be 'the hope of deriving some benefit from men whom he thinks he could not otherwise please, or to escape some injury at the hands of men whose displeasure or enmity he dreads'.[25] The trick was to collude in the deception, in the hope of helping the enquirer to actually become what she or he wished to seem to be – a person on whom Christian teaching had made a life-changing impression. To this end, Augustine advised, the process of instruction before admission to the catechumenate should include, in Kreider's phrase, 'a sixty-minute narration of salvation history from creation to the judgement day, culminating in exhortations to good behaviour'.[26] This *narratio* or 'summary of the Faith' would serve as a kind of public warning to the enquirer of what she or he was signing up to.

Augustine's *narratio* would offer a model for ambitious churchmen of later generations, particularly in the Carolingian period, though there is reason to believe that its function shifted from being a prelude to catechism to being all that was left of the catechism itself. For the children born to Christian families – those who did not come to the faith through conversion – there is no record of formal instruction in the early medieval period.[27] But this does not mean, of course, that there is no evidence for transmission of Christian ideas to the faithful. We will see below that hagiography may have taken over as the medium through which Christian 'content' was rehearsed for both new and hereditary members of the faith.

* * *

With this in mind, let us return to the *Passio Sebastiani*. Though the account purports to describe a martyrdom under Diocletian and Maximian, both of whom abdicated in 305, it is likely to have been written in the fifth or even the early sixth century. Therefore it is as a document of the imagination, rather than of the historical record, that it concerns us. Like the other *gesta martyrum*, martyr romances written

25 *De catechizandis rudibus*, 5.9, trans. and cit. Kreider, 'Changing Patterns', 32.

26 Kreider, 'Changing Patterns', 32, based on *De catechizandis rudibus*, 13.18 and 16.25–25.49.

27 Kreider, 'Changing Patterns', 41.

after the age of Constantine, the *Passio Sebastiani* has received little or no attention from scholars concerned with conversion and the miraculous in early Christianity. This is perhaps because there is an obvious time lapse of at least a century in these accounts between the author's day and that of the events recounted. The texts cannot, therefore, be read as an unmediated reflection of pre-Constantinian realities. But the process of mediation by which a fifth- or early sixth-century writer attempted to understand the heroism of Diocletian's generation holds a clue, it will be argued below, to the wider problem of how ancient and medieval Christians perceived the age which they understood as the great age of conversion.

There has long been a consensus among scholars and theologians that the post-Constantinian *passiones* of the martyrs were the product of fertile literary imaginations, based in at least some instances on names remembered in undifferentiated lists of the martyred handed down through the churches. The details of these texts are in all likelihood the product of invention, a point recognized by the Bollandist attempts to sift 'fact' from 'fiction' in the lives of the saints. Influential here has been Hippolyte Delehaye's maxim, drawing on Gregory the Great, that there is only one life of the saints, of which individual lives are mere instances. But however shaped by the forces of pious invention, the *gesta martyrum* served as one of the most important fora in which Christian thinkers could explore the historical process through which the Empire had become Christian.[28] It seems appropriate, therefore, to leave in suspension the question of whether the *gesta* are an accurate reflection of pre-Constantinian events, and to focus instead on how they reflect the concerns of post-Constantinian writers and audiences. Instead of seeing an ethical or rational approach to faith as standing in tension with belief in the miraculous, it is the ethical dimensions of the miraculous that the *Passio Sebastiani* stressed, reflecting the miraculous intervention in history that was the rise of Christendom. Signs and wonders were there to be found not only in the *virtutes* – the acts of miraculous power – but in the ethical life to which Christians were called, the every-day miracle of Christian fellowship, and the Word made flesh in the person not only of Jesus but of his saints.

In telling the story of Sebastian's career, from the time he is discovered as a Christian until his death and burial, the *Passio Sebastiani* shows

28 On the *gesta* as a response to earlier Christian literature, see Kate Cooper, *The Virgin and the Bride: Idealized Womanhood in Late Antiquity* (Cambridge, MA, 1996), 116–19.

a deep imaginative engagement with the problem of preaching and conversion, and with the effects of Christian belief on the household, both Christian and pagan. The *passio* centres on a sequence of conversions, and in each instance the new convert has a different constellation of family relationships which must be re-constituted in light of the conversion. What is noteworthy here is that it is not necessarily the *paterfamilias* who converts first, carrying his dependents along with him (although this paradigm is indeed present). Rather, different families are reached through 'first contact' with different members of the household.

The story opens with Sebastian, a military commander favoured by the emperors, giving solace to two Christian *viri inlustri*, the twins Marcus and Marcellianus, who have been imprisoned along with their slaves on the charge of being Christian. Their families obtain a stay of thirty days from the Urban Prefect, Agrestius Chromatius, in the hope that through pity or persuasion their wives and children can sway the young men to give up their folly. The *passio* thus takes up the conversion theme with the Christian twins attempting to hold firm in their conviction against the entreaties of their friends on behalf of their family responsibilities – the parents, wives, and children whom their death will leave bereft. In the face of persecution, the friends argue, it is the young men's responsibility to give up the faith, return to their homes, and fulfil their obligations. The *passio* emphasises the difficulty of holding firm in the face of this kind of pleading in greater detail than do any of the pre-Constantinian martyr *acta*, even the well-known prison diary of Vibia Perpetua which recounts at some length her father's pleas that she take pity on his grey head.

This leads to a verbal sparring match in which the families are pitted against Sebastian, who wins the day with his praise for the joys of eternity over the fleeting pleasures of this life. What saves the men from giving in to pity is the constant preaching of Sebastian, who reminds them again and again of how brief their earthly sufferings – and those of their families – will be, and how great their rejoicing in the realms of eternal light. There is uncertainty whether their father Tranquillinus and mother Marcia will follow the twins Marcus and Marcellianus to the faith, but they eventually do. Sebastian begins to have his effect first in the conversion of Zoe, the wife of the official in whose home the young men are held under arrest, and eventually on sixty-eight men and women gathered in the house, many of them future martyrs of Rome.

While the twins are imprisoned, Sebastian comes to preach to them and those gathered around them. The speech is accompanied by miraculous signs:

> for almost an hour he was illuminated by a tremendous light coming from Heaven. And beneath this very splendour, he was covered in an entirely white mantle by seven most bright angels. And a youth appeared next to him, giving him peace and saying, 'You will always be with me'.[29]

Sebastian then begins to heal the sick. First Zoe, who has been mute for six years. Sebastian says,

> If I am a true servant of Christ, and if everything was true which this woman heard and believed from my mouth, let my Lord Jesus Christ command that the faculty of speech should return to her, and let Him who opened the mouth of the prophet Zaccariah open her mouth.[30]

Zoe's first words are, 'blessed are you, and well-spoken is the sermon of your mouth!' The point here is that Zoe's miraculous speech echoes and reinforces that of Sebastian. The healing itself stands as a proof of the validity of Sebastian's preaching, a test of his status as a channel of divine power that is passed with flying colours. But the healing breaks Zoe's silence, and her miraculous echo amplifies the power of the martyr's word. Thus the miracle serves as spiritual punctuation to seal Sebastian's truth.

Zoe's confession of faith leads immediately to a development that seems to reflect the relational conversion pattern discussed by Stark. 'Moreover Nicostratus, her husband, when he saw that such was the virtue of Christ in his solemn wife, began to turn his feet towards Sebastian'.[31] Nicostratus then makes a speech to the young men who have been imprisoned in his house, asking to be allowed to hide them

29 *Passio Sebastiani* 23 (*ActaSS*, II Ian., 268): 'per unam fere horam splendore nimio de caelo veniente illuminatus est, & sub ipso splendore, candidissimo pallio amictus est ab angelis septem clarissimis, & iuvenis apparuit iuxta eum dans ei pacem, & dicens: Tu semper mecum eris'.

30 *Passio Sebastiani* 24 (ibid.): 'Tunc B. Sebastianus dixit: Si ego verus Christi servus sum, & si vera sunt omnia, quae ex ore meo haec mulier audivit & credidit, iubeat Dominus meus Iesus Christus, ut redeat ad eam officium linguae, & aperiat os eius qui aperuit os Zachariae Prophetae sui; & fecit crucem in os eius. Atque ad hanc vocem S. Sebastiani, exclamavit mulier voce magna, dicens: Beatus es tu, & benedictus sermo oris tui . . .'.

31 *Passio Sebastiani* 24 (ibid.).

or better yet to suffer in their stead. The twins respond with praise for his alacrity: '. . . your faith has arisen from the Master, and everything which an education of many years could scarcely confer, you have learned in the space of an hour'.[32] It should not go unnoticed that Nicostratus has in fact given no evidence whatever that he is aware of the 'content' of the Christian faith, and indeed there is no indication that he was present while Sebastian preached in his house.

With the next conversions, however, we seem to be squarely in MacMullen territory. When another high official, Claudius the *commentariensis*, converts, not only does he bring along his two sons for healing, but he is accompanied by his wife and extended family for baptism. Meanwhile, Nicostratus brings to the font thirty-three members of his own household. The model of conversion at play here is clearly that of the head of household who speaks for the members of his entourage – despite the fact that Nicostratus, of course, has been guided by the example of his wife. Tranquillinus, the father of Marcellianus and Marcus, converts too, this time in response to the example of his Christian sons. This represents a radical departure from his role as a Roman *paterfamilias* – in adopting the conviction of his sons, Tranquillinus has allowed youth to guide age rather than being guided by the older man's wisdom and authority. But in responding with alacrity to the revelation brought by his sons, Tranquillinus has shown that his wisdom is great indeed.

When the thirty days are over, the young men are brought before the urban prefect Agrestius Chromatius with whom we began. Now Tranquillinus must give account for his sons, and for his own performance in delivering them from their Christian superstition. When Chromatius asks Tranquillinus whether his sons are ready to offer sacrifice, Tranquillinus replies by revealing that he has converted to Christianity.

The conversation turns to a sparring match between the two men, with Chromatius accusing Tranquillinus of insanity and Tranquillinus boasting his good health of soul and body. Then Tranquillinus begins to extemporize on the failings of paganism as a religious system, followed by a debate between the two men over whether the histories of Livy show that the Gods failed to protect the Empire from attack even in the days where traditional cult was perfomed with care and precision. The scene seems intended almost as a text-book example of

32 *Passio Sebastiani* 26 (ibid., 269).

elite conversion, with two literate aristocrats testing each other's knowledge of Roman history and Roman ethics.

Chromatius is finally worn down by an elaborate explication of the metaphor of the soul as a ring lost in a sewer, which of course represents the body. (The irony that Sebastian's own body will be thrown into Rome's great sewer, the Cloaca Maxima, will not have been lost on the *Passio*'s audience.) Chromatius offers to pay Tranquillinus for his healing, but Tranquillinus tells him that his body can only be healed once his mind turns to the Truth. He then asks that Sebastian be brought to him. Once it becomes clear, however, that Chromatius intends to convert along with his son, Sebastian warns against an attempt to abuse his powers.

> Look to it lest you wish to be made a Christian, having been led only by the recuperation of your body. Rather let you make your mind pure so that you can see the reason for the truth. For unless you recognize who your Creator is, you will not be able to find the health which you seek.[33]

It is important to notice that despite the fact that he is speaking to the Urban Prefect of the city of Rome, one of the highest officials in the empire, Sebastian is precisely dealing here with the issue of conversion for the sake of access to advantages offered by membership in the faith community – that access to miraculous healing, once its efficacy is accepted, stands as a symbol for the benefits of belonging which Augustine and Stark saw important as a motivation within the conversion process. In the eyes of the *Passio*, MacMullen's distinction between 'elite' and 'mass' conversion wears thin indeed.

With this in mind, our final thoughts will be about the verbal and narrative characteristics of the martyr's preaching as represented in the *Passio*. The moment of 'ventriloquism', as I have called it – in which the martyr is portrayed as speaking with divine power or authority – is reflected in two distinct kinds of speech. The first type is that in which the speaker summarizes large swathes of information about the Christian faith drawn from biblical or liturgical sources, often using specialist vocabulary. This speech type resembles nothing so much as Augustine's *narratio*, the 'summary of the Faith' to which aspiring catechumens were to be treated before being admitted to formal

33 *Passio Sebastiani* 51 (ibid., 273).

instruction. The *narratio* rehearses the 'meaning' of the Christian tradition, over and over again for an audience who might well encounter the *Passio* annually on the feast day of the saint. It may be useful to understand the martyr's speech in this mode as an idealized account of conversion preaching, one which set in motion a 'feedback loop' involving the audience who would have heard or read the text.[34] In this sense, repeated exposure to the hagiographical narratives around Sebastian and the other Roman martyrs would have performed a function similar to the renewal of baptismal vows, reminding the Christian laity or monastic communities of the terms of the faith – or even instructing afresh those who were new to Christian belonging.

The second mode reflects a concern for 'plain speech', using short paratactic constructions and unpretentious vocabulary. The staccato effect of these short speeches is striking, and they often occur at the climactic moment of conversion or healing.[35] Both the words of miraculous power of the martyr and the words of confession by the newly healed or converted can take this form: the staccato speech can function as trigger or as punctuation. The staccato speeches give a vivid illustration of the power of the Christian word – often phrased in language drawn directly from the words of Jesus – which seems keyed to what is possibly a new concern to reach audiences with sharp and lively phrasing, in a way comparable to what can be seen in contemporary sermons.

To say that the miraculous was perceived as 'causing' belief, however, is not entirely accurate, because belief in turn was understood as a source of miraculous power. Early medieval writers were deeply interested in what they perceived as a synergy between God's extra-human agency and His ability to act through human beings. Their belief only whetted their interest in understanding the social structure of this process, and the post-Constantinian martyr narratives offer

[34] This point will be understood more clearly if and when a scholarly consensus emerges regarding the audience for the *gesta*: on this problem see now Clare Pilsworth, 'Reading the Roman Martyrs: Rome, Campania and the Case of Paris, Bibliothèque Nationale 12634 + St. Petersburg Q V I 5', in Kate Cooper and Julia Hillner, eds, *Dynasty, Patronage, and Lay Authority in a Christian City: Rome, c.350–850* (forthcoming).

[35] For comparanda, see Stanley Tambiah, 'The Magical Power of Words', *Man* 3 (1968), 177–206; P. L. Ravenhill, 'Religious Utterances and the Theory of Speech Acts', in W. J. Samarin, ed., *Languages in Religious Practice* (Rowley, MA, 1976), 26–39; Patricia Cox Miller, 'In Praise of Nonsense', in A. Hilary Armstrong, ed., *World Spirituality*, Vol. 15: *Classical Mediterranean Spirituality* (New York, 1986), 481–505.

direct evidence for their attempt to do so. Indeed, the belief of the miracle's recipient and the *virtus* or miraculous power of the martyr or holy man created a sort of virtuous circle in early Christian narrative, one whose force was amplified by the dynamics of narrative and representation when the story was re-told to a new audience.[36]

With this in mind, it may be appropriate to see the two types of speech proposed by the *Passio Sebastiani* as reflecting two different and complementary strategies vis-à-vis the *Passio*'s intended audience. The attempt to compress substantial Christian content into a summary which could bear frequent repetition must have served, in an extended way, a function not dissimilar to the liturgical repetition of the Creed. By contrast, the sharp and vivid language of the staccato speeches may have been designed to serve as a catalyst toward a new level of engagement – relationship might be a better word – with God through his saints. This may well echo a distinction made by Augustine between what he called 'the long, twisting lanes of speech' in the here and now[37] and the epiphany of discourse that will be possible in the heavenly Jerusalem.[38] (The *locus classicus* of this latter mode of eschatologically charged, transparent communication among Christians is Augustine's account in Book Nine of the *Confessions* of his conversation with Monica at Ostia just before her death.) The *Passio Sebastiani* can be said to make its own contribution to the post-Augustinian discussion of Christian *disciplina* by offering a distinction between what might be called credal and eschatological modes of didactic speech.

To be sure, the textual strategies of the *Passio* engage with a wider change in the attitude to rhetoric and authority during this period. Christians in late fifth- and early sixth-century Italy were deeply concerned by the difficulty of attaining in their speech what one writer called *puritatis index loquella*, 'the small voice which is the measure of purity'.[39] Sources as diverse as the *Rule of Saint Benedict* and the anony-

36 In a forthcoming essay on twelfth-century English miracle narratives, Simon Yarrow reminds us that 'the miracle is performed each time it is retold': 'The Negotiation of Community in Twelfth-Century English Miracle Narratives', in Kate Cooper and Jeremy Gregory, eds, *Elite and Popular Religion*, Studies in Church History 42 (Woodbridge, 2006), citing M. Gilsenan, *Recognizing Islam: Religion and Society in the Modern Middle East* (London, 1982, repr. 2000), 75.

37 The phrase is from *De catechizandis rudibus*, 10, 15, as cited in Peter Brown, *Augustine of Hippo* (London, 1967), 161.

38 This Augustinian binary, taken up by Gregory the Great, is discussed in Conrad Leyser, *Asceticism and Authority from Augustine to Gregory the Great* (Oxford, 2000), 177–81.

39 *Liber ad Gregoriam*, 4, ed. G. Morin, in *Etudes, texts, découvertes* (Paris, 1913), 383–439, 389, repr. in PL Supplement 3, 221–56.

mous *Handbook for Gregoria* written for a married laywoman, both probably from early sixth-century central Italy, attest that monks and married ladies alike habitually measured the number and tone of their words. By this means they showed themselves practitioners of the *sermo humilitatis*, the unpretentious style of speech that marked them as linguistic democrats.[40] In doing so, they stood as rebels against a Latin tradition which measured every syllable as an identifier of class, region, and literary accomplishment – or lack of it. A puritan aesthetic of the plain was emerging in devotional literature, so much so that Eugippius of Lucullanum, writing around 511 to the Roman deacon Paschasius to introduce his *Life* of the holy man Severinus, finds it difficult to refrain from boasting about his own inability to emulate the 'high style' of a fashionable *Life of Bassus* written by a learned layman of his day, known to Eugippius and now lost.[41]

In the world of monastic spirituality, anxiety that words of instruction should have the greatest possible impact on their listeners ran especially high, and again we see recourse to the idea of God speaking directly through his chosen intermediary. The preface to the anonymous *Regula Magistri*, for example, composed in central Italy around 500,[42] proposes a view of divine inspiration for the anonymous Master's teaching similar to the 'ventriloquist' passage of the *Passio Sebastiani* with which we began.[43] This is all the more significant when we remember that the *Regula Magistri*'s citations from the *Passio Sebastiani* offer what is in fact our earliest evidence for the latter text's composition.

This cluster of early sixth-century central Italian sources may well

40 Leyser, *Asceticism and Authority*, 59–61, with a summary of secondary literature since Eric Auerbach's *Literary Language and its Public in Late Antiquity*, trans. R. Mannheim (London, 1965).

41 On the relation between this text and the *Gesta martyrum*, see Kate Cooper, 'The Widow as Impresario: the Widow Barbaria in Eugippius' *Vita Severini*', in Walter Pohl and Maximilian Diesenberger, eds, *Eugippius und Severinus: Der Autor, der Text, und der Heilige* (Vienna, 2000), 53–64.

42 For discussion of the date and authorship of the *Regula Magistri*, see Leyser, *Asceticism and Authority*, 103, 108–17.

43 This is seen in the opening of the Rule, 'O homo, primo tibi qui legis, deinde et tibi qui me auscultas dicentem, dimitte alia modo quae cogitas, et me tibi loquentem et per os meum Deum te convenientem cognosce' (Prologus, 1), and again 'Et intellige tu, homo, cuius admonemus intuitum, quia te per hanc scribturam admonet Deus . . .' (Prologus, 16), *La Règle du maître* (vol. I, Prologue, Ch. 10), ed. Adalbert de Vogüé, SC 105 (Paris, 1964), 288 and 290.

reflect the concerns of a particular place and time, and yet the crucible of experience and experimentation from which all of these texts seem to emerge can be said to have had a far-reaching impact on Latin Christianity. Both the *Rule of Saint Benedict* and of *gesta martyrum* themselves, which stood as the pattern for subsequent Latin hagiography, exerted virtually immeasurable influence on the development of Latin devotional literature.

* * *

Attempts to understand the social function of religious ideas have traditionally been associated with reductionism and demystification – and indeed, as we saw in the case of Hume, the association has sometimes been significant. But as a result functional analysis is often dismissed with assertions that belief was 'genuine' or that motivations were 'religious' – as if this meant that genuine religious ideas and practices therefore had no social dimension. In the present case, we have seen that Hume and the author of the *Passio Sebastiani* had equal and opposite motivations for reflecting on the validity of second-hand knowledge where the supernatural was concerned, but both were deeply interested in the mechanics of the matter. Similarly, Rodney Stark and Augustine of Hippo have been shown to share a deep interest in whether or not new members of a religious community are likely to understand its 'ground rules' – though again for different reasons.

The present contribution has drawn on a functionalist analytical framework, with functionalism understood as the view that ideas are embedded socially in a communication system, through which individuals may attempt to influence – or even to control – one another's behaviour. Ideas in turn have been understood as being brought into play to encourage some tendencies and discourage others. We have assumed here that the charge of reductionism against functionalist analysis is ultimately a misdirected charge. Indeed, wrote Mary Douglas in 1970, 'the possibilities of functional analysis have not been exhausted. Like Christian ethics, it can be defended against its critics on the grounds that it has never really been tried'.[44]

Historically, we have tried to suggest, the most adept practitioners of structural-functional analysis have in fact been the historical agents themselves, the individuals charged with responsibility for institutions

44 Mary Douglas, 'Introduction', *Witchcraft Confessions and Accusations*, ASA Monographs 9 (London, 1970), xxv.

and communities. Within Christian discourse this desideratum of orchestrating energies and resources has usually been classed under the concept of stewardship. In this guise, what might be called 'pastoral functionalism' reflects the pragmatic thinking of religious leaders as they attempt to steer community members to direct their effort where it will be perceived as doing most good, or as 'multiplying' the efforts of others. 'Good stewards' have always engaged in functional analysis not because they do not 'believe', but because they do. Since institutional resources in Late Antiquity and the early middle ages were of course unimaginably slim by modern standards, the effort to foster even a rudimentary social continuity required as much ideological reinforcement as could be mustered.

Perhaps the greatest 'pastoral functionalist' within the Christian tradition was Augustine, who reminds us in Book 19 of the *City of God* that even robbers must attempt to establish peace among themselves – that even in the most dysfunctional corner of the social order, human beings will and must seek a basis of complicity within which to build structures of reciprocal obligation and mutual assistance, however doomed those structures may be to compromise and even failure. That Christians should use theological ideas to reinforce such structures was a matter of pastoral urgency. But Augustine knew well that motivation and even 'belief' were slippery to measure.

The approach to speech and the miraculous in the *Passio Sebastiani* may also reveal something about changing attitudes to Christian belonging and Christian conversion across our period. It has been suggested, as we saw above, that the generations after Constantine saw a progressive down-grading in the meaning of conversion, which is to say in the kind and quality of exposure to Christian teaching that could be expected in a convert presented for baptism. It may be, too, that the terms of Christian membership were changing in another sense, which is to say that the social function of Christian networks took on an enhanced importance as one by one the other established structures of reciprocity in the late and post-Roman period came under attack.

This leaves us, finally, with a paradox. In the fifth- or early sixth-century Italy of the *Passio Sebastiani*, to posit an opposition between a Christianity of ethical values and a Christianity comparatively poor in content but based on the more primitive value of allegiance, of *belonging*, is finally to miss the point. For the imaginative landscape of the *Passio Sebastiani* is one in which belonging *is* ethics. New and compelling forms of belonging, forms guaranteed by the

Word and its miraculous powers, emerge in the *Passio* as a new strategy of defence for the endangered social bonds of reciprocity and authority, as a ray of hope for the survival of a fragile world.

University of Manchester

THE DIABOLICAL POWER OF LETTUCE, OR GARDEN MIRACLES IN GREGORY THE GREAT'S *DIALOGUES*

by BARBARA MÜLLER

GREGORY the Great wrote his *Dialogues* between July 593 and October 594.[1] Like most scholars of Gregory the Great, I am convinced that the *Dialogues* are a genuine Gregorian work and do not share Francis Clark's opinion that the *Dialogues* are the rather clumsy product of a later forger.[2] The *Dialogues* are an extremely complex work on holiness, a skilful pastoral pedagogy, and a programme of mission as well. They contain Gregory's ideal of the Church which he developed during a time of crisis.[3] Some elements may even seem to be utopian.

Several of the miracle stories which Gregory presents in his *Dialogues* are set in gardens; some holy men are gardeners, do garden work or are concerned with gardens. In my perception Gregory used the motifs of the garden and the gardener as symbols to describe the ideal church leaders and their duties.[4] However, Gregory's gardens and gardeners should not exclusively be seen as metaphors. They are at the same time very real landscapes and actual people who are doing garden work.[5]

1 *Dialogorum libri quatuor seu De miraculis patrum italicorum*: Grégoire le Grand, *Dialogues*, ed. with French transl. Adalbert de Vogüé, 3 vols, SC 251, 260 and 265 (Paris, 1978–80) [hereafter: Greg.M., dial. (SC)] and Saint Gregory the Great, *Dialogues*, English transl. Odo J. Zimmermann (Washington, DC, 1959), from which quotations will be extracted for this article.

2 Francis Clark, *The Pseudo-Gregorian Dialogues*, 2 vols (Leiden, 1987); idem, *The 'Gregorian' Dialogues and the Origins of Benedictine Monasticism* (Leiden and Boston, MA, 2003).

3 According to Clark, *Pseudo-Gregorian Dialogues*, 1: 304 and 2: 450–1, the lettuce story [Greg.M., dial. I,4,7 (SC 260: 42–4)] is not of Gregorian origin as Equitius's 'marvellous activity' contradicts the 'inserted Gregorian passage' 5 [I,4,9 (SC 260: 46)] with its focus on grace. Clark misses the point of the story, which is God's power and not the supernatural power of an individual. In discussing a typical story of Gregory's *Dialogues* and showing it to be representative of Gregory's central concerns, my paper will also contribute to confirming the authenticity of the *Dialogues*.

4 Cf. Grégoire le Grand, *Règle Pastorale*, ed. with French transl. B. Judic, SC 381 and 382, 2 vols (Paris, 1992) [hereafter Greg.M., past. (SC)], III,25 (SC 382: 432).

5 On the topography of the *Dialogues*, cf. Georg Jenal, *Italia ascetica atque monastica: Das Asketen- und Mönchtum in Italien von den Anfängen bis zur Zeit der Langobarden (ca. 150/250–604)*, 2 vols (Stuttgart, 1995), 1: 192–214.

* * *

In many respects the following story is quite typical for other Gregorian miracle stories set in gardens:

> One day a nun of this same convent on entering the garden, found some lettuce (*lactucam*) there which appealed to her taste. Forgetting to say the customary blessing, she began to eat of it greedily. Immediately the Devil threw her to the ground in a fit of pain. The other nuns, seeing her in agony, quickly sent word to Abbot Equitius to come with all speed and help them with his prayers. As soon as the holy man entered the garden, the Devil, using the nun's voice, began to justify himself. 'I haven't done anything!' he kept shouting. 'I haven't done anything! I was sitting here on the lettuce when she came and ate me!' Full of indignation, the man of God commanded him to depart and vacate the place he held in this handmaid of almighty God. The Devil did so at once and after that could no longer exercise his powers over her.[6]

The garden of the lettuce story belongs to a monastery.[7] Gregory had a deep sympathy for the monastic life. He lived as a monk before he was elected pope. After his election he suffered from nostalgia for the quiet monastic life, as we can read, for example, in the prologue of his *Dialogues*.[8] However, as time went by he found ways to cope with his busy life without totally giving up his beloved contemplation. Still, the monastery always remained a perfect place for Gregory, and his best friends and most trustworthy bishops were monks.[9] So, it is not by accident that most of the miracles set in gardens or worked by gardeners are linked to the monastic life.

In our lettuce story the monastic garden is the place where the spiritual hero, abbot Equitius, and the devil fight. They represent the fight between good and evil. The monastic garden symbolises paradise,

6 Greg.M., dial. I,4,7 (SC 260: 42–4); cf. Palladius (monachus), *Historia Lausiaca* 38, 12: Palladio, *La storia Lausiaca*, ed. with Italian transl. G. J. M. Bartelink, *Vite dei Santi 2* (4th edn, Milan, 1990), 202 and the *Historia monachorum in Aegypto* 20,17: *L'Histoire des moines en Egypte*, ed. A. Festugière, Subsidia Hagiographica 53 (Brussels, 1961), 123.

7 On the history of the monastic garden, see Paul Meyvaert, 'The Medieval Monastic Garden', in Elisabeth Blair MacDougall, ed., *Medieval Gardens, 9th Dumbarton Oaks Colloquium on the History of Landscape Architecture, 1983* (Washington, DC, 1986), 23–53.

8 Greg.M., dial. I, prol. 3 (SC 260: 12).

9 For example abbot Probus, abbot Claudius, Peter the Deacon (the interlocutor of the *Dialogues*), bishop Maximian of Syracuse, bishop Marinian of Ravenna.

which the devil tries to conquer.[10] It is therefore a place of temptation.[11] There is another garden miracle where the paradisical character of the garden is even more obvious. It is the story of a holy man who used to work as a gardener of a monastery in Fondi.[12] This gardener caught a thief of vegetables with the help of a serpent that used to live in the garden of the monastery. The scenery, with its garden and the serpent, is obviously reminiscent of the biblical paradise described in the book of Genesis.[13]

The gardener's power over the serpent and Equitius's power over the devil identifies them both as holy men in a status of primordial purity. In the monastic tradition this status is called 'being like an angel'.[14] The counterpart to Equitius is the nun who was defeated by the devil. Typically for Gregory there are two main levels of actors: on one side, the leaders or rulers like Equitius, and on the other side, the submitted and dependent like the nun.[15] Gregory had a very hierarchical perception of society which runs throughout his works. This is also the case in the lettuce story: it is mainly a story about the spiritual power of Equitius whose successful healing testifies to and exemplifies his virtue and ultimately the power of God.[16]

Equitius was a 'free-lance preacher' and founder of several monasteries in the province of Valeria.[17] Gregory describes him as a charis-

10 The garden as paradise: C. Schneider, 'Garten', *Reallexikon für Antike und Christentum* 8 (1972), 1058–9; John Prest, *The Garden of Eden: the Botanic Garden and the Re-Creation of Paradise* (New Haven, CT, and London, 1981), 118–26.

11 Cf. Meyvaert, 'Garden', 50–1.

12 Greg.M., dial. I,3 (SC 260: 34–6); cf. Gregory of Tours, *Liber vitae patrum*, ed. B. Krusch, MGH, Scriptorum rerum Merovingicarum [hereafter: MGH.SRM] I,2 (Hannover, 1885), 14,2: 719; Ps. Venantius Fortunatus, *Vita sancti Amantii* 6, in *Venantii Fortunati opera pedestria*, ed. B. Krusch, MGH, Auctores Antiquissimorum [hereafter: MGH.AA] IV,2 (Berlin, 1885), 59–60 and idem, *Vita sancti Medardi* 4, ibid., 69.

13 Gen. 2, 8 and 3, 1. Cf. E. Bertaud, 'Hortus', *DSp* VII.1 (1969), 766–7.

14 Greg.M., dial. III,15,13 (SC 260: 322). Angelic examples of the Egyptian tradition: Arsenios 42 (PG 65, 105D–108B); Silvanos 12 (PG 65, 412C). Cf. K. Suso Frank, *ANGELIKOS BIOS. Begriffsanalytische und begriffsgeschichtliche Untersuchung zum 'engelgleichen Leben' im frühen Mönchtum* (Münster, 1964).

15 Greg.M., past. II,6 (SC 381: 202–4).

16 On the different addressees of the *Dialogues*: S. Boesch Gajano, 'Dislivelli culturali e mediazioni ecclesiastiche nei *Dialogi* di Gregorio Magno', *Quaderni storici* 41 (1979), 398–415.

17 Robert Markus, *Gregory the Great and His World* (Cambridge, 1997), 67. On Equitius: G. Marinangeli, 'Equizio Amiternino e il suo movimento monastico', *Bullettino della deputazione abruzzese di storia patria* 64 (1974), 281–343; idem, 'Influssi "Equiziani" nel monastero Gregoriano "ad Clivum Scauri"?', ibid. 71 (1981), 57–84; C. Rivera, 'Per la storia dei precursori di san Benedetto nella Provincia Valeria', *Bullettino dell'Istituto storico italiano e archivio muratoriano* 47 (1932), 25–49.

matic preacher of high spiritual authority and a rather unprepossessing rustic figure.[18] Like Equitius most of Gregory's garden heroes are monks. There is the simple anonymous garden monk,[19] the immigrated Syrian hermit Isaak[20] as well as the famous monastic father Benedict of Nursia.[21] Some of the garden miracle workers are bishops, amongst them the highly cultivated bishop Paulinus of Nola.[22]

In Gregory's garden miracles the holy man, or holy gardener, and his spiritual power and actions are the central part of the event. Hence, in Gregory's *Dialogues* we cannot find stories of the kind we read in Augustine's *City of God*. Here people are healed from blindness and paganism by the mere touch of flowers that had touched the relics of the glorious martyr Stephen.[23] Gregory's contemporary Gregory of Tours tells similar stories.[24] But in Gregory the Great's garden stories the plants or gardens are always linked to living holy men – and not to dead ones. This reflects Gregory's preference for living holy men over dead holy men or martyrs.[25]

18 Greg.M., dial. I,4 (SC 260: 38–58).

19 Neither the *Regula magistri* nor the *Regula Benedicti* mention a special office of a gardener. An early mention of a *hortulanus* can be found in Isidore's rule: Isidore of Sevilla, *Regula monachorum* 21, in *Santos Padres Españoles*, 2: San Leandro, San Isidoro, San Fructuoso, *Reglas monásticas de la España visigoda. Los tres libros de las 'Sentencias'*, ed. with Spanish transl. J. Campos Ruiz and I. Roca Melia (Madrid, 1971), 121. However, Meyvaert, 'Garden', 29, suggests that 'We can assume that throughout the Middle Ages each monastery had its own *hortulanus*, who was also a monk of the community'.

20 Greg.M., dial. III,14,6–7 (SC 260: 306–8).

21 Greg.M., dial. I,3 (SC 260: 34–6); II,6,1 (SC 260: 154–6); II,8,4 (SC 260: 162); II,8,11 (SC 260: 168); II,32,1–2 (SC 260: 226–8).

22 Bishop Bonifatius of Ferentis: Greg.M., dial. I,9 (SC 260: 88); Paulinus of Nola: III,1 (SC 260: 256–66). Gregory's story on Paulinus is set in Italy during the invasion of the Vandals, that is after 455. At this time the famous Paulinus of Nola (†431) had been dead for more than 20 years; cf. de Vogüé's note on Greg.M., dial. I,1 (SC 260: 256). Paulinus was very interested in gardening: in his letters he calls God *caelestis agricola, diligens hortulanus* and he perceives the soul as the *hortum animae nostrae* [Paulinus of Nola, *Epistulae*, ed. G. de Hartel and M. Kamptner, CSEL 29.1 (2nd edn, Vienna, 1999), ep. 39,6: 338 and ep. 44,6: 377 respectively].

23 Augustine of Hippo, *De ciuitate dei libri uiginti duo*, ed. B. Dombart and A. Kalb, CChr.SL 47 and 48, 2 vols (Turnhout, 1955) [hereafter: Aug., ciu. (CChr.SL)], 22,8 (CChr.SL 48: 821–2).

24 Gregory of Tours, *Liber in gloria martyrum*, ed. B. Krusch, MGH.SRM I,2 (Hannover, 1885), 70: 535; idem, *Liber de passione et virtutibus sancti Iuliani martyris*, ibid., 582–3.

25 For example, Greg.M., dial. II,16,1 (SC 260: 184–6). On Gregory's ideal of the man of God: G. Cracco, 'Uomini di Dio e uomini di chiesa nell'alto medioevo', *Ricerche di storia sociale e religiosa*, ns, 12 (1977), 163–202; idem, 'Ascesi e ruolo dei "Viri Dei" nell'Italia di Gregorio Magno', in *Hagiographie, cultures et sociétés, IVe–XIIe siècles. Actes du Colloque organisé à Nanterre et à Paris, 2–5 mai 1979* (Paris, 1981), 283–97; William D. McCready, *Signs of Sanctity: Miracles in the Thought of Gregory the Great* (Toronto, 1989), 89–90. For a comparison with the

* * *

In the lettuce story the miracle consists in the healing of a possessed nun. What other miracles occur in gardens? There is a miraculous removing of a rock in order to plant a small garden.[26] On the intervention of Benedict, the iron blade of a brush-hook used in the garden, which had fallen into a lake, rose from the bottom of the lake and slipped back onto the handle.[27] Furthermore an evil priest is crushed to death after having tried to destroy the souls of Benedict's disciples by sending seven naked women into the garden of Benedict's monastery.[28] Bishop Paulinus of Nola, when working temporarily as a gardener in Africa, prophesies the death of the king.[29] And there is the miraculous production of wine out of only a few grapes achieved by bishop Bonifatius of Ferentis.[30] Besides these clearly supernatural events, there are also less spectacular miracles like the change of attitude of thieves and the loss of arrogance of a servant of a Roman cleric.[31]

Most of Gregory's garden miracles are induced in a quite unspectacular way. Mostly, as in the case of Equitius and the nun, the miracle worker is simply praying.[32] In this way, Gregory stresses the divine origin of miracles strongly.[33] The part of the miracle workers consists primarily in believing in and asking for God's help and in showing humility and love towards the neighbour. The most spectacular example of self-denial is probably that of bishop Paulinus of Nola, who voluntarily lets himself be handed over into slavery to work as a gardener from then on.[34]

Gesta martyrum and Gregory of Tours: Joan M. Petersen, *The Dialogues of Gregory the Great in their Late Antique Cultural Background* (Toronto, 1984), 56–89 and 122–41.

26 Greg.M., dial. I,7,2 (SC 260: 66–8).

27 Greg.M., dial. II,6,1–2 (SC 260: 154–6); cf. II,8,8 (SC 260: 164–6).

28 Greg.M., dial. II,8,4 (SC 260: 162). On the pagan background of this story, cf. J. Laporte, 'Saint Benoît et les survivances du paganisme', in René Louis, ed., *Etudes ligériennes d'histoire et d'archéologie médiévales. Mémoires et exposés présentés à la Semaine d'études médiévales de Saint-Benoît-sur-Loire du 3 au 10 juillet 1969* (Auxerre, 1975), 233–46, 238–40.

29 Greg.M., dial. III,1 (SC 260: 256–66).

30 Greg.M., dial. I,9,2–4 (SC 260: 76–80).

31 Greg.M., dial. I,4,13 (SC 260: 50), he was the servant of a Roman *defensor* of the unnamed pope who challenged Equitius's authority as a preacher; cf. Adalbert de Vogüé, 'Le Pape qui persécuta saint Equitius. Essai d'identification', *AnBoll* 100 (1982), 319–25.

32 Greg.M., dial. I,4,7 (SC 260: 44); I,7,2 (SC 260: 66). Celebrating nocturnal *laudes*: dial. III,14,6 (SC 260: 306).

33 The miracles show God's power: Greg.M., dial. III,22,4 (SC 260: 358).

34 Greg.M., dial. III,1–3 (SC 260: 256–60). Paulinus behaved like Christ in sacrificing himself: III,1,8 (SC 260: 264), cf. Phil. 2, 7. Christ as a gardener has its biblical origin in John 20, 15, cf. Gregory the Great, *Homiliae in Euangelia*, ed. R. Étaix, CChr.SL 141 (Turnhout, 1999) [hereafter: Greg.M., euang. (CChr.SL 141)], II,25,4: 209–10; *Sancti Augustini in Iohannis*

Paulinus's story shows that what we call a miracle – in his own case the prophecy of the king's death – is only one of the holy gardener's numerous qualities. More often, these shine through ordinary pastoral activities. For example, Isaak the hermit admonishes thieves kindly not to steal vegetables anymore.[35]

In Gregory's miracle stories the transition from the miraculous to the ordinary is fluid. This reflects Gregory's general theory of miracles,[36] namely that daily life is full of God's miracles.[37] However, most people are unable to perceive how wonderful the world actually is; instead they ask for supernatural signs.

Concerning the men of God, Gregory explains:

> One cannot conclude that there are no great saints just because no great miracles are worked. The true estimate of life, after all, lies in acts of virtue, not in the display of miracles. There are many . . . who without performing miracles, are not at all inferior to those who perform them.[38]

His examples are Peter and Paul: 'Peter walked on the water, whereas Paul was shipwrecked on high seas'; despite this difference, both apostles 'have an equal share in the rewards of heaven'.[39]

The power to perform miracles is one of the many qualities of a saint or a church leader – and it is not even the most important one. In Gregory's view, it is a greater achievement to convert a sinner than to resurrect the dead.[40] Accordingly, Gregory's garden heroes act mostly in *non*-supernatural ways. They cultivate vegetables,[41] they cut hay,[42] they

evangelium tractatus CXXIV, ed. D. R. Willems, CChr.SL 36 (Turnhout, 1954), 121,3: 666; idem, *Sermones ad populum*, PL 38, 996–1484: sermo 246,3, col. 1154.

35 Greg.M., dial. III,14,6–7 (SC 260: 306–8); I,3 (SC 260: 34–6).

36 Greg.M., dial. I,12,4 (SC 260: 116).

37 Greg.M., euang. II,26,12 (CChr.SL 141: 227–8). As in Augustine's *City of God* the reflections on miracles start with the resurrection, Aug., ciu. 22,8 (CCh.SL 48: 815); on Augustine's understanding of miracles, see Petersen, *Dialogues*, 91–4; McCready, *Signs of Sanctity*, 8–15.

38 Greg.M., dial. I,12,5 (SC 260: 116).

39 Ibid.

40 Greg.M., dial. III,17,7 (SC 260: 340).

41 Greg.M., dial. I,3,2–4 (SC 260: 34–6); III,1,4 (SC 260: 260).

42 Greg.M., dial. I,4,12–3 (SC 260: 50); cf. Gregory the Great, *Registrum epistularum*, ed. D. Norberg, CChr.SL 140 and 140A, 2 vols (Turnhout, 1982) [hereafter: Greg.M., ep. (CChr.SL)], ep. 10,16 (CChr.SL 140A: 844–5).

do field work or are concerned with the church's vineyard;[43] some holy men plan and construct gardens.[44]

There are two reasons for their garden and field work: first, it occurs out of pure necessity – in order to provide food for the monastery and for other needy people. In this sense, garden work is part of the daily work of a church leader, or, to say it in a more Gregorian way, of the active life of a *rector*. Secondly, garden work has a spiritual aim: it teaches young monks and other people how to do something. It provides ascetic, spiritual and moral education. The part of the chief gardener or the holy gardener consists in instructing the inexperienced workers in the garden.

In one story, bishop Bonifatius of Ferentis sets a custodian over the church's vineyards to keep watch. The description of the guard's task, namely to guard 'with efficient watchfulness (*sollerti uigilantia*)', is the same as that used when Gregory describes the profile of a good bishop in his pontifical letters.[45]

Gregory's *Dialogues* are also a programme of conversion and mission.[46] So, not surprisingly, we find Benedict of Nursia doing missionary garden work. He performed it when he went to Monte Cassino, where formerly 'stood a very old temple in which the ignorant country people still worshipped Apollo as the pagan ancestors had done, and went on offering superstitious and idolatrous sacrifices in groves dedicated to various demons'.[47] One of the first actions of the man of God was to 'cut down the trees in the sacred groves'.[48] Benedict

43 Greg.M., dial. II,31,1 (SC 260: 226); I,9,2 (SC 260: 76).

44 Greg.M., dial. I,7,2 (SC 260: 66–8); II,6,1 (SC 260: 154–6); III,14,6–7 (SC 260: 306–8).

45 Greg.M., dial. I,9,2 (SC 260: 76); ep. 13,12 (CChr.SL 140A: 1011); cf. euang. I,17,14 (CChr.SL 141: 128–9) and idem, *Expositio in canticum canticorum*, ed. P. Verbraken, CChr.SL 144 (Turnhout, 1963), 40: 39–40. The issue of the custodian (*custos*) is close to the very important Gregorian theme of the *speculator* (Ez. 3, 17–21; 33, 1–20), cf. Gregory's first sermon as a pope, preserved in Gregory of Tours, *Historiarum libri decem*, ed. B. Krusch and W. Levinson, MGH.SRM I,1 (2nd edn, Hannover, 1951), 10,1: 479–81, and later his Homilies on Ezekiel, esp. I,11,4–11: *Homiliae in Hieziechelem prophetam*, ed. M. Adriaen, CChr.SL 142 (Turnhout, 1971), 1704. On Gregory and Ezekiel, see also Conrad Leyser, '"Let Me Speak, Let Me Speak": Vulnerability and Authority in Gregory's *Homilies on Ezekiel*', *Studia Ephemeridis Augustinianum* 34 (1991), 169–82. Considering the wider tradition: Christine Mohrmann, 'Episkopos – speculator', in eadem, *Etudes sur le latin des chrétiens*, 4 vols (Rome, 1958–77), 4: 231–52.

46 Miracles happen mainly for those who do not yet believe: Greg.M., euang. I,4,3 (CChr.SL 141, 30); idem, *Moralia in Iob*, ed. M. Adriaen, CChr.SL 143, 143A and 143B, 3 vols (Turnhout, 1979–1985), 27,36 (CChr.SL 143B: 1358).

47 Greg.M., dial. II,8,10 (SC 260: 168); cf. Laporte, 'Saint Benoît', 241–3.

48 Greg.M., dial. II,8,10 (SC 260: 168).

transformed the pagan landscape inhabited by demons into a powerful Christian site. This, according to his Rule, most certainly will have included the construction of a garden.[49]

* * *

In Gregory's *Dialogues*, only one garden story shows traces of the old Roman ideal of the garden as the place of leisure and philosophical conversation. This story about bishop Paulinus of Nola represents a mid fifth-century situation.[50] Apparently for Gregory philosophical *otium* and its location in the topical *locus amoenus* belong to the past.[51] In the story of Paulinus the king's son-in-law often comes 'into the garden to inquire about various matters, and soon realised that his servant was a very wise man. Before long he began to neglect the companionship of his old friends for that of his new gardener, whose conversation he enjoyed so much'.[52]

However, despite Paulinus's philosophical talents, he is also partly doing ordinary garden work. In Gregory's gardens there is no spiritual teaching or philosophical conversation without digging up or growing vegetables. In this Gregory differs not only from Cicero's philosophical Roman horticultural ideal[53] and at least partly from Augustine's attitude towards philosophy and work.[54] He also differs from his closer

49 According to the *Regula Benedicti* 66,6, a garden belongs to 'all the necessary things' of the monastery: *La Règle de Saint Benoît*, ed. with French transl. A. de Vogüé and J. Neuville, SC 181 and 182, 2 vols (Paris, 1972) [hereafter: RB], 182: 660; further mentions of gardens: RB 7,63 (SC 181: 488); 46,1 (SC 182: 594).

50 Greg.M., dial. III,1 (SC 260: 256–66). For the dating cf. above, n. 22; on the Roman background: A. R. Littlewood, 'Ancient Literary Evidence for the Pleasure Gardens of Roman Country Villas', in Elisabeth Blair MacDougall, ed., *Ancient Roman Villa Gardens, 10th Dumbarton Oaks Colloquium on the History of Landscape Architecture, 1984* (Washington, DC, 1987), 7–30; and, more generally, M. Conan, 'Nature into Art: Gardens and Landscapes in the Everyday Life of Ancient Rome', *Journal of Garden History* 6 (1986), 348–56.

51 Hence, the *secretum locum* of the prologue, where Gregory mourns, is less an equivalent to the classical *locus amoenus* than a place where a cultural and personal loss is felt more strongly. In this sense, the *locus amoenus* itself is a lost place: Greg.M., dial. I, prol. 1 (SC 260: 10). On the history of *otium*, see Jean-Marie André, *L'Otium dans la vie morale et intellectuelle romaine, des origines à l'époque augustéenne* (Paris, 1966); on *locus amoenus*: Ernst Robert Curtius, *Europäische Literatur und lateinisches Mittelalter* (2nd edn, Bern, 1954), 202–6.

52 Greg.M., dial. III,1,4 (SC 260: 260).

53 Cf. Littlewood, 'Evidence', 11–13.

54 For example, Augustine of Hippo, *Confessionum libri tredecim*, ed. L. Verheijen, CChr.SL 27 (Turnhout, 1981), 8,12: 130; cf. especially the setting of his early *Dialogues*: *Contra academicos libri tres*, I,4, in *Sancti Aurelii Augustini Contra academicos, De beata vita, De ordine, De magistro, De libero arbitrio*, ed. W. M. Green and Kl. D. Daur, CChr.SL 29 (Turnhout, 1970), 5 and 9 (two passages); *De ordine libri duo*, I,8, ibid., 101; some brief farming is mentioned in *Contra academicos* II,4: 23. Cf. S. MacCormack, 'The Virtue of Work: an

predecessor Cassiodorus who perceives the garden as a place of composure, especially for the less educated.[55]

Gregory's view of the garden is much closer to that of John Cassian and his Egyptian monastic friends. There the main function of the garden consists in providing food and not at all in enjoying the charming surroundings or in offering a pleasant place for philosophical conversations.[56]

* * *

The centre of Gregory's horticultural miracle stories is the person of the gardener, that is a living holy man. The miracles happen in order to demonstrate and confirm the spiritual power of the men of God and finally God's power.[57] At least after having witnessed a miracle people will know that they should trust in their spiritual leader, that is, a man who is capable to defeat not only a demon hidden in a lettuce but the Devil himself. Furthermore Gregory's spiritually gifted gardeners are fervent Christians whose power exceeds all pagan spirits of vegetation.

The group of the holy men linked with miraculous events in gardens is representative of Gregory's holy men in his *Dialogues*. They are mostly, but not exclusively, monks. They do have the spiritual power to perform miracles. However, very often they do not act in a supernatural way: instead they do actual garden work or fulfil their ordinary pastoral duties. In Gregory's view this is spiritually not less precious than performing miracles.

Gregory's not exclusively supernatural portrait of the gardeners reflects his ideal of a church leader as a person who is mainly caring for people's immediate ordinary and spiritual needs. Furthermore Gregory had a special interest in pedagogy and personal policy. His gardeners are not only spiritual leaders in a generic way, but more specifically they are also active in the education of monks and clerics. In this they do not differ from Gregory's ideas about leaders expressed in his other works.

Augustinian Transformation', *Antiquité Tardive* 9 (2001), 219–37. More generally, see Daniel Caner, *Wandering, Begging Monks: Spiritual Authority and the Promotion of Monasticism in Late Antiquity* (Berkeley and Los Angeles, CA, 2002).

55 Cassiodorus, *Institutiones diuinarum litterarum*, ed. R. A. B. Mynors (Oxford, 1937), I,29,1: 73; also I,28,6–7: 71–2; cf. Littlewood, 'Evidence', 29–30.

56 The Egyptian monks fled from the fertile places into the desert: John Cassian, Conlationes: Jean Cassien, *Conférences*, ed. with French transl. E. Pichery, SC 42, 54 and 64, 3 vols (Paris, 1955–9), 24,1–2 (SC 64: 171–4); cf. *Apophthegmata Patrum*: Silvanos 4 (PG 65, 409AB) and Johannes Kolobos 1 (PG 65, 204C).

57 The saints are one spirit with God (1 Cor. 6, 17): Greg.M., dial. II,16,3–7 (SC 260: 186–90).

Hence, contrary to Francis Clark, there is no reason to assume that the story of the lettuce miracle or similar miracle stories in the *Dialogues* are not authentic.

In Gregory's *Dialogues* we find only a slight trace of the old Roman horticultural ideal of philosophical leisure. In general in the *Dialogues* the garden is not a place of leisure but a place of work and education. Gardening in the *Dialogues* is literally a down-to-earth pedagogy, sometimes by means of miracles. If a person is too stubborn, ordinary pastoral guidance won't be sufficient and harsher lessons must be learned. If you can't even resist the temptation of a lush lettuce, you may find yourself struggling with a demon.

Universität Bern

*CONSTAT ERGO INTER NOS VERBA SIGNA ESSE**: THE UNDERSTANDING OF THE MIRACULOUS IN ANGLO-SAXON SOCIETY

by ANNA MARIA LUISELLI FADDA

THIS paper investigates two important themes which have not hitherto been fully appreciated: how the Anglo-Saxons, during the whole lengthy process of their reception of Christianity, interpreted the meaning of those extraordinary events commonly called *miracula*, and what reflection on the vernacular was carried forward by the knowledge achieved for purposes of communication. Although the question of the vocabulary of 'miracle' in Antiquity and early Christian times has been dealt with elsewhere,[1] any discussion of vernacular terminology is barely discernible and scarcely ever encountered. My intention is, therefore, to consider the intentional expressive activity of the Anglo-Saxons as a reflection of meaning on their language.[2]

What gives the enquiry a fitting start is that the word 'miracle', introduced into English from Norman French *via* Latin, first occurs in the *Anglo-Saxon Chronicle* under the famous entry for the year 1137.[3] Granted that five hundred years had elapsed between 597 (the coming of Christianity to England with St Augustine of Canterbury) and 1137, a most important question is what interpretation of the miraculous did the Anglo-Saxons achieve.

In the course of the conversion of England to Christianity,[4] Christian

* Augustine, *De magistro*, 2, 3, ed. K.-D. Daur, CChr.SL 29 (Turnhout, 1970), 159.

1 See especially C. F. D. Moule, *Miracles: Cambridge Studies in their Philosophy and History* (London, 1965), *excursus* 1 and 2, 235–8; Robert M. Grant, *Miracle and Natural Law in Graeco-Roman and Early Christian Thought* (Amsterdam, 1952).

2 I am quite conscious that this raises two crucial questions. The first involves the interpretation of the reality learnt by means of words. The second concerns the relationship between word and meaning. The topic is immense, with many strands leading in many directions, as all would readily acknowledge. But the discussion pursued here will be far narrower, corresponding only to those aspects dealing with Anglo-Saxon semantic activity within the selected subject matter.

3 This deals *inter alia* with the martyrdom of St William, crucified by the Jews of Norwich under King Stephen (1135–54).

4 On Christianity in southern England before and at the turn of the sixth century, in addition to Henry Mayr-Harting, *The Coming of Christianity to Anglo-Saxon England* (3rd edn,

missionaries faced enormous problems of interaction with pagan beliefs and ceremonies.[5] Anglo-Saxon secular law-codes contained prohibitions concerning heathen worship and behaviour, as well as penalties for sacrificing to pagan gods and devils.[6] A number of ecclesiastical documents were specifically concerned with ordering pagan rituals to cease and punishing anyone reluctant to abandon traditional ancestral superstitions.[7] Cubitt has recently underlined that practices condemned by the Church as pagan lingered into the eighth century,[8] to be condemned at the famous Council of Clofesho in 747;[9] in addition, we may focus on the report of the legates to Pope Adrian I in 786,[10] Alcuin's *Epistolae*,[11] or even the *Penitential* attributed to Bishop Ecgberht of York (735–66).[12] Such prohibitions must have seemed worth maintaining and perhaps also enlarging in the ninth and tenth centuries when, in the context of a well-known revival of paganism,[13] some

London and University Park, PA, 1991), see now J. Stevenson, 'Christianity in Sixth- and Seventh-Century Southumbria', in Martin Carver, ed., *The Age of Sutton Hoo: the Seventh Century in North-Western Europe* (Woodbridge, 1992), 175–83; R. Meens, 'A Background to Augustine's mission to Anglo-Saxon England', *Anglo-Saxon England* 23 (1994), 5–17; Robert A. Markus, 'Augustine and Gregory the Great', in Richard Gameson, ed., *St Augustine and the Conversion of England* (Stroud, 1999), 41–9; I. N. Wood, 'Augustine and Gaul', in ibid., 68–82; C. Stancliffe, 'The British Church and the Mission of Augustine', in ibid., 107–51; B. Yorke, 'The Reception of Christianity at the Anglo-Saxon Royal Courts', in ibid., 152–73.

5 On Anglo-Saxon paganism, see particularly D. G. Scragg, ed., *Superstition and Popular Medicine in Anglo-Saxon England* (Manchester, 1989); J. D. Niles, 'Pagan Survivals and Popular Belief', in Malcolm Godden and Michael Lapidge, eds, *The Cambridge Companion to Old English Literature* (Cambridge, 1991), 126–41; A. L. Meaney, 'Anglo-Saxon Idolators and Ecclesiasts from Theodore to Alcuin: a Source Study', *Anglo-Saxon Studies in Archaeology and History* 5 (1992), 103–24; Alexander Murray, 'Missionaries and Magic in Dark Age Europe', *P&P* 136 (1992), 186–205 [review article of Valerie I. J. Flint, *The Rise of Magic in Early Medieval Europe* (Oxford, 1991)]; David Wilson, *Anglo-Saxon Paganism* (London, 1992).

6 See, for example, 'The Laws of Wihtred of Kent' (695 AD), ed. Dorothy Whitelock, in *English Historical Documents, vol. I: c.500–1042* (London, 1955) [hereafter: *EHD*], chs 12 and 13, 363, or 'The Laws of Alfred' (871–99), in ibid., Int. 30, 373.

7 The earliest records, about AD 669, are found in Theodore's *Penitential*. See, I, xv, 2 (a section headed 'de cultura idolorum'); I, xv, 4; I, xiv, 16, in *Councils and Ecclesiastical Documents Relating to Great Britain and Ireland*, ed. Arthur West Haddan and William Stubbs [hereafter: *HS*], 3 vols (Oxford 1869–79), 3: 188–90.

8 Catherine Cubitt, *Anglo-Saxon Church Councils, c.650–c.850* (London and New York, 1995), 119.

9 Council of Clofesho, ch. 3, *HS*, 3: 363.

10 *EHD*, I, ch. 19, 772. A discussion of the legatine report is in Cubitt, *Councils*, 153–90.

11 Alcuin, *Epistolae*, ed. E. Duemmler, in *Epistolae Karolini Aevi*, II, *MGH*, *Epistolae* 4 (Berlin, 1895), nn. 2, 3, 290.

12 *HS*, 3: 413–31. In the form in which we have it, the Ecgberht *Penitential* was codified and expanded on the continent in Carolingian times (*c*.800). See Allen J. Frantzen, *The Literature of Penance in Anglo-Saxon England* (New Brunswick, NJ, 1983), 7–72.

13 In a well-known letter to the bishops of England, Pope Formosus (891–6) wrote that

remarkable indications of pagan behaviour may be found still existing side by side with Christian beliefs and customs. This situation is documented not only in the Canons of Edgar (about 960)[14] but also in the laws of Cnut (1020–23),[15] and in the Northumbrian Priests' Law (*c.*1020–23).[16] No wonder, then, that both secular and religious literature bear witness to a widespread and significant Anglo-Saxon belief in a number of evil powers or spirits – referred to as elves, dwarfs, fairies, goblins, giants, ogres, monsters, dragons, ghosts, demons[17] – who were frequently associated with hills, barrows, burial mounds, fens, water, and trees, and thought of as being thoroughly interwoven with the natural world and with people's lives. These spirits were thought not only to display unknown portents and terrors of various shapes but also to bring to the living disease and mortal wounds.[18]

Now, however, we may interpret this evidence in detail; when considered as a whole, it suggests that there was much common ground between Christians and pagan Anglo-Saxons in relation to the powers which controlled the visible world. The fundamental consequence of this shared belief in the supernatural was, according to Markus, that Christianity presented the pagan gods, and any other force that allowed men to communicate with them, as sinister powers of evil, thus subsuming them within the class of demons.[19] It is in this perspective

he had heard 'that abominable rites of the pagans have sprouted again . . . in the land of the English', *EHD*, I, 820.

14 *Wulfstan's Canons of Edgar*, ed. Roger Fowler, *Early English Text Society*, os 266 (Oxford and London, 1972).

15 *EHD*, I, 420 (II Cnut, no. 5 and 5.1).

16 Ibid., 437 (no. 47 and no. 48).

17 In Old English: *aelf, dweorg, puca, puce, orc, scinna, scucca, ent, fifel, thyrs, orcneas, draca, gigantes, eotenas.*

18 See, for example, the impressive sequence of Old English charms, as collected in Oswald Cockayne, ed., *Leechdoms, Wortcunning and Starcraft of Early England*, 3 vols, RS (London, 1864–6, repr. 1961), esp. vol. 2 (*Bald's Leechbook*) and 3 (*Lacnunga*). Editions of the O.E. charms are also to be found in Elliott van Kirk Dobbie, *The Anglo-Saxon Minor Poems*, Anglo-Saxon Poetic Records 6 (New York, 1942), cxxx, cxxxi, cxxxvi, 123–4; G. Storms, *Anglo-Saxon Magic* (The Hague, 1948), 196–203, 283, 295; J. H. G. Grattan and Charles Singer, *Anglo-Saxon Magic and Medicine: Illustrated Specially from the Semi-Pagan Text 'Lacnunga'* (London, 1952), 188–91. A useful discussion of the whole topic is in A. L. Meaney, 'Women, Witchcraft and Magic in Anglo-Saxon England', in Scragg, *Superstition*, 9–40; N. Thun, 'The Malignant Elves: Notes on Anglo-Saxon Magic and Germanic Myth', *Studia Neophilologica* 41 (1969), 378–96. See also *Felix's Life of Saint Guthlac*, ed. and transl. Bertram Colgrave (Cambridge, 1956, repr. 1985) and the heroic poem *Beowulf*, vv. 740–5: *Beowulf with the Finnesburg Fragment*, ed. C. L. Wrenn (London, 1958), 114.

19 R. A. Markus, *Signs and Meanings: World and Text in Ancient Christianity* (Liverpool, 1996), 130.

that the Anglo-Saxons understood all pagan rites, whether magical, divinatory or other.

Given that both religious acts and magical practices attained almost the same marvellous effects, the ecclesiastical hierarchy was of the opinion that it was crucially important to alert Christians to the role of magicians, healers and miracle-workers in pagan rituals and to inform them of differences between ecclesiastical and secular activities. One way of cutting the Gordian knot of uncertainty was to point out, as had St Augustine, that whereas magicians were concerned only with the bodies of the living, aiming for their own self-gratification, the saints, in imitation of Christ, performed wonders exclusively directed towards the salvation of souls and the glory of God.[20] Indeed, had not Jesus himself refused to perform gratuitous miracles unwarranted by redeeming efficacy?[21]

Certainly the Anglo-Saxons, in accepting Christianity, would expect of their new God and His intermediaries miraculous powers or virtues no less spectacular than those they had previously associated with their own gods and heroes.[22] Thus, taking the religious expectations of the pagans into account, and reminding themselves of Pope Gregory's thesis that miracles were intended to convert the heathen,[23] the missionaries so managed their strategies as to present miraculous events as *signs* of potent mystic influence stemming from God Himself. Further, in following Pope Gregory's teaching, they correlated these events with repentant sinners or with those persons willing to honour the Christian faith.[24] Indeed, there is much precious evidence to suggest that the Anglo-Saxon Church was concerned with the providential role of miracles. In relating the various stories of extraordinary healing effected through the relics of the saints at their shrines, or in assuring the mysterious occurrences of a number of afterlife visions, religious writers were cogently attempting to demonstrate that these events

20 Augustine, *De diversis quaestionibus octogintatribus*, 79, 4, ed. Almut Mutzenbecher, CChr.SL 44A (Turnhout, 1974), 228–9; see Markus, *Signs*, 133–4.

21 Matt. 4, 2–7; 12, 38; 16, 1–4; Luke 4, 23; 23, 8.

22 See Bertram Colgrave, 'Bede's Miracle Stories', in A. H. Thompson, ed., *Bede, his Life, Times and Writings: Essays in Commemoration of the Twelfth Centenary of his Death* (Oxford, 1935, repr. New York, 1966), 201–29, 203.

23 For example, *Homiliae in Evangelium*, I,4, I,3, II,29: PL 76, 1090–91, 1110 and 1215 respectively. The whole discussion is in William D. McCready, *Signs of Sanctity: Miracles in the Thought of Gregory the Great,* Pontifical Institute of Medieval Studies, Studies and Texts 91 (Toronto, 1989).

24 McCready, *Signs of Sanctity*, 81–3.

could have been exclusively performed through the direct or mediate intervention of God Himself.[25] It is especially appropriate, then, to compare and discuss the terminology employed both in Latin and in the vernacular.

Evidence from contemporary Latin literature reveals that the word *miraculum* was widely adopted in an extensive and generic sense of admiration or bewilderment, excited by what seemed to be strange and inexplicable. But because physical miracles could be performed also by magicians, whenever the circumstance of the miracle made it clear that under the visible effect, it involved the invisible working out of God's providence, mediated through the saints, the understanding of its religious significance was provided by means of other more pregnant words, such as *virtus, signum, indicium*, used either alone or in combination with *miraculum*. Let us consider, for example, Bede's evidence.[26] All Bedan material conforms perfectly to this picture. Nowhere does Bede use the word *miraculum* save in a general, non-technical sense. In contrast, given his deep concern for an authentically religious interpretation of 'miracle', he identifies the divine nature[27] of these *mira res*[28] by means of expressions endowed with functional meaning and a marked didactic significance.[29] Thus, the greatest and most efficacious miracles, associated with spiritual significance, are called *caelestia indicio*,[30] physical 'signs' evidencing supernatural power (*caelestium signa virtutum indicio sunt*),[31] an outward and visible indication of an inward and spiritual grace.[32] Indeed, the power of working authentic miracles could only be the privilege of God. Even the miracles performed by the saints must be ascribed to God: they do not possess any miraculous power in themselves, being only agents through whom God signifies His own power. It is their special proximity to God because of the sanctity of

25 Charles Thomas, *Bede, Archaeology, and the Cult of Relics*, Jarrow Lecture (Jarrow on Tyne, 1973), 2–7.

26 As Colgrave pointed out in 'Bede's Miracle Stories', 205, his miracle stories are almost confined to the *Historia Ecclesiastica* [hereafter: *HE*], the *Prose and Verse Lives of Cuthbert*, and the *Martyrology*.

27 *HE*, IV, 11, ed. B. Colgrave and R. A. B. Mynors, *Bede's Ecclesiastical History of the English People* (Oxford, 1969), 366–8.

28 Ibid.

29 Evidence in ibid., II: 2; III: 8, 10, 12, 15, 19; IV: 7, 10, 28, 30, 43; V: 2.

30 Ibid., IV: 6.

31 Ibid.

32 On Bede, William D. McCready, *Miracles and the Venerable Bede*, Pontifical Institute of Medieval Studies, Studies and Texts 118 (Toronto, 1994).

their life that naturally explains the transference to and recapitulation in them of God's own virtue (*virtutes ex meritis*).[33]

Further more illuminating testimonies of this attitude to 'miracle' can be found in the vernacular terms for 'miraculous events'. The first point to be underlined is the absence of the Latin word *miraculum* amongst the numerous Latin-Christian borrowings that entered the Anglo-Saxon language, rapidly becoming basic components of a newly-established vocabulary.[34] Whatever answer should be offered to the question of this omission, we can say for certain that Anglo-Saxon missionaries, in order to preserve Pope Gregory's teaching on miraculous deeds, as being God's works or *signs* given by Him for the salvation of mankind,[35] needed to provide an indispensable new system of signs and meanings, shared by the whole language-using community.

This attitude is at its clearest when we focus on a number of native words for 'miracle'. Firstly, any visible marvel that produces wonder is defined as *wundor*; but *wundor* is the effect, not the cause, the term conveying a basically neutral significance of the miraculous. But when the extraordinary outward manifestation is directly dependant on the misleading and illusive ability or performance of the wicked, the recorded vernacular words for these gratuitous miracles transmit the idea of superstitious practices and rituals either pertaining to demonic observances (*bealo-cræft, bealo-dæd*: 'art of evil, bale'; *scinn-cræft, scinn-lac*: 'art of evil spirits, phantoms'; *wiccecræft, wiccedom*: 'art of magicians') or strictly associated with demonic powers (*scinn/a*: 'phantom', 'demon'; *wicca*: 'wizard', 'magician', 'soothsayer'). Furthermore, although the effectiveness of magical deeds is not denied in Anglo-Saxon Christianity, the darker side of magic is specifically conveyed by the vernacular terminology.[36]

More importantly, a thorough contrast emerges whereby miracles are presented as ultimately dependent on the direct causality of God, or

33 *HE*, IV: 17.

34 Cf. Anna Maria Luiselli Fadda, 'The Vernacular and the Propagation of the Faith in Anglo-Saxon Missionary Activity', in Pieter N. Holtrop and Hugh McLeod, eds, *Missions and Missionaries*, SCH.S 13 (Woodbridge, 2000), 1–15.

35 See McCready, *Signs of Sanctity*, esp. 212–30.

36 For useful discussions on Anglo-Saxon magic, see N. Barley, 'Anglo-Saxon Magico-Medicine', *Journal of the Anthropological Society of Oxford* 3 (1972), 67–77; M. L. Cameron, 'Anglo-Saxon Medicine and Magic', *Anglo-Saxon England* 17 (1988), 191–215; Scragg, *Superstition*; Wilson, *Anglo-Saxon Paganism;* Bill Griffiths, *Aspects of Anglo-Saxon Magic* (Hockwold-cum-Wilton, 1996); Karen Louise Jolly, *Popular Religion in Late Saxon England: Elf Charms in Context* (Chapel Hill, NC, and London, 1996).

are invested with edifying meaning and purpose. In such cases *wundor,* under the pressures of communicating the Christian attitude towards the miraculous, is used only in combination with crucial verbal indicators such as 'divine', 'celestial', 'spiritual', and so on. It is in translating Latin texts that the Anglo-Saxon strategy, aiming at fostering the notion of 'miracle' as a significant act ultimately stemming from God, clearly emerges. In recounting the story of the Kentish princess Eorcengota, King Eorcenberct's daughter, Bede recounts that *multa quidem opera virtutum et signa miraculorum* were associated with this virgin by the people who lived in that place.[37] But in the Old English version of Bede's *Ecclesiastical History*, this passage is much more distinctively and significantly referred to as 'many works of spiritual powers (*monige weorc gastlicra mægna*) and many signs of celestial wonders (*monig tacon heofonlicra wundra*)'.[38] The implications of these alterations are surely relevant. Not only would they be more suitable to what the Anglo-Saxons might have expected from this story, but they also clearly reflect the interest of Anglo-Saxon Christianity in reminding people that any marvellous event performed by the saints is the visible manifestation of their personal link with God, who alone has the power to work wonders. In an even more striking example from the Latin *Vita* of St Giles,[39] we are succinctly informed that, after an act of healing accomplished by Giles, 'the fame of this miracle spread immediately'.[40] Conversely, the Anglo-Saxon rendering of this passage as *Godes wundor* strategically demonstrates that the ability to perform such miracles could only be a prerogative of God.[41] In another passage of the same *Vita*, where the Latin text points out that the power (*virtus*) of the holy man could not be kept hidden in the presence of its 'great magnitude',[42] the Anglo-Saxon text displays further details, including the overall significant assumption that the 'manifold wonders and powers'

37 *HE*, III: 8.

38 *The Old English Version of Bede's Ecclesiastical History of the English People*, ed. T. Miller, EETS os 95–6 [text] and 110–11 [glossary] (London, 1890–1 and 1898), 96: 531.

39 *ActaSS*, 1 Sept., I: 299–304; 'Catalogus codicum hagiographicorum Bibliothecae Civitatis Carnotensis', *AnBoll* 8 (1889), 86–208, 'Appendix ad cod. 84: Vita Sancti Aegidii', 102–20. Cf. Anna Maria Luiselli Fadda, ed., 'La versione anglosassone della *Vita sancti Aegidii abbatis*', *Romanobarbarica* 7 (1982–3), 273–352; the Latin text of the *Vita* is repr. in the appendix, at 342–52.

40 Luiselli Fadda, 'La versione anglosassone', 345.

41 Ibid., 310.

42 Ibid., 342.

(*manigfealde wundre ond mihte*) accomplished by St Giles were achieved from on high, by God Himself, through the agency of the holy man.[43] Miracles, then, are divinely produced events.

But nothing indicates more convincingly the Anglo-Saxon theocentric conception of the world than the recording of the most striking miracles as *tacn* (*fortacen*): 'token', 'afore-token', or *beacen* (*forebecen*): 'beacon', 'afore-beacon', 'sign'. In vernacular didactic and religious materials, these words significantly substitute the Latin *portentum, ostentum, prodigium,* so that the significance of the miracle is underlined and reinforced. Indeed, *forebecen* substitutes the Latin *prodigia* in the ninth-century Anglo-Saxon translation of the hymn 'canticum Exodii, feria Quinta' from the *Vespasian Psalter*;[44] and in the so-called *Vocabulary* of Archbishop Aelfric dating from the end of the tenth century,[45] the Latin terms *portentum, ostentum, prodigium* are glossed with *fortacen.* We can also observe that *tacn* and *beacen* are employed with the meaning of 'a supernatural sign', 'a miracle', every time the need for a spiritual interpretation of the event required it. When describing Jesus's miracle of turning water into wine in his homily for the Assumption of St John the Apostle, the most outstanding Anglo-Saxon homilist, Aelfric of Eynsham, a pupil of St Aethelwold, pointed to this miracle as being 'the first sign (*forme tacn*), that He openly wrought in His state of man'.[46] Even more clearly, by putting words into the mouth of the prophet Jeremiah in his homily *de natale Domini*, Aelfric explained that 'of the *wundrum* which Christ wrought . . . this is his *tacn*: he shall open the eyes of blind men, and to the deaf he shall give hearing, and with his voice he shall raise the dead from their sepulchres'.[47] Following the Biblical eschatological perspective, miracles are unrestrained gifts and efficacious signs of God's love for mankind.[48]

43 Ibid., 302.

44 References in Henry Sweet and T. H. Hoad, *A Second Anglo-Saxon Reader, Archaic and Dialectal* (2nd edn, Oxford, 1978), 122.

45 Richard Paul Wülcker and Thomas Wright, *Anglo-Saxon and Old English Vocabularies*, 2 vols (2nd edn, London, 1884, repr. Darmstadt, 1968), 1: 108, l. 17.

46 Aelfric brought out his work known as *Catholic Homilies* in two volumes, the first in 990, the second the following year. See *The Homilies of the Anglo-Saxon Church*, ed. Benjamin Thorpe, 2 vols (London, 1844–6, repr. 1971), 1: 58, l. 14. A similar reference is found in the homily '*Dominica II post Aepiphania Domini, nuptiae factae sunt in Chana Galileae*', in *Aelfric's Catholic Homilies,* ed. Malcolm Godden, EETS, 2nd ser., 5 (London and New York, 1979), 29.

47 *Catholic Homilies,* 8.

48 Ex. 15, 11; Deut. 6,10; Ps. 106, 7; 107, 8; 145, 9.

This conception of miraculous events as manifestations of the direct causality of God in the universe reveals significantly how Augustine's notion of signs was perceived in early Christian England. Augustine's strict concern to discover the meaning of the transcendent signs of God in the world,[49] signs being the words through which God interacts with humanity, gives us the key to understand the crucial role assigned to the signification in the training of Anglo-Saxon missionaries.[50] As is well-known, Augustine's main conception of the matter, given widely in his *de dialectica, de Genesis ad litteram, de Trinitate, de magistro, de doctrina Christiana*, was that words must be taken as signs *par excellence* of that which lies beyond,[51] or in addition to 'what it is perceived to be by the senses'.[52] Consequently, words having meanings on two levels,[53] the usual or primary sense, and the figurative sense, going beyond what exists, no communication should be possible for human groups, 'unless they could share, as it were, their minds and their thoughts'.[54]

But it is not difficult to envisage that it was within Gregorian pastoral activity that the Anglo-Saxon Church nurtured the Augustinian theory of meaning. According to McCready,

> it is generally acknowledged that Gregory was not a great speculative thinker, and that it is pointless to look for a theological or philosophical system in his writing. Rather than choosing to deepen a purely theological understanding of Christian dogma, for the most part Gregory limited himself to making doctrine as widely accessible as possible, so that Christians could have a firm grasp on what they were required to believe.[55]

[49] Augustine, *De doctrina Christiana*, I. 2, 2, ed. Josef Martin, CChr.SL 32 (Turnhout, 1962), 7–8; cp. Markus, *Signs and Meanings*, 86.

[50] See Helmut Gneuss, 'The Study of Language in Anglo-Saxon England', *Bulletin of the John Rylands Library* 72 (1990), 3–32; and Luiselli Fadda, 'The Vernacular and the Propagation of the Faith', 1–15.

[51] Augustine, *De doctrina Christiana*, II. 3, 4, ed. Martin, 33–4. Cp. idem, *Sermo* 288, 3, 4: PL 38, cols 1304–6 and *de Trinitate*, XIII. 1, 4, ed. W. J. Mountain and F. Glorie, CChr.SL 50A (Turnhout, 1968), 383–5.

[52] Augustine, *De doctrina Christiana*, II, 1, ed. Martin, 32; for further discussion see Markus, *Signs and Meanings*, 29 and 93–101.

[53] Markus, *Signs and Meanings*, 41.

[54] Augustine, *De catechizandis rudibus*, ed. I. B. Bauer, CChr.SL 46 (Turnhout, 1969), 155–78, at 122; further discussion in Markus, *Signs and Meanings*, 110.

[55] McCready, *Signs of Sanctity*, 63.

Essentially the same attitude towards the pagan audience in Anglo-Saxon England could be applied to the Gregorian missions. In fact, during the lengthy process of conversion to Christianity, the main problem that the missionaries had to cope with was how to bypass the many difficulties in interpreting the Christian message and how to carry out spiritual intercourse with pagans by means of language interaction. All our evidence testifies that the challenge of the Church in pagan England was to devise linguistic procedures and intelligible signifiers, suitable for conveying doctrinal information and guaranteeing a perfect competence in understanding the language of revelation, the language of God.[56] In fact, pagans did not have to struggle to recover the spiritual sense that was hidden in the deeply symbolic structure and nature of realities. Thus, the Anglo-Saxon missionaries aimed at illustrating how the biaxial language of the Gospels could be transposed into the present to teach pagans to read straight in the world the signs of the transcendent meaning just as the Gospels had taught. Moreover, they literally recast the lessons of the Gospels, where speaking the word actualizes a corresponding spiritual valence, and where the historical and material may be simultaneously spoken of as the spiritual and anagogic. In such a way, in the very act of communication, the word was appointed to read and to reveal the substance of the marvellous things signified, imprinting their form on pagan minds. In so far as they are seen as yielding a total Christian interpretation of the miraculous deeds or events, the significant words by which God's miracles were denoted appeared to be the recapitulation of both the acts of perceiving extraordinary things and of acquiring knowledge of the spiritual meaning 'which lies beyond what it is perceived to be by the senses'.[57]

In conclusion, according to the Anglo-Saxon perception of the Gregorian tradition, it was not the sensible effect of a miracle that was important so much as the promise of salvation conveyed by the miraculous deeds worked by God. Such wonders need not have raised any doubt as to their divine origin. Pagans were to be led to believe that miracles were worked for the purpose of teaching people to read and to understand the transcendent signs of God in the world. Thus, by pointing to miracles as *signs*, as celestial manifestations of God's power

56 See Luiselli Fadda, 'The Vernacular and the Propagation of the Faith', 1–15.

57 Augustine, *De doctrina Christiana*, II, 1, ed. Martin, 32.

and love for humanity, the audience would be allowed not only to read the story of Salvation as an open text written in created things, but to jump – as Robert Markus put it – 'straight to the "something else", *aliud aliquid*, signified, not by the word, but by the thing signified by the word'.[58]

Università degli Studi Roma Tre

58 Markus, *Signs and Meaning*, 65.

MIRACLES, MISSIONARIES AND MANUSCRIPTS IN EIGHTH-CENTURY SOUTHERN GERMANY

by CLARE PILSWORTH*

THERE was a certain poor little crippled girl, who sat near the gate of the monastery begging alms ... she committed fornication.... When her time came, she wrapped the child in swaddling clothes and cast it at night into a pool.... When day dawned, another woman came to draw water and seeing the corpse of the child, was struck with horror ... and reproached the holy nuns ... 'Look for the one who is missing from the monastery and then you will find out who is responsible for this crime'. [...] no one was absent except Agatha who ... had gone with full permission....

The blessed Leoba went straight to the altar and, standing before the cross, which was being prepared for the third procession, stretched out her hands towards heaven, and with tears and groans prayed, saying: 'O Lord Jesus Christ, King of virgins, Lover of chastity, unconquerable God, manifest Thy power and deliver us from this charge, because *the reproaches of those who reproached Thee have fallen upon us*'.

Immediately after she had said this, that wretched little woman, the dupe and the tool of the devil, seemed to be surrounded by flames, and, calling out the name of the abbess, confessed to the crime she had committed. Then a great shout rose to heaven: the vast crowd was astounded at the miracle, the nuns began to weep with joy, and all of them with one voice gave expression to the merits of Leoba and of Christ our Saviour.[1]

* This article is based on research supported by grants from the Leverhulme Trust, the British School at Rome and Manchester University. Special thanks to F. Lifshitz, M. Diesenburger, R. McKitterick, H. Reimitz, P. Nesteruk, N. Pilsworth, H. Williams, K. Cooper, B. Crostini, all members of the Centre for Late Antiquity, University of Manchester, all respondents at the 2003 Ecclesiastical History Socitety conference, and the staff of the libraries at Würzburg and Manchester.

[1] Rudolf of Fulda, *Vita Leobae*, ch. 12: *The Life of Saint Leoba*, transl. C. H. Talbot, in Thomas F. X. Noble and Thomas Head, eds, *Soldiers of Christ: Saints and Saints' Lives from Late Antiquity and the Early Middle Ages* (London, 1995), 255–77. For the Latin text, see the edition by G. Waitz, MGH.S 15.1 (Hannover, 1887), 127.

In this way Leoba, the eighth-century Anglo-Saxon abbess of the nunnery of Tauberbischofsheim in Southern Germany, dramatically clears the nuns of all wrongdoing in the concealment and death of a new-born baby. The *Life of Leoba* was written in the 830s, some fifty years after Leoba's death, by Rudolf of Fulda.[2] It is, however, on the eighth-century origins of the putative incident on which Rudolf may in part have based his miraculous account that I wish to focus here. It provides us, I shall argue, with a vivid snapshot of the social and religious context for the copying, reading, listening and interpretation of a key group of miracles in late antique and medieval culture, those of the Italian martyrs, by the nuns of Tauberbischofsheim and neighbouring communities in Leoba's lifetime.

Italian martyr narratives – rich in a wide variety of miracle stories – were composed by invariably anonymous authors throughout Italy between the fifth and seventh centuries, and were one of Italy's most successful early medieval exports, since they were distributed and read in relatively large numbers throughout Western Europe.[3] The miracle stories in the Italian martyr narratives were reused and reappropriated by one eighth-century female monastic community in the Würzburg region not, I shall argue, as exemplars for conversion, but for spiritual improvement. In other words, not for conversion in the sense of a nominal allegiance to the Christian faith, but, rather, Christianization in the broader sense of living out – in every aspect of life – the precepts of Jesus, whether within the monastery as a nun or in the local community as a devout lay Christian.[4] This might be termed part of a 'second

2 See C. Talbot, *The Anglo-Saxon Missionaries* (London, 1954); Ian Wood, *The Missionary Life: Saints and the Evangelisation of Europe 400–1050* (Harlow, 2001), 67–8; Stephanie Hollis, *Anglo-Saxon Women and the Church: Sharing a Common Fate* (Woodbridge, 1992), 283–8; Walter Berschin, *Biographie und Epochenstil III: Karolingische Biographie, 750–920 n. Chr.* (Stuttgart, 1991), 260–2.

3 On the Italian martyr narratives, the classic starting points are Albert Dufourcq, *Étude sur les Gesta martyrum romains*, 5 vols [Rome, 1988 (vols 1–4 originally published Paris, 1886–1910)], and Hippolyte Delehaye, *Étude sur le légendier romain: les saints de novembre et de décembre* (Brussels, 1936). For a more recent survey and further references, see Walter Berschin, *Biographie und Epochenstil im lateinischen Mittelalter*, 3 vols, Quellen und Untersuchungen zur Lateinischen Philologie des Mittelalters 8–10 (Stuttgart, 1986–91); Kate Cooper, ed., *The Roman Martyrs and the Politics of Memory, Early Medieval Europe* 9 (2000) and Clare Pilsworth, 'Vile Scraps: "Pamphlet" Manuscripts, Miscellanies and the Transmission and Use of the Italian Martyr Narratives in Early Medieval Western Europe', in preparation.

4 For a useful historiographical overview of the notion of conversion see N. J. Higham, *The Convert Kings: Power and Religious Affiliation in Early Anglo-Saxon England* (Manchester, 1997), 7–52. On Christianization in early medieval rural Europe in general, see the articles in *Cristianizzazione ed organizzazione ecclesiastica delle campagne nell'Alto Medioevo: espansione e*

phase' of conversion, perhaps focused on educated local elites in particular, using the universal *lingua franca* (in every sense) of the miraculous in the Latin Italian martyr narratives.[5] In order to demonstrate this, I shall use a combination of textual and manuscript-based analysis, beginning with our starting point for the broader social context in which manuscripts containing Italian martyr narratives were produced in eighth-century Southern German nunneries, namely the infanticide miracle in the *Vita Leobae*.

This miracle has been interpreted as a call by the author, Rudolf of Fulda, for stricter claustration of nuns in order to protect the 'missionary church . . . (from) the hostility and scorn of the largely uncoverted world that they inhabited'.[6] Rudolf might indeed have approved of strict claustration for female religious, but it is now recognized that the nunnery of Tauberbischofsheim, even at the time of its foundation between 732 and 735, did not lie deep in virgin 'pagan' territory but in an area south of Würzburg that was already Christianized by the end of the seventh century, albeit not to the standards demanded by the Anglo-Saxon missionaries. One such was Leoba's relative Boniface, who, from 736, at the behest of Odilo, the Frankish *dux* of Bavaria, had helped to found several monasteries in the region, including Tauberbischofsheim and Fulda, and established several dioceses, including Würzburg, by the early 740s.[7] Therefore, whether one is looking at this miracle from the perspective of the 830s when it was written, or at events in the eighth century which may have inspired Rudolf's account, one cannot talk of a 'largely unconverted world' and alternative interpretations and contexts must be sought.

Rudolf claimed that his work was based on the accounts of four nuns who knew Leoba, and this infanticide miracle is notable in that it specifically names a nun, Agatha, who, as we saw, inadvertantly became the centre of this scandal. It is therefore possible that Rudolf's account, however highly shaped and stylized for his own aims, may contain an

resistenze, Settimane di studio del Centro Italiano di Studi sull'Alto Medioevo 28, 2 vols (Spoleto, 1982). The most up-to-date survey of missionary work in early medieval continental Europe is Wood, *Missionary Life*, esp. 57–78 for Würzburg and the surrounding area.

5 On the problem of language and missionary work in early medieval Europe outside of Latin-speaking regions, see in particular Anna Maria Luiselli Fadda, 'The Vernacular and the Propagation of the Faith in Anglo-Saxon Missionary Activity', in Pieter N. Holtrop and Hugh McLeod, eds, *Missions and Missionaries*, SCH.S 13 (Woodbridge, 2000), 1–15.

6 Hollis, *Anglo-Saxon Women*, 282.

7 Wood, *Missionary Life*, 57–60, 67 and 159; idem, *The Merovingian Kingdoms 450–751* (London, 1994), 306.

echo of an event that took place at Tauberbischofsheim while Leoba was abbess.[8] If this is the case, and we place this event in the context outlined above, of a region already converted to Christianity when the Anglo-Saxon missionaries arrived in the 730s, then instead of hostile quasi-pagan locals, we may envisage people who to all intents considered themselves faithful Christians. Sections of the local community may therefore have very well resented being told by the incomers that they were not 'Christian' enough (or not the 'right' kind of Christian) and that it was Anglo-Saxon nuns who could demonstrate the exemplary Christian lifestyle to everyone else. In this context, it is entirely understandable that members of the local community would be quick to accuse the nuns in the case of a baby found in the river in order to pull them off the moral high ground, as it were.

It has been suggested by Rosamond McKitterick, however, that the role of Bonifatian nunneries such as Tauberbischofsheim, and nearby Kitzingen and Ochsenfurt, was not only to provide role models for Christian life (as defined by the Anglo-Saxon missionaries) but to produce manuscripts for use in the diocese to support the church's mission. Indeed, several eighth-century manuscripts which were identified by Bernard Bischoff as having been copied by nuns in the Würzburg region are preserved in Würzburg Cathedral library, but unfortunately we invariably do not know exactly when they were acquired.[9] These manuscripts might therefore have indeed been intended for use by clergy in the region, but could also originally have been for the use of the nuns themselves (both Anglo-Saxon and local), whether within the monastery, or, either via the local priest or prominent educated lay Christian aristocrat, for use in the parish. Some of the manuscripts in this group contain Italian martyr narratives – in particular, Würzburg, Universitätsbibliothek MS M.p.th.q. 28a (the other is Würzburg, Universitätsbibliothek MS M.p.th.q. 28b). I would like to argue that these manuscripts, and the miracle stories contained in them,

8 On the practice of infanticide in the Middle Ages, see W. Langer, 'Infanticide: a Historical Survey', *History of Childhood Quarterly* 1 (1973–4), 353–74 and E. Coleman, 'Infanticide in the Early Middle Ages', in Susan Mosher Stuard, ed., *Women in Medieval Society* (Philadelphia, PA, 1976), 47–71.

9 See above, n. 6; see also B. Bischoff, 'Manuscripts in the Age of Charlemagne', in idem, *Manuscripts and Libraries in the Age of Charlemagne*, ed. and transl. Michael Gorman (Cambridge, 1994), 20–55, 42–4. On the earliest Würzburg library catalogue, see E. A. Lowe, 'An Eighth-Century List of Books in a Bodleian Manuscript from Würzburg and its Probable Relation to the Laudian Acts', *Speculum* 3 (1928), 3–15, repr. in idem, *Palaeographical Papers 1907–1965*, ed. Ludwig Bieler, 2 vols (Oxford, 1972), 1: 239–50.

whether they were used by the nuns themselves or by the clergy in the diocese, should be viewed and interpreted, just like Rudolf's infanticide miracle in the *Life of Leoba*, in the context of a 'mission' that is not so much to convert but to 'improve' Christians in the region.

Therefore, the interpretation of the miracle stories copied into this manuscript depends both, in my view, on its immediate physical context, namely the codex into which it is copied, and on the wider social context into which the manuscript as a whole was intended to function.[10] MS M.p.th.q. 28a is one of the eighth-century manuscripts identified by Bischoff as being copied by nuns – in Anglo-Saxon majuscule and minuscule[11] – quite probably at Tauberbischofsheim, perhaps even under Leoba's abbacy, but the nearby Bonifatian nunneries of Kitzingen and Ochsenfurt cannot be completely discounted as alternative centres for the production of this manuscript.[12] It is relatively small (208 x 135 mm) and simply but attractively laid out, with some coloured initials.

The manuscript is a miscellany containing Isidore's *Synonyma*, the *Passio Potiti* and the *Passio Eugeniae*. Eugenia was born in the East, but, according to the Latin *passio*, spent the latter part of her life in Rome, where she was martyred – certainly there was a well-established cult dedicated to her memory in early medieval Rome, hence her designa-

10 For examples of this 'whole manuscript' approach, see F. Lifshitz, 'Gender and Exemplarity East of the Middle Rhine: Jesus, Mary and the Saints in Manuscript Context', in Cooper, ed. *The Roman Martyrs and the Politics of Memory*, 325–44; Laura Kendrick, *Animating the Letter: the Figurative Embodiment of Writing from Late Antiquity to the Renaissance* (Columbus, OH, 1999); Harry Y. Gamble, *Books and Readers in the Early Church: a History of Early Christian Texts* (New Haven, CT, and London, 1995); Rosamund McKitterick, *Books, Scribes and Learning in the Frankish Kingdoms, 6th–9th Centuries* (Aldershot, 1994); Helmut Reimitz, 'Ein Karolingisches Geschichtsbuch aus Saint Amand: Studien zur Wahrnehmung von Identität und Raum im frühen Mittelalter', unpublished Ph.D. thesis, University of Vienna, 1999; Rita Schlusemann, J. M. M. Hermans and Margriet Hoogvliet, eds, *Sources for the History of Medieval Books and Libraries* (Groningen, 2000).

11 On script types in general see Michelle P. Brown, *A Guide to Western Historical Scripts from Antiquity to 1600* (London, 1990), esp. 48–57, and Bernard Bischoff, *Latin Palaeography: Antiquity and the Middle Ages*, transl. Dáibhí Ó Cróinín and David Ganz (Cambridge, 1990), 90–5.

12 E. A. Lowe, *Codices latini antiquiores: a Palaeographical Guide to Latin Manuscripts Prior to the Ninth Century*, 11 vols (Oxford, 1934–66), 9: 55, no. 1435; see also R. McKitterick, 'The Anglo-Saxon Missionaries in Germany: Reflections on the Manuscript Evidence', *Transactions of the Cambridge Bibliographical Society* 9 (1989), 291–329, repr. in eadem, *Books, Scribes and Learning*, 300; Bernhard Bischoff and Josef Hofman, *Libri sancti Kyliani: die Würzburger Schreibschule und die Dombibliothek im VIII. und IX. Jahrhundert* (Würzburg, 1952), 7–8. For the earliest manuscript witnesses for the *Vita Leobae* itself, see G. Waitz's edition in MGH.S 15.1, 118–20, and the Namur hagiographic manuscript database at http://bhlms.fltr.ucl.ac.be (consulted: 22 October 2004).

tion as an Italian martyr.[13] Likewise Potitus is a Balkan saint whose cult is attested in Italy.[14] Isidore's *Synonyma* is an intriguing work that defies easy definition, having been described by different commentators as grammatical, ascetic, mystical or dogmatic in nature, or even, as Fontaine suggests, as a book of Christian wisdom.[15] Book one is a lamentation of the sinning soul;[16] Book two outlines the way a Christian life should be conducted. The *Passio Potiti* narrates the torture and martyrdom of the young Balkan saint Potitus whose cult is attested in Italy. The *Passio Eugeniae*, by contrast, tells the story of a woman from the East, Eugenia, who disguised herself as a man, became an abbot, successfully defended herself against an accusation of rape by baring her breasts, and subsequently travelled to Rome before finally being martyred.[17]

It might appear from this thumbnail sketch that the choice of texts in this manuscript was entirely random, but there is in fact, I argue, an overall theme and purpose to the manuscript, in which miracles play a leading role. The primary theme is not, however, in my view, that of conversion, as may be assumed at first sight, despite the fact that the *Passio Eugeniae* concerns the conversion of Eugenia, her family and others such as Basilla, an emperor's grand-daughter, and that the *Passio Potiti* includes several conversion miracles.[18] No designation of an

13 On Eugenia's cult, see Agostino Amore, *I martiri di Roma* (Rome, 1975), 125–6. On the textual history of the *passio*, see below, nn. 17 and 18.

14 Potitus' cult in the early middle ages appears to have been centred in Southern Italy, and Sardinia eventually appears to have acquired the relics. Potitus is attested in the ninth-century Neapolitan *Liber Pontificalis*. See *Biblioteca Sanctorum* 10 (Rome, 1968), 1072–4; *Passio Potiti*, BHL 6908, is the version found in Würzburg, Universitätsbibliothek, MS M.p.th.q. 28a and is edited in *ActaSS* Ian. 1, 754–7.

15 Jacques Fontaine, 'La Vocation monastique selon saint Isidore de Séville', *Studi medievali*, 3rd ser., 6 (1965), 163–95, 164–5 and 185, repr. in idem, *Tradition et actualité chez Isidore de Séville* (London, 1988), VII.

16 PL 83, 827, no. 474, ch. 5.

17 *Passio Eugeniae*, BHL 2666 is the version used in MS M.p.th.q. 28a and is edited in PL 73, 605–20.

18 One typical example is to be found in chapter two of the *Passio Potiti*, where a 'matrona' called Quiriaca is simultaneously cured of her leprosy and converted to Christianity: 'Et statim sana facta est mulier illa, et splenduit caro eius, sicut radij solis: et credidit Quiriaca', *Passio Potiti*, ch. 2, *ActaSS*, 756. See also, *Passio Eugeniae*, PL 73, 605–20 (BHL 2666). BHL 2667, which is believed to be the earliest version of the *passio* and has a more confused chronology than BHL 2666, is discussed and translated by H. I. Jones, 'The Desert and Desire: Virginity, City and Family in the Roman Martyr Legends of Agnes and Eugenia', unpublished M.A. thesis, University of Manchester, 1998. BHL 2666 may have been chosen by the compilers of MS M.p.th.q. 28a because it not only attempts a credible historical chronology, but also places more emphasis on education: see M. Humphries, 'Eugenia',

overall theme, however, and hence a primary aim for the whole manuscript, can be achieved without taking into account the presence of Isidore's *Synonyma* at the head of this codex.

Indeed, it is precisely the way in which the *Synonyma* has been edited by the anonymous compilers of the manuscript, I argue, that provides the key to understanding the principal aim and function of the codex. Only Book one (the sinning soul) and Book two, chapters 1–26 and 82 to the end have been included. The first selected section of Book two in the Würzburg manuscript (cc. 1–26) includes exhortations to remain continent, to avoid fornication, meat and wine, and to practise humility. The final selected chapters (cc. 82-end) focus on God's judgement and the importance of dispensing charity in the right spirit. Topics discussed in the second Book of the *Synonyma* that do not make it into this particular manuscript compilation include patience, peaceful relations with others, knowledge and wisdom, the correct usage of words, and sincerity. The work has therefore been deliberately trimmed to focus primarily on what might be described as a visibly ascetic or devout lifestyle (restricted diet, charitable works, abstinence from sex) and future judgement, with its promise of hoped-for salvation.[19] This impression is strengthened by the fact that Isidore's *Synonyma* was a popular text in eighth-century Germany, and it is therefore unlikely that the compiler of MS M.p.th.q. 28a did not have access to the full text.

It is in this context that the inclusion of the two *passiones*, and above all their miracles, should be viewed. This manuscript should therefore be characterized as a spiritual 'improvement' manual for either private devotional or communal reading for the intermediate or advanced devotee, rather than for 'beginners' being taught the ABC of faith. The

unpublished dossier from the British Academy funded *Gesta martyrum* project (1996–99) directed by Kate Cooper, University of Manchester.

19 Two other manuscripts of Isidore's *Synonyma* were in circulation in the Würzburg region by the ninth century: Würzburg, Universitätsbibliothek, MS M.p.th.f. 79, copied in Southern England in the eighth century but in use in the Würzburg region by the ninth century at the latest, and MS M.p.th.q. 28b, fols 43–64 (incomplete), copied in the Würzburg region (like 28a probably in a female scriptorium) at the end of the eighth century. The latter is therefore slightly later than MS M.p.th.q. 28a, but signals the great interest in this text in this region – a total of three surviving pre-ninth century manuscripts of a single text in one region is a large number! Certainly as far as the Prologue of the *Synonyma* is concerned, none of the copyists appear to be using any of these codices as direct exemplars, although it is possible that the commissioners/scribes themselves are adapting the Prologue. M.p.th.f. 79 is, unlike that of 28a, a complete text of Isidore: most of Book II in 28b is missing, so we cannot ascertain if it was following the structure of 28a or not.

other miracles in the *Passio Potiti* and *Passio Eugeniae* which might hitherto have been overshadowed by those relating to conversion, now take on a new significance.

Like many (but by no means all) martyr narratives, the finale of the *Passio Potiti* takes the form of an extended battle of wills between martyr and executioner: several attempts are made to kill Potitus and he is extensively tortured, but each time a miracle saves him – an angel cuts his bonds, or the emperor's henchmen are unable to touch him. In the final miracle before his death, his tongue is cut out but Potitus continues to speak, praising the Lord and taunting the emperor.[20] He is then beheaded. None of these miracles are unique to the *Passio Potiti* – what interests me is the way in which they might have been interpreted specifically in the context of the other texts in the miscellany. Despite the fact that Boniface did in fact manage to be killed in Frisia in 754 and was subsequently honoured as a martyr, this was a rare occurrence by the eighth century and therefore, given the contents of the preceding text, i.e. the *Synonyma*, these miracles should be interpreted as an exhortation not to martyrdom, but rather to protect the integrity of the body and at the same time test it through ascetic practices, in order to focus entirely on spiritual and not worldly matters and thereby obtain salvation, whether in a monastic or lay context.[21]

It might be said that it is precisely the fluidity of interpretation and use where the miraculous is concerned, particularly in the realm of devotional reading, that ensures, together with their ability to entertain, the martyr narrative's staying power as one of the most popular forms of religious literature centuries after the end of the persecutions. The *Passio Eugeniae* is a good example of this process, and survives in several other pre ninth-century manuscripts, as well as in MS M.p.th.q. 28a. This text, however, as I have outlined above, does not follow what might be termed a 'traditional' martyr narrative format, and there are fewer miracles in it than in the *Passio Potiti*. It is significant, however, that the miracles that are included are the parts of the text that are most directly relevant to the overall aims of the manuscript, and possibly also have resonance with the wider issue highlighted in the infanticide miracle in the *Vita Leobae* of a monastic community's relationship with the local lay community.

20 *Passio Potiti*, ch. 22, *ActaSS*, 757.

21 For a recent overview of the idea of purity in early medieval monasticism, see Albrecht Diem, *Keusch und rein: eine Untersuchung zu den Ursprüngen des frühmittelalterlichen Klosterwesens und seinen Quellen* (Amsterdam, 2000).

As in the *Passio Potiti*, several miracles occur just before Eugenia's death, when Eugenia is seized by Decius, prefect of the city, to sacrifice to the pagan Gods. She refuses, and when her persecutors attempt to throw her in the Tiber tied up, she survives, 'sitting upon the water'.[22] She is then kept in a dark prison without food and water, but Jesus appears to her before she is finally executed.[23] Like those in the *Passio Potiti*, these miracles highlight the virtues of faith, steadfastness, and unconcern for bodily needs. In the *Passio Eugeniae* perservance in virginity is also emphasized, which would have had particular resonance for the nuns who compiled the manuscript.

It is a sequence earlier in the narrative, however, which begins with a healing miracle and ends with one of vengeance, that may have addressed most directly the position in which the nunnery found itself in relation to the local community:

> A certain most prominent matrona of Alexandria, named Melantia . . . came to (Eugenia), having been strongly tormented many times through the year by quartan fever. When Eugenia had anointed her with oil, she immediately vomited forth with all vehemence poisonous liquid. And she was restored to the best of health.[24]

Not knowing that Eugenia is a woman, Melantia thereafter visits her assiduously, overcome by desire. Eventually Melantia propositions her, offering wealth including 'gold of a great weight'.[25] Having been spurned by Eugenia in no uncertain terms, Melantia then accuses Eugenia of rape and it is only when she 'tore . . . the tunic she was wearing' that she is 'seen to be woman' and therefore definitively proved her innocence.[26] Eugenia is reunited with her family – the Prefect happens to be her father – and Melantia is punished.

The central issue in this miracle sequence is not conversion, but the collision of secular and spiritual worlds and the vulnerability of nuns and monks to sexual accusations when they have close contact with lay Christians.[27] In the *Passio Eugeniae,* in stark contrast to many other

22 *Passio Eugeniae*, ch. 28, 620.

23 Ibid., ch. 29, 620.

24 Ibid., ch. 11, 612: 'Matrona quaedam Alexandrina, caeteris matronis praestantior, nomine Melanthia, . . . venit ad eam, quia quartana gravissime et iam per annum et eo amplius vexabatur. Quam cum beata Eugenia oleo perunxisset, omnem continuo violentiam fellis evomuit. Et sanissima reddita'.

25 Ibid., ch. 12, 612: 'auri pondus immensum'.

26 Ibid., ch. 15, 614: 'scidit . . . tunicam, qua erat induta, et apparuit femina'.

27 On the issue of sexual purity and ascetism in (male) monasticism, see Conrad Leyser,

martyr narratives, and indeed, also in the *Passio Potiti*, a healing miracle does not lead to general joy and mass conversions – Melantia is already a Christian. Instead, an increasingly difficult situation develops in which, in the normal course of events, a male abbot may not have been able to prove his innocence. I would like to suggest that this sequence of events may have reflected nuns' perhaps often fraught relations with a resentful local community as evoked in the infanticide miracle in the *Vita Leobae*. It may indeed have been one of the reasons the nuns chose to copy this particular *passio* rather than the many others that may have been available to them.[28] The dilemma was surely both the degree and type of engagement the nunnery should have with the local community, and whether this was compatible with the leading of an exemplary life devoted to God where the virginity and reputation of the nuns remained unquestioned.

We do not know precisely what conclusions the nuns may have reached on this vexed topic, but Würzburg MS M.p.th.q. 28a remains an evocative witness to how an analysis of miracle stories in their manuscript context can contribute to our understanding of early medieval spirituality, the complex notion of 'mission' in already notionally Christianized areas such as eighth-century Bavaria and the moral and practical dilemmas this 'mission' presented to all involved in it.

University of Manchester

'Masculinity in Flux: Nocturnal Emission and the Limits of Celibacy in the Early Middle Ages', in D. M. Hadley, ed., *Masculinity in Medieval Europe* (London and New York, 1999), 103–20; idem, *Authority and Ascetism from Augustine to Gregory the Great* (Oxford, 2000), esp. cc. 1 and 2, 2–61.

[28] Munich, Bayerische Staatsbibliothek, MS 4554, and Vienna, Österreichische Nationalbibliothek, MS 1556 (Lowe, *Codices latini antiquiores*, 9: 5, no. 1242, and 9: 19, no. 1502) are both roughly contemporary with MS M.p.th.q. 28a, while MS M.p.th.q. 28b was probably copied some decades earlier. All have been attributed to South or South-Western German scriptoria, and all include Italian martyr narratives, having no less than fourteen Italian *passiones* between them (including in some cases more than one version of each saint's *passio*). This indicates the wide circulation of a broad range of Italian *passiones* in early medieval Southern Germany.

MAPPING MIRACLES IN BYZANTINE HAGIOGRAPHY: THE DEVELOPMENT OF THE LEGEND OF ST ALEXIOS

by BARBARA CROSTINI

HAGIOGRAPHICAL narrative is often examined through the well-established text-critical principle according to which the earliest text is necessarily the most skeletal in outline, the least wondrous in plot, and therefore the most historically believable. According to this view, to the bare bones of truth, fanciful narrative and miraculous tales are added with time, as the tale grows in the telling.[1] The development of the Legend of St Alexios has been viewed as a case in point. The idiosyncratic life-story of this fourth-century ascete has been described as evolving from a nucleus of 'fact', essentially coinciding with the early Syriac *Life*, to a romanced complexity with the Byzantine version influencing the later versions in all major romance languages. Consequently, critics have isolated and, to a large extent, derided the 'miraculous' element in the plot, while failing to articulate an understanding of the role of miracles in Alexios's *Life*.

Here, I shall focus on two specific episodes and compare their treatment across four mid-Byzantine versions, in order to raise the question of what factors might have influenced the hagiographer's treatment of miracles in each specific instance. Far from being flight of fancy which ought to be dismissed by historians, the miraculous episodes form an essential element in the transmission and diffusion of Alexios's cult. Thus, not only is the search for the *Urtext* a restrictive approach to the study of hagiography, but the criteria for this quest need also to be revised in the light of a richer understanding of the text in its specific context(s).[2]

1 Arthur Amiaud, *La Légende syriaque de Saint Alexis l'homme de Dieu* (Paris, 1889), xliv: 'Que le fond d'une légende soit ou non authentique, la marche régulière de son développement n'est jamais du merveilleux au naturel, de la recherche à la simplicité; elle tend à s'amplifier plutôt qu'à se restreindre'.

2 Karl D. Uitti, 'The Old French *Vie de Saint Alexis*. Paradigm, Legend, Meaning', *Romance Philology* 20 (1966), 263–95, 266. Uitti departs from the 'genetically oriented studies of the Alexis Legend', to bring his own brilliant reading of the OF poem to the centre of the discussion.

* * *

The popularity, longevity and multiformity of the Alexios legend was fed by the extraordinary details of his adventures. Born in Rome of senatorial family, after his mother had begged for a child to end her sterility, Alexios relinquished his betrothed on their wedding night and fled to Edessa to live there as a beggar among beggars, sheltering in the narthex of a church dedicated to the Virgin. But after a vision revealed his sanctity to the church's sacristan, Alexios fled once more in order to preserve his anonymity. Fateful winds pushed his boat back to Rome, where he lived the rest of his days in his father's household, unrecognized by his parents, despite their desperate longing to find their lost son. Only at Alexios's death did a scroll he had written reveal posthumously both his identity and the story of his holy life.

While the majority of versions encompass the full outline of this story, the ancient Syriac texts transmitted by three sixth-century manuscripts present the story of an anonymous 'man of God', born in Rome, who, after leaving his bride, took up begging at Edessa and died there.[3] There are serious problems in establishing the precise relation of the Syriac legend to the Byzantine text.[4] While most scholars hold that the original version was written in Greek, they have reconstructed a hypothetical, lost original along the lines of the Syriac model, believing it did not include the saint's return to his native Rome.[5] When a version comprising the first part of the narrative only was found extant in a Renaissance Greek manuscript at Venice,[6] it was hailed as the *Urtext* by

3 Amiaud, *Légende syriaque*, i–vi. Later Syriac manuscripts also continue the story with Alexios's return to Rome.

4 It is not clear why the anonymous Syriac ascete is given the name of Alexios in Greek, how the accounts came to differ in a number of details, and how to reconcile a serious discrepancy in the chronology given for Alexios and for his Syriac antecedent; see Amiaud, *Légende syriaque*, lii: 'La légende byzantine [. . .] et la primitive légende syriaque sont en réalité deux œuvres distinctes'.

5 See Ch. E. Stebbins, 'Les Origines de la légende de Saint Alexis', *Revue belge de philologie et d'histoire* 51 (1973), 497–507.

6 Venice, Marcianus gr. App. VII. 33: see Elpidio Mioni, *Bibliothecae Divi Marci Venetiarum: Codices Graeci manuscripti*, 3 vols (Rome, 1960–72), 2: 60–2; see also C. Van de Vorst and H. Delehaye, 'Catalogus codicum hagiographicorum graecorum Bibliothecae Divi Marci Venetiarum', *AnBoll* 24 (1905), 169–256, 234–5. Both catalogues date the manuscript, written on Western paper, to the fifteenth century, while the editors consider it a twelfth-century manuscript. According to the catalogue, the manuscript is composed of two contemporary parts, perhaps in origin separate books: in the first part, comprising fols 1–161, there is a Life of Alexios that includes both parts (*BHG* 51, with a different ending); the version considered the *Urtext* is contained in the last folios of the second part (fols 177–179).

its first editor,[7] and proposed as such in English translation.[8]

The appeal of this Greek version, shorn of the wondrous elements included in the second half of the narrative, is that it endorses the classic reconstruction of the development of the Alexios legend from a simple core of truthful, believable events – his spurning marriage and living as a beggar – to the later, amplified versions that began with a ninth-century Byzantine canon by Joseph the Hymnographer,[9] and progressed through the tenth-century Latin versions[10] to the famous Old French poem.[11] As Gaston Paris neatly put it, 'Le merveilleux était à l'origine complètement absent de la vie [d'Alexis]'.[12]

But the adherence to the 'real' and the accompanying phobia of the extraordinary appears to reflect more the taste and sceptical mentality of modern scholarship, where miracles are 'at a discount',[13] rather than the likely development of the Alexios narrative. The later Greek version comprising only Alexios's sojourn in Edessa appears, upon closer inspection, an unlikely candidate for an *Urtext*: its omission of the mother sterility motif (present in the Syriac), its antiquarian slant,[14] its

7 *BHG* 56c: text first published by Margaret Rösler, 'Alexiusprobleme', *Zeitschrift für romanische Philologie* 53 (1933), 508–28, 508–11. See also eadem, *Die Fassungen der Alexius-Legende* (Vienna and Leipzig, 1905).

8 Auct *BHG* 56c: Carl Odenkirchen, *The Life of St Alexius in the Old French Version of the Hildesheim Manuscript*, Medieval Classics 9 (Brookline, MA, 1978), 21–9. Although the book received poor reviews – Maria Dominica Legge described it as a 'soggy sandwich', in *Medium Aevum* 50 (1981), 133 – this remains the only approach to any Greek version for non-Greek specialists.

9 *BHG* 56: see the list of liturgical printings of this poem in the list given in Louis Petit, *Bibliographie des Akolouthies grecques* (Bruxelles, 1926), 4–6; these versions, however, afford little philological accuracy. See also Stebbins, 'Les Origines de la légende', 504–5 and idem, 'Les Grandes versions de la légende de Saint Alexis', *Revue belge de philologie et d'histoire* 53 (1975), 679–95, 684.

10 Ulrich Mölk, 'Die älteste lateinische Alexiusvita (9./10. Jahrhundert). Kritische Text und Kommentar', *Romanistisches Jahrbuch* 27 (1976), 293–315; another Latin version, pr. *ActaSS* 17 July, IV: 251–3, is also pr. and transl. in Odenkirchen, *Life of St Alexius*, 34–51.

11 The latest edition of the French text is *La Vie de Saint Alexis*, ed. Maurizio Perugi (Geneva, 2000). Perugi summarizes the state of research concerning the origins of the legend in an excellent introduction. For a useful guide to further bibliography, see Christopher Storey, *An Annotated Bibliography and Guide to Alexis Studies (La Vie de Saint Alexis)* (Geneva, 1987).

12 This classic reconstruction was expressed, for example, by Gaston Paris, 'La *Vie de Saint Alexis* en vers octosyllabiques', *Romania* 8 (1879), 163–80, 164.

13 Benedicta Ward, 'Monks and Miracle', in John C. Cavadini, ed., *Miracles in Jewish and Christian Antiquity: Imagining Truth* (Notre Dame, IN, 1999), 127–37, 127.

14 The text specifies the time as 'when Emperors ruled at Rome', and describes the setting for the benefit of an audience unfamiliar with Rome: 'there is a river that flows through Rome; the sea is eighteen miles away, and ships come up by that river': Odenkirchen, *Life of St Alexius*, 21–2.

emphasis on the role of the sacristan in the story, its unsatisfactory conclusion, in which the body of the saint, though freshly buried, cannot be recovered by the search party,[15] are all elements that point to an *ad hoc* refashioning of the legend, perhaps for a local performance judging by the emphasis on dialogue.[16] Odenkirchen's own criteria of 'believability' fall short on such an examination.[17] Moreover, this version emphasizes Alexios's poverty by creating a refrain about his 'sitting with the poor' (καθήμενον ἐν μέσῳ τῶν πτωχῶν), which recalls mendicant ideals particularly consonant to the time of the manuscript's confection. Lastly, just as in the Syriac versions concerning the anonymous ascete, this version of the story leaves us a saint without relics, without a place for worship, and therefore without the essential elements for a cult.[18]

* * *

On the contrary, the subtle shadings of the miraculous in the tales narrated in medieval Byzantium belong to the dynamics of a living cult. While the relative emphasis on the miraculous depends on the particular circumstances of composition and audience, in the Greek tradition Alexios's sanctity remains an exceptional sign of the power of God, untamed into the example for imitation he becomes in the later Western tradition.[19]

Two miraculous episodes, one from each of the 'two parts' of the Legend, will be examined here: the apparition to the sacristan at Edessa and the surrender of the scroll at Alexios's death. The versions examined are:

15 Ibid., 28–9.

16 But see Uitti, 'The *Vie de Saint Alexis*', 277, n. 7, who, without endorsing Rösler's conclusions, does however appreciate some elements in this version.

17 Odenkirchen, *Life of St Alexius*, 29.

18 According to J. B. Segal, *Edessa: 'the Blessed City'* (Oxford, 1970), 173, the cult of Alexios was exploited to attract Christian pilgrims to Edessa, esp. to the site of his death in the 'xenodochion' and burial in that hospice's cemetery; see also ibid., 148 and 185, n. 7. Therefore, the later version may have been devised to 'bring back' the saint's cult to Edessa. I am grateful to Bernard Hamilton for bringing this issue to my attention.

19 For example, the inclusion of this text in the St Alban's Psalter is explained as endorsing Christina of Markyate's decision to spurn sex and high society in favour of an ascetic life; appropriately, the full-page miniature selected for this Psalter (p. 57) depicts the moment of Alexios's desertion of the marriage chamber and departure by sea, as can be seen online at http://www.abdn.ac.uk/stalbanspsalter/english/translation/trans057 (consulted: 4 February 2004).

(1) *BHG* 56d, from MS Mosquensis Saint Synod. 15, originally from the Iviron monastery on Athos, and dated 1023;[20]

(2) *BHG* 56e, a text from version A of the eleventh-century Imperial Menologion of Constantinople;[21]

(3) Auct. *BHG* 52m, a text from version B of the same Imperial Menologion;[22]

(4) *BHG* 53, from MS Monacensis gr. 3, written at the Constantinopolitan monastery of the Prodromos Petra by the scribe Arsenios in the first half of the twelfth century.[23]

I will be comparing the treatment of two episodes in each version, in order to reveal a spectrum of attitudes to the miraculous that are governed not by chronology, but by a complex set of different factors. I have kept the chronological sequence in the numbering of the witnesses, although I will draw together the monastic (nos 1 and 4) and the imperial (nos 2 and 3) versions in the analysis.

The first episode is the apparition to the sacristan of the church at Edessa, indicating to him the existence of the saint there. As this episode is contained in the first part of the life, to the four versions we may add the Venice manuscript that represents, in the view of current scholarship, the Byzantine original. In this version, the sacristan becomes the mouthpiece for the narrator's own scepticism, doubting his first two

20 F. Halkin, 'Une Légende grecque de Saint Alexis BHG 56d', *AnBoll* 98 (1980), 5–16, 5 at n. 8. The date of this manuscript coincides with the year of the translation of Alexios's relics from Rome to Montecassino: *Vie de Saint Alexis*, ed. Perugi, 21.

21 Vasilij Vasil'evic Latyshev, *Menologii anonymi Byzantini saeculi X quae supersunt: fasciculos duos sumptibus Caesareae Academiae Scientiarum e Codice Mosquensi 376 Vlad.*, 2 vols (St Petersburg, 1911–12; repr. Leipzig, 1970), 1: 245–52. On the dating of the Imperial Menologion to the reign of Emperor Michael IV (1034–41), see Francesco D'Aiuto, 'Nuovi elementi per la datazione del Menologio Imperiale', *Rendiconti dell'Accademia Nazionale dei Lincei*, ser. ix, 8 (1997), 715–47.

22 *Dix Textes inédits tirés du Ménologe Impérial de Koutloumous*, ed. and transl. François Halkin and André-Jean Festugière (Geneva, 1984), 80–93, with an introduction to the twelfth-century manuscript, Athos Koutloumous. 23, at 7–8.

23 The text was published by Hans Ferdinand Massmann, *Sanct Alexius Leben in acht gereimten mittelhochdeutschen Behandlungen: nebst geschichtlicher Einleitung sowie deutschen, griechischen und lateinischen Anhängen*, Bibliothek der gesammten deutsche National-Literatur 9 (Quedlinburg, 1843), 201–8; cf. C. Van de Vorst and H. Delehaye, *Catalogus codicum hagiographicorum graecorum Germaniae, Belgii, Angliae* (Brussels, 1913), 92–4. The catalogue description of this manuscript is still that of I. Hardt, *Codices graeci manuscripti* (Munich, 1804), 14–22, 15 (tenth century); but the hand of the scribe has been identified by E. Kakoulidi, 'The Library of the Prodromos-Petra Monastery at Constantinople', *Hellenika* 21 (1968), 3–39 (in Greek), shifting the dating of the codex forwards by two centuries. I would like to thank Dr Annaclara Cataldi Palau for this reference and for sharing with me her notes on this manuscript.

dream-visions of the Virgin as 'a figment of his imagination' (φαντασία); only when he is terrorized by a 'frightful man' on a third occasion does he start his search for Alexios.[24] In this case alone the divine instructions to the sacristan do not contain the order to bring Alexios into the church in order to improve his living conditions, a measure that would inevitably publicize his sanctity to all and precipitate the saint's departure, as in all the versions containing part two. To pre-empt such a consequence, Alexios's meeting with the sacristan in this version is worldly-wise from the start. At first, he refuses to provide any but the most basic information; when pressed by the sacristan's natural curiosity, the saint is cautious enough to bind his hearer by oath in a formal, legalistic way before disclosing his story.[25] This device allows the story to be (orally) preserved for posterity (by the sacristan), while at the same time guaranteeing that the saint may end his days in peace in Edessa, still unknown to the crowds. Thus, the dynamics of the revelation are manipulated in order to fit coherently with the story that belongs to this narrative.

By contrast, the version from Munich (no. 4) relishes a taste for the miraculous and accepts the apparition in an unquestioning manner. In this version, it is the icon of the Virgin, placed before the sacristan, that speaks to him during his night-prayer.[26] Her speech is simple and short, asking him to bring into her church the man of God, Alexios, because he is worthy of the kingdom of heaven and has been granted the Spirit. The sacristan has no practical difficulty in carrying out this order, but, the version underlines, he is struck with fear and wonder at the experience of the voice from the icon.[27] The emphasis on the prayerful interaction with the talking icon may be explained by the fact that this version was written for liturgical reading in a well-educated monastic community of the capital, as the sophisticated language and style also attest.[28]

The 1023 version (no. 1), displaying some idiosyncrasies in vocabulary, is more difficult to contextualize. In it, the Theotokos, who this

24 Odenkirchen, *Life of St Alexius*, 24; cf. Rösler, 'Alexiusprobleme', 520.

25 Ibid., 24–5.

26 Ulrich Mölk, 'Deux hymnes latines du XIe siècle en l'honneur de saint Alexis', in *Marche Romane. Mélanges de philologie et de littératures romanes offerts à Jeanne Wathelet-Willem* (Liège, 1978), 455–64, 460: this version is standard in the West in the eleventh century.

27 Massmann, *Sanct Alexius Leben*, 204.

28 Massman transcribes after the title a rubric, 'per eut', that should probably be understood as 'pater eulogesomen', indicating the liturgical destination of the piece.

time appears in person (φαίνεται) to the sleeping sacristan,[29] is given a longer, rhetorically adorned speech, that is nevertheless insufficient for the practical carrying out of her orders, making a second, more prosaic revelation necessary. The sacristan is in this version unfailingly pious, soliciting with his prayer the second speech, that comes to him as an unspecified '*apocalypsis*'. Just as the first speech dwelt poetically, but ineffectually, on Alexios's shining like the sun in the universe, so the information that he is 'the poor man sitting in the narthex' need not have been unequivocal, but the sacristan does not get it wrong.[30] Clearly, this narrative is more attuned to the general effect of the story, than careful in dealing sensibly with its nuts and bolts.

The Menologion A version (no. 2) is instead skilled at getting a plausible sequence together in a concise paragraph.[31] The completion of seventeen years of ascetic life outside the church is presented as the climax of Alexios's virtue, a time when he had achieved his aim of being fully pleasing to God. The vision the sacristan receives at this high point of Alexios's life is simply a dream (ὄναρ) of the Virgin, in which she orders the sacristan to take the saint into the church as the sign that the saint's prayer has indeed been pleasing to God, like the scent of myrrh (Ps. 141, 2). Despite busying himself with the search for the man, the sacristan fails, making a second apparition necessary: ἡ παντάνασσα . . . φαίνεται. This second speech is slightly more precise than that in the Moscow manuscript (no. 1), specifying that the poor man is the one sitting by the door of the church. All is now clear for the sacristan to take action.

The philosophical preoccupation of Menologion B (no. 3) is fully apparent even in the snippet from this episode, compressed in less than a paragraph. The theoretical precision is evident at the outset as the vision is defined 'a true vision, not a dream' (ὕπαρ οὐκ ὄναρ).[32] Evidently, a dream-vision might have had questionable status, and so the change to a 'true vision' of the Theotokos, standing before the sacristan, reassures the informed and critical reader, perhaps the emperor himself, that he can trust the event. This version of the legend privileges indirect over direct speech, so that the command of the

29 On the hypothesis that the apparition in person replaces the speaking icon motif at a later moment in the Life's evolution, see Mölk, 'Die älteste Lateinische Alexiusvita', 301 and n. 36.

30 Halkin, 'Une Légende', 10.

31 Latyshev, *Menologii*, 247.

32 Also cited in Mölk, 'Die älteste Lateinische Alexiusvita', 301, n. 36.

Virgin to bring 'the man of God' into the church is reported obliquely. But the sacristan is quick to ask, in this case, how to do this; and he gets an immediate, though brief, explanation, that Alexios is the poor man in the narthex of the church.[33]

Taste and audience, therefore, have an impact on the shaping of this visionary narrative in each case, and the variations are independent of any temporal progression. There appears to be a spectrum of sensibilities, from a less problematized, credulous version dwelling without qualms on the miraculous element in the narrative, to a more sophisticated approach. Even the latter, however, is not sceptical towards the miraculous narrative, but treats its subject matter in a lighter, smoother manner that does not let the wondrous element stand out.

A similar conclusion can be reached through the second example, the treatment of Alexios's surrendering at death the scroll containing the narrative of his life. This episode is in some respects the climax of the legend, and it is the moment commonly chosen for representation in art.[34] In reading the various versions of this story, one appreciates that this incident is not just an awkward, idiosyncratic feature of the legend, too embarrassing to be considered an integral part of it, and therefore better explained away as part of the later additions to the story; it is, in fact, the pivotal point in understanding the relationship between the saint and the community of faith that will perpetuate his cult.

The monastic version in the Munich manuscript (no. 4) constructs a lengthy, dramatic scene around this moment.[35] Though dead, the saint's appearance is shining and brilliant, so that his final surrender of the scroll 'as if he were alive' (οἵαπέρ ζῶν) does not come as a surprise. It is the earnest prayer of the emperors and the archbishop of Rome, prostrate at the saint's knees, that convince him to yield his life history for public knowledge, a publicity he had strenuously avoided during his lifetime. The first reading is already a liturgical act, with an appointed reader (Aetios), preceded by prayers, sealing the community's recognition of Alexios's sanctity.

33 *Dix Textes*, ed. Halkin and Festugière, 84–6.

34 See, for example, the scene depicted in the Imperial Menologion: Helen C. Evans and William D. Wixom, eds, *The Glory of Byzantium: Art and Culture of the Middle Byzantine Era, A.D. 843–1261* (New York, 1997), 101–2, fig. 56; and the quasi-contemporary frescoes in San Clemente, Rome: Federico Guidobaldi, *San Clemente: gli edifici romani, la basilica paleocristiana e le fasi altomedievali*, San Clemente Miscellany IV, 1 (Rome, 1992), fig. 230.

35 Massmann, *Sanct Alexius Leben*, 206.

A similarly ritualized, liturgically conscious reading of Alexios's scroll is found in no. 1.[36] Here too the drama builds up slowly to its climax, but with the added element that it is the spiritual leader alone who in the end succeeds in taking the scroll from the dead man's hands. The pope is defined in the prayer to Alexios as 'our father and shepherd of the whole ecumene' (πατὴϱ ἡμῶν καὶ ποιμὴν πάσης τῆς οἰκουμένης), an appellation that may not have passed unnoticed in the ecclesial climate of the first half of the eleventh century. A political edge is thus found in the saint's reticence and final choice of surrender, pointing to the correct mediation between holy man and community via ecclesiastical authority.

In Menologion A (no. 2), it is not a question of successive trials, but it is the collective power of prayer of all the spiritual and temporal leaders that is affirmed, together with the emphasis on the special status of this dead body, whose face shines brightly, like the sun.[37] In this version, the drama is minimized; the prayer to give up the scroll (χάϱτη) is accompanied by its rationale, 'so that from it it may be known who exactly he was, and from where, and what was written [in it]'.[38] The saint's consent is recorded in a matter-of-fact statement, appearing more like the granting of a first grace than a physical act of giving: 'the good Alexios consented to their prayer and gave them the scroll'.[39] There follows not the formal reading aloud of its contents, but a summary of that information. This version of the Imperial Menologion is much less concerned with the liturgical enactment and the ecclesial context of this scene, although it does preserve the episode as the first instance of fruitful interaction between the saint's bodily relics and the congregation's prayers.

Menologion B (no. 3), on the other hand, shies away from both the drama and the full enactment of this scene. The narrative is short, oblique, and contains only indirect speech; nevertheless, a genuine dialogue goes on between the emperor, patriarch and crowd, on the one hand, and the dead body on the other.[40] The initial struggle to obtain

36 Halkin, 'Une Légende', 14.

37 Latyshev, *Menologii*, 250.

38 Ibid.

39 Ibid.

40 *Dix Textes*, ed. Halkin and Festugière, 90. I disagree with the translation by Halkin and Festugière of the text at 90: 'ὁμοθυμαδὸν τοῦ μακαϱίου πάντες ἐπιδοῦναι τὴν χάϱτην ἐδέοντο', as: '[. . .] tous, d'un même mouvement, demandaient (au père) de leur remettre le papier du bienheureux' (*Dix Textes*, 91). The genitive, τουί μακαϱιςου, must be taken as the object of εθδεςοντο, a verb that is normally construed with the genitive in this

the scroll, that provided some dramatic moments in the other accounts, is here shrunk to the bare minimum: an adverb, μόλις, 'with difficulty', is meant to capture it all, with sublime concision. While the reading aloud of the scroll that follows is not formalized in liturgical fashion, this version concludes with a theological consideration, pointing to the crowd's amazement at this story as a sign of God's manner of glorifying his saints.

* * *

These examples show the degree of selectivity and sensitivity in treating the same subject matter that the authors of each version applied to their work, free to create from time to time the text that best suited their purposes, their audiences, their tastes and theological or political dispositions. In their attitude to the miraculous, these 'metaphrasts' do not show a univocal trend in adding more and more wondrous elements to a legend; on the contrary, their elaborations demonstrate a degree of reflection on the message behind such miraculous interventions, depicting a saint that is increasingly credible psychologically and emphasizing his role as intercessor, as a bridge between the ordinary and the supernatural, granted through his very exceptional life-story.

Despite the prologue in the Moscow manuscript offering the story 'to spur the souls who love virtue to the zeal and imitation of such wondrous deeds',[41] the Greek legend of St Alexios veers more towards the presentation of a single, exceptional man who, at his death, can act as intercessor, than to the holding up of an exemplum. The story of Alexios has been thus appropriately defined as a 'legend', rather than a *Vita*, by its editors, placing it in the framework of Delehaye's definition of hagiography as the result of an accumulation of folkloristic themes over an initial skeleton of historical fact. Yet Delehaye himself pointed out how the wondrous motifs in hagiography 'go back to a very remote antiquity'.[42] Alexios's story consists not only of his amazing refusal to consummate his marriage and of his choice of living among the poor at Edessa, but also integral to it are his divinely-appointed return to his father's home, his sojourn there unrecognized for many years until his secret death; and, climactically, the disclosure of his account of his deeds, found on the scroll eventually retrieved from his dead hand.

meaning and form, yielding the translation: 'Everyone together asked the blessed one to give up the scroll'.

41 Halkin, 'Une Légende', 6.

42 Hippolyte Delehaye, *The Legends of the Saints* (London, 1907), 32.

Nevertheless, the trend observed in the mid-eleventh century Constantinopolitan redactions, which limit the miraculous by reining in the story on tighter philosophical and theological tracks, recalls the contemporary phenomenon observed by Giulia Barone for Cluny.[43] If the intentional reduction of the miraculous from a saint's *Life* could serve the purpose of making the saint into an example more effectively held up for imitation, the development of hagiographical texts must be considered much more fluid and cannot be reduced to a linear, chronological pattern of additions. In such cases, the text-critical principle of lack of miracles as a sign of antiquity needs even more careful application. But, as Barone concludes, the ridding of the miraculous happens at a cost: the popularity of the saint is often harmed or curtailed by it.[44]

Rather than lamenting with Halkin that '*Aegre aliae ab aliis distinguuntur recensiones. Expectanda editio critica*',[45] the scholar who is not bound by Odenkirchen's 'interest in the "very first version" of the tradition'[46] may thrive on the very fluidity of approaches to the Alexios narrative, which guaranteed a relevance to this story and a richness to its tradition that a 'true account' devoid of miracles would never have managed to secure. The interest of the hagiographical tale depends on the editor's (and then on the reader's) looking carefully at the significance of what is done in each version, rather than on his (ab)use of the sceptical tools of the scholar's trade.[47] Rather than treating the hagiographer as a novelist with a fervid imagination, it may be more helpful to compare his work with the prophetic activity of a narrator of visionary apocalypses; and what appears at first absurd, or incomprehensible, may then reveal, in its proper context, its full meaning.

University of Manchester

43 Giulia Barone, 'Une Hagiographie sans miracles. Observations en marge de quelques Vies du Xe siècle', in *Les Fonctions des saints dans le monde occidental (IIIe–XIIIe siècle)*, Collection de l'École française de Rome 149 (Rome, 1991), 435–46.

44 Ibid., 446.

45 F. Halkin, *Bibliotheca hagiographica graeca. Novum Auctarium*, Subsidia hagiographica 64 (Brussels, 1984), 16.

46 H. S. Robertson, review of Odenkirchen, *Speculum* 55 (1980), 385–6, 386.

47 Gianfranco Contini, 'Filologia', in idem, *Breviario di Ecdotica* (Milan and Naples, 1986), 3–62, 7–8 and 31, speaks of a 'recensione aperta' in the case of multiple versions; see also his comments on Gaston Paris's editorial methods in 'La "Vita" francese "di Sant'Alessio" e l'arte di pubblicare i testi antichi', ibid., 67–97, 71–3. On editing hagiographies in general, see now the essays gathered in the new periodical *Sanctorum* 1 (2004).

'GOD WILLS IT': SIGNS OF DIVINE APPROVAL IN THE CRUSADE MOVEMENT

by BERNARD HAMILTON

ROBERT the Monk, who was present at the Council of Clermont in 1095 and heard Urban II preach the crusade sermon, reports that when he had finished speaking all who were there shouted: 'God wills it. God wills it'. The pope, Robert tells us, saw in this unanimity a sign of divine inspiration: 'I tell you that God has drawn this response from you to express the feeling which he has inspired in your hearts'.[1] Yet although Urban's arguments and eloquence convinced his audience at Clermont, reactions to the crusade were more ambivalent among some people in the West, even among some of those who took the cross. This was a legacy of the ambiguous attitude of Western churchmen towards violence and warfare. Western society in the early medieval centuries was very violent, and, as Guy Halsall has rightly pointed out, the Church helped to determine the norms of violence which Christian society found acceptable.[2] No doubt churchmen viewed their intervention primarily as a limitation exercise. From the later ninth century onwards, as the Carolingian Empire declined, the popes intermittently called on the warriors of the West to come to their aid.[3] Indeed, in some ways the campaign of the Garigliano, conducted by a league of Byzantine and Lombard forces organized by Pope John X, who himself took part in the fighting, and which achieved its objective of ridding the Papal States of bands of Muslim raiders who had settled there, was like a rehearsal for the First Crusade.[4] The Church further tried to influence the behaviour of Christian fighting men by encouraging the Truce and Peace of God

1 Robert the Monk, *Historia Iherosolimitana*, Bk. I, ch. 2 [hereafter RM], RHC Occ., 3: 729.

2 Guy Halsall, 'Introduction', in idem, ed., *Violence and Society in the Early Medieval West* (Woodbridge, 1998), 1–45, 11–12.

3 Paul Rousset referred to these wars as '*précroisades*' in *Les Origines et les caractères de la première croisade* (Neuchâtel, 1945), 27–42.

4 Girolamo Arnaldi, 'La fase preparatoria della battaglia del Garigliano del 915', *Annali della Facoltà di Lettere e Filosofia* IV (Naples, 1954), 123–44; Otto Vehse, 'Das Bündnis gegen die Sarazenen vom Jahre 915', *Quellen und Forschungen aus italienischen Archiven und Bibliotheken* 19 (1927), 181–204.

movements in the early eleventh century, and in some areas the liturgical blessing of swords was introduced.[5] Consequently, by 1095 the fighting men in Western Europe were accustomed to the Church hierarchy's calling on them for help.

At the same time the consciences of devout warriors were influenced by the western monastic tradition, particularly by the reformed communities that occupied so important a place in eleventh-century Western society. Monastic spiritual advisers counselled men guilty of sins of violence to undertake unarmed, penitential pilgrimages, and particularly favoured the pilgrimage to Jerusalem.[6] The monastic reformers taught that renouncing the world and entering the cloister was the true path of Christian perfection and the surest means of salvation.[7] Marcus Bull has traced the way in which the attitudes of the devout members of the warrior class in south-western France were formed by a variety of religious influences before the First Crusade.[8]

It is often assumed that the fact that Urban II was a former prior of Cluny and that St Hugh gave the First Crusade his full personal support together with that of his Order, drew together the two strands in the Western Church's traditional attitude towards warfare: that of fighting in the service of the Church, and that of renouncing physical violence for the spiritual warfare of the cloister. It is true that Urban's crusade combined the active ideal of fighting the enemies of the faith with the ascetic ideal of penitential pilgrimage. Yet Ambrogio Piazzoni has suggested that the Cluniac attitude towards the crusade was more nuanced, and that while supporting the crusade, members of the Order nevertheless continued to believe that the true service of Christ lay in entering the religious life, an ideal which was expressed forcefully by a later Abbot of Cluny, Peter the Venerable (1122–56).[9] In this paper I want to suggest that such ambivalent attitudes towards the crusade were more prevalent than the relatively little overt criticism which it

5 Thomas Head and Richard Landes, eds, *The Peace of God. Social Violence and Religious Response in France around the Year 1000* (Ithaca, NY, and London, 1992); Carl Erdmann, *The Origin of the Idea of Crusade*, tr. Marshall W. Baldwin and Walter Goffart (revised edn, Princeton, NJ, 1977), 79–87.

6 Cyrille Vogel, 'Le Pèlerinage pénitentiel', *Revue des sciences religieuses* 38 (1964), 113–53.

7 Richard W. Southern, *The Making of the Middle Ages* (London, 1953), 50.

8 Marcus Bull, *Knightly Piety and the Lay Response to the First Crusade: the Limousin and Gascony, c.970–c.1130* (Oxford, 1993).

9 Ambrogio M. Piazzoni, '*Militia Christi* e Cluniacensi', in *'Militia Christi' e Crociata nei secoli XI–XIII. Atti della undecima Settimana internazionale di studi, Mendola, 28 agosto–1 settembre 1989* (Milan, 1992), 341–72.

attracted might suggest.[10] It appears to me that even those who went on the First Crusade had doubts about whether God really did will this expedition and sought signs of divine approval to strengthen their faith in its validity.

The earliest crusading ventures did little to allay such doubts among the population at large. While the main armies were preparing to meet the official papal deadline for departure, 15 August 1096, other less well-prepared contingents set out for the East ahead of them. Between late June and mid-August 1096, the three German expeditions led by Folkmar, Gottschalk and Emicho were pulverized in Hungary. News of this soon reached the West as, subsequently, did that of the massacre of the so-called 'Peasants' Crusade', in which thousands took part, by the Turks of Nicaea in the early autumn of 1096. Albert of Aachen tells an anecdote about how unsettling people in the West found the news of such defeats: a parish priest in Lombardy, walking through the fields to his church, was approached by a pilgrim (i.e. a crusader), who asked him what he thought about the crusade (*iter*). He replied:

> Some people say this intention has been inspired in all pilgrims by God . . . others say that [the participants] have set out for superficial reasons. Because of this so many pilgrims have met with opposition in . . . Hungary. . . . And so I still have not made up my mind about it. . . .[11]

The stranger then revealed that he was St Ambrose, once Bishop of Milan, and assured the priest that the crusade would be successful and would capture Jerusalem in three years' time.

It was a widely held opinion among those who took part in the princes' crusade that all those who died on the expedition in God's service, whether in battle or from natural causes, were martyrs for the faith. The knight, Anselm of Ribemont, woke one morning and asked for the last rites. His companions were astonished, because he was in excellent health, but he related that his comrade, Engelrand of St Paul, who had been killed in battle, had appeared to him in a dream and had revealed that he was now living in Heaven, and that a home was being prepared there for Anselm, which would be ready 'tomorrow'. Anselm believed that his friend was now a saint and therefore was telling the

10 Elizabeth Siberry, *Criticism of Crusading, 1095–1274* (Oxford, 1985), 190–216.

11 Albert of Aachen, *Historia Hierosolymitana* [hereafter AA], Bk. IV, ch. 38, RHC Occ., 4: 415–16. For an account of the early crusading expeditions: John France, *Victory in the East: a Military History of the First Crusade* (Cambridge, 1994), 88–96.

truth; he received the sacraments and died in battle on the following day.[12] This opinion about the status of crusaders who died on the campaign was shared by some members of the hierarchy. Symeon, the Orthodox Patriarch of Jerusalem, who had made contact with the crusaders at Antioch, wrote to the Western Church claiming that he had had a vision of Our Lord, who promised him that all those who took part in the expedition would appear before him at the Last Judgement wearing crowns.[13]

The crusaders felt the need for re-assurance, not only about their personal salvation, but also about God's continuing support for their cause, particularly when they experienced setbacks. The most severe of these was at Antioch, which they besieged through the winter of 1097–8 when they suffered greatly from famine and disease. When they did finally capture the city in June 1098, they were almost immediately besieged in it themselves by a huge Muslim relief army, commanded by Kerbogha of Mosul.[14] During those months of crisis crusader morale was fortified by a series of dreams and visions which some of the participants claimed to experience. The priest, Stephen of Valence, had a vision of Christ and the Blessed Virgin Mary, who assured him that the crusade would receive divine aid if the Franks repented their sins.[15] Another priest, named Everard, had been in Tripoli while the crusade was besieged in Antioch. A Syrian Christian whom he met there told him that he had just had a vision of St Mark the Evangelist, who had called at Tripoli on his way from Alexandria to Antioch, and who told him: 'Christ now resides in Antioch and commands his disciples to join him and aid in the battle which the Franks must wage against the Turks'.[16]

The problem about claims to experiences of this kind is that they cannot be checked empirically, but a way was found of testing the authenticity of the revelations allegedly received by Peter Bartholomew. He was a young Provençal layman in the Count of

12 Raymond of Aguilers, *Historia Francorum qui ceperunt Iherusalem* [hereafter RA], RHC Occ., 3: 276–7; Ralph of Caen, *Gesta Tancredi* [hereafter RC], ch. 106, RHC Occ., 3: 680–1.

13 *Epistulae et chartae ad historiam primi belli sacri spectantes quae supersunt aevo aequalis ac genuinae. Die Kreuzzugsbriefe aus den Jahren 1088–1100*, ed. Heinrich Hagenmeyer (Innsbruck, 1901), no. VI, 142.

14 France, *Victory in the East*, 197–296.

15 RA, RHC Occ., 3: 255–6; *Fulcheri Carnotensis Historia Hiersolymitana (1095–1127)*, ed. Heinrich Hagenmeyer (Heidelberg, 1913) [hereafter: Fulcher], Bk. I, ch. xx, 244–7.

16 RA, RHC Occ., 3: 281; *Raymond d'Aguilers, Historia Francorum qui ceperunt Iherusalem*, trans. John H. Hill and Laurita L. Hill (Philadelphia, PA, 1968), 97–8.

Toulouse's army, who claimed to have had four visions of St Andrew telling him that the lance with which Christ's side had been pierced was buried near the high altar in Antioch cathedral. The princes ordered excavations to be made and a lance-head was found.[17] This seemed to prove that Peter Bartholomew's visions had been genuine, and that God really did support and approve of the crusade. The crusader leaders accepted the Lance as an authentic relic, and it undoubtedly boosted the army's morale. In a letter written to the Archbishop of Rheims shortly after its discovery, Anselm of Ribemont said of it: 'When this pearl of great price had been found, all our men took heart again'.[18] The Lance was carried into battle by Raymond of Aguilers, chaplain of the count of Toulouse, and the crusaders won a resounding victory.[19] Nevertheless, some of the leaders, including the papal legate, Bishop Adhemar, had, from the start, been sceptical about Peter's claims[20] and when, in the months that followed, he continued to have visions, many of which had a strong political content, he was examined by a church court and undertook to prove the authenticity of his claims by undergoing the trial by ordeal. This consisted of walking between two bonfires, carrying the Lance. He survived this test, but died a few days later. His supporters asserted that he had been mortally wounded by the enthusiastic spectators who surged round him after he had emerged unscathed from the flames, but his opponents saw in his death evidence that he had failed the ordeal.[21] Consequently the Holy Lance lost credibility in the eyes of much, though not all, of the army[22] and thereafter

17 RA, RHC Occ., 3: 253–5, 257–9. This is the fullest account of the discovery of the Holy Lance, which is mentioned in many other sources: Heinrich Hagenmeyer, *Chronologie de la première croisade* (Paris, 1902), 167–8, no. 284.

18 *Die Kreuzzugsbriefe*, ed. Hagenmeyer, 159, no. XV.

19 RA, RHC Occ., 3: 261; France, *Victory in the East*, 282–96.

20 When told of the visions, 'episcopus autem nihil praeter verba putavit', RA, RHC Occ., 3: 255. Ralph of Caen reports the accounts which he later heard of how Peter Bartholomew had 'salted' the excavations in Antioch cathedral, RC, ch. 100, RHC Occ., 3: 676–7.

21 RA, RHC Occ., 3: 279–88; FC, Bk. I, ch. xviii, ed. Hagenmeyer, 235–41. This trial may have been influenced by the practice which had developed in some parts of the West of authenticating relics through the ordeal by fire, Thomas Head, 'Saints, Heretics and Fire: Finding Meaning through the Ordeal', in Sharon Farmer and Barbara H. Rosenwein, eds, *Monks and Nuns, Saints and Outcasts. Religion in Medieval Society. Essays in Honor of Lester K. Little* (Ithaca, NY, and London, 2000), 220–38. I owe this reference to my daughter, Sarah Hamilton.

22 AA, Bk. V, ch. 32, RHC Occ., 4: 452. Guibert of Nogent, writing in 1106–9, defended the authenticity of the Holy Lance: *Guibert de Nogent, Dei Gesta per Francos et cinq autres textes*, ed. Robert B. C. Huygens, CChrCM 127A (Turnhout, 1996) [hereafter: Guibert], Bk. VII, ch.

relics played no significant role as indicators of divine approval of the Crusade, and were never subsequently used during the campaign to authenticate visions.[23] This is striking, because when they entered the Holy Land the crusaders were moving through a great treasure-house of potential relics.

Yet, although individual claims to have seen saintly helpers in visions were open to dispute, the ministry of the saints to the Church on earth was in principle accepted by all the crusaders as part of Catholic belief. The Patriarch Symeon of Jerusalem, writing to the Western Church in 1098, described how

> We do not put our trust in our numbers or our strength ... but we are protected by the shield and righteousness of Christ, and with the knights of Christ, George, Theodore, Demetrius and Blaise riding at our side, we have safely cut our way through the hosts of the enemy.[24]

There was at that time very little cult of these Byzantine military saints in the Western Church,[25] but the crusaders accepted that God had placed them in command of the spiritual defences of eastern Christendom. When the army reached Lydda, where St George was buried, they appointed Robert of Rouen as bishop to serve the shrine, because, said Raymond of Aguilers, 'we felt . . . that [St George] would be our intercessor with God and would be our faithful leader'.[26] Western saints, who were familiar to and well esteemed by the crusaders, were

xxxiv, pp. 332–3; Colin Morris, 'Policy and Visions. The case of the Holy Lance at Antioch', in John Gillingham and James C. Holt, eds, *War and Government in the Middle Ages. Essays in Honour of J. O. Prestwich* (Woodbridge, 1984), 33–45.

23 Raymond of Aguilers is the only eye-witness source for the First Crusade to mention other relics. St Andrew complained in a vision to Peter Bartholomew that the Count of Toulouse had neglected relics belonging to Andrew himself; the priest, Peter Desiderius, told Raymond of Aguilers that he had been ordered in a vision to collect the relics of Sts Omechius, Leontius and John Chrysostom from the church of St Leontius at Antioch; while looking for these, the count's representatives also found relics belonging to St George; in a later vision, Peter Desiderius was ordered by St George to collect the relics of St Thecla; RA, RHC Occ., 3: 265, 290. Since no other source mentions these relics, they evidently made little impact on the other crusaders.

24 *Die Kreuzzugsbriefe*, ed. Hagenmeyer, No. IX, p. 147. See also Christopher Walter, *The Warrior Saints in Byzantine Art and Tradition* (Aldershot, 2003).

25 The cult of St Blaise had been introduced in Rome by a Greek religious community in the tenth century and later became popular there, Bernard Hamilton, 'The City of Rome and the Eastern Churches in the Tenth Century', *Orientalia Christiana Periodica* 27 (1961), 6–26, 11.

26 RA, RHC Occ., 3: 292; trans. Hill and Hill, 115.

very seldom mentioned in the First Crusade sources.[27] The Byzantine military saints were rarely visible, though the author of the *Gesta Francorum,* who was present at the battle against Kerbogha fought on 28 June 1098, reports that a great host mounted on white horses, carrying shining banners, and led by Sts George, Demetrius and Mercurius swept down from the mountains to attack the Turks.[28] In describing this vision the author was almost certainly influenced by biblical imagery and precedent.[29]

Transcendental visions of this kind were rare, and the most favoured way of discerning God's will was by studying the heavens. This method was believed to be divinely sanctioned. The Book of Genesis records how on the fourth day of creation God said: 'Let there be lights in the firmament of the heaven to divide the day from the night; and let them be for signs and for seasons and for days and years' (Gen. 1, 14). The important word is 'signs'. These signs played a crucial role in preparing the world for the coming of Christ. Balaam, who was a gentile, prophesied: 'I shall see [the Almighty] but not now; I shall behold him, but not nigh: there shall come a star out of Jacob and a sceptre shall arise out of Israel' (Num. 24, 17). Medieval exegetes supposed that a knowledge of this gentile prophecy had enabled the Magi to recognize the significance of the star of Bethlehem and come to worship the infant Christ.[30]

Like the Magi, some learned men in eleventh-century Europe watched the skies to learn God's will, among them Bishop Gislebert of Lisieux. Walter of Cormeilles, a member of his household, later told Orderic Vitalis how in the spring of 1095 the bishop had observed a shower of shooting stars and had said to Walter: 'This signifies a movement of peoples from one kingdom to another'.[31] The crusade had not then been preached, so this phenomenon was later seen as a kind of

27 The only instance in the eye-witness accounts of the crusade is the appearance of Our Lady to the priest Stephen of Valence. St Agatha was in attendance, but did not speak, RA, RHC Occ., 3: 287.

28 *Anonymi Gesta Francorum et aliorum Hierosolimitanorum,* ed. and trans. Rosalind Hill (London, 1962) [hereafter: GF], 69.

29 Cf. II Kings, 6, 16–17. When reworking the account in GF, Robert the Monk included an explanation, which he attributed to Bohemond's chaplain, of how spiritual beings may become visible: 'assumant sibi aeria corpora . . . quia videri non possunt in spirituali essentia sua'. RM, Bk. V, ch. 9, RHC Occ., 3: 797.

30 Matt. 2, 1–11. See the commentary in the *Opus imperfectum in Matthaeum, Homilia Secunda,* PG 56, 636–46. This Latin work was wrongly attributed to St John Chrysostom and was read quite widely in the medieval West.

31 *The Ecclesiastical History of Orderic Vitalis,* Bk. IX, ch. 2, ed. and trans. Marjorie Chibnall, 6 vols (Oxford, 1969–80), 5: 8–10.

early warning system. After the Council of Clermont the skies were watched carefully for divine guidance. It was considered auspicious when an eclipse of the moon took place on 11 February 1096, while King Philip of France was meeting in Paris with his vassals to discuss the crusade, because the moon was traditionally held to symbolize Islam.[32]

As the main crusader army marched towards Syria they too watched the night skies. Fulcher of Chartres reports:

> When we reached the city of Heraclea [at the foot of the Taurus mountains on the western side], we beheld a certain sign in the sky, which appeared in brilliant whiteness in the shape of a sword, with the point towards the east.[33]

This was almost certainly a comet, and was interpreted as a good omen. Later, when the crusaders were besieged inside Antioch, the author of the *Gesta Francorum* describes how he saw 'a fire in the sky coming from the West, and it approached and fell upon the Turkish army, to the great astonishment of our men, and of the Turks also'.[34] This would seem to be the description of a meteor.

Communications between the crusade and Western Europe were very slow, and people in the West looked at the night skies as a kind of news bulletin, which might inform them of the crusade's progress. Ralph of Caen, who later became chaplain to Prince Tancred of Antioch, recalled how in 1098,

> when I was a little lad (*adulescentulus*) and still living in my father's house at Caen, I knew nothing about Antioch except the name. But one night the sky turned an horrendous red colour, and everybody who saw it said: 'There is a battle going on in the East'.[35]

Unlike visions, heavenly signs could be seen by everybody, and the Christian world speculated about how the Muslims had reacted to signs that in their own view so clearly foretold a victory for the crusade. Guibert of Nogent recounts how, while Robert I the Frisian, Count of

32 Guibert, Bk. II, ch. xvii, pp. 133–4.

33 Fulcher, Bk. I, ch. xiv, ed. Hagenmeyer, 203–5; *A History of the Expedition to Jerusalem, 1095–1127*, ed. Harold S. Fink, trans. Frances R. Ryan (Knoxville, 1969), 88–9.

34 GF, ed. Hill, 65; also reported by RA, RHC Occ., 3: 257. Robert the Monk makes Herluin, one of the envoys from the crusade to Kerbogha, claim: 'That star came as a warning to you and as an earnest of deliverance to us; for because of it we are assured that we have been given a mission by our God'. RM, Bk. VII, ch. 7, RHC Occ., 3: 826.

35 RC, ch. 57, RHC Occ., 3: 648.

Flanders, was staying in Jerusalem as a pilgrim in the 1080s, a great Muslim assembly was held on the Temple Mount, which lasted all day. The count's Muslim host told him the reason for this:

> We have seen unusual signs in the coming and going of the stars from which we have inferred with assurance that Christian men will come to these regions and will conquer us through persistence in warfare and frequent victories. . . .[36]

What the crusaders did not know was that there was one group of Christian observers who interpreted the signs in the heavens quite differently from themselves. The Armenian chronicler, Matthew of Edessa, reported

> Since the day the Frankish nation went forth, not one good or favourable omen appeared; . . . all the omens pointed to the calamity, destruction, ruin and disruption of the land, through death, slaughter, famine and other catastrophes.[37]

The experience of Frankish rule in Edessa, which culminated in the ruin of that ancient Christian city, must certainly have seemed to justify this gloomy prognostication.[38]

The decisive proof that God willed the crusade was its success in capturing Jerusalem in July 1099. Soon after that the Franks acquired the relic of the True Cross, which provided them with a perpetual reminder of God's approval of their conquest and settlement of the Holy Land. It was placed in a golden reliquary, encrusted with jewels, and became the standard of the kingdom.[39] When describing the Battle of Ramla in 1101, which the Franks of Jerusalem won against a numerically superior Egyptian army, Albert of Aachen remarked how 'the power of the Holy Cross was victorious not only over spiritual enemies, but also against the weapons of human enemies'.[40]

36 Guibert, Bk. VII, ch. xxvii, pp. 319–20.

37 Ara Edmond Dostourian, *Armenia and the Crusades, Tenth to Twelfth Centuries. The Chronicle of Matthew of Edessa* (Lanham, MD, New York and London, 1993), Pt. II, ch. 129 (*anno 1099–1100*), 175.

38 Monique Amouroux-Mourad, *Le Comté d'Edesse, 1098–1150* (Paris, 1988).

39 RA, RHC Occ., 3: 302; Fulcher, Bk. I, ch. xxx, ed. Hagenmeyer, 309–10; AA, Bk. VI, ch. 38, RHC Occ., 4: 488–9.

40 AA, Bk. VII, ch. 68, RHC Occ., 4: 550. Walter the Chancellor, in his account of how King Baldwin II brought the Holy Cross to Antioch in 1119 and saved the city after its army had been annihilated at the Field of Blood, attributed similar powers to the relic; *Galterii Cancellarii, Bella Antiochena*, Bk. II, ch. xii, RHC Occ., 4: 121–3; Thomas S. Asbridge and

Nevertheless, the continued well-being of the Crusader Kingdom was not automatic. Divine assistance was conditional on its recipients living righteous lives. This was a paradigm learned from those earlier rulers of the Holy Land, the Kings of Judah and Israel, for the medieval Church considered that the Old Testament was a prophecy of Christian history as well as an historical record of Jewish history.[41] This awareness had developed among those who settled in the Latin East while they were taking part in the First Crusade: the failure of the early expeditions which preceded the princes' crusade was attributed to the sinful lives of the participants, as were the serious checks which the main crusade experienced.[42] So the Franks who settled in the East remained vigilant about incurring divine disapproval and watched the night skies with care.

They came to understand that eclipses were part of the divinely constituted mechanism of the universe, and that those that could be accurately predicted were not portents at all.[43] The night skies of the Middle East produced unfamiliar phenomena. Fulcher of Chartres reports how on 23 February 1106

> from the third hour until noon we beheld in the sky two other suns, seemingly to the left and right of the real one. However, they did not shine like the actual sun, but glowed dimly in form and luminosity. Around these suns a circular whiteness appeared . . . inside this circle shone a half-circle resembling a rainbow.[44]

I thought this account fanciful, when I first read it; but on 27 June 2003 the writer of Weather Eye in *The Times* of London reported: 'A few days ago I saw three suns in the evening sky – the real sun was bordered on either side by lights splashed with the colours of the spectrum like small pieces of a rainbow'.[45]

The most spectacular phenomenon the Franks witnessed in the early

Susan B. Edgington, *Walter the Chancellor's 'The Antiochene Wars': a Translation and Commentary* (Aldershot, 1999), 156.

41 Beryl Smalley, *The Study of the Bible in the Middle Ages* (3rd edn, Oxford, 1983), specially ch. 1, 1–36.

42 AA, Bk. I, ch. 29, RHC Occ., 4: 234–5; RA, RHC Occ., 3: 256.

43 'In the following month, which was June, the moon appeared to us . . . entirely red. . . . This happened on the thirteenth of the month. If it had happened on the fourteenth we would certainly have thought it an eclipse. Therefore we regarded it as a portent': Fulcher, Bk. II, ch. lxi, tr. Ryan, p. 219; ed. Hagenmeyer, 604–5.

44 Fulcher, Bk. II, ch. xxxv, tr. Ryan, 189–90; ed. Hagenmeyer, 508–9.

45 Paul Simon, 'Weather Eye', *The Times*, Friday 27 June 2003.

years of their settlement was the aurora borealis seen in Jerusalem in December 1117. Fulcher of Chartres reports that

> we conjectured that either much blood would be shed in war, or that something no less threatening was forecast. . . . However, some people, prophesying, declared that this was a portent for those who were to die in the next year. And subsequently there died: Pope Paschal in January; Baldwin, King of Jerusalem, in April; . . . Arnulf, the Patriarch of Jerusalem; Alexius Emperor of Constantinople, and many others of the great men of the world.[46]

The belief that God communicated with men through heavenly signs was so strong at the time of the First Crusade that it even affected the symbolism of dreams. Albert of Aachen recounts that when Godfrey of Bouillon was travelling to the East in 1097, Canon Gislebert of Aachen dreamt that:

> The Duke sat enthroned in the sun, and there flocked around him a vast number of every kind of bird which exists. Then one group of them gradually flew away, but the greater part remained motionless on his right hand and on his left. After this the greater part of the sun was darkened and after a short time the throne of the Duke was entirely obliterated and almost all the birds who had stayed with him flew away.[47]

Albert understood this as a prophetic dream, foretelling Godfrey's brief reign in Jerusalem. It is significant that this prophecy, which augured the divine approval of the crusade, was formulated in terms of portents in the sky. It was there at the time of the First Crusade that Western people considered that the divine will might most securely be found written.

University of Nottingham

46 Fulcher, Bk. II, ch. lxiii, tr. Ryan, 220–1; ed. Hagenmeyer, 607–8.

47 AA, Bk. VI, ch. 36, RHC Occ., 4: 487–8.

STIGMATA ON THE FIRST CRUSADE

by WILLIAM J. PURKIS*

IN his eyewitness account of the First Crusade, Fulcher of Chartres described the shipwreck and drowning of a boatload of crusaders who were bound for the Holy Land in 1097. After the bodies of the dead were recovered, he explained how 'they discovered crosses evidently marked on the flesh above the shoulders'.[1] Fulcher supposed this incident to be a miracle, 'divinely revealed', and that the marking was a 'token of faith' (*pignus fidei*) bestowed by God upon his servants. It was a sign to the surviving crusaders that God favoured them and would fulfil the promise he had made that '*the just, though they shall be taken prematurely by death, shall be in peace*' (Wisd. 4, 7).[2]

Raymond of Aguilers, another participant in the crusade, recorded a similar incident. After a skirmish with the Muslims in which a number of crusaders were killed, an examination of the corpses revealed that 'all of the dead had crosses on their right shoulders'.[3] Prayers of thanksgiving were offered to God, 'who remembered his paupers' by this mark. In order to share with the rest of the crusade army the reassurance that this miracle brought, one of the survivors, who was also marked with the cross, was brought before them.

> And in that man we certainly saw a wonder – Raymond wrote – . . . he lasted through seven or eight days without sustenance, testifying that Jesus, to whose judgement he would go without doubt, was God, the creator of that cross.[4]

* I am grateful to the Arts and Humanities Research Board for supporting the research that led to this paper.

1 *Fulcheri Carnotensis Historia Hierosolymitana (1095–1127)*, ed. Heinrich Hagenmeyer (Heidelberg, 1913), 169–70. All translations by the author, except where indicated.

2 Ibid. For another treatment of the appearance of the sign of the cross upon the drowned crusaders and a discussion of similar events in Scandinavian sources, see Haki Antonsson, '*Insigne Crucis*: a European Motif in a Nordic Setting', in Thomas R. Liszka and Lorna E. M. Walker, eds, *The North Sea World in the Middle Ages: Studies in the Cultural History of North-Western Europe* (Dublin, 2001), 15–32. The symbolism of the cross is considered in Giles Constable, 'Jerusalem and the Sign of the Cross (with Particular Reference to the Cross of Pilgrimage and Crusading in the Twelfth Century)', in Lee I. Levine, ed., *Jerusalem: its Sanctity and Centrality to Judaism, Christianity, and Islam* (New York, 1999), 371–81.

3 *Le 'Liber' de Raymond d'Aguilers*, ed. John H. and Laurita L. Hill (Paris, 1969), 102.

4 Ibid.

Yet these were not isolated occurrences. In this paper, I shall explore the significance of the marks that appeared upon the bodies of some first crusaders, and argue that such 'stigmata' illustrate an important aspect of early crusade spirituality.

* * *

It was not until the French monk Guibert of Nogent completed his *Gesta Dei per Francos* (*c.*1111) that the miraculous events recorded by Fulcher of Chartres were elaborated upon further. Guibert had read Fulcher's *Historia* towards the end of the composition of his own work, and he chose to incorporate the story of the drowned crusaders into his narrative. He wrote of the recovery of their bodies and the discovery of the signs of the cross 'on the skin of their shoulders', describing the mysterious wounds as *sacrum stigma*, divinely imprinted as evidence of the crusaders' faith.[5] But Guibert also noted that the veracity of this miracle had been called into question because of a series of events that had occurred during the preaching of the crusade in 1096.[6] He described the hysteria with which Pope Urban II's appeal had been greeted and recounted a number of incidents in which men and women claimed that they had been touched by similar wonders:

> One man scratched his cheeks, drew a cross with the flowing blood, and showed it to everyone. Another showed the spot in his eye, by means of which he had been blinded, as a sign that a heavenly announcement had urged him to undertake the journey. Another, either by using the juices of fresh fruits, or some other kind of dye, painted on some little piece of his body the shape of a cross.[7]

Such claims had obviously arisen from a belief that those who bore the sign of the cross on their flesh were especially chosen by God. As Guibert put it, 'by means of this fraudulent and deceitful exhibition, they might claim that God had showed himself in them'.[8]

There are accounts of these events in many of the sources. In his *Chronicle*, Bernold of St Blasien reported for 1096 that '[Pope Urban]

5 *Guibert de Nogent, Dei Gesta per Francos et cinq autres textes*, ed. Robert B. C. Huygens, CChr.CM 127a (Turnhout, 1996) [hereafter: Guibert], 329.

6 See Jonathan Riley-Smith, *The First Crusade and the Idea of Crusading* (London, 1986), 34, 81–2, 114.

7 Guibert, 330; transl. Robert Levine, *The Deeds of God through the Franks: a Translation of Guibert de Nogent's* Gesta Dei per Francos (Woodbridge, 1997), 155–6.

8 Ibid.

made all those who devoted themselves to this journey mark themselves with the sign of the cross on their clothes; but the sign also appeared on the flesh itself of some of them.'[9] Baldric of Bourgueil described the 'countless numbers' of rumours that circulated about such discoveries:

> Many of the common people were displaying the cross which had itself grown divinely; and this same [miracle] was taken for granted by certain kinds of girls. This of course was seized upon as entirely fake. Some, in truth, had applied that likeness of a cross with a hot iron.[10]

Another writer recorded that

> the Western men, divinely inspired, some imprinted with the sign of the cross by a white-hot iron to their own flesh, others marked on the outside of their clothes, briskly and with one mind took to the way of God and the holy army.[11]

In his description of the 'various portents' that roused the Germans to undertake the crusade, Ekkehard of Aura wrote that:

> Some [of the crusaders] were . . . displaying the sign of the cross which had been divinely impressed either on their foreheads or their clothes or in any other place of the body, and they believed themselves by this same *stigma* to have been directed to the army of the Lord.[12]

And although written some thirty years after the successful recovery of Jerusalem, the crusade narrative Orderic Vitalis included in his *Ecclesiastical History* described how

> Walter of Poissy died at Philippopolis in Bulgaria; and after his death the sign of the holy cross appeared on his body. When the

[9] Bernold of St Blasien, *Chronicon*, ed. Georg Heinrich Pertz, MGH (Hannover, 1844), 5: 385–467, 464.

[10] Baldric of Bourgueil, *Historia Jerosolimitana*, RHC Occ., 4: 1–111, 17.

[11] *Historia de translatione sanctorum magni Nicolai . . . ejusdem avunculi alterius Nicolai, Theodorique . . . de civitate Mirea in monasterium S. Nicolai de Littore Venetiarum*, RHC Occ., 5: 253–292, 255.

[12] Ekkehard of Aura, *Hierosolymita, de oppressione, liberatione ac restauratione Jerosolymitanæ Ecclesiæ*, RHC Occ., 5: 1–40, 19.

> duke and the bishop of the city heard of this sign . . . they had Walter's body reverently brought into the city and buried.[13]

Guibert of Nogent was the only writer to consider one of these cases in detail. His subject was 'a certain abbot',[14] who attempted to fake a miraculous *stigma* out of a desire to secure funding to undertake the crusade:

> [He] cut into his forehead by I know not what means the sign of the cross, which ordinarily was made out of some kind of material and affixed to clothing. It did not look as though it had been painted on, but as though it had been inflicted, like a wound received in battle. After he had done this, to make the trick look authentic, he claimed that an angel had appeared to him in a vision and placed it there.[15]

This falsification paid dividends, and the abbot was soon inundated with gifts. However, he was eventually exposed as a fraud when his self-inflicted wound became infected.[16] Guibert's reaction is interesting for he did not condemn the abbot harshly, concluding that 'He had of course intended zealous imitation (*emulatio*) of God, but he had not carried this out wisely.'[17]

* * *

It is clear, therefore, that during the preaching and course of the crusade, there was a pattern of appearances, miraculous or otherwise, of the sign of the cross on the bodies of some participants. Although only two sources describe the marks using the actual word 'stigmata', many of these incidents do bear comparison with the later experience of the most famous of medieval stigmatics, St Francis of Assisi (d. 1226).

It was whilst in retreat on Mount La Verna in 1224 that Francis, immersed in a meditation on the Passion of Christ, was said to have

13 Orderic Vitalis, *The Ecclesiastical History*, ed. and transl. Marjorie Chibnall, 6 vols (Oxford, 1969–80), 5: 30. Orderic's version was based largely on the *Historia* of Baldric of Bourgueil but, as Chibnall notes, 'the information in this paragraph occurs only in Orderic': ibid., 30, n. 2.

14 The abbot can be identified as Baldwin, chaplain to Godfrey of Bouillon, and later archbishop of Caesarea (1101–8), from William of Tyre, *Chronique*, ed. R. B. C. Huygens, *CChrCM* 63–63a, 2 vols (Turnhout, 1981), 1: 472.

15 Guibert, 197; transl. Levine, *Guibert de Nogent*, 88, in part modified by author.

16 See Robert D. Smith, *Comparative Miracles* (St Louis, MO, 1965), 23–4, who noted that '[a] verified characteristic of [*bona fide*] stigmata is that the wounds do not become infected'.

17 Guibert, 197.

received an angelic vision in which the stigmata were marked upon his body.[18] Francis's religious life had been spent in close imitation of Christ, and the stigmata were perceived as an outward sign of his inner devotion and personal holiness. One of his contemporaries, James of Vitry (d. 1240), wrote that Francis had 'followed Him Who was crucified so explicitly that at his death the signs of the wounds of Christ were apparent on his hands, feet, and side'.[19] A later account described how

> Christ appeared to Saint Francis.... And these were His words: 'Do you know,' said Christ, 'what I have done to you? I have given you the Stigmata, which are the marks of My Passion.... In this way you shall be conformed to Me in My death as you have been during your life.'[20]

Whilst the stigmata of St Francis replicated the five wounds Christ had suffered during his Passion, and the miraculous marks found upon certain crusaders manifested themselves in the sign of the cross, both sprang from the same ideal of *imitatio Christi*.[21] Giles Constable has argued that 'until at least the twelfth century, the term stigmata was used in a general sense, rather than with specific reference to Christ's wounds', and he has demonstrated a number of instances in which 'stigmata' were reported to have appeared – or in which writers used the term figuratively – as an indication of the bearer's profound piety.[22] For example, in Peter Damian's *Vita* of Dominic *Loricatus* (d. 1060) it is recorded that 'Dominic carried the *stigmata* of Jesus on his body, and the banner of the cross was not only depicted on his forehead, but also impressed everywhere on his limbs'.[23] Caesarius of Heisterbach's

18 For a recent study, see Nitza Yarom, *Body, Blood and Sexuality: a Psychoanalytic Study of St Francis' Stigmata and their Historical Context* (New York, 1992).

19 James of Vitry, *Sermones ad fratres minores*, ed. Hilarinus Felder, Spicilegium Franciscanum 5 (Rome, 1903), 35, cited in Giles Constable, 'The Ideal of the Imitation of Christ', *Three Studies in Medieval Religious and Social Thought* (Cambridge, 1995), 143–248, 219.

20 *The Little Flowers of Saint Francis: with Five Considerations on the Sacred Stigmata*, transl. Leo Sherley-Price (London, 1959), 166.

21 For *imitatio Christi*, see especially Ernest J. Tinsley, *The Imitation of God in Christ: an Essay on the Biblical Basis of Christian Spirituality* (London, 1960); Constable, 'Imitation of Christ', *passim.*

22 Constable, 'Imitation of Christ', 199–201.

23 Peter Damian, *Vita Dominici Loricati*, PL 144, 1024A; see Constable, 'Imitation of Christ', 202–3: 'it is hard to tell how explicitly Damiani's words should be taken.... Since he was certainly familiar with the figurative use of the term stigmata, he may have been referring to the signs left on Dominic's body by his scourgings and other ascetic disciplines'. For

Dialogue on Miracles (composed *c.* 1220–35) contains a report of an incident that parallels the experiences of both St Francis and the stigmatics of the First Crusade. He described how 'a certain [Cistercian] novice . . . bowing his head with much reverence . . . felt a cross impressed upon his forehead, and I think that at that moment he was meditating on the Passion'.[24] It would appear, therefore, that it was only after the widespread fame of the 'stigmata' of St Francis that the term became specifically associated with the marks of Christ's Passion. As Herbert Thurston saw it,

> we have the striking fact that not a single case of stigmatization was heard of before the beginning of the thirteenth century. No sooner, however, was the extraordinary phenomenon which marked the last days of the seraphic St Francis published throughout the world, than other unquestionable cases of stigmata began to occur.[25]

Yet the idea that an individual bearing some kind of 'stigmata' should be regarded as a pious follower of Christ can be found in Scripture. In his Epistle to the Galatians, St Paul wrote 'let no-one cause me trouble, for I bear on my body the *stigmata* of Jesus'.[26]

* * *

It is with this background in mind that we can return to the crusade sources and, crucially, to the proclamation of the crusade itself by Pope Urban II in 1095.[27] Whilst there is no general agreement amongst historians about the exact content of his sermon at the Council of Clermont, there can be little doubt that Urban's preaching consisted of an exposition of two specific biblical passages in which Christ put

Dominic *Loricatus*, see Herbert J. Thurston and Donald Attwater, eds, *Butler's Lives of the Saints*, 4 vols (London, 1956), 4: 110–11.

24 *Caesarii Heisterbacensis monachi ordinis cisterciensis Dialogus miraculorum*, ed. Joseph Strange, 2 vols (Cologne, 1851; repr. Ridgewood, NJ, 1966), 2: 100.

25 See Herbert Thurston, *The Physical Phenomena of Mysticism* (London, 1952), 122; see also Constable, 'Imitation of Christ', 218–26.

26 Gal. 6, 17; see Christopher P. Jones, '*Stigma*: Tattooing and Branding in Graeco-Roman Antiquity', *Journal of Roman Studies* 77 (1987), 139–55, 150: 'It is probable that he actually refers to marks caused by ill-treatment, but regards them figuratively as the tattoos imposed on him as a slave of Christ. Out of St Paul grew the medieval use of the word *stigma* for marks received on the body by participation in Jesus' sufferings, either by self-laceration or mystic transmission'. See also Montague Summers, *The Physical Phenomena of Mysticism, with Especial Reference to the Stigmata, Divine and Diabolic* (London, 1950), 181–3.

27 See H. E. J. Cowdrey, 'Pope Urban II's Preaching of the First Crusade', *History* 55 (1970), 177–88, repr. in idem, *Popes, Monks and Crusaders* (London, 1984), XVI; Penny J. Cole, *The Preaching of the Crusades to the Holy Land, 1095–1270* (Cambridge, MA, 1991), 1–36.

himself forward as an exemplar for his disciples to follow. The anonymous author of the *Gesta Francorum* recorded the following:

> When that time had already come, of which the Lord Jesus warns his faithful people every day, especially in the Gospel where he says, '*If any man will come after me, let him deny himself, and take up his cross, and follow me*' (Matt. 16, 24), there was a great stirring of heart throughout all the Frankish lands, so that if any man, with all his heart and mind, really wanted to follow God and faithfully to bear the cross after him, he could make no delay in taking the road to the Holy Sepulchre as soon as possible.[28]

Robert of Rheims, who may well have attended the Council, offered a striking account of the wording of the sermon. He reported Urban saying:

> Whoever therefore shall carry out this holy pilgrimage, shall make a vow to God, and shall offer himself as a living sacrifice . . . and he shall display the sign of the cross of the Lord on his front or on his chest. When, truly, he wishes to return from there having fulfilled his vow, let him place the cross between his shoulders; in fact, by this twofold action they will fulfil that precept of the Lord which he prescribed himself through the Gospel: *He that does not carry his cross and come after me, is not worthy of me.* (Matt. 10, 38)[29]

Robert's version of the Clermont sermon was the only one to record these details about the position of the crusade badge and it is, of course, impossible to gauge whether Urban actually made such specific injunctions; they may have been documented in a lost conciliar decree.[30] It is worth noting that in a key part of Robert's report the exact meaning of the Latin is uncertain. Urban's instruction for the crusaders who were setting out was that the sign of the cross should be placed *in fronte sua*, a phrase translated here as 'on his front'. However, it could also be read as 'on his forehead'. It seems highly unlikely that this was what Urban intended, but if this does constitute an accurate report of his sermon

28 *Gesta Francorum et aliorum Hierosolimitanorum*, ed. and transl. Rosalind Hill (London, 1962), 1.

29 Robert of Rheims, *Historia Iherosolimitana*, RHC Occ., 3: 717–882, 729–30.

30 The *Gesta Francorum* records the positioning of the crusader cross as on the right arm or between the shoulders: 'Deferunt arma ad bellum congrua, in dextra uel inter utrasque scapulas crucem Christi baiulant', 7. Robert's *Historia* was itself based on the *Gesta*. Antonsson, '*Insigne Crucis*', 27, rightly notes that 'this particular positioning of the mark is naturally highly symbolic for it evokes the scene of Christ carrying the cross to Golgotha'.

the ambiguity may have contributed to some of the unusual events which unfolded as news of the proposed expedition was spread.[31] Baldric of Bourgueil described the response that Urban's sermon received:

> And immediately they all sewed the sign of the holy cross onto their clothes. This was, in fact, what the pope had ordered . . . because he had proclaimed the Lord to have said to his followers: *If anyone does not carry his cross and come after me, he cannot be my disciple.* (Luke 14, 27)[32]

At the heart of Urban's preaching was the idea that those who took part in the crusade were responding to the calls that Christ had made in Scripture. Encapsulating into a single image the Gospel passages he had cited, Urban instructed the crusaders to adopt the sign of the cross as an outward mark of their new commitment to follow Christ; Guibert of Nogent described the crusade badge as a *stigma passionis dominicae*.[33] Until the Clermont sermon, these passages had been inextricably linked with recruitment to the monastic profession,[34] but now Christians were being presented with an alternative model for imitating Christ, and a new form of religious observance specifically designed for the laity.[35] The impact of the idea that a layman no longer had to enter the cloister to become an imitator of Christ was recorded in the biography of the crusade leader Tancred:

> Day after day his prudent mind was in turmoil, and he burned with anxiety all the more because he saw that the warfare which flowed from his position of authority obstructed the Lord's commands. . . . But after the judgement of Pope Urban granted

31 Fulcher of Chartres, who may also have attended the council, certainly drew no connection between the sign of the cross appearing on the shoulders of those crusaders who drowned and the words of Urban's sermon; nor did he interpret those signs as an indication of vows being fulfilled.

32 Baldric of Bourgueil, *Historia*, 16.

33 Guibert, 117. For the adoption of the sign of the cross, see James A. Brundage, '*Cruce Signari*: the Rite for Taking the Cross in England', *Traditio* 22 (1966), 289–310; Colin Morris, 'Propaganda for War: the Dissemination of the Crusading Ideal in the Twelfth Century', in W. J. Sheils, ed., *The Church and War*, SCH 20 (Oxford, 1983), 79–101, 83–4.

34 On the use of Matt. 16, 24 as a '[stimulus] to a life of personal reform and withdrawal from the world', see Giles Constable, *The Reformation of the Twelfth Century* (Cambridge, 1996), 125.

35 Guibert, 87, depicted the crusade as 'a new way of gaining salvation'. For the crusade as 'a military monastery on the move', see Riley-Smith, *First Crusade*, 2, 26–7, 113–14, 118–19, 150–2, 154–5.

> remission of all their sins to all Christians going out to fight the gentiles, then at last, as if previously asleep, his vigour was aroused, his powers grew, his eyes opened, his courage was born. For before . . . his mind was divided, uncertain whether to follow in the footsteps of the Gospel or the world. But after the call to arms in the service of Christ, the twofold reason for fighting inflamed him beyond belief.[36]

These themes were echoed in a variety of sources. The idea of fulfilling Christ's precepts could be found in crusader charters,[37] and, in a letter to Urban II of 1098, the crusade leaders wrote that 'by your sermons . . . you taught us to take up crosses to follow Christ'.[38] In the same year, the Patriarch of Jerusalem wrote a general letter to the West exhorting the Christian knighthood to join the crusade: 'Come therefore, we pray, to fight in the army of the Lord in the same place in which the Lord fought, in which Christ suffered for us, leaving you an example that you should follow in his footsteps.'[39] And when Guibert of Nogent later described the hardship endured by the crusaders, he referred to it as 'cross-bearing' akin to Christ's Passion:

> Now they struggled to follow Christ, bearing a double cross, rejoicing that they had surpassed His commands, who had imposed upon them only one cross . . . what suffering do you think they endured, to what crosses were they constantly condemned. . . .[40]

* * *

The act of bearing the cross therefore reinforced the idea that through his actions the crusader was imitating Christ, and those who died on crusade were seen as martyrs who died for Christ as he had died for mankind.[41] A visible sign of *imitatio* was the appearance of the cross upon the bodies of some of the living and the dead: the 'token of faith' in the words of Fulcher of Chartres, and the *sacrum stigma* for Guibert of

36 Ralph of Caen, *Gesta Tancredi*, RHC Occ., 3: 587–716, 605–6.

37 See Jonathan Riley-Smith, *The First Crusaders, 1095–1131* (Cambridge, 1997), 62–3.

38 *Die Kreuzzugsbriefe aus den Jahren 1088–1100*, ed. Heinrich Hagenmeyer (Innsbruck, 1901), 164.

39 Ibid., 148.

40 Guibert, 178, 184; transl. Levine, *Guibert de Nogent*, 79, 82.

41 See H. E. J. Cowdrey, 'Martyrdom and the First Crusade', in Peter W. Edbury, ed., *Crusade and Settlement: Papers Read at the First Conference of the Society for the Study of Crusades and the Latin East and Presented to R. C. Smail* (Cardiff, 1985), 46–56; Shmuel Shepkaru, 'To Die for God: Martyrs' Heaven in Hebrew and Latin Crusade Narratives', *Speculum* 77 (2002), 311–41.

Nogent. It is only through appreciating the prominence of the ideal of imitating Christ in early crusade spirituality that these markings can be explained. They served to highlight the most pious of the crusaders, and their discovery led in turn to all manner of fraudulent attempts to replicate the miraculous. However, as Giles Constable has argued with respect to those individuals who later inflicted the wounds of Christ upon themselves, 'self-imposition . . . expresses even more clearly than supernatural intervention the stigmatic's devotion to Christ and desire to imitate His body'.[42] This is perhaps what Guibert of Nogent was describing when he wrote of the abbot who gouged the sign of the cross into his forehead that 'He had of course intended zealous imitation of God, but he had not carried this out wisely.'[43]

The hysteria that followed Pope Urban II's call for the Christian laity to 'take up their crosses' therefore provides a parallel to other incidents of stigmatism in the Middle Ages, incidents that were understood to demonstrate God's divine power at work through his most faithful followers.[44] As the examples considered here have shown, signs, wonders and miracles, such as the appearance of stigmata, not only reinforced the faith of those who witnessed them, but also inspired replication by fraudsters who, in this case, were motivated by a desire to imitate Christ. The pursuit of this most potent of spiritual ideals had previously been understood to lead to a life of monastic retreat, but in the eleventh and twelfth centuries the nature of religious life began to diversify dramatically.[45] It was in the wake of these changes that Francis and his followers appeared in the thirteenth century. And it was from out of this eleventh-century ferment that the crusade ideal emerged: another way for the people of Christendom to take up their crosses and follow Christ.[46]

University of Cambridge

42 Constable, 'Imitation of Christ', 201.

43 Guibert, 197.

44 The phenomenon of stigmatism has continued through to modern times. For a recent discussion, see Ted Harrison, *Stigmata: a Medieval Mystery in a Modern Age* (London, 1994).

45 See Constable, *Reformation, passim.*

46 Jonathan Riley-Smith, 'Crusading as an Act of Love', *History* 65 (1980), 177–92, 192: 'The charity of St Francis may now appeal to us more than that of the crusaders, but both sprang from the same roots'.

MONASTIC MIRACLES IN SOUTHERN ITALY, *c.*1040–1140

by G. A. LOUD

> ALMIGHTY God sometimes shows his miracles not only in great things but also in minor matters, so that the faith of believers shall be more and more increased and thus it causes all creatures to break out in praise of their Creator, since he is seen to have a care with fatherly piety in all those things that are granted to human endeavour.[1]

These words of Desiderius, abbot of Montecassino (1058–87) and briefly pope (as Victor III, 1086–7), are, of course, entirely conventional; they do however offer a succinct summary of the medieval view of miracles, signs and wonders. Yet the intrinsic historical interest of the subject is precisely because medieval authors, while they would all subscribe to the sentiments above, also deployed tales of miracles for more complex and varied reasons. South Italian monastic writers of the later eleventh and twelfth centuries, including Desiderius himself, offer an excellent example of the variety of such strategies. The miraculous remained an integral part of monastic life in southern Italy, perhaps to an even greater extent than in northern Europe, where by the twelfth century there was a tendency in hagiography to stress rather the importance of the virtue and personal qualities of the monastic saint than his wonder-working propensities.[2] Yet, to south Italian monastic writers the two strands were still inextricably linked – they held fast to a traditional view that miracles were a proof and corollary of virtue. Thus the biographer of Alferius, the Salernitan courtier turned hermit who founded the monastery of Cava, noted that:

> The name of his sanctity began to become famous, and this great reputation spread far and wide. And since the perfection of the saints is greater through merit than can be told through the mouths of men, the holy father not only behaved courageously but

1 Desiderius, *Dialogi de miraculis Sancti Benedicti*, ed. G. Schwarz and A. Hofmeister, MGH.SS 30.2 (Hannover, 1934), lib. II, ch. 21, 1138.

2 Ward, *Miracles and the Medieval Mind*, 171–80, esp. 174: 'a preference for virtue rather than miracles'.

> was illuminated with miracles, so that those whom fame enticed were made more sure by miracles. Some began to abandon the secular life and to subject themselves to his rule.[3]

Hagiographers assumed that reputation depended as much on miracles as virtue. Hence we are told of William of Vercelli, the founder of Montevergine, that word of his miracles spread throughout Apulia until it came to the ears of King Roger, and while it was his preaching that first made an impact at the royal court, and especially on the king's chief minister George of Antioch, the saint had to prove his chastity through a miracle before the king was convinced that he was a genuine holy man rather than a hypocrite.[4] Any historical basis for this tale is shaky indeed – Montevergine (and hence William's reputation) had already been founded at least a decade before Roger became king, although William retired from the house to become a hermit once again *c.*1127 – but to his first biographer, writing relatively soon after the saint's death in 1142, his wonder-working was integral to his fame and reputation.[5]

* * *

Of course, monastic writers from southern Italy, as elsewhere in Christendom, drew upon a common stock of 'conventional' miracles, or as we might say 'literary motifs'. Furthermore at Montecassino, the most productive centre of religious and hagiographical literature in the region, there was the particular influence exerted by the *Dialogues* of Gregory the Great, a work especially revered since it provided the earliest biography of the abbey's founder Benedict. A special *de luxe* illuminated edition of book II of the *Dialogues* (the Benedict biography) was prepared for Desiderius in 1075.[6] The abbot's own work on the miraculous was written in direct imitation, both in title and method, of

3 *Vitae quatuor priorum abbatum Cavensium*, ed. Leone Mattei-Cerasoli, Rerum Italicarum Scriptores 6.5 (Bologna, 1941) [hereafter: VQPA], 6. The probable author of this text was Peter II, abbot of Venosa 1141–56; see Hubert Houben, 'L'autore delle "Vitae quatuor priorum abbatum Cavensium"', *Studi medievali*, 3rd ser., 26 (1985), 871–9, repr. in idem, *Medioevo monastico meridionale* (Naples, 1987), 167–75.

4 *ActaSS*, 7 June, 110–11.

5 Hubert Houben, *Die Abtei Venosa und das Mönchtum im normannisch-staufischen Süditalien* (Tübingen, 1995), 70–1. For the composite nature of the biography, G. Mongelli, 'Legenda de vita et obitu S. Guilielmi confessoris et heremite', *Samnium* 23 (1960), 144–76 and 24 (1961), 70–119, esp. 81–112.

6 BAV, Vat. lat. 1202; Francis Newton, *The Scriptorium and Library at Montecassino* (Cambridge, 1999), 65–7, 291–307, esp. 292.

that of Gregory. Like its model it was intended to be written in four books (although the last of these does not now survive and may never have actually been written) and employed the device of an interlocutor, whom he called Theophilus, who fulfilled the same role as Gregory's deacon Peter. Furthermore, the scribe who wrote the only known copy of Desiderius's *Dialogues* also wrote, a few years earlier, the greater part of another Cassinese manuscript of those of Gregory.[7] The very first miracle recorded by Desiderius, of one of his predecessors walking across the River Liri without getting his clothes or feet wet, was a variant on a story of Gregory, concerning Benedict's disciple Maurus.[8] Further variants can be found in 'The Lives of the First Four Abbots of Cava' – in which Abbot Peter (ruled 1079–1123) was thrown into the sea when a ship capsized, but reached shore not only safely but entirely dry – and in the life of St John of Matera (d. 1139), the founder of Pulsano, where once again the holy man crossed a river without getting wet.[9] The author of this life was another who knew the *Dialogues* of Gregory well, and drew directly upon them.[10] Abbot Desiderius indeed occasionally referred expressly to the earlier *Dialogues*: thus he himself compared the story of a hammer miraculously recovered from the sea at Gaeta to Benedict's recovery of a metal scythe blade dropped into a lake by a careless Goth.[11] This story was in turn copied by Leo Marsicanus in the abbey's chronicle, once again with the reference to the precedent in Gregory.[12] Leo's 'Life of St Mennas', written after the translation of the saint's relics to Caiazzo in 1094, developed and expanded upon a chapter of Gregory to praise the eremitic life.[13] In addition, Leo IX recognized Montecassino's ownership of a Church at

[7] Newton, *Scriptorium and Library*, 67. This Gregory manuscript is now BAV, Vat. lat. 5735. The *Dialogi de miraculis* dates from 1076–9, although it has recently been suggested that the work may have been begun at least a decade earlier, W. D. McCready, 'Dating the *Dialogues* of Abbot Desiderius of Montecassino', *Revue Bénédictine* 108 (1998), 145–68.

[8] *Dialogi de miraculis*, I.1, 1118; cf. *Gregorii Magni Dialogi*, ed. Umberto Moricca, Fonti per la storia d'Italia 57 (Rome, 1924), II.7, 90.

[9] VQPA, 22; *ActaSS*, 5 June, 44.

[10] Francesco Panarelli, *Dal Gargano alla Toscana: il monachesimo riformato latino dei Pulsanesi (secoli XII–XIV)* (Rome, 1997), 27, 283–5.

[11] *Dialogi de miraculis*, II.13, 1133; cf. *Gregorii Magni Dialogi*, II.6, 89.

[12] *Chronica Monasterii Casinensis*, ed. H. Hoffmann, MGH.SS 34 (Hannover, 1980) [hereafter: *Chron. Cas.*,], lib. II.60, 284–5.

[13] G. Orlandi, '*Vita Sancti Mennatis*. Opera inedita di Leone Marsicano', *Rendiconti dell'Istituto Lombardo, Accademia di scienze e lettere* 97 (1963), 467–90 [text 479–90], based on *Gregorii Magni Dialogi*, III.26, 195–7. For the significance of this work, see H. E. J. Cowdrey, *The Age of Abbot Desiderius: Montecassino, the Papacy and the Normans in the Eleventh and Early Twelfth Centuries* (Oxford, 1983), 39–40.

Terracina after its historic rights had been proved by reading a passage from Gregory's *Dialogues*.[14]

Yet for all this reverence for Gregory's authority, Desiderius used his predecessor more as a model for style and phraseology than for content.[15] Furthermore, the purpose of his *Dialogues* was subtly different to that of Gregory. He was not just celebrating the wonders of an individual man of God but the power of the patron of a great monastery and the virtues of a community.[16] Hence there was relatively little stress on the curative powers of Benedict and his tomb, even though that tomb had been rediscovered during the rebuilding of the abbey church which Desiderius himself had undertaken in 1066.[17] Much more characteristic were the divine manifestations that marked the death of a conspicuously saintly monk: sweet smells and heavenly choirs, columns or balls of fire, or lights shining up to Heaven. Such testimony to the goodness of the individual brother was also a sign of the virtue of the community within which he lived, and these miracles were copied and imitated, both in the monastery chronicle and in later Cassinese hagiography such as Peter the Deacon's *Ortus et vita iustorum cenobii Casinensis* (*c*.1137).[18] Visions by dying monks, or concerning those recently deceased, were also a staple of Montecassino writers, and especially Peter the Deacon. Thus, in a story almost certainly derived from a (no longer extant) biography, a learned and saintly monk Guaiferius, who had joined the community at Montecassino after suffering persecution from Prince Gisulf of Salerno, appeared in a dream to a fellow 'master' after his death to reassure him that he was indeed enjoying eternal life. 'On the following morning the master

14 *Chron. Cas.*, II.84, 331–2; cf. *Gregorii Magni Dialogi*, II.22, 112.

15 For example, the demon 'hissing like a serpent, braying like an ass and roaring like a lion' in the *Dialogi de miraculis*, II.18, 1136, was derived from *Gregorii Magni Dialogi*, III.4, 144, although the subject of the former was a disobedient boy ignoring his father rather than a bishop casting out a devil.

16 Ward, *Miracles and the Medieval Mind*, 43–4. Cowdrey, *Age of Abbot Desiderius*, 32–3, suggests that the view of monasticism here was 'conventional and moderate', and not especially impressive.

17 *Chron. Cas.*, III.26, 395. See Paul Meyvaert, 'Peter the Deacon and the Tomb of St Benedict', *Revue Bénédictine* 65 (1955), 3–70, repr. in idem, *Benedict, Gregory, Bede and Others* (London, 1977).

18 *Dialogi de miraculis*, II.4, 1129, cf. *Chron. Cas.*, III.51, 434, and *Petri Diaconi Ortus et vita iustorum cenobii Casinensis*, ed. R. H. Rodgers (Berkeley, CA, 1972), 78; *Dialogi de miraculis*, II.7, 1130–1, cf. *Chron. Cas.*, III.43, 421; *Ortus et vita*, 68; *Dialogi de miraculis*, II.10, 1132, cf. *Chron. Cas.*, II.55, 270.

related this dream to the brothers, and from this they all experienced great joy'.[19]

* * *

Dreams and visions served many other functions as well. They might presage a death, especially of an abbot. Thus Abbot Gerard of Montecassino was forewarned of his own death (in 1123) by the miraculous appearance of one of his predecessors while the monks were celebrating mass on the anniversary of the latter's death.[20] Similarly, the death of Abbot Peter of Cava, in the same year, was announced to one of his monks by a vision of the three great Cluniac abbots, Odo, Maiolus and Odilo, coming to fetch him to join them.[21] Abbot Guido of St Clement, Casauria, in the Abruzzi (d. 1045) accurately foretold the very moment of his death, while the words from the Gospel, 'well done, thou good and faithful servant' (Matt. 25, 21 and 23), were being read.[22] Visions, particularly those revealed in dreams, might also predict other events. Both Desiderius and one of his predecessors, John III, had visions in which St Benedict foretold their appointment as abbot of Montecassino, and Desiderius had another some years later, in which the saint once again appeared, one night, to answer his prayers as to why the monastery was so often struck by lightning.[23] St Clement appeared in a vision to predict the downfall of a treacherous vassal of Casauria who had seized the abbey's animals.[24] Visions might also serve as a warning, as when Saints Benedict and Scholastica appeared in a vision to a Cassinese novice to prevent Desiderius's predecessor,

19 *Storia de' Normanni di Amato di Montecassino volgarizzata in antico francese*, ed. Vincenzo de Bartholomeis, Fonti per la storia d'Italia 76 (Rome, 1935) [hereafter: *Amatus*], lib. IV, ch. 45, 217–18, cf. *Ortus et vita*, 71. Deathbed visions, e.g. *Ortus et vita*, 74 (a vision of the Virgin), 94 (a dying monk is brought water by St Odilo of Cluny), 95 (a vision of St Stephen).

20 *Chron. Cas.*, IV.77, 541–2.

21 VQPA, 26. Peter had spent some time as a monk of Cluny and had attempted, not without considerable opposition, to introduce Cluniac customs to Cava, VQPA, 12–13. However, it has been argued that long-term Cluniac influence there was limited, see Giovanni Vitolo, 'Cava e Cluny', in Giovanni Vitolo and Simeone Leone, eds, *Minima Cavensia. Studi in margine al IX volume del Codex diplomaticus Cavensis* (Salerno, 1984), 19–44, and Hubert Houben, 'Il monachesimo cluniacense e i monasteri normanni dell'Italia meridionale', *Benedictina* 49 (1992), 341–61, repr. in idem, *Mezzogiorno normanno-svevo: monasteri e castelli, ebrei e musulmani* (Naples, 1996), 7–22.

22 *Chronicon Casauriense, auctore Johanne Berardi*, ed. Lodovico Antonio Muratori, *Rerum Italicarum Scriptores* II.2 (Milan, 1726), 853.

23 *Dialogi de miraculis*, II.3, 1128; *Chron. Cas.*, II.22, 206–7, III.8, 369 and III.20, 387. John III was abbot 998–1010.

24 *Chronicon Casauriense*, 885.

Frederick of Lorraine (who had been elected pope as Pope Stephen IX), from removing the abbey treasures to finance various political and military initiatives as pope. Here the vision, immediately reported to the pope, was important in convincing him of how unpopular this measure was among the monks, and it was instrumental in persuading him to return what had been taken.[25]

* * *

In 'The Lives of the First Four Abbots of Cava', visions and miraculous appearances were often connected with the enforcement of strict monastic discipline. Thus the founder, Abbot Alferius, appeared in a dream to a monk who was asleep while his fellows were singing the office, seized him by his cowl and dragged him into the choir. A brother from a cell in Calabria was on his way to the mother house when he unwisely accepted over-generous hospitality from a well-meaning layman, but while he slept this off, Abbot Peter appeared to him in a vision, ordering him to be flogged. Similarly, Peter appeared in a dream to a monk who had spoken disrespectfully of him after his death, beating him so hard that he cried out, and when this woke the other monks, the offender had the welts to prove the truth of his story.[26] Peter indeed comes across in this text as a stern and vengeful saint, whose austerity, and readiness to inflict condign and corporal punishment ('regular discipline'), is implicitly contrasted with the milder and more merciful ways of his short-lived successor Constable (abbot 1123–4), 'the friend of sinners... who was accustomed to conceal the faults of the delinquent'.[27] One monk indeed went so far as to spit on Peter's tomb, 'since he remembered not his merits but the sharpness of his correction'. He was duly punished with a swollen face and a painfully twisted mouth, only cured after he had begged for forgiveness at the tomb which he had profaned.[28]

The author comments here that this 'proved the justice and piety of the father against the mendacity of his detractors', which hints that such miracles were necessary to assure the reputation of one who in his lifetime had been unpopular. Earlier he had written that some were dubious about such stories, but 'since we desire to confound these

25 *Amatus*, III.50–1, 166–8; *Chron. Cas.*, II.97, 355.
26 VQPA, 11, 23, 27.
27 VQPA, 28, 30 (quote).
28 VQPA, 26–7.

enemies of the holy man, we shall produce excellent witnesses for nearly all his miracles, that is holy and venerable men'.[29]

For other monasteries, miracles were important not so much for convincing the doubters within their own ranks but to influence 'public opinion', especially among the laity in the area immediately surrounding the house. One of the key moments in the history of Casauria was the *inventio* of the relics of its patron, St Clement, in November 1104. The monks made the most of this with a solemn and public ceremony of rededication almost a year later.[30] But this would seem not to have entirely stilled doubts among local laymen – for the chronicle reported two miracles, one involving a man who had questioned the merits of the saint and the efficacy of burial in the monks' cemetery, whose body was lost for ever in the Pescara river as it was being ferried to the abbey for burial, the other the punishment of a noble youth from a family with whom the abbey had been in dispute and who had doubted the genuineness of the relics. In the second tale, the offender was saved from drowning by his pious companion who prayed to the saint for his rescue; but while he was submerged in the river, St Clement appeared, walking on the water, to reproach him for his disbelief and presumption. News of this second miracle, we are told, spread far and wide. Along with the rediscovery of the relics, it would seem to have been a factor in restoring the local influence of the abbey after a period of eclipse, when donations had fallen away and the abbey lands had been under threat from the Normans infiltrating northwards from Apulia into the Abruzzi.[31]

* * *

The instability caused by the arrival of the Normans in southern Italy posed considerable problems for both Montecassino and Casauria. Montecassino was under particular threat during the twenty years after the restoration of Pandulf IV to the principality of Capua in 1026.

29 VQPA, 20.

30 *Chronicon Casauriense*, 873–6.

31 These miracles were omitted from Muratori's partial edition of the chronicle; they have been edited by Hubert Houben, 'Laienbegräbnisse auf dem Klosterfriedhof. Unedierte Mirakelberichte aus der Chronik von Casauria', *Quellen und Forschungen aus italienischen Archiven und Bibliotheken* 76 (1996), 64–76. For the general context, see L. Feller, 'Casaux et *castra* dans les Abruzzes: San Salvatore a Maiella et San Clemente a Casauria (XI–XIIIe siècles)', *Mélanges de l'Ecole française de Rome – Moyen-Âge – Temps modernes* 97 (1985), 145–82, esp. 152–61, and idem, 'The Northern Frontier of Norman Italy, 1060–1140', in G. A. Loud and A. Metcalfe, eds, *The Society of Norman Italy* (Leiden, Boston, MA, and Köln, 2002), 47–74, esp. 59–64.

Pandulf had been deposed and imprisoned by the Emperor Henry II, and was not surprisingly hostile to an abbey ruled by an abbot, Theobald, whom the emperor had appointed. His Norman mercenaries, and later on other Normans operating independently, took over a substantial part of the *Terra Sancti Benedicti* until eventually expelled by Abbot Richer in 1045. The expulsion of the interlopers was made possible by the hire of soldiers from north of the Alps (Richer himself was a German) and by the provision of other troops by various friendly nobles from the Abruzzi, but (as presented by the monastery's chronicler Leo), 'everything that was done is indeed believed to have happened through the wish and with the help of Father Benedict'. The recovery of a fortress on the abbey's lands was presaged by the appearance of Benedict in dreams to two peasants, in the second of which the sleeper saw the saint beating the Normans with his staff, while at the height of the siege of Sant'Andrea it was alleged that a monk (clearly Benedict himself) appeared in the thick of the fighting encouraging the abbey's men. Furthermore, during the siege, the arrows and other missiles shot or thrown by the Normans were, again allegedly miraculously, blown back 'as though by a strong wind' to inflict many injuries on those who had launched them.[32]

Both Cassinese sources, and especially the abbey chronicle, and the chronicle of Casauria, emphasized what was perceived as the miraculous most strongly when it came to the prevention or punishment of those who sought to oppress the monastery or to steal its property. Thus a group of Capuan nobles who invaded the *Terra Sancti Benedicti* were led astray in the dark and ended up going round in circles 'through the merits of Father Benedict',[33] while thieves who broke into the monastery's cellar one night to steal provisions found these impossible to lift and then wandered through the precinct unable to find their way out until morning, when they were swiftly pursued and apprehended.[34] Whatever rational explanations we might find for such events, to both Desiderius and the abbey's chroniclers these were divinely inspired. Similarly monastic writers interpreted the deaths of those who had menaced their house as a consequence of divine

[32] *Chron. Cas.*, II.70–2, 308–14 (quotes from 311–12).

[33] *Dialogi de miraculis*, I.10, 1124; *Chron. Cas.*, II.80, 326–7.

[34] *Dialogi de miraculis*, I.12, 1124–5; *Chron. Cas.*, III.64, 446, with some differences in detail. Cf. *Ortus et vita*, 77. This appears to have been based upon Gregory of Tours, *Liber de virtutibus S. Iuliani*, ed. B. Krusch, MGH Scriptores Rerum Merovingicarum 1 (Hannover, 1885), ch. 20, 573.

vengeance. Thus a disease which carried off one of the (Lombard) Counts of Aquino and many other inhabitants of that town was a punishment for the counts' kidnapping of Abbot Richer and seizure of an abbey *castellum*. The count's surviving brothers,

> hastened to the monastery with ropes tied round their necks, confessed in a loud voice that they had gravely sinned against such a great man and had wickedly harmed such a venerable place, and they returned the aforesaid town of Sant'Angelo to the monks.[35]

Similarly a Norman count, Rodulf, died on the very day when he was planning to invade the monastery's territory; 'this event filled the rest of the Normans with such terror that in future they did not dare to launch an invasion of these lands nor to come here for plunder'.[36]

The problems of Casauria reached a peak about half a century later than those of Montecassino, for which the Norman conquest of the principality of Capua brought a welcome era of peace and protection. The major threat to the Abruzzese abbey in the 1080s and 1090s was a Norman called Hugh Mamouzet, whose eventual defeat was recounted with relish by the abbey's chronicler John Berard:

> God whom he had offended, and St Clement, overthrew his house, despoiled it of silver and gold, and did not permit him to fulfil his desires. For He made him suffer with a most serious illness which brought him to the grave, and in the year in which he died five of his sons followed him in death.[37]

Cava, much favoured by the Norman Dukes of Apulia, and the core of whose property lay within the area firmly under the control even of Robert Guiscard's relatively weak successors, was less troubled by greedy and acquisitive neighbours than some other monasteries. But when one of its subordinate cells (dedicated to St Michael) was under attack from a Norman nobleman, Roger of San Severino, Abbot Peter called on the archangel to protect it, and as a result the house where Roger was staying collapsed, killing his baby son, and bringing the sinner himself to repentance.[38]

Yet the punishments of those who offended the patron saints of these abbeys might involve a more direct and obvious supernatural

35 *Chron. Cas.*, II.69, 306–7.

36 *Chron. Cas.*, II.75, 317–18.

37 *Chronicon Casauriense*, 870.

38 VQPA, 21–2. The writer records that 'the innocent child was received into paradise'.

intervention than merely a conveniently timed death, however favourably interpreted by the monks. Overt acts of sacrilege might bring immediate retribution, as with the follower of Pandulf IV who was struck with an epileptic fit and temporary paralysis when he dared to take vestments and sacred vessels from the altar of St Benedict.[39] The Norman Count of Manopello who at the beginning of the twelfth century tried to hold Casauria to ransom and seized all its animals was struck down by St Clement in person as he feasted on the stolen meat, and died begging the saint not to hurt him any more.[40] And such punishment naturally extended to the hereafter. Desiderius of Montecassino recorded in his *Dialogues* that a servant of the duke of Naples was clearing up the nets after a hunt for wild boar when two monks appeared who took him to see the recently deceased Pandulf IV being tormented by demons for his 'innumerable crimes', but especially for the theft of a golden chalice from Montecassino.[41]

Sometimes divine protection might be benevolent rather than vengeful. John of Matera was wrongfully imprisoned, consoled by an angelic vision, miraculously freed from his chains, and walked free invisible to the guards.[42] A more interesting, and less conventional, example comes from the later part of the Casauria chronicle. After the takeover of the Abruzzi region by King Roger of Sicily in 1140, the monks naturally sought to secure royal protection, but were faced with the particular problem of vindicating the abbey's claim to a *castellum* which it had received from the Counts of Manopello, who had opposed the king and been dispossessed. As the abbot set off to meet the king, a laggard member of his party was intercepted by an elderly pilgrim, with a message that the king was well-disposed to the abbey, but on no account should they offer him money to secure what they wanted. The pilgrim subsequently disappeared, but when everything turned out as he foretold, it became clear that he was St Clement himself.[43]

Given the unstable conditions of southern Italy during much of the eleventh and twelfth centuries, it is hardly surprising that monastic writers often viewed divine intervention as protecting their houses, and saints took a personal role in the protection of the monks and their property, and vengeance on their enemies. But, as Abbot Desiderius

39 *Chron. Cas.*, II.59, 280–1.
40 *Chronicon Casauriense*, 873–4.
41 *Dialogi de miraculis*, I.13, 1125–6.
42 *ActaSS*, 5 June, 38.
43 *Chronicon Casauriense*, 888–9.

noted, God worked in small as well as in great matters, and divine assistance was sought for the mundane, and not just to defend against human foes. Thus the monks of Montecassino processed barefoot around all the churches on the mountain to implore God's help against the Normans in the 1040s; but they did the same to end a drought half a century or so later.[44] There were fasts and barefoot processions after the monastery was struck by lightning in 1063, and after a series of earthquakes in 1120.[45] After the *inventio* of the relics of St Clement in 1104, these were interred, carefully sealed, in the high altar of the abbey church, except for one tiny portion which was kept in a reliquary 'for the information of posterity, the certitude of the present day and the relief of the sick'. This was to be brought out in time of need. One occasion when it was produced was *c.*1118, when a plague of locusts was consuming the crops and causing famine – and the *virtus* of the saint drove the locusts into the Pescara river to perish.[46] John of Matera was asked by the people of Monte Gargano to help end a water shortage, and enjoined them, and especially the canons of the shrine of St Michael, to penitence. Here the saint decided that the drought had been caused by the sins of one particular canon, and after he had left the region rain duly fell.[47]

In addition, the relics of the saints, both of monastic patrons and holy abbots, had curative powers. Cures were reported at the tombs of the early abbots of Cava, and especially at those of the founder, Alferius, and Constable, the fourth abbot, although most of these concerned monks of the monastery.[48] There were also miracles at the tomb of Abbot Guido of Casauria, and these did not just involve members of the monastic community. But, after giving details of three such cures, the chronicler passed on with a cursory note that readers would be bored with any more, and thereafter such curative miracles are conspic-

44 *Chron. Cas.*, II.74, 316; *Ortus et vita*, 72 (in the time of Oderisius I, abbot 1087–1105).

45 *Chron. Cas.*, III.20, 386 and IV.65, 527. The penitential exercises on the first occasion were increased after Peter Damian visited the monastery, at the request of Desiderius; see J. Howe, 'Peter Damian and Monte Cassino', *Revue Bénédictine* 107 (1997), 330–51, 337–9.

46 *Chronicon Casauriense*, 876, 880.

47 *ActaSS*, 5 June, 39. The populace had wanted to burn the offending canon, but John would not permit this, desiring 'not the death of a sinner, but his conversion'.

48 A monk was cured of toothache and a mouth abscess, and another of fever, at the tomb of Alferius, VQPA, 11; a monk was cured of fever, another had a broken arm mended, and a third was cured of migraine at the tomb of Constable, while a smith was cured of eye problems by the dust from his tomb, ibid., 33–4.

uous by their absence.[49] This section of the chronicle was derived from an earlier *Vita* of Guido,[50] and it would appear that such cures were of relatively little interest to the late twelfth-century chronicler John Berard, even though the latter was more than willing to recount other wonders exercised in defence of the monastery and its material interests. While informing the reader that the reliquary containing a small portion of the relics of St Clement was used for the relief of the sick, he gave no details of any cures that resulted.[51] Similarly, although Desiderius in the *Dialogues* did report a few cures at the tomb of Benedict, primarily of lay people, these provided only a small proportion of the wonders he reported.[52] The same was true of the abbey chronicle, of which the original part, by Leo Marsicanus, written *c.*1100, anyway drew heavily on the *Dialogues* for the miracles it recounted. But even in the continuation, most of which was written by a monk called Guido in the 1120s, miracles associated with the tomb, while not entirely absent, were few.[53]

It is clear therefore that such curative miracles were no more than incidental to the purposes of these monastic chroniclers. To them, the power of St Benedict or St Clement was shown primarily by the defence of their monastery's interests against its local enemies, while to Desiderius and Peter the Deacon the real proof of God's favour was in the virtuous life of individual monks, as proven by miraculous events associated with them. Cures at a tomb were inevitably more important in overtly hagiographical texts, though even here we should note that the record of the miracles at the tomb of William of Vercelli was only added to the original *Vita* in the early thirteenth century, half a century or more after its composition.[54] However, such cures at Benedict's tomb were only minor incidents in the chronicle of Montecassino, and similar wonders were entirely absent from the Casauria chronicle. The

[49] *Chronicon Casauriense*, 854–5. The three cures involved a boy being educated in the cloister, with a high fever, a monk with gout, and a woman who had gone blind.

[50] Ibid., 843.

[51] Ibid., 876.

[52] *Dialogi de miraculis*, II.9, 1131, II.14–15, 1134–5, II.17–18, 1135–6.

[53] Thus, in the continuation, a peasant possessed by the devil, was cured at the tomb, as was a knight injured in a fall from his horse, while another knight whom Benedict had freed from captivity deposited his chains at the tomb, *Chron. Cas.*, III.38, 414, IV.44, 512–13, IV.58, 521–2. For the borrowings, Anna Maria Fagnoni, 'I "Dialogi" di Desiderio nella "Chronica monasterii Casinensis"', *Studi Medievali*, 3rd ser., 34 (1993), 65–94. There is a helpful summary of the complexities of the chronicle authorship by H. Bloch, *Monte Cassino in the Middle Ages*, 3 vols (Rome, 1986), 1: 113–17.

[54] *ActaSS*, 7 June, 114–16; cf. Mongelli, 'Legenda', Samnium 24 (1961), 97–112.

tomb of Clement was certainly the focus for devotion at the latter monastery – Abbot Grimoald, for example, 'poured out' his prayers before the tomb when faced with the oppression of Richard of Manopello, and thirty years later a vision promising divine aid against the latter's son was vouchsafed to two monks who rose before the early morning service to pray in front of the tomb[55] – but, despite some scepticism among the laity (as noted above), there was no need in the monks' mind for miraculous cures to authenticate the corporeal presence of the saint, especially once the relics had been uncovered and formally certified in 1104. It was new shrines, such as that of St Mennas (translated to Caiazzo in 1094 and a second time, to Sant'Agata dei Goti, in 1110) that needed curative miracles by way of authentication.[56]

* * *

However, there was one, highly significant, exception. This was the miraculous cure of the Emperor Henry II during his visit to Montecassino in June 1022. Clearly the exceptionally high status of the person who was healed, the generous gifts that he conveyed to the abbey, and the monks' pride in its historic connection with the western emperors, stretching (at least in their eyes) back to Charlemagne, meant that this miracle would have been valued by Cassinese writers. Yet there was a very significant shift in emphasis between the way in which the story was interpreted by Amatus, writing *c.*1080, and by Leo Marsicanus in his chronicle some twenty years later. The former stressed that Benedict wished to remain at Montecassino, and not to be translated elsewhere as the emperor desired.[57] To Leo, the miracle proved to the hitherto-dubious emperor that the saint was indeed buried at Montecassino. However, the real point of his version was not whether Henry had actually expressed such doubts, but (as Leo explained in the next chapter) to show the worthlessness of any claims that the relics of Benedict had been translated elsewhere, that 'the account of the translation is false, frivolous and worthless'.[58] Although no monastery is explicitly named, the abbey of Fleury is clearly implied.[59] By the time Leo was writing, the claims of Fleury to possess

55 *Chronicon Casauriense*, 874, 887.

56 B. de Gaiffier, 'Translations et miracles de S. Mennas par Léon d'Ostie et Pierre du Mont-Cassin', *AnBoll* 62 (1944), 5–32, 28–30. The authorship of these miracles, as opposed to the *Translatio*, is doubtful.

57 *Amatus*, I.30, 39–41.

58 *Chron. Cas.*, II.43–4, 247–52.

59 For the Fleury claims, see Ward, *Miracles and the Medieval Mind*, 46–51.

the body of Benedict were becoming increasingly strident, reaching their apogee with the dedication of the rebuilt church of Fleury by Paschal II in 1107, an event which was as significant to the French monastery as Alexander II's dedication of the rebuilt basilica in 1071 had been to Montecassino.[60] It was not therefore surprising that the continuation to the Montecassino chronicle later poured scorn on the Fleury claims, alleging that the pope had said publicly that these were false, and adding that when the bishops and French cardinals attempted to chant the festival mass, rather than the normal office for the day, they were miraculously prevented from doing so.[61] In these examples, the use of the miraculous was directed to a matter vital for Cassinese prestige and authority.

These miracles therefore display many different facets of monastic life and spirituality in eleventh- and twelfth-century southern Italy. They reflect the very different concerns of the writers of individual texts, and the differing circumstances of particular houses. At Cava, for example, a relatively untroubled external history allowed the biographer of the early abbots to focus upon the internal life of the house, although in doing so he revealed some of the tensions that undoubtedly existed there, especially under the austere Abbot Peter. At Montecassino and Casauria, both wealthy and long-established institutions that were correspondingly desirable targets at periods of social dislocation, the defence of the abbey and its lands was paramount, and the abbey chronicles were studded with miracles of power and vengeance, and visions of the patron saint. But though the emphases may have differed, all these monks would ultimately have agreed with the Cava author's view of its early leaders:

> We believe that through the prayers and merits of these men pristine and outstanding religion has to this day been preserved with holiness in this monastery, and will be free from and strengthened against attack and injury from all enemies, with the help of God, up until the end of the world.[62]

University of Leeds

60 For 1071, see *Chron. Cas.*, III.29, 398–402; Bloch, *Monte Cassino*, 118–21.
61 *Chron. Cas.*, IV.29, 494–5.
62 VQPA, 35.

MIRACLE, MEANING AND NARRATIVE IN THE LATIN EAST

by YVONNE FRIEDMAN

IN medieval narrative the First Crusade and the founding of the Latin kingdom were perceived as *Gesta Dei per Francos* – God's own deed.[1] Having no doubt that the success of the First Crusade was a miracle, God's intervention in history, the chroniclers' rendering of events was accordingly replete with miracles, such as the discovery of the Holy Lance in Antioch and the saints' taking an active role in the battle against Kirbogha of Mosul in 1098.[2] Even in the more level-headed historical narratives, military success was seen as a miracle and failures were attributed to the sins of the participants who were not pure enough to merit a miracle. Thus the miraculous intervention of God in history became the logical consequence of the prowess and religious behavior of the crusaders, an almost expected outcome of natural events.

Although everyday life in the Latin Kingdom was a more down-to-earth experience, its historians recorded many miraculous events. Fulcher of Chartres clearly viewed the existence of the kingdom as a miracle,[3] whereas William of Tyre explained the lack of miraculous deliverance in a later period as the outcome of the Franks' immoral behaviour.[4] The bringing of the True Cross into battle as a symbol of religious supremacy, as a sign that God was fighting with the host, was a public assertion of this atmosphere of miraculous expectations.[5] When the Cross was captured at the Battle of Hattin, 1187, this was perceived

1 *Guibert de Nogent, Dei Gesta per Francos et cinq autres textes*, ed. Robert B. C. Huygens, CChrCM 127a (Turnhout, 1996) [hereafter: Guibert], 80–4, 345 and *passim*.

2 *Raymond d'Aguilers, Historia Francorum qui ceperunt Iherusalem,* ed. and transl. John H. Hill and Laurita L. Hill (Philadelphia, PA, 1968), VII, 56–8, 63–7.

3 *Fulcheri Carnotensis Historia Hierosolymitana (1095–1127)*, ed. Heinrich Hagenmeyer (Heidelberg, 1913) [hereafter: Fulcher], III, 27, 6–8, 749: 'percipitis igitur esse hoc miraculum immensum et universo mundo valde stupendum'.

4 Guillaume de Tyr, *Chronique*, ed. Robert B. C. Huygens, CChr.CM 63–63a, 2 vols (Turnhout, 1981), 2: 27. Cf. Continuation of William of Tyre, *The Conquest of Jerusalem and the Third Crusade: Sources in Translation*, trans. Peter W. Edbury (Aldershot, 1996), 37.

5 Alan V. Murray, '"Mighty Against the Enemies of Christ": the Relic of the True Cross in the Armies of the Kingdom of Jerusalem', in John France and William G. Zajac, eds, *The Crusades and their Sources: Essays Presented to Bernard Hamilton* (Aldershot, 1998), 217–38.

as the greatest catastrophe, mentioned even before the downfall of the kingdom and the loss of life and limb.[6] Even when they were part of historical processes, military victory or defeat verged on the miraculous.

This paper proposes to examine the case of Bohemond of Antioch (*c.*1056–1111),[7] who, though released from captivity by ransom, in my opinion created a narrative of both romantic and miraculous deliverance. This paper focuses not only on the miraculous events recounted but also on the importance of their transmission via narrative. His case may help define the boundaries between the natural and supernatural events in the East as perceived by a society in which wonder was part of the narrative, or as Caroline Walker Bynum put it: 'Every view of things that is not wonderful is false.'[8]

In broad terms medieval miracles can be classified according to three categories: functional, polemical, and miracles of personal deliverance – these categories sometimes overlap. Some differences can be elicited between East and West regarding the frequency and importance of the different kinds of miracles, and for the relative importance of holy space and time in each.

I define functional miracles as those necessary because no alternative remedy to the situation was available. Such miracles were more usual in Europe, namely, miraculous healings and medical remedies in a period or situation when medicine seemed to lack adequate answers. Thus pilgrims flocked to holy shrines to seek miraculous cures for their ailments.[9] Such miracles were rarer in the Latin Kingdom, perhaps because medicine there was on a higher level than in Europe. Characteristic of such miracles was the importance of physical contact: direct contact with relics, a holy spring, or holy water or oil. One reason for the relative paucity of such miracles in the Holy Land as opposed to Europe was that the two most holy sites, the sepulchres of Jesus and Mary, were by definition empty, with no relics. The relics connected with their bodies, Mary's milk or hair, Jesus' foreskin, and so on, could be and were exported abroad.

[6] Penny J. Cole, 'Christian Perceptions of the Battle of Hattin (583/1187)', *Al-Masaq* 6 (1993), 9–39.

[7] For the debate regarding the date of his death see Anitra Gadolin, 'Prince Bohemund's Death and Apotheosis in the Church of San Sabino, Canosa di Puglia', *Byzantion* 52 (1982), 124–53.

[8] Caroline Walker Bynum, 'Wonder', *AHR* 102. 1 (1997), 1–26, 26.

[9] Finucane, *Miracles and Pilgrims*, 59–99.

The miraculous essence of these holy places lies rather in the historical or meta-historical events that took place there. The greatest miracle of all – the resurrection – remained unprovable by any relic. Walking in Christ's footsteps was in itself a testimony to and an experience of enacting the miracles of long ago. The expectations for miracles in these holy spaces were not of the private, functional kind common in Europe.

The second type of miracle is the polemical miracle – whose purpose was to prove theological supremacy. The holy places themselves bore witness to the Christian faith via signs given in the past. A contemporary miracle at the same place reinforced its authenticity, proving the truth of Christianity in the present. The most famous example is that of the Holy Fire descending in the Church of the Holy Sepulchre at Easter.[10]

Opinions regarding this annual miracle see-sawed, depending on whether or not the Christians had supremacy. The miracle started during the Muslim rule of the Holy Land, when a theological explanation for Muslim supremacy was needed. When the miracle failed to materialize in 1101, the patriarch Daimbert claimed that it was in fact unnecessary because the Christians ruled the holy places after the crusader conquest.[11] It continues as part of the Eastern Church's ritual to the present, but in 1238 Pope Gregory IX claimed that it was a fake, as the miracle was made redundant due to the renewed Christian sovereignty over Jerusalem.[12] For this kind of miracle publicity was crucial – the miracle had to happen in front of many and be told and retold by yet more. It is the narrative that anchors and disseminates the ongoing miraculous occurrence by combining holy time and space in the holy place. Contemporary Jewish miracles had the same qualities. Jewish *itineraria* tell about a miraculous wind that prevented Christians from entering the true place of King David's grave on Mount Sion or

10 Yvonne Friedman, 'The Status of the Church of the Holy Sepulchre in the Crusader Period', *Wilnai Book* 2 (1988), 58–66 [in Hebrew]; eadem, 'The City of the Kings of Kings', in Marcel Poorthuis and Chana Safrai, eds, *The Centrality of Jerusalem: Historical Perspectives* (The Hague, 1996), 209–12.

11 Caffaro de Cashifelone, *De liberatione civitatum orientis liber*, RHC Occ., 4: 255–6; Bartolf de Nangis, Appendix to Fulcher, 835.

12 *Acta Honorii III (1216–1227) et Gregorii IX (1227–1241), Pontificia commissio ad redigendum codicem iuris canonici orientalis. Fontes*, ser. III, 3 (Rome, 1950), no. 235; Friedman, 'The City of the Kings of Kings', 209–12.

the Tomb of the Patriarchs in Hebron.[13] Although place was crucial, the story was more important than physical contact with the holy.

We now come to the third category: personal deliverance from a quandary far from a holy place; for example, a prisoner's deliverance from captivity, a saint's intervention in a storm to save the one who prays to him, and the like.[14] This kind of miracle was the easiest to invent. There was no need for physical contact with the saint or his relics, nor were witnesses to the event necessary. The prayer answered, or rather the story about the prayer answered, was a private, personal experience. The only proof of the miraculous event was the narrative itself.

All three types of miracles share the importance of the narrative. It was not enough that a miraculous solution to a problem had occurred, only evidence for and recital of the story made the miracle meaningful. A miracle was not meant to be secret:

> It is the act of telling which constructs the miracle as such. The miracle has an impact through its telling and interpreting. The effect of a miracle is closely related to the way in which it is understood. A miracle cannot be separated from the discourse in which it is told.[15]

In Guibert of Nogent's opinion, the acceptable sign of a saint was the existence of a true, written tradition: '*scriptorum veracium traditio certa*'.[16] The miraculous event had to be told, recited and written down.

The story of Bohemond, the Norman prince of Antioch, may serve as an example of the different stages in the germination of a miracle from the event, via the oral narrative to the written testimony that established that it was indeed a miracle. As they emerge from the chronicles, the historical facts seem to be as follows: Bohemond was captured in an ambush in August 1100 by Malik-Ghazi ibn

13 Yvonne Friedman, 'Pilgrimage to the Holy Land as an Act of Devotion in Jewish and Christian Outlook', in Gilbert Dahan, Gérard Nahon and Elie Nicolas, eds, *Rashi et la culture juive en France du Nord au Moyen Âge* (Paris, 1997), 278–301; Elchanan Reiner, 'Overt Falsehood and Covert Truth: Christians, Jews, and Holy Places in Twelfth-Century Palestine', *Zion* 63. 2 (1998), 157–88 [in Hebrew].

14 E.g., Marcus Bull, *The Miracles of Our Lady of Rocamadour: Analysis and Translation* (Woodbridge, 1999), 121, 135.

15 Anne-Marie Korte, 'Introduction: Women and Miracle Stories', in eadem, ed., *Women and Miracle Stories: a Multidisciplinary Exploration* (Leiden, 2001), 1–28, 13.

16 Guibert de Nogent, *De sanctis et eorum pigneribus*, ed. Robert B. C. Huygens, CChr.CM 127 (Turnhout, 1993), 85–109: 87, 1.1, ll. 68–9. Cf. Julia M. H. Smith, 'Oral and Written: Saints, Miracles, and Relics in Brittany *c.*850–1250', *Speculum* 65 (1990), 309–43.

Danishmend (also known as Kumushtakin) and imprisoned at Niksar (Neocaesarea). The crusade of 1101 lost thousands of its members in a futile attempt to free him from jail by force. Two years later he was ransomed for the exorbitant price of 100,000 bezants, returned to Antioch, and after settling his affairs there set out for Europe to raise an army against Byzantine territories.[17] How was Bohemond released?

Matthew of Edessa, an Armenian chronicler close to the scene and conversant with Eastern usages of ransom, reports:

> In this same year [1103–4] the Frankish count Bohemond was ransomed from Danishmend for one hundred thousand *dahekans*; this was accomplished through the mediation and assistance of the great Armenian prince Kogh Vasil. This ruler donated ten thousand *dahekans* towards Bohemond's ransom money, while the count of Antioch, Tancred, gave nothing. Vasil collected the ransom money, doing all in his power to have it procured from every part of his territories. Finally he handed over the sum of one hundred thousand *dahekans* and had Bohemond brought to him.[18]

Matthew provides the pertinent facts usually found in ransom lists: the sum paid and by whom, and who negotiated the deal, usually a prominent individual. The sum in question, 100,000 *dahekans*, which is equivalent to a king's ransom in local bezants, fits Bohemond's status as the prince of Antioch. Therefore Matthew's report sounds reliable.

Other chroniclers, although they differ in detail, essentially support the version that Bohemond was ransomed. Fulcher of Chartres simply notes the ransom,[19] and Guibert of Nogent, who admits to copying the main facts from Fulcher, laconically states that Bohemond was ransomed by money and by pact.[20] Ralph of Caen claims that the people of Antioch, Prince Baldwin of Edessa, and the Latin patriarch of the city ransomed Bohemond for a hundred thousand gold pieces.[21] Albert of Aachen, who can be seen as the disseminator of the story as it reached Europe, has a very different narrative: he reports that

17 Ralph Bailey Yewdale, *Bohemond I, Prince of Antioch* (Princeton, NJ, 1924), 96–102; Carol Sweetenham and Linda M. Paterson, *The* Canso d'Antioca*: an Occitan Epic Chronicle of the First Crusade* (Aldershot, 2003), 8.

18 *Armenia and the Crusades, Tenth to Twelfth Centuries: the Chronicle of Matthew of Edessa*, ed. Ara Edmond Dostourian (Lanham, MD, and London, 1993), 3.14, 191.

19 Fulcher, II, 23, 457–60: 'After four years spent in the chains of the enemy, divine grace looked upon him, and on payment of a ransom he was released from his bonds'.

20 Guibert, 337, l. 1838: '. . . tandem cum pacto tum pecuniaria redemptione resolvitur'.

21 Ralph of Caen, *Gesta Tancredi in expeditione Hierosolymitana*, RHC Occ., 3: 147, 709.

Bohemond offered Danishmend an alliance against Kilij Arslan in return for his freedom and that it was through this alliance and the payment of 'only' 100,000 instead of 260,000 bezants that he obtained his release. The emir was willing to strike a bargain because the Seljukid sultan had demanded half of the 260,000 bezants offered by the Byzantine emperor to ensure that Bohemond would remain in jail. The funds were raised by the Latin patriarch of Antioch, the Armenian prince Kogh Vasil, and Baldwin of Edessa.[22] Albert's main addition lies in his description of the captive-captor relations and his demonstration of how Bohemond's diplomatic skills paved the way for his release via a military pact. All these accounts relate that Bohemond was ransomed in exchange for monetary payment, reflecting the actual practice of ransom, as we know it in the East.

I have shown elsewhere that ransom was not yet common usage in the home society of the crusaders.[23] Being a captive who had been ransomed for a huge sum was not a fitting résumé for a crusader hero. Orderic Vitalis, usually a levelheaded historian, lets romance invade his narrative of Bohemond's release and embellishes the historical facts to make them fit a hero of a *chanson de geste*.[24] In his story, Melaz, the beautiful daughter of Bohemond's captor Danishmend, frees the captives on condition that they fight on her father's side against his brother. After a long, adventurous story, Bohemond and his friends return triumphantly to Antioch, where Melaz receives baptism and marries a Christian knight. Orderic Vitalis's intricate, romantic story of the enamoured princess who frees Bohemond and uses his prowess to defeat her father's enemies differs from the above narratives and shows affinity to the vernacular chanson *Les Chétifs* in which the Muslim captor requires the assistance of the vanquished knights whom he has captured.[25] True to this genre, Bohemond gains his freedom fighting for his captor. If not completely fictitious, the story borders on the fantastic. We should, however, remember that Anna Comnena's description of Bohemond as a ferocious blond giant with flaring nostrils and light blue eyes shows

22 Albert of Aachen, *Historia Ierosolymitana,* ed. and transl. Susan B. Edgington, OMT (forthcoming); earlier edition in RHC Occ., 4: 9, 33–6.

23 *Encounter between Enemies: Captivity and Ransom in the Latin Kingdom of Jerusalem* (Leiden, 2002), 13–32. Cf. Jean Dunbabin, *Captivity and Imprisonment in Medieval Europe, 1000–1300* (Houndmills, 2002).

24 Orderic Vitalis, *The Ecclesiastical History*, ed. and transl. Marjorie Chibnall, 6 vols (Oxford, 1969–80) [hereafter: OV], 5: 10, 354–78.

25 *Les Chétifs*, ed. Geoffrey M. Myers (Tuscaloosa, AL, 1981), 65, 74–5, 77, ll. 3206–8.

that he might have been attractive to an Eastern princess.[26] After all, according to the genre, what did the Muslim enemy have beautiful daughters for if not to save brave Christian knights? The story's happy end is, however, a little unexpected: according to the conventions of the chansons Bohemond ought to have married the beautiful princess.[27] He avoids this by using the weak excuse that he is obligated to return to Europe to fulfil his religious vow to St Leonard of Noblac. He promptly whisks the lady over to one of his young nobles in Antioch. This tale might be seen as a 'literary refashioning of folkloric methods that have themselves been mapped onto a basic factual core'.[28]

The next stage of the story can be identified in a long and intricate narrative that appears as a miracle in an early twelfth-century manuscript of the *Vita* and miracles of St Leonard of Noblac.[29] Here the pious Saracen woman is the wife, not the daughter, of the captor,[30] and as is to be expected, the role of the saint in procuring the liberty of his protégé is more pronounced.[31] Not surprisingly, the canons of St Leonard of Noblac emphasized the efficacious role of prayer. The description of the conditions of Bohemond's captivity in the miracle story seems strange to say the least. Giving his word that he would not attempt flight, Bohemond is allowed to receive between ten and twenty visitors at a time. They encircle him, while he, reclining on a couch,

26 *The Alexiad of Anna Comnena*, transl. E. R. A. Sewter (Harmondsworth, 1969), 13, 10, 422; Matthew Bennett, 'Virile Latins, Effeminate Greeks and Strong Women: Gender Definitions on Crusade?', in Susan B. Edgington and Sarah Lambert, eds, *Gendering the Crusades* (Cardiff, 2001), 16–30, esp. 17, remarks that Anna's description better fits a horse than a man, which may well be, but nevertheless she seems to have been attracted to him.

27 Norman Daniel, *Heroes and Saracens: an Interpretation of the Chansons de Geste* (Edinburgh, 1984), 193–201; Jacques Le Goff, *The Medieval Imagination* (Chicago, IL, 1988), 159–61.

28 Marcus Bull, 'Views of Muslims and of Jerusalem in Miracle Stories, *c.*1000–*c.*1200: Reflections on the Study of First Crusaders' Motivations', in Marcus Bull and Norman Housley, eds, *The Experience of Crusading: I. Western Approaches* (Cambridge, 2003), 13–38, 35.

29 'Vita et miracula Sancti Leonardi (6.11)', *ActaSS*, 3 Nov., 148–73. The story is attributed to Waleran, a Saxon bishop and numbered as miracle II, 160–8. He is, however, not the author, but only the scribe of the manuscript, Paris, Bibliothèque Nationale, MS Lat. 5347.

30 'Danishmend's wife, secretly a Christian, had pity on the Christian man in all ways, and as befitted the noble duke, she sent to him by way of secret intermediaries food, clothing and other needful things. And also, if at any time she perceived that her husband was undertaking anything crueler against the prisoner, she [started to] soften his anger with wifely blandishments, and by coaxing, threatening and promising to ensure that the guards would not injure the captive nor annoy him with any insults': *ActaSS*, 6 Nov., iii, 163.

31 Céline Cheirézy, 'Hagiographie et société: l'exemple de saint Léonard de Noblat', *Annales du Midi* 107 (1995), 417–35.

converses with them at leisure about accepting God's will. Then comes the miraculous part, where St Leonard appears to Bohemond in a nocturnal vision and tells him:

> Indeed the power has been granted to me to deliver you, but it is not right for you just to escape from your fetters. Your deliverance will in no wise be advantageous unless he who has you in chains frees you. Now wait patiently for God's mercy and our promise.[32]

Bohemond resigns himself to await the saint's chosen *modus operandi*, namely, to let the captor's wife intercede for him. The saint then appears to Danishmend's wife, telling her it is God's will that Bohemond be released from prison. Negotiations for a pact between Bohemond and his captor begin and the sum of 5,000 bezants is mentioned. Even that seems too high a price for a miraculous deliverance. Danishmend's wife takes up a collection for him and she even provides him with funds for his personal needs. He returns triumphantly to Antioch. In 1912 Poncelet suggested, on the basis of the early manuscript tradition of the text, that the source for the miracle story was Bohemond himself, who disseminated this version of his release.[33] In actuality, we have seen the greater number and reliability of the chronicle sources that report he was ransomed, with the local princes taking a more active role, both in fundraising and in contributing sums, than Bohemond's compatriots. Upon his return to Europe to raise money and troops for a war against the Byzantines, Bohemond launched a propaganda campaign in which he portrayed himself as an invincible hero. The *Gesta Francorum* is one facet of this campaign, writing the history of the First Crusade as a panegyric to Bohemond.[34] Being a ransomed captive did not fit into this scheme, and a more heroic story, more in the nature of what befit a *chanson de geste* had to be invented.[35]

32 *ActaSS*, 6 Nov., iii, 165–6.

33 Albert Poncelet, 'Boémond et S. Léonard', *AnBoll* 31 (1912), 24–44.

34 Kenneth B. Wolf, 'Crusade and Narrative: Bohemond and the *Gesta Francorum*', *JMedH* 17 (1991), 207–16, claims that, by concentrating on the story of Antioch, the *Gesta* glossed over the fact that Bohemond was not among the conquerors of Jerusalem.

35 For the dissemination of the narrative, see William of Malmesbury, *Gesta Regum Anglorum*, ed. and transl. R. A. B. Mynors (Oxford, 1998), 692–3: 'Not long afterwards he came to Gaul, and there offered as a guerdon to St Leonard the gyves that had been such a burden to himself. For St Leonard is foremost, it is said, in power to loose a man from bondage, so that the captive is set free and bears away his chains, while his enemies look on and dare not say a word'. My thanks to Sue Edgington for this reference.

The miracle story gave a new meaning to the events. Captivity did not represent failure; the hero was tricked into captivity by treachery and his captivity was God's chastisement of his beloved son. The humiliating prison conditions were transformed into a court where visitors and friends were entertained, the ransom shrank into oblivion, and the real reason for Bohemond's release was his well-known prowess and wit, whereas his romantic charm was played down. Even his treacherous nephew Tancred, who in fact did nothing to help Bohemond, was transformed into a caring, contributing part of the *familia*.

According to Orderic, Bohemond himself related the various adventures in which he had played a part: 'referebat varios eventus quibus ipse interfuit'.[36] The discrepancy between fact and romance may in this case not have been the fault of the jongleurs who chant the deeds in a shameful song,[37] but may rather lie in a romanticized version related by Bohemond and his followers.

The boundaries between the natural and the miraculous were not always clear-cut. Thus the *Acta Sanctorum,* in Richard of the Principate's miracle story, blends natural and supernatural events. According to this version Alexius Comnenus ransomed and imprisoned Richard but was persuaded by St Leonard to release him.[38] Thus a perfectly natural act received a wondrous aura by having the saint intervene in history in the same way God did for the crusaders – via a natural act in unnatural circumstances.

A second, probably later version of Bohemond's miraculous release from captivity, found in a late-twelfth century manuscript, places the story in a more conventional framework. This shorter version glosses over the circumstances of falling into captivity. The main point is St Leonard's appearance after due prayers. The saint instantaneously releases Bohemond and his fellow captives by breaking their chains through the sign of the cross. The guards sense nothing, the doors open, and the fugitives escape, bringing their *vota* to St Leonard's tomb at Noblat.[39] That is the conventionally expected way such a miracle ought

36 OV, 6: 11, 12, 68.
37 OV, 6: 11, 25, 120: 'cantilena de vobis cantetur in urbe'.
38 *ActaSS*, 3 Nov., 159–60.
39 Ibid.

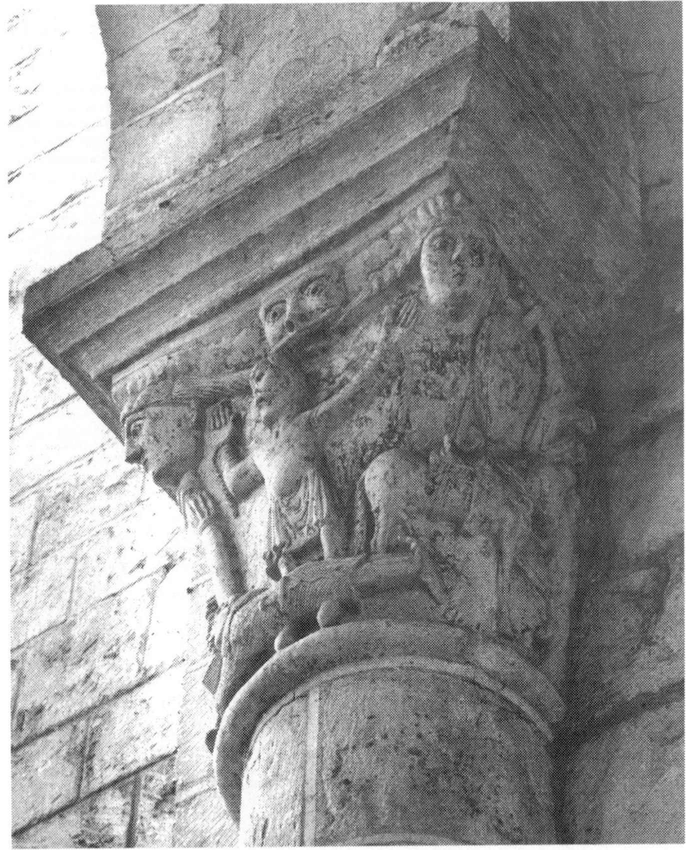

Fig. 1 St. Benedict frees a peasant prisoner miraculously
Photo: Phototèque Zodiaque, les Ateliers de la Pierre-qui-Vire

to occur, and the examples from hagiographies, from St Benedict[40] to St Foy[41] and St Eutropius,[42] are abundant.

A century later, when King Richard the Lionheart was taken prisoner on his return from the Holy Land, western mores had changed. It was no longer necessary to invent miraculous stories to explain his

40 *Miracula Sancti Benedicti*, in *Les Miracles de Saint-Benoit écrits par Adrevald, Aimoin, André, Raoul Tortaire et Hugues de Sainte Marie*, ed. E. de Certain (Paris, 1858), 356–71.

41 *The Book of Sainte Foy,* transl. Pamela Sheingorn (Philadelphia, PA, 1995), 102–3, 125–9, 148–9, 185–97, 235–9.

42 *ActaSS*, 30 April, iii: 742–8.

Fig. 2 Matthew Paris depicts the ransomed Frankish captives leaving their jail.

release from prison. Admired and revered in spite of his great fiasco, King Louis IX of France – Saint Louis – fell prisoner in Egypt and was ransomed for a huge sum paid by his subjects.[43]

The changed attitude toward ransom in the West also emerges from the shift in the prominence of miracles of deliverance by St Foy. In the eleventh century, according to Sigal, these were fifteen per cent of all the miracles. The twelfth century saw a reduction to nine per cent.[44] The miracles of St Benedict represented in the sculptures at the church at Fleury placed great emphasis on the attributes of the miracle of

43 Friedman, *Encounter between Enemies*, 213–38.

44 Pierre-André Sigal, *L'Homme et le miracle dans la France médiévale, XIe–XIIe siècles* (Paris, 1985), 268–9, 270. Sigal registers 159 miracles of deliverances out of a total of 4,756. Only five are miraculous escapes and none is a real act of the saint. Some saints seem to specialize in redemption: St Foy, St Leonard and St Mary Magdalen.

deliverance as we have noted them here: the chains break spontaneously via the agency of the victim's prayer to the saint, the saint himself is nowhere near the events, and his efficacious power works by remote control [fig. 1]. The miracle makes the unbeliever see the light and the captor lies at St Benedict's feet, praying.[45] Matthew Paris's illustration of deliverance fits the thirteenth century's acceptance of ransom: the captives leave prison with their handcuffs opened, but there is nothing miraculous about their hard-earned freedom – it is the result of negotiation and payment by their Christian compatriots [fig. 2].[46] In the thirteenth century, such dealings were an accepted aftermath of war. Like the literary narratives, these artistic representations of the release of captives reflect the mores of their time. To sum up: in the context of developing our understanding of the cultural assumptions and cognitive habits underlying the meaning of a miracle story, we may say that whereas modern sensibility would try to rationalize the miraculous, medieval discourse tried to 'miraculize' the natural, to elevate the shameful fact to a meaningful narrative, namely, a miracle. It appears that to Bohemond's mind, in the absence of a miracle, he could not have attained the status of a real hero.

Bar-Ilan University, Israel

45 Philippe Verdier, 'La Vie et les miracles de Saint Benoît dans les sculptures de Saint-Benoît-sur-Loire', *Mélanges de l'Ecole Française de Rome* 89 (1977), 117–53.

46 Cambridge, Corpus Christi College, MS 16, fol. 149r.

*MIRABILIS DEUS IN SANCTIS SUIS**: SOCIAL HISTORY AND MEDIEVAL MIRACLES

by MICHAEL GOODICH

PERHAPS our most learned and knowledgeable informant concerning both the heretics and their persecutors is the great inquisitor, hagiographer and Dominican historian Bernard Gui (1261–1331), who has been immortalized as the personification of evil by Umberto Eco in *The Name of the Rose*. In his manual for inquisitors, Gui issued the following caveat concerning the conduct of inquiries into heresy:

> It is worthwhile noting that if too many questions and answers are raised, the truth is distorted and destroyed as a result of the diversity of persons and events. Rather, it is suitable not to write down all the questions and answers, but only those which touch directly on the substance and character of the event and which more closely appear to express the truth. If in one deposition too many questions and answers are found, another deposition will appear thereby diminished since too little is recorded. When so many questions and answers are written down in a trial, agreement can scarcely be found in the depositions of the witnesses, which should be both considered and avoided.[1]

Gui's attempt to guarantee that no allegedly 'extraneous' information creeps into such hearings, indicates the desire on the part of the inquisi-

* Ps 67, 36 in the Vulgate, first used in Celestine III's canonization bull (1191) for Peter of Tarantaise, PL 206, 869–71, appears frequently in many subsequent bulls of canonization. I would like to thank participants at the 2003 meeting of CIHEC for their valuable suggestions.

1 Bernard Gui, *Manuel de l'Inquisiteur*, ed. G. Mollat and G. Drioux, 2 vols (Paris, 1926–7), 1: 32; Caterina Bruschi, '"*Magna diligentia est habenda per inquisitorem*": Precautions before Reading Doat 21–26', in Caterina Bruschi and Peter Biller, eds, *Texts and the Repression of Medieval Heresy* (York, 2003), 81–110. On Gui, see Bernhard Schimmelpfennig, 'Bernard Gui: Hagiograph und verhinderter Heiliger', in Dieter R. Bauer and Klaus Herbers, eds, *Hagiographie im Kontext. Wirkungsweisen und Möglichkeiten historischer Auswertung* (Stuttgart, 2000), 257–65; Bernard Guenée, 'Bernard Gui', in idem, *Entre l'Église et l'État. Quatre vies de prélats français à la fin du Moyen Âge (XIIIe–XVe siècle)* (Paris, 1987), 49–85; Antoine Thomas, 'Bernard Gui, frère prêcheur', in *Histoire littéraire de la France*, 42 vols (Paris, 1865–), 35 (1921): 139–232.

tors to gain complete control of their investigations in order to ensure their outcome. This expectation has no doubt been shared by law enforcement officials, policing agencies and secret services in modern times, whose methods have sometimes been compared to the darker days of the Inquisition.

Gui's suggestions however apply equally to the investigation of miracles and sainthood. As an active inquisitor and student not only of heresy, but also the author of an important legendary and biography of Thomas Aquinas, Gui was well acquainted with the drawbacks of such investigations.[2] His observation concerning the pitfalls of judicial inquiries is confirmed by the Dominican Ralph Bocking, whose life (*c.*1268–72) of the Oxford scholar, Bishop Richard of Chichester, was based on a canonization protocol. Ralph apologized for the unskilled, clumsy and confused style of his work on the grounds that it reflects the testimony of the deponents at the bishop's canonization process.[3]

In fact, between the twelfth and fourteenth centuries, the procedures used for the investigation of both heresy and the miraculous developed in tandem and often employed the same personnel. This parallel development has made trials for heresy and canonization important sources for medieval social history. In this paper, an attempt will be made to show how historians of the sacred and supernatural may profit from an awareness of the close ties between the investigation of heresy and of canonization, and from the issues that have already been raised by students of the Inquisition. Further, recognizing the difficulties encountered in reading such testimony, some specific miracles reported during the canonization processes will illustrate how they may serve as a rich source for the social history of the subaltern classes, whose voices may often be muffled or silenced in other kinds of historical sources.

Many of the questions raised in the study of medieval heresy and the Inquisition may be posed equally by students of the miraculous. For example, how reliable is the raw data provided by these trials? Does the intervention of court personnel taint the value of the deponents' testimony? Have the summaries and protocols that have reached us been altered to reflect the needs of the Church and its bureaucracy rather

2 The definitive essay is Antoine Dondaine, 'Le Manuel de l'Inquisiteur (1230–1330)', *Archivum fratrum praedicatorum* 17 (1947), 85–194. Gui was involved in the canonization of Thomas Aquinas and wrote a widely distributed *Speculum sanctorale*.

3 Ralph Bocking, *Vita et miracula S. Ricardi*, in *ActaSS*, 3 April, I: 283: 'rudi tamen stylo & incomposito, prout deponentium dicta testium continebant, confuse fuerunt conscripta'.

than the sentiments and facts reported by the speakers? In the case of miracles, are the surviving cases the product of a process whereby unreliable, unorthodox, and incomplete cases were filtered out early in the investigation? As the investigators increasingly refined their list of questions and the speakers were not given free reign to tell their stories uninterrupted, what is now left unsaid, or at least unrecorded? Who conducted the trials, and was their aim to simply provide credible documentation for the conviction of prejudged heretics or the canonization of already well-regarded putative saints? Can such court records help us to reconstruct the lives of rural and urban members of the subaltern classes, whose voices are rarely heard in traditional narrative sources, or do we hear only what we were intended to hear, while some more embarrassing details may be left out, in accordance with Gui's caveat?

* * *

Although many canonized saints had done battle in the struggle with heretics, pagans, Jews, schismatics, Muslims or other non-believers, the link between heresy and sainthood was most clearly voiced for the first time in the canonization bull of the merchant Homobonus of Cremona issued by Innocent III in 1199. Innocent stressed that by means of: 'signs and miracles . . . the perversity of the heretics is confounded when they witness the prodigies that abound at the tombs of Catholics'.[4] But the tie between the personnel and procedure in trials for heresy and canonization predates Innocent's pontificate. Both the first papal legislation concerning the pursuit of heretics, *Ad abolendam* (1184), and the first protocol of a papal canonization trial *in partibus*, the case of the hermit Galgano of Chiusdino (1185), date from the pontificate of Pope Lucius III.[5] The use of the inquisitorial method of investigation for a wide variety of cases, including simony, heresy, excommunication, marriage cases, and episcopal appointments, among others, was probably initi-

4 Roberto Paciocco, '"Virtus morum" e "virtus signorum". La teoria della santità nelle lettere di canonizzazione di Innocenzo III', *Nuova rivista storica* 70 (1986), 597–610; Jürgen Petersohn, 'Die Literae Papst Innocenz' III zur Heiligspechung der Kaiserin Kunigunde (1200)', *Jahrbuch für frankische Landesforschung* 37 (1977), 1–25; *Die Register Innocenz' III*, ed. Othmar Hageneder *et al.*, 5 vols (1964–97), 1: 762.

5 Yves Dossat, *Les Crises de l'Inquisition toulousaine au XIIIe siècle (1233–1273)* (Bordeaux, 1959), 106; PL 201, 1297–1300; Fedor Schneider, ed., 'Der Einsiedler Galgano von Chiusdino und die Anfänge von San Galgano', *Quellen und Forschungen aus italienischen Archiven und Bibliotheken* 17 (1914–24), 61–77.

ated under Innocent III and entered canon law in about 1206.[6] Innocent's pontificate was especially active in setting precedents for both the persecution of heretics and canonization of saints. The recently reconstructed 1210 trial of the heretical Paris theologian Amaury de Bène is perhaps the earliest evidence for the application to an ecclesiastical court of the new inquisitorial procedures found in Innocent's *Compilatio tertia*.[7] During Innocent's pontificate the rubric '*inquisitio*' was first applied to canonization inquiries, while under his successor Honorius III the term inquisitor referred to those who conducted the hearings.[8]

Both the earliest extant manuals for the guidance of inquisitors and papal lists of questions to be posed by commissions investigating canonization cases date from the 1230s, when the use of the same personnel in both heresy and sainthood trials emerges.[9] The participation of a narrow circle of experts guaranteed the imposition of a uniform ideology to both the understanding of heresy and of its allegedly most effective antidote, the Christian miracle. Conrad of Marburg (1180/90–1233), who was probably the first official papal inquisitor, was entrusted by Pope Gregory IX with the investigation of heresy in Germany in around 1227. He was responsible for a veritable reign of terror in pursuit of Cathars, Waldensians, and Luciferians, in addition to the rural Stedingers, who lived in Germany's northern marshlands and were accused of heresy and witchcraft. Conrad's close involvement in the case of Elizabeth of Thuringia (d. 1231) likewise set important precedents. He served as her spiritual guide and in 1232 provided the first summary of her miracles, including a record of the points of agreement and discord among the witnesses. This represents an early documented effort to distinguish between credible and doubtful miracles.[10]

6 Lothar Kolmer, *Ad capiendas vulpes. Die Ketzerbekämpfung in Südfrankreich in der ersten Hälfte des 13. Jahrhunderts und die Ausbildung des Inquisitionsverfahrens* (Bonn, 1982), 59, 109–12; Dossat, *Les Crises*, 111–13; Raoul Naz, 'Inquisition', in *Dictionnaire de droit canonique*, 7 vols (Paris, 1935–65), 5: 1418–26.

7 J. M. M. H. Thijssen, 'Master Amalric and the Amalricians: Inquisitorial Procedure and the Suppression of Heresy at the University of Paris', *Speculum* 71 (1996), 43–65.

8 Roberto Paciocco, *"Sublimia negotia": le canonizzazioni dei santi nella curia papale e il nuovo Ordine dei frati Minori* (Padua, 1996); Simon Tugwell, 'Notes on the Life of St Dominic', *Archivum fratrum praedicatorum* 66 (1996), 5–100, esp. 177 for the term *inquisitio*. See Kenneth Pennington, *The Prince and the Law, 1200–1600: Sovereignty and Rights in the Western Legal Tradition* (Berkeley, CA, 1993), 64, on how reason, oral argument and written evidence now replaced the ordeal as the foundation of adjudication.

9 Dondaine, 'Le Manuel', 85–194.

10 Kolmer, *Ad capiendas vulpes*, 113–22; Alexander Patschovsky, 'Konrad v. Marburg',

Conrad and Elizabeth's close association is attested by their posthumous appearance together in a vision to a man sentenced to death in order to allegedly revive him after the hanging.[11] The other papal investigators in Elizabeth's case themselves often provided their own testimony of the supernatural by testifying to having seen the victims in good condition after their miraculous cure. Four cases were reported by Conrad himself, and had therefore passed the highest scrutiny. One important miracle was experienced by the Cistercian Abbot Raymund of Eberbach, one of the commissioners in her case. He was in such pain from a diseased leg on the way to Marburg that he was almost prevented from continuing, had it not been for Elizabeth's posthumous intervention.[12] The personal testimony of one of the investigators himself would, presumably, substantially enhance Elizabeth's chances before the curia.

Elizabeth's canonization trial provides us with the first extant list of questions or *formula interrogatorii*. The preparation of such a list of questions followed a series of cases in which both Honorius III and Gregory IX had earlier expressed dissatisfaction with the method of inquiry. In Elizabeth's case the involvement of the canonist, papal chaplain and penitentiary Raymund of Penyafort, the editor of Gregory IX's *Decretals*, would insure closer adherence to the rules of evidence in the

Lexikon der Mittelalter 5 (1990), 1360–1; idem, 'Zur Ketzerverfolgung Konrads von Marburg', *Deutsches Archiv für Erforschung des Mittelalters* 37 (1981), 641–93; see the Bull of Gregory IX, *Ut ceci viam*, 13 October 1232, in *Les Registres de Grégoire IX*, ed. Lucien Auvray, 4 vols (Paris, 1896–1955), 1: 548: '. . . quomodo sciunt, quo tempore, quo mense, quo die, quibus presentibus, quo loco, ad cujus invocationem, et quibus verbis interpositis, et de nominibus illorum circa quos miracula facta dicuntur, et si ante cognoscabant, et quot diebus ante viderunt eos infirmos et quanto tempore fuerunt infirmi, et de qua civitate sunt oriundi et interrogantur de omnibus circumstantiis diligenter'. For less precise inquests see the contemporary case of Odo of Tagliacozzo in 'Documenta de B. Odone Novariensi ordinis Carthusiani', *AnBoll* 1 (1882), 323–54; and Hildegard of Bingen in 'Acta inquisitionis de virtutibus et miraculis S. Hildegardis', *AnBoll* 2 (1883), 116–29. Other contemporary cases under Gregory IX concern Virgil of Salzburg, Dominic, Anthony of Padua and, of course, Francis of Assisi.

[11] James of Voragine, *Legenda aurea*, ed. Giovanni Paolo Maggioni, 2 vols (2nd edn, Florence, 1998), 2: 1175. This comes from the 1233 miracle collection in Albert Huyskens, *Quellenstudien zur Geschichte der hl. Elisabeth, Landgräfin von Thüringen* (Marburg, 1908), 155–239, n. 17. On her process see *Sankt Elisabeth, Fürstin, Dienerin, Heilige. Aufsätze, Documentation, Katalog* (Sigmaringen, 1981), 123–36.

[12] Huyskens, *Quellenstudien*, 246–7. On the popularity of Elizabeth's cult, see Matthias Werner, '*Mater Hassiae—Flos Ungariae—Gloria Teutoniae*. Politik und Heiligenverehrung im Nachleben der hl. Elisabeth von Thüringen', in Jürgen Petersohn, ed., *Politik und Heiligenverehrung im Hochmittelalter* (Sigmaringen, 1994), 449–540, esp. 455–68.

deposition of witnesses.[13] A list of ninety miracles reported in 1232 by the archbishop of Mainz and other local ecclesiastics in a postulatory letter asking for Elizabeth's canonization stresses the role of the miracle as a divine tool to 'assist the universal church and confound the heretics'.[14] These correspondents apologized for not providing more information about the witnesses because of the pressure of the crowd at Marburg during Conrad's sermon on the occasion of the consecration of two altars in Elizabeth's honour. Most of the elements of the fullest miracles are already present in Elizabeth's inquest, allowing us to draw a portrait of her constituents, including their gender and geographical origin, although professional and class background may still be lacking in such reports.

The overlapping use of personnel trained in the inquisitorial processes for the adjudication of both heresy and canonization continued. I will cite just a few more examples. Odo of Châteauroux (d. 1273), cardinal-bishop of Tusculum, who took part in the trial of the Talmud and of the radical Joachite Gerard of Borgo San Donnino, was then directly involved in the canonization cases of Louis IX of France, Hedwig of Silesia, Richard of Chichester and Philip of Bourges. After taking part in the canonization process of Thomas of Hereford in 1307, William Durand the Younger (*c.*1271–1330), bishop of Mende, in the following year, served as a member of the commission examining the notorious charges against the Templars. In a third example, Jacques Fournier, later elevated to the papacy as Pope Benedict XII (1334), conducted the series of inquisitorial trials that were to become the basis of Le Roy Ladurie's study of the peasants of Montaillou.[15] He continued to serve as a judge in several trials of heretics and other ideological deviants;[16] and in 1330 he examined the canonization dossier of the Breton lawyer Yves of Tréguier (d. 1303).[17]

13 Josef Leinweber, 'Das kirchliche Heilsprechungsverfahren bis zum Jahre 1234. Der Kanonisationsprozess der hl. Elisabeth von Thuringen', in *Sankt Elisabeth,* 128–36.

14 *Hessisches Urkundenbuch. I. Urkundenbuch der Deutschordens-Ballei Hessen, 1207–1299*, ed. Arthur Wyss (Leipzig, 1879), 25–9, esp. 28: 'in subsidium universalis ecclesie et hereticorum confutandam'.

15 Emmanuel Le Roy Ladurie, *Montaillou: Cathars and Catholics in a French Village, 1294–1324*, trans. Barbara Bray (Harmondsworth, 1980).

16 Guy Mollat, *Les Papes d'Avignon (1305–1378)* (10th rev. edn, Paris, 1964), 74–88. The culprits included the Fraticello Conrad, the former inquisitor Jean Garland, the Breton priest Yves de Kérinou, the English Dominican Thomas Walleys and the knight Adhémar de Mosset.

17 *Monuments originaux de l'histoire de Saint Yves*, ed. A. de la Borderie *et al.* (Saint-Brieuc, 1887).

Such inquisitors were assisted by papal, royal or imperial notaries, like the well-known papal notary Berardo of Naples (1231–93), who were trained in classical literature, Scripture, canon and Roman law and thereby guaranteed adherence to suitable procedures and legal formulae.[18] The oral testimony in such trials was copied down, rewritten, summarized and read back to the deponents by a group of skilled professionals trained in both law and the liberal arts.[19] Such notaries also drew up a large number of affidavits concerning miracles not directly related to canonization inquests, such as those of Simon of Todi and Ambrose of Siena;[20] while several appear as star witnesses in support of the miracles attributed to Pope Celestine V and Clare of Montefalco.

Nevertheless, despite their professional training, considerable criticism, much of it justified, has recently been levelled at those who view these inquisitors and notaries as neutral ethnographers. This jaundiced view of the judiciary in the service of the state has no doubt been influenced by some of the darker episodes of twentieth-century history. The records of the Inquisition were clearly tainted by the politics of domination, by the censorious intervention of the inquisitor, his attempt to pigeonhole the deponents into neat ideological categories, to disregard the nuances of belief and practice, and to prove the officials' abilities as persecutors of heretics.[21] Some have criticized what might be termed the 'constructionist hegemonism' of both the inquisitors and those who

[18] F. Kaltenbrunner, 'Die Briefsammlung des Berardo de Neapoli', *Mitteilungen des Instituts für österreichische Geschichtsforschung* 7 (1886), 21–118, 555–635, esp. 557; D. Lohrmann, 'Caraciolo, Berardo', in *Dizionario biografico degli italiani*, ed. A. Ghisalberti *et al.*, 54 vols (Rome, 1960–2000), 19: 313–17.

[19] Natalie Zemon Davis, *Fiction in the Archives: Pardon Tales and their Tellers in Sixteenth-Century France* (Stanford, CA, 1987), argues in favour of the conscientiousness of the notaries. On the other hand, James B. Given, *Inquisition and Medieval Society: Power, Discipline and Resistance in Medieval Languedoc* (Ithaca, NY, 1997), 144–7, provides examples of venal notaries in the service of the Inquisition.

[20] David Foote, 'How the Past Becomes a Rumor: the Notarization of Historical Consciousness in Medieval Orvieto', *Speculum* 75 (2000), 794–815 on the civic role of the professional notaries. Notaries are given an especially central role in the case of Thomas Aquinas. See *ActaSS*, 7 March, I: 686; *Thomae Aquinatis vitae et fontes praecipue*, ed. A. Ferrua (Alba, 1968), 204.

[21] See e.g. Renato Rosaldo, 'From the Door of his Tent: the Fieldworker and the Inquisitor', in James Clifford and George E. Marcus, eds, *Writing Culture. The Poetics and Politics of Ethnography* (Berkeley, CA, 1986), 77–97. Further criticism of the willingness to read inquisitorial documents uncritically is found in Natalie Zemon Davis, 'Les Conteurs de Montaillou (note critique)', *Annales: Économies, Sociétés, Civilisations* [hereafter: *Annales*] 34 (1979), 61–73.

accept their reports at face value.[22] John Arnold, James Given and Mark Gregory Pegg have recently undertaken the difficult task of separating the multiple discourses of participants in the inquisitorial trial.[23]

If we turn from the investigation of heresy to miracles reported at canonization inquests, we are likewise hampered by the intrusion of the inquisitor, canon lawyer, notary or biographer. As in heresy cases, the witnesses were often expected to recall events that had occurred years earlier, with its inevitable distortions of memory. For example, in the 1250s case of Stanislaus of Cracow (*c.*1036–79) doubts were raised about the ability of two centenarians who had been asked to recall their knowledge of a long-dead saint.[24] In addition to the perennial vagueness of deponents about their age, witnesses often disagreed about the precise time and date of a miracle, especially after many years had passed. Such difficulties were aggravated by the emotional atmosphere often accompanying both heresy and canonization trials. Thousands might testify within a short period of time, as during the 202 days of heresy hearings held at Toulouse in 1245–6 involving deponents from the Lauragais.[25] The earliest record of posthumous miracles of a particular saint was also often simultaneously accompanied by the sensational performance of miracles at the site of the saint's tomb, when spectators might view a dramatic exorcism or the unanticipated mass cure of disabled pilgrims. This is well documented in the daily record of pilgrims reported at Thomas of Hereford's shrine, when thirty-two eyewitnesses allegedly witnessed the restoration of speech to one

22 See, e.g., Kathleen Biddick, 'The Devil's Anal Eye: Inquisitorial Optics and Ethnographic Authority', in eadem, *The Shock of Medievalism* (Durham, NC, 1998), 105–34.

23 John H. Arnold, *Inquisition and Power: Catharism and the Confessing Subject in Medieval Languedoc* (Philadelphia, PA, 2001); Given, *Inquisition and Medieval Society*; Mark Gregory Pegg, *The Corruption of Angels: the Great Inquisition of 1245–1246* (Princeton, NJ, 2001).

24 Vincent Kadlubek, *Vita majora S. Stanislai*, ed. Wojciech Ketrzynski, in *Monumenta poloniae historica,* 6 vols (Warsaw, 1960–1), 4: 319–438, esp. 434–5; *Bullarium franciscanum romanorum pontificum*, ed. Johannes Hyacinthus Sbaralea, 3 vols (Rome, 1759–65), 1: 610 (26 May 1252: letter of Innocent IV to James of Velletri).

25 Walter Wakefield, 'Inquisitorial Assistants. Witnesses of Confessions in Manuscript 609', *Heresis* 20 (1993), 58–69; Mark Gregory Pegg, 'Questions about Questions; Toulouse 609 and the Great Inquisition of 1245–6', in Bruschi and Biller, eds, *Texts and the Repression of Medieval Heresy*, 111–25; Grado G. Merlo, *Eretici e inquisitori nella società piemontese del Trecento* (Turin, 1977), 11–15. Some problems are discussed in Guy P. Marchal, 'De la Mémoire communicative à la mémoire culturelle. Le passé dans les témoignages d'Arezzo et de Sienne (1177–1180)', *Annales* 56 (2001), 563–89; Jacques Paul, 'Expression et perception du temps d'après l'enquête des miracles de Louis d'Anjou', in *Temps, mémoire, tradition au Moyen-Age* (Aix-en-Provence, 1983), 19–41.

miraculé.[26] Exorcisms at the site of a tomb were probably the most theatrical and effective demonstrations of the saint's power and the vengeance wrought against those who unpatriotically failed to honour his or her reputation. Such events were often the first public demonstration of a cult. In order to enhance the *fama* or reputation of the saint, many miracle collections highlight in particular the miracles that occurred during the translation of the putative saint's relics and its attendant religious enthusiasm. These theatrical events may well have become distorted in the memories of deponents.

In the light of such difficulties, the conscientious historian may well raise doubts about any effort to read canonization records and miracle stories as the genuine, uncensored voice of the peasants and urban folk. The critical reader must be aware that the inquisitors and notaries translated, selected, edited, rewrote, dissected, rearranged and summarized the deponents' testimony. Studies of eyewitness testimony suggest that when witnesses are allowed to report freely rather than respond to specific questions, they provide the most accurate but least complete initial recall. This is precisely what the inquisitors – according to Bernard Gui – discouraged them from doing by the use of a prepared list of questions.[27] The presence of ten or more witnesses, who had travelled together from the same village to reach the hearing room in order to testify about one miracle, may often have also led to collusion in the depositions and a rather monotonous uniformity in their testimony. The cases of Elizabeth of Thuringia, Stanislaus of Cracow and others often state that the various witnesses were 'in concord' about the events, without fleshing out the testimony of each deponent.

The inquest concerning Louis of Toulouse (d. 1297) illustrates the difficulties faced in interpreting such tainted testimony. One woman from a village near Nîmes testified that 'the people, having seen the frequency of the miracles he performed, regarded him as a saint'. A lame man said that his cure 'was a great miracle beyond [the laws] of nature'; while a woman said, 'they consider it to be a great miracle since they believe that such a cure is [otherwise] impossible'. A soldier who had been cured of a fever had stated that, 'the physicians were extremely surprised, they said that such a thing could not happen in accordance with their skill unless God had miraculously intervened'.

26 See Oxford, Exeter College, MS 158, for the summary record of Thomas's miracles recorded at Hereford cathedral beginning in 1286.

27 Elizabeth F. Loftus and James M. Doyle, *Eyewitness Testimony: Civil and Criminal* (2nd edn, Charlottesville, VA, 1992), 74.

These remarks sound suspiciously like rehearsed or coaxed testimony reflecting the views of the court officials concerning the nature of the miraculous rather than the spontaneous reactions of the deponents themselves.[28] Nevertheless, a comparison of the words of different deponents in the same inquiry may reveal slips of the tongue, non-ideologically charged details and unrehearsed diversions from the standard miracle script, which are of special interest to the social historian, such as the ethnic mix that characterized many frontier communities.[29] For example, the survival of vernacular in the protocol of Thomas of Hereford reveals the presence of English, French, Welsh, and Latin speakers at the hearings.[30] Margaret of Hungary's hearing involved the use of Italian, Latin, Hungarian, German and probably several Slavic dialects.[31]

Nevertheless, social historians, particularly those associated with the French school of the *Annales*, have accumulated a rich experience in filtering out the trappings of formal procedure and official ideology from evidence of the mores, social and family structure, and underlying long-term beliefs in traditional rural and urban societies. Evelyne Patlagean has pointed out with respect to the Byzantine period that by contextualizing saints' lives and miracles it is possible to exploit hagiography to fill in historical gaps that might otherwise be inaccessible to the historian.[32] By focusing on less ideologically charged secondary details and reading between the lines, historians of the miraculous have made remarkable contributions to social history, despite being hampered by Gui's caveat to inquisitors to avoid the extraneous.[33] Just as trials for heresy have been used to reconstruct the community of non-believers by shedding light on, for example, family ties, popular belief and practice, and the dynamics of community life, in the same way, canonization inquests can paint a portrait of the community of the faithful and the constituency of a particular cult. The aim is to rescue

28 *Processus canonizationis et legendae variae Sancti Ludovici O.F.M., episcopi Tolosani*, ed. Benvenutus Bughetti, *Analecta franciscana* 7 (1951), 164, 181, 184, 200.

29 Bruschi, '"*Magna diligentia est habenda*"', 83–4.

30 Christian Krötzl, 'Zu Übersetzung und Sprachbeherrschung im Spätmittelalter am Beispiel von Kanonisationsprozessen', *Das Mittelalter* 2 (1997), 111–18.

31 *Inquisitio super vita, conversatione et miraculis beatae Margarethae virginis*, ed. William Fraknoì, in *Monumenta romana episcopatus Vesprimiensis*, 4 vols (Budapest, 1896–1907), 1: 163–384, esp. 181, 200, 232, 246, 274, 275, 301, 315, 317, 322, 325, 331, 353, 367, 371, 375.

32 Evelyne Patlagean, 'Ancienne hagiographie byzantine et histoire sociale', *Annales* 23 (1968), 106–26.

33 Peter Assion, 'Die mittelalterliche Mirakel-Literatur als Forschungsgegenstand', *Archiv für Kulturgescichte* 50 (1968), 172–80.

such folk from the anonymity of history, and to move from the pious generalities of hagiography to the circumstances of a particular miracle and its social climate.[34]

One example drawn from the 1276 canonization trial of Margaret of Hungary illustrates the graphic detail provided by such miracle reports.[35] Three deponents testified about the alleged revival from death of a twin infant named Sebastian born to a couple from a village in the diocese of Vàc near Budapest. Each one was allowed to summarize the miracle at the beginning of his or her testimony. But thanks to the probing questions of the inquisitors we have inherited a lively visual recreation of the setting and dramatic moments surrounding the child's cure. We learn that when the miracle was performed the victim's family lived on a small farm, containing at least two buildings, which had been abandoned by the time of the hearing in 1276. It was situated some distance from other residents of the local village (*villa*), which was inhabited by both free and bonded persons dwelling in five homesteads (*mansiones*). The three deponents, namely the child's father, mother, and his by now married older sister, had witnessed his revival after several hours early one morning around the feast of St Andrew on November 30, in 1269 or 1270. It is reported that after the twins' birth, the infant boy's sister had lived for several months from Shrovetide until the feast of St Martin, i.e. November 11, when she perhaps suffered crib death. Neither the victim himself nor an older brother named Alexander, who was also present at the time of the miracle, was to testify at the canonization hearing.

The door to the house where the child Sebastian was found dead in bed lying beside his mother was apparently locked from the inside, since his father had to shout several times to be let in from the outside by his daughter, after hearing his wife Cunig's wailing. We are provided with the names of the neighbours who later heard of the miracle, since at the time only members of the immediate family had been present. The investigators inquired about the family's status. The mother described herself as free and *nobilis*. She characterized her husband as rather wealthy (*satis dives*). He, on the other hand, simply said he was not bonded (*non sum servus*) and not rich (*non sum dives*). The daughter spoke of herself as neither rich nor poor (*nec dives, nec pauper*).

34 Michael Sot, 'Le Miracle et le temps d'histoire (haut Moyen Age occidental)', in Denise Aigle, ed., *Miracle et Karama. Hagiographies médiévales comparées* (Turnhout, 2000), 197–216.

35 *Inquisitio*, ed. Fraknoì, 1: 325–31.

Since the mother generally provided more precise answers, it would appear that her husband was perhaps suspicious of revealing too much to the court, particularly his income.

This case suggests that the natural taciturnity of some witnesses could only be broken down through the persistence of the inquisitors, who have willed us a valuable legacy. The exact words of members of the subaltern classes found in Margaret's and other protocols – even if only paraphrased or summarized – are presumably more reliable than the stereotypical hagiographical *topoi* as a reflection of the local community.[36] In the absence of an extant canonization protocol, it is also possible to reconstruct the inquiry by comparing the contents of a contemporary biography with the questions posed by Rome at such inquests, as in the cases of Hedwig of Silesia and Richard of Chichester.[37] Furthermore, in cases for which we are fortunate enough to possess both the raw material of the trial and later biographies based on it, we can trace the process through which the unsifted statements of the deponents were selected and turned into a theologically orthodox biography, a canonization bull, liturgy, sermon, visual illustrations and a host of other media through which the saint's message reached a wider public.[38]

Sharon Farmer, Jean-Claude Schmitt, Pierre-André Sigal, Ronald Finucane, Laura Smoller, Robert Bartlett, Paolo Golinelli, Stanko Andric and others have successfully sought to harness this material concerning miracles in the service of social history. They have read between the lines in order to separate the genuine daily concerns of the deponents from the ideological interests of the notaries, clerks, inquisitors, canon lawyers, theologians and commissioners who populated canonization hearings.[39] The micro-historian, by reducing the scale of

36 Edward Muir, 'Observing Trifles', in Edward Muir and Guido Ruggiero, eds, *Microhistory and the Lost Peoples of Europe*, trans. Eren Branch (Baltimore, PA, 1991), xvi. This volume contains a selection of articles from the *Quaderni storici* written by micro-historians.

37 Simon of Trebnitz, *Vita majora Hedwigis*, ed. A. Bielowski, in *Monumenta poloniae historica*, 4: 510–633, esp. 621; Ralph Bocking, *Vita Ricardi ep. Cicestrensis*, in *ActaSS*, 3 April, I: 283–317; *Saint Richard of Chichester. The Sources for his Life*, ed. David Jones, Sussex Record Society 79 (Lewes, 1993). As their authors admit, such biographies closely follow the testimony elicited at the canonization trial, with the addition of the rhetorical and narrative conventions of contemporary hagiography; including citations of Scripture and literary models as Gregory of Tours, Sulpicius Severus and the *Vitae patrum*.

38 Michael Goodich, 'The Use of Direct Quotation from Canonization Hearing to Hagiographical *Vita et Miracula*', in Gerhard Jaritz and Michael Richter, eds, *Oral History of the Middle Ages: the Spoken Word in Context* (Budapest, 2002), 47–57.

39 Christian Krötzl, *Pilger, Mirakel und Alltag. Formen des Verhaltens im skandinavischen*

his observation to a particular miracle or cult, hopes to reveal historical factors that have otherwise been overlooked and to unearth the individuals and events that lay hidden behind the rhetoric of ideology.[40] Farmer, for example, has graphically traced the insecurities of unemployment, single motherhood, vagabondage and marginal existence in thirteenth-century Paris reflected in the miracles of St Louis.[41] Finucane and Bartlett have pieced together exciting tales of childhood accidents, coroners' inquiries and political treason from the voluminous files of Thomas of Hereford's canonization trial.[42] Smoller has attempted to reduce the alleged gap between elite and popular notions of the supernatural in the case of Vincent Ferrer, and to reveal the individuals hidden behind the formulae of legal testimony.[43]

An important question raised by the social historian is whether notions of the sacred and the supernatural differ among different social groups, in order to test the supposed divide between learned and popular culture in the Middle Ages.[44] Was Christian faith in the miraculous imposed by the clerical elite, or was it endemic among all social classes? Recent anthropological research, for example, has revealed the decline of certain ritual practices, such as the veneration of sacred trees

Mittelalter (12.–15. Jahrhundert) (Helsinki, 1994); Jean-Claude Schmitt, *The Holy Greyhound: Guinefort, Healer of Children since the Thirteenth Century*, trans. Martin Thom (Cambridge, 1983); Pierre-André Sigal, *L'Homme et le miracle dans la France médiévale (XIe–XIIe siècle)* (Paris, 1985); idem, 'Maladie, pèlerinage, et guérison au XIIe siècle. Les miracles de Saint Gibrien à Reims', *Annales* 24 (1969), 1522–39; Paolo Golinelli, *Città e culto del medioevo italiano* (Bologna, 1991); Stanko Andrić, *The Miracles of St John Capistran* (Budapest, 2000).

40 Giovanni Levi, 'On Microhistory', in Peter Burke, ed., *New Perspectives on Historical Writing* (Cambridge, 1991), 92–113; see also Carlo Ginzburg, *The Cheese and the Worms*, transl. John and Anne Tedeschi (London, 1980); Natalie Zemon Davis, *Women on the Margins: Three Seventeenth-Century Lives* (Cambridge, MA, 1995); Jacques Revel, 'Micro-analyse et construction du social', in Jacques Revel, ed., *Jeux d'échelles. La micro-analyse à l'expérience* (Paris, 1996), 15–36.

41 Sharon Farmer, *Surviving Poverty in Medieval Paris: Gender, Ideology, and Daily Lives of the Poor* (Ithaca, NY, 2002).

42 Robert Bartlett, *The Hanged Man. A Story of Miracle, Memory and Colonialism in the Middle Ages* (Princeton, NJ, 2004); Ronald Finucane, *The Rescue of the Innocents: Endangered Children in Medieval Miracles* (New York, 1997).

43 Laura Smoller, 'Miracle, Memory, and Meaning in the Canonization of Vincent Ferrer, 1453–54', *Speculum* 73 (1998), 429–54; eadem, 'Defining the Boundaries of the Natural in the Fifteenth Century: the Inquest into the Miracles of St Vincent Ferrer (d. 1419)', *Viator* 28 (1997), 333–59.

44 The theme of 'Elite and Popular Religion' has been chosen as the topic for the Ecclesiastical History Society Conference, 2004, by the President, Prof. Eamon Duffy, and will be the subject of SCH 42.

and ponds in the movement from rural to urban society.[45] The *exempla* of Stephen of Bourbon reveal the persistence of pre-Christian beliefs and practices in rural areas and efforts to root out pagan survivals, which was one of the goals of the inquisitors and Dominican preachers. In addition, hagiographers and scholastic apologists recognized the continuing presence of doubters concerning the miracles of the saints. But, paradoxically, it was only through miracles, not through words or deeds, that these very same infidels, like the legendary twelve Jewish elders who had debated St Silvester, would be converted.[46] Those groups whom R. I. Moore has noted were being increasingly demonized and excluded from society, such as Jews, lepers, Muslims, heretics, sexual minorities and others, are most graphically portrayed as the objects of conversion or retribution in medieval miracles. And it is such miracles that often best illustrate the complexity of medieval society.[47]

Examples of mockery in the face of the supernatural, in which sceptics are invariably rewarded with divine retribution, abound in miracle collections and raise doubts about the myth of a Catholic consensus which allegedly held sway in the central Middle Ages. Their doubts may be attributed to a number of causes, such as: (1) anger against the clerical greed which some observed behind the promotion of saints' cults; (2) rivalry between religious orders, leading to doubts about the skills of one's opponents; or (3) political opposition to the alleged miracle worker, sometimes a by-product of local patriotism. In the case of Cardinal Peter of Luxemburg (d. 1387), one observer suggested during the Great Schism that Peter's false cult had been created in order to attract pilgrims to his tomb at Avignon, instead of attending the rival

45 Amots Dafni, 'Why are Rags tied to the Sacred Trees of the Holy Land?', *Economic Botany* 56 (2002), 315–27.

46 As William of Auvergne (*De fide*, ch. 3) said, 'Prophetis et apostolis non est creditum in articulis fidei nisi miraculorum testimoniis; unde rebelles et increduli, qui sermonibus sanctorum virorum credere non volebant, miraculis inducebantur et usque hodie inducuntur ad fidem', cited in Albert Lang, *Die Wege der Glaubensbegründung bei den Scholastikern des 14. Jahrhunderts* (Münster, 1930), 6, n. 3. Engelbert of Admont, *Tractatus de gratiis et virtutibus beatae virginis Mariae*, in Stift Admont, Admont MS 181, fol. 72v, notes that the role of contemporary saints is to perform miracles in order to rekindle the faith which has grown cold, frighten evil persons and comfort the good. I would like to thank the Hill Monastic Manuscript Library for allowing me access to their copy of this manuscript. For some cases of doubt, see Gábor Klaniczay, 'Miracoli di punizione e maleficia', in Sofia Boesch Gajano and Marilena Modica, eds, *Miracoli: dai segni alla storia* (Rome, 1999), 109–35, for cases taken from the contemporary case of Margaret of Hungary.

47 R. I. Moore, *The Formation of a Persecuting Society: Power and Deviance in Western Europe, 950–1250* (Oxford, 1987).

church of Notre Dame de l'Espérance.[48] Such doubt might be based on some prior personal acquaintance with the saint, as in the case of a local curate noted in the protocol of Philip of Bourges.[49]

The most persistent voices of scepticism were Jews, Waldensians and Cathars. In the case of Empress Cunegunda, one of the earliest cases of a saint's cult confirmed by Rome under the new regulations, it is reported that the chief rabbi of Bamberg had observed the crowds as they flocked to her tomb seeking divine aid. He questioned whether she could cure a child severely mauled by a marauding wolf. Because of his intemperate words doubting Cunegunda's abilities, he suffered divine vengeance and, as a consequence, converted.[50] The ability to convert such Jewish doubters is stressed in the miracles of many contemporary saints.[51] Heretics also serve as straw men to highlight the efficacy of Christian miracles. A century and a half after Peter Martyr's death, a Cathar detractor cast doubt on the sanctity of the Dominican inquisitor, saying:

> Peter . . . was an evil man and a sinner and was damned to Hell because he persecuted Christ's servants, namely the Waldensians and Cathars by whom St Peter was killed. The death of [a certain] Brother Jacopo Bechi was more valuable in God's eyes than the death of the blessed martyr Peter.[52]

But such sentiments appear to be more ideologically than class-based, since Catharism touched all social classes. The rare cases specifically

48 *Vita beati Petri de Luxemburgo*, in BN, MS Paris. lat. 5379, fol. 17r: 'Non credens quod per eum deus operatur miraculose immo tenens firmiter quod esset quaedam fictio adinventa ad populum alliciendum maxime propter scismatis factum . . .'. This quotation is based on the canonization hearing. See also *ActaSS*, 2 July, I: 582C. Other cases of doubt are reported here.

49 See the summary in see *Processus supra vita et miraculis domini Philippi archiepiscopi Biturcensis,* BN, MS Paris. lat. 5373A, fol. 3r.

50 *Vita et miracula Cunegundis*, in *ActaSS*, 3 March, I: 278.

51 Thomas Aquinas's polemical battles with Jews, Averroists, William of St Amour, Siger of Brabant, the Fraticelli, Brethren of the Free Spirit and Greek schismatics are emphasized in the *Vita* by Willam of Tocco, in *ActaSS*, 7 March, I: 663–6. One of the witnesses at the canonization hearing of Thomas of Hereford said of Thomas: 'videns quod iudei multa mala perpetrabant in regno Anglia procuravit cum rege quod praedicaretur eis et quod illi qui nollent converti exirent regnum Anglie . . .' (BAV, MS Vat. lat. 4015, fol. 104r; see also fol. 88r). Richard of Chichester, Angelo of Trapani and Raymund of Penyafort also actively converted the Jews.

52 Grado Merlo, 'Pietro di Verona – S. Pietro martire. Difficoltà e proposte per lo studio di un inquisitore beatificato', in Sofia Boesch-Gajano and Lucia Sebastiani, eds, *Culto dei santi: istituzioni e classi sociali in età preindustriale* (L'Aquila, 1984), 417–88, 480, taken from a 1395 trial of heretics in Piedmont.

cited in bulls of canonization, in which people were punished for doubting a saint's miracles, concern a man who choked on his food for mocking the miracles of Peter Martyr, a stone mason in the case of Louis of Toulouse, and a man whose motives are unclear in the case of Thomas Aquinas.[53]

* * *

Participants at canonization trials may be divided into several groups. The first group, the court personnel, selected the witnesses, drew up the questions, determined the limits of the investigation, and voiced the official definition of the miraculous within the parameters of Christian theology and canon law. The second group, largely drawn from the clerical and noble elite, encompassed witnesses who were personally acquainted with the putative saint, often members of the candidate's monastery, the court, or episcopal *familia*. They stressed the putative saint's virtues, and presumably only reported those successful miracles that would aid the campaign for canonization that they themselves may have initiated and financed. A third group represented a wider constituency of both urban and rural folk who could enhance the saint's *fama*, and who voiced a more textured view of the circumstances in which the supernatural might intervene. Here, all social classes might be represented, but as reliable and trustworthy witnesses their notion of the supernatural presumably conforms to clerical demands for orthodoxy. A suitable measure of a cult's popularity is the continuous record of miracles taken down by clerks at a pilgrimage site, in which the identities of the votaries and a summary of each miracle are recorded. For example, the list of hundreds of pilgrims to Thomas Cantilupe of Hereford's tomb beginning in 1286 found in Exeter College, Oxford, MS 158, or a similar list for the shrine of Leonard of Inchenhofen in Bavaria beginning in 1258, allow us to expand the constituency beyond those who participated in a canonization hearing.

Nevertheless, certain kinds of miracles may be more class or gender-based. For example, the recovery of pet animals, a specialty of Thomas of Hereford, is more common among the aristocracy. Assistance to children accidentally injured or drowned when they fell under mill wheels or into a pond occurs among the rural peasantry. Rescue

53 *ActaSS*, 29 April, III: 702B. For the miracle of a Cathar who drew his sword before a fresco illustrating the assassination of Peter Martyr, turned mute, and converted, see Stift Admont, Admont MS 781, fol. 90r; for the skeptic in Louis of Toulouse's 1317 canonization, see *Bullarium romanum*, IV: 145–8; for Thomas, ibid., IV: 186–90.

from the rigors of war is more often experienced by soldiers or merchants who suffered from cruel imprisonment or were unable to pay an unreasonable ransom.[54] Women appear to be more often the victims of possession than men. Accessibility to physicians before resorting to the supernatural is greater among urban folk and the elite classes in the developed south as opposed to the rural north.[55] Some medical conditions are clearly more gender-specific. But whatever its origin or genre the structure of the miracle remains uniform, whether imposed by judicial or folkloristic precedent.[56]

The late thirteenth-century unpublished canonization enquiries of Bishop Philip of Bourges and Bishop Thomas Cantilupe of Hereford, for example, illustrate what social historians may glean from miracles. Thomas' miracles have been unsatisfactorily edited and rearranged in narrative form by the Bollandists and have been studied by Finucane, Bartlett, Christian Krötzl, and Michael Richter, among others. Philip's case has been cursorily examined by Vauchez, but has been otherwise neglected.[57] These dossiers allow us to chart the constituency, geographical distribution, genres of miracle and invocations characteristic of the burgeoning cults. Thomas' extensive dossier has allowed us

54 Michael Goodich, 'Die wundersame Gefangenenbefreiung im mittelalterlichen Kanonisationsdocumente', in Bauer and Herbers, eds, *Hagiographie im Kontext*, 69–84.

55 Joseph Ziegler, 'Practitioners and Saints: Medical Men in Canonisation Processes in the Thirteenth to Fifteenth Centuries', *Social History of Medicine* 12 (1999), 191–225.

56 See for example J. H. Ross and Meryl Jancey, 'The Miracles of Thomas of Hereford', *British Medical Journal* 295 (19–26 December 1989), 1590–4; Michael Goodich, 'Filiation and Form in the Late Medieval Miracle Story', *Hagiographica* 3 (1996), 1–18; André Jolles, *Einfache Formen* (Halle, 1930), 23–8; R. I. Moore, 'Between Sanctity and Superstition: Saints and their Miracles in the Age of Revolution', in Miri Rubin, ed., *The Work of Jacques Le Goff and the Challenges of Medieval History* (Woodbridge, 1997), 55–67, provides a simple structure to the miracle: (1) a cure is sought; (2) the circumstances are established; (3) conditions for a cure are stated; (4) a blessing is pronounced; and (5) a miracle is proclaimed.

57 Bartlett, *The Hanged Man*; Michael Richter, *Sprach und Gesellschaft in Mittelalter. Untersuchungen zum mündlichen Kommunikation in England von der Mitte des elften bis zum Beginn des vierzehnten Jahrhunderts* (Stuttgart, 1979), 171–217; idem, 'Walser und Wündermänner um 1300', in Susanna Burghartz *et al.*, eds, *Spannungen und Widersprüche: Gedenkschrift für František Graus* (Sigmaringen, 1992), 23–36; idem, 'William ap Rees, William de Braose and the Lordship of Gower, 1289 and 1307', *Studia celtica* 32 (1998), 189–200; Finucane, *Rescue of the Innocents*; idem, *Miracles and Pilgrims: Popular Beliefs in Medieval England* (2nd edn, Basingstoke, 1995); Michael Goodich, 'Foreigner, Foe and Neighbor: the Religious Cult as a Forum for Political Reconciliation', in Albrecht Classen, ed., *Meeting the Foreign in the Middle Ages* (New York, 2002), 11–26; idem, 'Liturgy and the Foundation of Cults in the Thirteenth and Fourteenth Century', in Yitzhak Hen, ed., *De Sion exibit lex et verbum domini de Hierusalem. Essays on Medieval Law, Liturgy and Literature in Honour of Amnon Linder* (Turnhout, 2001), 145–57; André Vauchez, *Sainthood in the Later Middle Ages*, transl. Jean Birrell (Cambridge, 1997), *passim.*

to reconstruct village life in Hereford and the Welsh border regions at a time of economic distress, forced anglicization, internecine warfare and growing royal power under Edward I. Each miracle is attested by family members, neighbours and bystanders, who provide living illustrations of such issues as the mix of Welsh, English and Anglo-Norman residents, the role of the coroner and the changing status of royal, episcopal and seigneurial rights, the geography of the sacred and affective ties within the family. In Philip's case, we possess a kind of checklist reporting the areas of agreement and disagreement among witnesses to the miracles, similar to those in the earlier cases of Elizabeth of Thuringia and Stanislaus of Cracow. These stenographic remarks are however not as full as a contemporary curialist's study of one of Louis IX's miracles (*c.*1295–7), summarizing contradictions in the testimony and reliability of the deponents based on the principles of canon and Roman law.[58] The fullest document of this kind is a 1318 curialist's detailed analysis of miracles attributed to Thomas of Hereford, in order to determine whether there are any Biblical or historical precedents to each miracle and the extent of their theological and medical reliability. This text has been more thoroughly addressed by Vauchez and Finucane.[59]

One example will illustrate the richness of such canonization dossiers. The case of Bishop Philip of Bourges (d. 1261), nephew of William of Bourges (d. 1218), who had been canonized by Honorius III in 1218, was heard in 1264–6 at Beaugency, Bourges and Orléans.[60] The commissioners call themselves '*inquisitores*' and the material relating to this abortive trial was read and collated by Odo of Châteauroux, who also delivered two unpublished sermons on Philip's virtues.[61] The

58 Louis Carolus-Barré, 'Consultation du cardinal Pietro Colonna sur le IIe miracle de Saint Louis', *Bibliothèque de l'Ecole des chartes* 117 (1959), 57–72; *Miracula S. Stanislai*, ed. Zbigniew Perzanowski, in *Analecta Cracoviensia* 11 (1979), 68–141.

59 Ronald Finucane, 'Authorizing the Supernatural: a Curialist's Analysis of Some English Miracles around 1318', unpublished paper presented at International Medieval Congress, University of Leeds, 14–17 July 2003.

60 On Philip, see *Bibliotheca sanctorum*, 12 vols (Rome, 1980), 3: 87–8; A. Baudrillart, ed., *Dictionnaire d'histoire et de géographie écclésiastiques*, 27 vols (Paris, 1912–99), 8: 92–8; for the canonization inquest see *Processus supra vita et miraculis domini Philippi archiepiscopi Biturcensis*, in BN, MS Paris. lat. 5373A, fols. 1v–61v; BAV, MS Vat. lat. 4019. The commissioners were Peter de Minci, bishop of Chartres, Robert de Marzy, bishop of Nevers, and the Dominican prior of Paris with the assistance of the Dominican prior of Bourges.

61 Rome, Biblioteca Angelica, MS 157 (B.6.10), fols 93v–95v for his sermons. I would like to thank both the Biblioteca Angelica and the Institut de Recherche et d'Histoire des Textes for their assistance. This stress on virtues rather than miracles by preachers is clear in

absence of any reference to Philip's miracles in these sermons reveals the tension between popular and learned views of sanctity: the people needed 'signs and miracles', while the learned demanded a virtuous life. This distinction reflects a long hagiographical tradition. John of Salerno in his life of Odo of Cluny (878–942) had said: 'Those who like to heap praise on exorcists, on those who raise the dead and on others famous for their miracles may do so. I would rather praise Odo for patience as his prime virtue.'[62]

In these sermons, Odo of Châteauroux likewise prefers to survey Philip's career and lineage, his ties to the Cistercian order, his chastity, service to the poor and other virtues, rather than his miracles. At the canonization process forty-five miracles were recounted by a hundred and forty witnesses, of whom forty-five were female, forty-six male laymen, and forty-nine clergy. This preference for miracles reported by the clergy is reflected in the contemporary biography drawn from the protocol and suggests that Philip's cult appealed to a more local and ecclesiastical audience. His miraculous discovery of the relics of St Severa, reported by only one cleric, is given pride of place. Many of his miracles demanded confirmation by a clerical witness, in addition to the laity. On the other hand, papal bulls of canonization markedly prefer miracles performed among the laity as evidence of a wide constituency and as a means of spreading and maintaining the cult. This presumably reflects the audience for whom the saints' cults were intended and may explain Philip's failure to achieve medieval canonization, despite efforts to revive the case in 1331.[63]

Philip's miracles are less varied and rich than other contemporary cases (such as those of Margaret of Hungary and Richard of Chichester), since nearly all of them concerned the thaumaturgical cure of the blind, paralysed, lame, mute and others. Nevertheless, by breaking down each one to at least thirty schematic elements reflecting the traditional 'who, what, when, where, why, and how' of any miracle narrative, it is possible to draw out the social environment of the cultic community.[64]

the over sixty sermons concerning Clare of Assisi examined in Marina Soriani Innocenti, 'I sermoni latini in onore di Santa Chiara', in *Chiara di Assisi. Atti del XX Convegno internazionale, Assisi, 15–17 Ottobre 1992*, Società Internazionale di Studi Francescani, ns 3 (Spoleto, 1993), 357–80.

62 John of Salerno, *Vita Odonis*, in PL 133, 49.

63 This was the occasion for the production of the Vatican ms., which is a copy of the original, including an account of its treatment by Rome.

64 See n. 11 for the list of questions in Elizabeth's case. For Philip's questions, see BAV, MS Vat. lat. 4019, fol. 9r–v: 'Testos legitimos quos super vita conversationem et miraculis

A map may be drawn up of the geographical boundaries of the cult and its adherents, where they were born and lived, how far they were willing to travel in pursuit of a cure, and whether the cures occurred in close proximity to the tomb or elsewhere (an increasing characteristic of late medieval piety).[65] Professional background, age, kind of affliction, symptoms, access to medical care, marital status and personal acquaintance with the saint are among the details provided. Since several family members frequently testified, we are able to learn about the dynamics of family structure and ties of affection. For example, the cure from insanity, apparent post-natal depression, and paralysis in 1263 of the thirty-year-old Jeanne Laboyssans from the village of Crosses, about six miles from Bourges, was reported by twelve witnesses, including the victim herself, her husband, mother, the local curate and a Benedictine prior. Jeanne's pilgrimages to such far-away shrines as Notre-Dame de Rocamadour, St-Gilles-du-Gard, near Nîmes, and St Vrain near Orléans, before achieving a cure for her various afflictions at St Étienne de Bourges, are also reported. A series of visions of the saint punctuate Jeanne's serial cures.[66]

Although the investigators were presumably interested in maximizing points of agreement among witnesses, in Jeanne's case and others this was not always the case. The separate curial list summarizing the points of discord among deponents reflects greater scepticism about the supernatural among experts than among the lay witnesses. Because of inconsistencies, seventeen miracles were singled out for further scrutiny. More difficulties would no doubt have been discovered had the

recolende memorie Philippi bituricensis archiepiscopi recipere prius ab eis prestito iuramento diligenter examinare curetis et de omnibus que dixerint interrogetis eosdem quomodo sciunt quo tempore quo mense quo die quibus presentibus quo loco ad cuius invocationem et quibus verbis interpositis et [de] nominibus illorum circa quos miracula facta dicuntur et si ante cognoscebant et quot diebus ante viderunt eos infirmos et quanto tempore fuerunt infirmi et quanto tempore visi sunt sani et de quo loco sint oriundi et interrogetis de omnibus circumstanciis et circa singula capitula . . .'. The questions posed by Innocent V in the 1276 case of Margaret of Hungary are identical. See *Inquisitio*, ed. Fraknoì, 1: 161–2.

65 Christian Krötzl, 'Miracles au tombeau – miracles à distance: approches typologiques', in Aigle, ed., *Miracle et Karama*, 557–76, notes the greater frequency of miracles far from the shrine in the thirteenth and fourteenth centuries. This parallels the substantial rise of miracles which occur in the presence of movable altarpieces, particularly in Italy.

66 BAV, MS Vat. lat. 4019, 56v–63v; BN, MS Paris. lat. 5373A, *Processus supra vita et miraculis domini Philippi archiepiscopi Biturcensis,* fols 16r–19r; *Vita sancti Philippi archiepiscopi Biturcensis*, in Edmond Martène and Ursin Durand, eds, *Thesaurus novus anecdotorum*, 5 vols (Paris, 1717–26), 3: 1927–46, here 1942–3, 'xii: De alienatis a sensu, intellectu, memoria et loquela liberatis'.

case not been discontinued. In the case of Pope Celestine V, the summary of his miracles examined by the curia indicates that some cardinals were highly critical of miracle stories; however, given the pro-French bias of the cardinals and their clear detestation of Celestine's alleged persecutor and successor Boniface VIII, his canonization was probably a foregone conclusion. For example, the future Pope John XXII rejected many of his predecessor's proposed miracles, perhaps due to political rather than theological considerations.[67] Even Celestine's biographer Gaetano Stefaneschi and his promoter Richard of Siena voiced sharp doubts. All those miracles, which were even minimally questionable according to Richard, were rejected for inclusion in the final bull of canonization.

We may now return to the caveat voiced by Bernard Gui about the dangers of allowing his witnesses too much free rein. As I hope I have demonstrated, we owe a debt of gratitude to those officials who investigated the miracles of Margaret of Hungary, Philip of Bourges and others. The social historian has inherited an unparalleled record of the role of faith in the supernatural among the subaltern classes. At the simplest level, the required record of the witnesses' name, age, origin, family ties, place of residence, profession, time and site of the miracle, and the names of those present, permits us to draw a picture of the cult and its constituents. At the same time, despite the ideological commitments of the court's personnel, their probing questions allow us to recreate the otherwise lost private worlds of a host of otherwise silent denizens who populate our historical imagination. This includes an infant revived from death in a village near Budapest, and an emotionally distressed woman from the village of Crosses near Bourges. Rural and urban folk, women, children, criminals, the disturbed and others are given a voice, however fleeting and sometimes marred by the intrusive intervention of the clerical elite. It is often precisely when the court strays from Gui's demand to stick to the essentials that we are able to slip through the cracks into the otherwise hidden world of our deponents. Following the lead of historians of religious dissent, if we avoid focusing on the standard *topoi* of the miracle and try to minimize the more ideologically charged issues of the canonization trial, we may profitably exploit these miracle tales as a rich source for the more mundane environment of our deponents. We may learn how time and

[67] Franciscus van Ortroy, ed., 'Procès-verbal du dernier consistoire secret préparatoire à la canonisation de Pierre Célestin', *AnBoll* 16 (1897), 475–87.

distance were measured, the geographical limits of the community of faith, the medical knowledge of the witnesses and their access to physicians, and the roles played by members of the family, friends, neighbors and the clergy as participants in manifestations of the sacred. Such micro-historical reconstructions may help to liberate us from the stereotypical and return us to the complex, concrete environment in which those too often left out of the historical narrative experienced the miraculous.[68]

University of Haifa

68 Carlo Ginzburg, 'Morelli, Freud and Sherlock Holmes: Clues and Scientific Method', *History Workshop* 9 (1980), 5–36, 15–16.

SIGNS, WONDERS, MIRACLES: SUPPORTING THE FAITH IN MEDIEVAL ROME

by BRENDA BOLTON

JUDGING by the quantity of surviving texts – whether *vitae* or saints' lives, *libelli miraculorum* or narratives of miracles for public reading in church, lectionaries or collections of liturgical readings, *inventiones* and *translationes* or accounts of relics found and later moved to a new location, popular receptivity to signs, wonders and miracles had reached a high point by the turn of the twelfth century.[1] Whilst ordinary laypeople remained fascinated by supernatural phenomena, intellectuals were already beginning to challenge the preternatural in a process described by Chenu as the 'desacralizing' of nature.[2] In the first book of his treatise, *De sanctis et eorum pignoribus* (*c.*1120), Guibert, Abbot of Nogent, had contrasted the credulity of the faithful towards pseudo-miracles with the growing unease experienced by many scholars at inadequate written evidence for the authentication of relics.[3] Andrew of Saint-Victor (*d.*1175), in an exposition on the literal interpretation of Scripture, found himself arguing for a natural explanation of events before any recourse to the miraculous.[4] In the School of Pastoral Theology at Paris, Master Peter the Chanter (*d.*1197) vehemently criticized trial by ordeal as a flagrant tempting of God whereby a supposedly miraculous intervention was allowed to intrude into the regular legalistic operation of the courts.[5] In the years immediately

[1] Jacques Dubois and Jean-Loup Lemaître, *Sources et méthodes de l'hagiographie médiévale* (Paris, 1993); A. Dierkens, 'Réflexions sur le miracle au haut moyen âge', in *Miracles, prodiges et merveilles au moyen âge: XXVe Congrès de la Société des historiens médiévistes de l'enseignement supérieur public (Orléans, juin 1994)*, Série Histoire ancienne et médiévale 34 (Paris, 1995), 1–30; Marcus Bull, *The Miracles of Our Lady of Rocamadour: Analysis and Translation* (Woodbridge, 1999), esp. 3–25. I am most grateful to Dr Christoph Egger for sharing information with me.

[2] M.-D. Chenu, *Nature, Man and Society in the Twelfth Century: Essays on New Theological Perspectives in the Latin West*, ed. Jerome Taylor and Lester K. Little (Chicago, IL, 1968), 14.

[3] Guibert of Nogent, *De sanctis et eorum pignoribus*, PL 156, 607–80, 621–4; Colin Morris, 'A Critique of Popular Religion: Guibert of Nogent on *The Relics of the Saints*', in G. J. Cuming and Derek Baker, eds, *Popular Belief and Practice*, SCH 8 (Cambridge, 1972), 55–60.

[4] Andrew of Saint Victor, *Expositio in Ezechielem*, ed. M. A. Signer, CChr.CM 5E (Turnhout, 1991), 6, ll. 106–9; Beryl Smalley, *The Study of the Bible in the Middle Ages* (Notre Dame, IN, 1970), 388–9.

[5] Peter the Chanter, *Verbum abbreviatum*, PL 205, 228; John W. Baldwin, *Masters, Princes*

following the Chanter's death, his former students, led by Pope Innocent III (1198–1216) and like-minded clerical associates, developed a significant agenda, emphasizing rationality and record keeping to sustain the faith of the Church within a new and more firmly pastoral context.

Thus, in November 1215, when well over a thousand ecclesiastics descended on Rome to attend the Fourth Lateran Council on which Innocent III set such store,[6] they would have been relieved to hear previous prohibitions re-enforced against the ordeal,[7] in accordance with the Chanter's castigations, and to witness the enactment of legislation against the increasingly inappropriate veneration of relics[8] – both decrees being subsequently incorporated into canon law.[9] Nor ought these delegates to have been surprised to find other miraculous phenomena at the very heart of conciliar proceedings. For Innocent and his circle of close advisors, all matters regarding popular religiosity were to be treated with sensitivity – but none more so than the prevailing current of belief in signs and wonders.[10] In his dual role as bishop of Rome and impresario of this great ecumenical event, Innocent's obligation was to heal the deep divisions between a learned and an unlettered definition of the miraculous. An outward sign of the healing process was to be his powerful, image-making consecration of the Church of S. Maria in Trastevere on the first Sunday of the Council, demonstrating to all those present the significance to the faith of Rome's first accepted Christian miracle – the fountain of oil which gushed from the Tiber bank at the very moment of Christ's birth.

Innocent III's attitude to the miraculous has not received the detailed attention it undoubtedly deserves. His four canonization

and Merchants: the Social Views of Peter the Chanter and his Circle, 2 vols (Princeton, NJ, 1970), 1: 326–7; 2: 218–19.

6 A. Luchaire, 'Liste des évêchés représentés au Concile de 1215', in K. J. Hefele and H. Leclercq, eds, *Histoire des Conciles d'après les documents originaux*, 11 vols in 22 (Paris, 1907–52), 5.2 (1913): 1723–33.

7 Canon 18, *Conciliorum Oecumenicorum Decreta*, ed. G. Alberigo (Bologna, 1973), 244.

8 Canon 62, ibid., 263–4.

9 *Corpus iuris canonici*, ed. E. Friedberg, 2 vols (Leipzig, 1879), 2: X 3.42.2, 650; 2: X 3.50, 659–60.

10 Cf. Acts 2, 22: '. . . Jesus of Nazareth, a man approved of God among you by miracles and wonders and signs'. Miracles are designated as *virtus*, *prodigia* and *signa* in the Vulgate; elsewhere as *mirabilia*, *magnalia* or *miraculum*: see the chapter 'The Vocabulary of Miracle', in C. F. D. Moule, *Miracles,* Cambridge Studies in their Philosophy and History (London, 1965), 235–8; Robert M. Grant, *Miracle and Natural Law in Graeco-Roman and Early Christian Thought* (Amsterdam, 1952), 153–220; Benedicta Ward, *Miracles and the Medieval Mind*, 221, n. 4.

processes, of Homobono of Cremona (*d.*1197),[11] the Empress Cunigunda (*d.*1033),[12] Gilbert of Sempringham (*d.*1189),[13] and Wulfstan of Worcester (*d.*1095),[14] took place between 1199 and 1203. A possible fifth candidate, Procopius of Sázava (*d.*1053), may have been canonized in 1204 but no precise documentation survives.[15] Whether Innocent's last canonization took place in 1203 or 1204 is immaterial: quite suddenly, his encounters with any elements of the miraculous are deemed to have ceased.[16]

The present essay will demonstrate that this is far from being the case. Innocent's interest in and concern for the faith in Rome, as revealed by his conciliar legislation on the appropriate use of relics and the ordeal, continued to focus on two urgent requirements. The first was the need to curb popular credulity lest the simple faithful should be led astray by an excessive and unquestioning enthusiasm; the second was to create a common evidential base against which to judge the credibility of miracles.[17] In what follows, I discuss both these requirements and set them in the context of two events which, at first sight, appear somewhat at variance with Innocent's usual measured approach to the miraculous – the *inventio* or discovery in 1209 at Veroli of relics of Mary Salome, one of Christ's aunts, and the transformation in 1215 of the church of S. Maria in Trastevere into a second Roman Bethlehem

11 1 January 1199, *Die Register Innocenz' III., 1. Pontifikatshjahr, 1198-99. Texte*, ed. Othmar Hageneder and Anton Haidacher, Publikationem der Abteilung für historische Studien des Österreichischen Kulturinstituts in Rom 2 (Graz, 1964) [hereafter: *Reg. Inn. 1*], no. 528 (530), 761–4 [henceforth *Reg. Inn. I*]; Roberto Paciocco, '"Virtus morum" e "virtus signorum". La teoria della santità nelle lettere di canonizzazione di Innocenzo III', *Nuova Rivista Storica* 70 (1986), 597–610, 599–600; André Vauchez, *La Sainteté en Occident aux derniers siècles du Moyen Age: d'après les procès de canonisation et les documents hagiographiques*, Bibliothèque des Écoles françaises d'Athènes et de Rome 241 (Rome, 1988), 412–14; idem, 'La Canonisation de Saint Homobon', in Andrea Sommerlechner, ed., *Innocenzo III: Urbs et Orbis, Atti del Congresso Internazionale, Roma, 9–15 settembre 1998*, 2 vols (Rome, 2003), 1: 435–55.

12 J. Petersohn, 'Die Litterae Papst Innocenz' III. zur Heiligsprechung der Kaiserin Kunigunde (1200)', *Jahrbuch für Landesforschung* 37 (1977), 1–25.

13 *The Book of St Gilbert*, ed. Raymonde Foreville and Gillian Keir, OMT (Oxford, 1987).

14 J. Fontanini, *Codex constitutionum quas Summi Pontifices ediderunt in canonizatione Sanctorum ab anno 993 ad annum 1729* (Rome, 1729), n. 30, 40–1; 14 May 1203, *Die Register Innocenz' III., 6. Pontifikatsjahr, 1203-04. Texte und Indices*, ed. Othmar Hageneder, John C. Moore and Andrea Sommerlechner, Publikationem der Abteilung für historische Studien des Österreichischen Kulturinstituts in Rom (Vienna, 1995), no. 63 (62), 86–9.

15 Jaroslav Kadlec, 'Procopio', *Bibliotheca Sanctorum* 10 (Rome, 1968), 1167–74.

16 Cf. Michael Goodich, 'Vision, Dream and Canonization Policy under Pope Innocent III', in John C. Moore, ed., *Pope Innocent III and his World* (Aldershot, 1999), 151–63, 161.

17 Grant, *Miracle and Natural Law*, 41–86, for valuable discussions of credibility and credulity. Cf. R. A. Markus, 'Augustine on Magic', in idem, *Signs and Meanings: World and Text in Ancient Christianity* (Liverpool, 1996), 125–46.

and cult centre. Innocent's consecration sermon on that day – in so far as it can be reconstructed – reflected the pastoral theologian's view that, of all miracles, the greatest was the eucharistic sacrifice of Christ himself, repeated every day by simple priests at the altar, and thus deeply significant for the faith of the whole Church.

Not since the pontificate of Gregory the Great (590–604) had another pope displayed such a keen appreciation of the combined power of Scripture and appropriate legend to support the faith.[18] A former pupil of Peter the Chanter, and a considerable theologian in his own right, Innocent was thoroughly conversant with Gregory's ideas on sanctity and miracles. In common with Gregory, he frequently cited Christ's commission to the apostles (Mark 16, 15–18), promising that signs would accompany those who believed and regarding spiritual miracles to revive souls as more significant than physical ones.[19] By recognizing the need to persuade the scholars of his day to accept as normative the simple piety of ordinary people, Innocent promoted a critical awareness of popular devotion by fully embracing the ideals of the *vita apostolica*.[20] Representing a return to practices common in the Apostolic Church – poverty and preaching, in particular – this movement was expanded and strengthened by lay groups of penitents proclaiming their personal witness to the absolute value of the Gospels. Hence, any event reminiscent of the continuity between miracles of the Apostolic Age and those occurring in their own day would possess a special value for those who knew their scriptural texts.

Such spiritual currents in the Church had profoundly influenced the Chanter and his pupils. In particular, their support for a reformed and pastoral episcopate ensured that Thomas Becket (*d.*1170), canonized at Segni in 1173 by Alexander III (1159–81), was the hero and model bishop for this group. The youthful Lotario dei Conti di Segni, later Innocent III, is known to have interrupted his studies at Paris in the 1180s to visit the martyr's tomb at Canterbury.[21] Whilst the full effects

18 Christoph Egger, '*The Growling of the Lion and the Humming of the Fly*: Gregory the Great and Innocent III', in Frances Andrews, Christoph Egger and Constance M. Rousseau, eds, *Pope, Church and City: Essays in Honour of Brenda M. Bolton* (Leiden and Boston, MA, 2004), 13–46.

19 William D. McCready, *Signs of Sanctity. Miracles in the Thought of Gregory the Great*, Pontifical Institute of Mediaeval Studies, Studies and Texts 91 (Toronto, 1989), 16–20.

20 E. W. McDonnell, 'The *Vita Apostolica*: Diversity or Dissent?', *ChH* 24 (1955), 15–31; Chenu, *Nature, Man and Society*, 239–69.

21 *Willelmi Chronica Andrensis,* ed. I. Heller, MGH. SS 24 (Hannover, 1879), 690–773, 737–8.

of this pilgrimage on the future pope cannot be known, Anne Duggan has shown how rapidly Alexander III's unhesitating canonization of Becket in 1173 at Segni helped to consolidate his image into an object of cult supported by a powerful liturgical office.[22] The unswerving faith and courage of the martyr bishop created an exemplar throughout Christendom and nowhere more so than in papal circles. Lotario would certainly have seen the splendid new Trinity Chapel awaiting the saint's translation,[23] and would probably have heard the impressive liturgical rhymed office, constructed in time for the first celebration of Becket's feast on 28–29 December 1173.[24]

The rhymed office, or *historia*,[25] a short account of highlights in a saint's life, commemorated on a certain day, functioned as a set of liturgical readings, interspersed with sung psalms. In canonical communities, the nocturns of Matins of solemn feast days were arranged in nine numbered lections, divided into three nocturns, that is, sections of three psalms and three lections in each.[26] Two such *historiae*, '*Cum orbita solis*' – the earliest life of Homobono of Cremona (*d.* 13 November 1197) – and the *Acta consecrationis* of Santa Maria in Trastevere, are significant for their lections, which provide original insights into attitudes to miracles, signs and wonders during Innocent III's pontificate. Lection VII of '*Cum orbita solis*' is a short treatise expounding and explaining the concept of the miracle.[27] We will see below that evidence of behind-the-scenes activity at the Fourth Lateran Council has recently emerged from MS Vat. lat. 10999, the *Acta consecrationis* of Santa Maria in Trastevere compiled to mark the anniversary of the church's consecration.[28] The last two lections of this *historia*, VIII and

22 Anne Duggan, 'The Cult of St Thomas Becket in the Thirteenth Century', in Meryl Jancey, ed., *St Thomas Cantilupe* (Hereford, 1982), 21–44; eadem, *Thomas Becket* (London, 2004), 230–5.

23 William Urry, 'Some Notes on the Two Resting Places of St Thomas Becket at Canterbury', in Raymonde Foreville, ed., *Thomas Becket, Actes du Colloque International de Sédières, 19–24 août 1973* (Paris, 1975), 195–209, 198.

24 Anne J. Duggan, 'A Becket Office at Stavelot: London, British Library, Additional MS 16964', in Anne J. Duggan, Joan Greatrex and Brenda Bolton, eds, *Omnia disce. Medieval Studies in Memory of Leonard Boyle, O.P.* (Aldershot, 2005), 161–82, 164.

25 R. Jonsson, *Historia. Études sur la genèse des offices versifiés*, Studia Latina Stockholmiensis 15 (Stockholm, 1968); Duggan, 'A Becket Office', 163, n. 15.

26 The monastic office was arranged in eight numbered lections.

27 Daniele Piazzi, *Omobono di Cremona. Biografie dal XIII al XVI secolo. Edizione, traduzione e commento* (Cremona, 1991), 30–43.

28 *Legenda in consecratione sancte Marie transtiberim lecta ex diversis ystoriarum libris*, BAV, MS Vat. lat. 10999, fols 143r–153r. The most recent provenance appears to be the Archivio di S. Callisto in Trastevere.

IX, show that the miraculous was central to local preparations for the Council and to Innocent III's consecration of the church itself.[29] (MS Vat. lat. 8429, which contains a partial transcription of the original *Acta* by Pietro Moretti, the eighteenth-century antiquarian and canon of S. Maria in Trastevere, also offers important evidence.)[30]

It was at the instigation of his Cathedral Chapter that Sicard, bishop of Cremona (1185–1215),[31] composed '*Cum orbita solis*', both for liturgical use and to promote Homobono, his strong local candidate, for canonization. In Lection VII, Sicard, who was not only a canonist but also an historian and liturgist, speaks of supernatural phenomena.

> Wonderful is God who works wonderfully in all things, and more wonderfully in those which happen beyond the course of nature, so that the faith of the saints may be for a proof to posterity and their life an example of the course of right living, confirming these things by miracles, that is, works unfamiliar to men, happening not contrary to nature which is always obedient to its Creator, but beyond nature, which does not usually work in such a way by its own force. For since faith is of those things which are not seen, nor do they have merit if human reason provides experience of them, it requires a power in things that are apparent that a sharpness of

29 MS Vat. lat. 10999, fol. 152r–v; Bernhard Schimmelpfennig, '"Mitbestimmung" in der Römischen Kirche unter Innocenz III.', in Stanley Chodorow, ed., *Proceedings of the Eighth International Congress of Medieval Canon Law. San Diego, University of California at La Jolla, 21–27 August 1988*, Monumenta iuris canonici, ser. C, Subsidia 9 (Vatican City, 1992), 455–70; idem, 'Jesus, Maria und Augustus. Ein Text zur Weihe von S. Maria in Trastevere (1215) und zur Geschichte Trasteveres in Antike und Mittelalter', in Lotte Kéry, Dietrich Lohrmann, Harald Müller, eds, *Licet preter solitum: Ludwig Falkenstein zum 65. Geburtstag* (Aachen, 1998), 119–41; idem, 'Ein Text zur Kirchweihe von S. Maria in Trastevere', in Nicholas Bock, Sible de Blaauw, Christoph L. Frommel and Herbert Kessler, eds, *Kunst und Liturgie im Mittelalter, Akten des internationalen Kongresser der Bibliotheca Hertziana und der Nederlands Instituut te Rome, Rome, 28–30 September 1997*, Römisches Jahrbuch der Bibliotheca Hertziana 33 (Munich, 2000), 33–45.

30 Pietro Moretti, *De Postrema Dedicatione Insignis Basilicae S.e Mariae Transtyberim . . . ann. 1215 . . . Excerpta . . . de perantiquo Lectionario MS: in pergameno composito ab Auctore Innocentij III Coevo, quod asservatur in Archivio S.e Mariae, quodque premittit narrationi de consecratione historiam aedificationis Basilicae sub Innocentio II . . .*, BAV, MS Vat. lat. 8429, fols 160r–162r. The transcription ends on fol. 165v with the initials P. M. S. M. T. C. (Petrus Morettus Sanctae Mariae Transtiberim Canonicus). Cf. Dale Kinney, 'S. Maria in Trastevere from its Founding to 1215', unpublished Ph.D. thesis, New York University, 1975, 213–23, 335–47.

31 E. Brocchieri, *Sicardo di Cremona e la sua opera letteraria. Introduzione allo stato attuale delle richerche* (Cremona, 1958), Annali della Biblioteca Governativa e Libreria Civica di Cremona 11, fasc. 1; Piazzi, *Omobono di Cremona*, 44–8; Vauchez, 'La Canonisation de Saint Homobon', 435–55.

> mind may be awakened for the invisible things which are to be of service for salvation.[32]

Sicard then provides a brief history of miracles in the Church. According to this, many miracles took place in the Apostolic Age, but their frequency diminished as time passed. At the turn of the twelfth century, in what he saw as the old age of the world, where faith was sleeping, where wickedness was rife, and where, for many Christians, charity grew cold, then the supreme goodness of God repeated miracles, so that faith might be born and grow strong with the food of miracles. Finally, Sicard confirms that the greatest miracle of all is that which is accomplished every day by simple priests – even if they are morally unworthy – in offering the eucharistic sacrifice.

> Accordingly, at the beginning of the birth of the Church, the Most High gave frequent signs among the faithful but, as faith grows cool, wickedness abounds and the charity of many is cold. Then, the supreme goodness of God repeats miracles, so that faith may be born and grow strong with the food of miracles. Even in miracles, men are sometimes deceived by the appearance of what is right. Often miracles occur, not by the merits of individuals but through the power of names and sacraments. What is more marvellous than that bread is changed into flesh and wine into blood?[33]

* * *

While Innocent's first encounter with the credulity of the faithful and the vigour of miracle stories probably took place at Becket's tomb, amidst those seeking healing cures and *ampullae* of Canterbury water, evidence exists to show that the Pope exercised caution in regard to signs and wonders transmitted through dreams or visions. In the early summer of 1198, he informed Octavian, cardinal bishop of Ostia, of the visions of an elderly priest. The priest reported three separate appearances by the Apostle Peter, who had warned him that certain altars in the eponymous Basilica were in dire need of attention.[34] In a measured approach, Innocent maintained that even should the priest's revelations

32 Piazzi, *Omobono di Cremona*, 36–7. My translation.

33 Ibid., 37–8.

34 19 July 1198, *Reg. Inn. 1*, no. 359, 540–1; Christopher R. Cheney, 'The Letters of Pope Innocent III', *Bulletin of the John Rylands Library* 35 (1952), 23–43, repr. in idem, *Medieval Studies and Texts* (Oxford, 1973), 16–38, 19–20; Goodich, 'Vision, Dream and Canonization Policy', 154–5.

be untrue, it was still better to show 'pious faith than rash incredulity', especially since what was being suggested was pertinent to the proper celebration of the divine mysteries.[35] The Pope also treated the proliferation of wonder-working relics at Sainte-Colombe de Sens – in this case, the various duplicated body parts of St Loup – with deep suspicion, and insisted, in a letter to the Abbot and community there, that 'deceit should not be tolerated under the veil of piety'.[36] However, his most sceptical statements were reserved for those miracles *in vita*, still occurring in his own day, which held such sway in popular religion and hagiography. These he considered as both useless and positively dangerous in that they risked deluding the faithful.

Innocent expressed serious reservations over popular credulity, not only in his letter to Octavian but also in each of the extant bulls for those he canonized. In these letters, as in that to Octavian on visions and in a privilege of 1201 to the first order of the Humiliati,[37] Innocent included a strongly rhetorical citation, borrowed from Scripture, which summed up his attitude to the dangers of credulity. Warning that Satan's messenger frequently transformed himself into an angel of light in order to deceive believers (2 Cor. 11, 14),[38] he stressed that certain people were presently in possession of the power to perform miracles in the world, although these were utterly without value. He compared the delusion thus created with that caused by Pharoah's magicians (Ex. 7, 8–13), Balaam's ass (Num. 22, 28) or the Antichrist, who possessed the ability to lead even the chosen faithful into error.

Following his election, Innocent established clear guidelines, bringing canonization under strict papal control for the first time and circumscribing the exclusive role of miracles.[39] Significantly, *Audivimus*, the letter by which Alexander III had claimed the exclusive papal right to canonize, was already beginning to enter into canon law collections.[40] The gain for the Church was considerable. Henceforth, it alone

35 *Reg. Inn. 1*, 541, l. 18: '. . . et melius est pie credere quam temere dubitare'.

36 12 May 1212, PL 216, 549–50; or see Cheney, 'The Letters of Pope Innocent III', 17–18.

37 H. Tiraboschi, *Vetera Humiliatorum monumenta*, 3 vols (Milan, 1766–8), 2: 139.

38 Goodich, 'Vision, Dream and Canonization Policy', 156–9; idem, 'Innocent III and the miracle as a weapon against disbelief', in Sommerlechner, ed., *Innocenzo III: Urbs et Orbis*, 1: 456–70.

39 S. Kuttner, 'La Réserve papale du droit de canonisation', *Revue historique de droit français et étranger* 17 (1938), 172–228.

40 Goodich, 'Vision, Dream and Canonization Policy', 156. For the text of *Audivimus* see *Corpus iuris canonici*, 2: X 3.42.1, 650.

was empowered to establish a relationship between cause and effect, between signifying and signified, between posthumous miracles and preceding virtues. Innocent's insistence that reliable evidence alone could distinguish genuine miracles from the false and worthless first appears in *Quia pietas*,[41] his letter of canonization for Homobono, which established rigorous criteria for a saint's official recognition by the Church. Kuttner and others have shown that Innocent deserves particular credit for having introduced into the canonization process the interdependence of moral virtues in life, *virtus morum*, and supernatural phenomena occurring after death, *virtus signorum*, as a means of validating each other.[42] Innocent's judgement was that neither good works nor posthumous miracles were sufficient in themselves to prove sanctity, and that in future, both would be required.

Innocent further ordered that, to be proven, miracles in the canonization process would henceforth require not merely attestations but actual witnesses ready to give their evidence under oath.[43] In the case of Homobono, the witness was his godfather, the priest Osbert, who had already acted as his confessor for twenty years. For Gilbert of Sempringham's canonization process, for which the dossier has survived, the procedure was more rigorous. Innocent imposed a three-day fast on the whole community, in the presence of Hubert Walter, archbishop of Canterbury, Eustace, bishop of Ely, and Acharius, abbot of Peterborough, who travelled in person to Sempringham to examine the sworn witnesses.[44] Statements of evidence were copied down, sealed and transmitted to the Curia.

* * *

A miraculous event with which Innocent seems only too happy to associate himself was to become the preface to an existing Cistercian *Liber miraculorum* at the special request of his close friend, Gerald, abbot of Casamari.[45] Gerald, abbot of this important house at the southern

41 12 January 1199, *Reg. Inn. 1*, no. 528 (530), 761–2.

42 Kuttner, 'La Réserve papale', 207–8; Goodich, 'Vision, Dream and Canonization Policy', 151–63, 156; Paciocco, '"Virtus morum" e "virtus signorum"'.

43 *The Book of St Gilbert*, cvii.

44 Ibid., 241–53.

45 On Gerald I, abbot of Casamari (1182/3–?1209/11) and bishop of Reggio Calabria (?1209/11–?1217), see Federico Farina and Igino Vona, *L'abate Giraldo di Casamari*, Bibliotheca Casaemariensis 3 (Casamari, 1998); Brenda Bolton, 'Gerald of Casamari between Joachim of Fiore and Innocent III', *Florensia* 13/14 (1999–2000), 31–43, 37–8.

frontier of the Patrimony, had adapted *De miraculis libri tres*, three books of miracles originally compiled by the Spanish Cistercian, Herbert, archbishop of Torres (*c.*1178),[46] updating them for use by his Order.[47] Gerald now prefaced *De miraculis libri tres* with his own letter of 25 May 1209 to Innocent, dedicating the whole miracle collection to him.[48] While the other miracles concerned conversions within the Cistercian Order, the exceptional evidential base of this one miracle was completely in line with Innocent's own insistence on authenticity and credibility and, furthermore, referred back to the Apostolic Age, when the grace of miracles was more widely distributed. Abbot Gerald's letter[49] provided Innocent with the ideal means by which to link this historic site to the faith of the Early Church, and to demonstrate the working of new guidelines on the authenticity of relics and validation of miracles.[50]

In 1209, Veroli, a small but ancient town of the Ernici, on the Via Casilina between Rome and Capua, just inside the boundary of the Patrimony, was at the centre of an important – some said miraculous – find. St Peter, appearing in a vision to a local youth called Tommaso, told him of a hidden treasure and directed him to a most difficult site, a harsh and arid place, just outside the Cyclopean walls of the town, almost inaccessible because of its rocks and precipices. Tommaso reported the Apostle's instructions to Odo, bishop of Veroli, who, believing the vision, sent along a team of workmen. Their task was to break up and move the massive rocks by using crowbars and iron hammers. When this had been done – with the greatest difficulty – a cave, almost as high as a man, came to light and yielded up – a collection of bones! In the cave was a stone, under which was another stone with the bone relics identified by an inscription. The inscription read: 'MARY THE MOTHER OF JOHN THE APOSTLE AND JAMES IN THIS'. A charter written on parchment was found together with the

46 Herbert, novice and monk at Clairvaux under Fastredus (1157–62); third abbot of Mores (diocese of Langres); archbishop of Torres in Sardinia (*c.*1180): see Bruno Griesser, 'Herbert von Clairvaux und sein *Liber miraculorum*', *Cistercienser-Chronik* 54 (1947), 21–39, 118–48, 134–8.

47 Herbert of Torres, *De miraculis libri tres*, PL 185, 1271–1384.

48 P. Lehmann, 'Ein Mirakelbuch des Zisterzienordens', *Studien und Mitteilungen aus dem Benediktiner- und dem Cistercienser-Orden* 14 (1927), 72–93.

49 Biblioteca Vallicelliana, MS Cod. H. 6, fols 143v–144r. Two other copies exist: one in the Archivio di Stato di Pistoia, and the other in Weimar, pr. in Lehmann, 'Ein Mirakelbuch', 72–5; *ActaSS*, Aprilis I, 813; Vincenzo Caperna, *Storia di Veroli* (Veroli, 1907, repr. Sala Bolognese, 1989), 270–1.

50 Brenda Bolton, 'Gerald of Casamari between Joachim of Fiore and Innocent III', 37–8.

stone, repeating the inscription on the stone. The charter and the bones were wrapped up together in a cloth and were in perfect condition – whole and undefiled as if just placed there.

The machinery of official identification was then set in motion. Bishop Odo and his team requested the presence at the site of three significant witnesses of good repute. One was Gerald of nearby Casamari, just seven kilometres away from Veroli; the other two were also Cistercians – one, the abbot of S. Anastasius (present-day Tre Fontane) in Rome,[51] the other, Gualterico, bishop of Penne, near Pescara.[52] Together these three appeared as requested to inspect and authenticate the find. In the cave, Odo lifted up the bones and handed them to Gerald. Gerald, using techniques of 'medieval archaeology', that is, examining them, handed the bones back to Odo who handed them to his Deputy who handed them to abbot Gerald's monk, who found his hand covered with fresh blood. Gerald himself saw the blood-soaked cloth in which the relics had been wrapped and experienced a sweet smell which pervaded the cave. Then, a great earthquake occurred, or so Gerald was told, although surprisingly he did not feel it.[53] He simply remembered seeing pure and recent blood on the bones, identifying one bone in particular as a tibia.

The relics were claimed to be those of Mary Salome, the wife of Zebedee and mother of their sons, John the Apostle and James the Greater (of Compostella). A variation on this account placed the bones of Mary Cleophas there too, but she seems rapidly to have disappeared from view. The remains – whether of one or two of the Marys who had come to the Sepulchre to anoint the body of Christ, their nephew – were recovered from the site and placed in a new shrine near the high altar of the cathedral of S. Erasmo at Veroli. A church was erected soon after 1209 in honour of Santa Salome where Tommaso seemed to have been entrusted with some sort of honorary churchwardenship in order to guard the relics.[54]

A manuscript from Pistoia provides one further stage in the process

51 Name unknown, see Filippo Caraffa, *Monasticon Italiae*, 1, *Roma e Lazio: eccettuate l'arcidiocesi di Gaeta e l'abbazia nullius di Montecassino* (Cesena, 1981), 84–5.

52 Conrad Eubel, *Hierarchia Catholica medii aevi, sive summorum Pontificum. S.R.E. Cardinalium, ecclesiarum antistitum . . .*, 9 vols (Regensburg, 1898–1958), 1: 394.

53 *Chronica romanorum pontificum et imperatorum ac de rebus in Apulia gestis (781–1228), auctore ignoto monacho Cisterciensi*, ed. A. Gaudenzi, Società Napoletana di Storia Patria 1 (Naples, 1888), 35: 'terremotus magnus . . . ita quod in provincia valvina et teatina turres et alta hedificia diruerunt'.

54 Even today, Veroli possesses a treasury of 643 relics.

of attestation of the Veroli relics.[55] Vethosus, a papal notary, appended a wax seal to authenticate Gerald of Casamari's letter and faithfully copied the account word for word, *de verbo ad verbum*, to which he attached the appropriate seal and signed his name to it. Soffredo, bishop of Pistoia (1208–23), and Leto, Odo's successor as bishop of Veroli (1212–24), attested to the veracity of this relic invention, placing it under their seals. Interestingly, both bishops state that although the relics were small in quantity, they were very much respected for their quality and were to be venerated *qua decet* – as is fitting.[56] The letters of verification together with Gerald's original were to be forwarded to Lotario, archbishop of Pisa. At all stages, Innocent himself was informed by appropriate members of the clergy and extreme caution was taken to test the veracity of what was claimed.

The accounts of some of the healing miracles provide vivid local details.[57] Aldruda of Pistoia, suffering from elephantiasis, betook herself to Veroli at the instigation of Mary Salome through a vision, where she was healed. Aufreda, from Naples, suffered from such severe arthritis of the hands and feet that she could no longer walk but, when taken to Veroli, found herself cured. Gregory of Puglia, a youth who had suffered a stroke and contortion of the mouth, had made a fruitless journey to the hot baths of Pozzuoli but found no cure there.[58] Needless to say, a visit to Veroli was just what this youth needed to restore his speech and straighten his mouth.

In the case of the miraculous relics of Veroli, it is clear from the documentation that very careful authentication was made. It would have been unthinkable to have a fraudulent shrine so close to Rome, and Innocent was clearly kept abreast at every stage of events. Even the seals of the bishops involved were double-checked and the verification of a succession of witnesses was carefully noted down. Innocent incidentally did much to lay down the principles by which forgeries could be detected and throughout his pontificate was on the look-out for cases of forged documents bearing spurious seals.[59] These relics seem subsequently to have been used as a focus for a lay confraternity for the

55 Partially pr. by F. A. Zaccaria, *Anecdotorum medii aevi . . . collectio* (Turin, 1755), 209.

56 Farina and Vona, *L'abate Giraldo di Casamari*, 47–9.

57 *ActaSS*, Aprilis I, 814–5.

58 C. M. Kauffmann, *The Baths of Pozzuoli: a Study of the Medieval Illuminations of Peter of Eboli's Poem* (Oxford, 1959), 1–23.

59 Patrick Zutshi, 'Innocent III and the Reform of the Papal Chancery', in Sommerlechner, ed., *Innocenzo III: Urbs et Orbis*, 1: 84–101.

cult of Mary Salome, centred on the cathedral chapter of Veroli. The Chapter Archives for 1210, 1211 and 1225 record money gifts for the construction of a chapel in the place where the tomb had been found. The support of Gerald, the high-status abbot of Casamari, one of the leading Cistercian houses of the Patrimony, did much to promote the saint's cult. The name of Innocent III probably did more. Mary's head was soon enclosed in an impressive silver-gilt reliquary and her invention was widely diffused through its inclusion as the preface to *De miraculis libri tres*.

* * *

We turn now to a previously over-looked text from a manuscript codex in Giessen which makes clear that the first formal session of the Fourth Lateran Council (11–30 November 1215) came to a close with a *processio*,[60] one of those spectacular acts of ritualized 'outdoor' religious manifestations so popular in Rome.[61] It was a really memorable event, occurring on 15 November, the first Sunday of the Council, and was witnessed by an anonymous German cleric. He gives a description in detail of a *letania* or *collecta processionalis*, that is, a procession with a strong and distinctively popular component, bringing together many groups of diverse status.[62] The destination of the *collecta* was S. Maria in Trastevere, the old *titulus Calixti (et Juli)*, on the far bank of the River Tiber.[63] The aim and objective was that participants should witness the consecration after its reconstruction by Innocent II (1130–43) of this, the oldest of all Roman churches dedicated to the Virgin. Decked out in all their festive finery, the lay nobility of Rome conducted Innocent III, *honorificentissime*, through the City of which he was bishop, to the accompaniment of drums, strings, organs, raucous trumpets and

60 Giessen, Universitätsbibliothek, MS 1105, fols 59r–60v; Stephan Kuttner and Antonio García y García, 'A New Eyewitness Account of the Fourth Lateran Council', *Traditio* 20 (1964), 115–78; 'Eyewitness Account of the Fourth Lateran Council (1215)', trans. Constantin Fasolt, in Julius Kirshner and Karl F. Morrison, eds, *Medieval Europe*, University of Chicago Readings in Western Civilization 4 (Chicago, IL, 1986), 369–76, 371–2.

61 Sible de Blaauw, 'Contrasts in Processional Liturgy. A Typology of Outdoor Processions in Twelfth-Century Rome', in Nicolas Bock, Peter Kurmann, Serena Romano and Jean-Michel Spieser, eds, *Art, cérémonial et liturgie au Moyen Âge*, Études lausannoises d'histoire de l'art 1 (Rome, 2002), 357–95.

62 Ibid., 359: 'participatory procession'; John F. Baldovin, *The Urban Character of Christian Worship: the Origins, Development, and Meaning of Stational Liturgy*, Orientalia Christiana Analecta 228 (Rome, 1987), 158–66.

63 Mariano Armellini, *Le Chiese di Roma dal secolo IV al XIX*, ed. Carlo Cecchelli, 2 vols (Rome, 1942), 2: 786.

chorus.[64] The litany – possibly an invocation to previous martyr-saints of Rome – was the truly popular part of this procession, but such was the tumult that the German cleric could distinguish only the incessant customary chanting of *Kyrie eleison, Christe eleison* by the people.[65] The unrivalled enthusiasm of the crowd was displayed on every street and from every tower, with innumerable lights and banners from the Ponte Cestio, crossing the river Tiber, right up to the Church of Santa Maria. The ceremonial progress of Innocent through Rome to Trastevere was likened by the cleric to Christ's entry into Jerusalem.[66] The conciliar delegation following the Pope included not only bishops and abbots but also members of the lesser clergy, high-status visitors and a throng of eager citizens.[67] For Innocent, however, the centrepiece of the Council on this occasion was to be his consecration of the 'Church of Our Lady of the flowing oil'.[68]

The miracle of the *fons olei* or fountain of oil,[69] which gushed from the ground near the Tiber bank at the *taberna meritoria*, or charitable hospice for retired soldiers, in the reign of Octavian Augustus, was a credible sign by which God could be recognized. The Christian argument was about 'signification',[70] that is, what was signified and how it could be interpreted as a sign from God. Thus, this signification was of Christ's birth to the Gentiles in the West, even as the Star was shining for others in the East. It was Cassius Dio who first recorded Trastevere's most distinguishing feature, the marvellous fountain of oil, in a non-Christian context. This third-century historian, in his *Roman History*, placed it as occurring sometime before 38BC.[71] For Dio, the spurting of oil on the bank of the Tiber was just one of many events of

64 Kuttner and García, 'New Eyewitness Account', 125, ll. 60–78.

65 Ibid., 125, l. 67: 'sicut sui moris est'; Baldovin, *Urban Character of Christian Worship*, 162–4; de Blaauw, 'Contrasts in Processional Liturgy', 359, n. 7.

66 Kuttner and García, 'New Eyewitness Account', 125, ll. 66–8, suggest similarities with the first antiphon for the distribution of the palms on Palm Sunday.

67 Michele Maccarrone, 'Il IV Concilio Lateranense', *Divinitas* 2 (1961), 270–98; Brenda Bolton, 'A Show with a Meaning: Innocent III's Approach to the Fourth Lateran Council, 1215', *Medieval History* 1 (1991), 53–67, repr. in eadem, *Innocent III: Studies on Papal Authority and Pastoral Care*, Variorum Reprints, CS 490 (Aldershot, 1995), XI.

68 Kuttner and García, 'New Eyewitness Account', 125, ll. 60–1: '. . . ad consecrandam ecclesiam beate Marie que ad Oleum fundentem'.

69 Carlo Cecchelli, '*Fons olei*', in *Capitolium* 1 (1925/6), 535–9, unhelpfully suggests the existence of petroleum deposits in Trastevere.

70 Averil Cameron, 'The Language of Images: the Rise of Icons and Christian Representation', in Diana Wood, ed., *The Church and the Arts*, SCH 28 (Oxford, 1992), 1–42, 37. Cf. Markus, *Signs and Meanings*, 69.

71 Cassius Dio, *Historiarum Romanarum quae supersunt* (Berlin, 1898), 280 (Lib. XLVIII, ch.

a portentous nature contained in a whole list of omens or portents. Julius Obsequens, in his *Book of Prodigies*, produced in the fourth century, left an inexplicable and disappointing gap in events between 42BC and 17BC.[72] It was to be Jerome, interpolating into Eusebius's *Chronici Canones*, which he translated into Latin around 381, who first located the phenomenon at the old soldiers' hostel, site of the so-called *taberna meritoria*, across the Tiber in Trastevere.[73] According to Jerome, it was from this hostel that oil spurted out of the ground, flowing ceaselessly all day and signifying the grace of Christ.[74] Jerome's translation seems to have provided Paul Orosius with material for inclusion in his *Seven Books of History against the Pagans*, completed in 418, but Orosius went on to elaborate the legend further.[75]

For Orosius, this oil was of the greatest significance, flowing, as it did, throughout the day in a very large stream. His commentary stressed the interpretation of the miracle as an explicit foretelling of the coming of the Saviour:

> And when the Emperor ruled the whole world, what sign could be more obvious, if it was not to mean the forthcoming birth of Christ? Christ, in fact, in the language of his people, amongst whom and from whom he was born, meaning the Anointed one. And thus, while the Emperor was granted tribunician power in perpetuity, this oil gushed out in Rome for the whole day. Signs in the sky and wonders on earth indicated very clearly to those people who were not accustomed to listen to the voice of the prophets that for the whole day, that is, for the whole duration of the Roman Empire, Christ and from him, the Christians, namely the Anointed and those anointed from him, would be produced copiously and perpetually – from a hostel, namely from the Church which is both hospitable and generous.[76]

43, 4); Ernest Cary, *Dio's Roman History*, Loeb Classical Library 5 (London and New York, 1917), 311.

72 Grant, *Miracle and Natural Law*, 57; Kinney, 'S. Maria in Trastevere', 172–3 and n. 217.

73 Kinney, 'S. Maria in Trastevere', Appendix II, 354–9.

74 *Sancti Eusebii, Hieronymi, Opera Omnia*, 8, PL 27, 431–2: 'E taberna meritoria trans Tiberim oleum terra erupit, fluxitque tota die sine intermissione, significans Christi gratiam ex gentibus'.

75 Paolo Orosio, *Le Storie contro i pagani*, ed. Adolf Lippold, 3 vols (Milan, 1976), Book VI,18–20, 2: 203–13.

76 Ibid., Book VI,20,6, 2: 221–2. My translation.

Orosius makes specific the association of the function of the place or hostel, the *taberna meritoria*, with that of the Church, and the fountain of oil flowing, as it did, all day long in Rome, so marking the continuing stream of conversions to Christianity. The fountain also occurs in the *Historia Romana* of Paul the Deacon (766–74),[77] who drew passages word for word from both Jerome and Orosius, referring not only to the very considerable quantity of oil from the *taberna meritoria*, saturating the ground, but also to a heavenly rainbow which encircled the sun. Importantly, the Deacon reinforced the association of the fountain with the preparation for the Nativity in Bethlehem. He moved the date forward and placed the event in 29BC instead of 40BC, as Orosius had done, and in so doing, linked it with the peace of Octavian Augustus.

The miraculous fountain of oil did not, however, come to be associated with the church of S. Maria in Trastevere itself until the ninth century, when Anastasius, *bibliothecarius* of the Holy Roman Church under Popes Nicholas I (858–67), Hadrian II (867–72) and John VIII (872–82), wrote to Ursus, sub-deacon and doctor of Nicholas I.[78] In his letter, Anastasius styled himself as 'insignificant abbot' of the monastery of S. Maria in Trastevere 'in the place where once, around the time of Christ's birth, oil had flowed'.[79] Anastasius's reference to Jerome's translations from Greek and Hebrew indicate his acquaintance with this author's works, while the marvellous fountain had become one of S. Maria's distinguishing features. By 1073, it appears as the official epithet of the church, 'the venerable *titulus* which is in Trastevere and is called *fundens oleum*'.[80] The *Acta consecrationis* imply that the exact site of the oil well had not been located before the rebuilding by Innocent II,[81] when the source of the oil was revealed – 'in that same spot where moist earth was found, which when pressed, exuded oil rather than water'.[82] By the mid-twelfth century, the *fons olei* had come to be

77 Paolo Diacono, *Historia Romana*, ed. Amedeo Crivellucci, Fonti per la Storia d'Italia 51 (Rome, 1914), Book VII,8, 100–1.

78 'Anastasii Bibliothecarii epistolae sive praefationes', ed. E. Perels and G. Laehr, in *Epistolae Karolini Aevi*, MGH 5 (Munich, 1978), 395–442, 398–400.

79 Ibid., 399: 'Anastasius exiguus abbas monasterii sanctae Dei genitricis Mariae Virginis siti trans tiberim, ubi olim circa Domini nativitatem fons olei fluxit'; Karin Bull-Simonsen Einaudi, '*Fons Olei* e Anastasio Bibliotecario', *Rivista dell'Istituto Nazionale d'Archeologia e Storia dell'Arte* 13 (1990), 179–222, esp. 209–21.

80 BAV, Galletti MS Vat. lat. 8051, fol. 13.

81 MS Vat. lat. 10999, fol. 151r.

82 Ibid.: 'in eodem quoque loco in fundamento terra madida inventa est, que expressa magis oleum quam aquam emittebat, quousque ad hec tempora, sicut expressa fuit, reservata apparet'.

considered as an on-going miracle, not merely something that happened on one particular day – the day of Christ's birth – but as a manifestation, either sign or wonder, which had a fixed beginning but no foreseeable end!

S. Maria in Trastevere was originally the ancient oratory or *titulus* of Pope Calixtus I (218–22),[83] close to which another pope, Julius I (337–52), may have erected a basilica church.[84] Not only did Gregory IV (827–44) build a *praesepium* chapel there in imitation of that at Santa Maria Maggiore,[85] but, in 1123, Calixtus II (1119–24) created a new liturgical station for the feast of the Circumcision on 1 January, the Octave of the Nativity,[86] effecting this by means of a rare stational transfer from S. Maria *ad Martyres*, where it had been celebrated since the seventh century.[87] S. Maria in Trastevere was transformed between 1138 and 1143 in a monumental building campaign[88] by the Papareschi pope, Innocent II, who died before he could consecrate it.[89] That this church, or at least its high altar, still remained to be officially consecrated some seventy years after its most recent restoration was not at all exceptional.[90]

The *Acta consecrationis* provide a unique record of those miraculous events leading to the consecration of S. Maria in Trastevere.[91] This reveals the prime mover to have been Guido de Papa (Papareschi), a close relation of Innocent II, an influential figure in both Rome and the

83 *Liber Pontificalis*, 1: 141; Kinney, 'S. Maria in Trastevere', 1–59.

84 *Liber Pontificalis*, 1: 8; Kinney, 'S. Maria in Trastevere', 24–65, for discussion of this complex problem.

85 *Liber Pontificalis*, 2: 78; Kinney, 'S. Maria in Trastevere', 106–15, esp. 115: 'itself an "authentic" simulation of the Grotto of the Nativity'.

86 Vittorio Peri, '*Nichil in Ecclesia sine causa*. Note di vita liturgica romana nel XII secolo', *Rivista di Archeologia Cristiana* 50 (1974), 249–73.

87 Johann Peter Kirsch, *Die Stationskirchen des Missale Romanum: mit einer Untersuchung über Ursprung und Entwicklung der liturgischen Stationsfeler*, Ecclesia orans 19 (Freiburg im Breisgau, 1926), 232–3.

88 Kinney, 'S. Maria in Trastevere', 223–333, for the complex and detailed changes to the structure; see her article, 'The Apse Mosaic of Santa Maria in Trastevere', in Elizabeth Sears and Thelma K. Thomas, eds, *Reading Medieval Images: the Art Historian and the Object* (Ann Arbor, MI, 2002), 19–26.

89 Kuttner and García, 'New Eyewitness Account', 144–5; Kinney, 'S. Maria in Trastevere', 215–17.

90 Kuttner and García, 'New Eyewitness Account', 144–5, n. 85. Cf. Leonard Boyle, 'The Date of the Consecration of the Basilica of San Clemente', *Archivum Fratrum Praedicatorum* 30 (1960), 417–27.

91 *Le Liber Pontificalis: texte, introduction et commentaire*, ed. L. Duchesne and C. Vogel, 3 vols (Paris, 1886–1957), 2: 78; Kinney, 'S. Maria in Trastevere', 335–47.

Patrimony, and an almost exact contemporary of Innocent III.[92] A leading member of the *Romana fraternitas*,[93] Guido ruled over the canonry of S. Maria in Trastevere for almost thirty years from 1191, when Clement III created him cardinal priest of the church, until his death in 1221. Between 1191 and 1193, he was legate in Lombardy for Celestine III (1191–8). In the summer of 1199, he served Innocent III by acting against Markward of Anweiler at Veroli with Octavian of Ostia and Hugolino.[94] Following his elevation by Innocent in 1206 as cardinal bishop of Palestrina, he remained deeply involved in the care and administration of his title church, to which no successor was appointed in his lifetime. Uniquely, a document of 1211 from the *Tabularium* of the church names Guido as both cardinal priest and bishop.[95] To hold both offices simultaneously was most unusual, indicating his importance to this region just across the Tiber.

The *Acta*, which describe Guido in glowing terms – handsome, tall, much admired for his grey hair, and continually active up to the time of the Council[96] – confirm his unique role in the *collecta processionalis* and consecration of 15 November 1215. His affection and concern for his title church was reflected in the outcome of a meeting with the canons of S. Maria in Trastevere following vespers on Tuesday 13 October, the vigil of the Feast of St Calixtus. The matter under discussion was the consecration of their church, which had not previously been mentioned, but Guido, divinely informed by a mysterious voice that the ceremony would be deemed particularly appropriate at this time, subsequently retold many times in old age how this sign had come about.[97] On the following Sunday, 18 October, before Mass, he summoned all the people of Trastevere together to decide how the

92 Guido de Papa, cardinal priest of S. Maria in Trastevere (1191), cardinal bishop of Palestrina (1206–21): see Werner Maleczek, *Papst und Kardinalskolleg von 1191 bis 1216 : die Kardinäle unter Coelestin III. und Innocenz III* (Vienna, 1984), 99–101.

93 Tommaso di Carpegna Falconieri, *Il clero di Roma nel medioevo* (Rome, 2002), 241–72; Susan Twyman, 'The *Romana fraternitas* and Urban Processions at Rome in the Twelfth and Thirteenth Centuries', in Andrews, Egger and Rousseau, eds, *Pope, Church and City*, 13–46, 16.

94 *Gesta Innocentii PP. III*, PL 214, I–CL, cols xvii–ccxxviii, at XXIII, col, xliv; *The Deeds of Pope Innocent III by an Anonymous Author*, transl. James M. Powell (Washington, DC, 2004), 25.

95 Galletti MS Vat. lat. 8051/1, fol. 134: 'Ego Guido dei gratia presbiter cardinalis venerande ecclesie Sancte Marie tituli Calixti et Penestrinensis (*sic*) episcopus'.

96 MS Vat. lat. 10999, fol. 152v: 'canitie admirabilis . . . continuo faciente usque ad tempora vixit concilii'.

97 Ibid.: '. . . sed cum tempus instaret concilii, sicut ab eodem sepe audivi'.

consecration should be carried out.[98] When Guido had explained matters to them, they unanimously agreed that, after nones that very day, they would jointly go to seek the Pope's consent.

Hence, the whole delegation – clergy, soldiers and parishioners – went in great excitement to put their case to him. Nor did they have far to go! The Sunday after the feast of St Calixtus was, by long tradition, S. Maria's annual *statio* (an occasion established before 587), when the pope sat at his 'watching post' in the church.[99] They found Innocent at the 'watch tower', *in loco speculi*, where the church's past history, including an impressive collection of popes, 'the holy bodies of Calixtus, and Cornelius (251–3) and the priest Calepodius, joined with those of Julius'[100] (and were commemorated in its apse mosaic).[101] This would certainly have been brought to Innocent's attention while on duty that day. When he received the delegation, he heard them kindly even though his other arduous commitments towards the forthcoming Lateran Council must have been much on his mind.[102] The people's spokesman, the eloquent James John Crassi, put forward an elaborate statement to explain that they were there as a result of Guido's divine vision and, following a very public consultation, all implored Innocent to grant the gift of consecration to their church. It was in keeping with his faith that Innocent's assent to the consecration was made on the grounds that divine providence and God's will had brought all of them together at this point and in this place.

The Pope's reply to the request of the people of Trastevere, recorded in direct speech in the *Acta*, is highly significant. Adapting Psalm 117, verse 23, he first replied:

98 Ibid.; Kinney, 'S. Maria in Trastevere', 338–9.

99 Ugonio, *Historia delle stationi di Roma*, 134. Tertullian saw '*statio*' as derived from military use, standing on post or guard: see Baldovin, *Urban Character of Christian Worship*, 143; C. Mohrmann, 'Statio', *Vigiliae Christianae* 7 (1953), 1–15, repr. in eadem, *Études sur le latin des chrétiens*, 4 vols (Rome, 1965), 3: 307–30.

100 MS Vat. lat. 10999, fol. 151r.

101 Kinney, 'The Apse Mosaic of S. Maria in Trastevere', 23–5; William Tronzo, 'Apse Decoration, the Liturgy and the Perception of Art in Medieval Rome: S. Maria in Trastevere and S. Maria Maggiore', in idem, ed., *Italian Church Decoration of the Middle Ages and Early Renaissance: Functions, Forms and Regional Traditions*, Villa Spelman Colloquia 1 (Bologna, 1989), 167–93; Ursula Nilgen, 'Texte et image dans les absides des XIe–XIIe siècles en Italie', in Robert Favreau, ed., *Épigraphie et iconographie. Actes du colloque tenu à Poitiers les 5–8 octobre 1995* (Poitiers, 1996), 153–65.

102 For example, his concern to protect his curial officials from the fever sweeping Rome in autumn 1215: cf. E. Heller, 'Der kuriale Geschäftsgang in den Briefen des Thomas von Capua', *Archiv für Urkundenforschung* 13 (1935), 198–313, 259.

> *It is the Lord's doing* that you have asked for the consecration of that church, and *it is marvellous in our eyes* (Ps. 117, 23)[103] that an Innocent made the body and an Innocent will put in the soul. For nothing else sounds right except that he restored it and I will consecrate it.[104]

This said, he cheerfully consented to the prayers of those making the request and added, 'It is right that the place should be honoured by all men in which the Lord deigned to show the sign of the oil at the time of his birth'.[105] And then, as the author of the *Acta* reports, the Pope was at pains to recount briefly to the assembled crowd other signs which had come to light in the City. By so concurring, he demonstrated that he fully appreciated the unique history and appropriateness of S. Maria's site. Rejoicing and exulting, Innocent returned to his quarters in Rome and prepared for the consecration.[106]

* * *

That the theory and ceremonial of a consecration was of great importance to Innocent is clear from his three surviving model sermons; for the solemn dedication of a church, for the consecration of the altar and for appropriate gospel readings on those occasions.[107] We obtain an even stronger sense of the significance from the many local consecrations he carried out as he itinerated through the Patrimony of St Peter, uniting communities and bringing spiritual food to the people.[108] Having brought to S. Maria in Trastevere on 15 November more than one thousand patriarchs, archbishops, bishops, cardinals and other ecclesiastics who had come to the Lateran Council, Innocent consecrated the church of 'Our Lady of the flowing oil' in their presence.

While his consecration sermon has unfortunately not survived, some elements can be reconstructed using evidence from three sources. The first is a letter from Innocent to the abbot and convent of Fossanova, containing the burden of his sermon at the consecration of

103 Cf., 'In nativitate Domini', PL 217, 456, for an identical citation.

104 MS Vat. lat. 10999, fol. 152v; Kinney, 'S. Maria in Trastevere', 343: 'And the conceit was delicious: *quia Innocentius fecit corpus, et Innocentius inmittet anima*'.

105 Ibid.

106 MS Vat. lat. 10999, fol. 153v: 'Gaudens et exultans versus est ad propria'.

107 *Sermones de Tempore XXVII–XXIX*, PL 217, 433–50.

108 Brenda Bolton, '"The Caravan Rests": Innocent III's Use of Itineration', in *Omnia disce*, 41–60, 51–2 and 54–5.

the high altar on 19 June 1208.[109] The second is Lection VII of the *Acta consecrationis* which assimilates Innocent II, who rebuilt the church, to King David who built a temple for the Lord.[110] The third source is a letter of 22 June 1234 from Gregory IX (1227–41) to the Chapter of S. Maria in Trastevere which Moretti transcribed immediately following the *Acta*.[111] In this, Gregory informs the canons that he himself had witnessed the consecration of 1215, together with all those who had come to the General Council and grants remission of penance to all the faithful visiting the church on the day of its consecration and up to eight days thereafter.

It seems highly likely that Gregory is repeating and reusing Innocent's lost sermon as the basis for his letter to the canons. The first part develops the association between David as Innocent II, who rebuilt S. Maria in Trastevere, and Solomon, his son, as Innocent III, who instilled the soul, echoing Lection IX of the *Acta*. Humorous and quick-witted, Innocent knew that his fellow curialists frequently referred to him as Solomon and played on the joke.[112] Might we see in this his lightness of touch? Perhaps so. Parts of this letter are almost a word for word version of Innocent's 1208 sermon at Fossanova. Speaking of Christ, 'who was himself sacrifice and priest, and who as both ransom and reward gave himself so that dying he might redeem all the faithful from death, and gave himself as food on the altar so that living he might feed the same faithful for life', Innocent stressed how great and arduous this sacrifice was which brought all mankind, indissolubly united into one body, head and limbs.[113] His message echoed that of Sicard. Nothing was more marvellous – even in the place of the flowing oil – than the eucharistic miracle which alone could bring an end to divisions between the learned and unlearned by demonstrating the significance to the faith.

* * *

Innocent III's attitude to the use of miracles, signs and wonders reveals an awareness of identifiable problems in supporting the faith through the miraculous. The Veroli case clearly demonstrates the requirement

109 PL 215, 1435–7.

110 MS Vat. lat. 10999, fol. 151v.

111 Moretti, *De postrema dedicatione*, fols 162r–163v.

112 K. Hampe, 'Eine Schilderung des Sommeraufenthaltes der Römischen Kurie unter Innocenz' III in Subiaco 1202', *Historische Vierteljahrsschrift* 8 (1905), 509–35.

113 PL 215, 1436: 'Cum ergo magnum et arduum sit sacramentum altaris'.

of authenticity and justification. Abbot Gerald's letter of 1209, so publicly enshrined in the Cistercian manual of miracles, demonstrates the need for such proof and verification. The question of validity was, therefore, ever present and the Lateran decrees were to lay a strong emphasis on replacing credulity with credibility. Innocent's caution over the canonization process and its use of the miraculous certainly led on to a much stricter procedure, with notaries under pressure from the Papal Curia to produce an exact version of a witness's testimony, and to swear to the accuracy of their records. So strictly was this provision subsequently enforced, that out of forty-eight inquests held between 1199 and 1276, no fewer than eighteen of them were rejected for the reason that the words were not so reported.[114]

Innocent would certainly not have been altogether pleased at the chronicle entry of the Anonymous Cistercian from the monastery of Santa Maria di Ferraria near Teano in the Campania for the year 1216. He solemnly recorded the death and burial of the Pope in Perugia,[115] asserting 'that with God's favour, the blind, the insane and those suffering from other ailments have been cured at the papal tomb'.[116] These supposed *post-mortem* healing miracles are corroborated by no other source, nor does Innocent's name appear subsequently amongst the so-called 'flexible oligarchy' of local Perugian saints.[117] At least, events did not allow credulity to succeed in this instance.

Formerly University of London, Queen Mary & Westfield College

114 Vauchez, *La Sainteté en Occident*, 60–4.

115 *Chronica romanorum pontificum . . . ignoto monacho Cisterciensis*, 36: 'Idem dominus papa Innocentius iij us obiit xvij Kal. Augusti'.

116 Ibid.: '. . . ad cuius tumulum, sicut dicitur, ceci, maniaci et aliis infirmitatibus detenti Deo favente sanati sunt'.

117 Gary Dickson, 'The 115 Cults of the Saints in Later Medieval and Renaissance Perugia: a Demographic Overview of a Civic Pantheon', *Renaissance Studies* 12 (1998), 6–19, repr. in idem, *Religious Enthusiasm in the Medieval West: Revivals, Crusades, Saints*, Variorum Reprints, CS 695 (Aldershot, 2000), X, 18. But Innocent's biographer does speak of the *fons papalis* which flowed in Spoleto following his visit in 1198, *Gesta Innocentii*, X (bis), col. xxvi; *Deeds of Pope Innocent III*, transl. Powell, 12.

MODERNIZING ST CUTHBERT: REGINALD OF DURHAM'S MIRACLE COLLECTION

by SALLY CRUMPLIN

AROUND 1200, the Church of St Cuthbert in Durham produced an illustrated copy of Bede's *Life of St Cuthbert.*[1] Opulently decorated with illustrations rich in colour and gold, this book crowned a century that had seen Cuthbert's church grow in power and stability. After the seventh-century Northumbrian golden age, centuries of upheaval had characterized the Cuthbertine church: it changed immensely in location and religious observance, moving across Northumbria and adapting the community to suit difficult situations. By contrast, the twelfth century saw the building of the imposing Durham cathedral and castle, and the ornamentation of the church with many riches. The church was led by a sequence of very influential bishops and a thriving monastic community.[2] This power and prosperity of the Durham church was marked at the start and end of the twelfth century with great manifestations of Cuthbert's cult. An illustrated *Life of Cuthbert* was produced in the early years of the century;[3] in 1104 Cuthbert's body was translated into its current position in the cathedral and found to be just as incorrupt as it had been in 698, eleven years after his death; several hagiographical works on the cult and church were produced during this century;[4] and its end was

1 London, BL, MS Yates Thompson 26: see Dominic Marner, *St Cuthbert: his Life and Cult in Medieval Durham* (London, 2000). Bede's *Vita sancti Cuthberti* [hereafter: *VCB*] is published in *Two Lives of St Cuthbert*, ed. Bertram Colgrave (Cambridge, 1940), 142–306.

2 The Cuthbertine community moved from Lindisfarne, possibly to Norham, and wandered (from *c*.875) before settling at Chester-le-Street in 883. The church was finally established at Durham in 995. During its travels, the community lost elements of its monastic identity, but in 1083 the clerical community of Durham was replaced wholesale with Benedictine monks. For an excellent discussion of the church's history, see William M. Aird, *St Cuthbert and the Normans: the Church of Durham, 1071–1153* (Woodbridge, 1998).

3 Oxford, Bodleian Library, MS University College 165: discussed in Anne Lawrence-Mathers, *Manuscripts in Northumbria in the Eleventh and Twelfth Centuries* (Cambridge, 2003), 89–108 and in Barbara Abou-El-Haj, 'Saint Cuthbert: the Post-Conquest Appropriation of an Anglo-Saxon Cult', in Paul E. Szarmach, ed., *Holy Men and Holy Women: Old English Prose Saints' Lives and their Contexts* (New York, 1996), 177–206.

4 These were: a collection of twenty-one miracles, *Capitula de miraculis et translationibus sancti Cuthberti* [hereafter: *De miraculis*], ed. Thomas Arnold, in *Symeonis Monachi Opera Omnia*, RS 75, 2 vols (London, 1882, 1885), 1: 229–61 and 2: 333–62; a tract on the origins

marked with the beautifully illustrated Bedan *Life*. Cult and church were intrinsically linked, and provided the basis upon which Durham's twelfth-century power was built – a power which was to continue into the ensuing centuries.

Cuthbert's cult and church were thriving in the late twelfth century and at this time Reginald, a monk of Durham, produced his *Libellus de Admirandis beati Cuthberti Virtutibus*, a large miracle collection of 141 chapters.[5] Reginald began to write the *Libellus* in the 1160s and completed this first phase of the miracle collection, consisting of 107 chapters, before 1167. He wrote in his introductory chapters that Aelred of Rievaulx was its patron and was to peruse the *Libellus* after its production: Aelred died in 1167 and thus the first phase must have been completed by that year. After 1170, Reginald added a second phase of 34 chapters; the dating of this can be specified on the basis of references to the cults of Thomas Becket and Godric of Finchale who both died in that year.[6]

Explanations for the production of this grand miracle collection have focused on this latter phase, emphasizing the threat from the new saints Thomas and Godric, and on the notion that Durham was a peripheral area, unable to keep up with the vibrant south of England. Victoria Tudor, echoed by Dominic Marner, speculated that 'the rise of the Canterbury cult in particular spelt the end of the peak in Cuthbert's popularity'.[7] Donald Matthew disparagingly remarked that 'Cuthbert was a saint of a bygone era', and described the 'brave and baffled efforts' of the Durham monks to deal in vain with the 'new age' of the twelfth

and progress of the church, Symeon of Durham, *Libellus de exordio atque procursu istius, hoc est Dunhelmensis, ecclesie: Tract on the Origins and Progress of This Church of Durham* [hereafter: *LDE*], ed. and transl. David Rollason (Oxford, 2000); and an abbreviated form of this *LDE*, the *Brevis relatio de Sancto Cuthberto et quomodo corpus eius Dunelmum venerit, et excerpta de vita et miraculis sancti Cuthberti*, ed. J. Hodgson Hinde, in *Symeonis Dunelmensis opera et collectanea*, Surtees Society 51 (Durham, 1868), 223–33.

5 *Reginaldi monachi Dunelmensis libellus de admirandis beati Cuthberti virtutibus* [hereafter: *Libellus*], ed. J. Raine, Surtees Society 1 (Durham, 1835). I am greatly indebted to Robert Bartlett for generously sharing his notes on this text.

6 My phases differ slightly from those of Victoria Tudor, who tentatively suggested the first as ending somewhere around chapter 110. Based on stylistic evidence, particularly the length of chapter headings, the second phase began with ch. 108. See Victoria M. Tudor, 'Reginald of Durham and St Godric of Finchale: a Study of a Twelfth-Century Hagiographer and His Major Subject', unpublished Ph. D. thesis, University of Reading, 1979, 91–2.

7 Victoria Tudor, 'The Cult of St Cuthbert in the Twelfth Century: the Evidence of Reginald of Durham', in Gerald Bonner, David Rollason and Clare Stancliffe, eds, *St Cuthbert, his Cult and his Community to AD 1200* (Woodbridge, 1989), 447–67, 467; Marner, *Life and Cult*, 54.

century. Matthew extended this image of decline to encompass the Durham Church as a whole, stating that 'Durham had been relegated to the periphery of the powerful new kingdom shaped by the Angevins'.[8]

Was Reginald's *Libellus* written to salvage a waning, outmoded and outranked cult? There are two main problems with this depiction of impotence. First, it negates the fact that Reginald's miracle collection was conceived and completed some time before these new cults began, at a time of greater stability than had been enjoyed since Northumbria's seventh-century golden age. Second, it reflects a southern English bias, which requires discussion before the original and overarching reasons for the *Libellus*' production may be examined.

A southern bias to English history underplays the semi-independent power of the north. Recent scholarship has shown that, during much of the medieval period, connections within northern England and southern Scotland to the Forth formed a unit rather more distinct than a border on a map may indicate. As Robert Bartlett puts it, 'Durham and Dunbar had different lords but were part of the same world'.[9] Durham was essential to this unit at the north of England: its bishops, although under the nominal control of the Kings of England, were able to exercise largely autonomous power so far from the English royal centre – particularly notable was Hugh du Puiset whose episcopate lasted over forty years from 1154 to 1195.[10] Far from being on the periphery and at the mercy of two bordering nations, threatened by events at the English political centre, Durham was in fact the heart of its own immense political power.

This power manifested itself in saints' cults as well as secular politics: there was a vibrant network of saints' cults, stretching across southern Scotland and northern England, which was particularly active during the twelfth century.[11] But a southern leaning is also evident in studies

8 Donald Matthew, 'Durham and the Anglo-Norman World', in David Rollason, Margaret Harvey and Michael Prestwich, eds, *Anglo-Norman Durham, 1093–1193* (Woodbridge, 1994), 1–22, 19–21.

9 Robert Bartlett, *England under the Norman and Angevin Kings, 1075–1225* (Oxford, 2000), 78. An example of this recent scholarship is Aird, *Cuthbert and the Normans*, esp. 227–75; see also William E. Kapelle, *The Norman Conquest of the North: the Region and its Transformation, 1000–1135* (London, 1979).

10 For discussion of this episcopate, see G. V. Scammell, *Hugh du Puiset, Bishop of Durham* (Cambridge, 1956).

11 The cults of saints such as Kentigern, Ninian, Margaret, David and Aebbe were linked through institutional, political and personal ties between monasteries, particularly Cistercian

of cults. David Knowles, listing the chief pilgrimage cults in pre-conquest England, chose Bury for Edmund, Evesham for Egwin and Malmesbury for Aldhelm. He wrote that, by the late twelfth century, these sites had been usurped by Edward the Confessor at Westminster, Wulfstan at Worcester and Thomas at Canterbury[12] – never a mention of Cuthbert, the saint who had received patronage from most Anglo-Saxon kings after Alfred, and from William of Normandy.[13] Whilst these cults were undoubtedly important, all were based in the southernmost third of England; it seems necessary to redress the balance somewhat in Cuthbert's favour, to recognize the power of this northern cult, and that it existed in a semi-independent social and political sphere.

Whilst Becket's cult was a concern of the *Libellus*, there is no evidence to indicate that the new St Thomas debased Cuthbert's popularity, particularly as Canterbury and Durham are at opposite ends of England. Indeed, plotting the geographical spread of St Thomas's pilgrims, Ronald Finucane shows the cult's popularity markedly thinning in northern England, and not really encroaching into Cuthbert's saintly territory that was concentrated across northern England and southern Scotland from Perth to the Humber.[14] It is difficult to gauge the relative popularity of two such different cults. Certainly Becket's martyrdom inspired crowds of pilgrims almost instantaneously, and numerous *vitae* and miracle collections were produced, but the cult was new and explicitly connected with events at the heart of ecclesiastical and dynastic power in England.[15] By contrast, Cuthbert's cult had been strong for nearly 500 years and required no such flurry of hagiographical writing.

All that was required was for Reginald to adapt and update the

houses, and episcopal seats. Cf. Lawrence-Mathers, *Manuscripts in Northumbria*, 194–216; Robert Bartlett, 'Cults of Irish, Scottish and Welsh Saints in Twelfth-Century England', in Brendan Smith, ed., *Britain and Ireland 900–1300: Insular Responses to Medieval European Change* (Cambridge, 1999), 67–86, 81–3.

12 David Knowles, *The Monastic Order in England: a History of its Development from the Times of St. Dunstan to the Fourth Lateran Council* (2nd edn, Cambridge, 1963), 481.

13 See for example *Historia de sancto Cuthberto: a History of Saint Cuthbert and a Record of his Patrimony* [hereafter *HSC*], ed. Ted Johnson South (Cambridge, 2002), cc. 25–28, 64–6, and ch. 32, 68, and *LDE*, iii.20, 196–200.

14 Ronald Finucane, *Miracles and Pilgrims. Popular Beliefs in Medieval England* (2nd edn, London, 1995), 163–6. I am grateful to Simon Taylor for his guidance with locating place names.

15 Ward, *Miracles and the Medieval Mind*, 89–109; Michael Staunton, *The Lives of Thomas Becket* (Manchester, 2001).

miracle collection that he had recently completed: he duly added a group of Cuthbert miracles reported since he completed the first phase of his work. Included in this group of miracles were six references to St Thomas, all of them confidently stating Cuthbert's dominance over the Canterbury saint. Here, Reginald updated the claims of his earlier section. Before 1170, Reginald wrote how a noble leper from southern England called upon the three most excellent English saints to cure him:

> And thus he took counsel by offering to the blessed Cuthbert, and to the saint King Edmund, and to the glorious queen Aethelthryth [an interesting choice compared with Knowles's trio]; and by thus lighting three candles of the same width and length to their honour, he wished to prove from the merits of which saint he should hope for an agreeable cure.[16]

After 1170 Reginald told how the friends of a woman suffering from gout and lumbago similarly sought the agency of one of the three principal English saints by drawing lots, but this time they were Cuthbert, Edmund and Thomas.[17] Needless to say, in both these cases Cuthbert was the victor: Reginald wrote with confidence, not desperation, about the cults with which Cuthbert co-existed and sometimes competed. It is significant here to also mention Godric of Finchale: he was seen as the local pretender to Cuthbert's dominance, but, as with Becket, the spread of the cult shows that Cuthbert would not have been threatened. Godric's cult had a very local following, and his *Vita*, also written by Reginald, shows that Godric was styled to complement, not threaten Cuthbert: he developed as a champion of women, a social group with which Cuthbert had limited contact.[18]

If Reginald did not write to bolster a wavering cult, why, then, did he write his *Libellus*? He was primarily responding to local issues. The cult and church were increasingly stable and rich, but this was a highly textual community: important needs were met with an appropriate text – for example the *Historia de sancto Cuthberto* was a charter-history to assert land claims, whilst Symeon's *Libellus Dunelmensis ecclesie* [*LDE*] was an overtly monastic-toned history of the church to establish its new monastic identity at Durham after 1083. Most pertinently to

16 *Libellus*, ch. 19, 37–44.

17 *Libellus*, ch. 115, 260–1.

18 Finucane, *Miracles and Pilgrims*, 168. On women see Victoria Tudor, 'The Misogyny of St Cuthbert', *Archaeologia Aeliana*, ser. 5, 12 (1984), 157–67.

Reginald, the early twelfth-century *De miraculis*, the most recent miracle collection, showed Cuthbert as a fierce protector and political figure, but beneficent, particularly to the community, in the increasingly settled circumstances. By Reginald's time, several decades later, Cuthbert's depiction needed modernizing, to suit the firm stability of his church and cult. As Benedicta Ward has shown, while unstable times were often accompanied by miracles showing the saint's power, such as through punishment, stability was usually reflected through beneficent miracles: cures and non-violent tales.[19] Reginald needed to remove the fierce elements of Cuthbert that had appeared in the most recent depictions.

Further to this local need, Reginald was responding to wider pressures, in the western Church. The cult of the saints developed particularly rapidly during the twelfth century, becoming more and more formalized. While the focus on saints' cults at the end of the twelfth century has often rested with canonization, it is important to recognize that formalization was a far broader development of which papal recognition of saints was only a part. Describing the 'Age of Growth' of the Western Church from *c.*1050 to *c.*1300, Sir Richard Southern wrote that 'increasingly complex problems demanded more refined solutions than old rituals could provide'.[20] Well-established 'old rituals' were not obliterated, but maintained within a growing overarching legal framework, personified by the lawyer popes who dominated papal rule from the mid-twelfth to the end of the thirteenth century.[21] This legal structure had inevitable ramifications for the cult of saints and its accompanying hagiography. Thus, by the later twelfth century, a formal, legally tinged pattern for the proclamation and depiction of saints was developing. The key to this was the demonstrability of sanctity; the result was hagiography dominated by miracles with visible, tangible results, supported by identified witnesses.

There are two developments in hagiography and saints' cults associated with this formalization. The growth in cults led to an increase in pilgrimage. As pilgrimage grew, cures and other beneficent miracles were increasingly sought from saints, and were recorded to encourage

19 Ward, *Miracles and the Medieval Mind*, 34.

20 R. W. Southern, *Western Society and the Church in the Middle Ages* (London, 1970), 35.

21 Robert Bartlett, 'The Hagiography of Angevin England', in P. R. Coss and S. D. Lloyd, eds, *Thirteenth Century England* 5 (Woodbridge, 1995), 37–52, 48–9. See also C. Duggan, 'From the Conquest to the Death of King John', in C. H. Lawrence, ed., *The English Church and the Papacy in the Middle Ages* (2nd edn, Stroud, 1999), 65–116, 65.

further patronage.[22] Not only was this pattern of recording beneficent miracles clearly followed by Reginald, evidence for pilgrimage to Cuthbert's cult centres was clear in the *Libellus*.[23]

Furthermore, this same period saw an increasing number of medical miracles. This is hardly surprising, as the miracles which most clearly represent formalization and pilgrimage are cures: one would travel many miles to experience the disappearance of a hernia, the healing of broken bones or the dismissal of an evil spirit, and one could see the results. But this increase in cures, and particularly in medicalized miracles, must also be attributed to the wealth of medical texts which emerged during the twelfth century: translations of classical texts previously preserved only in the Muslim world, and new works from new centres of learning. Notably, Durham had a particularly good selection in its library.[24] The use of such texts is exemplified by the increasing inclusion of technical detail, a trait very much evident in the *Libellus*.[25]

Cures tended to dominate hagiographical works particularly from the later twelfth century: over half of Pierre-André Sigal's sample in his magisterial survey of 5,000 miracles, and ninety per cent of Finucane's 3,000 English and French miracles were tales of healing.[26] Reginald's *Libellus* shows a similarly large proportion of cures. This tied together the local needs and the demands of the wider church trends. Cures were not only demonstrable, part of pilgrimage growth, and in Reginald's reach due to the Durham medical library; they also were the very type of beneficent miracle that would display the confidence and stability of Cuthbert's church. Thus nearly forty per cent of Reginald's miracles are cures: perhaps a smaller proportion than those of Sigal and Finucane, but this figure should be put into the context of Cuthbert's cult. It makes for a striking contrast with the proportions seen in the

22 Jonathan Sumption, *Pilgrimage: an Image of Mediaeval Religion* (London, 1975), 160; see also Finucane, *Miracles and Pilgrims*, 39–55.

23 E.g. *Libellus*, ch. 48, 98–101 and ch. 125, 270–1.

24 A twelfth-century Durham catalogue shows that the church possessed works from the great medical centres of Montpellier and Salerno, and from Constantine the African's translations: Cambridge, MS Jesus College 44; National Library of Scotland, MS Advocates 18.6.11. Cf. *Catalogues of the Library of Durham Cathedral*, Surtees Society 7 (Durham, 1838), 6–8. On centres of medical learning, see Nancy G. Siraisi, *Medieval and Early Renaissance Medicine: an Introduction to Knowledge and Practice* (Chicago, IL, 1990).

25 E.g. *Libellus*, ch. 98, 217–219, ch. 101, 224–225 and ch. 119, 264–265. I am grateful to Simone Macdougall and Iona McCleery for sharing their ideas on the increasing medicalization of miracles.

26 Pierre-André Sigal, *L'Homme et le miracle dans la France médiévale: XIe–XIIe siècles* (Paris, 1985), 255; Finucane, *Miracles and Pilgrims*, 59.

other texts: a tenth in Symeon's *LDE* and a quarter in *De miraculis*, a complete absence of cures in the *Brevis Relatio* and the single cure in the *HSC*.[27] Healing miracles are thus a good departure point from which to illustrate the changes made by Reginald to the cult of Cuthbert, to modernize it for the late twelfth century and beyond.

That Reginald's modernization was part of a wider trend can be shown by comparison with two other twelfth-century cults. The three *Vitae* of Edward the Confessor show a similar progression towards the dominance of cures: the first, produced around 1066, contained far fewer cures than Osbert of Clare's work of the 1130s, which in turn included fewer cures than Aelred's version of the 1160s.[28] The medical emphasis of Reginald's Cuthbertine miracles is echoed in the hagiography of Thomas Becket.

The long-term importance of Reginald's modernization can be demonstrated by comparing his cures with an account of a much more recent saint:

> In May 1998, Mrs Besra was suffering from a painful, gigantic tumour in her uterus. Leaving her husband and five children behind in her village, she hobbled into the home for the destitute run by the Missionaries of Charity, Mother Teresa's order, in the West Bengal town of Patiram. 'For two months I had severe pain, terrible pain, and I was crying. I was not able to sleep; I could only lay on the left side and I couldn't stand straight', she said.
>
> . . . 'The sisters gave me medicine but the pain was still there. I was always praying to Mother Teresa whose picture was on the wall just opposite my bed'.
>
> After several unproductive trips to the hospital, two of the nuns caring for Mrs Besra – sisters Bartholomea and Ann Sevika – decided to take matters into their own hands. On 5 September 1998 – the first anniversary of Mother Teresa's death – the nuns tied a silver oval-shaped medallion to Mrs Besra's stomach using a piece of black thread.
>
> The medallion had been placed on Mother Teresa's body after

27 See above, nn. 4 and 13.

28 *The Life of King Edward who Rests at Westminster: Attributed to a Monk of Saint-Bertin*, ed. and transl. Frank Barlow (2nd edn, Oxford, 1992); 'La Vie de S. Édouard le Confesseur par Osbert de Clare', ed. M. Bloch, *AnBoll* 41 (1923), 5–131; *The Life of St Edward, King and Confessor*, transl. Jerome Bertram (2nd edn, Southampton, 1997). I am grateful to Joanna Huntington for sharing her research on Edward the Confessor. On St Thomas's medical cures, see Finucane, *Miracles and Pilgrims*, 67.

> her own death. Mrs Besra then fell asleep while the sisters prayed – and wept – holding her stomach. When she woke up the next morning the tumour had miraculously disappeared. 'My stomach became smaller and smaller', Mrs Besra recalled.
> 'In three days it was completely all right. I am sure that Mother Teresa made me all right'. She became well enough to start helping in the garden, and eventually went back to her village.[29]

This miracle displays several key elements: the sufferer was named and her ailment described. She made her pilgrimage to the cult centre. She prayed repeatedly to the venerated figure. She was given medical treatment that failed to help. Eventually two members of the religious community acted as intermediaries. They used a secondary relic of Mother Teresa, on the anniversary of her death, and it cured the sufferer upon contact with her affected parts. Mrs Besra was able to return to her normal life. The two sisters were named and therefore available as witnesses.

Reginald's miracle accounts display the same characteristics. He described the infected hand of the son of Ranulf, poor toll-gatherer and citizen of Durham. The boy was taken to Cuthbert's tomb where his hand was wrapped in the cloth in which Cuthbert's body had lain, whereupon the hand was cured. Ranulf was careful to inform the custodians of the saint's body who would give testimony.[30] In another miracle, the wife of a sheriff of Northumbria was suffering from a minutely described illness of the womb. Medicine failed to help, but she was cured when she invoked Cuthbert at Farne.[31] Finally, Durham monks bore immediate witness to the injury of Wictred by a bell clapper, and to his miraculous recovery (except for a dented head). He was soon, like Mrs Besra, able to continue with his work.[32] Details of people, ailment and place were all essential to Reginald's miracle tales.

The healing accounts of Reginald have far more in common with Mother Teresa, a twentieth-century saint, than with the healing Cuthbert depicted by Bede. A typical example from Bede's *Life of Cuthbert* serves to illustrate this point. It took place when Cuthbert was travelling around during a time of plague:

29 L. Harding and P. Willan, 'Mother Teresa's "miracle" ', *The Observer*, 19 August 2001.
30 *Libellus*, ch. 131, 279–80.
31 *Libellus*, ch. 119, 264–5.
32 *Libellus*, ch. 92, 201–4.

> In one village he exhorted everyone he found and said to the priest, 'Do you suppose there is anyone else left in the place who needs visiting and speaking to, or can I now move on to the next?'
>
> The priest looked all round and pointed out a woman some distance away, who had just before lost one son and was now holding another, dying, in her arms. Her tear-stained face gave ample proof of both past and present ills. Cuthbert went up to her without delay, blessed the boy, and kissed him.
>
> 'Have no fear', he said to the mother. 'Do not grieve. The child will get better and live, and you will lose no more of your family.'
>
> Mother and child both lived long afterwards, thus proving the prophecy true.[33]

Bede identified no people, places or symptoms. The miracle was more concerned with biblical overtones than with specific detail.[34] Significantly, Reginald did use Bede's text as a model, including similar proportions of miracle types and in particular recounting animal miracles very similar to those of Bede, but he changed the tone and style for a new era.[35] The contrast between this Bedan miracle and Reginald's cures, which bear a far closer resemblance to the miracle of Mother Teresa, emphasizes the fact that Reginald was indeed modernizing his saint.

The predominance of beneficent miracles as evidence of the confidence and stability in Cuthbert's cult can be augmented by two further characteristics of the *Libellus*. First, the absence of political figures is striking: it echoes Bede's lack of temporal information and contrasts with all other Cuthbertine texts. The *HSC*, Symeon's *LDE* and *De miraculis*, communicating the survival of Cuthbert's church through dangerous times, mentioned the church's triumph over a vast army of Scots, and punishments of William of Normandy, Earl Robert Cumin (d. 1069), and the bishop of Durham, Ranulf Flambard (1099–1128).[36] Reginald's omission of such important figures does not mean that turbulence had departed from the north of England. Indeed, a miracle late in the collection occurred during Henry the Young King's rebel-

33 *VCB*, ch. 33, 258–60.

34 Cf. 1 Kings 17, 17–24.

35 E.g. *VCB*, ch. 19, 220–2 and ch. 20, 222–4; *Libellus*, ch. 78, 162–3. On Bede's Cuthbertine animal miracles, see Paul Cavill, 'Some Dynamics of Story-Telling: Animals in the Early Lives of St Cuthbert', *Nottingham Medieval Studies* 43 (1999), 1–20.

36 *HSC*, 32, 68; *De miraculis*, ch. 4, 240–2 and ch. 6, 245–7; *LDE*, ii.13, 120–6, iii.15, 182–8, iii.19–20, 196–200.

lion against Henry II in 1173, when his supporters attacked from the north of England backed by William the Lion, king of Scots.[37] The miracle, however, did not refer to any of these dynastic characters, nor did it become embroiled in the partisan spirit of the time. Rather it told of an unnamed supporter of Henry II who was punished for spurning the sanctity of Cuthbert by riding his horse into the church precinct. Reginald's disassociation from the secular politics, so heavily ingrained into earlier texts, reflected the confidence of the church by the late twelfth century.[38]

Second, Cuthbert's power was conveyed in Reginald's *Libellus* through the wide dissemination of his cult. The pilgrims to Cuthbert's tomb at Durham came from all over the north of England and southern Scotland, but devotees also visited other cult centres. Lindisfarne was mentioned in all the texts since Bede's as the historical home of the Church, and safe haven, and this identity was continued in the *Libellus*.[39] But the *Libellus* showed Lindisfarne far more as a centre for worshipping Cuthbert, than as a location for cures or as a place to gather for liturgical feasts.[40] The more ascetic centre on Farne, where Cuthbert had lived as a hermit, could not be the scene of such large gatherings in his honour; and yet Reginald was particularly enthusiastic in publicizing Farne as a pilgrimage centre, recounting seventeen miracles there. These either involved stricken sailors[41] – accidental pilgrims – or individual devotees seeking a cure. While the majority of ailing Cuthbert devotees went to Durham, it seems logical that those with easier access to Farne would go there for Cuthbert's assistance.[42]

The dissemination of Cuthbert's cult beyond the locale of Durham,

37 *Libellus*, ch. 127, 272–3. These events are described in Bartlett, *England under the Norman and Angevin Kings*, 55.

38 This makes an interesting comparison with St Benedict's miracles, which display a similar shift in levels of secular detail: see D. Rollason, 'The Miracles of St Benedict: a Window on Early Medieval France', in Henry Mayr-Harting and R. I. Moore, eds, *Studies in Medieval History Presented to R. H. C. Davis* (London, 1985), 73–90, 81–4.

39 *Libellus*, ch. 13, 19–20, ch. 16, 28–32 and ch. 105, 234–6.

40 *Libellus*, ch. 22, 47–50.

41 E.g. *Libellus*, ch. 28, 63–5 and ch. 30, 67–9.

42 *Libellus*, cc. 118–119, 263–5; see also ch. 102, 226–9. Geoffrey of Durham's *Vita Bartolomei*, concerning a Farne hermit, and the anonymous collection of Farne miracles, both written around the end of the twelfth century, enhanced the reputation of Farne as a cult centre. These texts are bound with Reginald's *Libellus* in BL, MS Harley 4843. *Vita Bartolomæi Farnensis*, ed. Thomas Arnold, *Symeonis Monachi Opera Omnia*, RS 75, 2 vols (London, 1882, 1885), 1: 295–325; Edmund Craster, 'The Miracles of St Cuthbert at Farne', *AnBoll* 70 (1952), 5–19; Edmund Craster, 'The Miracles of Farne', *Archaeologia Aeliana*, ser. 4, 29 (1951), 93–107.

Farne and Lindisfarne was dependent upon three factors: the use of relics, the dedication of local churches and St Cuthbert's feast day. Reginald's *Libellus* gave plentiful evidence for all of these. Durham monks sometimes carried a relic with them and this could be used to give relief to the sick far from Durham. Cuthbert's relics were also carried with the intention to publicly spread the cult. Alan, a monk of Durham, travelled around south-eastern Scotland, curing people in Perth, Dunfermline and Haddington in Lothian with the aid of Cuthbert's relics, and publicly displaying them in a procession on St Margaret's Day in Dunfermline.[43]

In addition to these itinerant relics, permanent centres of worship for Cuthbert were established throughout northern England and southern Scotland. Miracles at these centres appeared in groups in the *Libellus*, and were often written in a common style, implying that they had been written at the centre in question and then the record had been sent to Durham for Reginald's compilation. These centres were spread as far afield as Cheshire, Galloway, Lothian and Teviotdale. Two of them are particularly significant in the *Libellus* for the timing of their miracles. Aelred of Rievaulx related a miracle in Kirkcudbright that took place on St Cuthbert's Day, 1164. And two miracles at a church dedicated to Cuthbert in Lothian happened during the period of Cuthbert's feast, just as Mrs Besra was cured on the anniversary of Mother Teresa's death. It seems that in the absence of relics, the feast day was increasingly becoming a suitable focus for miracles. Furthermore, these miracles are evidence that Cuthbert was part of the strong network of saints' cults across northern England and southern Scotland.[44]

Reginald's *Libellus* was the product of a church and cult confident in its own sphere of power. The stability of the later twelfth century demanded that Cuthbert's image be updated. Conveniently, this updating for local needs also allowed Reginald to modernize in accordance with the Western Church as a whole. That Reginald's *Libellus* did not mark the apogee of Cuthbert's cult is evident not only from the

43 *Libellus*, cc. 97–101, 215–25; see also ch. 53, 109–11, in which a monk habitually carries around a secondary relic.

44 See also the Scottish emphasis of the *Libellus de nativitate sancti Cuthberti*, ed. J. Raine, in *Miscellania Biographica*, Surtees Society 8 (Durham, 1838), discussed in Thomas Owen Clancy, 'Magpie Hagiography in Twelfth-Century Scotland: the Case of *Libellus de nativitate sancti Cuthberti*', in Jane Cartwright, ed., *Celtic Hagiography and Saints' Cults* (Cardiff, 2003), 216–31.

highly decorated *Life of Cuthbert*, but also from the continuing presence of Cuthbert's cult in ensuing centuries: the manuscript production which continued in Durham and elsewhere;[45] the production of new Cuthbertine hagiography;[46] the fourteenth-century window in York Minster, the fifteenth-century paintings in Carlisle cathedral stalls (to give only a few examples).[47] Reginald modernized St Cuthbert to maintain the popularity built since the seventh century and to ensure the continuation of this devotion.

University of St Andrews

45 For example, insular and continental manuscripts of Bede's *Vita sancti Cuthberti* are listed in *Two Lives*, ed. Colgrave, 20–39.

46 For example the fourteenth-century verse *Life*: *The Life of St. Cuthbert in English Verse, c. A.D. 1450: from the Original MS. in the Library at Castle Howard*, ed. J. T. Fowler, Surtees Society 87 (Durham, 1891).

47 These were copied from the manuscript of Bede's *Vita*, illustrated *c.*1200: see Bertram Colgrave, 'The Saint Cuthbert Paintings on the Carlisle Cathedral Stalls', *The Burlington Magazine* 73 (1938), 16–21.

MULTOS EX MEDICINAE ARTE CURAVERAT, MULTOS VERBO ET ORATIONE: CURING IN MEDIEVAL PORTUGUESE SAINTS' LIVES

by IONA McCLEERY

THE following is a description of a miracle attributed to the Portuguese friar-physician, Gil de Santarém (d. 1265):

> . . . Domingas Pires . . . had a great abscess on her left hand and for more than forty days had suffered pain so strong that she could not bear it. She went to Gil's tomb and, scattering some of its earth on her hand and arm, she prayed in supplication and with tears to the blessed man that, since in life he had been a physician not only of souls but also of bodies and had cured many through the art of medicine and through word and prayer and now that he was powerful with God, he would deign to cure this his supplicant. As soon as she had prayed, her very serious abscess burst spontaneously.[1]

Domingas seems to have believed that the saint to whom she was praying excelled as an intercessor because he had once been a physician both of the soul and of the body. He had 'cured many through the art of medicine and through word and prayer' (*multos ex medicinae arte curaverat, multos verbo et oratione*). The aim of this paper is to examine the processes at work in some medieval miracles and to consider the relationship between curing by 'the art of medicine' and by 'word and prayer'.

The relationship between physician and saint has attracted the attention of historians for some time, but it is sometimes forgotten that both usually had the same aim: the cure of the sick.[2] It is important to investigate at greater length how each went about their healing work

[1] André de Resende, *Aegidius Scallabitanus: um Diálogo sobre Fr. Gil de Santarém. Estudo Introductório, Edição Crítica, Tradução e Notas*, ed. Virgínia da C. Soares Pereira (Lisbon, 2000) [hereafter: *AS*], 498–9. A version can also be found in *ActaSS*, 3 May, 400–36. I am responsible for all translations.

[2] The forerunner of this approach was Henry J. Magoulias, 'The Lives of the Saints as Sources of Data for the History of Byzantine Medicine in the Sixth and Seventh Centuries', *Byzantinische Zeitschrift* 57 (1964), 127–50. See also Valerie I. J. Flint, 'The Early Medieval 'Medicus', the Saint – and the Enchanter', *Social History of Medicine* 2 (1989), 127–45.

and how they interacted at both a professional and a spiritual level. It is also important to think about how people like Domingas might have viewed their various healers. Miracle accounts are one of the few methods available to historians of accessing the lives of otherwise undocumented medieval people. This study focuses on a number of miracles drawn from four relatively little-known Portuguese saints' cults. Hagiography is a fledgling discipline in Portugal and these cults have not previously undergone comparative analysis. However, it is clear that they compare well with other European examples and deserve much greater attention.[3]

The four cults in question are those of: the early Christian martyr Vincent whose remains were translated from the Algarve to Lisbon cathedral by King Afonso Henriques in 1173;[4] the five Franciscan martyrs of Morocco, killed in 1220, venerated at the Augustinian house of Santa Cruz de Coimbra;[5] Gil de Santarém, thirteenth-century physician and Dominican friar, whose cult centred on the Dominican convent of Santarém;[6] and finally, Isabel of Aragon, Queen of Portugal (d. 1336), celebrated for her Franciscan piety, and venerated in the nunnery of Santa Clara de Coimbra.[7] In order to illustrate some of the fascinating questions raised by miracles, a series of related 'blood' miracles has been selected for analysis. This is just one method of researching these cults, and using them to investigate healing beliefs and practices further.

3 Mário Martins, *Peregrinações e Livros de Milagres na nossa Idade Média* (Coimbra, 1957); Maria Clara de Almeida Lucas, *Hagiografia Medieval Portuguesa* (Lisbon, 1984); José Mattoso, 'Saúde Corporal e Saúde Mental na Idade Média Portuguesa', in idem, *Fragmentos de uma Composição Medieval* (2nd edn, Lisbon, 1993), 233–52; Giulia Lanciani and Giuseppe Tavani, eds, *Dicionário da Literatura Medieval Galega e Portuguesa* (Lisbon, 1993), 279–81, 307–10, 384–9, 458–63.

4 *S. Vicente de Lisboa e seus milagres medievais*, ed. Aires Augusto Nascimento and Saul António Gomes (Lisbon, 1988) [hereafter: *Vicente*]. The two Latin *Vitae* date from shortly after 1173 (seventeen miracles) and from the mid-thirteenth century (seven miracles).

5 Maria Alice Fernandes, 'O Livro dos Milagres dos Santos Mártires (Edição e Estudo)', unpublished M.A. thesis, University of Lisbon, 1988. This is a collection of twenty-six miracles recorded in the vernacular during the fifteenth century.

6 The Latin *AS* contains eighty healing miracles. See I. McCleery, 'Life and Death in Medieval Portugal: the Cult and Miracles of Gil de Santarém', in Maria João Branco, ed., *Shaping the State in Medieval Portugal: Administration, Church and Society* (forthcoming).

7 J. J. Nunes, ed., 'Vida e Milagres de Dona Isabel, Rainha de Portugal', *Boletim da Segunda Classe da Academia das Sciências de Lisboa* 13 (1918–19), 1293–1384. Also found in *ActaSS*, 2 July, 169–213. The *Vita* was written in the vernacular shortly after Isabel's death and records twenty miracles.

* * *

The first miracle is again one attributed to Gil de Santarém:

> In Santarém in the parish of Marvila, Maria Domingas, wife of D. Estêvão, a rich merchant and honest citizen, suffering from a continuous haemorrhage for five years, had abandoned all idea of conceiving. . . . Thus, after the useless and empty care of many physicians, as many of the laity as of the Dominican convent, namely brothers Andre and Bernardo, she came to despair of her health . . . on a certain Saturday . . . she was troubled by a haemorrhage so excessive that, from the depletion of her blood, she lost her strength and thought she would die.[8]

Maria's mother advised her to go and pray at Gil's tomb and she made a vow to keep vigil there on the eve of his feast for the rest of her life:

> . . . her health followed without delay. The same day the previously unstoppable haemorrhage was staunched and the next day, the redundant humour completely dried up. . . . And she who had for five years of trouble been prevented from having children, soon conceived and gave her joyful husband a new baby.[9]

A similar story can be found in one of Vincent's miracles:

> A certain woman . . . suffered for many years from a flow of blood and great disturbance. After having spent all her money on the ignorance of physicians, she declared nothing to be of use, and went with faith and prayer to St Vincent, asked for health and received it in this way. After having prayed, St Vincent appeared to her while asleep, advising that if she dressed in clean, washed clothes nothing that she had suffered for ten years would she have any longer. As soon as she had been bound to these words, health followed.[10]

Of great interest are the parallels between these cases of bloody flux and another type of miracle. The book of the Martyrs of Morocco tells

> . . . of how a canon swallowed a leech and carried it around for an unknown period of time. And after some days blood came out of his nose for twenty-one days to such an extent that everyone

8 *AS*, 550–3.
9 Ibid.
10 *Vicente*, 46.

> despaired of his life. . . . so much so that the wife of the knight Vasco Anes, his god-mother, commended him to those holy martyrs. Then the leech came out through one of his nostrils and he received back his health and he is alive now.[11]

Compare this story with one of Isabel's miracles. Domingas Rodrigues

> had a leech inside her and she was yellow and dry by reason of the harm and damage that she received by carrying around that leech, and many masters of medicine and others tried with their wisdom and knowledge to get it out of her but they could not. Hearing them talk where she lived of the mercy that God had done to many through this queen, she came to [Isabel's tomb] and standing crying by that monument . . . began to say very weakly that she had that leech in her lip. And a chandler of the queen, who looked after the candles, seeing the leech in the lip, went at it with his tongs but could not pull it out . . . and then at that moment, with everyone present, they saw the leech come out through a nostril and fall on the ground. [. . .] And what happened is in a document made by the hand of Martim Afonso, notary of Coimbra.[12]

This is the story as found in Isabel's official *Vita*; unusually though the document written by Martim Afonso has survived the passage of time. Dated 27 July 1336, thus just two weeks after Isabel's death on 4 July, the document records the cures of two women, one of which did not make it into the official *Vita*. In the original account, the woman with the leech explained that she

> did not know for certain at what time she had eaten or drunk a leech nor how but for eight days and more she had had great clots of blood coming from her throat, and she did not know for certain what it was and some told her that she had some bad illness and others said that she had a leech in her and they told her that she had gone to the Alfafar spring, which in truth has leeches that attach themselves to things. . . .

Domingas claimed she went to several shrines in Coimbra seeking help, including the Martyrs of Morocco at Santa Cruz, before she visited Isabel's tomb at Santa Clara. She said that while she was there,

11 Fernandes, 'Livro dos Milagres', 118.
12 Nunes, 'Vida e Milagres de Dona Isabel', 1374.

> Pouring out blood, she could feel something moving in her nose and she saw the leech appear in her right nostril and they seized it and everyone praised the name of God. . . .

The notary appended a list of witnesses, including 'mestre Geraldo phisico', who was

> present when the said leech came out of the said nostril; the which leech I the said notary saw hung up alive [at the tomb] for a good two days. . . .[13]

Comparison between this document and the version of events in the official *Vita* reveals a fascinating process of selectivity. Why was Domingas's cure accepted and that of another woman who had a cyst on her eye rejected? Why did the author of the *Vita* add the chandler and the sentence that 'many masters of medicine' failed to extract the leech? This last addition contrasts with the actual presence of a physician amongst the witnesses. What was his role in this miracle? We also need to ask questions of the other blood-related miracles. The haemorrhaging women stories are based on one found in the gospels of Matthew, Mark and Luke, in which a woman, who had been bleeding for twelve years, managed to touch Jesus' cloak and was cured. According to Mark and Luke she had previously spent all her money on physicians in vain.[14] This is probably the earliest mention in a Christian context of what would become a widespread *topos* of medieval miracles: the expensive physician unable to heal those later cured by divine power.[15]

* * *

To what extent then can we accept the two Portuguese miracles as descriptions of real sick women? The bleeding has clear connotations of menstrual impurity going back to ancient taboos encapsulated in religious law: note that Vincent advised his supplicant to dress in clean clothes. The leech miracles resemble stories about a priest who swallowed a horrible spider that had fallen into the consecrated wine. In one

13 António G. Ribeiro de Vasconcelos, *Evolução do Culto de Dona Isabel de Aragão, Esposa do Rei Lavrador Dom Dinis de Portugal (a Rainha Santa)*, 2 vols (Coimbra, 1894, repr. 1993), 1: 259–63.

14 Matt. 9, 20–21, Mark 5, 25–34, Luke 8, 43–48; Gerd Theissen, *The Miracle Stories of the Early Christian Tradition*, transl. Francis McDonagh (Edinburgh, 1983), 91–2; Howard Clark Kee, *Medicine, Miracle and Magic in New Testament Times* (Cambridge, 1986), 51, 115.

15 Finucane, *Miracles and Pilgrims*, 60–71.

example in the *Cantigas de Santa Maria* of Alfonso X of Castile (d. 1284), the spider came out of a vein during blood-letting, and in another it came out from under a finger nail.[16] Is the leech in the Portuguese miracles similarly symbolic of sin or the devil? In the case of the miracle attributed to Isabel, it would be possible to argue this if one only had access to the official *Vita*. However, there is a level of realism in the notarial document – the leech-filled spring for example – that rings true. Equally, in the case of the haemorrhaging woman whom Gil cured, there is such a wealth of personal data that it is almost as if the recorder wanted to emphasize that the circumstances were real.

It may be that religious *topoi* were powerful enough to persuade scribes to alter miracle accounts to lend them the weight of tradition, but their presence does not imply that the people involved did not exist. If miracle collections were to work as successful advertising for shrines, then the people had to be real and the stories plausible. It is possible that leeches, or rather serious nosebleeds, were problems, and that 'bloody flux' was a catch-all term for women who presented themselves at shrines with undisclosed gynaecological problems.[17] Excessive menstrual flow and chronic bloody discharge were conditions treated in texts like the twelfth-century gynaecological work, the *Trotula*, and also in the *Treasury of the Poor*, a thirteenth-century compendium attributed to the Portuguese physician Petrus Hispanus.[18] The Bolognese surgeon, Teodorico Borgognoni (d. 1298), discussed internal and external haemorrhage in some detail in his *Chirurgia*, dedicated to the Bishop of Valencia.[19] In the thirteenth-century health guide of Aldobrandino of Siena, leeches were collected for blood-letting

16 Alfonso X, *Cantigas de Santa Maria*, ed. Walter Mettman, 3 vols (Coimbra, 1959–64), nos 222 and 225.

17 The condition could have been caused by a number of things. A haemorrhaging nun in the early Middle Ages was said to have 'suffered from what the doctors call haemorrhoids': *The Life of Saint Leoba*, transl. C. H. Talbot, in Thomas F. X. Noble and Thomas Head, eds, *Soldiers of Christ: Saints and Saints' Lives from Late Antiquity and the Early Middle Ages* (London, 1995), 255–77, 271. This episode is quoted in this volume by Clare Pilsworth, 'Miracles, Missionaries and Manuscripts in Eighth-Century Southern Germany', 67–76. For some understanding of the vagueness of 'women's problems' in more recent times see Edward Shorter, *Women's Bodies: a Social History of Women's Encounter with Health, Ill-Health and Medicine* (London, 1991).

18 *The* Trotula: *a Medieval Compendium of Women's Medicine*, ed. and transl. Monica H. Green (Philadelphia, PA, 2001), 80–3, 118–19, 124–5, 132–3; *Obras Médicas de Pedro Hispano*, ed. Maria Helena da Rocha Pereira (Coimbra, 1973), 348–51.

19 *The* Surgery *of Theodoric, ca A.D. 1267*, transl. Eldridge Campbell and James Colton, 2 vols in 1 (New York, 1955–60), 1: 55–65, 2: 143–5.

precisely from the kind of spring described by Domingas Rodrigues.[20] According to all these works, nosebleeds were indeed immediately life-threatening and more likely to be suffered by men, since women normally lost excess blood through menstruation, and bloody flux weakened women over a long period of time. Miracles can therefore be backed up by contemporary medical theory to some extent.

The fact remains that the account of Domingas Rodrigues's cure appears to have been manipulated – the addition of the chandler, 'the masters of medicine' – which suggests that hers and the hagiographer's understanding of illness may have differed. To return to the first miracle cited, that of Domingas Pires who prayed to Gil de Santarém as a physician of the soul and the body: was it her emphasis or the shrine recorder's that he had cured many by 'the art of medicine' and 'word and prayer'? The problem with Gil's cult is that he and many of his fellow brethren were physicians. Remember that some of the 'useless' physicians consulted by the bleeding Maria Domingas had been friars. In fact numerous people in Santarém went to the convent seeking medical treatment rather than a miracle cure. For example, another Domingas Pires brought her son João to the friar-physicians Andre and Bernardo because he was suffering a violent nosebleed. They ordered her to go home and prepare a prescription they gave her, adding as an afterthought that she could also get some earth from Gil's tomb and tie it in a bag around the child's neck. This she did (though she also intended to take the medical advice) but 'they had not gone more than thirty paces when the boy's stream of blood stopped'.[21]

Miracles like this suggest that people, in Santarém at least, did know what to expect from 'the art of medicine': prescriptions, examination, health advice and even counselling – a woman called Maria Soeira, terrified by demonic visions, confessed regularly to brother Andre, whose role, whether as priest, counsellor, physician, appears ill-defined.[22] Words of guidance and learning, and a form of ritual interaction, were expected elements in the patient-practitioner relationship in the Middle Ages as today.[23] The Dominican Order also knew what 'the

20 Peter Murray Jones, *Medieval Medicine in Illuminated Manuscripts* (London, 1998), 98.

21 *AS*, 504–7.

22 Ibid., 500–3.

23 Darrel W. Amundsen and Gary B. Ferngren, 'Evolution of the Patient–Practitioner Relationship: Antiquity through the Renaissance', in Earl E. Shelp, ed., *The Clinical Encounter: the Moral Fabric of the Patient-Physician Relationship* (Dordrecht and Boston, MA, 1983), 1–46; Michael R. McVaugh, 'Bedside Manners in the Middle Ages', *Bulletin of the History of Medicine* 71 (1997), 201–23.

art of medicine' meant because on several occasions they prohibited friars from examining the pulses and urines of the laity and proscribed the use of compound medicines such as laxatives and electuaries.[24] These prohibitions appear to express anxiety about medical professionalism – as represented by expensive drugs and urine analysis –, rather than a ban on medical practice *per se*. Numerous friars had medical interests and the surgeon Teodorico Borgognoni, mentioned above, was himself a Dominican. Gil's brethren, who evidently ran an effective local medical practice, were perhaps the target of Dominican legislation. It is possible then that Domingas Pires understood what she was talking about when she mentioned Gil's dual role, but it also seems likely that the friars emphasized Gil's medical identity. His miracles are unusually positive about physicians: although the hagiographer used the *topos* of the failed practitioner, only once was he described as ignorant.[25] Several patients tried a combination of religious and medical healing at the same time, and were sometimes responsible for the failure of treatment: for example, a surgeon successfully treated a child with a skull fracture, but Gil had to miraculously heal the haemorrhage provoked later by the infant's restlessness.[26]

The medical emphasis in Gil's cult means that it may not be typical. However, it can be argued that the *topos* of the despairing physician found in all four cults analysed here could not work unless there was viable local competition in the form of medical practitioners. Why add the reference to 'masters of medicine' to the record of Domingas Rodrigues's cure at Isabel's tomb otherwise? Evidence from across Europe suggests that many sick people accessed medical care before going to the shrine and by reading between the lines we can put together a reasonable picture of local health provision.[27] The fact that a physician witnessed Domingas's cure suggests that there was a level of cooperation in shrines that we cannot always determine. We should remember that many physicians were clerics during this period and

24 *Acta capitulorum provincialium ordinis Fratrum Praedicatorum: première province de Provence, province romaine, province d'Espagne (1239–1302)*, ed. C. Douais, 2 vols (Toulouse, 1894), 1: 34, 61; 2: 493, 610, 543; *Acta capitulorum generalium ordinis praedicatorum*, ed. Benedikt Maria Reichert, Monumenta Ordinis Fratrum Praedicatorum Historica 3, 9 vols (Rome, 1898–1904), 1: 58.

25 *AS*, 492–4.

26 Ibid., 484–5.

27 Finucane, *Miracles and Pilgrims*, 60–99.

they were increasingly involved in canonization processes in the late Middle Ages.[28]

* * *

Medical influence also appears in medieval cults in subtler form. The giving of tomb earth or dust in water and the tying of little bags of dust around the neck, found in these Portuguese cults, is reminiscent of medical preparations and amulets.[29] Saints could also appear in visions to carry out quasi-surgical operations or give medical advice. Certainly Gil acted like this but so did Thomas Becket and Dominic, for whom no medical interests can be documented.[30] There are other examples of the saint touching impaired organs. A deaf and dumb woman had her ears tapped by Vincent in a vision,[31] a man with toothache was given a blow in the mouth by one of the Martyrs of Morocco,[32] and Isabel healed a wounded leper with egg white.[33] After curing a blind man by anointing his eyes with oil and making the sign of the cross, Gil was asked by a friar-physician why he went against medical advice. Gil answered that faith was stronger than art, comparing himself to Christ who also anointed the eyes of the blind *contra medicorum regulas*.[34] What is interesting is that the following century the French surgeon Henri de Mondeville (d. *c.*1320) understood this biblical image to mean that Christ acted as a surgeon.[35] We have here the very old image of *Christus medicus* (or *Chirurgicus*) that can be traced back at least to the second century CE. Throughout the Middle Ages, theologians, even those who disapproved of complex medical treatments, used medical analogies in their writings. What happened in the late Middle Ages was that physi-

28 Cornelius O'Boyle, *The* Art of Medicine: *Medical Teaching at the University of Paris, 1250–1400* (Leiden, 1998), 45–52; William J. Courtenay, 'Curers of Body and Soul: Medical Doctors as Theologians', in Peter Biller and Joseph Ziegler, eds, *Religion and Medicine in the Middle Ages* (York, 2001), 69–75; Joseph Ziegler, 'Practitioners and Saints: Medical Men in Canonization Processes in the Thirteenth to Fifteenth Centuries', *Social History of Medicine* 12 (1999), 191–225.

29 Valerie I. J. Flint, *The Rise of Magic in Early Medieval Europe* (Oxford, 1991), 243–50, 301–28; Finucane, *Miracles and Pilgrims*, 62–3, 89, 94.

30 *AS*, 520–1; *Legenda sancti Dominici*, ed. A. Walz, Monumenta Ordinis Fratrum Praedicatorum Historica 16 (Rome, 1935), 355–433, 432–3; Finucane, *Miracles and Pilgrims*, 67–8.

31 *Vicente*, 82–5.

32 Fernandes, *Livro dos milagres*, 134.

33 Nunes, 'Vida e milagres de Dona Isabel', 1378–9.

34 *AS*, 414–5.

35 Simone C. Macdougall, 'The Surgeon and the Saints: Henri de Mondeville on Divine Healing', *Journal of Medieval History* 26 (2000), 253–67, 257–8.

cians and surgeons like Mondeville, Borgognoni, Petrus Hispanus, and the Catalan surgeon, Arnau de Vilanova (d. 1311), began to use these images to promote their own professions.[36] This was a time when the medical profession was growing in confidence and prestige, but prominent physicians had always attracted negative attention: the adverse criticism in miracles compares well with that found in Pliny's *Natural History* in the first century or Chaucer's *Canterbury Tales* in the fourteenth.[37] This is another reason why we should beware of accepting scathing comments in miracles at face value. Physicians and saints competed for clients in what historians have called a 'medical marketplace', so we should expect a certain amount of lampooning and self-promoting.[38]

Indeed, it is now established that the criticism went both ways. A recent article on Mondeville revealed his highly critical attitude towards the cult of the saints. He condemned the credulity of the common people who attributed the cures of specific ailments to the saints.[39] In this he pre-empted the arguments of the sixteenth-century surgeon and reformer Paracelsus (d. 1541) who denounced common beliefs about the diseases of St Vitus's Dance and St Anthony's Fire.[40] It is possible that other medieval physicians shared these beliefs, but it should not be forgotten that popular medical compendia included prayers, amulets, incantations and magic stones, and both these and more learned treatises often began with theological prefaces.[41] Medical and surgical cures that occurred against all expectation could be attributed to the skill of the practitioner, but ultimately their cause was God. In these cases the practitioner interceded with God on the patient's behalf in much the same way as the saint interceded on a supplicant's. One of the most influential biblical texts in this debate, Ecclesiasticus

36 Joseph Ziegler, *Medicine and Religion c.1300: the Case of Arnau de Vilanova* (Oxford, 1998), 176–267.

37 Pliny the Elder, *Natural History: a Selection*, transl. John F. Healy (London, 1991), 263–7; Geoffrey Chaucer, *The Canterbury Tales*, ed. A. C. Cawley with revisions by Malcolm Andrew (1st publ. 1958, revised edn London, 1996), 13–14.

38 Michael R. McVaugh, *Medicine before the Plague: Practitioners and their Patients in the Crown of Aragon, 1285–1345* (Cambridge, 1993), 35–67, 136–8; Katharine Park, *Doctors and Medicine in Early Renaissance Florence* (Princeton, NJ, 1985), 85–117.

39 Macdougall, 'The Surgeon and the Saints', 263.

40 Charles Webster, 'Paracelsus Confronts the Saints: Miracles, Healing and the Secularization of Magic', *Social History of Medicine* 7 (1995), 403–21.

41 Cornelius O'Boyle, 'Medicine, God and Aristotle in the Early Universities: Prefatory Prayers in Late Medieval Medical Commentaries', *Bulletin of the History of Medicine* 66 (1992), 185–209.

38, 1–15, declares that the physician and the herbs of the earth were created by God to heal the pains of humankind and should therefore be honoured. Physicians of the soul interpreted these words spiritually in sermons, and physicians of the body interpreted them both literally and spiritually in medical writings. Many less learned people could well have been confused by these complex arguments.[42]

It seems likely that whatever the problems are with miracle analysis, Domingas Pires did have an understanding of what it meant to pray to someone who had healed by 'the art of medicine' and 'word and prayer'. Essentially, the difference between these things appeared largely cosmetic through much of the Middle Ages. This does not mean that some theologians and physicians did not try to demarcate the difference, but the fact remains that there was a blurring of the lines at many levels of understanding, including that of the majority of people who went to shrines. A lot of research has been done on the relationship between the academic physician and the theologian; it is now necessary to focus future investigations on the attitudes and experiences of more ordinary people in their pursuit of health. Miracles provide historians with one of the few opportunities to do this.

University of Durham

42 Ziegler, *Medicine and Religion*, 231–40.

MIRACULOUS CRUCIFIXES IN LATE MEDIEVAL ITALY

by KATHERINE L. JANSEN*

IN the year 1206, as Saint Francis was walking near the church of San Damiano, just outside the walls of Assisi, he was suddenly overcome by an urge to enter the dilapidated sanctuary. Upon entering, in the words of his first hagiographer,

> he fell down before the crucifix in devout and humble supplication; and smitten by unusual visitations, he found himself other than he had been when he entered. While he was thus affected, something unheard of before happened to him: the painted image of Christ crucified moved its lips and spoke. Calling him by name it said: 'Francis, go repair my house, which as you see, is falling completely to ruin'.[1]

The actual crucifix, whose head is angled in slight relief from the body, has hung in the church of Santa Chiara since 1260 [fig. 1]. Wishing to honour the miraculous object, the impending saint inaugurated a tradition of devotion to the enormous painted crucifix: 'Right away he gave a certain priest some money to buy a lamp and oil, lest the sacred image should be deprived of the due honour of a light even for a moment'.[2]

The account describes the events of that day as nothing short of miraculous:

> What a wonderful thing and a thing unheard of in our times! Who is not astonished at these things? Who has ever heard like things? Who would doubt that Francis, returning now to his native city, appeared crucified, when, though he had not yet outwardly

* I am grateful to Catholic University of America for a faculty grant-in-aid which subsidized the publication of the photographs for this article.

[1] Thomas of Celano, *Vita secunda*, transl. Placid Hermann, O.F.M., *The Second Life of St Francis*, in Marion A. Habig, ed., *St Francis of Assisi, Writings and Early Biographies: English Omnibus of the Sources for the Life of St. Francis* (4th rev. edn, Chicago, IL, 1983), 359–543, ch. vi, par. 10, 370. The Latin text can be found in multiple editions; I have used *S. Francisci Assisiensis vita et miracula additis opusculis liturgicis auctore fr. Thoma de Celano*, ed. Édouard d'Alençon (Rome, 1906). For the other versions of the *Life*, see *BHL* 3095–3136.

[2] Celano, *Vita secunda*, 370.

Fig. 1 Unknown Artist. Painted crucifix, S. Chiara, Assisi, Italy. Photo: Alinari/Art Resource, NY

completely renounced the world, Christ had spoken to him from the wood of the cross in a new and unheard miracle?[3]

It is worth noting that these words are drawn not from Thomas of Celano's first *Life* of St Francis, written for the saint's canonization in 1228, but from the same author's second *Life* of the saint composed between 1246 and 1247 at the behest of the master general of the Franciscan Order, Crescentius of Jesi, in order to take into account new biographical materials that had come to light during the intervening years.[4]

It was clearly a crucial moment in Francis's conversion narrative and Celano's revised *Vita* emphasizes this point through editorial intervention that stresses the singular and miraculous nature of the event. He was also careful to highlight how it fortified Francis with a mission – to repair the universal Church, as Bonaventure would later interpret it.[5] Significantly, Bonaventure also included an account of the miraculous crucifix in his *Legenda Maior*, which became the official *Vita* of the saint in 1263. From the *Legenda Maior* the episode passed quickly into visual representations of Saint Francis's *Life*, most notably into the Assisi master's *Vita*-cycle (comprising twenty-eight scenes of which the San Damiano speaking crucifix is the fourth), painted in the upper church of the Basilica of San Francesco at Assisi between 1295 and 1310 [fig. 2].[6] Celano also fashioned this moment as one that irrevocably altered Francis's being, indeed his very identity – 'he found himself other than he had been when he entered'. A new man, transformed and armed with a mandate from Christ, Francis was now equipped to endure the forthcoming struggles with his family, which would inevitably ensue over the renunciation of his patrimony.

This type of miraculous narrative – passages that hagiographers and artists often depict as transformative moments in the lives of the saints – is the focus of this essay, which will examine later medieval hagiography that recounts the words and deeds of miraculously animated

3 Ibid.

4 For the addition of the new material, see Habig, ed., *Omnibus*, 186–9.

5 *Legenda Maior*, transl. *Major Life of St. Francis*, in Habig, ed., *Omnibus*, 627–787, ch. 2, 640, of which over four-hundred manuscripts survive; see John Fleming, *An Introduction to the Franciscan Literature of the Middle Ages* (Chicago, 1977), 45.

6 For a discussion of the dating, see James Stubblevine, *Assisi and the Rise of Vernacular Art* (New York, 1985), 16 and 39, n. 2.

Fig. 2 School of Giotto. Scene from fresco cycle: St Francis in prayer before the speaking crucifix of S. Damiano. Upper Church, Basilica of S. Francesco, Assisi, Italy. Photo: Alinari/Art Resource, NY

crucifixes and their interlocutors.[7] To frame the problem even more tightly, my evidence will be limited to literary accounts depicting actual physical, tangible artifacts, objects perceived as works of art – not mystical visions of Christ crucified – which intruded suddenly in the

7 The fundamental work on painted crosses in Italy is still Evelyn Sandberg Vavalà, *La croce dipinta italiana e l'iconografia della passione* (Verona, 1929, repr. 1980).

lives of the saints, serving as agents of the sacred.[8] My aim is to tease out the meanings of these stories for contemporaries and to show in what manner they are revealing of the textual communities for whom they were written. In so doing, this paper will demonstrate that these narratives should be read on at least two levels. The first tells us what the hagiographer wants his audience to know about the saint. It highlights the critical junctures – moments of doubt and crisis – in which miraculous crucifixes were believed to have intervened in the lives of the saints to resolve the spiritual exigencies at hand. The narratives furthermore demonstrate the human frailty of the saints and how even their footsteps sometimes faltered on the arduous path to sanctity. The second level of reading, focusing more on the literary production of the narrative, discloses something of the underlying politics and the larger spiritual landscape that shaped the resulting *Vita* or legend. Such an approach perforce suspends judgement on the historicity of the miracle: I accept miracles as such because medieval audiences accepted them as such. Hagiography, then, can and should be read as a vital witness to the spiritual aspirations of both its authors and audiences.[9]

The hagiographical texts under consideration here are mainly of Italian provenance but the phenomenon they represent is not unique to Italy.[10] Nonetheless, I will argue that it is not insignificant that many of these narratives emerge from the soil of the Italian peninsula in the thirteenth and fourteenth centuries, that rich matrix which gave rise to the mendicant movement.

[8] André Vauchez has looked at the phenomenon of animated sacred images – not speaking crucifixes, however – in 'Les Images saintes: représentations iconographiques et manifestations du sacré', in idem, *Saints, prophètes et visionnaires: le pouvoir surnaturel au Moyen Age* (Paris, 1999), 79–91, Italian transl. as 'Le immagini sante: rappresentazioni iconografiche e manifestazioni del sacro', in *Santi, profeti e visionari: il soprannaturale nel medioevo* (Bologna, 2000), 81–94, for which reference I am grateful to Nicole Bériou. On this topic, particularly for the wonder-working image of the Madonna dell'Impruneta, see Richard Trexler, 'Florentine Religious Experience: the Sacred Image', *Studies in the Renaissance* 7 (1972), 7–41. For sculpted Umbrian miraculous crucifixes in particular, see Elvio Lunghi, *La Passione degli Umbri: crocifissi di legno in Valle Umbra tra Medioevo e Rinascimento* (Foligno, 2000), for which I thank Joanna Cannon.

[9] Jeffrey Hamburger makes a similar point in relation to visual devotional material; see 'The Visual and the Visionary: the Image in Late Medieval Monastic Devotion', in idem, *The Visual and the Visionary: Art and Female Spirituality in Late Medieval Germany* (New York, 1998), 111–48.

[10] I am grateful to the audience at the Ecclesiastical History Society conference, and particularly to Michael Goodich, who suggested a number of other miraculous crucifix narratives, which I shall consider more fully when I return to this topic at a later date.

* * *

Notwithstanding Thomas of Celano's claims to the contrary, the San Damiano crucifix is not our first example in hagiographical literature of a polychrome Christ-figure animated by a sacral presence. The earliest example of which I am aware is told in relation to the dramatic conversion of the young knight, Giovanni Gualberto (*c*.995–1073) sometime in the early decades of the eleventh century. One of Giovanni's earliest vitae, written by Atto of Pistoia circa 1140, recounts what at first seems to be yet another tale of Italian violence and vendetta in medieval Florence.[11] One day while Giovanni was outside the city, riding in the hills with his retainers, he came across the killer of one of his close relatives. According to the rules of vendetta still very much operative in this period, Giovanni, as the descendant of the murdered man, could have avenged the death of his relative, killing the murderer with impunity on the spot. It would have been easy for him to have done so: the encounter seems to have taken place in a rather narrow passageway and the assassin, seeing no way out, had dismounted from his horse, prostrated himself face down upon the ground and flung his arms out in the form of a cross. But instead of inflicting the mortal blow, Giovanni, moved by the sight of the terrorized man splayed out before him, invited his sworn enemy to rise and pass by in peace, assuring him of forgiveness. After this incident, Giovanni and his party arrived at the church of San Miniato where the young knight knelt before a crucifix to pray. The crucifix, for its part, nodded his head toward Giovanni, 'as if to render thanks for having had mercy on his enemy out of reverence for Him'.[12] Atto concludes the account by remarking that the cross, 'on account of such a great miracle, is even now preserved with great vigilance at the monastery of San Miniato'.[13] It should be noted that, like the San Damiano crucifix, this one also has a head angled in relief from its body [fig. 3].[14]

11 *BHL* 4397–4406. For the tangled relationship between the earliest *Vitae*, see Raffaello Volpini, 'Giovanni Gualberto', *Bibliotheca Sanctorum*, 13 vols (Rome, 1961–70), 6: 1012–29. For editions of the *Vitae*, see the edition by F. Baethgen, MGH.S 30.2 (1934), 1076–1110. Atto's opening paragraphs are interpolated into Baethgen's edition of the *Vita Iohannis Gualberti auctore abate Strumensi* because the first few folio pages of Strumi's *Vita* (contained in a unique exemplar) have been lost.

12 Ibid., par. 2–3, 1080.

13 Ibid.

14 Visual representation of the nodding crucifix does not seem to have entered the iconography of Giovanni Gualberto until the fourteenth century, well after the scene was established for Saint Francis's *Vita* cycles. According to recent research, the miraculous crucifix, translated in 1671 with great solemnity from San Miniato to the principal Vallombrosan

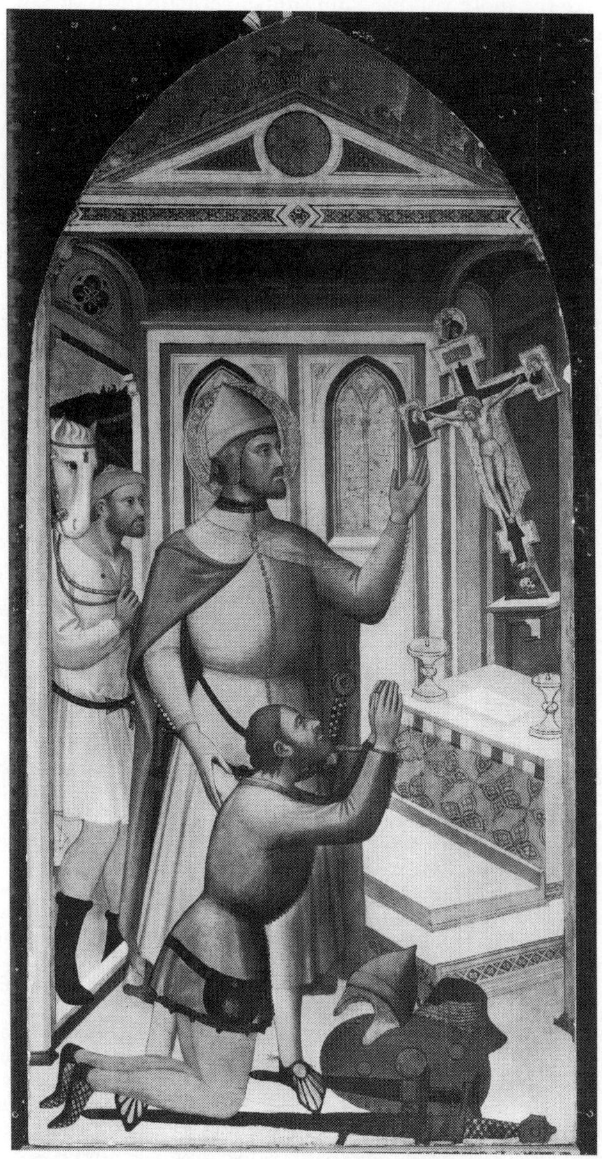

Fig. 3 Niccolò di Pietro Gerini. Panel painting: San Giovanni Gualberto and his enemy make peace before the miraculous crucifix of S. Miniato. Photo: The Metropolitan Museum of Art, NY, Gynne Andrews Fund, 1958

Unlike the more voluble San Damiano crucifix, that of San Miniato tacitly registered its approval of Giovanni's deed of Christian mercy in the language of gesture.[15] The results, however, were the same. Like Francis, after his miraculous encounter with a crucifix Giovanni's thoughts turned immediately and entirely to God. And although his family fiercely opposed his decision, Giovanni decided to enter the monastic life at San Miniato. Thus we have two miraculous crucifixes of central Italy that spoke to the saints – one in words, one in gesture – each of which either precipitated or authorized conversions to the religious life. Both seem to have intervened in the saints' lives to confirm their conversions and to steel them for the subsequent dramas, which in the medieval world inexorably followed when sons withdrew from the lives for which their families had destined them.[16]

Perhaps because the early manuscript tradition of the *Vita* of San Giovanni Gualberto was so circumscribed, his encounter with a miraculous crucifix seems not to have made a great impression on either the period's saints or their hagiographers, as we hear no more about this type of miraculous phenomenon until the thirteenth century, the age of the mendicants. But, beginning with Francis's supernatural experience at San Damiano, miraculous crucifixes now almost routinely intervene in the lives of the saints. Thus while André Vauchez is surely right to see the rise of animated sacred images in the later Middle Ages

church of the Santissima Trinità in Florence, turns out to be datable to no earlier than the thirteenth century; see Raffaello Volpini and Antonietta Cardinale, 'Giovanni Gualberto, Iconography', *Bibliotheca Sanctorum*, 6: 1029–32. For a description of the translation ceremony, see Emiliano Lucchesi, O.S.B., *Il crocifisso di S. Giovanni Gualberto e lo stendardo della Croce di S. Francesco di Sales* (Florence, 1937), 31–2.

15 It should be noted that in the same period, Bernard of Clairvaux (d. 1154), an author noted for his affective piety, received a much more affectionate gesture from a crucifix beneath which he was praying. Although his first hagiographers do not mention the event, Conrad of Eberbach in his *Exordium Magnum*, written at the turn of the century, describes the moment when Bernard, rapt in prayer, was received into the arms of the crucifix, which had detached its arms from the cross in order to embrace the supplicant saint. Conrad of Eberbach, *Exordium Magnum Cisterciense*, ed. B. Griesser (Rome, 1961), ch. vi, 102–3: 'De monacho spirituali qui vidit imaginem crucis sanctum patrem in oratione constitutum amplexantem', cited by Jean-Claude Schmitt, 'La Culture de l'imago', *Annales: Histoire, Sciences Sociales* 1 (1996), 3–36. For a catalogue of forty wooden crucifixes which have detachable arms enabling the deposition of the Christ-figure for Good Friday lamentation scenes, see G. and T. Taubert, 'Mittelalterliche Kruzifixe mit schwenkbaren Armen', *Zeitschrift des Deutschen Vereins für Kunstwissenschaft* 23 (1969), 79–121.

16 Tellingly, in the chapter immediately preceding his visit to San Damiano, Thomas of Celano recounts that Francis had to fend off questions from his friends about whether he was ready to marry: see *1 Cel.*, Habig, ed., *Omnibus*, ch. iii, 7.

as a substitute for the cult of relics,[17] I would suggest that the phenomenon of speaking crucifixes is a bit more complicated: mirroring the mendicants themselves, whose stock-in-trade was speech (specifically, preaching), the crucifixes of the later Middle Ages became in some sense the bearers of mendicant identity, as I will now endeavour to show.

* * *

To continue with the Franciscan Order, let me begin with Margaret of Cortona (1247–97), a penitent associated with the *Ordo Fratrum Minorum*. Like many of her penitent sisters of the period, Margaret divided her post-conversion life between prayer, religious devotions and performing works of charity. Notably, she was one of the founders of a hospital dedicated to succouring the poor and needy of Cortona. Margaret had come to the life of penance at about the age of twenty-five after having lived a somewhat unorthodox life. Possibly of peasant descent herself, she had lived openly and in some luxury in Montepulciano with her lover, a nobleman, with whom she had borne a son. After witnessing her lover's murder, she converted to the religious life. In 1272, with her son in tow, she arrived in Cortona and was taken in by two pious penitent women. She earned her keep there as a midwife.

In addition to her nursing and charitable activities, Margaret had a richly rewarding mystical life which took the form of visions in which she interacted with Christ, the Virgin and the saints. The progress of her spiritual life from penitential conversion to mystical perfection was the primary subject of her *Vita*, completed in 1307 by one of her intimate friends, also her spiritual director, the Franciscan Fra Giunta Bevegnati.[18]

It is noteworthy that an image of the crucified Christ played a central role in the development of Margaret's spiritual life.[19] Unlike the

[17] Vauchez, 'Le immagini sante', 83–4.

[18] *BHL* 5314. A critical edition, now superseding that in *ActaSS*, 3 February, 298–357, is *Legenda de vita et miraculis Beatae Margaritae de Cortona*, ed. Fortunato Iozelli, O.F.M. (Grottaferrata, 1997) [hereafter *Legenda BMC*].

[19] Recent scholarly opinion attributes it to a thirteenth-century Spanish master. It now hangs in a nineteenth-century altar, in the Church of Santa Margherita in Cortona, dedicated to the saint. It was translated there on 14 December 1602, as a prelude to yet another attempt by the commune to have its local holy woman canonized, which finally succeeded in the year 1728. For the sources and recent scholarship on the crucifix, see Laura Corti and Riccardo Spinelli, eds, *Margherita da Cortona: una storia emblematica di devozione narrata per testi e immagini* (Milan, 1998), and esp. Lunghi, *La Passione degli Umbri*, 65–90, for Margaret's rela-

flat painted *Christus triumphans* type associated with San Giovanni Gualberto and Saint Francis; it was, rather, a sculpted and polychrome *Christus patiens* – or more specifically a suffering gothic type that was then gaining prominence throughout the Italian peninsula. Fra Giunta tells us that sometime in the year 1277, when Margaret had been newly admitted to the Third Order of Saint Francis by Fra Ranaldo of Arezzo, the same friar witnessed Margaret in prayer before a crucifix which suddenly addressed her with these words: '*Quid vis, paupercula*?', to which Margaret, having been illuminated by the Holy Spirit, replied: 'I neither seek nor desire anything other than you, my Lord, Jesus'.[20]

Margaret, as we know from Fra Giunta's *Vita*, was generally a bundle of insecurities, most of them probably stemming from her somewhat chequered past. The encounter with the speaking crucifix initiated a number of visions that seemed to help her work through her relation to her notorious past, her penitential status, and its relationship to her salvation – all of which eventually culminated in a vision that would finally ease her anxious conscience. Fra Giunta's *Legenda* recounts that one day, while Margaret was taking communion, she heard Christ's voice encouraging her thus: 'Daughter, I will place you with the seraphim where the virgins aflame with love are found.'[21] Staggered as she was, Margaret nevertheless managed to summon a reply: 'Lord, how is this possible if I was so great a sinner?' To which the Lord responded: 'Daughter your many punishments will purify your soul of every impurity . . . your contrition will restore your virginal purity.'[22] Margaret, chary even at the promise of such great consolation, turned to Christ and posed yet another question, this one disclosing all her anxieties about personal salvation. 'Lord', she asked, 'have you also put the Magdalen in celestial glory among the virgins?' To which the Lord replied reassuringly: 'With the exception of the Virgin Mary and the martyr Catherine, no one in the chorus of virgins is greater than the Magdalen.'[23] I have written elsewhere that hagiography and the

tionship to this crucifix. See also John Paoletti, 'Wooden Sculpture in Italy as a Sacral Presence', *Artibus et Historiae* 26 (1992), 85–100, with thanks again to Joanna Cannon. For the canonization, see Joanna Cannon and André Vauchez, *Margherita of Cortona and the Lorenzetti: Sienese Art and the Cult of a Holy Woman in Medieval Tuscany* (University Park, PA, 1999), 5.

20 *Legenda BMC*, I, 1a, 180. One post-medieval source (Pietro Strozzi) dates the event to the year 1267, an impossibility as Margaret had yet to arrive in Cortona by that year; see Corti and Spinelli, *Margherita da Cortona*, 197.

21 *Legenda BMC*, IV, 15, 231–2.

22 Ibid.

23 Ibid.

visionary accounts it contains reveal that Mary Magdalen's apotheosis among the virgins provided comfort for many women troubled over the (apparently) irretrievable loss of their own virginity.[24] The model of the penitent Mary Magdalen provided hope that this loss was not an insurmountable obstacle in the quest for salvation and its divine rewards. Mary Magdalen's presence among the virgins seems to have provided inspiration for Margaret of Cortona's claim to a place in the heavenly choir of virgins, despite her scandalous past. It was the second of three visions invoking Mary Magdalen in which Christ reassures Margaret of her status. In the final vision, the Lord introduces Margaret to Mary Magdalen with the words, 'this is my beloved daughter'.[25] And Margaret's conscience was at peace at last. Tellingly, it was the speaking crucifix of Cortona that seems to have prompted this series of mystical colloquies with Christ, which, in the event, confirmed for the anxious Margaret that her new identity as a penitent was acceptable to the Lord.

In addition to reassuring Margaret, the speaking crucifix of Cortona also served Fra Giunta's purposes in making Margaret a truly Franciscan saint. Joanna Cannon has argued that one of the goals of Fra Giunta's *Vita* was to exalt the Franciscan Order and to claim Margaret as its own.[26] Clearly, the literary construction of the miraculous crucifix narrative bears out this assertion. Indeed, this episode is so important to Fra Giunta's narrative structure that he opens his *Legenda* with it. A Franciscan audience would have immediately associated Margaret's miraculous speaking crucifix with that of their founder, particularly when the Order is not once but twice invoked in that first paragraph. And if that were not enough, Christ's salutation of Margaret as '*paupercula*' (poor little one) resonates with associations to holy poverty that in turn call to mind Francis's familiar term of endearment, 'il poverello', less familiar perhaps in the Latin as '*pauperculus*', but important nonetheless as it is an appellation that from the earliest period was associated with Francis himself.[27]

All this was Fra Giunta's way of claiming Cortona's holy woman for

24 'Like a Virgin: the Meaning of the Magdalen for Female Penitents of Later Medieval Italy', *Memoirs of the American Academy in Rome* 45 (2000), 131–52.

25 *Legenda BMC*, VII, 32, 344.

26 Cannon and Vauchez, *Margherita of Cortona*, 25.

27 The first evidence of the appellation comes from Francis himself in a letter written to Lady Jacoba of Settesoli (*13 Ep. 1*) as he lay dying at the Porziuncola. The salutation reads: 'Dominae Iacobae, servae Altissimi, frater Franciscus, pauperculus Iesu Christi, salutem et societatem spiritus sancti in Domino Iesu Christo': *Concordantiae verbales opusculorum S. Francisci et S. Clarae Assisiensium*, ed. I. Boccali (Assisi, 1976), 121.

the Franciscan Order. For it must be remembered that despite Fra Giunta's claims otherwise, the Third Order of Franciscan penitents had not yet formally been instituted at the time that Margaret was casting her life in a penitential mode. That did not occur until 1289, when the bull *super montem* endeavoured to impose order on the disorderly penitential movement.[28] It bears remarking that the penitential movement of Margaret's day was still very much in a fluid stage, and those who undertook to live in that fashion were very much 'free-lancers', as Augustine Thompson memorably describes them.[29] Given this rather *ad hoc* situation, it is not surprising then that Fra Giunta should have taken care to pour the unconventional contents of Margaret's life into a decorous Franciscan mould. In fashioning a Franciscan saint, Fra Giunta in this one passage modelled Margaret's *Life* directly on two pillars of Franciscan identity: the founder's relationship to Christ and to holy poverty. Fra Giunta's miraculous crucifix narrative bestowed on Margaret's rather improvised and irregular life a truly Franciscan identity.

* * *

From early Franciscan hagiography, we now turn to three important saints' *Vitae* produced by the Dominican Order, beginning with the *Life* of Thomas Aquinas (*c.*1225–74) written by William of Tocco.[30] William's *Vita* of Thomas, published in 1323 for the canonization of St Thomas, was based on evidence that he had collected beginning in 1317, when he was commissioned by the Order (along with Robert of Benevento) to gather depositions for the canonization inquest.[31] Tocco's narrative is based on the testimony of one Dominic of Caserta, a lay sacristan at the church of San Domenico Maggiore in Naples, where Thomas made his profession and spent both the early and final years of his career.[32] Chapter 34 of the *Vita* recounts that one night Dominic of Caserta noticed Thomas's absence from both his studio and

28 See Cannon and Vauchez, *Margherita of Cortona*, 2–3.

29 I cite from Thompson's new and important book, which he has kindly shared with me in manuscript, *Cities of God: the Religion of the Italian Communes, c.1125–c.1325*, (University Park, PA, 1995).

30 *BHL* 8149–68. I have learnt much about the cult of Saint Thomas from the work of Charlotte Allen, Ph.D. candidate at the Catholic University of America.

31 Edmund Colledge, O.S.A., 'The Legend of St. Thomas Aquinas', in *St. Thomas Aquinas 1274–1974: Commemorative Studies* foreword by Etienne Gilson, 2 vols (Toronto, 1974), 1: 13–28, 18.

32 *Ystoria sancti Thome de Aquino de Guillaume de Tocco (1323)*, ed. Claire le Brun-Gouanvic (Toronto, 1996), 162, n. 3.

Fig. 4 Unknown Artist. Panel painting: crucifixion scene from S. Domenico Maggiore, Naples, Italy. Photo: Archivio dell'Arte/Luciano Pedicini, Naples

the office of matins, an event so unusual that it aroused the sacristan's suspicions. Undertaking to investigate the matter, he happened into the chapel of San Nicola, where to his astonishment he found Thomas rapt in tearful prayer, levitating two cubits in the air. As if the sight of the corpulent angelic doctor hovering weightlessly above the ground were not miracle enough, the sacristan also reported to William of Tocco that the crucifix in the chapel spoke the following words: '*Thoma, bene scripsisti de me, quam recipies a me pro tuo labore mercedem?*', to which Thomas replied: '*Domine, non nisi te*' [fig. 4].[33] Not insignificantly, his hagiographer added, Thomas then wrote the third part of the *Summa* which treated Christ's passion and resurrection, a fitting response to this miraculous encounter. Tocco further noted that it was one of the last things he wrote, a miraculous sign, which clearly signalled Christ's approbation of Thomas's *magnum opus*.[34] From Tocco's *Vita*, this scene very quickly found its way into Thomas's iconography, particularly the imagery that issued from southern and central Italy, notably the Kingdom of Naples and Tuscany, both provinces which housed important Dominican *studia generalia*, institutions which had an interest in promoting the sanctity of their learned patron [fig. 5].[35]

Unlike the youthful Giovanni Gualberto, whose conversion to the religious life was sparked by the gesture of the Christ-figure on the cross, or Francis of Assisi whose agonizingly slow religious conversion was hastened by the lapidary words of the San Damiano crucifix that crystallized his mission for him, or even Margaret of Cortona who needed reassurance that her penitential life was pleasing to the Lord, Thomas Aquinas was near the end of his life, more than thirty years of it spent in the habit of the Dominican Order, when he experienced a miracle of the crucifix.[36] But it was a point in his life when he too seems to have been beleaguered by doubts – doubts of a different order, but doubts all the same. His worries centred on his theological writings,

33 Ibid.

34 Ibid., 161–2.

35 For the *studia* see M. Michèle Mulchahey, *'First the Bow is Bent in Study': Dominican Education before 1350* (Toronto, 1998). For Thomas's iconography, see George Kaftal, *Iconography of the Saints*, 4 vols (Florence, 1952–85), 1: *Iconography of the Saints in Tuscan Painting*, 977–88; 2: *Iconography of the Saints in Central and Southern Italy*, 1088–96; 3: *Iconography of the Saints in the Painting of North East Italy*, 973–84; 4: *Iconography of the Saints in the Painting of North West Italy*, 640–2.

36 Thomas made his profession at San Domenico Maggiore in Naples sometime in the years between 1238–44. From 1252–6 he studied at Paris and during the period 1256–9 and again in 1269–72 he lectured there as regent master. In 1272–4 he returned to Naples where he finished the *Summa*.

Fig. 5 Sassetta. Panel painting: St Thomas Aquinas presents his work to the crucifix of S. Domenico Maggiore. Pinacoteca, Vatican Museums, Vatican City. Photo: Alinari/Art Resource, NY

which his peers had neither accepted unequivocally during his lifetime, nor indeed immediately after his death. The most recent controversy in which he had become embroiled was in Paris in 1270 when some of his Aristotelian positions were attacked vigorously by John Pecham, Thomas's Franciscan counterpart at the university during his regency as Master of Theology from 1269–72. His propositions were condemned yet again three years after his death in 1277, this time in both Oxford and Paris.[37] Hence, the miracle in William of Tocco's *Vita* served a double narrative purpose. The speaking crucifix at San Domenico Maggiore surely provided the troubled theologian with much needed

[37] For the condemnations, see John F. Wippel, 'The Condemnations of 1270 and 1277', *Journal of Medieval and Renaissance Studies* 7 (1977), 169–201 and Roland Hissette, *Enquête sur les 219 articles condamnés à Paris le 7 mars 1277* (Louvain and Paris, 1977).

consolation and assurances about the veracity of his writings, intervening in Thomas's life at a moment of existential crisis, brought on perhaps by his effort to conclude his great work. The words of the incarnate Christ – the topic on which Thomas was then not incidentally engaged in explicating – provided the doubtful theologian with much needed reassurances from the ultimate judge himself. Such timely consolation, according to Tocco, sanctioned the completion of Thomas's defining and enduring text, the *Summa theologiae*, after which he wrote no more. Tocco's narrative also served to underscore the orthodoxy of Thomas's writings, which by this time – 1323 – had at last been accepted by the universal Church, clearing the way for the canonization of the Dominican theologian. Thus, this passage can be read as the Order's public vindication of the writings of Saint Thomas Aquinas. It is important to note that Thomas's canonization hinged not only on his virtuous life but also on his theological teachings. And what better judge of his theological corpus was there than Christ himself, who commended Thomas with the words: 'Thomas, you have written well about me.' It is probably not insignificant that Christ's praise of Thomas's theology appears not once but twice in Tocco's *Vita*, albeit in a slightly different form. In Chapter 52 of the *Vita*, Tocco describes an event that seems to have taken place perhaps in Rome at a time when the Parisian masters were disputing questions pertaining to eucharistic theology. Thomas brought his own writings on the matter into the chapel and placed them upon the altar. He then prayed beneath the crucifix for guidance. No sooner had he begun to pray than he was again elevated into the air. This time Christ appeared to him standing on his manuscript proclaiming, '*Bene de hoc mei corporis sacramento scripsisti*', yet another commendation of Thomas personally, to say nothing of the Dominican Order which his theological writings represented.[38]

Just as the speaking crucifix in Naples served the double function of assuaging the doubts of Thomas Aquinas and providing his writings

38 *Ystoria*, ed. Le Brun-Gouanvic, ch. 52, 187–9. A later, early-modern tradition claims yet a third '*bene scripsisti*' commendation for Thomas, this one occurring at Orvieto, where he is said to have written the office of *Corpus Domini*, on which see Colledge, 'The Legend', 24, who cites Giovanni Michele Pio, *Delle vite degli uomini illustri di San Domenico* (Bologna, 1607–13), 226–7. A mid fourteenth-century scene from the fresco cycle by Ugolino di Prete Ilario in the Cappella del Corporale in the Duomo at Orvieto also suggests an Orvieto miracle of this sort. Thomas is here represented in an act of prayer beneath a cross that hangs above an altar on which a chalice and the eucharistic wafer are prominently displayed. The scene is reproduced in Lunghi, *La Passione degli Umbri*, fig. 21.

with an '*imprimatur Christi*', as it were, so too did the crucifixes which spoke to another celebrated Dominican, Peter of Verona, also known as Peter Martyr (1205–52). There are two accounts of separate incidents in which crucifixes spoke to Peter; it should be noted, however, that none of the earliest *Vitae*, which date from the second half of the thirteenth century, mentions these miraculous events.[39] But in an account of the saint's miracles, which Dondaine dates to circa 1316, Bérenger of Landore recounts an episode that took place in Milan, presumably at the Dominican convent of Sant'Eustorgio. Just as William of Tocco was careful to report a witness to the miracle of the speaking crucifix at San Domenico Maggiore, so too Bérenger scrupulously prefaces his miracle account by explaining that this wondrous event was witnessed by a friar, who happened to be standing near the threshold of the chapel on the night when the crucifix spoke to Friar Peter. Bérenger further relates that Peter had prostrated himself before an image of the crucified one and commended himself to Christ lamenting that he was unsure that he would be able to withstand the tribulations that awaited him. And from the cross Christ responded to him with this rhetorical query: 'Friar Peter, what did I do to suffer on the cross? Thus you must have faith because I am with you and you will come to me with the crown of honour and glory'.[40] The crown to which the speaking crucifix referred was of course the martyr's crown, which Peter would

39 *BHL* 6721–6. Among the earliest *Vitae*, based almost entirely on Innocent IV's canonization bull, are those by Tommaso Agni da Lentini, of which I have used the fourteenth-century Italian edition, *S. Pietro Martire da Verona Leggenda di Fra Tommaso Agni da Lentini nel volgare trecentesco*, ed. Stefano Orlandi, O.P. (Florence, 1952) and Jacobus de Voragine, *Golden Legend.* For the most recent Latin critical edition, see Iacopo da Varazze, *Legenda Aurea*, ed. Giovanni Paolo Maggioni, 2 vols (Florence, 1998), I: 421–2. The standard English translation is *The Golden Legend: Readings on the Saints*, transl. William Granger Ryan, 2 vols (Princeton, NJ, 1993), I: 254–66. A. Dondaine, 'Saint Pierre Martyre', *Archivum Fratrum Praedicatorum* 23 (1953), 66–162, unravels the relationship between these and subsequent *Vitae.*

40 I wish to thank Donald Prudlo, Ph. D. candidate at the University of Virginia, Charlottesville, who is currently writing a dissertation on the cult of Saint Peter Martyr, for sharing with me the text from Trèves, Bibliothèque de la Ville, MS 1168, fol. 134r–v. On this manuscript, see Dondaine, 'Saint Pierre Martire', 128–30, who calls this anonymous tract after Bérenger of Landore, the Master General of the order 1312–17, under whom the miracle collection was probably compiled. The crucifix itself is mentioned in Galvano Fiamma's fourteenth-century chronicle of the Dominican Order as having been at the convent of Sant'Eustorgio in Milan at the 1229 chapter meeting: 'in capitulo erat ymago crucifixi, que interdum locuta est sancto Petro martyri' (Dondaine, 'Saint Pierre Martire', 160, n. 70). I have not yet been able to ascertain whether or not a crucifix associated with this miracle still survives at Sant'Eustorgio.

earn in 1252 when on the road from Como to Milan he was ambushed by two Cathar assassins who cleaved his head in two with an axe.[41]

Like Thomas, Peter seems to have been suffering from a crisis of confidence about his mission, particularly about the office of inquisitor that he had assumed in 1251. His years of disputations and preaching against the heretics had stirred up so much hostility and animosity that angry threats against him had almost become a routine event in his life. The words of the Milanese crucifix ministered to Peter at a moment of intense self-doubt. Bérenger tells us that Peter found Christ's words so heartening that his fears evaporated and he was henceforth able to tolerate the perils of office, to say nothing of the death-threats, which he regularly received. The speaking crucifix of Milan, then, served to alleviate Peter's fears by prophesying his martyrdom. But it also re-fashioned Peter in the Lord's image by likening his fate as a martyr to Christ's own passion.

Significantly, Antonino Pierozzi, Dominican archbishop of Florence, writing in about 1455, enriched the hagiographical tradition with yet another account of a speaking crucifix in his *Chronicae*, a world history to which a catalogue of saints' *Vitae* is appended. He relates a story of how the Order, in an effort to avoid scandal, had exiled Peter to a convent in Jesi in the Marches because certain brothers had claimed to have overheard female voices in his cell. In the spirit of humility, Fra Peter accepted his sentence without contest, but upon arriving in Jesi he threw himself on the mercy of the convent's crucifix, seeking to know why the Lord had allowed an innocent man such as himself to be judged and indeed punished so unjustly. To which the Lord responded: 'Peter, what crimes did I commit to be condemned to the cross with such opprobrium and faithlessness? Learn to bear all [your trials] equably by my example'.[42] Peter was comforted by these words and in the fullness of time the inquest revealed that those who had thought that they had heard 'women of the street' in his cell were mistaken; rather, what they had heard turned out to be the voices of the celestial virgin-martyrs of the Lord in colloquy with the future martyr.[43]

41 Perhaps because artists used Jacobus de Voragine's *Golden Legend* as source material which, as we have just seen, did not recount this episode, the scene does not appear in the iconography of the saint, who is nonetheless elsewhere readily identifiable by the knife plunged into his skull. For the iconography, see Kaftal, *Iconography of the Saints,* 1: 818–32; 2: 900–10; 3: 843–54; 4: 548–53.

42 Antoninus, *Chronicae*, 3 vols (Lyons, 1576), 'de Beato Petro Martyre', 3: 640.

43 Antonio Vivarini, in a mid fifteenth-century polyptych panel now in Berlin, illus-

Antonino closes his account of the miraculous crucifix of Jesi by informing his readers that 'to this day the image of that crucifix in the aforesaid convent is held in reverence and veneration'.[44]

Tellingly, the crisis narratives in the lives of the mendicant saints contemporaneously serve to emphasize Dominican identity. That is, the miraculous crucifixes which spoke to friars Thomas Aquinas and Peter of Verona each authorized functions by which Dominican identity was constructed. In the first case, the San Domenico Maggiore crucifix validated the teaching-function of Thomas Aquinas by commending his writings. From the outset, Saint Dominic had envisioned his new Order as teachers and preachers well schooled in theology, who thus armed with erudition and authority could preach the message of the Gospels. Thomas Aquinas embodied this mission, something that the Order itself had recognized as early as 1265 when it commissioned him to establish a *studium* in Rome at Santa Sabina. This *studium* was the Order's first attempt in the Roman Province to offer a programme in advanced theological instruction to its friars.[45] It is not without significance that Brother Thomas was chosen to create this programme: by the mid-1260s there was no one who better personified this aspect of Dominican mission or identity than Thomas Aquinas himself.

But it is also important to remember that the Order of Preachers emerged against the backdrop of Catharism, which also served to crystallize the Dominicans' identity as disputants of heresy, yet another important aspect of mendicant identity. Over the course of the thirteenth century, as the inquisition developed, they became even further identified as enemies of heresy, as the office of inquisitor fell to the Order whose training had best prepared them for the job. It was not an office beloved by the populace, as Peter of Verona well knew. Bérenger of Landore and Archbishop Antonino each demonstrate how the words of the Christ-figure assuaged Peter's anxieties about his role as inquisitor by promising him the honour and glory bestowed by the martyr's

trates the visitation by the holy virgins overheard by Dominican friars. The image is reproduced as fig. 1109 in Kaftal, *Iconography of the Saints*, 3: 846.

44 Ibid. In a *furtum sacrum* carried out in 1479, a Dominican friar spirited the crucifix away from Jesi to the convent of San Domenico in Chioggia where it is still venerated. An image of the crucifix, which is over four metres high and hangs over the high altar awaiting funds for restoration, can be seen on line at http://www.savevenice.org/site/pp.asp?c=9eIHKWMHF&b=6807, then click under current projects, then crucifix (consulted 27/12/04). For the 'theft', see Dondaine, 'Saint Pierre Martire', 160, n. 69.

45 For the Santa Sabina mission, see Mulchahey, *'First the Bow is Bent'*, 278–306.

crown. Bérenger's narrative explicitly, and Antonino's implicitly, each cast Peter as an imitator of Christ, whose ultimate sacrifice would testify to the power of the Faith. Each of these narratives strive to show the reader some very human aspects of the saints – how even they succumbed to self-doubt about their missions – but were rescued from the depths of spiritual despair by the soothing words of Christ. But the passages also reveal a Dominican context that was intent on fashioning its saints as learned teachers and guardians of orthodoxy whose vocations had been authorized by the words of Christ himself.[46]

The two-tiered theme of personal crisis and Dominican self-fashioning at the foot of the cross continues in the final *Vita* under consideration, that of Saint Catherine of Siena (1347–80).[47] Like Margaret of Cortona, Catherine was a penitent or what in fourteenth-century Siena was known as a *mantellata*. Other than the Orders with which they were associated, what made Catherine's penitential life quite distinct from Margaret's was that by the time Catherine entered the Dominican Sisters of Penance in the second half of the fourteenth century, the institutional framework for her to do so actually existed. Nonetheless, she certainly seems to have tailored the existing penitential garment to her own particular specifications. Catherine too was an ecstatic mystic who carried out an active ministry in the world. Among many other charitable activities, she nursed lepers as well as the sick and dying, comforted prisoners awaiting execution, served as a peace-maker amongst feuding families, and even advised local notables and crowned heads of Europe, including several popes.[48] When she met her confessor and future hagiographer Raymond of Capua she was a woman of twenty-seven, and already renowned.[49]

46 Lunghi cites the case of Giacomo da Bevagna, a thirteenth-century Dominican saint, whose *Vita* records the intervention of yet another miraculous crucifix who came to the aid of its supplicant. It seems that once when Giacomo was praying before the cross, he asked for a sign to confirm that he was among the elect. In response the crucifix replied: 'Let this very blood be a sign and a certainty to you', after which blood began to flow from the wound in the crucifix's side, three drops of which spurted onto Giacomo's lips. The Latin text is published in an appendix to E. Paoli, 'La vita del beato Giacomo Bianconi scritta da Ventura da Bevagna: un testo ritrovato?', *Hagiographica* 4 (1997), 253–99, cited in Lunghi, *La Passione degli Umbri*, 49, n. 6.

47 *BHL* 1702–9.

48 For Catherine's apostolate in the world, see Karen Scott, 'St Catherine of Siena, *Apostola*', *ChH* 61 (1992), 34–46.

49 For Raymond's Latin *Vita*, see *ActaSS*, 3 April, 853–978; I use (sometimes silently amended) the English translation of Raymond of Capua, *The Life of St Catherine of Siena*, transl. George Lamb (London, 1960) [hereafter, *LCS*].

Raymond's *Life* of the saint is replete with stories of Catherine's encounters with a speaking Christ; these encounters, however, were of a visionary nature, that is, Christ appeared to Catherine in order to converse with her not through a painted or sculpted figure on the cross, but in human form, a man seemingly conjured out of flesh and blood. Raymond reports that soon after she joined the *mantellate*, Catherine enclosed herself in a cell, devoting herself to vigils, prayers, and meditations whereupon 'He would deign to appear to her and reveal things useful to her soul'.[50] In describing her visions to Raymond, Catherine herself had said that when they 'first began to appear to her they generally came into her imagination but that sometimes she could also perceive them with her physical senses, so that she actually heard our Lord's voice'.[51] She had so many visions and revelations of the Lord, that as Raymond recalled: 'it would be difficult to find two human beings who have so continually enjoyed each other's company as this holy virgin did that of her Bridegroom'.[52]

Raymond's prose limpidly describes Catherine's colloquies with Christ as visionary experiences; nonetheless, artists, perhaps influenced by the iconographic tradition already well established for Saints Francis, Giovanni Gualberto and Thomas Aquinas, and their speaking crucifixes, insisted on representing Catherine's mystically embodied encounters with Christ as those with a crucifix [fig. 6]. Of countless colloquies that Catherine exchanged with her bridegroom, I have found only one in which a miraculous crucifix played a part. It should be noted that the episode took place shortly before she joined the Sisters of Penance, while Catherine was still living at home under the worldly influence of her family. Raymond reports that once, while Catherine was praying before a crucifix, a devil appeared holding a silken dress with which he tried to entice her. For her part, Catherine made the sign of the cross and the devil quickly vanished; but he left her with the foul desire to adorn herself in luxurious finery, a profane indulgence she had previously foresworn. Distressed by her weakness when confronted with temptation, Catherine cried out for comfort from the Lord. But it was the Virgin Mary who appeared to her and removed a radiant garment from the wound in the side of the crucified Christ-figure on the cross, and then began to embroider it with

50 *ActaSS*, Part I, ch. 5, par. 84 and 86, 874; *LSC*, ch. 9, 72–3.
51 Ibid.
52 Ibid.

Fig. 6 Vecchietta. Painted door of reliquary cabinet: St Catherine of Siena in prayer before a crucifix. Pinacoteca Nazionale, Siena, Italy. Photo: Alinari/Art Resource, NY

precious gems. Meanwhile she placated Catherine's agitated spirit with these words: 'Remember, daughter, that the garments that come from the side of my Son exceed all others in beauty and charm'.[53] Raymond concludes the episode by remarking that with this miracle, all Catherine's anxieties melted away, notably relieving her conscience.

This episode is positioned at the beginning of the *Vita*, which means that in terms of Catherine's chronology she was about the age of twelve.[54] It occurred before she had joined the Sisters of Penance and while her mother Lapa still dreamed of making a good marriage for her youngest daughter. The devil's offer of a silken dress is significant. Catherine's family had tried to entice her to remain in the secular world and marry, offering her an embarrassment of riches, particularly the promise of sumptuous clothing. Indeed, Raymond recounts how Catherine's sister Bonaventura tried to cajole her younger sister into attiring herself in sumptuous finery, but in the words of her hagiographer, she refused, for 'she could never get herself to feel an inclination for any man or even to be voluntarily seen by men'.[55] Fine garments, then, for both Catherine and Raymond were associated with attracting suitors for marriage, which of course would jeopardise the cherished vow of virginity that Catherine had made when she was still a mere child.

The miraculous crucifix interceded in Catherine's life when, under assault from her family, her resolve to maintain her vow of virginity began to waver. It taught her that everything she ever needed was contained in the sacred body of Christ, strengthening her resolve to hold out against her family's entreaties and increasingly desperate measures to lure her into an unwanted marriage. Soon after her encounter with the miraculous crucifix, she felt emboldened enough to lecture family members on the error of their ways and to inform them that she was betrothed to the Lord, her only spouse.[56] Shortly thereafter she joined the Dominican Sisters of Penance.

Raymond's *Vita* of Catherine dwells on her virginal state; indeed, he frequently refers to her as the 'holy virgin', whom he defends against those who would cast aspersions otherwise. For Raymond, Catherine's identity as a virgin was the lynchpin upon which all else hinged. The

53 *ActaSS*, Part III, Ch. 7, par. 402, 952–3; *LSC*, Epilogue, 362–3.

54 Raymond reports that young women were considered marriageable at the age of twelve, *ActaSS*, Part I, ch. 2, par. 41, 863; *LSC*, ch. 4, 36.

55 *ActaSS*, Part I, ch. 2, par. 45, 864; *LSC*, ch. 4, 37–40.

56 *ActaSS*, Part I, ch. 3, par. 54, 866–7; *LSC*, ch. 5, 48.

purity of her body signified the purity of her soul: her virginity authorized her mission as a Dominican. Raymond could only defend Catherine's extremely active apostolate in the world, an anomaly for women, so long as her body remained intact. Thus for Raymond, who was intent on having his spiritual charge canonized, Dominican female identity was bound up first and foremost with the state of virginity. Raymond's narrative of Catherine's encounter with a miraculous crucifix served to accentuate Catherine's virginal state, that essential condition which marked out for women their Dominican identity as virgins of the Lord.[57] Raymond's discursive text worked like those of William of Tocco and Bérenger of Landore: it first endeavoured to show how the crucifix erased Catherine's doubts about her vocation, but more importantly for the benefit of the Dominican community it also inscribed Catherine amongst the ranks of holy virgins, an integral aspect of female Dominican identity.

* * *

Ultimately, then, miraculous crucifix episodes served the hagiographical narrative in two ways. For the protagonists, a sacred image of Christ crucified intervened at critical moments in their lives – either during conversion or moments of severe self-doubt – in order to authorize or fortify their spiritual progress, thereby demonstrating to the textual community the humanity of God's saints. But these narratives are also revealing of the mendicant contexts in which they were produced. Miraculous crucifix stories also serve to seal or highlight specific aspects of mendicant identity, which the hagiographer as the voice of his textual community divined his readers would both desire and expect from a *Vita*.

But why should real, tangible, physical crucifixes serve as a device around which hagiographical narrative constructed identity? 'Imageless devotion' was the condition to which monastic authors had once aspired. But as Jeffrey Hamburger and others have shown, much had changed by the later Middle Ages.[58] Now even the mendicant orders themselves were promoting visual imagery as a means to devotion. Thus in the body-focused piety of the later Middle Ages, a piety that centred on the crucified body of Christ, corporeal images, particularly

57 There is a large literature on the theme of virginity in the lives of female saints; for a good example, see Karen A. Winstead, *Virgin Martyrs: Legends of Sainthood in Late Medieval England* (Ithaca, NY, and London, 1997).

58 See Hamburger, 'The Visual and the Visionary', 111–48.

crucifixes, were perforce one of the most if not *the* most important of devotional aids. As a devotional agent of the sacred, the crucifix represented the reality of the presence of the holy in the world.[59] A miraculous crucifix was even more efficacious: it collapsed the distance between the sacred and its representation. A miracle that was effected through the likeness of Christ's physical body sealed on the saint a mark of personal sanctity, the confirmation of a privileged relationship with Christ. But it also marked out the crucifix itself as a wonder-working object of devotion through which others might hope to have their own faith sustained.

Ultimately, miraculous crucifixes interacted with the saints by conferring upon them powerful Christian identities. And identity, as we have seen, was often (and of course still is) forged in the crucible of crisis. What also bears remarking is that the crucifixes of the later Middle Ages were also quite a garrulous lot, as crucifixes go. And that I think is what sets these miracle accounts apart as those particular to the mendicant Orders. It is probably no coincidence that in these stories Christ's words – the preaching of which was the vocation of the friars – served to inscribe the defining features of mendicant identity on the souls of their saints.

Catholic University of America

59 Hans Belting, *The Image and its Public: Form and Function of Early Passion Paintings*, transl. Mark Bartusis and Raymond Meyer (New Rochelle, NY, 1989), 302.

BLOODY MIRACLES OF A POLITICAL MARTYR: THE CASE OF THOMAS EARL OF LANCASTER

by DANNA PIROYANSKY*

THE blood of Thomas, earl of Lancaster, executed in March 1322 under King Edward II, was central to his representation as a political martyr. In this paper I shall discuss the miraculous flow of blood from Lancaster's tomb, which occurred on two occasions, and shall suggest two interpretations, symbolic and political, of the meaning of these miracles.

Thomas of Lancaster was King Edward II's first cousin,[1] and the richest magnate of his day.[2] This status enabled – indeed required – him to take part in the political life of the kingdom. He participated in Edward II's coronation ceremony and in May 1308 received the Stewardship of England, an office that made him 'viceroy of England'.[3] He was part of a vast coalition, which aimed to banish Edward's favourite, Piers Gaveston, from court.[4] Lancaster was one of the Ordainers, who presented their political demands to the king in the York parliament of 1311,[5] and in January 1312 he was involved in the capture, trial and execution of Gaveston.[6] Gaveston's replacement as King Edward's

* I would like to thank Miri Rubin, Bettina Bildhauer and Thomas Freeman for their helpful comments.

1 Born *c.*1277, Thomas was the son of Edmund – Henry III's son and Edward I's younger brother – and Blanche of Navarre (mother to Queen Isabella). 'De ortu et nobilitate Thomae, Comitis Lancastriae' is given in *Johannis de Trokelowe: et Henrici de Blaneforde, monachorum S. Albani . . .*, ed. Henry Thomas Riley, RS 28 (London, 1886), 70–1. The most complete study of Lancaster's life and activity is John Robert Maddicott's biography, *Thomas of Lancaster, 1307–1322: a Study in the Reign of Edward II* (London, 1970).

2 Lancaster inherited the earldoms of Lancaster, Leicester, Derby, Lincoln and Salisbury. Maddicott roughly valuates Lancaster's yearly income to £11,000: ibid., 9–10, 22.

3 L. W. V. Harcourt, *His Grace the Steward and Trial of Peers* (London, 1907), 124. For a Lancastrian tract which defines the office of Stewardship, see ibid., 164–7.

4 Maddicott, *Thomas of Lancaster*, 84.

5 The Ordinances are printed in *Rotuli Parliamentorum, ut et petitiones, et placita in Parliamento . . . (1278–1503)*, ed. J. Strachy, 7 vols (London, 1767–1832), 1: 281–6; for a discussion of the Ordainers and Ordinances see, for example, James Conway Davies, *The Baronial Opposition to Edward II: its Character and Policy. A Study in Administrative History* (1st edn, Cambridge, 1918, repr. London, 1967), 357–93.

6 *The Anonimalle Chronicle, 1307 to 1334, from Brotherton Collection MS 29*, ed. Wendy R. Childs and John Taylor, Yorkshire Archaeological Society 147 (Leeds, 1991), 86; Maddicott, *Thomas of Lancaster*, 129.

favourite by the Despensers created new tensions between Edward and Lancaster, which were dealt with in the Treaty of Leake (August 1318).[7] The culmination of the hostility between king and earl was reached in October 1321, after Edward's siege and capture of Leeds castle (Kent). Earlier in the summer two 'pseudo-parliaments' were held by the northern barons in Pontefract and Sherburn, where they decided upon a confederation for mutual defense against the Despensers.[8] While the king was advancing towards the rebels' army, Lancaster and his men set fire to Burton (Staffordshire), then moved on to Tutbury and Pontefract, hoping to continue further to the north.[9] Arriving at the crossing of Boroughbridge they found it blocked. The earl of Hereford was killed while trying to force a way through and Lancaster surrendered in the morning.[10] He was taken to York and then to the king at Pontefract, where he was tried.

The accusations in Lancaster's trial included general charges of murder, robbery, arson and other felonies, as well as more specific ones, such as displaying his banner contrary to his homage, coming armed to parliaments, and allying with Robert Bruce and other enemies of the king and kingdom.[11] Lancaster was not given the chance to answer these allegations, and was convicted and sentenced to be hanged, drawn, and beheaded, although the first two punishments were commuted, due to his noble status.[12] On 22 March 1322 Lancaster was taken to a hill outside the town of Pontefract, where he was decapitated. His body was handed over to St John the Evangelist's priory at Pontefract, where he was buried close to the high altar.[13] Following his execution, devotion to the earl promptly gathered momentum. While Lancaster's voice was eternally silenced by the beheading, it was also endowed with permanence.[14]

Although Lancaster was never officially canonized, we can trace

7 *The Life of Edward the Second: by the So-Called Monk of Malmesbury*, ed. and trasl. Noel Denholm-Young (London, 1957), 85, 88; for the Treaty of Leake, see Michael Prestwich, *The Three Edwards: War and State in England, 1272–1377* (2nd edn, London, 2003), 78–9.

8 Maddicott, *Thomas of Lancaster*, 268–9.

9 *The Life of Edward*, 123.

10 For the armies' manoeuvers, see ibid., 115–25.

11 *Johannis de Trokelowe*, 112–24.

12 'Gesta Edwardi de Carnarvan', in *Chronicles of the Reigns of Edward I and Edward II*, ed. William Stubbs, RS 76, 2 vols (London, 1882–3), 1: 77.

13 *The Anonimalle Chronicle*, 108.

14 This is often emphasized in martyrologies. See Sarah Kay, 'The Sublime Body of the Martyr: Violence in Early Romance Saints' Lives', in Richard W. Kaeuper, ed., *Violence in Medieval Society* (Woodbridge, 2000), 3–20, 18.

cultic activity related to him from 1322 until as late as 1536, when Henry VIII's visitors of monasteries in the north recorded that Lancaster's belt and hat were still working wonders at Pontefract, the former by helping lying-in women, the second, by treating headaches.[15] Although Lancaster's adherents were mainly men, most of them knights and monks, the cult must have had some appeal for women too, since one of its relics offered relief to women in labour. Though it had its epicentre in Pontefract, the geographical spread of the cult stretched to Lincolnshire, Leicestershire, Norfolk, Suffolk, Oxfordshire, London, Essex, Hereford, and as far as Kent and Somerset.

At least some of Lancaster's miracles were recorded in chronicles, especially in the pro-Lancastrian chronicle *The Brut* and in those influenced by it, as well as in a *Vita* that was compiled sometime in the fourteenth century.[16] These sources furnish us with examples focusing on Thomas's blood. *The Brut* tells us about a healing miracle that occurred to a blind priest, who dreamed for three nights running that he should go to the hill where Lancaster was martyred and there be healed:

> And when he come to þat place þat he was martred on, deuoutely he made þere his prayer, and prayede God and Seynt Thomas þat he might haue his sight aȝeyne. And as he was in his prayers, he laide his right hand oppon þe same place þere þe Gode man was martred on; and a drope of dry bloode and smal sande cleued on his honde, and þerwiþ he striked his eyne, and anone, þrouȝ þe might of God and of Seynt Thomas of Lancastre, he hade his sight aȝeyn, and þankede þo Almighty God and Seynt Thomas.[17]

The priest's sight was not restored as a direct consequence of doing the pilgrimage to the shrine, or even praying to Lancaster. The healing

15 *Letters and Papers, Foreign and Domestic, of the Reign of Henry VIII*, ed. James Gairdner, J. S. Brewer and Robert Henry Brodie, 38 vols, RS 120 (London, 1862–1932), 10: 137, 141.

16 Lancaster's *Vita* survived in two fifteenth-century non-English collections of saints' lives. One of these was compiled by the martyrologist Herman Greven while living in the Carthusian monastery in Cologne, probably during the 1460s or 1470s. It is extant in a manuscript in Berlin's Stadtbibliothek as MS Theol. lat. fol. 706, and it brings together the legends of about two hundred and fifty saints from different countries, that of Lancaster on fols 109r–111r. This text was copied in John Gielemans's (d. 1487) *Novale Sanctorum*, a collection of *Vitae* of saints who lived after 1300. This text survives as manuscript Vienna, Österreichische Nationalbibliothek, MS Ser. n. 12.708 (Lancaster's life on fols 38r–40r), and was printed in *Anecdota ex codicibus hagiographicis Iohannis Gielemans: canonici regularis in Rubea valle prope Bruxellas*, Subsidia hagiographica 3a (Bruxelles, 1895), 92–100.

17 *The Brut or The Chronicles of England*, ed. Friedrich W. D. Brie, 2 vols, EETS os 131 and 136 (London, 1906, 1908), 1: 228–9.

occurred only when he touched his eye with a drop of Lancaster's blood that remained on the ground, much like Longinus's miraculous healing from blindness by Christ's blood during the Crucifixion.[18]

The other miracles involving blood, however, yield less readily to typological classification, and they do not end in a straightforward healing. *The Brut*, Thomas Walsingham's (d. *c.*1422) *Historia Anglicana*[19] and John Capgrave's (d. 1464) *Abbreuiacion of Cronicles* (completed *c.* 1462–63),[20] all report that blood flowed from Lancaster's tomb at Pontefract in 1359. Walsingham and Capgrave mention the episode quite briefly, the first stating that 'Hoc anno, sanguis effluxit de tumba Domini Thomae, quondam Comitis Lancastriae, apud Pontem Fractum',[21] the second that 'In þis ȝere blod ran owt of þe toumbe of Thomas, duk of Lancastir, at Poumfreit'.[22] The unknown author of *The Brut* adds that the blood was 'as ffresshe as þat day þat he was done to þe deþe'.[23] We can tell that this bleeding was indeed seen as miraculous from a later report on a similar event, described as the greatest of a '*coruscacione miraculorum*' (a flash of miracles) performed by the martyr.[24] Quite disappointingly, this is all the information and we are left without a fuller description, the reasons for it, or the reactions it elicited. Did the blood flow from the tomb for hours, or days, or weeks? Were there just a few drops, or was it a trickle of blood, or a gushing forth?

Blood, flowing from martyrs' bodies, tombs or places of execution, varied in significance. It could have represented what Henry Platelle called 'la voix du sang', that is when the body of a victim of violence bled in the presence of its murderer, as '*l'accusation suprème de la victime*'.[25] In other cases, it could have been related, more generally, to

18 See Rose Jeffries Peebles, *The Legend of Longinus in Ecclesiastical Tradition and in English Literature, and its Connection with the Grail* (Baltimore, PA, 1911), 37–43.

19 For the dating, see Antonia Gransden, *Historical Writing in England. Part II: c.1307 to the Early Sixteenth Century* (Ithaca, NY, 1982), 124–6.

20 John Capgrave, *John Capgrave's Abbreuiacion of Cronicles*, ed. Peter J. Lucas, EETS os 285 (Oxford, 1983), xv–xviii.

21 Thomas Walsingham, *Historia Anglicana*, ed. Henry Thomas Riley, 2 vols, RS 28 (London, 1863–4), 1: 288.

22 *John Capgrave's Abbreuiacion*, 171.

23 *The Brut*, 309.

24 *Abbreviata Cronica: ab anno 1377 usque ad annum 1469*, ed. J. J. Smith, Publications of the Cambridge Antiquarian Society 1 (Cambridge, 1840), 10: 'et de aliis miraculis variis'.

25 Henri Platelle, 'La Voix du sang: le cadavre qui saigne en présence de son meurtrier', in Étienne Delaruelle, ed., *La Piété populaire au Moyen Age: Actes du 99e Congrès National des Sociétés Savantes, Section de Philologie et Histoire jusqu'à 1610* (Paris, 1977), 161–79, 161.

the shedding of the martyr's innocent blood, in each case that the bleeding occurs without an apparent prompt.[26] Sometimes, as in the flowing of fluids such as blood, milk or oil from the bodies – either alive or dead – of women saints it represented nourishment, a 'quasi-sacerdotal feeding', as Caroline Walker Bynum has observed,[27] whereas in the early modern period it was occasionally attributed to demons or witches.[28]

It seems that Lancaster's blood, and especially that spilt at the place of execution, had special meaning to his followers. Its flow represented simultaneously several things: an accusation for the injustice and wrong done to him, which caused the spilling of his innocent blood, and at the same time its nourishing legacy for people. This idea is implicit in a letter sent under Edward III's seal to Pope John XXII in 1327, requesting an inquiry into a possible canonization of Lancaster.[29] In this letter, the martyr's blood was likened both to a heavenly river flowing in different parts of England, and to the falling of heavenly dew, health-giving and fertilizing.[30]

For Lancaster's adherents, such as one William Leuere from Leicestershire who went on a pilgrimage to Pontefract in Easter week of 1333,[31] rumours about blood flowing from Lancaster's tomb were probably good news. Those who heard the story about the blind priest

26 See, for example, the cases of the Spanish virgin martyrs Nunilo and her sister Alodia (d. 851, celebrated 22 October), or that of Abbot Follian (d. *c.*655, celebrated 31 October): C. Grant Loomis, *White Magic: an Introduction to the Folklore of Christian Legend* (Cambridge, MA, 1948), 38; *ActaSS*, October 9, 639, and October 13, 418; *Butler's Lives of the Saints*, ed. Herbert Thurston and Donald Attwater, 4 vols (2nd edn, London, 1956), 4: 178, 230. See also examples in Herbert Thurston, *The Physical Phenomena of Mysticism*, ed. J. H. Crehan (London, 1952), 283. The explanation Thurston suggested for blood flowing from corpses is that it was triggered by an attempt to cut away parts of the dead body for their use as relics: ibid., 286.

27 Caroline Walker Bynum, *Holy Feast and Holy Fast: the Religious Significance of Food to Medieval Women* (Berkeley, CA, and London, 1987), 123, 273–4.

28 Stuart Clark, *Thinking with Demons: the Idea of Witchcraft in Early Modern Europe* (Oxford, 1997), 274, 590–1.

29 Possible reasons for the effort of canonization at this period may have been political, such as a need to counterweight the rising popularity of the cult evolving around Edward II, and to make a conciliatory gesture towards Henry of Lancaster. A. R. Echerd, 'Canonization and Politics in Late Medieval England: the Cult of Thomas of Lancaster', unpublished Ph.D. thesis, University of Chapel Hill, NC, 1983, 140.

30 Thomas Rymer, *Foedera, conventiones, litterae, et cujuscunque generis acta publica . . .*, ed. John Caley and Frederick Holbrooke, 4 vols, Record Commission (London, 1816–30), 2: 695: 'Qui jam, velut fluvius, de loco voluptatis, ad irrigandum egrediens paradisum, in partes divisus, terram Angliae, sancti sui sanguinis effusione rubricatam, rore coelesti temperat salubriter & foecundat'.

31 *Calendar of Inquisitions Post Mortem and Other Analogous Documents Preserved in the Public Record Office*, 21 vols, RS 154 (London and Woodbridge, 1898–2002), 10: 177–8.

healed with just one dry drop of Lancaster's blood may have been impressed by the potential for healing which this freshly flowing blood offered. But the blood's significance seems to have been linked to both private and public aspirations: the personal restoration to health, and the communal healing of the people.

It is not clear from the sources what triggered the miraculous flow of blood. Since Edward II was long dead, Lancaster's blood was not pointing at the murderer. Perhaps the miracle was a product of a single person's imagination; or perhaps St John's priory sought to encourage Lancaster's adherents to visit the tomb. It may also have been a reaction to contemporary events. In 1359, as Walsingham and other chroniclers report, the marriage of John of Gaunt, Edward III's son, and Blanche of Lancaster, the daughter of Henry duke of Lancaster, was celebrated. Following Simon Walker's reading of cults of political saints as encouraging political appeasement and re-integration,[32] a link between the flow of blood and the wedding of Edward II's grandson and Lancaster's great niece may have been attempted here. The miracle could have been seen as a sign of approval from the martyr for the marital union of the two families and the healing of the political breach between the Plantagenets and the Lancastrians.

More than a century after Lancaster's execution, in 1466, Lancaster's tomb bled again. 'Hoc etiam anno' – tells John Herryson, Chancellor of the University of Cambridge –

> has began a great rumor in England about a flash of miracles by . . . blessed Thomas Earl of Lancaster at Pontefract . . . and principally the bubbling up of blood (*ebullacione sanguinis*) from his tomb in the feast of St Luke the Evangelist [October 18].[33]

While the main event in 1466 was the coronation of Elizabeth Woodville, wife of Edward IV, at Westminster, the answer probably lies elsewhere, in earlier events in Yorkshire. During 1464 Henry VI was humiliated by his adversaries in the north and was finally taken to the Tower of London: the humiliation of his pious name-bearer Henry VI, also at Pontefract,[34] may have been a trigger for the 'bubbling

32 Simon Walker, 'Political Saints in Later Medieval England', in R. H. Britnell and A. J. Pollard, eds, *The McFarlane Legacy: Studies in Late Medieval Politics and Society* (Stroud, 1995), 77–106, esp. 90.

33 *Abbreviata Cronica*, 10.

34 When 'the lord montagu presented the kyng [Edward IV] . . . with kyng Henryes

up of blood'. The traumatic executions, at Exham, Newcastle, Middlham and York, of a later generation of Lancastrian supporters could have called to mind the wave of executions following the battle of Boroughbridge, of which Lancaster's was the most memorable: the significance for the dead earl's memory may have caused his blood to flow. The reform of the English coinage by the king could also have been interpreted as triggering response from Lancaster's blood. In one of the chronicles, that of John Warkworth, reporting on the first thirteen years of Edward IV's reign, it is written that 'Kynge Edwarde changed the coyne of Englonde, by whiche he hade grete getynge; . . . to the grete harme of the comene peple.'[35]

Lancaster was represented after his death as the defender and tutor of the English people. His generosity – already in life – was elaborated in hagiographical sources, and his good treatment of the poor and needy is referred to time and again. In one of the *memoriae* to him, for instance, after the *Versicle* '*Ora pro nobis beate Christi miles*', the *Response* is '*Qui pauperes nunquam habuisti viles*'.[36] He is referred to as '*generose miles Christi*',[37] while the *Vita* also elaborates the theme of Lancaster's kindness.[38] Perhaps in the flowing of blood of 1466 was Lancaster's reaction to these political events, and the troubles of the 'comene peple'.

Bloody miracles, as we have seen, were the recognition of innocence, and a sign of nourishment and care. They responded to contemporary events, political and fiscal, allowing the re-make of the martyr as a relevant figure of political culture. But in Lancaster's case there was an even more specific significance to the miraculous blood flowing: for, as we shall see, much of Lancaster's representation concentrated on his blood.

Lancaster's blood was central to his martyrological image, and we find references to it in hagiographical sources, chronologies, iconography, and in the diplomatic letters requesting his official canonization. In the liturgical office in his honour, contained in BL, MS Royal 12

bycoket (a seal of the King's customs?)': *Chronicles of London*, ed. Charles Lethbridge Kingsford (Oxford, 1905), 178.

35 John Warkworth, *A Chronicle of the First Thirteen Years of the Reign of King Edward the Fourth*, ed. James Orchard Halliwell, Camden Society (London, 1839), 4.

36 Baltimore, Walters Art Gallery, MS W. 105, fol. 13v (dated to the 1340s), and Cambridge, Clare College, MS 6, fol. 144r (thirteenth-century manuscript, but the *memoria* to Lancaster was added in a fourteeth-century hand).

37 Norwich, Norfolk Museums and Archaeology Service, MS 158.926/4f, fol. 152r (compiled *c.*1339).

38 *Anecdota ex codicibus hagiographicis Iohannis Gielemans*, 94.

St Peter *ad vincula* Church, South Newington (Oxfordshire):
The Execution of Thomas earl of Lancaster

C XII, fol. 1, dated between 1320 and 1340, there is an emphasis on the precious blood of Thomas, the flower of knighthood. In the parish church of the village of South Newington, Oxfordshire, a wall painting, dated to *c.*1330, survived, which shows – significantly, next to the martyrdom scene of Thomas of Canterbury – that of Lancaster's beheading. While the executioner raises both one leg and one armed hand in the air, just about to deliver the final blow, Lancaster kneels with his back turned to the executioner, his hands (now no longer visible) joined in prayer. On his neck are two bleeding gashes. The dominant colour in this mural is red, not only because of the centrality of Lancaster's bleeding neck in the scheme, but also because of his red cloak. The scene was identified by the art historian E. W. Tristram as the earl's beheading precisely because of the bleeding cuts, since in the *Vita Edwardi Secundi* the author reported that Lancaster 'stretched his head as if in prayer, and the executioner cut off his head with two or three strikes'.[39] Historical realism was not the only thing that concerned the painter of this depiction of the martyred earl. The fact that his blood was seen as 'precious' – as claimed in the office in his honour – is meaningful and calls for further attention. Why was Lancaster's blood so important?

The obvious answer is that since Lancaster was unjustly sentenced to death, and since his '*sanguis innocens*' was shed,[40] it possessed beneficial qualities. Thomas's nephew, Henry duke of Lancaster (d. 1361), wrote in 1354 *Le Livre de Seyntz Medicines*, an Anglo-Norman treatise dealing with the healing powers of Christ's suffering body.[41] In this text, Christ is represented as the divine doctor, who heals the patients (sinners) from their malady through his sufferings, bringing healing not only to the author himself, but to humanity as a whole. One type of healing described, for instance, is the washing of the patient in a bath of 'le sank precious, quant de la lance'.[42] Similarly, the healing that Lancaster's blood offered was not only that of individuals, such as the blind priest discussed earlier, but also the healing of the 'English nation' as a whole.

39 *The Life of Edward*, 126; E. W. Tristram, 'The Wall Painting of South Newington', *Burlington Magazine* 62 (1933), 114–29, with 4 pls, see 123 and detail of Thomas's head, pl. IV, B.

40 *Flores Historiarum*, ed. Henry Richards Luard, 3 vols, RS 95 (London, 1890), 3: 206.

41 Henry of Lancaster, *Le Livre de Seyntz Medicines: the Unpublished Devotional Treatise of Henry of Lancaster*, ed. E. J. Arnould, Anglo-Norman Texts 2 (Oxford, 1940).

42 Ibid., 202, l. 18.

Lancaster's death, following his active opposition to the King, was also explained as an altruistic deed, a sacrifice for the profit of the community. His death benefited the state of England ('*statum anglie*'), justice in general ('*Iustus pro iusticia fuit decollatus*'), or the peace and tranquillity of England's inhabitants ('*pro pace et tranquillitate regnicolarum Angliae*').[43] This altruistic suffering – a sort of unintentional *imitatio Christi* – endowed Lancaster's miracles, especially the ones linked to his blood, with the power to heal, if not to save.

Lancaster's death in defence of the English people, however, is not the only reason for the centrality of blood in his representation. Lancaster's distinguished pedigree was also noted,[44] the fact that such a high-born noble was executed, as the *Lanercost Chronicle* commented, 'like any thief or vilest rascal'.[45] Contemporaries, so it seems, were traumatized by the summary manner in which the greatest magnate of the time was put to death. 'O calamity!' – exclaimed the writer of the *Vita Edwardi Secundi* – 'To see men lately dressed in purple and fine linen now attired in rags, bound and imprisoned in chains!'[46] Lancaster's 'gentle' blood is mentioned repeatedly in the sources. The author of *The Brut,* for instance, laments: 'Allas þat euer soche a gentil blode shulde ben don to deþ with-outen cause and resoun!'[47] The link between Lancaster's noble blood and the martyrological shedding of it is evident in these lines, from *A Chronicle of the Civil Wars of Edward II,* written about 1327: 'Oh princely blood, extraordinary blood, noble blood, and precious blood also, why [were you] so contemptibly shed?'[48]

Only when juxtaposed and interwoven, these meanings and significances of blood – as nourishing, noble, healing, and sympathetic – may reveal to us why Lancaster's blood was cherished for more than a century after his execution. The outpourings of blood from the tomb in 1359 and 1466 linked past and present, private and public, noble and common, and were thus significant and memorable. They not only emphasized Lancaster's unjust individual past suffering, but also linked

43 Baltimore, Walters Art Gallery, MS W. 105, fol. 13v; Oxford, Bodleian Library, MS e. mus. 139, fol. 85r (late fourteenth century); BL, MS Royal 12 C XII, fol. 1r.

44 See n. 2 above.

45 *Chronicon de Lanercost* (Edinburgh, 1839), 244.

46 *The Life of Edward,* 124–5: 'O monstrum! uidere uiros purpura et bisso nuper indutos nunc attritis uestibus incedere, et uinctos in compedibus recludi sub carcere!'.

47 *The Brut,* 223.

48 'O sanguis/regius, sanguis egregius, sanguis generosus, sanguis eciam preciosus, cur tam contemptibiliter/effusus?': George L. Haskins, ed., 'A Chronicle of the Civil Wars of Edward II', *Speculum* 14 (1939), 73–81, 79.

it to his noble status, and to the therapeutic power of his suffering. Lancaster's flowing blood promised his adherents, and the English people as a whole, care, compassion and protection from private and collective hardships.

University of London

MIRACLES AND VISIONS IN *DEVOTIO MODERNA* BIOGRAPHIES

by MATHILDE VAN DIJK

SISTER Liesbeth of Heenvliet (d. 1450) was a scion of a high ranking noble family in the county of Holland. Her parents had named her after Saint Elizabeth of Hungary, from whom they were descended. Liesbeth was born blind. Her mother did not dare to inform the child's father, Johan of Heenvliet. Instead, she appealed to God and His Mother. Contrary to what she should have done, she did not vow her daughter to God's service. Despite her mother's laxity, Liesbeth's eyes healed completely. She grew into a beautiful and most intelligent girl – a further sign that God and the Virgin had extended their mercy to her.

At the age of ten, Liesbeth's 'inner self began to be drawn towards God's service', against the wishes of her parents.[1] They tried everything to dissuade her. They forced her to change confessors, from a pious man who might have stimulated her in her wish to embrace the religious life to her parents' creature, a worldly priest. He was to use all his cunning to find out whether she had any plans for the conventual life. Furthermore, they put Liesbeth's playmate to the same use: she was to serve as an informer on their daughter's religious leanings. Liesbeth was not to be moved.

A first attempt to run away to a convent failed, as God intended for her to enter into a different community. She got her chance when her cousin Katharina of Naaldwijk made her vows at the regular canonesses of Saint Agnes and Mary at Diepenveen, a convent of the Chapter of Windesheim. Liesbeth and her mother were to attend the ceremony. On their way there Liesbeth fell ill. Upon arrival, she exaggerated her illness, forcing her mother to leave her with the sisters. Before long, it became obvious that Liesbeth had no intention whatsoever of leaving the convent.

Once more, her parents tried everything to dissuade her. They

[1] Cited after the manuscript Deventer, Stads- en Atheneumbibliotheek, MS 101 E 26, commonly known as DV, fol. 269r: 'Sij began seer getrect toe worden van bijnen onsen leven heren toe dienen'. I am grateful to Wybren Scheepsma for allowing me to work with his transcription. Furthermore, thanks are due to Thomas Head, Koen Goudriaan, Sabrina Corbellini, Arjo Vanderjagt and Hildo van Engen.

stopped at nothing. When persuasion failed, they engaged the services of an eligible bachelor. He was to kidnap Liesbeth and to force her into marriage. Somehow the sisters got wind of this evil plan. They put the child out of his reach by making her stay inside the convent's enclosure. Desperate, Liesbeth's mother forced her way into the convent with the family's knights. They discovered her in an attic. When the knights put up ladders, she tried to amputate her ear. Furthermore, she threatened to cut her nose and mouth off and to send these items to her father. The mother backed off. She reported these events to Liesbeth's father, who had threatened to kill his wife if she were to return without their daughter. He decided to put up with the situation, but with bad grace. He gave his wife a hard time and did not give a penny to the convent for many years.[2]

* * *

The life of Liesbeth of Heenvliet provides a good introduction to the subject of this article: the role of signs and wonders in the *Devotio Moderna* biographies. It is included in the sisterbook of Diepenveen, a collection of lives of exemplary sisters. The sisterbook survives in two versions, both from the sixteenth century.[3] The authors, sisters from the same community, wrote it for the education of their fellow sisters. Such sets of lives of both male and female adherents were an important genre in the *Devotio Moderna*, the religious reform movement to which Diepenveen belonged.

Among scholars of such biographies, it has long been common opinion that brushes with the supernatural are for the most part absent. This is supposed to be true for miracles, worked by the subjects of the biographies before or after their deaths, and for other signs of divine intervention, such as visions. The usual explanation for the biographers' caution with regard to supernatural experiences is their common sense. In older publications, this was sometimes connected to the national character of the Dutch, which is supposed to be characterized by

2 The account of Liesbeth's entry into the convent is paraphrased after DV, fols 266v–278v.

3 Next to DV, there is manuscript D: Zwolle, Rijksarchief, Collectie Van rhemen, inv. nr. 1. Manuscript D has been edited in *Van den doechden der vuriger ende stichtiger susteren van Diepen Veen (Handschrift D)*, ed. D. A. Brinkerink (Leiden, 1904). Both versions have been used for this paper. For an outline of the differences between the two versions, see W. F. Scheepsma, *Deemoed en devotie. De koorvrouwen van Diepenveen en hun geschriften* (Amsterdam, 1997), 135–41. For an assessment of the genre of sisterbook, see Anne M. Bollmann, *Frauenleben und Frauenliteratur in der Devotio Moderna. Volkssprachische Schwesternbücher in literaturhistorischer Perspektive* (Groningen, 2004).

level-headedness.[4] Next to this, the Windesheim canons appear to share the common suspicion of female visionaries.[5] In 1455 the Chapter forbade its sisters to publish about revelations.[6] Therefore, as far as lives by female authors are concerned, it would have been only natural if their authors had kept their mouths shut about such matters.

The odd thing is that they did not. In separate articles, the Antwerp scholar Thom Mertens and his Leiden colleague Wybren Scheepsma uncovered many examples of miracles and visions.[7] Liesbeth's tale is a case in point. Her recovery from blindness is an obvious miracle. Furthermore it is striking that her entire life is described as being driven by God. For instance her beauty, her intelligence and her failed attempt to run away are all results of grace. At the same time, it is equally clear that, when miracles or visions are described, they are toned down. In particular, the miracles that were worked by the subjects of the biographies are not very exciting. The sisterbook tells a tale about a sister who, when she was suffering from temptation, went to pray at the grave of a prioress and was then healed.[8] Slightly more spectacular is a similar story about another sister who took the same problem to the grave of the first rector of the convent, Johannes Brinckerinck. He spoke to her from beyond the grave and advised her to take her trouble to another sister, Liesbeth's cousin, Katharina of Naaldwijk.[9] Generally, not much is made of the person who experiences the miracle or vision. Moreover, the contents of the visions are seldom revealed, except for the revelations in which a deceased member of the community appears. This is striking, especially in view of the fact that the tales are modelled on the lives of the saints. For instance, Liesbeth's tale takes after the legend of a virgin martyr.

4 F. W. J. Koorn, 'Hollandse nuchterheid. De houding van de Moderne Devoten tegenover vrouwenmystiek en -ascese', *Ons geestelijk erf* 66 (1992), 97–114.

5 Rosalynn Voaden, *God's Words, Women's Voices: the Discernment of Spirits in the Writing of Late-Medieval Women Visionaries* (Woodbridge, 1999), 66–71.

6 *Acta Capituli Windeshemensis. Acta van de kapittelvergaderingen der Congregatie van Windesheim*, ed. S. van der Woude (The Hague, 1953), 53.

7 Thom Mertens, 'Het Diepenveense zusterboek als exponent van gemeenschapstichtende kloosterliteratuur', in Wybren Scheepsma, ed., *Het ootmoedig fundament van Diepenveen. Zeshonderd jaar Maria en Agnesklooster 1400–2000* (Deventer, 2002), 77–94, and Wybren Scheepsma, 'Illustere voorbeelden. De invloed van de *Legenda Aurea* op de geschriften van de koorvrouwen van Windesheim', in *'Een boec dat men te Latine heet Aurea Legenda: Beiträge zur niederländischen Übersetzung der Legenda Aurea* (Münster, New York, Munich and Berlin, 2002), 261–82. Incidentally, the same is true for communications at the other end of the spectrum, i.e. diabolical delusions.

8 DV, fol. 225r.

9 DV, fol. 17r–v.

Threats of a forced marriage and self-mutilation are common features in the legends of such saints.[10] Moreover, in similar sets of biographies from different religious circles experiences of the supernatural are much more frequent.[11]

Mertens suggests that there was some discussion at Diepenveen about the status of revelations. He cites the example of Liesbeth's cousin, who, after her demise, appeared to an Observant Franciscan rather than to her own sisters. When he asked her why, she answered: 'They [the sisters] take all revelations as fallacies or signs of mental illness'.[12] Katharina's words imply criticism of those who did not take supernatural experiences seriously. The accounts of miracles and visions are the result of a compromise. The two versions of the sisterbook were completed in the sixteenth century, long after oral and written traditions about the exemplary sisters must have been established. Therefore, it was impossible entirely to leave out the stories that everybody in the convent knew, but these could be minimized, in deference to the prohibition against revelations or possible scepticism about such matters in the convent itself.[13]

These explanations do not seem to be entirely satisfactory. The level-headedness of the sisters seems limited. The sisters themselves and their biographers were always ready to conclude that a miracle had indeed happened. The latter present miracles and visions as relatively common occurrences in the lives of these exemplary sisters, not as embarrassments which are inserted only grudgingly. Scheepsma cites the example of a sister who heard the signal that the *elevatio* was about to take place, just when she was tapping beer. In her eagerness to look at the body of our Lord, she forgot to put the plug back into the barrel. When she ran back, no beer had been spilled. For both the sister and her biographer, it was obvious that a miracle must have happened.[14] Yet neither Mertens nor Scheepsma addresses the question of why the

10 For a typology of the legends of virgin martyrs, see for instance Birte Carlé, 'Structural Patterns in the Legends of the Holy Women of Christianity', in eadem, ed., *Aspects of Female Existence. Proceedings from the Saint Gertrud Symposium 'Woman in the Middle Ages'* (Copenhagen, 1980), 79–86.

11 For instance, the Dominican sisterbooks from the fourteenth century: G. J. Lewis, *By Women, for Women, about Women. The Sisterbooks of Fourteenth-Century Germany* (Toronto, 1996).

12 DV, fol. 256v.

13 Mertens, 'Het Diepenveense zusterboek', 90.

14 Scheepsma, 'Illustere voorbeelden', 267. The anecdote is included in DV, fol. 356r and *Van den doechden*, fol. 157r.

authors of the sisterbook included such supernatural experiences, at least not specifically.

In the following sections, I shall look at the purposes of the accounts of miracles and visions. I shall argue that such tales were as important a part of the educational rhetoric of the sisterbook as the accounts about the sisters' virtues. Like the virtues, they served as tools to create a corporate and an individual identity at Diepenveen. Mertens mentions this aspect as the primary aim of the sisterbook as a whole.[15] I shall ask the following questions: why do the authors insert miracles and revelations? What kinds of miracles and revelations were inserted? How do the authors describe such occurrences? What was their view about the presence of God in their lives? How does this relate to their status as women in the *Devotio Moderna*, particularly in the Chapter of Windesheim? How does this connect to other views inside the movement about God's intervention? First, I shall give a sketch of the status of women in the *Devotio Moderna*. Secondly, I shall compare the sisterbook to the lives of the brothers at Windesheim in Johannes Busch, *De viris illustribus*.[16] I shall concentrate on his chapters on the nature of miracles and on the visionary Brother Hendrik Mande. As members of the same chapter, brothers and sisters shared the same ideological context and it is clear that the two communities had close mutual ties. In both sets of biographies, there are references to members of the other community. Yet, in *Devotio Moderna* studies, simultaneous research on both communities has seldom been attempted.

* * *

Devotio Moderna started in the 1370s in the city of Deventer. Eventually, it was to dominate religious life in the Low Countries and the Rhineland until the Reformation. It was a typical late-medieval reform movement. Its aim was to return to the piety of the Early Church. Apart from Jesus Christ and the apostles, the primary examples for imitation were the Desert Fathers. According to Busch, these hermits, monks and nuns had found the best way to imitate Christ and the apostles after persecution ended. Although he praised later attempts to recreate this form of piety by the Poverty Movement, he felt that the initial fervour

15 Mertens, 'Het Diepenveense zusterboek', 93–4.

16 Johannes Busch, *De Viris Illustribus*, in *Des Augustinerpropstes Johannes Busch Chronicon Windeshemense und Liber de reformatione monasteriorum*, ed. Karl Grube (Halle, 1866) [hereafter: *DVI*].

had died.[17] The adherents of *Devotio Moderna* were very critical of contemporary religious, particularly of the Mendicants.

From the first, women were a major target group of the *Devotio Moderna*. Geert Grote (1340–84), the founding father of the movement, worried particularly about the Beguines. When he himself created a community of women living without vows, he attempted to provide an improvement on them. Aware that many Beguines had been condemned for heresy,[18] he understood this to be due to a lack of proper spiritual guidance. He placed his own community of Sisters of the Common Life under the care of the parish priest as to make sure that this would never be a problem for them. Grote was only partially successful. Sisters of the Common Life were repeatedly accused of being Beguines and, therefore, heretics.[19] The same went for male adherents of the *Devotio Moderna* who lived without vows.

Such difficulties were a major reason why, from the 1390s, so many brothers and sisters adopted a rule and organized themselves in chapters. The purpose of such a congregation was to exert strict control on its members. Evidence suggests that women got the worst of this.[20] The Windesheim prohibition against visions is a case in point. Undoubtedly, the canons wanted to avoid the havoc that, in their eyes, had been caused by Beguine visionaries like Marguerite Porete.

* * *

In the concluding chapter of *De viris illustribus* Busch claims that the brothers whom he has just described are saints, despite the fact that they did not work any miracles (*exteriora miracula*).[21] He goes on to say that his assertion is in accordance with the authority of the Church. Miracles and signs are by no means indispensable proofs of sanctity. He cites the examples of biblical figures, whom he calls canonized saints: Noah, Abraham and others. From the New Testament, he mentions the Virgin Mary, Saint John the Baptist and 'various other confessors and virgins'. Following Gregory the Great, Busch adds that miracles were

17 *DVI*, ch. 3.

18 Walter Simons, *Cities of Ladies: Beguine Communities in the Medieval Low Countries, 1200–1565* (Philadelphia, PA, 2001), 19–34, 118–20.

19 L. Peeters, ed., 'Den beghinne des Cloesters Jerusalems', *Limburgs Jaarboek* 7 (1900), 260–90, 264.

20 This appears to be true all over Europe. Cp. for instance: Alison Weber, *Teresa of Avila and the Rhetoric of Femininity* (Princeton, NJ, 1990), 18–33.

21 *DVI*, ch. 72.

needed to convert the pagans.[22] Now, this type of miracle is no longer necessary. Instead God works spiritual miracles. These miracles of the heart have as specific a purpose as the original kind had: they educate the faithful on how to progress in the faith. These were the kind of miracles that Busch's brothers worked. The entire life of an exemplary brother is conceived of as a miracle.

In Busch's context, there could be no other explanation for the brothers' perfection. The adherents of the *Devotio Moderna* were convinced that all humankind was contaminated by original sin. Men and women should rid their hearts of carnality in order to restore themselves to Adam's original perfection. No human being could accomplish such a task by himself. The only chance of success was if God provided an act of grace. Therefore, if the brothers are perfect, a miracle is the only explanation.

* * *

The authors of the sisterbook did not assume as much as Busch did. Much as the sisters may look like saints, it is obvious that they were not. They are struggling mortals who have a hard time fighting their natural inclination to sin. If they are exemplary, it is because of their perseverance in attempting to clean their hearts from all carnality. As saints, Busch's brothers do not need such agonizing struggles. They are perfect all along thanks to the workings of divine grace.

Amongst others, the difference between the brothers and the sisters is illustrated by the way in which the period before entry into the convent is described. In the lives of the sisters, the life before is always considered as something to get rid of. If they were serious about embracing a religious life, that is a life that was focusing on God, they needed a radical break with their former worldly existences. With Busch's brothers, the picture is entirely different. Their former position is no obstacle to their spiritual progress. In the case of a brother who had been a sheriff before, Busch asserts that this came in handy for the monastery, as he was good at negotiating privileges. He knew all people in authority.[23]

Despite the difference in the biographers' view of the subjects, the sisterbook is part of the same economy of grace as *De viris illustribus*. Miracles are played down, but on the other hand the biographers

22 William D. MacCready, *Signs of Sanctity: Miracles in the Thought of Gregory the Great* (Toronto, 1982), 16–32.

23 *DVI*, ch. 37.

present the lives of their sisters as being driven by divine grace entirely. God is omnipresent, in a very active role. Liesbeth's story is a good example. First of all, she descends from at least one saint. For a medieval audience, it would have been obvious that she was bound to have some inherited sanctity.[24] When her inner self starts to have leanings towards the religious life, this is not presented as the decision of an individual, but as something caused by an external force. This must be God – in the rest of the story it is obvious that He keeps an eye on all further events. Several occurrences are ascribed to the working of His mercy, for instance Liesbeth's recovery from blindness. However, the Liesbeth-is-a-saint motif is not extended beyond this point: she does not work miracles herself, before or after her death. She does, however, experience a vision. While she is embroidering the wrapping of some relics of Saint Ursula and the 11,000 virgins, she is spoken to by one of the skulls.[25] In line with the sisterbook's common practice, this is not highlighted. And indeed, why should the authors want to do such a thing? The point of a sisterbook is to provide an example for the Christian faithful. Miracles of the heart, like the lives of the exemplary sisters, were enough for that.

* * *

As for the accounts of visions, the same rule applies. If revelations make it into the sisterbook, they should have some use for the education of the sisters. This is why the appearance of a sister after her death is the only type of vision, of which the contents are always revealed. For instance Katharina of Naaldwijk told the Observant Franciscan friar that she had been in Purgatory for a few hours only. Now, she was on her way to heaven. The reason for this light sentence was that she had suffered so much in her last illness that she had had her Purgatory before death. Such messages helped the readers to make sense of the harsh fate of an excellent sister like Katharina.[26] Other deceased sisters report the same. Thus they give reassuring messages to the ones left behind: the sisters' perseverance, their toil and suffering in this life is rewarded. Furthermore, they advocate the usefulness of prayer. Several deceased sisters thank the living for their efforts to speed them on their way.

24 Cp. Gabor Klaniczay, *Holy Rulers and Blessed Princesses. Dynastic Cults in Medieval Central Europe* (Cambridge, 2002), 12, 209–20, 227–32.

25 DV, fol. 285r.

26 DV, fol. 256v and *Van den doechden*, fol. 65v.

Interestingly, visions of sisters and brothers after their deaths are also a speciality of the Windesheim brother Hendrik Mande (d. 1431), at least according to Busch.[27] Unlike most of the Diepenveen sisters, he is constructed as a visionary, as a brother with a special talent for contact with God. Mande had started out as a scribe of the count of Holland. Eventually, after a series of visions of the suffering Lord, he understood God's intentions: he was to become a regular canon at Windesheim. Like other visionaries, Mande suffered from a chronic illness. Furthermore, he was constantly in floods of tears. Like the visions of the deceased in the sisterbook, those of Mande have a reassuring purpose. They tell the readers that they too are on the right track to perfection, if only they follow the examples of their predecessors. Their toil and suffering will have a purpose. In the end, if they persevere, they become eligible for eternal life. At the end of Mande's biography, Busch gives us one account of another type of vision. Here too, the message is reassuring. One day, Mande encountered a boy just outside the monastery's gate. The boy told Mande that he was called Lamb and that he had just visited his father's house. Upon this, he vanished.[28] To Busch's readers, it would have been obvious that the visionary must have seen the Lamb, i.e. Jesus Christ. The home that He visited was their very own monastery. The anecdote confirmed that God really dwelt with them. Thus, they could self-assuredly conclude that they were on the right track.

* * *

In the preceding paragraphs, I focused on the special instances of God's intervention, which cause the recipients to experience direct contact with the supernatural. This should not obscure the fact that the authors of the Diepenveen and Windesheim biographies perceived the lives of their subjects as being directed by God, every step of the way. In view of the depravity of humankind, there could be no other explanation for their exemplariness or even sanctity. According to the Dutch medievalist Johan Huizinga, this omnipresence of the divine is typical of Late Medieval piety.[29] It is also an instance of the *Devotio Moderna*'s

27 See for the life of Hendrik Mande: *DVI*, ch. 43–45. Mande's surviving work presents a more varied picture. See, for more information: Thom Mertens, *Hendrik Mande (?–1431). Teksthistorische en literairhistorische studien* (Nijmegen, 1986).

28 *DVI*, ch. 45.

29 Johan Huizinga, *The Waning of the Middle Ages: a Study of the Forms of Life, Thought, and Art in France and the Netherlands in the Fourteenth and Fifteenth Centuries* (3rd edn, London, 1990), 147–8, 184–5, 217.

identification with the Desert Fathers. The *Collationes patrum* advocate that religious people should relinquish their wills and submit to God's.[30] Obviously, this is what the exemplary sisters and brothers did.

Busch focuses on the fact that whenever God works miracles, He does so for a purpose. Since '*miracula exteriora*' are no longer necessary as everybody is a Christian, the Windesheim brothers worked '*miracula interiora*', which are useful in the education of the faithful. Like Busch, the Diepenveen authors wrote the lives of their sisters in order to educate them into the religious life: miracles of the heart are enough for this.

The same applies to visions. However, the female authors of the sisterbook faced many more difficulties when they attempted to describe them, even if they were convinced that such things were bound to happen in the life of an exemplary sister. They had to juggle the prohibition against women writing about revelations with their educational aims. It did not serve any purpose to reveal the contents of visions or to make much of the sisters who have them. In view of women's well-known moral weakness, their claims that they had visions might be false, or these visions might be diabolical delusions. Though it is obvious that neither was true for the exemplary sisters in the sisterbooks, it would not do to encourage their successors to think that they could be as special as these sisters were. This restriction does not apply to the Windesheim brothers such as Hendrik Mande. Yet it is striking that Busch focuses on his visions of the deceased. In the sisterbook too, these are the only visions of which the contents are revealed. It is obvious why. Such visions help the sisters (and, for that matter, the brothers) to persevere on their ways to spiritual perfection and tell them that they are on the right track.

University of Groningen

30 John Cassian, *Conférences*, ed. E. Pichery, 3 vols, SC 42, 54, 64 (Paris, 1955–9), 1: 1.

A VULCANOLOGICAL JOACHIM OF FIORE AND AN AERODYNAMIC FRANCIS OF ASSISI IN COLONIAL LATIN AMERICA

by JAIME LARA

CATACLYSMS of nature and apocalyptic beliefs have always gone hand in hand. While Christians have had no monopoly on such beliefs, expectations of this kind have been an important part of the Western religious tradition both in Christian Europe and in the 'millennial New World', the latter a time and place of heightened eschatological anticipation. One of the 'best-sellers' among Christians in medieval Europe was *The Fifteen Signs before Doomsday*, a work that detailed the cataclysms which would occur before the end.[1] But in another region of the world – a new world replete with frequent seismic and volcanic activity – it became even more so a type of prophecy that would captivate the religious imagination of colonizers and missionaries.

The last fifty years of scholarly research on the discovery and evangelization of the Americas have demonstrated the presence of pervasive eschatological, apocalyptic, and chiliastic thinking among the New World colonizers and the colonized alike, which coloured both the initial evangelization and the subsequent development of Church policy. In many ways, the New World of the sixteenth century cannot be considered the first blossoming of the Early Modern Period, as much as the last flowering of a medieval culture that began with St Augustine's *City of God*.[2] There, among newly discovered lands and peoples, it was hoped that a final golden age of world history – a millennial kingdom of the mendicant friars and their new Christians – would be inaugurated.[3] The medieval foundation of this millennial belief had

1 See the modern edition: William Watts Heist, *The Fifteen Signs before Doomsday* (East Lansing, MI, 1952).

2 On the continuation of the Middle Ages into the sixteenth-century New World, see Luis Weckmann, *La Herencia medieval de México* (Mexico, 1984), Engl. transl. by Frances M. López-Morillas, *The Medieval Heritage of Mexico* (New York, 1992).

3 See, for example: John Leddy Phelan, *The Millennial Kingdom of the Franciscans in the New World: a Study of the Writings of Gerónimo de Mendieta (1525–1604)* (2nd edn, Berkeley, CA, 1970); Alain Milhou, *Colón y su mentalidad mesiánica en el ambiente franciscanista español* (Valladolid, 1983); idem, 'Apocalypticism in Central and South American Colonialism', in

been provided by the twelfth-century prophet of history, Joachim of Fiore, and it experienced a revival among the first generation of Franciscans, Augustinians and Dominicans who evangelized the native peoples of America. The Franciscans were particularly enamoured of Joachim because of his supposed prediction of the advent of St. Francis as an eschatological figure. When a cataclysmic event occurred in the first year of the seventeenth century, it challenged the friars to rethink Joachim's prophecies, as well as to respond to newly ignited and dangerous prophecies of the Indians. This paper attempts to bring together some of this millennial research. By considering historical, mythic, theological, and anthropological texts side by side with visual images, I shall attempt to arrive at a three-dimensional representation of the period and its preoccupations. Hopefully, the end result will be to make evident the intellectual richness of colonial Latin America, and to stimulate further investigation into this area of ecclesiastical history.

Like the very individuals with whom I shall deal in this article, I am a picture-thinker. As an art historian, I think in terms of visual history and visualized narratives; so let me begin this inquiry into a millennial moment by relating a story, a true story both of coincidence and of deeper concerns.

* * *

In the year of our Lord 1600, on the second Friday in the season of Lent, sometime between noon and 3:00 in the afternoon, that is, at the hour of the accustomed Lenten penitential processions, the Peruvian volcano of Huaynaputina began a protracted series of explosions and eruptions.[4] It was the largest recorded volcanic eruption in the Western

The Encyclopedia of Apocalypticism, 3 vols (New York, 1998–2000), 3: 3–35; Marcel Bataillon, *Erasmo y España: estudios sobre la historia espiritual del siglo XVI* (2nd edn, Mexico, 1966); Georges Baudot, *Utopía e Historia en México: los primeros cronistas de la civilización mexicana (1520–69)* (Madrid, 1983); Juana Mary Arcelus Ulibarrena, 'La esperanza milenaria de Joaquín de Fiore y el Nuevo Mundo: trayectoria de una utopia', *Florensia* 1 (1987), 47–78; Delno West, 'Medieval Ideas of Apocalyptic Mission and the Early Franciscans in Mexico', *The Americas* 45 (1989), 293–313; the articles in Gian Luca Potestà, ed., *Il profetismo gioachimita tra Quattrocento e Cinquecento: Atti del III Congressso Internazionale di Studi Gioachimiti, San Giovanni in Fiore, 17–21 settembre 1989* (Genova, 1991); Frank Graziano, *The Millennial New World* (Oxford, 1999); Jaime Lara, *City, Temple, Stage: Eschatological Architecture and Liturgical Theatrics in New Spain* (Notre Dame, IN, 2004).

[4] The volcano is located 70 km southeast of the city of Arequipa, Peru. The eruption of Huaynaputina ranked a number 6 on the intensity scale of volcanic eruptions. The maximum, a number 8, has only been recorded for the eruption of Krakatou. Tom Simkin and Lee Siebert, *Volcanoes of the World: a Regional Directory, Gazetteer, and Chronology of Volcanism during the Last 10,000 Years* (2nd edn, Tucson, AZ, 1994), 143.

Hemisphere, greater by far than that of Vesuvius in 79 CE, or Mount St Helens, U.S.A., in 1980, and only slightly smaller than the colossal eruption of Krakatou, Indonesia, in 1883. It sent both Christian Spaniards and neo-Christian Indians searching for answers to apocalyptic questions.[5]

On that Friday, 18 February 1600, several violent earthquakes levelled buildings and the first eruption occurred accompanied by deafening explosions and flashes of light apparently coming from the caldera. On Sunday, 20 February, another explosion occurred, spewing ash and pumice. The sky turned red, then darkened to the black of midnight – and all this at high noon. It was not until six days later that the sun and stars returned to be seen. But on the following Friday, 25 February, a new series of eruptions commenced, and the ear-shattering noise and the earthquakes continued. The blast was so strong that it was reported to have been heard within a radius of one thousand kilometres. In the nearby city of Arequipa the ground gave way, rising or sinking two metres in some places. The stone vaulting of the cathedral collapsed, crushing to death the faithful who were attending Mass. On Monday, 28 February, at 3 o'clock in the afternoon the darkness was again total and continued so until 1 March, when Huaynaputina opened its eastward side in what is known as a 'lateral eruption' and a river of fire flowed out into the nearby Tambo river.[6] The river backed upstream and created two temporary lakes twenty-eight kilometres long. Fish were either boiled alive or soon died because of the high content of mercury in the contaminated water. Throughout the ordeal, during the long pitch-black days that spread like a belt across South America, the terror was heightened by red-hot bombs of molten lava, the size of a man's head, which were ejected with such force that they rained fire from heaven for miles around. What began on 18 February continued until 2 April when the sun finally reappeared. By that time, the suffocating ash had completely buried several Indian towns and their entire populations. In August of that year, there was another eruption, and finally in November, ten months later, the event – which had all the elements of the Apocalypse – ended, not to be repeated until 1667. The news of the event was spread rapidly throughout the

5 Thérèse Bouysse-Cassagne and Philippe Bouysse, 'Volcan indien, volcan chrétien: à propos de l'eruption du Huaynaputina en l'an 1600 (Pérou Méridional)', *Journal de la Société des Américanistes* 70 (1982), 43–68.

6 The river of hell-fire is typical of Byzantine and Italian depictions of the Last Judgement; see, for example, Desanka Miloševic, *The Last Judgment* (Vaduz, 1964), esp. 29–59.

American colonies by the *Cartas Anuas* of the Jesuits and by several chroniclers.[7] Fear of similar cataclysms abounded because, in the faulty science of the time, it was thought that volcanoes communicated with one another underground and that the eruption of one could presage the eruption of another.[8]

The Spaniards in Peru reacted in a predictably Christian way, discerning the displeasure and wrath of God, especially in light of the lascivious Carnival that they had ended only a few days prior to the first eruption. As *The Fifteen Signs before Doomsday* reminded the reader, earthquakes, eruptions, and the poisoning of the waters would presage the end of days. Indeed, rivers of molten fire had always been familiar elements in visual depictions of punishment and the Last Judgement in the European and Byzantine traditions, as at Torcello, or in Giotto's interpretation of the theme in the Scrovegni Chapel at Padua.[9]

The neo-Christian natives of Peru, on the other hand, reverted to the mythology of their Inca past and saw the volcano as a *huaca*, a deity who was fighting on their side against the European invaders and the Christian God. The conquest of Peru had been particularly cruel, chaotic, and prolonged; and only ten years earlier the Incas had participated in a bloody and futile rebellion against the Spanish overlords.[10] In their Quechua language the eruption of Huaynaputina was the moment of *pachacuti*, literally 'the world turned upside down', which heralded a rupture or reversal of the given order, the return of the mythical Inca, and the commencement of a third and final age of world history.

My purpose in relating this story is not to offer a lesson in vulcanology, but to say that it is shortly after this cataclysmic occurrence that Joachim of Fiore was first seen in the Americas; and, not surprisingly,

7 It was later incorporated into the *Historia del Nuevo Mundo* of Fray Bernabé Cobo (1653); Martín Murúa, *Historia del origen y genealogía real de los reyes inças del Perú* (1611); and the travelogue of Fray Diego de Ocaña (MS no. 215 in the Library of the University of Oviedo) in modern transcription as *Un viaje fascinante por la América Hispana del siglo XVII* [1605] (Madrid, 1969).

8 Other volcanoes erupted in the vicinity of Huaynaputina: Urbinas in 1600, 1662, 1677, 1784; Misti in 1677, 1784, 1787; Sabancaya in 1750 and 1784. Popocateptl, in central Mexico (see below), has experienced almost continuous eruptions both large and small throughout recorded history.

9 The Last Judgement is located on the interior west wall of both buildings. The river of fire flows from beneath Christ's throne, off to his left, and down to hell.

10 The rebel Inca lord, Túpac Amaru, had been publicly executed in 1572. Uprisings continued sporadically until 1590.

he was usually accompanied by a flying Francis of Assisi.[11] This was no coincidence, but directly related to the explosion of Huaynaputina, and in response to the incendiary political-social-religious situation posed by the conquest of the Andes.

* * *

Joachim of Fiore is one of the most interesting but understudied figures of the medieval world. He was considered for several centuries to be a *magnus propheta* and the greatest picture-thinker of the Middle Ages. Born about 1135 in Calabria, he was the son of a wealthy merchant.[12] After a pilgrimage to the Latin Kingdom of the Crusaders in the Holy Land, he dedicated his life to the pursuit of God. For a time he lived as a hermit in Sicily upon the dangerous slopes of Mount Etna, an active volcano that had recently erupted.[13] Hence, he had a certain association with volcanic eruptions, a connection that continues today in his homeland where he is a local saint and protector against disasters.

He was a wandering preacher in his native Calabria before being ordained and entering the Benedictine monastery of Corazzo. Joachim soon became abbot, and during the 1180s was involved in a campaign

11 For the presence or influence of Joachim of Fiore in European art see: Guido Bondatti, *Gioachinismo e francescanesimo nel Dugento* (S. Maria degli Angeli, 1924), 147–64; Jean Rousset, 'Il più antico ritratto di Gioacchino da Fiore', *Archivio Storico per la Calabria e la Lucania* 3 (1933), 321–4; F. D. Klingender, 'St Francis and the Birds of the Apocalypse', *Journal of the Warburg and Courtauld Institutes* 16 (1952), 13–23; Franco Prosperi, *La mistica gioachimita prefrancescana nella simbologia delle sculture: la facciata della cattedrale di Assisi* (Perugia, 1968); Marjorie Reeves, *The Influence of Prophecy in the Later Middle Ages: a Study in Joachimism* (Oxford, 1969; 2nd edn, Notre Dame, IN, 1993), 73, 96–100, 164–5, 230, 266, 460, 479; Edith Pásztor, 'Architettura monastica, sistemazione urbanistica e lavoro del Novus Ordo auspicato da Gioacchino da Fiore', in *I Cistercensi e il Lazio: Atti delle giornate di studio dell'Istituto di storia dell'arte dell'Università di Roma, 17–21 maggio 1977* (Rome, 1978), 149–56; Malcolm Bull, 'The Iconography of the Sistine Chapel Ceiling', *Burlington Magazine* 130 (1988), 597–605; Ferdinando Batazzi, 'L'iconografia francescana nel chiostro di Ognissanti di Firenze secondo gli Spirituali e nelle cronache manoscritte', *Vivens homo* 2 (1991), 277–84; Josephine Jungic, 'Joachimist Prophecies in Sebastiano del Piombo's Borgherini Chapel and Raphael's Transfiguration', in Marjorie Reeves, ed., *Prophetic Rome in the High Renaissance Period* (Oxford, 1992), 321–44; *Gioacchino Abate di Fiore*, ed. Mariolona Bitonti (San Giovanni in Fiore, 1998), 9–14 and 47–76.

12 Robert Lerner, 'Joachim of Fiore's Vision of Irenic Conversion', unpublished lecture delivered at Columbia University, 26 October 1996, wherein he speculated on a Jewish origin for Joachim, based on new evidence.

13 Mount Etna had erupted in 1163 accompanied by an earthquake and tsunami. This event was incorporated into the apocalyptic prophecy known as the *Vaticinium Sibillae Erithraeae*; see Bernard McGinn, *Visions of the End: Apocalyptic Traditions in the Middle Ages* (New York, 1979; 2nd edn, 1998), 122–5.

to have his monastery incorporated into the stricter Cistercian order.[14] It was during this time that he first came to the attention of Pope Lucius III, who encouraged him to write down his apocalyptic theories and to expound a mysterious prophecy attributed to the Sibyls that had recently come to light in Rome.[15]

In 1188 Joachim and his followers separated themselves from the monastery, and by 1192 had founded a new house at San Giovanni in Fiore, in the high Sila plateau. Despite the remoteness of the new establishment, during the final decade of his life, Joachim had numerous contacts with the great and powerful.[16] By the time of his death in 1202, he was one of the most noted religious figures of his day.[17] He shared much with the Jewish and Christian apocalyptic prophets of the biblical period, and identified himself with Ezekiel, the prophet of the exile. A sense of immediately impending crisis provided the motive for the proclamation of his message from the book of Revelation that 'the sixth seal is about to be broken open'.[18]

Joachim was a first-rate visual thinker, graphic artist, and biblical exegete whose scriptural hermeneutic was based upon a distinction between allegory and concordance. As Marjorie Reeves states:

> Concord is not allegory; it is a similitude of proportion between actual historical events which exist in their own right, each in its own dispensation. The concords are inbuilt in their very historical existence by the hand of God. . . .[19]

14 Corazzo was first a Benedictine and then a Cistercian monastery during Joachim's lifetime; hence, the different colour habits worn by Joachim in works of art.

15 McGinn, *Visions of the End*, 126. For the text and interpretation of the Sibylline oracles, see Bernard McGinn, 'Joachim and the Sybil', *Cîteaux* 24 (1973), 97–138. According to McGinn, the 1180s were a time of great upheaval in Europe and many people turned to signs, stars, and Sibyls.

16 Richard the Lionheart had just come from concluding the peace treaty of 1192 with the caliph Saladin after the defeat of the Latin Kingdom of Jerusalem by the Muslims. For the political significance of these encounters, see Reeves, *Influence of Prophecy*, 3–15.

17 The order that he founded experienced such an expansion in the following decade that it was hailed by the Fourth Lateran Council in 1215 as one of the four pillars of the Church. Innocent III had opened the Council with a homily, based on Ez. 9, 4, in which the signing with the *Tau* became a symbol for spiritual renewal in the church. Francis of Assisi, thought to have been present at this event (and whose personal signature was the *Tau* symbol), became the figure of renewal who carried out Innocent's programme both literally and spiritually. See below.

18 Stephen Wessley, 'The Role of the Holy Land for the Early Followers of Joachim of Fiore', in R. N. Swanson, ed., *The Holy Land, Holy Lands, and Christian History*, SCH 36 (Woodbridge, 2000), 181–91.

19 Marjorie Reeves and Beatrice Hirsch-Reich, *The Figurae of Joachim of Fiore* (Oxford, 1972), 6.

These letter-by-letter similitudes and symmetries between Testaments were not used merely to understand the past – as in traditional scriptural allegory – but, far more daringly, to reveal the future. Joachim believed that he could anticipate the future from the remembered past.[20]

The abbot's unique contribution is his use of the Trinity as the key to the meaning of world history,[21] and it was this trinitarian scheme that would be so attractive to later religious thinkers in the New World. For Joachim, exegesis of Scripture reveals not only the grand plan of the two Testaments, but also a scheme of three periods of time called states (*status*).[22] These are complex, organic, progressive, and interlocking in character. The first *status* began with Adam and lasted until Christ: it was ascribed to God the Father and was defined as the time of the order of the married people. The second *status* overlapped the first. It began to bear fruit in Christ, and lasted until Joachim's century. It was credited to the Son and was the time of the order of clerics. The third *status*, the time of the monastic orders – when all Christendom will be a monastic community – was ascribed to the Holy Spirit. It would make its full appearance in the thirteenth century, and would bear fruit in the last age down until the end of the world.[23] As his schematic drawings illustrate, Joachim's mind moved according to the rich combinations of pictorial and symbolic thought rather than the clarity of discursive mentality.[24]

20 Henri Mottu, *La Manifestation de l'Esprit selon Joachim de Fiore: herméneutique et théologie de l'histoire d'après le Traité sur les quatre évangiles* (Neuchâtel, 1977), 101–13.

21 Bernard McGinn, 'Influence and Importance in Evaluating Joachim of Fiore', in *Il profetismo gioachimita tra Quattrocento e Cinquento*, 15–36; 18: 'If there is one thing that modern research on Joachim's view of history has shown us, it is that his views on historical periodization are highly complex, a combination of binary, ternary and multiple patterns involving elements of finality, progression and recurrence. . . . The notion of *concordia* involves not just a synoptic attempt to harmonize texts, or to compare a parallel series of events from the Old and New Testaments, but also the working out of the structural conformity or correlation of the two Testaments necessary to understand a coming third stage of history'.

22 Joachim divides the three periods differently in different contexts according to the image that he is developing at the moment. In general, they conform to (1) Old Testament, (2) New Testament, (3) The Age of the Holy Spirit, an approaching moment in the thirteenth century, *c.*1260, according to his calculations. See Reeves and Hirsch-Reich, *Figurae*, 248–55.

23 Bernard McGinn, *Apocalyptic Spirituality* (New York, 1979), 102–3; Augustine Thompson, 'A Reinterpretation of Joachim of Fiore's *Dispositio Novi Ordinis* from the *Liber Figurarum*', *Cîteaux* 33 (1982), 194–205; Delno C. West and Sandra Zimdars-Swartz, *Joachim of Fiore: a Study in Spiritual Perception and History* (Bloomington, IN, 1983), 93.

24 See Bernard McGinn, 'Symbolism in the Thought of Joachim of Fiore', in Ann Williams, ed., *Prophecy and Millenarianism: Essays in Honour of Marjorie Reeves* (Harlow, 1980),

According to abbot Joachim, the third age would be prefaced by an imminent crisis of history. During this time, two new religious orders of spiritual men would arise to confront Antichrist and his forces: an order of preachers in the spirit of Elijah (symbolized by the colour white), and an order of hermits in the spirit of Moses or Enoch (symbolized by the colour black).[25] (We shall meet these figures again in America.) Despite the vagueness of the abbot's descriptions, it would be hard for future generations not to see here a prophecy of the two mendicant orders that were born in the decade after Joachim's death, the Dominicans and the Franciscans.[26] These were also the first two religious orders to arrive in the New World, and it was the Franciscans who most developed this *mythos* there.

By the time of Francis and Dominic, several Joachimite texts were in circulation, and more would appear in the coming decades. Indeed, for the next several centuries prophetic texts concerning the Sibylline oracles, the visions of Merlin concerning the Holy Grail, the return of the lost tribes of Israel, the Last World Emperor, the Second Charlemagne, the Angelic Pope, the Islamic menace and proximity of Antichrist, and the rediscovery of the Terrestrial Paradise of Adam and Eve (in the New World) were often attributed to the Calabrian abbot.[27] Furthermore, many of the treatises ascribed to Joachim, but actually composed in the thirteenth century, originated in Franciscan circles. A distinctive Franciscan Joachimite apocalyptic was developing with three subplots: (1) the identification of the Franciscans and the Domini-

143–64. Joachim's many drawings and analyses using flora can be seen as vitalistic renewal in the general sense: see Gerhard Ladner, 'Vegetation Symbolism and the Concept of the Renaissance', in Millard Meiss, ed., *De artibus opuscula XL: Essays in Honor of Erwin Panofsky* (New York, 1961), 303–22.

25 *Expositio in Apocalypsim*, fols 175v–176r, on Rev. 14, 15–16. Additionally, Joachim associates these two individuals with the two witnesses of Rev. 11, 1–14. See Herbert Grundmann, *Neue Forschungen über Joachim von Fiore* (Marburg, 1950), 106–7.

26 The Augustinian Observants also saw themselves as the spiritual sons of Joachim. See Marjorie Reeves, 'Joachimist Expectations in the Order of Augustinian Hermits', *Recherches de théologie ancienne et médiévale* 25 (1958), 111–41.

27 For the Sibylline Oracles, see McGinn, 'Joachim and the Sibyl', 98–100. For Joachim and Merlin, see De Lubac, *La posteridad espiritual de Joaquín de Fiore*, 2 vols (Madrid, 1988), 1: 15 and 78 [first published as *La postérité spirituelle de Joachim de Fiore* (Paris, 1981)]. For the reappearance in the late fifteenth century of prophecies related to Merlin, the Grail legend and the Grail castle, see *Baladro del sabio Merlín (Burgos, Juan de Burgos, 1498): Guía de lectura*, ed. Paloma Gracia (Madrid, 1998). The Grail was supposedly a possession of Charlemagne, and the Grail legend later passed into the mythology surrounding the Hapsburg dynasty, especially Charles V of Spain. See Marie Tanner, *The Last Descendant of Aeneas: the Hapsburgs and the Mythic Image of the Emperor* (New Haven, CT, 1993), 207–14. For a possible Joachimite origin of the Grail legend, see Reeves, *Influence of Prophecy*, 71–95.

cans with the two groups of spiritual men prophesied by Joachim; (2) the specification of radical poverty as the prophetic sign of the new spiritual men; (3) and the belief that Saint Francis was, in reality, the Angel of the Sixth Seal of Revelation, chapter 7, whose advent had marked the beginning of the critical period of history, the third *status*.[28] St Bonaventure saw the symbolic equation of Francis and the Angel of the Apocalypse and incorporated this interpretation into the official biography of the saint and into the liturgical hymns for Francis's feast, which made it safe for the orthodox.[29]

Later, these and other Joachimite texts were being read by Christopher Columbus and the first friars who would travel to the New World. When printing was invented and Joachim's works were published by the mendicant friars in Venice, beginning in 1516, his thought and graphic images became available to the New World missionaries and members of their native flock.[30] At least one

[28] Stephanus Bihel, 'S. Franciscus fuitne angelus sexti sigilli?', *Antonianum* 2 (1927), 59–90; Stanislao da Campagnola, *L'Angelo del sesto sigillo e l'alter Christus: genesi e sviluppo di due temi francescani nei ss. XIII–XIV* (Rome, 1971), 7–48; John Fleming, *From Bonaventure to Bellini: an Essay in Franciscan Exegesis* (Princeton, NJ, 1982), 129–57. On Francis as the initiator of the third state, see Raoul Manselli, *La 'Lectura super Apocalypsim' di Pietro di Giovanni Olivi: ricerche sull'escatologismo medievale* (Rome, 1955), 211, n. 1; and Stanislao da Campagnola, 'Dai *viri spirituales* di Gioacchino da Fiore ai *fratres spirituales* di S. Francesco d'Assisi', *Picenum Seraphicum* 11 (1974), 24–52.

[29] Bonaventure, *Legenda maior S. Francisci Assisiensis et eiusdem Legenda Minor* (1263), ed. Collegii S. Bonaventurae (Florence, 1941), col. 13, Prologue: 'And so not without reason is he considered to be symbolized by the angel who ascends from the sunrise bearing the seal of the living God, in the true prophecy of that other friend of the Bridegroom, John the apostle and evangelist. For "when the sixth seal was opened", John says in the Apocalypse, "I saw another Angel, ascending from the rising of the sun, having the seal of the living God".' The orthodox equation was also made in the papal bull of Leo X, *Ite vos in vineam meam* (1517), for the official recognition of the Observant Reform and the effective suppression of the Conventual Franciscans. See P. Di Fonzo, 'La famosa bolla di Leone X *Ite vos* non *Ite et vos*', *Miscellanea Francescana* 44 (1944), 164–71; and De Lubac, *La posteridad*, 1: 164. See also Fleming, *From Bonaventure to Bellini*, 18.

[30] The schema of world history, first explained in the *Book of Concordance*, was later summarized and included in the printed version of his commentary on the Apocalypse (1527). I used the copy in the Biblioteca Nacional de México. It is also found in a compilation of his thought – with tracts on the Sibylline Oracles, Antichrist, and the temporal *status* of the Church – published as *Abbas Joachim magnus propheta. Hec subiecta in hoc continentur libello. Espositio magni prophete Ioachim: in librum beati Cirilli de magnis tribulationibus & statu Sanctae matris ecclesie: ab hiis nostris temporibus vsque ad finem seculi vna con compilatio ex diversis prophetis Noui ac Veteris Testamenti . . . Item explanatio figurate & pulchra in Apochalypsim de residuo statu Ecclesie . . . Item Tractus de Antichristo . . . Item Tractus septem statibus Ecclesie* (Venice, 1516; repr. by Bernardinum Benalium, 1520).

Fig. 1 Francisco de Escobar, convent of San Francisco, Lima, seventeenth century. 'Joachim directs the painting of St Francis in San Marco, Venice'. Photo: author

Joachimite text was translated into Náhuatl, the ancient language of the Aztecs.[31]

I said before that Joachim of Fiore and flying Francis of Assisi were seen in Latin America shortly after the eruption of Huaynaputina. I should really have informed the reader that they were seen in colonial painting. Between the years 1601 and the late eighteenth century, at least twelve extant series of cloister paintings of the life of Francis of Assisi were created containing scenes in which Joachim may have appeared.[32] Unfortunately, certainty cannot be attained because several of the individual canvases have disappeared and several others are so severely damaged that it is impossible to be sure. I shall examine the most important examples without keeping to a strict chronology, beginning with those from the Andean region within earshot of the volcano Huaynaputina.

31 The text is known as the *Floreto de Sant Francisco* (not to be confused with the more familiar *Little Flowers*). See *Floreto de Sant Francisco, Sevilla 1492*, ed. Juana Mary Acelus Ulibarrena (Madrid, 1998), 149–58.

32 The only known cloister painting in Europe containing Joachim's portrait is that of the convent of Ognissanti, Florence. Interestingly enough, it was painted in 1601, one year after the eruption of Huaynaputina. See Bondatti, *Gioachinismo e francescanesimo*, 163–4; Batazzi, 'L'iconografia francescana', 278–80.

One of the earliest cycles was painted by the layman, Francisco de Escobar, for the cloister of the convent or friary of San Francisco, Lima, sometime in the seventeenth century [fig. 1]. Abbot Joachim, dressed in black, stands directing an artist to paint St Francis. Both seem to be privileged to look into the future where, to the right, the apocalyptic Francis flies by above St John the Evangelist, depicted upon the island of Patmos writing his visions, and below a balcony from which St Bonaventure and another doctor observe and write at their desks. I speculate that the second figure might well be that of the Franciscan scholar Peter John Olivi the primary theorist of the Spiritual Franciscans, a fervent Joachite, and author of a *Commentary on the Apocalypse* (1295). Olivi's exaltation of Francis as the angel of the Apocalypse comes closest to the later *De conformitate* of Bartholomew of Pisa in considering Francis to be a perfect *alter Christus*.[33] In his exposition of St Francis' *Rule*, Olivi incorporated a Joachimite scheme of history into it by expanding on Francis' statements about missionary activity and had Francis speak of an expectation of global salvation during the transitional days between the second and third statuses.[34] Olivi's 'franciscanizing' Apocalypse commentary was particularly admired by the Observant Franciscans (the group that evangelized America) who had it printed at their own expense in Venice in 1513.[35] Hence, contrary to the opinion of some commentators such as Professor Joseph-Ignasi Saranyana,[36] I think that John Peter Olivi is the best candidate for the identity of the figure in this painting and in another that I will mention below.

Here the scene represents the famous legend narrating that Joachim had travelled to Venice, where he had prophetically directed the depic-

33 In spite of the opposition of the Inquisition, Peter John Olivi's Joachimist ideas circulated in Europe, especially Spain. See Manselli, *La 'Lectura super Apocalypsim'*, 211; idem, 'La resurrezione di san Francesco dalla teologia di Pietro de Giovanni Olivi ad una testimonianza di pietà popolare', *Collectanea Francescana* 46 (1976), 309–20; idem, 'L'Apocalisse e l'interpretazione francescana della storia', in W. Lourdaux and D. Verhelst, eds, *The Bible and Medieval Culture* (Louvain, 1979), 157–70.

34 Peter John Olivi, *Expositio super regulam fratrum minorum: Peter Olivi's Rule Commentary*, ed. David Flood (Wiesbaden, 1972), fols 123v–124r.

35 See West, 'Medieval Ideas of Apocalyptic Mission', 297.

36 See Josep I. Saranyana and Ana de Zaballa, *Joaquín de Fiore y América* (2nd edn, Pamplona, 1995), 143; and Saranyana's subsequent objection to my thesis, 'Joaquín de Fiore y el joaquinismo', in Ana de Zaballa Beascoechea *et al.*, eds, *Utopía, mesianismo y milenarismo: experiencias latinoamericanas* (Lima, 2002), 57–71. Not only does Saranyana deny the presence of Peter John Olivi in these paintings, he further denies the presence of Joachim of Fiore in any of them, or the influence of Joachim's theology of history in colonial Latin America.

Fig. 2 Gregorio Vásquez Ceballos, mid-17th century.
'Joachim displays the portraits of saints Francis and Dominic'.
Photo: courtesy of the Museo Colonial de Bogotá, Colombia

tion of the two spiritual men of the Third Age, that is, St Francis and St Dominic Guzman, in the sacristy of San Marco.[37] Indeed, the image of Francis which is being painted here is later hung above the open doorway through which we see a priest and acolyte ready to begin Mass.[38] The legend is found in a number of writings, but I will venture to guess that here it derives from the *De conformitate*, *The Conformity of the Life of St Francis to that Our Lord*, written by Bartholomew of Pisa circa 1390 and published in the sixteenth century.[39] This version of the story was the most accessible to American audiences and is probably the textual source.

A related painting of the mid-seventeenth century is found in

37 See Bondatti, *Gioachinismo e francescanesimo*, 147–57. On the Joachimite theme of the *viri spirituales*, see da Campagnola, 'Dai *viri spirituales*', 24–52.

38 Hector H. Schenone, *Iconografía del arte colonial: los santos*, 2 vols (Buenos Aires, 1992), 1: 330–9.

39 Printed editions: Milan 1510, 1513. I consulted the 1513 edition. Two later editions from Bologna 1590 and 1620 are defective and appear to display deliberate omissions and tampering. The *De conformitate* has been reprinted with notes and commentary in *Analecta Francescana* 4–5 (1906 and 1912).

Fig. 3 Juan Zapaca Inka, convent of Santiago de Chile.
'The Prophecy of St John on Patmos'.
Photo: courtesy of the Museo de la Orden Franciscana, Santiago

Bogotá, Colombia [fig. 2]. It depicts the same legend, but the protagonists are now outdoors in the Piazza San Marco: Joachim holds two paintings or models of the spiritual leaders, Francis and Dominic.[40] As in the Lima painting, this artist, Gregorio Vasquez y Ceballos, has chosen to dress Joachim in a black robe as a Benedictine, even though, as a former Cistercian, he should really be vested in white, as we shall see below.[41]

Joachim appears again in a series of cloister paintings by the Indian artist Juan Zapaca Inka in Santiago de Chile shortly after a devastating earthquake of 1647 [fig. 3]. At least two additional copies of this painting were made by other Indian artists: one for the Franciscan convent in Cuzco, Peru, in 1668 (one year after another eruption of Huaynaputina), and another for their convent in the Indian town of Ocopa, Peru, in 1768. Both locales are within the general area of Huaynaputina and other active volcanoes.

The three paintings represent a scene of the 'Prophecy' or prediction

40 This legend corresponds to the version as told by St Antoninus of Florence. See *Divi Antonini archiepiscopi Florentini Chronicorum opus* (Lyons, 1586), part III, 559.

41 Schenone, *Iconografía*, 337. See note 14 above.

Fig. 4 Basilio de Santa Cruz, convent of San Francisco, Cuzco, Peru, 1668. 'The Prophecy of St John on Patmos'. Photo: author

of the coming of St Francis as the sixth angel of the Apocalypse who rises up from the East.[42] On the right, the Eritrean Sibyl observes from a hilltop, with St Bonaventure below her. On the left, John of Patmos is inspired to write his Apocalypse, whilst above in a hut the diminutive figure of Joachim with a long beard is barely visible. In the Cuzco version of the painting, we can see him better. Once again, he is painting; but this time he sits below three suns, symbolic of the two ages that have come and gone and of the now-dawning third age [fig. 4].[43]

42 On Francis of Assisi as the sixth angel of the Apocalypse, see Bihel, 'S. Franciscus fuitne'; da Campagnola, *L'angelo del sesto sigillo*. Unfortunately, the authors do not treat the Counter-Reformation era.

43 Gabriel Guarda *et al.*, *Barroco hispanoamericano en Chile: Vida de San Francisco de Asís* (Santiago de Chile, 2002), 30–1; and Schenone, *Iconografía*, 334–5.

Joachim also appears in at least three representations of the birth of St Francis. In Mexico, the lay artist Luis Berrueco painted two elaborate canvases sometime before 1750, and possibly a third.[44] The first painting was housed in the Franciscan church of the Indian town of Huaquechula located at the foot of yet another active volcano, Popocateptl.[45] The work was commissioned by a wealthy Indian chief [fig. 5]. The birth of St Francis is witnessed not only by Joachim (correctly dressed in white at the extreme right), but also by St Bonaventure, the Sibyl, St John the Evangelist, the archangel Raphael, and by the prophets of the Last Days, Enoch and Elijah. The Sibyl, placed on the lower left, writes these words in her book: 'There will be a fearful beast who will come from the East and two stars will rise up against it'. The beast, a dragon with a long tail depicted next to Joachim, is falling headlong whilst two stars seem to be pursuing it.[46] The figure on the lower right, who I identify once again as Peter John Olivi, writes in his book the familiar quote from Revelation 7, 2: 'I saw another angel who came up from where the sun arises . . .'.

The background of the canvas may further relate to the Book of Revelation, chapter 6, verses 12–13: 'And the sun went as black as coarse sackcloth; the moon turned red as blood, and the stars of the sky fell upon the earth'. The details seem to describe events similar to those of a volcanic eruption; indeed, something like an eruption is occurring behind the figure of Joachim.[47] In the *De conformitate*, Bartholomew of Pisa explicitly likened the coming of Francis of Assisi to an earthquake by reference to this biblical verse: [*Franciscus*] *factus est terremotus magnus*.[48]

Recently, I have had the good fortune to discover a second painted version of this theme that was originally housed in the conventual church of the Franciscans in the nearby city of Atlixco, which is also within the potential destruction area, or 'red zone', of the Mexican

44 Elisa Vargas Lugo and Marco Días, 'Historia, leyenda y tradición en una serie franciscana', *Anales del Instituto de Investigaciones Estéticas*, Universidad Nacional Autónoma de México 44 (1975), 59–82. I have made some preliminary investigation of a series on the life of St Francis in San Martín Texmelucan, Puebla (also near the Mexican volcano), that leads me to believe there was another identical painting.

45 In the Mexican state of Puebla. The painting was stolen in 2000 when its iconographic value was discovered. Lamentably, it is now lost.

46 The beast is identified with Mohammed in the *De conformitate* (Milan, 1513), fol. 12r.

47 The possible visual reference to 'sackcloth' might hint at the *ordo saccis vestitus* mentioned by Joachim of Fiore. See Reeves, *The Influence of Prophecy*, 168 and 182.

48 See 'De conformitate', *Analecta Francescana* 4 (1906), 77.

Fig. 5 Luis Berrueco, church of San Martín, Huaquechula, Mexico, before 1750. 'The Nativity of St Francis'. Photo: author

volcano.[49] Here we see a youthful and handsome Joachim (extreme left), together with St Bonaventure and the evangelist John (upper left), the Sibyl and John Peter Olivi (lower left), and an Old Testament prophet [fig. 6]. The defeated seven-headed dragon and the pursuing stars are more clearly evident at the lower right; whilst the smiling face of a dawning sun – a new age – appears over the horizon.

The earliest treatment of this theme appears to have been in 1601 at Potosí, Bolivia – again, near to Huaynaputina, and only one year after the first eruption, but it has unfortunately lost its auxiliary figures.[50] A

49 Vargas Lugo and Díaz, 'Historia, leyenda y tradición', 66. There was a third and earlier series in the convent of San Francisco, Mexico City. A later series in Zacatecas may have had a similar scene, as also the series at the Franciscan church of Antigua, Guatemala, a city destroyed in an earthquake. See Luis Luján Muñoz, 'Nueva información sobre la pintura de Cristóbal de Villalpando en Guatemala', *Anales del Instituto de Investigaciones Estéticas* 57 (1986), 113–37; and Juana Gutiérrez Haces *et al.*, *Cristóbal de Villalpando (ca. 1649–1714): catálogo razonado* (Mexico City, 1997), 261–3, 385–7.

50 According to Mgr Bernardino Rivera, OFM, auxiliary bishop and historian of Potosí, there were originally thirty-six paintings of the life of St Francis in the cloister by the painter Francisco Navarro. Many were lost in 1880 when cloister walls and ceilings were replaced. The 'Nacimiento' was cut down to make room for the installation of a new stairway.

Fig. 6. Luis Berrueco, from Atlixco, Mexico, before 1750. Private collection. 'The Nativity of St Francis'. Photo: author

later version of the theme of Francis's birth in Santiago de Chile, again by Juan Zapaca Inka, does not depict Abbot Joachim. It does, however, include the defeated demons, the archangel Raphael, dressed as a pilgrim, who seals the infant Francis with the cross, and again the same archangel who carries the news and image of the saint's birth to Enoch and Elijah in Paradise.[51] In Joachim of Fiore's writings on the Book of Tobit, the archangel Raphael represents both the person and the inspiration of the Holy Spirit in the third age. The archangel Raphael also acted as godfather at Francis's baptism in popular legend and art.[52]

* * *

[51] Saint Bonaventure, *Legenda Maior*, prologue. For the Chilean iconography, see Guarda, *Barroco hispanoamericano*, 34–5.

[52] Lerner, 'Joachim of Fiore's Vision of Irenic Conversion', and Guarda, *Barroco hispanoamericano*, 36–9.

It is obvious from these images that the proper subject of the paintings is not Joachim of Fiore but rather Francis of Assisi, and one could understand Joachim's appearance here as merely a moment in popular Franciscan eschatology or an 'ornamental use' of Joachim of Fiore, as one author has stated.[53] Granted, the authentic works of Joachim would not be determined until the twentieth century, and Joachimite texts were commonly accepted as part of his canonical works.[54] But the fact is that, in addition to his image in art, Joachim's three ages of world history were known in the Americas, and with some precision of thought amongst the christianized Incas and Maya.

Twentieth-century anthropologists have been able to document beliefs in the ages of the Father, Son and Holy Spirit, among indigenous people in mountain villages and remote hamlets of the Andes.[55] The precise locations are important because they are more or less coextensive with the ancient Inca empire, but the epicentre of the belief can be situated around Huaynaputina. This area is also replete with images of the winged Francis of Assisi.

The Trinitarian legends to which I am referring have several variations all of which show an imprecision or popularization when compared to Joachim's *three ages* as articulated in his authentic writings. They also demonstrate a syncretic convergence between the three pre-Hispanic ages and a later trinitarian reinterpretation.[56]

In brief, the first Andean age is that of *Dios Yaya,* God the Father, and the time of the *machu*, meaning Gentiles. The second is that of *Dios Churi*, God the Son, Jesus Christ, understood as the new solar deity who, during the evangelization, replaced the Aztec sun god, Inti.[57] Solar

53 See Saranyana and Zaballa, *Joaquín de Fiore y América*, 143.

54 Cf. Saranyana, 'Joaquín de Fiore y el joaquinismo', 67. To say, as Saranyana does, that Joachim's thought was never known in America because his authentic works circulated together with Joachimite texts is just as ludicrous as to say that Thomas Aquinas's ideas were unknown to eighteenth- and nineteenth-century scholars because they came through secondary sources and commentaries.

55 Henrique-Osvaldo Urbano, 'Del sexo, incesto y los ancestros de Inkarrí: mito, utopía e historia en las sociedades andinas', *Allpanchis* 17–18 (1981), 77–103; Fernando Fuenzalida, 'El mundo de los gentiles y las tres eras de la creación', *Revista de la Universidad Católica*, Pontificia Universidad Católica del Perú, ns 2 (1977), 59–84; Olivia Harris, 'De la fin du monde: notes depuis le nord-Potosí', *Cahiers des Ameriques Latines* n.s. 6 (1987), 93–118; Manuel M. Marzal *et al.*, *The Indian Face of God in Latin America* (Maryknoll, NY, 1996), 86.

56 Henrique Osvaldo-Urbano, '*Dios Yaya, Dios Churi* y *Dios Espíritu*: modelos trinitarios y arqueología mental en los Andes', *Journal of Latin American Lore* 6 (1980), 111–27.

57 See Jaime Lara, 'The Sacramented Sun: Solar Eucharistic Worship in Colonial Latin America', in Peter Casarella and Raúl Gómez, eds, *El Cuerpo de Cristo: the Hispanic Presence in the U.S. Catholic Church* (New York, 1998), 261–91.

imagery and metaphors were used by the missionaries from the earliest moments of the New World evangelization to create an indigenous Christology. In Mexico, for example, the Franciscans inserted black obsidian mirrors in their outdoor crosses, not only to catch the sunlight, but also to retain the pre-Hispanic connotations of sacred blood, human and divine, offered in sacrifice to the solar deity.[58] In Peru, on the other hand, a common feature of evangelization churches is a solar eucharistic balcony at the east end of the building behind the high altar. Some of these balconies were lined with mirrors and used for the exposition of the Blessed Sacrament in its monstrance at the hour of sunrise. Thus, the age of *Dios Churi*, Jesus Christ the *sol iusticiae*, was ingeniously crafted as a new solar era; and this belief continues today. For the majority of those interviewed over the last thirty years by the anthropologists, the second age is the present moment in which we live.

The third age is that of *Dios Espíritu*, God the Holy Spirit, and for many of those interviewed, it was to begin in the millennial year 2000. The transition from one age to the other occurs through a catastrophe, a tragedy with cosmic dimensions, a universal cataclysm, which is the aforementioned *pachacuti*, the upheaval of world, time, and space.[59] For example, between the first and second ages the Gentiles are said to have risen in insurrection against the newborn sun, and were subsequently burnt to death by its heat.[60] We can now understand why the natives reacted to the eruption of Huaynaputina in the way they did, and the fact that the conquered Incas saw the event as the end of one age and the beginning of another: they anticipated the defeat of the European invaders and their god.

Both the concept of *pachacuti* and of three world ages can be traced back to pre-Hispanic times by way of the early chroniclers, such as the Jesuit historian Anello Olvia, who approvingly recorded and published this Inca version of providential history in 1601, significantly only one year after the eruption of Huaynaputina.[61] Another written source is

58 See Lara, *City, Temple, Stage*, 41–69.

59 Thérèse Bouysse Cassagne, *La identidad Aymara: aproximación histórica (siglo XV, siglo XVI)* (La Paz, 1987), 174–95; Manuel Burga and Alberto Flores Galindo, 'La utopía andina', *Allpanchis* 17–20 (1982), 85–102; Sabine MacCormack, '*Pachacuti*: Miracles, Punishments and Last Judgment: Visionary Past and Prophetic Future in Early Colonial Peru', *American Historical Review* 93–4 (1988), 960–1006; eadem, *Religion in the Andes: Vision and Imagination in Early Colonial Peru* (Princeton, NJ, 1991), 281–331; and Milhou, 'Apocalypticism', 27–30.

60 In another version, a judgement by water or deluge had occurred at the end of the first *age*. See Fuenzalida, 'El mundo de los gentiles', 63–4.

61 MacCormack, '*Pachacuti*', 980–1.

that of the christianized Inca, Felipe Guaman Poma de Ayala, an Andean picture-thinker and social commentator.[62] In his *New Chronicle and Good Government* (1615), he identified the eruption of Huaynaputina and the destruction of the city of Arequipa as divine chastisement and as one of the signs of the approaching end of the world.[63] In Guaman Poma's schema, there are several world epochs, each represented by a historical figure as in Joachim's exegesis.[64] It seems more than coincidental that the fourth epoch commenced with King David, whom Guaman Poma depicts playing a ten-stringed harp,[65] in accordance with the title of one of Joachim's major theological works, the *Psalterium Decem Chordarum*.[66]

Furthermore, Guaman Poma's half-brother, Martin de Ayala, was a secular priest who later became a hermit. The holiness of hermits held a special attraction for the author, and one could speculate that he knew of Joachim of Fiore, the holy hermit of Mount Etna, and admired him for precisely that reason (see http://www.kb.dk/elib/mss/poma/index-en.htm; fol. 645).[67]

The description of the third age in modern Andean mythology is particularly striking. In remarkable consistency with the colonial anti-Spanish feelings, today's descendants of the Incas hope for a return

62 The autograph manuscript of Guaman Poma, housed in the Royal Library of Denmark, Copenhagen (GkS 2232 4to) consists of nearly 1200 pages, including 398 full-page drawings.

63 See the author's manuscript illustration at http://www.kb.dk/elib/mss/poma/index-en.htm at fol. 1061 [consulted 6 December 2004]. See also, Guaman Poma de Ayala, *Nueva corónica y buen gobierno*, ed. J. Murra, Rolena Adorno and Jorge L. Urioste (Madrid, 1987); Rolena Adorna, *Guaman Poma: Writing and Resistance in Colonial Peru* (2nd edn, Austin, TX, 2000); Jan Szeminski, 'From Inca Gods to Spanish Saints and Demons', in Steven Kaplan, ed., *Indigenous Responses to Western Christianity* (New York, 1995), 56–74.

64 Juan Ossio, 'Las cinco edades del mundo según Felipe Guaman Poma de Ayala', *Revista de la Universidad Católica* ns 2 (1977), 43–58.

65 See http://www.kb.dk/elib/mss/poma/index-en.htm, fol. 28 (consulted 6 December 2004).

66 Joachim of Fiore, *Psalterium decem chordarum* (Venice, 1527). The *Psalterium* was earlier known through the mendicant publication *Abbas Joachim magnus propheta*: see above, n. 30. Also see MacCormack, 'Pachacuti', n. 59.

67 The association of holy hermits to Joachim of Fiore's third age of the Holy Spirit was explicitly made by Pedro de Quiroga, canon of the cathedral of Cuzco, Peru. Joachim is frequently mentioned in relation to the holy hermit, Cyril of Mt Carmel (of the Sibylline Oracles), and with Enoch and Elijah in the *De conformitate* (Milan, 1513), fol. 12r. See MacCormack, '*Pachacuti*', 975, who believes that Guaman knew of Joachim's works through his close working relationship with the Jesuits. Even if he never mentions Joachim of Fiore by name, his contemporaries in Peru certainly did. The Jesuit, José de Acosta, and the Augustinian friar, Antonio de la Calancha, both cite Joachim's *Treatise on the Apocalypse* and other writings.

of Inca Viracocha, the great creator god and culture hero. The third age will supposedly be a utopian and paradisiacal time when human beings will become *runas*: they will sprout multi-coloured wings and fly like hummingbirds (or like the flying Francis). They will be vegetarians, and there will be no disease or injustice.

Flying men were not unknown in pre-conquest Peru; they appear to have been Inca priests who dressed in flying costumes. But it appears that the myth was contaminated or deliberately altered early on by the mendicant friars' stories of their spiritual men like flying Francis of Assisi or flying Dominic de Guzmán.[68] The reinterpretation through a Christian lens seems more than coincidental.

It also seems more than coincidental that in seventeenth- and eighteenth-century literature both the Jesuits and the mendicant orders were aggressively claiming Joachim of Fiore as the visionary who foresaw their particular orders' founding. In the Andes, Francis of Assisi flies as the herald of the Inca-Christian third age. Francis also flies in other Andean painting with multi-coloured wings as another Michael the Archangel defending the dogmas of the Catholic Church against the charges of the Protestant heretics – often in a visual defence of the doctrine of the Immaculate Conception.[69]

Nor is it by coincidence that Protestants were particularly critical at this moment of literary works that exalted Francis of Assisi, such as the *De conformitate*, which they considered blasphemous and they virulently ridiculed. One such stinging satire had been written by Erasmus Alber (1500–53), a student of Martin Luther. The work first appeared in Wittenberg in 1542. It was translated into several European languages, among them an English edition of 1679 popular among Protestants in North America.[70]

68 On Andean angels, see Teresa Gisbert, *Iconografía y mitos indígenas en el arte* (La Paz, 1980, repr. 1994), 86–8. A flying St Vincent Ferrer – who had declared himself to be the angel of the Apocalypse – also appears in Latin American colonial art. By coincidence, a bust of a flying Vincent Ferrer is found in Cosenza, Italy, in the church which marks the site of Joachim's birthplace.

69 The role of St Francis as a new Michael the Archangel, who has been given the empty throne of Lucifer in heaven, is expounded in the *De conformitate*. See *Analecta Francescana* 4 (1906), 53; also John V. Fleming, *An Introduction to the Franciscan Literature of the Middle Ages* (Chicago, IL, 1977), 47. Due to publication restrictions, I was unable to include the images of these paintings in this study.

70 Alber's satire was popular well into the eighteenth century through the French translation, *L'Alcoran des Cordeliers* (1556), extant in several colonial Latin American libraries. The English edition, *The Alcoran of the Franciscans, or a sink of lies and blasphemies, collected out of a*

In response to Alber's disparagement, a Peruvian Franciscan, a *mestizo* (half-Indian, half-Spaniard) by the name of Pedro Alva y Astorga defended and amplified the *De conformitate*, and went to the opposite apologetic extreme. In 1651 he published the *Naturae prodigium gratiae portentum*, in which he went far beyond Bartholomew of Pisa to discover more than four thousand similarities between Francis and Christ.[71] The frontispiece of the work was one of the iconographic inspirations for flying Francis, who has merged totally with Christ, the crucified seraph.[72] Alva y Astorga's text for the 'Nativity of Saint Francis' corresponds to the saint's depiction and details in the paintings at Huaquechula and Atlixco. Indeed, the text was, no doubt, that used by the painter Luis Berrueco as his inspiration:

> At the birth of Francis, many rejoiced and were glad; to wit, the mother, the parents, and the relatives of the child, as well as the neighbours and friends and the whole household of his father. And those three, Joachim the Abbot, Enoch the Patriarch, and Elias the Prophet, when they heard about his nativity, rejoiced with great gladness.[73]

* * *

In sum, the few paintings we have examined in which Joachim and Francis appear together must be considered representative of several more now lost or yet to be discovered – an enterprise that this writer is actively pursuing. Joachim and the flying Francis appear in Franciscan

blasphemous book belonging to that Order called 'The Book of the Conformities' (London, 1679), was an early textbook at Yale University.

71 *Naturae Prodigium gratiae Portentum hoc est Seraphici P.N. Francisci vitae acta ad Christi D.N. Vita & mortem regulata, & coaptata...* (Madrid, 1651). Fray Pedro, Minorite, later worked in Rome on the cause of the sainthood of Francisco Solano, the only other Franciscan saint who occasionally flies in Latin American art. See *Scriptores Ordinis Minorum*, ed. Luke Wadding (Rome, 1650; repr. Bologna, 1978), 184, 187, 275.

72 See Pamela Askew, 'The Angelic Consolation of St Francis of Assisi in Post-Tridentine Italian Painting', *Journal of the Warburg and Courtauld Institute* 32 (1969), 280–305; and *Lexikon der Christlichen Ikonografie*, 8 vols (Rome, 1968–76), 6: 311–12 and fig. 16.

73 In his objection to the presence of Joachim in these paintings and to a significant influence of the abbot's thought in Latin America, Prof. Saranyana seems to be unaware of these sources. See notes 36 and 54 above. The Latin text of the *Naturae Prodigium* (p. 19) reads: 'In Nativitate Francisci multi laetati, & gauissi sunt, videlicet Mater, parentes, & cognati pueri, atque vicini, & amici, ac tota paterna domus; & tres illi, Ioachimus Abbas, Enoch Patriarcha, & Helias Propheta, audientes eius nativitatem gauissi sunt gaudio magno'. I have made use of the copy extant in the Biblioteca Nacional de México, Mexico City (No. 922, 245 FRA. a).

establishments located in highly volcanic or seismically active regions. Earthquakes and volcanoes appear to have been the stimuli for the depiction of these eschatological scenes. Joachim and the flying Francis appear more often than not in paintings either created by native artists or commissioned by wealthy indigenous nobles. Several were commissioned for Indian towns.

Joachim's presence should be seen in relation to depictions of the flying Francis of Assisi who, as the Angel of the Apocalypse, is in a defensive posture against attacks from within the Catholic Church and from without: rival claims on the part of the Dominicans and Jesuits that *their* founders were the prophesied Angel of the Apocalypse, and Protestants who satirized the excesses of Franciscan filial fervour. Rooting Francis of Assisi in Joachim's prophetic literature was an ingenious counter-measure in the polemics of the Counter-Reformation.

But it also was a visual response to Indian unrest, and an implicit approval of the political status quo in the face of a 'war of prophecies'. The seventeenth and eighteenth centuries were a time of native uprisings throughout the Spanish colonies in the Americas.[74] The astute Indian leaders of these insurrections were making use of Christian imagery and rhetoric – frequently taken from the Book of Revelation – to justify their rebellion against the Spanish Antichrist. They predicted the return of the Great Inca and the violent ousting of the interlopers.[75] The revived *mythos* of pre-Hispanic heroes like flying men of the third age were becoming more and more bellicose and dangerous to the claims of both state and church.[76] Therefore, as a counter-measure to the subversive native-inspired apocalyptic, the winged man of the third age, Francis of Assisi, was also able to re-channel native fears and aspi-

74 Antonio Porro, 'Un nuevo caso de milenarismo maya en Chiapas y Tabasco, México, 1727', *Estudios de historia novohispana* 6 (1978), 109–17; Alonso Zarzar, *Apo Capac Huayna, Jesús Sacramentado: Mito, utopia y milenarismo en el pensamiento de Juan Santos Atahualpa* (Lima, 1989), 62–3; José Luis Milafuentes Galván, 'Agustín Ascuhul, el profeta de Moctezuma. Milenarismo y aculturación en Sonora 1737', *Estudios de historia novohispana* 12 (1992), 123–41; David Timmer, 'Providence and Perdition: Fray Diego de Landa Justifies his Inquisition against the Yucatecan Maya', *ChH* 66 (1997), 477–88; D. D. Gow, 'The Roles of Christ and Inkarrí in Andean Religion', *Journal of Latin American Lore* 6 (1980), 279–98; MacCormack, '*Pachacuti*', 982–87; and Milhou, 'Apocalypticism', 26–30.

75 See Graziano, *Millennial New World*, 89–131 and *passim.*

76 In their teaching addressed to the Indians, most missionaries during the late sixteenth and seventeenth centuries, far from hastening the age of the Holy Spirit, sought to support the colonial order of society. See Sabine MacCormack, 'The Heart Has its Reasons: Predicaments of Missionary Christianity in Early Colonial Peru', *Hispanic American Historical Review* 67 (1985), 443–66.

rations into a Christian eschatology and the expectation of a fully Christian utopian third age in a world beset by apocalyptic eruptions and tremors, both geological and metaphorical. This vulcanological Joachim of Fiore and this aerodynamic Francis of Assisi were a testimony to the signs, wonders, and miracles of an age that was yet to come.

Yale University

MIRACLES IN POST-REFORMATION ENGLAND

by ALEXANDRA WALSHAM*

TO speak of miracles in post-Reformation England may seem like something of an oxymoron. The sense of internal contradiction in my title springs from the fact that sixteenth- and seventeenth-century Protestant ministers consistently maintained that this category of extraordinary events had long since ceased. They did not deny that supernatural acts of this kind had taken place in biblical times. As set down in the books of the Old Testament, God had vouchsafed many wonders to His chosen people, the Hebrews, including the parting of the Red Sea, the raining of manna from heaven, and the metamorphosis of Aaron's rod into a serpent.[1] Equally, the New Testament recorded the prodigious feats performed by Christ and his apostles to convince the disbelieving Gentiles and Jews: from the raising of Lazarus and the transformation of water into wine at the marriage at Cana to curing lepers of their sores and restoring sight to the blind, not to mention the great mysteries of the Incarnation and Resurrection.[2] But dozens of sermons and tracts reiterated the precept that God no longer worked wonders above, beyond, or against the settled order and instinct of nature – the standard definition of miracle inherited from the scholastic writings of St Thomas Aquinas.[3] Such special dispensations were the 'seales and testimonials' of the Gospel.[4] They had been necessary to sow the first seeds of the faith, to plant the new religion centring on the redemption of mankind by Jesus of Nazareth. But this gift, stressed John Calvin and his disciples, was only of 'temporary duration'.[5] Miracles were the swaddling bands of the primitive Church, the

* I am grateful to Michael Duffy, Sarah Hamilton and Andrew Spicer for support while this essay was being written and to Patrick Collinson and Tom Freeman for comments on an earlier draft.

1 Ex. 14, 26–29; Num. 11, 9; Ex. 7, 8–12.

2 See John 11, 43–44 and 2, 1–11; Mark 1, 40–42; Matt. 8, 2–4; John 9, 1–7.

3 Aquinas's views are enshrined in his *Summa Theologiae*, Ia, q. 110, a. 4. See also Ia, q. 105, a. 6–8. Key passages from his *Summa Contra Gentiles* are extracted in Richard Swinburne, ed., *Miracles* (New York and London, 1989), 19–22.

4 Fernando de Texeda, *Miracles Unmasked* (London, 1625), 4–5.

5 Ibid.; John Calvin, *Institutes of the Christian Religion*, IV/19/18–19, ed. John T. McNeill, transl. F. L. Battle, 2 vols (London, 1961), 2: 1466–7. The passage concerns the apostolic gift of healing, but Calvin also made the point in other contexts.

mother's milk on which it had been initially weaned. Once the Lord had begun to feed His people on the meat of the Word, he expected them to believe the truth as preached and revealed in Scripture rather than wait for astonishing visible spectacles to be sent down from heaven. Although there was some uncertainty about exactly when such wonders had come to an end, Protestant divines were in general agreement that, as a species, miracles were now extinct. Christians could and should not expect to see such occurrences in the course of their lifetimes.[6]

By the early seventeenth century the cessation of miracles was not merely a doctrinal precept but also a cultural commonplace. William Shakespeare alluded to it in *Alls Well that Ends Well* and the axiom that 'Miracles are ceast' was also reiterated (rather anachronistically) by the bishop of Ely in a scene in *Henry V*.[7] By the reign of James I, it had attained the status of a proverb instantly familiar to theatre audiences. And yet the vocabulary of the miraculous did not disappear from the English language. The word miracle and its derivative forms did not lapse into linguistic oblivion, redundancy or disuse. Despite repeated claims that miracles were a thing of the past, people from all spheres of society continued to use this terminology to describe strange phenomena that baffled, astonished and amazed them. The word can be found in print and manuscript no less than in the realm of ephemeral speech and idle conversation, and in the pages of learned treatises of theology and natural philosophy as well as in the inexpensive pamphlets and broadside ballads which flooded from London presses in the wake of dramatic events.

This essay seeks to explore the significance of this ostensible discrepancy, to investigate what appears to be an interesting area of inconsistency at the heart of sixteenth- and seventeenth-century religious culture. It suggests that these tensions and ambiguities cannot simply be explained away as a symptom of the failure of the English Reformation to effect more than a superficial transformation of the

[6] See for example *Later Writings of Bishop Hooper*, ed. Charles Nevinson, PS 21 (Cambridge, 1852), 44–5; James Calfhill, *An Answer to John Martiall's Treatise on the Cross*, ed. Richard Gibbings, PS 11 (Cambridge, 1846), 333; Edward Dering, *XXVII Lectures, or Readings, upon Part of the Epistle Written to the Hebrues* (London, 1590), sigs G3v–G5r; Robert Tynley, *Two Learned Sermons* (London, 1609), 59–60, 63–5; Richard Sheldon, *A Survey of the Miracles of the Church of Rome, Proving them to be Antichristian* (London, 1616), esp. 50–1; John Downame, *The Summe of Sacred Divinitie* (London, [1620?]), 377.

[7] William Shakespeare, *All's Well that Ends Well,* II. iii. 1–6; *Henry V*, I. i. 68–70. References are to the first folio of 1623.

outlook of the ordinary laity, as a measure of the perennial gap between clerical ideals and parish realities, and as a function of the stubborn resilience of traditional piety, although undoubtedly these factors did play their part. Rather it argues that miracles persisted in early modern England as much *because* of the Reformation as *in spite* of it. This is a topic that offers insight both into the ideological ruptures and dislocations which accompanied the onset of Protestantism and into the undercurrents of continuity and the unspoken, half-conscious processes of negotiation, accommodation and re-contextualization which helped to mitigate, temper and ease these iconoclastic changes. It sheds light upon a series of delicate transactions between medieval Catholicism and the new religion, between ecclesiastical discourse and popular literature, religious controversy and practical divinity, together with the confessional frictions and sectarian conflicts which the issue helped to exacerbate between Catholics, Protestants, and later Dissenters. In the process, my discussion may serve to unsettle some still prevalent assumptions about the critical role which the Reformation played in facilitating what the German sociologist Max Weber called 'the disenchantment of the world' and to reinforce Bob Scribner's well-known critique of this desacralization thesis.[8] As we shall see, if in some respects Protestantism was deeply corrosive of inherited ways of understanding the workings of the universe and sceptical about the intervention of supernatural forces in human affairs, in others it buttressed them, even as it subtly and rhetorically redefined existing opinions. Above all, I want to emphasize that we need to understand Protestantism not as a static body of dogma and doctrine dictated by the clergy but rather as a dynamic living organism, a tissue of belief and practice which the laity played a large part in shaping and which was shifting and pluralistic in tone and content in different contexts and climates.

* * *

[8] Max Weber, *The Protestant Ethic and the Spirit of Capitalism*, transl. Talcott Parsons (London, 1930), 105 (though Parsons translates '*Entzauberung der Welt*' as 'the elimination of magic from the world'). Robert W. Scribner, 'The Reformation, Popular Magic and the "Disenchantment of the World" ', *Journal of Interdisciplinary History* 23 (1993), 475–94; idem, 'Reformation and Desacralisation: from Sacramental World to Moralised Universe', in R. Po-Chia Hsia and R. W. Scribner, eds, *Problems in the Historical Anthropology of Early Modern Europe*, Wolfenbütteler Forschungen 78 (Wiesbaden, 1997), 75–92.

It would be a mistake to underestimate the importance of the miraculous in the sacramental world inhabited by late-medieval Catholics. The idea that God performed miracles upon the intercession of saints and in response to vows and promises made by the laity underpinned devotion to statues and images and the thriving practice of pilgrimage; it sustained a vast repertoire of ritual practices involving relics and sacramentals; and it was utterly central to the celebration of the mass, at the heart of which was the ineffable act of transforming mere bread and wine into the body and blood of Christ. Saturating the didactic and hagiographical literature of the later Middle Ages, miracles were a vital component of what Eamon Duffy has christened 'traditional religion'.[9] Yet, at the same time, they were an area of Catholic piety that was not without its blemishes and cracks. Anxieties about restraining lay enthusiasm for the supernatural within the parameters of orthodoxy had long been a preoccupation of the clerical hierarchy and the scandal caused by cases of corrupt monks and priests who touted false relics and miracle stories for monetary gain did raise questions about the Church's integrity, if only temporarily. By the fourteenth century, satirists like Langland and Chaucer were exploiting these points of weakness and vulnerability for comic effect.[10]

Building upon these existing strands of scepticism and criticism, the early Reformation witnessed a sustained and powerful assault upon the late-medieval culture of miracles. First of all, humanist embarrassment about popular credulity and clerical corruption, as reflected in the writings of Desiderius Erasmus and Thomas More, exercised considerable influence.[11] The determination of these humanists to distance themselves from the 'fictions' and 'fabrications' contained in works like the famous *Golden Legend* converged with an emerging strand of evangelical polemic flowing from the pens of men like William Tyndale and

9 See Thomas, *Religion and the Decline of Magic*, 27–59; R. W. Scribner, 'Cosmic Order and Daily Life: Sacred and Secular in Pre-Industrial German Society' and 'Ritual and Popular Belief in Catholic Germany at the Time of the Reformation', in idem, *Popular Culture and Popular Movements in Reformation Germany* (London, 1987), 1–16, 17–47; Eamon Duffy, *The Stripping of the Altars: Traditional Religion in England c. 1400–1580* (New Haven, CT, and London, 1992), esp. 155–205, 266–98; Finucane, *Miracles and Pilgrims*.

10 See Finucane, *Miracles and Pilgrims*, 191–202; Jonathan Sumption, *Pilgrimage: an Image of Mediaeval Religion* (London, 1975), 35–40; Peter Marshall, 'Forgery and Miracles in the Reign of Henry VIII', *P&P* 178 (2003), 39–73, 46–7.

11 See 'The Shipwreck', 'The Apparition' and 'The Religious Pilgrimage', in *The Whole Familiar Colloquies of Desiderius Erasmus of Rotterdam*, transl. Nathan Bailey (London, 1877); *The Dialogue concerning Heresies*, bk. I, chs 14–15, in *The Complete Works of St Thomas More*, ed. Thomas M. C. Lawler *et al.*, 15 vols (New Haven, CT, and London, 1981), 6.1: 85–92.

John Bale.[12] Echoing the savage words hurled by Luther and other Continental reformers at the cult of saints and its 'superstitious' adhesions, these propagandists poured venomous scorn on notorious manifestations of the miraculous. As Peter Marshall has recently shown, this was a theme taken up with considerable relish by government publicists and, in the wake of the campaign to despoil the monasteries and discredit the papacy, much effort was devoted to exposing forged and fraudulent miracles such as the mechanical contraption that moved the eyes and lips of the Rood of Boxley in Kent, the relic of the Holy Blood preserved at Hailes Abbey in Gloucestershire (which was said to come not from Christ but a duck), as well as the feigned visions and prophecies of Elizabeth Barton, the 'maid' or nun of Kent, who was executed for treason in April 1534.[13] The early Protestant attack on false miracles also owed something to the legacy left by the Lollards, to a vigorous native tradition of fierce contempt for veneration of 'stokkis and stones', 'worme-eten bonys', 'olde raggis' and other tangible manifestations of traditional belief in the physical immanence of sacred power in material artefacts.[14] The 'corrosive capacity' of this evolving body of discourse may well help to explain the 'perplexing fragility' of late medieval Catholicism in the face of the legislative offensive launched against it by the Henrician and Edwardian regimes.[15]

By the Elizabethan period these various elements of critique had crystallized into the precept that miracles had ceased. The slight hesitation that had surrounded the issue in John Calvin's *Institutes of Christian Religion* hardened into a categorical assertion that such events were now obsolete.[16] This was to become an insistent slogan repeatedly invoked by Protestant apologists in their unending war against Roman Catholi-

12 See for example, William Tyndale, *Doctrinal Treatises and Introductions to Different Portions of the Holy Scriptures*, ed. Henry Walter, PS 42 (Cambridge, 1848), 195, 232–5, 286–9; John Bale, *The Actes of English Votaryes* (2nd edn, Wesel [Antwerp], 1546).

13 Marshall, 'Forgery and Miracles', *passim*; see also Finucane, *Miracles and Pilgrims*, 203–16.

14 *The Works of a Lollard Preacher: the Sermon 'Omnis plantacio', the Tract 'Fundamentum aliud nemo potest ponere' and the Tract 'De oblacione iugis sacrificii'*, ed. Anne Hudson, EETS, os 317 (Oxford, 2001), 231.

15 Marshall, 'Forgery and Miracles', 72–3, 40.

16 See D. P. Walker, 'The Cessation of Miracles', in Ingrid Merkel and Allen G. Debus, eds, *Hermeticism and the Renaissance: Intellectual History and the Occult in Early Modern Europe* (London and Washington, DC, 1988), 111–24, 112. For the complexity of Calvin's thinking on the issue, see also Carlos M. N. Eire, *War against the Idols: the Reformation of Worship from Erasmus to Calvin* (Cambridge, 1986), 221–4; Moshe Sluhovsky, 'Calvinist Miracles and the Concept of the Miraculous in Sixteenth-Century Huguenot Thought', *Renaissance and Reformation* 19 (1995), 5–25, 9–11.

cism. The great advantage of this principle was that it allowed Protestants to demolish all Catholic miracles with a single stroke: each individual case could be automatically dismissed as an emblem of popish deceit without going to the trouble of demonstrating it in detail. The dramatic supernatural interventions cited in support of Catholic doctrines such as purgatory, transubstantiation, clerical celibacy and the immaculate conception were no more than the 'lying wonders' of Satan and the false prophets which Christ had warned would proliferate in the last days (Matt. 24 and 2 Thess. 2). Their very abundance provided patent proof that the Church of Rome was the Antichrist, the Seven-Headed Beast delineated in the Book of Revelation (Rev. 17, 11). They were either 'cunning devices' and 'juggling tricks' contrived by popish priests to delude the laity for their own profit and gain or they were examples of the extraordinary ingenuity of Lucifer, that skilled manipulator of nature, that master of the arts of optical illusion and disguise. In short, since neither the devil nor man could perform truly supernatural acts, these counterfeit marvels were not miracles at all.[17]

The argument that miracles had ceased was intimately linked with Protestantism's attempt to align itself with the forces of enlightenment and knowledge. It was part of a rhetoric of liberation from the 'superstitions' with which the medieval Church had glazed the eyes of ignorant laypeople and drugged them into servile submission and obedience. Furthermore, in consistently comparing miracles with the pap fed to infants, Protestants like Edward Dering were seeking to associate their own religion with adulthood and maturity. To require miracles in the modern era was a mark of weakness, 'infirmitie' and imperfection.[18] As Robert Tynley, archdeacon of Ely declared in a sermon preached at the Spittle in 1609,

[17] Such arguments are expounded with particular clarity in Sheldon's *Survey of the Miracles of the Church of Rome* (see n. 6 above). For a close study of how the miracles associated with St Dunstan were redefined as diabolical magic and fabricated legends, see Helen L. Parish, '"Impudent and Abominable Fictions": Rewriting Saints' Lives in the English Reformation', *Sixteenth Century Journal* 32 (2001), 45–65. For the devil as a natural magician, see Stuart Clark, *Thinking with Demons: the Idea of Witchcraft in Early Modern Europe* (Oxford, 1997), 161–78. On the theme of 'lying wonders', see also Rob Iliffe, 'Lying Wonders and Juggling Tricks: Religion, Nature, and Imposture in Early Modern England', in James E. Force and David S. Katz, eds, *Everything Connects: in Conference with Richard H. Popkin* (Leiden, 1999), 185–209.

[18] It was, he alleged, to 'doo injurie to our Saviour Christ': Dering, *XXVII Lectures*, sigs G4v–5r.

> as props which are needefull for Children to learne to goe by, are a hindrance unto them, when they are growne to mans estate, so . . . if Miracles were wrought now adaies, men would be offended by them.[19]

The Reformation critique of such spectacles also reflected a deep distrust of the visual: it reflected the consuming fear of idolatry that was such a tell-tale feature of Protestant thinking. Dering, for instance, insisted that it was by miracles that the Egyptians, Persians, and Assyrians in turn had been brought to worship mere material 'stockes and stones' and warned that by signs of this kind Satan 'carieth us indeede into deadlie blindnese'.[20] Like images, visible wonders could all too easily be false and misleading teachers. Scripture should be the sole anchor of a Christian's belief, not 'forged traditions' buttressed by these flimsy and deceptive conceits.[21] Turning the taunt that Protestantism was an upstart, new-fangled religion quite on its head, reformed ministers stressed that their faith needed no such external struts to support its verity and purity. Confirmed by the miracles worked in the time of Christ, it needed no new marvels to prove its authenticity.[22]

The doctrine of the cessation of miracles was a recurring refrain in the anti-Catholic literature of sixteenth- and seventeenth-century England, but it was reiterated with particular urgency in the Jacobean period in such tracts as Richard Sheldon's apocalyptic *Survey of the Miracles of the Church of Rome* (1616) and John Gee's *The Foot out of the Snare* (1624), a scurrilous exposé of the full range of 'Mountebanke trumpery' used by the papists in their desperate attempt to uphold their Antichristian hierarchy and seduce the simple people to serve the Scarlet Whore of Babylon.[23] The heightened temperature of claims that 'miracles had ceased' reflected the fact that, like their counterparts on

19 Tynley, *Two Learned Sermons*, 64. Seeking to refute his Catholic adversaries from their own mouths, Tynley was, in fact, quoting from the Spanish Franciscan theologian Diego de Estella (1524–78). At pp. 64–5, Tynley also cited similar assertions by Ambrosius Catharinus, John Fisher and Thomas Stapleton, whose comments reflected the distinct ambivalence of mid sixteenth-century Catholic apologists about the miraculous, as alluded to below.

20 Dering, *XXVII Lectures*, sig. G5r.

21 Sheldon, *Survey*, 35.

22 See Tynley, *Two Learned Sermons*, 66: 'we therefore thinke miracles superfluous unto us . . . because we professe the same doctrine which our Saviour and his Apostles . . . have confirmed to our hands, by so many true signes, and divine miracles . . . As for the faith of the Church of Rome, as it is new and strangely degenerating from the ancient Catholike faith, so it is no marvell if it bee confirmed by new miracles . . .'.

23 John Gee, *The Foot out of the Snare* (London, 1624); idem, *Hold fast: a Sermon Preached at Paules Crosse* (London, 1624), 38.

the Continent, the English Jesuits and seminary priests, who trained in the Low Countries and returned to England as missionaries from the mid 1570s, were actively utilizing the miraculous as an evangelical tool. Taking advantage of Protestantism's tactical decision to disarm itself of such supernatural spectacles, the Tridentine priesthood set out to advertise Catholicism's superior thaumaturgic capacities.[24] By the late sixteenth century, the mood of defensive wariness about traditional effusions of the cult of saints that had characterized the first generation of Catholic reform had begun to wane.[25] Cardinal Robert Bellarmine and other controversialists vigorously reasserted the precept that visible signs were a perpetual mark of the true Church, as well as a necessary endorsement of any 'extraordinary mission' it launched.[26] Conversely the absence of such heavenly testimonials in heretical countries was regarded as telling evidence that the Protestant Church was 'the conventicle of Satan'.[27] This energetic reaffirmation of the miraculous often involved an implicit challenge to the Reformation principle of *sola scriptura*: miracles were held to be a clearer endorsement of disputed doctrines than the Bible itself. Every sect could wrest the obscurer passages of Scripture for its own ends, wrote the Irish Jesuit Richard Archdekin in 1667, but when the Lord 'speaks by works . . . they cannot be controverted'.[28]

Accordingly, the English Catholic missionaries eagerly promoted the miracles wrought by the Virgin Mary at shrines on the Continent, including the Holy House at Loreto and the wonder-working image of

[24] See my 'Miracles and the Counter Reformation Mission to England', *HistJ* 46 (2003), 779–815. For parallel strategies on the Continent, see Philip M. Soergel, *Wondrous in his Saints: Counter-Reformation Propaganda in Bavaria* (Berkeley, CA, 1993), 159–216, and Trevor Johnson, 'Blood, Tears and Xavier-Water: Jesuit Missionaries and Popular Religion in the Eighteenth-Century Upper Palatinate', in Bob Scribner and Trevor Johnson, eds, *Popular Religion in Germany and Central Europe, 1400–1800* (Basingstoke, 1996), 183–202.

[25] See Walsham, 'Miracles', 785; Lucy E. C. Wooding, *Rethinking Catholicism in Reformation England* (Oxford, 2000), 116–17.

[26] Robert Bellarmine, *Disputationes . . . de controversiis christianae fidei* (3rd edn, Ingolstadt, 1590–3), bk. 4, ch. 14, no. 11, cols 1347–54. See also Richard Bristow, *A Briefe Treatise of Diverse Plaine and Sure Waies to Finde out the Truth* (Antwerp, 1574; repr. 1599), fols 15a–39a; Thomas Hill, *A Quartron of Reasons of Catholike Religion* (Antwerp, 1600), 33–9.

[27] George Musket, *The Bishop of London his Legacy* (Saint Omer, 1623), 64–76, 65; Philips Numan, *Miracles Lately Wrought by the Intervention of the Glorious Virgin Marie, at Mont-Aigu*, transl. Robert Chambers (Antwerp, 1606), sigs A2v–C7v.

[28] Richard Archdekin, *A Treatise of Miracles . . . obtained by the sacred reliques of S. Francis Xaverius, exposed . . . at Mechlin* (Louvain, 1667), 9. See also Chamber's dedicatory epistle in Numan, *Miracles*, sig. B7v: 'miracles are more evident proofes of a true religion then are the Scriptures'.

the Madonna and child lodged in an oak tree at Montaigu, near Sichem, on the battle-scarred frontier of the Spanish Netherlands. They also actively circulated stories of the strange prodigies and judgements which had signified divine disapproval of the execution of their captured colleagues, as well as the remarkable thaumaturgic cures worked by Edmund Campion's girdle and rib, the thumb of Edmund Geninges, and a wide range of other gory martyrs' relics. They made much mileage out of Protestant patients who were converted after recovering from dangerous illnesses reversed by the application of sacramentals imported from the Continent, like wax tablets bearing the figure of the *agnus dei* and bottles of holy water blessed in the name of Saints Francis Xavier and Ignatius of Loyola.[29] And they became adept at transforming the rite of exorcism into a dramatic spectacle symbolizing the expulsion of the unclean spirit of the Calvinist heresy itself, most notably in the case of the group of servants and adolescents dispossessed at Denham and Hackney by a team of priests led by the Jesuit William Weston in 1585–6.[30]

The skill and success with which the Counter-Reformation priesthood deployed the miraculous as a vehicle for teaching Tridentine dogma and for instructing the laity how to behave in the face of persecution does much to explain the frequency and vehemence with which Protestants repeated the mantra that miracles had ceased. It also accounts for the outpouring of pamphlets dedicated to exposing the 'egregious impostures' perpetrated by these runagate priests. John Gee, for instance, devoted nearly an entire tract to unmasking the fake apparitions created by paper lanterns, transparent glasses and Jesuits dressed in white sheets which had persuaded innocent Protestant girls to enter overseas convents.[31] In another example of this viciously satirical genre, *The Jesuits Miracles, or New Popish Wonders*, Robert Pricket set out to unmask as a machiavellian fraud an ear of straw stained with the blood of the Gunpowder Plot martyr Henry Garnet, upon which had subsequently appeared an exquisite portrait of the dead Jesuit's visage [fig. 1]. Pricket and other Protestant writers were merciless in their mockery of

29 See Walsham, 'Miracles', 788–99.

30 Ibid., 800–5. These exorcisms were the subject of a devastating attack by S[amuel] H[arnset], *A Declaration of Egregious Popish Impostures* (London, 1604), which incorporates extensive summaries of the content of the 'book of miracles' prepared by Weston. See also D. P. Walker, *Unclean Spirits: Possession and Exorcism in France and England in the Late Sixteenth and Early Seventeenth Centuries* (London, 1981), 43–9; F. W. Brownlow, *Shakespeare, Hausnett and the Devils of Denham* (Newark, DA, 1993).

31 John Gee, *New Shreds of the Old Snare* (London, 1624).

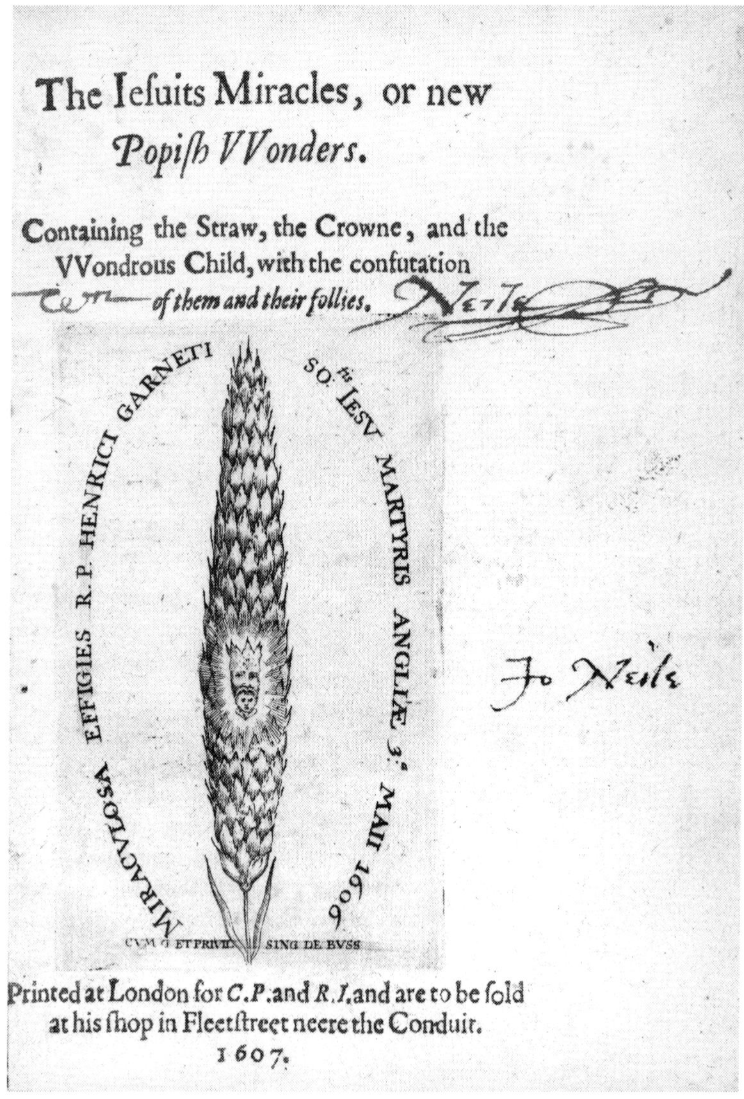

The Ieſuits Miracles, or new *Popiſh VVonders.*

Containing the Straw, the Crowne, and the VVondrous Child, with the confutation *of them and their follies.*

Printed at London for *C.P.* and *R.I.* and are to be ſold at his ſhop in Fleetſtreet neere the Conduit. 1607.

Fig. 1 R[obert] P[ricket], *The Jesuits Miracles, or new Popish Wonders. Containing the Straw, the Crowne, and the Wondrous Child* . . . (London, 1607), title-page. By permission of the British Library. Shelfmark: C117.b.13.

this effigy, which they alleged to be the work of an ingenious engraver, and did not fail to point out that Garnet, a well-known defender of equivocation, was depicted with a double face. Thomas Coryate sarcastically ranked this incident among 'the merry tales of Poggius the Florentine' and the same tactic was employed by many other propagandists.[32] It became conventional to dismiss the many miracles contained in the medieval legends of the saints as 'old wives' tales' and to compare the 'Ignatian fables' circulated by the Jesuits with the fictitious histories of Guy of Warwick and Bevis of Southampton – entertaining stories which might be suitable reading by a winter fireside 'to drive a man out of a melancholie fit', but not matters which intelligent and rational Protestants would regard with any seriousness.[33] But the hilarious tone of such pamphlets should not deceive us into thinking that they regarded the threat which Catholic miracles presented as feeble or negligible: on the contrary they believed that laughter was the most devastating weapon they could mobilize against it. Protestantism's repeated reiteration of the doctrine of the cessation of this class of supernatural acts embodied a frank awareness that no loophole could be left unclosed if the seductive appeal of these 'new popish wonders' was to be successfully countered.

It is important to underline the polemical context in which the assertion that miracles had ceased almost invariably occurred. As the post-Reformation period progressed, spokesmen for the Church of England strategically invoked the same precept to discredit other dissenting groups whose activities involved an implicit or explicit claim to this kind of divine vindication. It was a weapon in the acrimonious disputes that surrounded the celebrated dispossessions by fasting and prayer carried out by John Darrell and other puritan exorcists in the 1580s and 90s[34] and it reared its head in much mid seventeenth-century propaganda against the thaumaturgic exploits of enthusiastic sects, including the Ranters, Muggletonians, and especially the Quakers,

32 R[obert] P[ricket], *The Jesuits Miracles, or new Popish Wonders* (London, 1607), esp. sigs B1v–3v; Thomas Coryate, *Coryats Crudities* (London, 1611), 625.

33 Sheldon, *Survey*, 23; Sir Edward Hoby, *A Letter to Mr T. H[iggons] late Minister: Now Fugitive* (London, 1609), 101–2. Such allegations were commonplace. See, e.g., Barnaby Rich, *The True Report of a Late Practise Enterprised by a Papist* (London, 1582), sigs B1r, E1r; Reginald Scot, *The Discovery of Witchcraft* (London, 1665 edn; first publ. 1584), bk 8, ch. 7, 87–8.

34 See Walker, *Unclean Spirits*, 66–9; Thomas Freeman, 'Demons, Deviance and Defiance: John Darrell and the Politics of Exorcism in Late Elizabethan England', in Peter Lake and Michael Questier, eds, *Conformity and Orthodoxy in the English Church, c.1550–1660* (Woodbridge, 2000), 34–63.

whose leader George Fox later compiled a 'book of merakells' worked by himself and his disciples as a natural accompaniment to 'the first breaking forth of the Truth'.[35] To orthodox Protestant heresiographers like William Prynne, Ephraim Pagitt and Thomas Edwards, the pretensions of the sectaries in this area were further proof that they were simply papists in disguise, the old enemy Antichrist dressed in a new set of clothes.[36]

* * *

But what exactly did Protestants mean when they said that miracles had ceased? This question becomes all the more pressing when one turns to the technical theological treatises in which reformed ministers examined the attributes and properties of God. In the course of their explications of the doctrine of providence, we find that their attitude to this category of events was rather more complicated than I have hitherto implied. Here, significantly, they seem reluctant to rule out completely the possibility that miracles might still be manifested. This would have been to bind the hands of God and to impose limits on the prerogative of a deity who was, by definition, omnipotent. Divine omnipotence was one of the keynotes and capstones of Protestant theology, a traditional feature of Augustinian Christianity upon which the reformers, especially John Calvin, placed fresh, if not unprecedented emphasis. This preoccupation with the supreme majesty and sovereignty of God was a side-effect of Protestantism's fierce determination to eliminate all intermediaries between the Almighty and the individual believer and to strip away the pantheon of wonder-working saints venerated by the populace as minor deities. It was also a function of the central Reformation tenet of justification by faith alone, a corollary of the notion that human beings could take no steps of their own to achieve salvation but were helplessly dependent upon the Lord's mercy and grace. Accordingly, Protestants envisaged a universe ruled over by a God who foreknew all events and dynamically intervened to bring them about. It was a commonplace that not a single sparrow perished, not a drop of rain, nor a leaf from a tree, nor a hair from one's head fell to the ground

35 This was probably only compiled in the late 1680s, towards the end of Fox's life. The manuscript is now lost but its contents are ingeniously reconstructed by Henry J. Cadbury in *George Fox's 'Book of Miracles'* (Cambridge, 1948).

36 See William Prynne, *A Fresh Discovery of some Prodigious New Wandring-Blasing-Stars, and Firebrands, Stiling Themselves New-Lights* (2nd edn, London, 1646), 13; Thomas Edwards, *Gangraena* (3rd edn, London, 1646), pt I, 32; Ephraim Pagitt, *Heresiography* (2nd edn, London, 1654), 140.

without His express permission. His finger could be detected in the most mundane and trivial occurrences no less than in earth-shattering events – in a painful bee-sting on the nose or a spider discovered swimming in the family porridge bowl no less than in an earthquake, volcano, fire, or flood.[37]

The question of miracles arose in the context of discussion of the precise mechanisms by which Providence worked. It was widely agreed that God could operate both mediately and immediately. He could employ the intricate network of instruments and forces which He had established at the time of the Creation, but equally, as the Oxford divine William Pemble insisted, He was able to work 'either against or beside that order so appointed'.[38] According to the Essex vicar Ralph Walker, the Lord was not 'so tied to second causes, as that when they faile, his Providence ceaseth unto us'.[39] Yet, paradoxically, in acting thus God was not subverting His original plan: miracles were not spontaneous improvisations in response to human actions or invocations but rather events for which the Almighty had foreseen the need in His infinite wisdom and built into His scheme from the very beginning of time.

One of the particular difficulties which confronted the theologians was distinguishing between events which did in fact transgress or contradict nature and those which merely seemed to do so – those which, as the exiled puritan theologian William Ames wrote in his *Marrow of Sacred Divinity*, were merely 'by a metonymy of the effect called a Miracle'.[40] What he meant was that in using this term one was simply employing a figure of speech. In other words, such occurrences only appeared miraculous in the eye of the beholder: their actual 'natural' causes remained cloaked and hidden from the view of imperfect human beings. Technically they were preternatural rather than supernatural, *miranda* rather than *miracula*, wonders or marvels rather than miracles. This theme of the subjectivity of the miraculous reflected a significant strand within the thinking of St Augustine, for whom Creation was the sole, all-encompassing miracle, a system into which God had integrated stupendous signs and wonders which would strike

37 For a fuller discussion, see my *Providence in Early Modern England* (Oxford, 1999), 8–15.

38 William Pemble, *A Treatise of the Providence of God*, in *The Workes of that Learned Minister of Gods holy Word, Mr. William Pemble* (3rd edn, London, 1635), 259–79, 279, and see 278–9 *passim*.

39 Ralph Walker, *A Learned and Profitable Treatise of Gods Providence* (London, 1608), 54.

40 William Ames, *The Marrow of Sacred Divinity* (London, 1642), 47.

awe and admiration into the hearts of feeble mankind, but which were in essence no less 'natural' than the daily rise and setting of the sun or the regular turn of the tides.[41] By a semantic sleight of hand, some theologians thus subsumed miracles into the category of 'special' or 'extraordinary providences'. Others, though, separated this kind of happening out into a class of its own, carving out a small space for them on the outer fringes of Reformed cosmology and conceding that they might very occasionally occur. Yet, however defined, in practice the line between the merely prodigious and the truly miraculous remained very blurred and hazy indeed – a problem compounded by the fact that advances in natural philosophy were constantly pushing back the frontiers of scientific knowledge.[42]

Collapsing the boundary between nature and supernature was one way of reconciling the doctrine that miracles had ceased with orthodox providential theology. Linked with this was a tendency to draw a distinction between physical, thaumaturgic miracles and mystical or spiritual ones that transpired within the realm of the soul. This had its roots in a sermon preached by Martin Luther in 1535, which insisted that the material variety of wonders had been a feature only of the early days of Christ's Church, a concession to the needs of converting the idolatrous heathens, but maintained that the miracles which the Holy Spirit wrought in the hearts and consciences of true believers continued in perpetuity. Taken up by Calvin and later writers, this interiorization of the concept of the miracle[43] allowed Protestants to have their cake and eat it too. It enabled them to dismiss cures wrought by Roman Catholic images, relics, sacramentals and other inanimate objects as fraudulent and false and to deny that priests and other individual persons could be conduits of supernatural power (a gift which had

41 St Augustine, *Concerning the City of God against the Pagans*, bk 21, ch. 8 and bk 22, ch. 8, transl. Henry Bettenson (Harmondsworth, 1972), 979–83 and 1033–47 respectively. John A. Hardon provides a useful, if somewhat apologetic, survey of changing conceptions of the miraculous in 'The Concept of Miracle from St. Augustine to Modern Apologetics', *Theological Studies* 15 (1954), 229–57. For medieval views, see Ward, *Miracles and the Medieval Mind*, 3–19. 'The blending of the miraculous and the natural in Calvinist cosmology' is central to Sluhovsky's argument in 'Calvinist Miracles', 20 and *passim*.

42 See Clark, *Thinking with Demons*, esp. 153–5, 161–78, 262–6, 279; Lorraine Daston, 'Marvelous Facts and Miraculous Evidence in Early Modern Europe', *Critical Inquiry* 18 (1991), 93–124. On contemporary understandings of the relationship between natural and miraculous causation, see also Paul H. Kocher, *Science and Religion in Elizabethan England* (San Marino, CA, 1953), 93–118, esp. 104–14.

43 See Bernard Vogler, 'La Réforme et le miracle', *Revue d'histoire de la spiritualité* 48 (1972), 145–9; Eire, *War against the Idols*, 221–4.

ceased when the 'Lords apostles, and Extraordinary Messengers fell asleep')[44] and yet simultaneously to claim that God had not stopped demonstrating His mighty power to the elect. The intangible mysteries of evangelical renewal and justifying faith were the real miracles of the modern age. As the Nottinghamshire minister Charles Odingsells asserted in a sermon delivered in 1619, in the guise of the conversion of intransigent sinners and profane unbelievers 'invisible miracles' were 'wrought daily and plentifully in the visible Church'.[45] The Lord's providential intercessions in the lives of those He had predestined to a place in heaven were likewise evidence of His unceasing miraculous interventions. Only by the miracle of His love, preached Paul Baines, could God melt the hard and frozen hearts of unregenerate human beings.[46]

Miracles, then, occupied a decidedly grey area in Protestant theology. The tangled complexity of reformed thinking on this topic must be underlined, but it is also vital to recognize that reformed clergymen were not unwilling to exploit the fundamental ambiguity which surrounded the category of the supernatural to win the populace round to the Protestant cause. In a context of confessional rivalry, they often glossed over the technical, polemically driven distinction between a miracle and a providence and exploited popular incomprehension of the hair-splitting intricacies of these scholarly definitions. By declaring that miracles had ceased, Protestants were (in a sense) cutting off their nose to spite their face, but in the guise of providence they were conveniently able to reclaim essentially the same kind of divine approbation. Like their Catholic rivals, they too needed to be able to demonstrate that God was on their side. Furthermore, few could resist the temptation to slip into the emotive and potent language of the miraculous for rhetorical effect. Thus, determined 'to stop the mouths of our insolent adversaries, which are alwaies craking of their miracles', Robert Tynley insisted that the advent of Protestantism itself was a miracle: the 'restoring of the puritie of religion . . . from the drosse and corruptions

44 To use the words of a mid-seventeenth-century writer: London, BL, MS Sloane 1926, fol. 1r.

45 Charles Odingsells, *A Discourse of Miracles*, in *Two Sermons Lately Preached at Langar in the Valley of Belvoir* (London, 1620), 59.

46 Paul Baynes, *The Mirrour or Miracle of Gods Love unto the World of his Elect* (London, 1619), 9–10 and *passim*.

of Antichrist', he said, could not have been achieved 'without the extraordinary and powerful working of almighty God'.[47]

Dozens of patriotic sermons and tracts used the same terminology to describe the special blessings which the Lord had bestowed upon England since 1559, proclaiming that the nation's many providential deliverances from popish plots and conspiracies were equally miraculous. They cited the failure of repeated attempts to assassinate Elizabeth I (who was herself posthumously celebrated as 'a mirrour and miracle of princes')[48] and the collapse in 1623 of the projected match between Prince Charles and the Habsburg Infanta, and they laid particular emphasis on the defeat of the Spanish Armada in 1588 and the discovery of the Gunpowder Plot in 1605. In engravings like Samuel Ward's *Double Deliveraunce* of 1621, they depicted Philip II's invincible flotilla of ships being dispersed by a heaven-sent wind and the supernatural shaft of light revealing the dastardly Guy Fawkes to the authorities on his way to blow up the Houses of Parliament.[49] In due course, the Restoration of Charles II to the throne and the Glorious Revolution which had rescued England from the tyranny of Stuart Catholicism and from the jaws of arbitrary power, would similarly be celebrated among what came to be termed the 'great miracles of this latter age'.[50] In practice, then, Protestant preachers and ministers frequently employed the words miracle and providence almost interchangeably.

* * *

With these observations in mind, we must now turn to examine in more detail some of the events which contemporaries identified and loosely referred to as miracles, principally as reported in the inexpensive news pamphlets and ballads combining journalistic description and moralistic commentary which flowed from English, as from many

47 Tynley, *Two Learned Sermons*, 66.

48 See *A Most Excellent and Remarkable Speech Delivered, by that Mirrour and Miracle of Princes, Queen Elizabeth of Famous Memory* (London, 1643).

49 See Walsham, *Providence*, 243–7. Samuel Ward, *To God, In Memorye of his Double Deliveraunce from the Invincible Navie and the Unmatcheable Powder Treason* (Amsterdam, 1621).

50 *The Diary of Sir Simonds D'Ewes (1622–1624): journal d'un étudiant londinien sous le règne de Jacques 1er*, ed. Elisabeth Bourcier (Paris, 1975), 164. See also Alexander Brome, *A Congratulatory Poem on the Miraculous, and Glorious Return of that Unparallel'd King Charles the II., May 29. 1660* (London, 1660); *A Proclamation . . . a Miraculous Deliverance from Popery and Arbitrary Power* (London, 1689). The Civil War defeats of the King were celebrated by Parliament's supporters in similar terms: see, e.g., *A Miraculous Victory Obtained by the Right Honourable Ferdinando, Lord Fairfax* (London, 1643); *[E]nglands Miraculous Preservation Emblematically Described* (London, 1647).

European presses in the sixteenth and seventeenth centuries. It is necessary to recognize the element of sensationalism implicit in this genre and to take account of the commercial instincts of booksellers who packaged these leaflets and broadsides with catchy titles and intriguing woodcuts with the aim of luring people to buy them. At the same time it is a mistake to interpret cheap print of this kind as inherently disconnected from the realm of serious clerical discourse: the same stories appear in both sermons and three-halfpenny pamphlets and there was constant two-way traffic between the pulpit and the ephemeral press.[51] Differences of emphasis, tone and theological sophistication cannot disguise the fact that these texts share many points of overlap. Both provide evidence of the nature and contours of popular Protestantism; both reveal how far the Reformation was able to assimilate aspects of traditional piety and to rehabilitate them in a new guise; both embody a cosmology that accommodated, even enhanced expectations about the intercession of supernatural forces in the earthly world.

Many of the occurrences described as miracles in sixteenth- and seventeenth-century England were of a punitive and admonitory character. Thus when a minor tremor shook London and the southern counties in April 1580, damaging buildings and killing a young shoemaker's apprentice and a maidservant, clergy and laity alike interpreted it as 'a rare and unaccustomed miracle'.[52] Similarly a pamphlet entitled *Miracle upon Miracle* described the floods which ravaged Coventry in 1607 and warned that only an unbeliever would search for natural causes.[53] Grotesquely deformed infants were often explained as 'miraculous' interventions by the deity to alert humanity to the consequences of sin and ingratitude, and the plight of an elderly Welsh woman who sprouted a crooked horn on her forehead in 1588 was also seen as a spectacle sent directly by God to punish her for cuckolding her husband and to deter others from doing the like [fig. 2].[54] When three

51 For a more detailed exposition of this argument, see Walsham, *Providence*, 32–64.

52 Arthur Golding, *A Discourse upon the Earthquake that Hapned throughe this Realme of Englande* (London, 1580), sig. B3v. This tract was incorporated into the official order of prayer issued to appease divine wrath: 'A godly Admonition for the time present', in William Keatinge Clay, ed., *Liturgical Services: Liturgies and Occasional Forms of Prayer Set Forth in the Reign of Queen Elizabeth*, PS 30 (Cambridge, 1847), 572.

53 *Miracle upon Miracle or A True Relation of the Great Floods which Happened in Coventry, in Lynne, and other Places* (London, 1607), esp. 6.

54 See for example, *Gods Handy-worke in Wonders. Miraculously Shewen upon Two Women, Lately Delivered of Two Monsters* (London, 1615); *A Myraculous, and Monstrous, but yet, most True, and Certayne Discourse of a Woman . . . in the Midst of whose Fore-head. . . . There Groweth out a Crooked Horne . . .* (London, 1588).

A myraculous, and Monſtrous, but yet moſt true, and certayne diſcourſe, of a Woman (now to be ſeene in London) of the age of threeſcore yeares, or there abouts, in the midſt of whoſe fore-head (by the wonderfull worke of God) there groweth out a crooked Horne, of foure ynches long.

Jmprinted at London by Thomas Orwin, and are to be ſold by Edward White, dwelling at the little North dore *of Paules Church, at the Signe of the Gun.* 1588.

Fig. 2 *A myraculous, and Monstrous, but yet, most true, and certayne discourse of a Woman . . . in the midst of whose fore-head . . . there groweth out a crooked Horne . . .* (London, 1588), title-page.
By permission of the Huntington Library, San Marino, CA.

bodies rose out of their graves in the Danish city of Holte in 1616, a pamphlet appeared announcing this 'Miraculous News' and a mysterious vision of clashing armies seen in the sky above Berkshire in 1628 was likewise described as a 'miraculous' apparition.[55] A Jacobean compilation of news items entitled *A Miracle of Miracles* contained the stories of a young German girl resurrected from the dead to prophesy woe against vanity and pride and of the appearance of the devil disguised as a headless black bear in rural Somerset, as well as an account of the 'great deluge' which had drowned villages in Lincolnshire, Norfolk, Suffolk and Kent in 1613 [fig. 3]. The first two of these reports of allegedly recent events were actually Elizabethan favourites which the unscrupulous publisher John Trundle (whose trademark was 'Read and Tremble') had quite literally updated to satisfy the voracious appetite of the English book-buying public for wonders.[56]

Both preachers and pamphleteers heralded such events as 'visible sermons' and 'tongues of heaven'. They interpreted them either as 'extraordinary preachers' sent by God to warn mankind of the imminent end of the world or as portents of the interim plagues He regularly visited upon wicked communities and countries to induce them to repent. God's three arrows of war, famine and pestilence were not only devastating catastrophes in and of themselves; they were also signs of the Apocalypse and the Second Coming. Like Israel before it, England was an ungrateful and iniquitous nation which had to be shaken out its stupor, indifference and apathy with the aid of astonishing miracles.[57]

Alongside these collective calamities we may situate cautionary tales of the divine judgements which the Almighty meted out to incorrigible sinners. Stories of adulterers and drunkards struck down in the height of their vice and impiety and of perjurers, murderers and sabbath-breakers who came to spectacularly sticky ends were not only a standard feature of the cheap print of the period. They were also obsessively collected by godly Protestant ministers such as Oliver Cromwell's schoolmaster, Thomas Beard, as sources of moral instruction and

55 *Miraculous Newes, from the Cittie of Holdt . . . Where there were Plainely Beheld Three Dead Bodyes Rise out of their Graves . . .*, transl. T. F. (London, 1616); *Looke up and See Wonders. A Miraculous Apparition in the Ayre, Lately Seene in Barke-shire . . .* (London, 1628).

56 T. I., *A Miracle, of Miracles . . .* (London, 1614). See Gerald D. Johnson, 'John Trundle and the Book-Trade 1603–1626', *Studies in Bibliography* 39 (1986), 177–99.

57 Walsham, *Providence*, 116–224.

A Miracle, of Miracles.

As fearefull as euer was ſeene or heard of in the memorie of MAN.

Which lately happened at *Dichet* in Sommerſetſhire, and ſent by diuers credible witneſſes to be publiſhed in LONDON.

Alſo a Propheſie reuealed by a poore Countrey Maide, who being dead the firſt of October laſt, 1613. 24. houres, reuiued againe, and lay fiue *dayes weeping, and continued propheſying of ſtrange euents to come, and ſo died the 5. day following.*

Witneſſed by M. *Nicholas Faber*, Parſon of the Towne, and diuers worthy Gentlemen of the ſame countrey. 1613,

Withall, Lincolneſhires Teares. For a great deluge, in which fiue Villages were lamentably drowned this preſent month.

At London printed for *John Trundle*: and are to be ſold at Chriſt Church gate. 1614.

Fig. 3 T. I., *A Miracle, of Miracles* (London, 1614), title-page. By permission of the British Library. Shelfmark: C39.d.5.

edification.[58] And in the pages of Beard's famous *Theatre of Gods Judgements* (1597) the word miracle appears not infrequently. A section devoted to detailing the awful fates of those who had persecuted God's faithful children, for instance, contains the story of one Doctor Whittington, an ecclesiastical official who presided over the burning of 'a certaine godly woman' from Chipping Sudbury in Gloucestershire only to be gored to death shortly afterwards by a furious bull which broke loose and, 'pricked forward with some supernatural instinct', ran straight through him with his horns, trailing his guts 'all the street over, to the great admiration and wonder of all that saw it'. '[N]one can be so dull and ignorant', declared Beard, 'but must needs confesse a plaine miracle of Gods almightie power, and a worke of his owne finger'.[59] This story came from John Foxe's 'Book of Martyrs' and was itself a piece of Protestant folklore, an oral tradition passed down from father to son before being related to the martyrologist half a century later. This helps to explain the element of embellishment that is all too evident in its narrative structure; in fact reports of the death of this particular bishop's chancellor were somewhat premature: he outlived the alleged accident by more than a decade and a half.[60] Such stories were part of a long tradition of punitive miracles, the roots of which stretch far back into the didactic literature of the medieval past – a tradition of anthologies of sermon exempla dating from the twelfth century onwards which Protestants like Beard ruthlessly plundered for additional examples of divine indignation against evil-doers, incorporating them into their own collections with little sense of ideological inconsistency or embarrassment and only the minimum of theological sterilization.[61]

Tridentine writers were not slow to highlight the apparent hypocrisy of their enemies in this regard. Writing in 1565, the Louvain exile Thomas Stapleton made the point with unusual acuity. Protestants might fulminate against the ridiculous occurrences found in such texts as Bede's *Ecclesiastical History*, but

58 Ibid., 65–115.

59 Thomas Beard, *The Theatre of Gods Judgements* (1st edn, London, 1597; 3rd edn, 1631), 60–1.

60 John Foxe, *Actes and Monuments* (4th edn, London, 1583), 775–6. On Foxe's errors in connection with this case, see James Frederic Mozley, *John Foxe and his Book* (London, 1940), 163–4.

61 See Walsham, *Providence*, 71–2.

> let them shewe a reason why the Actes and Monuments of M. Fox, deserve not the lyke. Are there not also in that donghell heaped a number of miserable miracles to sette forth the glory of their stinking Martyrs?[62]

'Iff the Crosse of saint Oswalde seme a superstitious tale', asked Stapleton, 'how much more fonde and fabulous is the tale of one that suffred at Bramford, with a greate white crosse, appearing in his brest?' He concluded that the 'upstert sectaries' had not a single leg to stand upon.[63] This polemical theme was developed at much greater length by Nicholas Harpsfield in his Latin treatise *Dialogi sex* published the following year.[64] In fact most of the 'straunge wonders' Foxe incorporated were either psychological or naturalistic in character. They did not demand the kind of willing suspension of disbelief that was necessary in the case of the frankly fantastic miracles reported in much medieval hagiography, the rigorous humanist revision of which was one key manifestation of the Counter Reformation itself. But it is certainly true that the accounts of heroic heretics who died at the stake that he acquired from a variety of sources did contain occasional references to prodigious phenomena like incombustible organs and bizarre spectral tokens which were strikingly similar to those contained in the traditional lives of the saints. Foxe did not always edit these out.[65] These were aspects of the Catholic culture of the miraculous which popular Protestantism, despite the sceptical rhetoric of its own controversialists, did not so much undercut or erode as perpetuate, albeit in a restrained and modified guise.

Similar themes emerge when we turn to other occasions on which the interventions of the Almighty bore a more benevolent face. We have already seen the word miracle creep into descriptions of God's

62 Bede, *The History of the Church of Englande*, trans. Thomas Stapleton (Antwerp, 1565), sig. C1r.

63 Ibid.: Bramford was a mistake for Brentwood.

64 [Nicholas Harpsfield] Alan Cope (pseud.), *Dialogi sex* (Antwerp, 1573; first publ. 1566), esp. 540–1, 666–8, 680–1, 688. Harpsfield's comments also referred to miracles mentioned by Luther and other Protestant writers.

65 Foxe, *Actes and Monuments* (1563 edn), 95, 433, 444, 520, 881, 1040, 1355, 1669. A number of these 'miracles' were left out of the second and later editions. See also Patrick Collinson, 'Truth, Lies and Fiction in Sixteenth-Century Protestant Historiography', in Donald R. Kelley and David Harris Sacks, eds, *The Historical Imagination in Early Modern Britain: History, Rhetoric, and Fiction 1500–1800* (Cambridge, 1997), 37–68, 55–7. This is a complex topic, to which it is impossible to do justice in a single paragraph. I am grateful to Tom Freeman for comments that saved me from a serious lapse of judgement.

intercessions on behalf of the English monarchy and state. It also appears regularly in stories of men and women rescued from imminent danger of death. Thus in 1631 the survival for nine months of eight sailors left behind by mistake in the inhospitable, ice-bound climate of Greenland was attributed to 'Gods power and providence' and celebrated as a 'miraculous preservation', notwithstanding their Robinson Crusoe-like ingenuity in searching out food and fending off ravenous beasts.[66] So too was the deliverance of Edmond Pet and his crew from the peril of a violent storm at sea in 1613, after all on board knelt and earnestly prayed that the Lord might save them from a watery grave, just as in the Bible He had preserved Jonah in the belly of the whale and snatched Daniel from the jaws of the lions.[67] Once again it is possible to detect curious echoes of the miracle tales of the late Middle Ages, in which the traveller delivered from maritime danger by the intercession of the Virgin Mary or another saint is a familiar motif.[68] Here, though, several typical elements have been silently excised: God alone acts to rescue these hapless human beings and the ritual repetition of the *Ave Maria* and *Pater Noster* which is often central to such exempla is no longer a feature. To reconcile the episode with the Protestant theology of providence it is also necessary to assume that the Lord was not spontaneously responding to the importunate pleas of these people, but rather carrying out a decision He had made at the time of the Creation. Such stories are suggestive of the transmutations of the miraculous that accompanied the onset and entrenchment of the Reformation.

Even more revealing of this process of cultural migration is a news pamphlet reporting the 'strange miracle' of John Jones, an upright and innocent Protestant youth from the thoroughly Calvinist city of Dort in the northern Netherlands. Falsely accused of robbing an innkeeper, Jones was sent to his death on the gallows at Christmas 1612, but preserved alive for five days by God, who placed beneath his feet an invisible stool and fed him with the ethereal aid of one of His angels. Despite his ordeal, when taken down from the gibbet the young man was discovered to be in perfect health, his robust resilience a testimony

66 *Gods Power and Providence: Shewed in the Miraculous Preservation and Deliverance of Eight Englishmen, Left by Mischance in Green-land Anno 1630* (London, 1631).

67 *Lamentable Newes, Shewing the Wonderfull Deliverance of Maister Edmond Pet Sayler* (London, 1613).

68 Caesarius of Heisterbach, *The Dialogue on Miracles*, transl. H. von E. Scott and C. C. Swinton Bland, 2 vols (London, 1929), 1: 515–16; 2: 59, 209–10; Johannes Herolt, *Miracles of the Blessed Virgin Mary*, transl. C. C. Swinton Bland (London, 1928), 64–7.

Fig. 4 *A True Relation of Gods wonderfull mercies, in preserving one alive, which hanged five dayes, who was falsely accused* (London, [1605?]), title-page. By permission of the British Library. Shelfmark: C143.b.19. The running head of this pamphlet reads 'A strange miracle'.

A Wonder of Wonders.

BEING

A faithful *Narrative* and true *Relation*, of one

Anne Green, Servant to Sir *Tho. Reed* in *Oxfordshire*, who being got with Child by a Gentleman, her Child falling from her in the house or Office, being but a span long, and dead born, was condemned on the 14. of *December* last, and hanged in the Castle-yard in *Oxford*, for the space of half an hour, receiving many great and heavy blowes on the brests, by the but end of the Souldiers Muskets, and being pul'd down by the leggs, and was afterwards beg'd for an Anatomy, by the Physicians, and carried to Mr. *Clarkes* house, an Apothecary, where in the presence of many learned Chyrurgions, she breathed, and began to stir; insomuch, that Dr. *Petty* caused a warm bed to be prepared for her, let her blood, and applyed Oyls to her, so that in 14 hours she recovered, and the first words she spake were these; *Behold Gods Providence! Behold his miraculous and loving kindness!* VVith the manner of her Tryal, her Speech and Confession at the Gallowes; and a Declaration of the Souldiery touching her recovery. *Witnessed by Dr. Petty, and Licensed according to Order.*

Fig. 5 W. Burdet, *A Wonder of Wonders. Being A faithful Narrative and true Relation, of one Anne Green* (London, 1651), title-page. By permission of the British Library. Shelfmark: E. 621 [11].

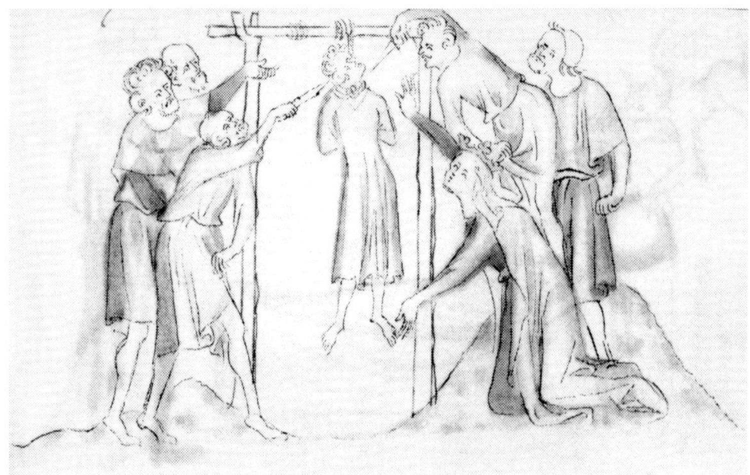

Fig. 6 Queen Mary Psalter (early 14th century), British Library, MS Royal 2 B. vii, fol. 206r: Ebbo the thief supported on the gallows by the Virgin for two days. By permission of the British Library.

to this stupendous act of divine vindication [fig. 4].[69] More than a generation later, a servant named Anne Green was executed at Oxford in December 1650 for the crime of infanticide. When removed to an apothecary's house for dissection, her body showed unexpected signs of life and, after strenuous efforts lasting fourteen hours by the surgeons (involving blood-letting, the application of plasters to her breasts and the insertion of a clyster pipe), she regained consciousness and reputedly spoke the words: 'Behold Gods Providence! Behold his miraculous and loving kindness!' [see fig. 5].[70] Her extraordinary recovery was interpreted by many commentators, respectable students of medicine among them, as evidence of her innocence of the charge of murdering the infant in her womb and supernatural proof that she had merely suffered a miscarriage.[71] Once again these cases have intriguing medieval antecedents: the tale of the hanged man or woman miraculously

69 *A True Relation of Gods Wonderfull Mercies, in Preserving One Alive, which Hanged Five Dayes, who was Falsely Accused* (London, [1605?]). A ballad on the same topic survives in manuscript: Andrew Clark, ed., *The Shirburn Ballads 1585–1616* (Oxford, 1907), 159–63.

70 *Newes from the Dead. Or A True and Exact Narration of the Miraculous Deliverance of A. Greene . . .* (Oxford, 1651), title-page. See also W. Burdet, *A Wonder of Wonders. Being a Faithful Narrative and True Relation, of one Anne Green . . .* (London, 1651); *A Declaration from Oxford, of Anne Green* (London, 1651).

saved is a topos which repeatedly reappears in hagiographical compilations associated with the Virgin, St James of Compostella, and St Thomas Cantilupe of Hereford too [fig. 6].[72] In these post-Reformation examples, though, there is no suggestion, as there is in some earlier versions, that a hardened criminal can be delivered solely because of his pious devotion to Our Lady or other celestial patron. Instead the occurrences (which probably reflect the blundering inefficiency of contemporary methods of capital punishment!) have been re- contextualized, and in the case of John Jones, who is said to have stoically resisted the proselytizing assaults of the Jesuits, given a sharply anti-Catholic and confessional edge.[73] Pruned of their overtly Marian and popish allusions, these miracles survived the ruptures of the Protestant Reformation in a refined form. It would be wrong, however, to interpret these strands of apparent continuity too swiftly or simplistically as evidence of stubborn Catholic survivalism, of a kind of cultural dissimulation beneath which lay a hard core of religious conservatism. It may be more appropriate to see them as emblematic of the complex processes by which English society made the transition to a new theological environment.

Some of the same points apply to the patterns of underlying continuity that can be discerned when one turns to examine other medical miracles. These had always formed the majority of thaumaturgic wonders wrought at medieval pilgrimage shrines[74] and the abolition of the cult of saints in the 1530s and '40s removed a vast network of heavenly specialists in areas from gynaecology and obstetrics to plague and the toothache, which had hitherto occupied an important place within the eclectic health care culture of the populace. Notwithstanding

71 *Mercurius Politicus*, 28 (12–19 December, 1650) and 32 (9–16 January 1650[1]), pr. in Joad Raymond, ed., *Making the News: an Anthology of the Newsbooks of Revolutionary England 1641–1660* (Moreton-in-Marsh and New York, 1993), 182–4, and see Raymond's commentary on 170–3.

72 Caesarius of Heisterbach, *Dialogue on Miracles*, 1: 53–5; 2: 60–1, 74; Herolt, *Miracles*, 22–3; *Acta SS Octobris I*, 682. See the article by Michael Goodich in this volume, 135–56.

73 *A True Relation*, sigs A3v–4r. Distinctively Tridentine variations on this theme also survive from seventeenth-century France. See Roger Chartier, 'The Hanged Woman Miraculously Saved: An *Occasionnel*', in idem, ed., *The Culture of Print: Power and the Uses of Print in Early Modern Europe*, transl. Lydia G. Cochrane (Cambridge, 1989), 59–91. A similar broadsheet about an innocent maiden who survived her hanging near Rheims in 1589 was published in Augsburg: Walter L. Strauss, *The German Single-Leaf Woodcut 1550–1600: a Pictorial Catalogue*, 3 vols (New York, 1975), 3: 1194.

74 Finucane calculates that nine tenths of the late medieval miracles reported were medical: *Miracles and Pilgrims*, 59.

Protestantism's massive assault upon the resources of supernatural power sanctioned and supplied by the Catholic Church, 'miraculous' cures continued to be witnessed and documented in the sixteenth and seventeenth centuries. This is apparent not least at sites which had formerly been venerated as holy wells and which enjoyed a second life in this period as healing spas and springs. Doctors and Protestant divines tried hard to wean people from the idea that the waters of such wells derived their virtue from the saints to whom they had once been dedicated and stressed instead the salutary effects of their mineral properties. Writing about one such resort at Newnham Regis in Warwickshire, Walter Bailey, Regius Professor of Physic at Oxford, complained that too many were convinced that their remedial qualities 'were supernaturally given from God without any ordinarie meanes. . .. Much like unto the superstition of our forefathers'.[75] But it would be wrong to imply that physicians and ministers were allies in a process of secularization which denuded these sites of spiritual or sacred meaning; on the contrary, they continued to interpret them within a framework of firmly religious assumptions. The discovery of new healing wells was itself frequently regarded as an extraordinary divine dispensation: thus a pamphlet about a fountain recently 'found out' in Cheshire in 1600 heralded it as evidence of the magnanimity of Providence and urged readers to praise God, the 'great Guider of nature, and over ruler of naturall causes'.[76] Doctors sometimes spoke of springs as a kind of divine NHS for poor people who could not afford their charges and 'perish for want of outward meanes' and the catalogues of cures they compiled to advertise them are scattered with explicit (if often parenthetical) references to their 'miraculous' character.[77] The theological ambiguity of such writers about the status of these cures was symptomatic of the equivocal and evasive nature of Protestant thinking on this critical subject.

Nor can we ignore the continuity in post-Reformation England of the traditional ceremonies in which the monarch touched for the king's

[75] Walter Bailey, *A Briefe Discours of certain Bathes or Medicinall Waters in the Countie of Warwicke neere unto a Village called Newnam Regis* ([London?], 1587), sig. A3v.

[76] G. W., *Newes out of Cheshire of the New Found Well* (London, 1600), sig. D2v. See also sig. A3v and *passim*.

[77] M[ichael] St[anhope], *Newes out of York-shire* . . . (London, 1627), 20. On the language used to describe cures, see my 'Reforming the Waters: Holy Wells and Healing Springs in Protestant England', in Diana Wood, ed., *Life and Thought in the Northern Church c.1100–c.1700: Essays in Honour of Claire Cross*, SCH.S 12 (Woodbridge, 1999), 227–55, 252.

evil or scrofula.[78] Dating back to the time of King Edward the Confessor in the eleventh century, the survival and powerful later seventeenth-century revival of this form of thaumaturgic healing may also be seen as a symbol of the ideological ambivalence I have been underlining. Purified of its more conspicuously 'popish' features under Edward VI and Elizabeth I, demand for this royal rite of magical healing remained high throughout the period under discussion. Elizabeth initially discontinued the practice, doubting both its lawfulness and its effectiveness, but, anxious to counteract Catholic taunts about the illegitimacy of her claim to the throne as an excommunicated heretic, was said to have 'soon quitted that Fitt of Puritanisme'.[79] By the end of her reign official apologists were celebrating the miraculous cures wrought 'by the sacred hands of the Queenes most Royall Majesty' in extravagant tones.[80] Even James I, who thought the ritual a superstitious relic of popery in flat contradiction of the Calvinist precept that miracles had ceased, found himself obliged to satisfy the desire of the populace for access to the supernatural power of which, as an anointed king, he was believed to be a conduit. At least at first, however, he hedged the ceremony about with casuistical qualifications – preceding it with a sermon and exhorting his audience to consider the rite he was about to perform as no more than an earnest prayer to heaven on behalf of the sick, lacking any hint of intrinsic efficacy.[81] A monarch who clung so tenaciously to the doctrine of the divine right of kings could hardly afford to relinquish a spectacle that enhanced the sacred aura and dignity of the English Crown. In this way, the royal miracle was integrated into Protestant culture, growing to a peak of popularity under Charles II, who touched over 100,000 people in the course of his reign.[82]

In the guise of this practice we may perhaps see English Protestantism edging gently away from its earlier rejection of the idea that individual persons could be actual vessels or instruments of divine

78 Raymond Crawfurd, *The King's Evil* (Oxford, 1911) should be supplemented by Marc Bloch, *The Royal Touch: Sacred Monarchy and Scrofula in England and France*, transl. J. E. Anderson (London, 1973), esp. 181–92, 207–13.

79 Henry Stubbe, *The Miraculous Conformist*... (Oxford, 1666), 9.

80 See the royal surgeon William Clowes's *A Right Frutefull and Approoved Treatise, for the Artificiall Cure of that Malady, called in Latin Struma, and in English, the Evill, Cured by Kinges and Queenes of England* (London, 1602), sig. A2v, and also the royal chaplain William Tooker's *Charisma: Sive Donum Sanationis* (London, 1597).

81 For James I, see Bloch, *Royal Touch*, 188, 191–2; Crawfurd, *King's Evil*, 83–8.

82 Bloch, *Royal Touch*, 212.

influence and grace.[83] At a popular level, this had always been a powerful tendency, as had the belief that the gold coins called angels bestowed upon patients in the course of the ceremony were more than a mere token or pledge. Scrofula sufferers often supposed that if they lost or misplaced these specially inscribed items they might suffer a relapse.[84] Such objects thus became a kind of Protestant amulet or sacramental. The Long Parliament's earlier determination to abolish this remnant of popish idolatry seems to have served only to enhance demand for it. Crowds flocked to the captured monarch and after his execution in January 1649 stories circulated of handkerchiefs soaked in the royal martyr's blood which had worked miraculous cures, 'to the comfort of the Kings friends, and astonishment of his Enemies'.[85] According to Royalist propaganda, visitors apparently travelled for miles to see a fifteen-year old girl from Deptford whose eyesight had been restored by the application of one such gory rag, and who in turn became a kind of relic herself.[86] Such cases are inescapably evocative of Roman Catholic reverence for sacred objects and were vehemently denounced in these terms by puritan propagandists, but once more we should hesitate before instinctively echoing their judgement. What these episodes reveal is seventeenth-century Protestantism's ability to absorb and accommodate tendencies which the passionate polemical battles of the early Reformation had hitherto relegated far beyond the pale.

This analysis may also help to explain why the mid-seventeenth century saw such a dramatic resurgence of claims by ordinary persons to be able to work miraculous effects on the ailing individuals upon whom they laid their healing hands. The Irish 'stroker' Valentine Greatrakes, who 'cured' many people of scrofula and other diseases in the 1660s by means of a technique which sceptical opponents described

83 There was, however, some theological ambiguity on this point. Protestant writers admitted that God did employ human beings as the mechanisms of His Providence but emphatically insisted that His omnipotent power could not be communicated to any creature: see Arthur Dent, *A Sermon of Christes Miracles* (London, 1610 edn, first publ. 1608), sigs B2r–3r.

84 Bloch, *Royal Touch*, 183.

85 *A Miracle of Miracles: Wrought by the Blood of King Charles the First, of Happy Memory, upon a Mayd at Detford . . .* (London, 1649), title-page.

86 Ibid., *passim.* For the polemical content and purpose of this pamphlet, see Andrew Lacey, *The Cult of King Charles the Martyr* (Woodbridge, 2003), 62–4. In the 1680s, reports of cures wrought by the Duke of Monmouth and his sister were publicized as part of the campaign in support of his rival claim to succession to the Stuart throne. See *A True and Wonderful Account of a Cure of the Kings-Evil* (London, 1681).

in terms resonant of modern physiotherapy, is perhaps the most famous of these Protestant thaumaturges. Many leading lights of the Church and Royal Society were convinced by Greatrakes's assertion that his gift was given by God 'to convince this Age of Atheism' and to 'abate the pride of the Papists, that make miracles the undeniable Manifesto of the truth of their church', even if they quibbled about the precise status of these events.[87] Greatrakes was somewhat unusual in being an orthodox member of the Church of England; most of his rivals belonged to enthusiastic sects like the Society of Friends. As mentioned above, George Fox recorded dozens of 'merakells' wrought on the deaf and dumb, crippled and chronically ill, among which the alleged resurrection of Dorcas Erbury from the dead by James Nayler in Exeter gaol in 1656 became a notorious legend of sectarian blasphemy and pretension.[88] Such episodes remind us that the miraculous had once again become a highly contentious category of occurrence, a weapon of controversy and a target of fresh accusations of popery, fraudulence and diabolism.

Even so miracles continued to proliferate towards the end of the century at an apparently growing rate – that is if the incidence of pamphlets describing them can be given any interpretative weight. The story of Marie Maillard, a thirteen-year-old lame Huguenot girl who was instantly healed while reading a Bible in November 1693 was particularly celebrated. As she was perusing the passage in Mark 2 in which Christ cures a man afflicted by the palsy, she heard her tumorous thigh bone snap and 'a Voice saying unto her, *Thou art healed*' and presently she was able for the first time to walk about freely and easily.[89] The episode inspired a number of copy-cat cases among Baptists and

87 *A Brief Account of Mr. Valentine GREATRAKS, and Divers of the Strange Cures by him Lately Performed* . . . (London, 1666), 30–1. See also *Wonders if not Miracles, or A Relation of the Wonderful Performances of Valentine Greatrux* (London, 1665), and Stubbe, *Miraculous Conformist*. Greatrakes's opponents marshalled the usual arguments to counteract these claims, insisting his cures were fraudulent, diabolical or purely natural wonders and reiterating the claim that miracles had ceased: see [David Lloyd], *Wonders no Miracles* (London, 1666) and BL, MS Sloane 1926. For a detailed discussion, see Eamon Duffy, 'Valentine Greatrakes, the Irish Stroker: Miracle, Science and Orthodoxy in Restoration England', in Keith Robbins, ed., *Religion and Humanism*, SCH 17 (Oxford, 1981), 251–73.

88 Cadbury, ed., *George Fox's 'Book of Miracles'*, 5–6 and see plate II. It should be noted that the allegation that such events were 'miracles' often came from the early Quakers' opponents, who sought thereby to discredit them for their presumption. Only retrospectively did Fox and other Friends embrace this categorization. By the end of the century the Quakers were seeking to distance themselves from this aspect of sectarian enthusiasm. See Rosemary Moore's essay in this volume, 336–45.

89 James Welwood, *A True Relation of the Wonderful Cure of Mary Maillard* (London, 1694).

Anglicans, all involving an encounter with key sentences in Scripture, some in ways reminiscent of the popular puritan practice of bible divination.[90] Occurring a century and a half after the Henrician break with Rome, these were miracles with impeccable Protestant credentials. Having fled France in the wake of Louis XIV's revocation of the Edict of Nantes, Marie Maillard was a living emblem of the continuing power and relevance of international Calvinism and of the bookish piety that we tend to regard as a distinctive hallmark of zealous Protestantism.

* * *

These and other incidents lend strength to a general impression that by the 1680s and 90s some learned Protestants were relaxing their harsh line on the cessation of miracles and beginning to make concessions with regard to the question of their perpetuity. A defender of Valentine Greatrakes, the Stratford physician Henry Stubbe can be found declaring in 1666 that 'to say that Miracles are ceased is a groundless folly, if not a disingenuous impudence in giving the Lye to several Histories of various Religions',[91] while in 1713 Bishop William Fleetwood of Wales told Catholic readers of his polemical attack on the life of the Celtic virgin St Winifred: 'We are no Enemies to Miracles, but we desire to be assured that they were wrought, before we believe them'.[92] Finally, in his *Compleat History of . . . Remarkable Providences*, published in 1697, the Sussex vicar William Turner incorporated multiple examples of 'miraculous cures of diseases in this present age' and of miracles giving testimony to 'Christianity, Orthodoxy and Innocency'.[93]

The popularity of miracles in late Stuart England may at first sight seem something of a puzzle, coinciding as it does with the growth of mechanical philosophy and the first stirrings of ideas which would lay

Quotation from the summary in William Turner, *A Compleat History of the Most Remarkable Providences, both of Judgment and Mercy . . .* (London, 1697), 109–10.

90 See *A Relation of the Miraculous Cure of Susannah Arch, of a Leprosy and Ptysick* (London, 1695); *A Relation of the Miraculous Cure of Mrs Lydia Hills, of A Lameness of Seventeen or Eighteen Years Continuance* (2nd edn, London, 1696). See also the case of a shepherd cured while listening to a sermon at a nonconformist meeting: *A True Copy of a Letter of the Miraculous Cure of David Wright* (London, 1693[4]).

91 Stubbe, *Miraculous Conformist*, 26.

92 William Fleetwood, *The Life and Miracles of St Wenefrede* (London, 1713), 11, and see 39–40, 63, and his declaration that 'no understanding Protestant did ever maintain, that Miracles Ceased after the Apostles Preaching', 95.

93 Turner, *Compleat History*, pt I, ch. 82, 109–20 and ch. 148, 160–3.

the intellectual seeds of the Enlightenment. But this is to assume an anachronistic polarity between science and religion which revisionist historiography over the last decade and a half has seriously qualified and undermined. If we recognize that experimental enquiry was frequently not so much an agent of secularization as a buttress of traditional Christian truth and an ally in the discernment of the benevolence of divine Providence, it no longer becomes so difficult to explain why the leading natural philosophers of the period – Robert Boyle, Isaac Newton and others – were among the foremost advocates of belief in the existence of miracles. It is not necessary to speak of unresolved contradictions and discrepancies, of collisions and conflicts in the thinking of these figures[94] to account for the prominence of discussions of the miraculous in their scientific writings, though we should recognize that the concept was undergoing yet another subtle shift of definition, in which St Augustine's notion of nature as the sole and supreme miracle would rise to renewed prominence. Moreover, if miracles were violations of the natural order, then it followed that those most familiar with these processes were best placed to judge the veracity and authenticity of the miraculous.[95]

If the late seventeenth century saw a growing willingness to defend and document supernatural occurrences this was because they were seen as a bulwark against the tide of scepticism and deism which the Christian establishment believed was sweeping England. Just as spirits, witches, angels and demons were investigated in an effort to garner evidence that God Himself existed, so too was the careful recording of providences and miracles seen as one of the most powerful barriers which could be erected against what William Turner called 'the abounding Atheism of this Age'.[96] Now that the battle with the papists for dominance was over and the nonconformists and sectaries had been

94 See Richard S. Westfall, *Science and Religion in Seventeenth-Century England* (New Haven, CT, 1958), 70–105, esp. 85–91, and 203–4.

95 Westfall is convincingly criticized by R. M. Burns, *The Great Debate on Miracles: from Joseph Glanville to David Hume* (Lewisburg, PA, 1981), esp. 52–7 and 247–51. The argument is further developed in Peter Harrison, 'Newtonian Science, Miracles, and the Laws of Nature', *Journal of the History of Ideas* 56 (1995), 531–53, and J. J. MacIntosh, 'Locke and Boyle on Miracles and God's Existence', in Michael Hunter, ed., *Robert Boyle Reconsidered* (Cambridge, 1994), 193–214.

96 Turner, *Compleat History*, dedicatory epistle. Joseph Glanvill's *Saducismus Triumphatus* (London, 1681) is the leading example of the attempt to use witchcraft and other manifestions of the supernatural in support of the existence of God. For the ways in which providentialism developed in the context of advances in natural philosophy, see Michael P. Winship, *Seers of God: Puritan Providentialism in the Restoration and Early Enlightenment* (Balti-

tamed and contained by toleration, the real challenge was holding back the flood of irreligion. In this struggle the visible spectacles of divine majesty that had initially converted the Jews and Gentiles and planted the faith in biblical times might once again assume a critical role. In this sense, David Hume's corrosive attack on miracles in his *Enquiry Concerning Human Understanding* (1748) was by no means representative of contemporary learned opinion.[97] As Dr Jane Shaw shows in a forthcoming monograph, the eighteenth century was still very much an age of miracles, and not merely at the level of the 'meaner' and 'vulgar' sort of people.[98]

Yet it would be wrong to end with the suggestion that the late seventeenth century marked the end of a hiatus inaugurated by the Reformation. For, as argued in this essay, miracles had always retained a place in both Protestant theology and in popular practice and belief: they should not be read as an un-Protestant anomaly. Their presence and the complex processes by which their meanings and forms evolved, migrated and mutated have much to tell us about the ways in which England became a reformed nation. They also offer us a way of accounting for the interesting and enduring paradox that Protestantism presented itself as a movement designed to remove the magical and miraculous elements from religion but ended up fostering its own rich and thriving culture of the supernatural.

University of Exeter

more, MD, 1996), esp. 93–110; William E. Burns, *An Age of Wonders: Prodigies, Politics and Providence in England, 1657–1727* (Manchester, 2002), esp. 57–96.

97 Nor was it as original as has often been alleged. R. M. Burns sees it as 'a tail-end contribution to a flagging debate' about the miraculous that was initiated by advocates of belief in their perpetuity. He argues that the attack on miracles was 'a defensive reaction to this development': *Great Debate*, quotations at 10 and 12 and see esp. chs 6–8, 131–246. See the essay in this volume by Françoise Deconinck-Brossard, 356–75.

98 Jane Shaw, *Miracles in Eighteenth-Century England* (New Haven, CT, and London, forthcoming). For a foretaste of her arguments, see eadem, 'The Late Seventeenth and Eighteenth Centuries', in Richard Harries and Henry Mayr-Harting, eds, *Christianity: Two Thousand Years* (Oxford, 2001), 162–91.

THROUGH A VENICE GLASS DARKLY: JOHN FOXE'S MOST FAMOUS MIRACLE

by THOMAS S. FREEMAN

ON New Year's Day, 1578, Sir John Langley, a wealthy alderman of the City of London, lay dying. Present at his deathbed were three of the most eminent preachers in the capital: Robert Crowley, who held four London livings, Alexander Nowell, the dean of St Paul's cathedral and John Foxe, the martyrologist. As Langley's life ebbed away, Foxe went up to the dying man and 'used both godly councell unto him and some devote prayers'.[1] Since Langley could no longer speak, Foxe urged him to signify his belief in Christ by holding up his hands:

> Ymmediatly so he did and then . . . Mr Fox was verie gladd, and told him that he had done ynoughe to show him self both a Crystian and to depend only uppon the merittes of Chrystes passione.[2]

The details of Langley's deathbed help to establish the background for a miracle that Foxe was credited with performing and which would be celebrated for over a century. Because of his fame as the author of the *Acts and Monuments* (popularly known as 'Foxe's Book of Martyrs') and because the only living which he held was a prebend in Salisbury cathedral, Foxe's extensive pastoral work in London is often forgotten. Foxe's appearance at Langley's demise is a reminder of his status as one of London's most famous and active preachers. It also serves as a reminder that much of Foxe's reputation rested on his role as a spiritual physician, treating the ailing consciences of the godly.

As the Protestant Reformation gained strength and momentum in England, it swept away many of the institutions and practices which had anchored believers in an assurance of their salvation, and carried

[1] The National Archive, C24/134, depositions of Francis Langley, Christopher Hunt and Thomas Bradshaw. All dates are new style. The punctuation in all quotations has been modernized but the original spelling has been retained, although the letters i, j, u and v have been modernized. All of the manuscript archives consulted for this paper are in London. All places of publication are London unless otherwise noted.

[2] Ibid.

the godly into the uncharted expanses of soteriological uncertainty. The greater the emphasis on justification by faith and predestination, the greater the potential for believers to despair about the possibility of attaining their salvation. Many devout Protestants, in both early modern England and in New England, were tormented by fears and doubts as to whether they were among the reprobate or elect.[3] A number of eminent clergymen gained fame for their skill in treating these crises of conscience: John Bradford, Richard Greenham, Edward Dering, John Dod, Robert Bolton, William Perkins and Richard Baxter among them.

In her article in this volume, Alexandra Walsham has comprehensively summarized the complexities and ambiguities of English Protestant attitudes towards the miraculous.[4] One area, however, where the Protestant clergy was relatively quick to discern, and to proclaim, the existence of miracles in the post-apostolic era was in recounting the healing wonders which attended the activities of those ministers who gained acclaim as physicians of the soul. There were two fundamental reasons for the absence of the usual wariness towards the miraculous in these accounts. First, they were directed almost exclusively at fellow Protestants and their authors were thus able to abandon some of the defensive postures of works designed to cross the confessional divide. Secondly, such accounts were written by clergy and the wonders related in them tended to glorify fellow clergy.

In this contribution, I will examine one of the most famous of the miracles which occurred in the course of a minister comforting an afflicted conscience. The historiography of this miracle, which was recounted in numerous works for over a century, epitomizes both fundamental shifts in Protestant attitudes towards the miraculous in sixteenth- and seventeenth-century England and the glorification of spiritual physicians as thaumaturges.

3 See John Stachniewski, *The Persecutory Imagination: English Puritanism and the Literature of Religious Despair* (Oxford, 1991), esp. 27–61, and Peter Iver Kaufman, *Prayer, Despair and Drama: Elizabethan Introspection* (Champaign, IL, 1996). For religious despair among Marian Protestants, see Thomas S. Freeman, '"The Good Ministrye of Godlye and Vertuouse Women": the Elizabethan Martyrologists and the Female Supporters of the Marian Martyrs', *JBS* 39 (2000), 16–21. For religious despair in New England see David D. Hall, *Worlds of Wonder, Days of Judgement: Popular Religious Belief in Early New England* (New York, 1989), 131–7.

4 See in this volume, Alexandra Walsham, 'Miracles in Post-Reformation England', 273–306.

* * *

John Foxe provides a striking and early example of how a reputation for skill in treating afflicted consciences could foster a reputation as a miracle-worker. His younger son, Simeon Foxe, in a memoir of his father, of which much more will be said shortly, described John Foxe's popularity as a spiritual healer and its consequences:

> There repaired to him, both citizens [of London] and staungers, noblemen and common people of all degrees, and almost all for the same cause: to seek some salve for a wounded conscience. At length some who were likewise sick in body, would needs be carried to him, but this to stop rumours, he would not suffer to be used. For because they were brought thither, they were by some reported to be cured.[5]

Simeon's description is fascinating for the way in which it reveals how Foxe's activities as a spiritual physician readily acquired a quasi-miraculous aura. Simeon's description is corroborated by a number of letters surviving among John Foxe's papers. One 'T. H.' wrote to John Foxe, thanking him for the comfort he received from Foxe in wrestling with despair over his sins and also for 'the great consolation and fatherly councell I receaved att your handes beynge the [*sic*] sore deceased in sowle and body also'.[6] Even clergy turned to Foxe for spiritual counsel: Thomas Croke, the rector of Great Waldingfield, Suffolk, wrote to Foxe in 1575, confessing his fears that his godliness was mere hypocrisy and received a long letter of consolation from the martyrologist.[7] And one Thomas Dollman begged Foxe's help because he was possessed by an evil spirit and tempted to despair.[8] This last example provides the link between Foxe as a spiritual physician and the most spectacular of Foxe's pastoral activities: his career as an exorcist.[9]

5 John Foxe, *Acts and Monuments of matters most speciall . . .*, 3 vols (1632–41), STC [Wing] F2035, II, sig. B2r. Simeon's memoir of his father was first printed in the second volume of the 1641 edition of John Foxe's martyrology, the *Acts and Monuments*: hereafter cited as *Memoir*.

6 BL, Harley MS 416, fol. 120r–v. There is also a letter to Foxe begging for his advice on overcoming a 'temptacion of blasphemy': ibid., fol. 131r.

7 BL, Harley MS 417, fols 126r–127v.

8 BL, Harley MS 416, fol. 116r–v.

9 Foxe's most celebrated exorcism is described in Kathleen R. Sands, *An Elizabethan Lawyer's Possession by the Devil: the Story of Robert Briggs* (Westport, CT, 2002), a book which, unfortunately, is poorly researched and superficial. For an overview of Foxe's career as an exorcist, see the article on him in the *Oxford Dictionary of National Biography* (Oxford, 2004).

* * *

John Foxe's role as a spiritual physician also lay behind his involvement in the most celebrated miracle he would be credited with performing. In many ways, moreover, his patient (for lack of a better term), Mary Honeywood, was as remarkable a figure as the martyrologist. If Foxe was a celebrated healer of afflicted consciences, Mary Honeywood was a very notable sufferer from one. She was born in 1527 and in 1543 she married Robert Honeywood, a wealthy gentleman of Charing and later, of Marks Hall, Essex. During Mary's reign she aided imprisoned Protestants and corresponded with the martyr John Bradford. She forced her way through the spectators to witness his execution, losing her shoes in the press of the crowd, and was forced to walk barefoot from Smithfield to St Martins before she could obtain a new pair.[10]

Three letters from Bradford to Honeywood survive; in all three Bradford assuaged her doubts about her salvation and urged her to trust in God's love.[11] During Elizabeth's reign, Honeywood turned to Edward Dering, the famed puritan preacher, for spiritual solace. According to Patrick Collinson, 'Dering's letters to Mrs. Honeywood are entirely occupied with the comforting of what he calls her 'heavie estate' and with assuring her that her afflictions were a singular token of God's favour'.[12] In 1591, the self-proclaimed Messiah, William Hacket, performed an exorcism on Mary Honeywood, to free her of the demon which she believed had been possessing her for fourteen years.[13] Yet about four or five years earlier, John Foxe had come to comfort Honeywood, and – if several generations of godly writers were to be believed – a miracle had taken place.[14]

10 See Thomas Fuller, *The History of the Worthies of England*, ed. P. Austin Nuttall, 3 vols (1840), 2: 158–9, and the article on Mary Honeywood in the *Oxford Dictionary of National Biography*. I am grateful to Dr Jacqueline Eales for sending me a copy of her article on Honeywood in advance of publication.

11 *Certain most godly, fruitful, and comfortable letters of such true saintes and holy martyres* . . ., ed. Henry Bull (1564), STC 5886, 298–305 and 426–7. Cf. Susan Wabuda, 'Henry Bull, Miles Coverdale and the Making of Foxe's *Book of Martyrs*', in Diana Wood, ed., *Martyrs and Martyrologies*, SCH 30 (Oxford, 1993), 245–58.

12 Patrick Collinson, 'A Mirror of Elizabethan Puritanism: the Life and Letters of "Godly Master Dering" ', in idem, *Godly People: Essays on English Protestantism and Puritanism* (London, 1983), 289–324, 318.

13 Henry Arthington, *The Seduction of Arthington by Hacket* . . . (1592), STC 799, 14–15, and Richard Cosin, *Conspiracie for pretended Reformation* (1592), STC 5823, 5 and 64. Also see Alexandra Walsham, ' "Frantik Hacket": Prophecy, Sorcery, Insanity and the Elizabethan Puritan Movement', *HistJ* 41 (1998), 27–66.

14 A marginal note in the manuscript of Simeon Foxe's memoir states that the incident

The first printed narrative of the marvel occurred about three decades after the event, in *God's Arraignment of Hypocrites*, a work by the puritan minister John Yates.[15] (In the absence of a printed account and since he had no discernable ties to the Foxe or Honeywood families, it seems probable that Yates drew upon a manuscript which described the incident. Manuscript accounts of the incident may have been circulating among the godly for years). According to Yates, 'a vertuouse gentlewoman ... doubting verie often of her salvation' complained to 'a worthy minister' who advised her to trust in God's mercy. One day, the minister was trying to console the woman while she lay in bed drinking from 'a venice glass'. Suddenly the woman cried out:

> 'You have often told me, that I must seeke no further then God's word, but I have been long without comfort, and can indure no longer; therefore if I must be saved let this glasse be kept from breaking' and so she threw it against the walls. Here myght the Lord's hand, for the tempting of his majestie have left her to the everlasting woes of her distrustful heart, yet the Lord that is rich in mercie . . . was content to satisfie the lanquishing soule with a miracle: The glasse rebounds againe and comes safe unto the ground, which the minister having gotten into his hand sayeth, 'Oh, repent of this sinne, bless God for his mercie, and never distruste more of his promise: for now you have his voyce from heaven in a miracle, telling you of your estate'.[16]

One feature of this remarkable narrative is worth emphasizing: Yates did not hesitate to call what transpired a miracle.

The terminology is important. Many English Protestant writers and preachers insisted, particularly when attacking Catholic beliefs and practices, that miracles had ceased with the end of the apostolic era. A strict theoretical distinction was maintained between wonders, which could be created through divine or diabolical manipulation of

took place when Honeywood was sixty (BL, Lansdowne MS 388, fol. 36v). This would be in 1586–7. John Foxe died on 18 April 1587.

15 Since *God's Arraignment* was, in part, an attack on Arminianism, it seems safe to characterize Yates as a puritan, at least at the time he wrote the book. However, later in life, Yates would align himself with that most anti-puritan prelate, Bishop Richard Montagu (whom Yates had previously criticized). For the details of Yates's career, see Matthew Reynolds, 'Puritanism and the Emergence of Laudianism in City Politics in Norwich, *c.*1570–1643', unpublished Ph.D. thesis, University of Kent, 2002, 72–3, 92–8, 108–12, 123–41 and 171–2.

16 John Yates, *Gods arraignment of hypocrites* (Cambridge, 1615), STC 26081, 356–7.

secondary causes or elemental forces, and miracles, which were divine interventions resulting in violations of natural laws.[17] At times this distinction could be quite rigidly observed; at her trial in Newton, Massachusetts, in 1637, Anne Hutchinson declared that even if she were condemned, she would be delivered 'by miracle as Daniel was'. Pressed by the court on her use of the term 'miracle', her supporter, the eminent divine John Cotton, said that it was unclear whether by miracle she meant 'a work above nature or . . . some wonderful providence'. Cotton further declared that if the former was meant, he disbelieved in them, but that he could accept 'some special providence of God to help her'.[18]

Yet the distinction was not always strictly observed, and often the terms 'miracle', 'wonder' and 'special providence' could be used loosely or even interchangeably by clerical writers.[19] That Yates called the Honeywood incident a miracle may not be particularly significant *per se*, but the fact that a number of other clerical writers in the early seventeenth century also hailed it as a miracle is important.

Yates's book enjoyed brief but considerable popularity, going through three editions in 1615–16. Yet it was the inclusion of Yates's account in Robert Bolton's *Instructions for a right comforting of afflicted consciences* which secured the popularity of this tale in puritan circles and, indeed, among Calvinists in Europe.[20] Bolton was another of the great spiritual physicians of the era; his contemporary biographer praised his 'singular dexterity in comforting wounded and afflicted spirits'.[21] Almost all of Bolton's works were steady sellers and the *Instructions* was no exception; published in 1631, it went through three editions through the following decade, before it was incorporated into Bolton's collected works in 1640.

Bolton had reprinted Yates's version of the 'miracle' virtually word

17 See Alexandra Walsham, *Providence in Early Modern England* (Oxford, 1999), 226–30.

18 *The Antinomian Controversy, 1636–1638: a Documentary History*, ed. David D. Hall (Middletown, CT, 1968), 273 and 340–1.

19 For example, Samuel Clarke, in the course of two pages, variously described the rescue of William Bradshaw from drowning as 'a miracle', 'a wonder of wonders' and 'a special providence of God': Samuel Clarke, *The lives of two-and-twenty English divines* (1660), STC [Wing], C4540, 29–30.

20 Robert Bolton, *Instructions for a right comforting [of] afflicted consciences* (1631), STC 3258, 5. The Dutch scholar Voetius mentioned the incident, citing Bolton, in a work on miracles written in 1640: see G. Voetius, *Selectae disputationes theologicae*, 3 vols (Utrecht, 1655), 2: 1024. I am grateful to Dr Aza Goudriaan for this reference.

21 Edward Bagshaw, *Mr. Boltons Last And Learned Worke of the Foure last Things, . . . together with the life and death of the authour* (London, 1635), STC 1190, 16.

for word. Samuel Clarke reprinted this account in a popular collection of providential stories published in 1646.[22] He cited both Yates and Bolton as his sources and reprinted their account, only omitting the minister's remonstrance of the gentlewoman. As Yates and Bolton had done, Clarke unhesitatingly hailed the unbroken glass as a miracle; in fact, he would be the last author to do so. And like Yates and Bolton, Clarke did not relate the names of either the worthy minister or the suffering gentlewoman; but that deficiency had been made good in another account of the incident.

* * *

A memoir of John Foxe's life, written by his youngest son Simeon, was printed as a preface to the 1641 edition of the *Acts and Monuments*.[23] It contained another version of the story of the despairing woman and the miraculously unbroken glass. In this story, 'Mistris Honiwood, an honourable Gentlewoman who had almost twenty years lain sick of a consumption through melancholy' sent for John Foxe. He prayed with her, and tried to console her but she remained convinced that her death was imminent:

> At length . . . he then told her that she should not onely grow well of that consumption, but also live to an exceeding great age. At which words, the sick gentlewoman, a little moved and earnestly beholding Master Fox, 'As well might you have said', quoth she, 'that if I should throw this glasse against the wall, I might beleeve it would not break to pieces' and holding a glasse in her hand, out of which she had newly drunk, she threw it forth. Neither did the glasse, first by chance lighting on a little chest standing by the bed side, and afterward falling upon the ground, either break or crack, in any place about it, and the event fell out accordingly.[24]

There are a number of important differences between Simeon Foxe's version of events and the version of Yates (and subsequently Bolton and Clarke). In Simeon's account Honeywood is tormented by fears of death, not of damnation. By the time this account was written, the Foxe

22 Samuel Clarke, *A Mirrour or looking-glasse both for saints and sinners* (London, 1646), STC [Wing] C4548, 10–11.

23 For a persuasive argument identifying Simeon Foxe as the author of this anonymous memoir, see J. F. Mozley, *John Foxe and his Book* (London, 1940), 1–11.

24 *Memoir*, sig. B3r–v.

and Honeywood families were closely linked.[25] It is very likely that Simeon deliberately transformed Mary Honeywood's doubts about her salvation into doubts about her survival in order to protect her reputation. Yet despite the differences in the narratives, and the silence of Yates on who the participants in his story were, it is clear that Simeon Foxe and Yates were describing the same event. Did it actually happen? Or did Simeon simply graft his father's name onto an evergreen tale of the miraculous?

There must have been some factual basis to the story. As we have seen, the mention of Mary Honeywood was fraught with familial complexities for Simeon. These complexities were increased by the mention of Grace Heneage (still alive in 1641) as an eyewitness to the veracity of Simeon's narrative.[26] Neither name would have been casually invoked by Simeon. Moreover, the narrative printed in 1641 was the tip of a textual iceberg and a little exploration of its submerged mass will yield some insights into the incident and the reactions of John Foxe's family to it.

Simeon Foxe stated in the printed version of the memoir that it had been written 'about thirty yeers' before its publication, that is around 1611.[27] The original manuscript account has not survived, but a scribal copy of it in Latin remains among the Foxe family papers.[28] Internal references in this copy indicate that it was certainly written before 1614.[29] The scribal copy is corrected and annotated throughout in two hands, those of Simeon and his elder brother Samuel Foxe. Samuel's

25 The Heneage brothers, Sir Thomas and Michael, were close friends of John Foxe, who had a particular regard for Michael (*Memoir*, sig. B6r). Michael Heneage married Grace Honeywood, the daughter of Robert and Mary Honeywood. Grace and her brother Robert Honeywood (the younger) were executors of Michael's will; its overseer was Sir Moyle Finch: cf. P. W. Hasler, *The House of Commons, 1558–1603*, 3 vols (1981), *s.v.* 'Heanage, Michael' [hereafter: *Hasler*]. In addition to being Sir Thomas Heneage's son-in-law, Sir Moyle was the godfather of Samuel's eldest daughter, with Lady Anne Heneage being her godmother (*Hasler* and BL, Lansdowne MS 679, fol. 39r). Sir Thomas Heneage was the godfather of Samuel's eldest son Thomas, with Lady Finch acting as godmother (ibid., fol. 39r). In fact, Samuel Foxe's marriage was held in Sir Moyle's house (ibid., fol. 47r). The capstone was placed on this network of happy families when John Foxe's grandson Thomas, eldest son of samuel Foxe, married Anne Honeywood, one of the numerous grandaughters of Mary Honeywood.

26 *Memoir*, sig. B3v.

27 Ibid., sig. A3r.

28 BL, Lansdowne MS 388, fols 1r–51v.

29 Mozley, *John Foxe*, 4. Mozley ignores a statement in the manuscript that Mary Honeywood 'hodieque vivit annis nonagenaria' [is alive today at the age of ninety] (Lansdowne MS 388, fol. 36v). Honeywood was ninety in 1617. Nevertheless, Simeon probably miscalculated or exaggerated her age.

annotations were definitely written after 1620.[30] What very probably happened was this: Simeon's memoir was originally written sometime before 1614. Sometime after 1620, it was decided to publish the memoir (possibly to be included in what would be the 1631 edition of the *Acts and Monuments*). In preparation for this a scribe copied Simeon's original memoir and this was then revised and corrected by both brothers. Samuel's death in 1630 probably prevented the memoir from being included in the 1631 edition. The memoir was, however, resurrected and reprinted (with Samuel's revisions included) in the next edition of the *Acts and Monuments.* This was done by Simeon himself, who translated his original Latin memoir into rather stilted English.[31]

Samuel's revisions drastically altered Simeon's original version of the Honeywood incident. Two facts become crystal clear when reading Simeon's memoir in any of its redactions: that Simeon was forced to confront a flourishing legend of his father as a thaumaturge and that he heartily disapproved of it. According to Simeon, John Foxe's reputation as a wonderworker originated because people saw that he

> did many things many things beyond the opinion of an ordinary good man [and] believed that he could not be voide of some divine inspiration, and now some began, not as a good man to honour him, but as one sent from heaven, even to adore him, through the folly of mankinde, madly doting upon any thing, whatsoever their own will hath set it up to be worshipped.[32]

In his manuscript memoir, Simeon had mentioned the '*fama*' of his father's reputation for supernatural healing; one of the corrections he made to his work was to cross this word out and replace it with the more negative '*rumoribus*'.[33] Simeon's distaste for such rumours was not shared by other members of his family. Where Simeon reported, but refused to endorse, a story that John Foxe had prophesied the death of Mary Tudor, his niece, Samuel's daughter, boasted of the same

30 Unfortunately, Mozley did not realize that this manuscript was a scribal copy (see *John Foxe*, 8) and he ignored the annotations in it. In the original text Honeywood is referred to as still living (see the previous note). Yet Samuel crossed this passage out and declared that she lived to be over ninety. He also changed a reference to her in the present tense to the past tense (Lansdowne MS 388, fol. 36v). Mary Honeywood died in 1620.

31 Both the original Latin memoir, and its English translation were printed in the 1641 *Acts and Monuments.* Mozley has demonstrated that it was Simeon who did this translation (*John Foxe*, 8–9).

32 *Memoir*, sig. B3r.

33 Lansdowne MS 388, fol. 30v.

prophecy and her grandfather's divine inspiration at a Christmas dinner in 1634.[34] Simeon's original account of the Honeywood incident merely had John Foxe predicting that she would recover and live to a great age. The story of the unbroken glass was written in the margin of Simeon's manuscript by Samuel and later included, with Samuel's other revisions, in the printed memoir.[35]

The fact that Simeon wrote a narrative of an encounter between his father and Mary Honeywood before Yates's printed version appeared helps confirm that such an encounter did take place. Samuel's additions may have been based on Yates, but he also added the note, already mentioned, citing Grace Heneage as a witness to the incident.[36] And Yates's account, of course, was written long before Simeon's memoir was printed and was completely independent of it.

Probably thanks to the popularity of the *Acts and Monuments*, the account of the Honeywood incident contained in Simeon's memoir seems to have become even more widely known. In 1647, Henry Jessey, the Baptist minister, referred to what 'that famous Mrs. Honeywood had said and done with a Venice glasse'.[37] Since Simeon's was the only narrative of the wonder, available at the time, which supplied Mary Honeywood's name, it must have been one of Jessey's sources. (Interestingly, Simeon does not mention that the glass Honeywood threw was Venetian, so Jessey must have been aware of at least one of the other narratives as well). In any case, Jessey's casual reference would seem to indicate that by the mid-seventeenth century both Mary Honeywood and her glass had indeed become famous.

* * *

That fame was only increased when Thomas Fuller wrote an account of the incident in his *Worthies of England*, first printed in 1662. Fuller drew on Simeon's memoir, the narrative printed by Bolton and oral sources to construct his account. Yet Fuller's account is significantly different from previous versions. Even more than Yates and Bolton he emphasized the spiritual despair Honeywood felt. According to Fuller,

34 *Memoir*, sig. A8r and George Atwell, *An apology, or defence of the divine art of natural astrologie* (1660), STC [Wing] A4162, 32–3.

35 *Memoir*, fol. 36v.

36 Lansdowne MS 388, fol. 36v. Actually Samuel's note cites Anne Heneage, the widow of Micheal Heneage as the witness. This was an error (Grace Heneage was Michael's widow) probably caused by the fact that a preceeding anecdote in the memoir described Foxe predicting the recovery of Anne Heneage from illness.

37 Henry Jessey, *The exceeding riches of grace advanced* . . . (1647), STC [Wing] J687, 11–12.

Honeywood cried out the bleak words: 'I am as surely damned as this glass is broken' as she threw the glass. But, although he praises Foxe for his skill in healing 'a broken spirit', Fuller marginalizes the role of the minister in the story. Not only does Fuller omit the minister's remonstrance to Honeywood, but he also makes a point of observing (correctly) that she took no lasting comfort from the episode. And although Fuller declares that the incident was 'a wonder', he was even more wary of invoking the supernatural than Simeon Foxe had been. After conceding that the famous Venetian glass had rebounded undamaged, Fuller continued: 'I confess it is possible (though difficult) so casually to throw as brittle a substance, that, lighting on the edges, it may be preserved; but happening immediately in that juncture of time, it *seemed* little less than miraculous'.[38]

The next significant recounting of the story, that by the Presbyterian minister John Flavell, in 1673, is a reaction against Fuller's version. Although he repeats Fuller in having Honeywood cry out that she was surely damned, Flavell restores the minister to his central role by resurrecting the rebuke of Honeywood from Bolton (whom Flavell cites as his source). But although Flavell must have known from Fuller that this divine was Foxe, he simply refers to him as 'a worthy minister'. Although Flavell did not call the event a miracle but simply described it as a 'wonder', he nevertheless pointedly failed to repeat Fuller's wary strictures on how the event seemed miraculous. And the Presbyterian flatly contradicted Fuller by maintaining that far from the 'wonder' having no effect on Honeywood, it 'greatly altered the temper of her mind'.[39]

Above all, Flavell's motives for printing the story were new. It was one of a number of incidents related to demonstrate not the ways of Providence, but its very existence. In the dedication of his book, Flavell claimed that 'We are fallen into the dregs of time, sensuality runs everywhere into Atheism. . . . The largess of Providence have so blinded, and perfectly stupified the minds of some, that they neither own a Providence nor a God'.[40] Elsewhere Flavell declared that proving that Providence existed was one of the most effective ways of combating atheism.[41] Identical considerations impelled William Turner to

38 Fuller, *Worthies*, II: 158–9. My emphasis in the last quotation.

39 John Flavell, *Divine Conduct: or the mysterie of Providence* . . . (1673), STC [Wing] F1158, 73.

40 Ibid., sigs A4v–A5r.

41 Ibid., sig. A8v.

compile a massive collection of providential judgements which he published in 1697.[42] It is not surprising, therefore, that Turner repeated Flavell's account word-for-word (except for Flavell's citation of Bolton which Turner omitted).[43]

A year before Turner's collection was printed another version of the Honeywood story appeared in the *Miscellanies* of the noted antiquarian John Aubrey. Apart from Simeon Foxe, who was a physician, Aubrey was the only non-cleric among the authors we have discussed and therefore it is probably not surprising that he was unconcerned with the issue of religious despair or with the role of the minister. In fact, Aubrey declares that Robert Bolton was the minister counselling Honeywood when she threw the glass.[44] Aubrey's concern with the story arose solely from its interesting and unusual qualities; Mary Honeywood's unbroken glass had moved from being a miracle to being an anecdote.

* * *

The Honeywood 'miracle' is only an isolated incident but it does call into question assumptions many scholars still hold about the survival of the miraculous in post-Reformation England. The story was not a folk survival nor was it the product of popular culture; rather it was related and disseminated by university-educated writers. Yet – and this is very suggestive of the symbiotic relationship between elite and popular cultures – it does seem to have become widely known and even to have spawned imitations. Two notorious sufferers from afflicted consciences in the 1640s, Sarah Wight and Joyce Dovey, both flung earthenware cups, one at a wall, the other at an iron pot, only to have the cups miraculously rebound without breaking or cracking.[45]

Nor does the Honeywood miracle readily conform to any facile attempts to equate Protestantism with scepticism towards the miraculous. In fact, the only authors unequivocally to hail the Honeywood incident as a miracle were puritan or non-conformist writers such as

42 Turner stated that he had been inspired to begin his project by Increase Mather's call for a record of providential events to refute sceptics: William Turner, *A compleat history of the most remarkable providences . . .* (1697), STC [Wing] T3345, sig. B1r. He also declared that 'to record Providences seems to be one of the best methods that can be pursued against the abounding atheism of this age': ibid., sig. B1v.

43 Turner, *Compleat history*, 123 in the first of seven separate paginations.

44 John Aubrey, *Miscellanies* (1696), STC [Wing] A4188, 100.

45 Jessey, *Exceeding riches*, 11–12, and Dr. William's Library, Baxter Treatises, VI, no. 211, fol. 321v.

Yates, Bolton and Clarke. They did so partly from a desire to show God's mercy towards those suffering from soteriological despair and His ability to ease their sufferings. Yet the story, at least in these versions, also buttressed the role of the godly minister and contained an implicit moral to sufferers like Mary Honeywood: it was vital to follow the guidance of the godly minister. The whole purpose of the miracle, in these versions, was in the manifestation of divine support for the opinion of the minister.

But it was not in support of a particular minister. Simeon Foxe's memoir, which expresses the desire of the Foxe family to glorify their famous forebear, and Thomas Fuller's *Worthies* are the only versions of the story to name Foxe as the divine present when Honeywood threw her glass cup. And even in Fuller's version, Foxe's role is even marginalized. It is striking that the miracle (or wonder) came to be associated with Bolton as much as Foxe, so much so that Aubrey thought that Bolton was the minister involved. It is even more striking that Flavell, who knew that Foxe was the 'worthy minister', still did not bother to name him. In fact, it was preferable that the minister not be named, as that made it easier for the example to be applied to all clergy and not simply one godly thaumaturge.

There is also an interesting chronological pattern to the various versions of the Honeywood story. Even in the Foxe family version of the story there was a tension between Samuel and Simeon over the extent to which the event was a supernatural occurrence. Simeon's guarded scepticism foreshadowed later attitudes. No one writing about the Honeywood incident after 1650 went so far as to call it a miracle. This wariness corresponds to larger transformations within English attitudes towards miracles and supernatural wonders. As several communications within this volume demonstrate, belief in miracles continued unabated among some Protestants well into the eighteenth century.[46] Nevertheless the terms of discussion of the supernatural had fundamentally changed. Earlier the possibility that miracles had occurred in the post-apostolic era was challenged, now the possibility that miracles had ever occurred was being challenged. Where tales of the miraculous had earlier been related for various didactic, polemical or homiletic purposes, now they were used to demonstrate the very existence of the supernatural.

[46] See in particular the papers by Alexandra Walsham, Robert Webster and John Tomlinson printed in this volume.

The narratives of the Honeywood incident in the second half of the seventeenth century mirror these transformations. They went from being a triumphant vindication of the pastoral work of the ministry to being a rearguard action against the advancing forces of scepticism. The importance of the story now was not in the purpose of the wonder but in the fact that a well-witnessed and verified wonder had taken place at all. From miracle to wonder to curiosity, we can see reflected in Mary Honeywood's Venice glass the course and development of tales of signs and wonders in early modern England.

University of Sheffield

MIRACLES WITHIN CATASTROPHES: SOME EXAMPLES FROM EARLY MODERN GERMANY

by HARTMUT LEHMANN

ON September 11, 2001, a small church next to Ground Zero survived almost unharmed, adjacent to the place where the famous Twin Towers had once stood. Journalists who reported the disaster and who saw the location of this little church talked of a miracle.[1] This was the only word available to them in order to explain what seemed to be inexplicable otherwise. But in our secularized age, in none of the reports which I have read was a connection made between the possible causes of the catastrophe of 9/11 and the possible meaning of the survival of the little church which was called a 'miracle'. People in early modern Germany would have been able to draw such connections, and this is the topic of my essay. In recent years, some historians have discovered the crucial role of catastrophes in pre-modern times.[2] As they point out, catastrophes changed people's lives drastically and in unforeseen ways. This was also true for early modern Europe and in particular for early modern Germany. With two exceptions, however, the importance of religion in coming to terms with the consequences of catastrophes has not been discussed.[3] Moreover, in these studies miracles were not mentioned, even though the belief in miracles is a significant element of almost every account concerning a catastrophe.

1 Personal memory.

2 Wolfgang Breidert, ed, *Die Erschütterung der vollkommenen Welt: die Wirkung des Erdbebens von Lissabon im Spiegel europäischer Zeitgenossen* (Darmstadt, 1994); Andreas Schmidt, *'Wolken krachen, Berge zittern, und die ganze Erde weint . . .': zur kulturellen Vermittlung von Naturkatastrophen in Deutschland 1755 bis 1855* (Münster, 1999); Manfred Jakubowski-Tiessen, *Sturmflut 1717: die Bewältigung einer Naturkatastrophe in der Frühen Neuzeit* (Munich, 1992); Ulrich Löffler, *Lissabons Fall – Europas Schrecken: die Deutung des Erdbebens von Lissabon im deutschsprachigen Protestantismus des 18. Jahrhunderts* (Berlin and New York, 1999); Dieter Groh, Michael Kempe and Franz Mauelshagen, eds, *Naturkatastrophen: Beiträge zu ihrer Deutung, Wahrnehmung und Darstellung in Text und Bild von der Antike bis ins 20. Jahrhundert* (Tübingen, 2003). I am very grateful to Marie Luisa Allemeyer and Manfred Jakubowski-Tiessen for drawing my attention to some of the sources which I have used.

3 Hans-Ferdinand Angel, *Der religiöse Mensch in Katastrophenzeiten: religionspädagogische Perspektiven kollektiver Elendsphänomene* (Frankfurt a. M., 1996); Manfred Jakubowski-Tiessen and Hartmut Lehmann, eds, *Um Himmels Willen: Religion in Katastrophenzeiten* (Göttingen, 2003).

Before I attempt to explain why, how, and with what consequences people in early modern Germany were able to make a connection between a catastrophe which they experienced and a miracle which they believed they had witnessed, I will give some examples of miracles within catastrophes, that is of miracles within natural disaster.[4]

On the night before Christmas of 1717, the coast of the Netherlands and Northern Germany was hit by a powerful flood. Thousands of people died in the waves that night, tens of thousands of cattle perished. Whole villages were wiped away. Unheard of misery ensued.[5] In reading the numerous reports about this event which were published in the course of 1718 and the following years,[6] we find that, within the context of extensive damage and enormous loss of life all along the coast, there were remarkable, unexpected, that is to say miraculous, examples of human rescue; in short: there were miracles. These events were interpreted as unmistakable signs of God's providence, mercy and kindness. In one case, a man, his wife and their three children were drifting in the water holding tight to some beams from the roof of their house which had collapsed under the impact of the waves. After two of the children had died in the cold water, and as the parents and their remaining last child were expecting that they would die soon as well, a white pigeon appeared and sat down next to them on a piece of wood. Remembering Noah's story, the family began to have some hope. Not in vain, as we are told in the report about this event. The pigeon began to fly slowly in one direction, and the man paddled as well as he could behind the pigeon, until he led his family to an elevation above water-level, where they were safe and could be rescued.[7]

In another report about the same great flood of Christmas 1717, after a house had collapsed in the waves some small children were drifting in the water in their crib. In the ferocious storm, and amidst high waves, the crib did not overturn, until a current in the water swept the crib to the shore where the children were saved by people at once full of joy and completely amazed. It was an angel, the writer of this report explained, who had saved the young innocent children and who

[4] The general background is discussed in: Jakubowski-Tiessen and Lehmann, eds, *Um Himmels Willen*, 7–13; Groh, Kempe and Mauelshagen, eds, *Naturkatastrophen*, 11–33.

[5] Jakubowski-Tiessen, *Sturmflut 1717*, 57–78.

[6] Jakubowski-Tiessen, *Sturmflut 1717*, 8–11.

[7] Georg Johann Hencken, *Historische Nachricht von merckwürdigen Exempeln der göttlichen Providence und Vorsehung in wunderbahrer Errettung der Menschen bey der Wasser-Fluth in der Christ-Nacht des vorigen 1717. Jahrs* (Halle, 1718), 19.

had guided them until they were rescued.[8] These are just two of a number of reports in which we are told of examples in which God had miraculously saved people in that night, which was remembered by the people on the coast for many generations.[9]

In early modern Germany, just as in contemporary Europe, floods were just one form of natural disasters which threatened people's lives.[10] The earthquake that destroyed Lisbon in 1755 was perhaps the most powerful in a series of earthquakes in the epoch between Luther and Voltaire. Much more frequent were large fires which endangered the lives of people in many cities and which in some cases levelled all the houses.[11] And then there were large-scale cases of plague well into the eighteenth century, often preceded by harvest failure and periods of hunger.[12] Many people in early modern Europe also experienced war almost like a flood, or an earthquake, that is like a natural disaster, a catastrophe sent by God, and in the course of war, as is well known, disastrous fires were an ever-recurring event.

Let me explain now, step by step, the religious message as well as the context of those miracles, encapsulated, so to speak, in catastrophes. What was their meaning according to the conviction of simple minds, and of learned theologians? First and foremost, we have to recognize that people in pre-Enlightenment Europe were well aware of the distinction between a catastrophe and other cases of misfortune. Catas-

8 Johann Friderich Jansen, *Historisch-Theologisch Denckmahl der Wunder-vollen Wegen Gottes in den grossen Wassern / welche sich anno 1717 den 25. December, zu vieler Länder Verderben / so erschröcklich ergossen* (Bremen and Jever, 1722), 255.

9 Johann Christian Hekelius, *Ausführliche und ordentliche Beschreibung derer beyden erschrecklichen und fast nie erhörten Wasserfluthen in Ost-Frießland und denen meisten an der Nord-See gelegenen schönen Ländern . . . und bey jedes Ortes Beschreibung angeführet wird, wie wunderbahrlich der liebe Gott einige Menschen daselbst aus der Fluth errettet, und wieder aus den Wassern heraus gezogen habe* (Halle, 1719).

10 Hartmut Lehmann, *Das Zeitalter des Absolutismus: Gottesgnadentum und Kriegsnot* (Stuttgart, 1980), 105–69; Hartmut Lehmann and Anne-Charlott Trepp, eds, *Im Zeichen der Krise: Religiosität im Europa des 17. Jahrhunderts* (Göttingen, 1999); Manfred Jakubowski-Tiessen, ed., *Krisen des 17. Jahrhunderts* (Göttingen, 1999); see also Thomas, *Religion and the Decline of Magic.*

11 Marie Luisa Allemeyer, '"Daß es wohl recht ein Feuer vom Herrn zu nennen gewesen . . .". Zur Wahrnehmung, Deutung und Verarbeitung von Stadtbränden in norddeutschen Schriften des 17. Jahrhunderts', in Jakubowski-Tiessen and Lehmann, eds, *Um Himmels Willen*, 201–34.

12 Heinrich Dormeier, 'Pestepidemien und Frömmigkeitsformen in Italien und Deutschland (14.–16. Jahrhundert)', in Jakubowski-Tiessen and Lehmann, eds, *Um Himmels Willen*, 14–50; Otto Ulbricht, 'The Experience of Violence in the Thirty Years War: a Look at the Civilian Victims', in Joseph Canning, Hartmut Lehmann and Jay Winter, eds, *Power, Violence and Mass Death in Pre-Modern and Modern Times* (Aldershot, 2004), 97–127.

trophes, they believed, were sent, and administered, by God.[13] Not so other cases of misfortune, however. If a hail-storm destroyed the harvest in a certain region, for example, or if a cow died unexpectedly, or if mother and infant died in childbed, some people might believe in a special act of God, but not all. Many would see in these events a devil‘s wicked deed, or the work of witches, the devil‘s agents. Even smaller misfortunes, such as a broken arm, would have been attributed not to witches, but simply considered as a case of ill luck. None, however, doubted that a large-scale disaster, such as the great flood of Christmas 1717, had been caused by God. Witches, or even the devil, could not have brought about such a massive disturbance of the natural order of things, even if the witches might have wished to harm as many people as possible, and even if the devil had intended to destroy as much of God‘s creation as possible. In this respect, Catholic and Protestant theologians were of one mind with simple folk.[14]

But why would God do something so terrible as killing thousands of people and depriving thousands more of their livelihood? How could such cruelty be understood in the light of God's mercy? In all the sources available to us we find one and the same answer: a serious flood, or a violent earthquake, or a devastating fire, were means through which God punished his disobedient and sinful children. Such disastrous events were the expression of God's wrath. But God's wrath did not come down on humankind unexpectedly, nor was it exerted without prudence. It is very important, therefore, to contextualize the explanation of catastrophes as the result of God's anger and disappointment.

* * *

One basic assumption was that God never punished people before he had warned them. If men's actions angered God, he had several ways of admonishing and of warning them.[15] Most conspicuous were the comets which were understood as a torch which God held out of one of the windows of heaven in order to tell people to stop sinning.[16] Other signs of warning were the birth of deformed children, or unusual signs

13 Jakubowski-Tiessen, *Sturmflut 1717*, 88–93.

14 Jakubowski-Tiessen, *Sturmflut 1717*, 94–5.

15 Benigna von Krusenstjern, 'Prodigienglaube und Dreißigjähriger Krieg', in Lehmann and Trepp, eds, *Im Zeichen der Krise*, 53–78.

16 Hartmut Lehmann, 'Die Kometenflugschriften des 17. Jahrhunderts als historische Quelle', in Wolfgang Brückner, Peter Blickle and Dieter Breuer, eds, *Literatur und Volk im 17. Jahrhundert: Probleme populärer Kultur in Deutschland*, 2 vols (Wiesbaden, 1985), 2: 683–700.

of light in the sky, or the appearance of strange animals, and the like. In all of these cases, it was believed that God manipulated some aspect of nature in order to catch the attention of people and to instill in them fear. People were convinced that such prodigies – *prodigia* – always preceded catastrophes, considered as the very act of severe punishment. There is an extensive literature on prodigies in many countries of early modern Europe, and all of these prodigies, people believed, or were made to believe, carried the same message: God was disappointed that people did not cherish the blessings He had bestowed on humankind through creation; He was angered because His children did not follow His commandments as revealed to Moses and as explained by Christ. In particular, pastors would preach, God was upset because some people sinned in a most frivolous way. But since God was kind, they would add, He warned his children before punishing them, in the hope that they would stop sinning and obey his commandments. However, should the various signs of warning be ignored, the argument continued, God may decide to punish, just as a father would have to punish his disobedient children.[17]

Yet another aspect is equally important: God never punished relentlessly; even if He punished severely, people believed, He also demonstrated prudence and mercy. Following Noah's rescue, God had sent the rainbow as a sign of hope. Even in their own times, with many people sinning in a most provocative manner, theologians argued that God would keep this promise. In the disasters understood and explained as catastrophes in early modern Germany, therefore, God never killed all the people, or destroyed everything. Even though He caused large-scale death, He always observed some limits: He punished some as an example for all others, who were not hit by the disaster despite the fact that their sins were no less glaring than the sins of those who died in an earthquake, who lost all of their possessions in a fire, or who drowned in a flood. What we find in the tracts concerning each of these catastrophes, and what people were told by the theologians, is that God used the means of exemplary punishment in order to stop sin: He punished some, or even quite a few, in the hope that all of those who witnessed the disaster, but had remained unharmed, would redirect their lives by confessing their sins, praying to God for forgiveness, and beginning to live the lives of good Christians again. They could do this by following

17 Jakubowski-Tiessen, *Sturmflut 1717*, 95–8.

the example of the lives of good Christians that were explained to them in the edifying literature of their times.[18]

Such repentance and remorse was believed to have yet another effect. It was, as people were told, the one and only way to quell God's wrath and thereby overcome the effects of the catastrophe, because God would reward repenting and committed Christians with tranquil waters; for them God would control the forces inherent in fire and in earthquakes.[19]

But what, then, is the meaning, or should I say the function, of miracles within catastrophes? Let me give, before answering this question, some more examples, this time from miracles which occurred in the course of some of the devastating fires in seventeenth-century German cities. In the fire which raged in Rostock in 1677, for example, it was considered a miracle that all churches except one remained unharmed,[20] just as in the fire which had destroyed the city of Eisleben in 1601 the one and only house that had not been touched by fire was the house in which Luther had been born.[21] In the city of Fraustadt in 1685 everything was lost in the flames except the library of the pious Protestant theologian and hymn-writer Valerius Herberger (1562–1627).[22] These kinds of miracles were, if we are to believe the edifying tracts written after destructive fires, not limited to Protestant Germany. In Catholic Passau, for example, a picture of Mary was found completely intact among the ashes after the great fire of 1662.[23] Miracles in the course of fire were not limited to sacred objects, moreover. In the city of Freystadt the fire destroyed everything except the records of the local court in 1637.[24] This was considered not only as a miracle

18 See Rudolf Lenz, ed., *Leichenpredigten als Quelle historischer Wissenschaften* (Stuttgart, 2004).

19 Hartmut Lehmann, 'Zur Erforschung der Religiosität im 17. Jahrhundert', in Monika Hagenmaier and Sabine Holtz, eds, *Krisenbewußtsein und Krisenbewältigung in der frühen Neuzeit. Festschrift für Hans-Christoph Rublack* (Frankfurt a. M., 1992), 3–11; see also Willem Frijhoff, 'Predestination and the Farmer. An Incident of Life and Faith in Early Seventeenth-Century Holland', in idem, *Embodied Belief. Ten Essays on Religious Culture in Dutch History* (Hilversum, 2002), 93–110.

20 Christopherus Stahlius, *Brand-Predigt von dem Ursprung schädlicher Feuersbrunsten* (Rostock, 1678), 34.

21 Johann Henrich Kindervater, *Curieuse Feuer- und Unglücks-Chronica* (Nordhausen, 1712), 81.

22 Kindervater, *Curieuse Feuer- und Unglücks-Chronica*, 139.

23 Stadtarchiv Passau II A 252: 'Beschreibung des Stadtbrandes von 1662 durch den Ratsherren und Goldschmid Wilhelm Schmid', 18; Stadtarchiv Passau II A 279: 'Auszüge aus den Jahrbüchern des Jesuitenkollegiums von 1662–1664 über den Stadtbrand von 1662', 7.

24 Andreas Gryphius, *Fewrige Freystadt* (Lissa, 1637), 51–2.

but also as a sign that God expected due legal procedures from those who had survived. In another city everything went up in flames except some fishing-boats and the oil mill.[25] Again people spoke of a miracle, and in this case they believed that God had given them the means to rebuild the city after the fire. Just as in the case of floods, also in the case of big fires many more examples could be given.[26]

As in the case of floods, people believed that a punishing God had sent the fire; they were convinced that God would be able to burn even houses which were made out of stone; but they also believed that just as God had started the flames he was able to limit their range, while human attempts to extinguish the fire were futile as long as God had not decided to stop the flames. Most importantly, Protestant as well as Catholic Germans were sure that even in the case of the most disastrous fire, the punishing God would give a sign of hope: in short, that he would produce a miracle.

* * *

We are able, then, to determine exactly the place as well as the role of miracles within catastrophes. Miracles are the third in a sequence of three steps. First, people believed, God admonished his disobedient children so that they would begin to lead a Christian life. Second, if people failed to do so, and if they ignored God's warnings, God decided to punish. As a God of love and mercy, God would not punish indiscriminately. Even while exacting extreme punishments, he would set an example of restraint, we are told, in the hope that people would change their way of life. Thirdly and finally, in addition to limiting the scope of his punishment, God would also send an extra message to his children so they would not despair, and he would do so in the form of a miracle.

By miraculously saving some people's lives even within a terrible flood, or by preserving sacred objects even in the midst of a disastrous fire, God's message was clear to those who were ready to listen, and this message had several aspects. In performing a miracle, God gave proof of his continued supreme power as a Creator. Just as he had created the natural order, he was the one and only who could modify, even break the laws of nature, as in the case of a miracle. Miracles demonstrated to people that God's power to act was not exhausted, and that he was able

25 Jan Adriaansz Leegwater, *Een Kleine Chronyke . . . van de Dorpen von Graft en de Ryp* (Amsterdam, 1710), part 10.

26 Allemeyer, 'Wahrnehmung, Deutung und Verarbeitung von Stadtbränden', 209–14.

to interfere with laws of nature which he had created; he had not only done so in biblical times, but he would continue to do so up to the present. Miracles possessed, moreover, yet another quality: they were the proof of God's unlimited goodness and mercy. In sending a miracle, even as he punished severely, God let his children know that he had not given up on them and that he trusted that they would listen. Miracles within catastrophes, therefore, were God's way of saying that he planned to continue his work of salvation with humankind, even though he was at times so angered that he had to punish. But through the means of a miracle people who had experienced a catastrophe should retain hope and trust in God.

In retrospect, it is not surprising that Protestants in early modern Germany believed in these kinds of miracles no less than Catholics. True, Protestant reformers had criticized Catholic belief in miracles as a kind of superstition which should be abolished. But under the broad theological umbrella of belief in God's providence, belief in signs, wonders and miracles could and did continue to prosper also in Protestant circles.[27] In fact, considering the examples which we find in sixteenth- and seventeenth-century Protestant broadsheets and tracts, there seems to have existed a kind of longing for divine intervention also on the Protestant side.[28] If they heard of a wonder, if they were able to observe a strange sign, or if a miracle was reported to them, the background of the persons involved in these events was not questioned, nor were the attendant circumstances critically scrutinized. Rather, Protestants too seemed to be relieved that God had sent a signal of his presence in their own time, and such signals could refer to a surprisingly wide range of matters. They could involve health, that is miraculous healing, or the rescue of life in a dangerous situation, or the preservation of sacred objects like a Bible with Luther's German translation. And perhaps one could go even a step further: while Catholics had begun to institutionalize relatively strict measures with regard to the acceptance of an unusual event as a miracle in the decades after the Council of Trent, given that a person who had produced a miracle was a candidate for sanctification, Protestants lacked such control mechanisms. Therefore, Protestant belief in miracles was very often quite naïve until the Enlightenment, and, since according to Protestant

27 Willem Frijhoff, 'Signs and Wonders in Seventeenth-Century Holland: an Interpretive Community', in idem, *Embodied Belief*, 137–52.

28 Willem Frijhoff, 'Votive Boats or Secular Models? An Approach to the Question of the Figurative Ships in the Dutch Protestant Churches', in idem, *Embodied Belief*, 137–52.

theology it was God and God alone who was able to effect miracles, all kinds of wonders and strange events could be interpreted as a miracle. There was nothing, so the argument went, which God was not able to do.[29]

There is yet another aspect which I should mention. The reports about miracles within catastrophes did not attempt in any way to demystify or to demythologize the notion of miracle, quite the contrary. What we have are stories of 'wunderbare Errettung' (miraculous rescue), stories about the 'wundervolle Wege Gottes' (God's wonderful ways), and stories about 'Gottes große Barmherzigkeit' (God's unlimited mercy).[30] By the end of the seventeenth and in the early eighteenth century, some philosophers discussed the possibility and the probability of miracles also in Germany and the neighbouring countries. Benedict de Spinoza (1632–77), for example, in his *Tractatus theologico-politicus*, published in 1670, argued that nothing could happen which was contrary to the laws of nature and to the forces inherent in nature.[31] He contended that, even when something looked strange and seemed miraculous, it had a natural cause. For Spinoza, therefore, events considered miraculous were unsuited as proof for Gods power and providence, including those instances in the Old and New Testaments which were called miracles. As Spinoza explained, we should see in these events extraordinary natural powers according to the laws of creation, but nothing which interfered with the order of creation. A few decades later, the German philosopher Christian Wolff (1679–1754), in discussing miracles and wonders, came to much the same conclusion.[32] Both Spinoza and Wolff were not able to convince the theologians of their time, not to mention the wider public. In describing miracles within the great flood of 1717, happening in Christian Wolff's own time, no one doubted the reality of miracles in the course of this disaster.

[29] Hartmut Lehmann, 'Stendal 1601: Eine mißgebildete Totgeburt als Göttliches Warnzeichen', in Wolfgang Breul-Kunkel and Lothar Vogel, eds, *Rezeption und Reform. Festschrift für Hans Schneider* (Darmstadt, 2001), 157–63.

[30] See pamphlets mentioned in nn. 7, 8, 9.

[31] Benedictus de Spinoza, *Tractatus theologico-politicus*, in *Spinoza Opera*, ed. Günter Gawlick and Friedrich Niewöhner (Darmstadt 1979), vol. 1.

[32] For complete survey of the discussion about wonders and miracles in the seventeenth and eighteenth centuries, see Johann Heinrich Zedler, *Großes Vollständiges Universal-Lexikon* (Leipzig and Halle, 1749), 59: 1997–2086.

* * *

I am tempted to continue by saying that in early modern Germany there was no flood, no fire, no earthquake without a miracle. Such a statement is, of course, incorrect, in that we have many reports about catastrophes in which miracles are not mentioned. But there are a remarkable number of reports about catastrophic events in which it is typical that we are informed first about prodigies and then about miracles, which shows that many contemporaries believed that both prodigies and miracles were something like constitutive parts of any natural disaster.

We must explain, therefore, what the religious and social function of this sequence – characterized by prodigy, by the disaster understood as a divine punishment, and by the accompanying miracle – may have been. Most important is the fact that conditions of life in early modern Germany were very unfavourable. There were outbreaks of plague, there was a series of wars, the Reformation resulted not in peace but in new controversies, new forms of repression, renewed warfare. Furthermore, beginning in the 1570s, the climatic conditions in Central Europe began to deteriorate. In some years, ice and snow did not melt until April, in other years the summer was wet and cold, in yet others frost set in before the fields had been harvested.[33] Not all years were the same, but the overall effects of the change of climate, which is appropriately labelled a 'Little Ice Age' in recent literature,[34] were most severe. Bad harvests resulted in widespread lack of food-supply; lack of food led to hunger, especially among the poor, but later also in other segments of society; those weakened by hunger were easy victims of all kinds of illnesses, including plague; the need to secure the food-supply produced much additional local and regional hostility. In the decades after 1570–80, therefore, in Central Europe the vicious cycle of hunger, plague and war was renewed with ever increasing destructive force.[35] As demographic statistics tell us, well before the outbreak of the Thirty

33 Christian Pfister, *Wetternachhersage: 500 Jahre Klimavariationen und Naturkatastrophen 1496–1995* (Bern, 1999); Rüdiger Glaser, *Klimageschichte Mitteleuropas: 1000 Jahre Wetter, Klima, Katastrophen* (Bern, 1999).

34 Wolfgang Behringer, Hartmut Lehmann, Christian Pfister, eds, *Kulturelle Konsequenzen der 'Kleinen Eiszeit'* (forthcoming: Göttingen, 2005), 7–30.

35 Wolfgang Behringer, '"Ettlich Hundert Herrlicher und Schöner Carmina oder gedicht / von der langwirigen schweren gewesten Teurung / grossen Hungersnot / und allerlay zuvor unerhörten Grausamen Straffen / und Plagen" – Zwei Krisengedichte', in Jakubowski-Tiessen and Lehmann, eds, *Um Himmels Willen*, 294–356.

Years War the population in Central Europe had begun to decline.[36] Death was omnipresent; sudden unexpected death without the certainty of salvation was something many people feared. *Memento mori* became the slogan of the time.

Pastors and priests were challenged by this unfortunate turn of events more than anyone else in early modern German society. They had to explain why God no longer provided good harvests, why prayers for enough food and for good health remained unanswered.[37] In Catholic regions, many questioned why the processions and saints no longer gave the kind of protection one was used to. In Protestant as well as in Catholic regions of Germany people asked what had happened and why they were no longer able to enjoy the divine blessings which their forefathers had been allowed to enjoy. What had gone wrong? Why had God withdrawn his favour?

In this situation, both Protestant and Catholic theologians came up with three distinctly different answers. The first answer was the appeal for awareness of the devil. Psychologically speaking, it was a call to look out for scapegoats. The devil had recruited more people as witches than ever before, theologians, magistrates and lawyers argued, and it was witches who had caused widespread misfortune and misery.[38] What this meant was clear: if one succeeded in hunting down and in eliminating all witches, one could rid Christian society of this special menace and this particular kind of demonic plague. As is well known, witch-hunting reached its climax in Germany in the decades after 1570.[39]

The second answer was especially popular among German Protestants. In the generation after Luther many Protestant theologians

36 Christian Pfister, 'The Population of Late Medieval and Early Modern Germany', in Bob Scribner, ed., *Germany: a New Social and Economic History, I: 1450–1630* (London and New York, 1996), 33–62; Neithard Bulst and Christian Pfister, 'L'Allemagne', in Jean-Pierre Bardet and Jaques Dupâquier, eds, *Histoire des populations de l'Europe*, 3 vols (Paris, 1997–9), 1: 509–27.

37 Hartmut Lehmann, 'Frömmigkeitsgeschichtliche Auswirkungen der "Kleinen Eiszeit"', in Wolfgang Schieder, ed., *Volksreligiosität in der modernen Sozialgeschichte* (Göttingen, 1986), 31–50.

38 Wolfgang Behringer, 'Die Krise von 1570: ein Beitrag zur Krisengeschichte der Neuzeit', in Jakubowski-Tiessen and Lehmann, eds, *Um Himmels Willen*, 51–156; see also Stuart Clark, *Thinking with Demons: the Idea of Witchcraft in Early Modern Europe* (Oxford, 1997).

39 Wolfgang Behringer, *Hexenverfolgung in Bayern: Volksmagie, Glaubenseifer und Staatsräson in der frühen Neuzeit* (München, 1987); Gerhard Schormann, *Der Krieg gegen die Hexen: das Ausrottungsprogramm des Kurfürsten von Köln* (Göttingen, 1991).

argued that they lived at the very end of the fourth monarchy as prophesied by Daniel. While some insisted that the millennium had already gone by and that what remained was to wait for the day of the Last Judgement, others believed in the imminent return of Christ who would inaugurate his glorious realm of a thousand years.[40] For members of both groups, the misfortunes and strange events of all kinds which they witnessed and experienced were special signs, *Zeichen der Zeit*, as they were called in German, that is, eschatological signs which were sent by God so that people would recognize that the divine order of salvation had progressed quickly and that the final judgement was approaching rapidly. In this context, disasters were sometimes considered not the work of a punishing God but the result of the devil's rage on whom God had bestowed more power in the last period before Christ's Second Coming so as to test the firmness of people's belief. Along this line of argument, the expected reaction was obvious: people should search for redemption, theologians explained, and in doing so they should concentrate on the growth of their spiritual lives. The mass of edifying literature produced and consumed in seventeenth-century Germany is a telling sign of the strength of this conviction.[41]

The third and final answer can be seen in the arguments connected with the sequence of prodigies as divine warnings, of punishment administered by a prudent and just God, and of miracles as divine signs of hope. This answer implied not the easy way of looking for scapegoats, that is of accusing and denouncing other people with the intention of killing them if it could be proven that they were indeed witches. Nor did this answer arouse eschatological expectations and dwell on apocalyptic fantasies. Rather, with the sequence of divine prodigies, of limited punishment and of miracles as part of the punishment, theologians had found a new and convincing way of coming to terms with the deep-felt effects of great disasters. This answer had several very attractive features: whoever believed in this answer was able to renew trust in God's mercy. In this way, belief in prodigies and in miracles almost had a kind of therapeutic effect. God's power no longer appeared threatening but as the expression of his wise guidance and of his just govern-

40 Manfred Jakubowski-Tiessen, Hartmut Lehmann, Johannes Schilling and Reinhart Staats, eds, *Jahrhundertwenden: Endzeit- und Zukunftsvorstellungen vom 15. bis zum 20. Jahrhundert* (Göttingen, 1999), 73–161.

41 Hartmut Lehmann, *Das Zeitalter des Absolutismus: Gottesgnadentum u. Kriegsnot* (Stuttgart, 1980), 114–23.

ment over the world. There was no need to despair or to despise God. In complete contradiction to the misery caused by natural disasters, belief in their function as divine punishment and, even more importantly, belief in the miracles which God had sent at the same time, succeeded in creating new hope, and in sustaining the will to rebuild what had been destroyed in the course of God's punishment.

* * *

In conclusion, I should like to add three remarks. First, one may argue that every miracle is a divine intervention meant to help someone who is in despair or in a dangerous situation. There are many such examples also in early modern Germany. I should like to add that natural disasters, in the course of which hundreds and sometimes thousands of people were killed, can hardly be compared to personal misery or to individual misfortune. Miracles within catastrophes have to be considered as a special theological answer to this very special human challenge. This theological answer may not have been as fascinating as hunting witches, or as compelling as observing the signs of the last times with the intention to determine the exact date of Christ's Second Coming. Most certainly, moreover, looking back from our own time, the belief in miracles as part of catastrophes may have been just as speculative as the other two answers. In the context of seventeenth-century Christian theology and Christian tradition, however, belief in prodigies and belief in miracles was demanding as well as rewarding. It was demanding because those who accepted these ideas put their lives under God's strict rule. But it was rewarding because in doing so their trust in God's justice and mercy was immensely strengthened.

Second, I should like to point out that people in early modern Germany were not so naïve that they did not know the difference between various kinds of natural disasters and how to protect themselves against them. They were well aware that nothing could be done against earthquakes, except perhaps saying prayers regularly. But people living on the coast were used to building dikes and keeping existing dikes in good repair. Almost all of the cities had fire ordinances which regulated how to build chimneys and stoves and what to do in case of a fire. Damage caused by fire or flood was not taken as fateful, but when such disasters occurred, it was believed that it was God who was punishing men. After the events, the question of responsibility was nevertheless raised. We have reports about heated debates in which some people asked who had been in charge of supervising the dikes and why they had broken, or why someone had been careless in handling fire and how one could be sure that this would not occur again.[42]

As I mentioned before, and this is my third concluding remark, in some countries of Europe belief in miracles had been contested well before 1700. The discussion about miracles was focused on the miracles mentioned in the New Testament, and it was closely linked to the emergence of modern biblical criticism. This discussion was especially lively in Great Britain and in France.[43] In Central Europe, the notion of miracles within catastrophes was upheld much longer than in Western Europe. As far as I can tell, the first big crisis which was no longer explained as a punishment by God, and in which miracles were no longer observed, was the great famine of 1770–2.[44] It is true that even in 1770–2 some German pastors spoke of the need for repentance. But the majority of those who discussed the causes and consequences of this event, including many pastors, argued that the crisis had become so severe because people had forgotten to use the rational powers entrusted to them by God in order to improve social and economic conditions, and in particular agriculture. Not repentance, but rather the introduction of new forms of crop rotation, of new methods of ploughing, of new and better forms of storage, was necessary. With some delay, the Enlightenment had also reached Central Europe. This was the end of belief in miracles within catastrophes.

Max-Planck-Institut für Geschichte

42 Jakubowski-Tiessen, *Sturmflut 1717*, 242–8; Allemeyer, 'Wahrnehmung, Deutung und Verarbeitung von Stadtbränden', 211–14.

43 Paul Hazard, *La Crise de la conscience européenne: 1680–1715* (Paris, 1934).

44 These previous remarks are based on research by my doctoral student Anne Staff (unpublished); see also Wilhelm Abel, *Massenarmut und Hungerkrisen im vorindustriellen Europa* (Hamburg and Berlin, 1974).

LATE SEVENTEENTH-CENTURY QUAKERISM AND THE MIRACULOUS: A NEW LOOK AT GEORGE FOX'S 'BOOK OF MIRACLES'

by ROSEMARY MOORE

GEORGE Fox, chief among the founders of Quakerism, died in 1691, leaving a huge mass of papers for publication together with funds to support the project. In the event, some of his papers were never published and were lost, and little was known about them until the discovery in 1932 of an annotated list of all Fox's papers, which had been compiled in the 1690s, and which included references to two unknown books, a 'Book of Miracles' and a 'Book of Examples of God's Judgements on Evildoers'. The finder was Henry J. Cadbury (1883–1974), who is best known in non-Quaker circles as a New Testament scholar, and the skills he needed for the analysis of New Testament documents were invaluable in handling the Fox corpus.[1] He was able to gain an idea of the contents of these lost books, particularly the 'Book of Miracles', and his partial reconstruction of it, published in 1948 with a comprehensive introduction, is still an important source for any study of the miraculous element in early Quakerism.[2]

The 'Book of Miracles' was a compilation of accounts of over one hundred and fifty Quaker miracles, mostly healings, many performed by George Fox himself. Internal evidence suggests that it was put together over a period of time and not completed until 1689, two years before Fox's death.[3] In the political circumstances of the late seventeeth century, there were good reasons why the leading Quakers of that time would have hesitated to publish such material, which might have revived old controversies about extravagant Quaker behaviour, and

[1] Henry Joel Cadbury was Hollis Professor of Divinity at Harvard University and author of many books and pamphlets on the Bible and on Quakerism. Cadbury edited the list of Fox's papers, and published it as *The Annual Catalogue of George Fox's Papers: Compiled in 1694–1697* (Haverford, PA, and London, 1939).

[2] *George Fox's 'Book of Miracles'*, ed. Henry J. Cadbury, with a foreword by Rufus M. Jones (Cambridge, 1948, repr. with additional forewords, Philadelphia, PA, and London, 2000). Cadbury's conclusions regarding the 'Book of Examples' were more tentative, and were included in *The Narrative Papers of George Fox*, ed. Henry J. Cadbury (Richmond, IN, 1972), 209–32.

[3] *'Book of Miracles'*, 59.

little needs adding to Cadbury's explanations for the non-appearance of the 'Book of Miracles'.[4] What does need more critical attention are the questions, first, concerning the authenticity of these stories, and second, why Fox made such a collection. Cadbury ignored the question of historicity, although he was well aware of the poor contemporary evidence for early Quaker miracles.[5] As a consequence, he had no problem regarding Fox's reasons for writing these books, namely that he:

> felt clearly that the miracles that surrounded his life and the beginnings of the Quaker movement were too numerous and too significant to be ignored. A collection of these was worth making to have upon record.[6]

An alternative view, presented here, is that the absence of early and independent evidence for miracles suggests that this collection embodies Fox's own interpretation of certain happenings, which he saw as actual miraculous interventions of God.

Now there is no question about the importance of signs and wonders in popular British religion in the mid-seventeenth century.[7] Some of it lay on the borderland between religion and witchcraft, and accusations of being concerned in such weird events were normally denied by Quakers immediately they came to light, though sometimes the same story would be brought up time and again for years. One of the most startling and circumstantial was the tale of how a Quaker turned a woman into a bay mare, buggered her, and rode her about the country near Colchester. This story was publicized in a popular ballad, and recurs a number of times in the anti-Quaker literature.[8] On

4 Ibid., 73–85.

5 The Introduction to the *'Book of Miracles'*, 4–32, contains a full account of the evidence for early Quaker miracles, performed by Fox and others. Barry Reay and Larry Ingle, scholars who might have been expected to be sceptical, also ignored the problem of historicity: see H. Larry Ingle, *First among Friends: George Fox and the Creation of Quakerism* (New York and Oxford, 1994), 64, 102, 240; Barry Reay, *The Quakers and the English Revolution* (London, 1985), 36–7.

6 *'Book of Miracles'*, 55.

7 See for instance Thomas, *Religion and the Decline of Magic*. For Quakers, in addition to the introduction to the *'Book of Miracles'*, see Kenneth Carroll, 'Sackcloth and Ashes and Other Signs and Wonders', *Journal of the Friends' Historical Society* 54 (1957), 314–25; idem, 'Early Quakers and "Going Naked as a Sign"', *Quaker History* 67 (1978), 69–87: summary in Rosemary Moore, *The Light in their Consciences: Early Quakers in Britain, 1646–1666* (University Park, PA, 2000), 91, 126.

8 This story can be found in John Gilpin, *The Quakers Shaken* (2nd edn, London, 1655), in *Strange and Terrible Newes from Cambridge being a relation of the Quakers bewitching M. Philips*

another occasion, Quakers were said to have been involved in an attempt to resurrect a dead man near Worcester, although the Quakers said that the people concerned were nothing to do with them.[9]

Then there were miraculous deliverances, especially healings, cures that were otherwise unexplained. The performance of such miracles was considered to be a sign of the presence of the True Church, as described in Matt. 11, 5 and in the Acts of the Apostles. People who declared that they possessed the spirit of God, as Quakers did, were expected to perform miracles in proof of their claims. The difficulty was that opponents of Quakers could, and did, make use of reports of such cures as evidence of witchcraft or popery. Claims of miracles in Quaker pamphlet literature are couched in very general terms, and when challenged to perform miracles Quakers prevaricated, offering lengthy fasts, or making the suggestion that Quaker miracles were spiritual rather than physical.[10] It is quite likely that an unofficial 'fringe' Quakerism was less cautious, and was responsible for some of the allegations of pretended Quaker miracles in the anti-Quaker pamphlets.[11] Such healings might be scorned as merely the action of divine providence, a distinction that Quakers, unlike some seventeenth-century groups, did not use.[12] I know of just one first-hand claim by a Quaker, in the 1650s, to have successfully performed a healing, and that was made in 1652 by the young and excitable Richard Farnworth.[13] No contemporary records have been found of George Fox performing successful healings at this time, though an opponent, Francis Higginson, referred to his failure to heal a cripple, and Fox was once

(London, 1659) and in [John Denham], *A Relation of a Quaker that attempted to Bugger a Mare near Colchester* (London, 1659).

9 London, Society of Friends, Swarthmore MSS 1.217, also known from other references: cited in *'Book of Miracles'*, 11–12.

10 Thomas More, *An Antidote against the spreading Infection of Antichrist* (London, 1655), 8; [John Camm and Francis Howgill], *Answer to a Book that Samuel Eaton put up to Parliament* (London, 1654), 16, and George Fox, *The Great Mistery of the Great Whore* (London, 1659), 31, repr. of the 1831 edn in *The Works of George Fox*, ed. T. H. S. Wallace, New Foundation Edition, 8 vols (State College, PA, 1990), 3: 80. All these examples and others are cited in the *'Book of Miracles'*, 23–32.

11 For 'fringe' Quakerism, see Moore, *Light in their Consciences*, 28, 45, 52, 133–4, 195, 222–3.

12 See for instance, Jonathan Clapham, *A Full Discovery and Confutation of the wicked and damnable doctrines of the Quakers* (London, 1656), cited in *'Book of Miracles'*, 19–21. For 'providences', see *'Book of Miracles'*, 15–16.

13 Swarthmore MSS 1.372, Farnworth to Nayler, July 1652.

asked to advise on a failed healing attempted by one of his followers.[14] In effect, Quakers needed proper miracles to support their claims, but the evidence suggests that they were not good at performing them.

Prophetic signs, which, as in the Old Testament, may have been thought by their actors to have an actual effect, were definitely in the early Quaker tradition. 'Walking naked as a sign', sometimes varied by wearing sackcloth and ashes, was a common Quaker practice in the early days, being a warning of coming disaster, but there are very few instances of this practice after 1660. Even before the Restoration, the Quaker leadership was trying to distance itself from the more eccentric manifestations of Quakerism, having learnt that such happenings did not help the Quaker image in the public eye. Similarly, the quaking of the early charismatic meetings, which the first Quakers certainly saw as a wondrous sign of the presence of God, practically vanished within a few years of the foundation of the movement.[15]

The idea that God might intervene directly in human affairs was much more persistent. A disaster to oneself would be understood as the punishment of God for one's own misdoing, or as necessary training, and Quakers, like others, took such happenings very seriously. In the public sphere, Quakers looked for instances of unpleasant things happening to their enemies, and Quaker Meetings were asked to report annually to the Yearly Meeting: 'What signal Judgements have come upon Persecutors?' But towards the end of the seventeenth century people were becoming less inclined to interpret such events as the result of God's direct intervention, while with the increase of toleration there was less persecution. In 1701 the Yearly Meeting decided to stop collecting reports of 'signal Judgements' or, as they were also called, 'examples'.[16]

As the seventeenth century progressed, Quakers became increasingly concerned to present themselves as normal useful citizens, thus erasing memories of the 1650s. To quote Norman Penney, editor of the original manuscript of Fox's 'Journal', 'The mantle of respectability that has so often stifled the spirit of prophecy was already beginning to be wrapped round the Society of Friends'.[17] Quaker theology was also

14 Francis Higginson, *Brief Relation of the Irreligion of the Northern Quakers* (London, 1653), 29, cited in *'Book of Miracles'*, 19; London, Society of Friends, A. R. Barclay MS 21.

15 Moore, *Light in Their Consciences*, 148–9.

16 *The Journal of George Fox*, ed. Norman Penney, 2 vols (Cambridge, 1911), 1: 394, n. 1 [hereafter: *Cambridge Journal*] from the Minutes of London Yearly Meeting.

17 *Cambridge Journal*, Introduction, 1: ix.

changing. Recent studies have shown that many of the first Quakers, especially Fox and Nayler, took their claim to unity with Christ very literally, to the point that the distinction between Christ and the believer could become blurred.[18] This trend can be seen in the number of trials of Quakers for blasphemy up to 1653, after which time they learnt to moderate their language and express their beliefs in strictly Biblical terms.[19] When Fox talked of his relationship to Christ as being 'flesh of his flesh and bone of his bone', he meant precisely that.[20] The 'light in the conscience' that the first Quakers knew was not a vague feeling of guidance, but the experience of being wholly taken over, physically as well as spiritually, by the risen Christ.[21] Fox and Nayler, moreover, were acknowledged as having more of the 'measure' of Christ in them than their followers and on occasion were treated with something very like divine honours.[22] Therefore miracles, as has been seen, were expected from such people.

Twenty years later the works of Robert Barclay show an attenuation of this faith. He used the same terminology of 'the light in the conscience', but meant something subtly different, for he was trying to relate Quaker ideas to standard Protestant Christianity. For Robert Barclay, the Light was like a seed, which 'draws, invites and inclines to God', and he carefully distinguished between Christ and the human:

> We do not at all intend ... to equal ourselves to that holy man the Lord Jesus Christ. ... For though we affirm that Christ dwells in us, yet not immediately, but mediately, as he is in that seed, which is in us: whereas he, to wit, the Eternal Word, which was with God, dwelt immediately in that holy man [Jesus].[23]

18 Richard Bailey, *New Light on George Fox and Early Quakerism: the Making and Unmaking of a God* (San Francisco, CA, 1992), esp. 92–9; Nigel Smith, 'Hidden Things brought to Light', in Thomas N. Corns and David Loewenstein, eds, *The Emergence of Quaker Writing: Dissenting Literature in Seventeenth-Century England* (London, 1995), 63–8; Moore, *Light in Their Consciences*, 76–9; Lawrence S. Kuenning, 'The Bunyan-Burrough Debate of 1656–57 Analyzed Using a Computer Hypertext', unpublished Ph.D. thesis, Westminster Theological Seminary, Philadelphia, PA, 2000, 169–95, online at http://www.qhpress.org/texts/bvb/lkbbda.html), ch. 7 (consulted: 14 February 2004).

19 Moore, *Light in Their Consciences*, 78–9.

20 Fox, *'Great Mistery'*, 9, 11, in *Works*, 3: 46, 51. The reference is to Eph. 5, 30b (now considered spurious and not found in modern versions) and to Gen. 29, 14.

21 Smith, 'Hidden Things', 65–6, for mid-seventeenth century ideas of the body.

22 Bailey, *New Light*, 75–136, presents persuasive arguments for Fox and Nayler being regarded as divine, though one may regret his choice of the word 'avatar' in this connection.

23 Robert Barclay, *An Apology for the True Christian Divinity*, ed. Licia Kuenning (S. I., 1678; repr. Glenside, PA, 2002), Fifth and Sixth propositions, par. XIII, 120–1.

The first Quakers did not make this distinction. James Nayler at his trial is reported as saying that he was of the same nature as Christ, though not of the same stature, and he suffered for it. George Fox was probably always clearer than Nayler about where God ended and humanity began, and he adapted his language and remained on good terms with the new Quaker theologians.[24] But he never changed his deepest beliefs, and they can be traced in his published writings to the end of his life.[25]

Similarly, and connected with the changing Christology, the Quaker attitude to miracles was likewise changing. Whether or not they could succesfully perform them, early Quakers had believed that miracles were a necessary sign of the presence of the True Church. But the new generation of intellectual Quaker leaders, Robert Barclay, George Keith and William Penn, considered that miracles were not necessary for such evidence. Barclay accepted what he called the 'common Protestant answer', that, 'We need not miracles because we preach no new gospel, but that which is confirmed by all the miracles of Christ and his apostles'.[26] Keith and Penn made similar statements.[27] They repeated this view in Holland in 1677, when Penn took the lead in disputing with the Mennonite Galenus Abrahamz, who said that messengers of Christ should perform miracles. Penn conceded that he did know of healings through faith in the power of God, and Barclay and Keith would have said the same, for they must have heard of the widely reported healing, in a Quaker context, of a Dutch woman in 1676, a story which was also known to and accepted by their acquaintance Henry More.[28] However, unlike More, who made and published a collection of miracles, the new Quaker intellectuals did not consider modern miracles, if they

24 See Moore, *Light in Their Consciences*, 40–7, for the breach between Fox and Nayler and its aftermath. The best book for the interpretation of Nayler is probably Leo Damrosch, *The Sorrows of the Quaker Jesus: James Nayler and the Puritan Crackdown on the Free Spirit* (Cambridge, MA, and London, 1996).

25 See for instance Fox's pugnacious Quaker version of the traditional creed, *Something in answer to such as falsely say the Quakers are no Christians* (London, 1682), but written earlier, esp. the final page, 28.

26 Barclay, *Apology*, Tenth Proposition, par. XII, 251.

27 Examples, cited *'Book of Miracles'*, 26, are George Keith, *Immediate Revelation . . . not ceased* (London, 1668), 4, 11; William Penn, *A Serious Apology for the Principles and Practices of the People called Quakers* (London, 1671), Part II, 86–8.

28 *'Book of Miracles'*, 27, 54, 66. More heard the story from Mercurius van Helmont, and included it in his own collection of miracles. More and van Helmont, together with Keith, Barclay and Penn, were all members of Lady Conway's circle of friends at her home at Ragley.

occurred, to be of any great interest or importance to them. Penn's preface to the published version of Fox's Journal contains no mention of miracles.

At this time the English Church's attitude to miracles was more relaxed, perhaps, than earlier in the century, and tales of spiritual healings and events such as miraculous escapes from danger were quite acceptable in many church circles up to and beyond the end of the seventeenth century. This also applied in popular Quakerism; Cadbury found a number of accounts of spiritual healing by or connected with Quakers during the later part of the seventeenth century, though few were recorded at the time they were supposed to have occurred.[29] In contrast, the Quaker intellectuals held firmly to a traditional Protestant viewpoint and were probably quite consciously trying to distance themselves from early charismatic Quakerism.

George Fox's attitude to miracles chimes more closely with popular religion than with the theology of Barclay, Keith and Penn. He dictated the main manuscript of his Journal in 1676. It was somewhat more restrained than his 'Short Journal' of 1664, in that he no longer described himself as 'the son of God', but it abounded in healing miracles, visions, and signal judgements, passages that would, if published untouched, have brought Quakers into disrepute at a time when they were particularly anxious to stand well in society.[30] During the years following, probably in cooperation with others, he put together his 'Book of Examples', a collection of God's judgements on evildoers.[31] Although opinion was beginning to turn against the concept of 'signal judgements', the book was not entirely out of place in the context of later seventeenth-century Quakerism, when Quakers were still suffering persecution and making organised collections of such 'examples'.

The 'Book of Miracles' took shape at the same time. Some of the happenings it describes are also mentioned in the 'Journal', but, except for the Dutch incident and a few relating to Fox's American journey in the 1670s, none are at present known from contemporary records and

29 *'Book of Miracles'*, 62–72: see, in this volume, Alexandra Walsham, 'Miracles in Post-Reformation England', 273–306.

30 *The Short Journal and Itinerary Journals of George Fox*, ed. Norman Penney (Cambridge, 1925), 17, 32–3, and note. These passages were omitted from the corresponding passages in later versions of the 'Journal'.

31 Cadbury, *Narrative Papers*, 216.

few were noted in any other sources.[32] It is true that the ephemeral Quaker tracts and manuscripts of the later seventeenth century have not been as well studied as the earlier ones, but even so, if all the incidents described in the 'Book of Miracles' occurred as described, and were recognized as miraculous, then one would expect that traces would have been found elsewhere. In brief, the great majority of all records of Quaker miracles come from the writings of George Fox, and most of these miracles were allegedly performed by George Fox himself.[33] Many of them were cures that might have happened from natural causes, especially if aided by faith in Fox. In the course of the telling, accounts of natural events seem to have turned into 'miracles'.

The body responsible for Quaker publications was the Second Day Morning Meeting, a group of senior Quakers, set up by Fox in 1672, which had acquired considerable authority, to the point of editing, and even in one case turning down, papers by Fox himself.[34] Fox must have been perfectly aware of the hesitations that the Morning Meeting would have about publishing the 'Book of Miracles'. During his later years Fox was under serious attack from within Quakerism, as a result of objections to the administrative system that he had set up, and his position as charismatic leader was challenged.[35] His belief in a real union with God was, under the influence of Barclay and Penn, becoming outmoded. The compilation of the 'Book of Miracles' begins to look like an act of defiance, reiterating Fox's original message that Christ had returned. To Fox, the healings he described in the 'Book of Miracles' were demonstrations of the power of God within him. In the uncongenial setting of the late seventeenth century, he was trying to maintain the faith of the original Quakers and his own position as leader. In his 'Journal', and in the 'Books of Miracles and Examples', George Fox hoped to ensure that his own record of true Quakerism would be left for his heirs, even if unpublished in his lifetime.

Events turned out otherwise. Quakers had gained toleration for their meetings in 1689, but they had plenty of problems remaining. They

32 One that does have another mention is the healing of John Banks's arm, *'Book of Miracles'*, no. 62a, 120, which was described in circumstantial detail in Banks's journal. However, this was not published until 1712, and his account appears to have been written a long time after the event.

33 Bailey, *New Light*, 195, 265–9, analyses these reports according to date, and suggests that there is a pattern showing that most 'miracles' occurred during periods when Fox was particuarly self-confident.

34 Ingle, *First among Friends*, 256.

35 Ibid., final chapters.

were seeking relief on the taking of oaths and the payment of tithes. William Penn was held under suspicion by William III's government for having been too close to James II. Robert Barclay, the most able Quaker intellectual, died in the same year as Fox. Not long afterwards, George Keith became disillusioned with Quaker theology, quarrelled very publicly with the Quaker leadership, and ended his life as an Anglican priest. One Francis Bugg, an ex-Quaker who detested Fox and had a venomous turn of phrase, was alert to any openings that might come his way, and 'pretended' Quaker miracles were one of his favourite lines of attack. In these circumstances, Fox's manuscripts could not be published in their original form.

The Morning Meeting entrusted the editing of Fox's 'Journal' to Thomas Ellwood, whose version, published in 1694, is still the one included in Fox's *Collected Works*.[36] Ellwood omitted or smoothed over political references favourable to Cromwell, and dealt similarly with passages suggesting the direct intervention of the Almighty, or associating Quakers too closely with biblical happenings. 'Examples' of the fates of evildoers were edited, and likewise Fox's claims to psychic insight and prophetic dreams. Many of Fox's healings disappeared. A dozen healings did remain, and were listed as 'Miracles' in the index, but with the suggestion that the Lord was responsible for them, thus removing the human agency one degree from God.[37] But even so, they provided an immediate *casus belli* for Francis Bugg. They were counterfeit miracles, he said, like those allegedly performed by Papists, certainly not performed in the name of Christ, and mostly plain lies.[38]

A collection of Fox's Epistles was published a few years later, probably having been edited in a similar manner to the 'Journal', though in the absence of most of the original manuscripts one cannot be sure.[39] Finally, a number of Fox's previously published papers were reprinted.[40] This left a good deal of problematic material, notably the 'Books of Miracles and Examples'.

36 *A Journal or historical account of the life, travels, sufferings, Christian experience and labour of love in the work of the ministry, of that ancient, eminent and faithful servant of Christ, George Fox . . .*, ed. Thomas Ellwood (London, 1694). The Journal makes up vols 1–2 of the *Works of George Fox*.

37 See the Introductions to the *Cambridge Journal*, esp. 1: xiii–xxvi (by T. Edmund Harvey) and 1: xl–xli, for details of Ellwood's alterations; cf. also *'Book of Miracles'*, 35–8.

38 For a summary of Bugg's attacks, see *'Book of Miracles'*, 75–8.

39 First published by Sowle in 1698, now making up vols 7–8 of *The Works of George Fox*.

40 Vols 4–6 of *The Works of George Fox*, known as *Gospel Truth Demonstrated*, or the 'Doctrinals'.

So what happened to them? They were an embarrassment. After the turn of the century, 'examples' were no longer collected. The miracles in the Journal, even as edited by Ellwood, had caused quite sufficient furore. Perhaps the Morning Meeting followed its usual practice with works about which it had doubts. They were put 'in the drawer', to await further consideration, and after that, they rarely saw the light of day again.[41] Someone, sometime, must have thrown away the contents of the drawer.

University of Birmingham

[41] This practice was described by Christine Trevett in her presidential address to the Friends' Historical Society in 2001, published as 'Not fit to be printed: the Welsh, the Women and the Second Day's Morning Meeting', *Journal of the Friends' Historical Society* 59 (2001, issued 2004), 115–44.

RECLAIMING GHOSTS IN 1690S ENGLAND

by SASHA HANDLEY

ON Wednesday 1 June 1692, a young man, about fifteen years of age, went to his bed. He had no sooner lain down than he heard 'a Hand sweeping on the wall'. Then it came 'with a rushing noise on his beds-head' and 'stroaked him over the face twice very gently'. Opening his eyes he saw before him 'an apparition of a woman cloathed in black apparel'. Following this eerie encounter, other members of the family claimed to have seen the apparition 'in the same room with a lighted candle'. Perplexed by these unexplained visits the mistress of this 'Civiliz'd Family' wrote to the editors of the bi-weekly periodical the *Athenian Mercury* desiring to know 'what should be the occasion of the disturbance' and 'whether it be advisable to ask the question of the apparition'.[1] Samuel Wesley (father of John), Church of England minister and co-editor of the *Athenian Mercury*, advised the woman to have a chat with the ghost, to find out its purpose and to discover how it might be satisfied.[2]

Wesley's support for this episode may seem surprising since the reality of ghosts and apparitions was highly contested in the religious polemic of post-Reformation England. According to the new Protestant regime, ghosts had no 'middle place' from which to return to the living since Purgatory was now abolished and each individual was powerless to affect his or her spiritual fate. For many Protestant reformers the notion of a dynamic afterlife lacked currency, and to believe in ghosts represented a heretical adherence to the principles of the Catholic Church. If spirits did appear they were not to be conceived as spirits of the dead but as angelic messengers from God or evil spirits sent to do the Devil's work.

In spite of official objections, however, souls of the dead continued to visit their friends and relatives on a regular basis. Moreover, Peter Marshall has shown that Elizabethan and Jacobean ministers often diluted or even reversed the orthodox rejection of ghosts at parish level and determined to put these preternatural episodes to good doctrinal

1 *Athenian Mercury*, no. 28, Saturday 2 July (1692), 2.

2 Although individual editorial responses were anonymous, questions relating to religion were most likely to be answered by Samuel Wesley.

use.[3] Such *ad hoc* local accommodations ensured a more fruitful exchange of clerical and lay knowledge about ghosts than has generally been allowed by historians, but it was not until the 1690s that the relationship between Protestantism and ghosts blossomed into one of more thoroughgoing reciprocity. It was against this relatively harmonious background that Samuel Wesley was able to openly endorse tales of the wandering dead in one of the most widely circulated publications of the day.

Keith Thomas and Ronald Finucane have tackled Restoration-era ghost beliefs as part of broader chronological spans,[4] but little has been said about the institutional fortunes of the Church and discussions of the preternatural world. In seeking to fill some of these gaps, this discussion largely focuses on the 1690s, and more particularly on Richard Baxter's *The Certainty of the World of Spirits* (1691), and the *Athenian Mercury* (1691–7) under the editorship of John Dunton. Baxter's treatise provides one of the most comprehensive clerical vindications of ghosts in this period and his work usefully highlights the shifting religious priorities of Restoration Protestantism that saw ghosts publicly reinstated as valid sources of spiritual reflection. Baxter's work also highlights clerical interaction with lay perceptions of ghosts that filled the pages of the *Athenian Mercury*.

* * *

The *Athenian Mercury* ran from 1691 to 1697 and set out to resolve any curious questions that its readers cared to submit. Unlike any other periodical of its generation, the *Mercury* devoted its energies entirely to its readers. The journal was based around an interactive question and answer format, which engaged with the real-life issues of the ordinary men and women who chose to write in. As an Anglican Minister and co-editor of the journal, Samuel Wesley answered questions relating to religion and much of his time was spent responding to queries about ghosts. 'Do the Deceased walk?', asked one reader in issue twenty-eight. 'Where go the Souls of Good Men immediately after Death?' 'Where are the souls of men to remain till the last day?' Was the soul 'in an active or unactive state' after its separation from the body?[5] These were

3 Peter Marshall, *Beliefs and the Dead in Reformation England* (Oxford, 2002), 254.

4 Thomas, *Religion and the Decline of Magic*, 701–24; R. C. Finucane, *Appearances of the Dead: a Cultural History of Ghosts* (London, 1982), 117–50.

5 *Athenian Mercury*, no. 29, vol. 1 (1691), 1; no. 28, vol. 1 (1691), 1; no. 7, vol. 2 (1691), 2; no. 28, vol. 4 (1691), 2.

just a few of the questions put to the *Mercury* by readers who were clearly unsure what lay in store for them beyond the grave. Protestant teaching on this subject was ambiguous and had failed to satisfy curiosity about the exact nature of life after death. As a result, considerable slippage was envisaged between the natural and preternatural worlds; if the souls of the dead could not be definitively placed, then what was to stop them from returning to earth?

The links between this world and the next had not been severed and ghosts continued to fascinate *Mercury* readers throughout the six years of its publication. In fact this journal received so many tales of the wandering dead that its editors took the unusual step of devoting an entire issue to reports of their appearances amongst the living. The issue was fittingly published on All Souls' Night, 1691, and according to the editors it served a dual function: first, to reduce 'the many Proselytes of Sadducism and Hobbism amongst us', but also, secondly, to give 'great satisfaction to all our Querists in general'.[6]

* * *

The campaign against 'Atheists' and 'Sadducees' followed the growth of radical religious dissent during the years of civil war. In their most extreme guise, the materialist philosophies which flowered at this time denied the existence of an afterlife and sometimes even of God. Following the accession of Charles II in 1660, fear of materialist heresies was supplemented by a perceived threat from men of science whose new empirical philosophies shifted emphasis away from the spiritual realm and focused man's contemplation on the physical world. Restoration England thus presented new challenges to a Church seeking to re-establish its authority and a polemical battle duly ensued. Henry More and Joseph Glanvill were among the first to recognize that ghost stories could act as crucial weapons in the campaign to re-enchant the world and to reinstate religion at the heart of civil society.[7] Ghosts were, after all, visible manifestations of the soul's immortality, evidence of God's providential activity and convincing justifications of the Christian faith. For those who placed their trust in demonstration

6 *Athenian Mercury*, no. 10, vol. 4, Saturday 31 October (1691), 1.

7 Fear of these heresies was evidenced by a series of measures against nonconformity in this period. See Philip C. Almond, *Heaven and Hell in Enlightenment England* (Cambridge, 1994), 40–3, and John Spurr, 'Religion in Restoration England', in Lionel K. J. Glassey, ed., *The Reigns of Charles II and James VII & II* (Basingstoke, 1997), 92–4.

alone, ghostly visitations could provide immediate and persuasive evidence that religious sceptics had got it wrong.

Richard Baxter shared these convictions and his *World of Spirits* directly addressed sceptics who claimed 'that could they be certain of Spirits and Apparitions', it would do more to convince them of the existence of God 'than the Assertions of the Scriptures'.[8] Baxter therefore set out to guide these doubters back to the path of righteousness by providing fresh and credible evidence that ghosts continued to appear – and only with divine permission. Catering for new empirical tastes, Baxter rejected antiquated ghost stories in favour of fresh reports that were nearest 'both for Time and Place'.[9] Samuel Wesley and his co-editors John Dunton and Richard Sault clearly approved of Baxter's methodology, reporting ghost sightings from correspondents and adding tales of their own. The *Mercury* told of a house in Lancashire where a ghost had haunted the grounds for a number of years. Following some excavation work 'there was found the skeleton of a man, which was seen by the Minister' and by 'Mr. Moss, a very intelligent Gentleman'. This report was accompanied by a ghost from Puddle-Dock in London who haunted the tenants of a house until human remains were discovered in the cellar with 'a great nail driven into the skull'.[10] The bones were reburied in St Gregory's churchyard and the ghost appeared no more. Revelations of murder, wrongdoing and improper burial were familiar motifs of the early modern ghost story; the *Athenian Mercury* explicitly engaged with these popular themes and sought to exploit the ghost narrative as a means of communicating important religious messages.

* * *

In 1690s England, churchmen appropriated ghosts to reassert the authority of the Church in its broadest sense, but also for more consistent pastoral purposes. In 1691, the *Mercury* reported the appearance of Mr Lunt's ghost (formerly a servant) to his brother in Derbyshire. Having led a sinful life, Lunt now wished to provide a better example to his relation and asked that his brother 'woul'd go to one with whom he had lived as a Servant, and demand some money which was due to him'. He was to give it to a woman in the same town 'whom he had

8 Richard Baxter, *The Certainty of the World of Spirits fully Evinced* (London, 1691), 17.
9 Ibid., 1.
10 *Athenian Mercury*, no. 28, vol. 7, Saturday 2 July (1692), 2.

promised marriage to, and got her with child' before deserting both his service and her. When the ghost offered to reward his brother for his efforts, the man insisted that he 'would ask nothing'.[11] The tale exemplified the moral fortitude of this poor man who prized the duties of Christian charity and familial duty more than his own personal enrichment. In the style of a parable, ghost stories were promoted as moral exemplars, advancing a practical moral theology that was increasingly emphasized by Restoration clerics as a necessary supplement to an introspective faith.

Despite the upheavals of Reformation, ghosts continued to be invested with important religious and emotional meanings. By scrapping purgatory and prayers for the dead, Protestantism officially outlawed an extended process of mourning for the dead in which the living could play an active role.[12] Extra-liturgical comfort was sought and ghosts provided one outlet for expressions of loss by grieving relatives. The *Athenian Oracle* (a spin-off from the *Mercury*) printed a tale from Smithfield in London where the ghost of Mr Watkinson appeared to his daughter about six months after his death to comfort her during her grieving.[13] Other *Mercury* readers also required assurance that the dead still remained connected to the living in some way. In June 1691 one reader asked 'Whether separated Souls have any knowledge of the Affairs in this World'. In issue twenty, another wondered if 'we shall know our Friends in Heaven' and 'Whether the Departed have any Knowledge of, or ever concern themselves with the affairs of their Friends in this Life?' To this last question, Wesley clearly recognized the use to which personal anxieties could be put, replying that 'either some departed Souls have particular Commissions . . . or that all of them have a Cognizance of our Affairs.'[14]

Restoration ghosts were not hangovers from an age of superstition but were clearly relevant to the religious climate of the day. Calvinist orthodoxy taught that all were bound either to heaven or to hell; a pious life of good works might be interpreted as a 'sign' of election but no earthly deeds could materially alter one's ultimate destination. Recognizing the fear that was borne out of these uncertainties, a number of prominent divines challenged the uncompromising

11 *Athenian Mercury*, no. 10, vol. 4, Saturday 31 October (1691), 1.
12 Marshall, *Beliefs and the Dead*, 128.
13 *The Athenian Oracle*, vol. IV (1703–10), 288.
14 *Athenian Mercury*, no. 7, vol. 2 (1691), 1; no. 25, vol. 1 (1691), 2; no. 20, vol. 1 (1691), 1.

doctrines of predestination and eternal torment over the course of the seventeenth century. The archbishop of Canterbury John Tillotson promoted a God 'who was not obliged eternally to torment the wicked' and William Whiston claimed that wicked souls would be annihilated rather than suffer hell's torments in perpetuity.[15] Plagued by fears of damnation as a young boy, the Cambridge Platonist Henry More preferred to advance a more liberal theology that concentrated on moral values and introduced a measure of free will into the formula for salvation. Ghosts formed part of More's vision of a dynamic afterlife and as Calvinist extremes were increasingly tempered by Arminian influences in the Church, wandering spirits achieved greater acceptability with the value of human agency reasserted.

In October 1691, the *Athenian Mercury* gave a very specific example of how ghosts soothed the anxieties created by an uncertain process of salvation. The journal printed an account from a gentlewoman whose son had taken 'ill courses' during his life. The lady's efforts to reprove her son had made some impact since the young man did eventually reform, but following his untimely death soon afterwards, this pious mother still feared that her son would be denied entrance to heaven as punishment for his sins. Convinced that his repentance had come too late, the lady was 'extreamly afflicted' and 'fear'd he was in Hell'.[16] Her worries were allayed though when just a month later 'the young man's spirit came to his mothers bed' and reassured her that he was at rest.[17] Ghost stories could be moulded to fit with a broader clerical project to steer a middle path between the extremes of heaven and hell. If a repentant sinner could be welcomed into Abraham's bosom then it gave some hope to ordinary men and women that they might hope for a similar reward.

Richard Baxter's appropriation of ghosts represented a similar attempt to reconcile the idea of a loving and benevolent God with the image of a cruel and vengeful Lord. Baxter's ghosts encouraged moral reformation on this side of the grave and showed that God had a care to purge sinners before it was too late. His *World of Spirits* provided practical guidance on the workings of the spirit world and aimed to instil godly principles in its readers. Although Baxter sought to admonish his

15 Almond, *Heaven and Hell*, 156; D. P. Walker, *The Decline of Hell: Seventeenth-Century Discussions of Eternal Torment* (Chicago, IL, 1964), 9, 108.

16 *Athenian Mercury*, no. 10, vol. 4, Saturday 31 October (1691), 1.

17 Ibid.

audience by claiming that evil spirits were more frequently seen than angelic ones, those that were visited by the Devil's minions were not to despair but to look upon such appearances as a test of faith, a call to righteousness by a compassionate God without whose will and permission 'no Spirits can do any thing'.[18]

Baxter's treatise included several letters about one such terrifying ghost that haunted the house of Lieutenant Colonel Bowen in Glamorgan. Bowen rose to prominence in the army during the late civil wars and his occupation introduced him to mortalist philosophies that eventually led him to be labelled 'an absolute Atheist'.[19] Bowen led 'a careless and sensual Life' which was no doubt a reflection of his spiritual degeneracy since he denied the existence of an afterlife, of God and the Devil and accounted 'Temporal Pleasures all his expected Heaven'.[20] In December 1656, an apparition in Bowen's shape appeared to his wife when in her chamber one evening. The ghost requested conjugal favours but this 'Godly Gentlewoman' was not to be fooled since she was lately estranged from her husband and knew him to be in Ireland at that time. Nonetheless, this malicious spirit was not easily deterred and it returned to torment the household on several occasions. That this was an evil spirit provoked by the sins of Bowen was not hard to fathom and Baxter underlined the point with descriptions of the spirit's violent antics and by including popular (and no doubt unscriptural) motifs of ghost stories in his commentary. When the spirit appeared, Mrs. Bowen felt something 'like a Dog under her Knees' that lifted her from the ground; the candles burned blue at its approach and the ghost introduced 'an unsufferable Stench' into the house 'like that of a putrified Carcase'.[21]

To combat this spirit Mrs Bowen called on others to join her in prayer and when Mr Miles (an Anabaptist minister) and four other 'Godly Men' answered her plea the household rested peacefully. Maurice Bedwell, minister of Swansea, investigated the case and having quizzed Bowen's maidservant he judged her to be 'thoroughly Godly' and could find nothing to invalidate the tale. The opinions of learned and unlearned, clerical and lay, combined to bring this relation to public notice and because the apparition had assumed the very form

18 Baxter, *World of Spirits*, 3–4.
19 Ibid., 23.
20 Ibid.
21 Ibid., 25.

and countenance of Bowen, all were agreed that it brought a clear message from God that the atheist was headed straight for hell unless he repented.

If Bowen was a lost cause, then a gentleman of rank from London who had fallen into 'the sin of drunkenness' offered a better prospect for reform. This man received numerous visits from a concerned ghost who knocked at his bed's head every time he lay down drunk. His brother, a sober and 'pious Man' and a member of Richard Baxter's congregation, resolved to watch while he slept and restrained his brother's hands 'lest he should do it himself'.[22] He could only confirm the actions of this spirit, however, when a pair of shoes levitated from underneath the bed. Clerical guidance was sought and the sinner was brought before Baxter himself who interpreted the ghost as an urgent sign from God that the drunkard must kick his habit before it was too late. God clearly took care of this man's soul and when Baxter asked him 'how he dare so sin again, after such a warning', the gentleman was sobered by his preternatural messenger and could offer no excuse for his wayward behaviour. Reflecting on this marvellous providence, Baxter was himself unsure what kind of spirit would take

> such a care of this man's soul.... Do good spirits dwell so near us? Or are they sent on such messages? Or is it his Guardian Angel? Or is it the soul of some dead friend, that suffereth, and yet, retaining Love to him, as Dives to his brethren, would have him saved?[23]

* * *

If Richard Baxter was convinced that a colourful spirit world lay on the other side of the grave then he was in good company. Baxter was joined in his attempts to re-enchant Restoration England by a network of clergymen who were similarly keen to promote godliness among the laity. Baxter's treatise included tales from John Hodder, minister of Hauke-Church in Dorset, who told of 'the actings of Spirits in a House, yea, a Religious House of that Country, of which he was himself an Ear and Eye Witness'.[24] Thomas Tilson, minister of Aylesworth in Kent, told Baxter of an apparition at Rochester and as a postscript to his letter begged 'that God would bless your pious Endeavours for the Convic-

22 Ibid., 60.
23 Ibid.
24 Ibid., 88.

tion of Atheists and Sadduces, and for the promoting of true Religion and Godliness'.[25] Bishop of Gloucester Edward Fowler was also known to supply his friend Henry More with a steady stream of ghost stories that led Shaftesbury to describe him as 'a zealous Defender of Ghosts'.[26] Moreover, Protestant ministers were also active in the marketplace of cheap print. A minister from Devon was the most likely author of a *Narrative of the Demon of Spraiton* in 1683 and a pamphlet of 1712 concerning the ghost of Edward Ashley was accompanied by 'an excellent sermon preach'd by a Reverend Divine of the Church of England on that Miraculous Occasion'.[27]

So why did ghosts play such a key role in campaigns for godly reformation in the 1690s when few Protestant clerics dared to publicly support their appearances just a few decades earlier? The changing religious climate of Restoration England provides some explanation for this accommodation. Despite the suppression of nonconformity that marked the age and the triumph over popery in 1688, the dominance of the Church of England was somewhat illusory. After William III ascended the throne in 1689, the Church lost political protection and faced increasing criticism over the forms of Anglican worship and the effectiveness of the liturgy. The Prayer Book was described as 'dry stuff' that 'failed to move or to satisfy'.[28] One way to engage the lay community was to provide more lively vehicles of religious instruction and tales of the preternatural certainly helped to dramatize the familiar moral exhortations that emanated from pulpit and pen. When a Cambridge haunting captured local attention in the summer of 1694, a local minister seized the opportunity 'to make a long sermon the next Sunday to his people in the Round Church about it, and to tell them the whole story of the same'.[29] In 1691 a short chapbook told of the 'dreadful ghost' that appeared to John Dyer in Southwark. The 'affrightful shapes' assumed by the apparition were described with relish and the visual spectacle of this account was heightened by a crude

25 Ibid., 147.

26 Anthony Ashley Cooper, 3rd Earl of Shaftesbury (1671–1713), 'A Letter Concerning Enthusiasm to My Lord *****', in *Characteristics of Men, Manners, Opinions, Times*, ed. Lawrence E. Klein (Cambridge, 1999), 5.

27 *A Narrative of the Demon of Spraiton* (London, 1683); *The Wonderful and Strange Apparition and Ghost of Edward Ashley* (London, 1712).

28 Spurr, 'Religion', 113.

29 Ibid., 112. For ghost story in Cambridge, see *The Diary of Abraham De La Pryme, the Yorkshire Antiquary*, ed. Charles Jackson, Surtees Society 54 (Durham, 1870), 39–42.

woodcut of the ghost in its winding sheet. Dyer's tale was given greater reverence however by the appendix of two appropriate prayers with which to combat the actions of malignant spirits. Despite the sensational details of the story, the Southwark ghost was judged a worthy vehicle through which to convey religious teachings.[30] Whether accompanied by visual stimuli or set to music, ghost stories had the capacity to instruct and to entertain and this flexibility ensured commercial success in the competitive marketplace of print. Indeed, in Restoration England ghosts made more frequent appearances in ballads and cheap printed pamphlets than ever before or since and their starring roles in narratives of love and murder reflected their prominence in the contemporary imagination.

By the final decade of the seventeenth century ghosts had been largely stripped of their popish associations. Henry More and Joseph Glanvill advanced the process of reintegration that saw ghosts move into the foreground of religious instruction, but the anti-catholic hysteria that accompanied the Exclusion Crisis and the reign of King James II was still to come. By the 1690s these tensions had not disappeared but they had subsided sufficiently to allow the ambiguous figure of the ghost to be convincingly re-clothed in a Protestant guise.

The story of the Devil of Masçon provides the best example of the process of deconfessionalisation from which ghosts profited in these years. At the start of the seventeenth century a troublesome spirit that went on to terrify the whole neighbourhood haunted the house of French Protestant Minister François Perrauld. The town of Masçon was a hotbed of religious conflict between warring Catholic and Protestant factions, but this evil spirit was indiscriminate in its attacks which led 'Friends and Enemies, papists and Protestants' to swear the truth of the episode. The spirit united the community against a common enemy and this salutary tale was recounted by Richard Baxter and by the *Athenian Mercury*, crediting the relation on the basis of this confessional consensus.[31] It is surely significant that the tale was not printed in England until 1659. Further editions followed in 1669 and 1679 and this publication success reflected the revived interest in ghosts that marked these years of religious change.

Apparitions of all persuasions (whether angels, devils or departed

30 *A true relation of the dreadful ghost appearing to one John Dyer* (London, 1691).

31 *Athenian Mercury*, no. 26 (1692).

souls) were reincorporated into religious schemas because they served a contemporary purpose and fitted with the broad based Protestantism encompassed by the Restoration Church. Old orthodoxies were increasingly breaking down and ghost stories sat alongside a wide diversity of doctrine, polity and ways of worship that increasingly catered for the tastes of a rapidly changing society. The rehabilitation of ghost stories as respectable conduits for religious reformation reached its climax in the final decade of the seventeenth century and it is no coincidence that these years also saw the foundation of the Society for Promoting Christian Knowledge along with numerous societies for the Reformation of Manners.

By teaching that the spirits of the dead might yet appear to the living, the work of Richard Baxter and Samuel Wesley illustrates the conscious and sustained reintegration of ghosts into Protestant theology by the close of the seventeenth century. This process of accommodation reflects the shifting priorities of churchmen who were actively and openly engaging with persistent themes in popular belief in order to cement the relationship between Protestantism and the people. The re-appropriation of ghosts by a cross-section of Protestant divines in 1690s England was a pragmatic response to a changing climate of religious belief and, potentially, a site of confessional and social unity that could help to heal the internal divisions of an increasingly fragmented Protestant Church.

University of Warwick

ACTS OF GOD, ACTS OF MEN: PROVIDENCE IN SEVENTEENTH- AND EIGHTEENTH-CENTURY ENGLAND AND FRANCE

by FRANÇOISE DECONINCK-BROSSARD

A HEADLINE in the *Daily Telegraph* once read: 'Vicar is "act of God" victim'.[1] The article explained:

> A vicar has become a victim of an 'act of God' after a thunderbolt wrecked his car during a storm. Dennis Ackroyd, vicar of St Luke's ... in Cleckheaton, near Bradford ... now faces problems claiming compensation from his insurance company.

The dramatic irony derives from the fact that English-speaking insurance companies still use the phrase 'act of God' when referring to what is known in French as a 'natural disaster', i.e. the action of uncontrollable natural forces in causing an unexpected accident such as an earthquake, a fire, a flood, an epidemic among men or cattle, in which 'human agency, by act or negligence, has had no part'.[2] Many such events took place in seventeenth- and eighteenth-century England and France. Among the national calamities that have left a mark in our collective memories, we may remember the great fire of London, the plague epidemics of 1665 in England and 1720 in Provence, and the Lisbon earthquake of 1 November 1755. Many other fires, storms, and misfortunes caused great distress. A highly infectious epizootic disease decimated the cattle in mid-eighteenth-century England. The earth shook several times, in different parts of the world: tremors were felt in 1692 in Jamaica, in 1727 in New England, and in 1746 in the capital city of Peru, Lima. In 1750, Londoners felt the earth quake twice, on 8 March and 8 April, and more or less expected a third seismic vibration to take place the following month. Last but not least, European history in the late seventeenth and early eighteenth centuries is but a long list of protracted wars. Man-made though it may now seem to a historian, armed conflict had traditionally been regarded, together with famine and disease, as yet another 'act of God'. Like the four horses of

1 *The Daily Telegraph*, 21 July 1997, 10.

2 OED online, *s.v.* '*force majeure*' (consulted on 20 December 2003).

the Apocalypse, war and starvation, plague and distemper, earthquakes and floods, fires and storms thus revealed the Lord's wrath.

Such providentialism,[3] however, was gradually challenged in the period under review. Scientific investigation and philosophical enquiry highlighted the 'natural causes' that could explain awful phenomena, theodicy was no longer acceptable, and in some cases man's hand became as conspicuous as the hand of the Lord behind some terrible disasters. Such a gradual change in outlook implies a re-assessment of evil, anomaly, risk, and the interpretation of history. Whilst an 'act of God' is often excluded by definition from insurance coverage, as the Yorkshire vicar mentioned in the *Daily Telegraph* soon realized, man's malicious intent is not. The whole issue about compensation for the 2003 blackout in North America turns on whether negligence is found to have caused the power cut.[4]

This essay argues against a linear history of ideas and mentalities. Both the providential and the rational, 'enlightened' approaches to disaster long existed side by side in the religious discourse on public calamities. I shall first explore conventional interpretations of natural disasters as providential 'acts of God'. Most of the investigation will be based on sermon literature, therefore on discourse *stricto sensu*. The second part will deal with the debate on optimism, miracles and natural philosophy. The conclusion will discuss the response of religious language to scepticism and suggest that providentialism may not have disappeared completely at the dawn of the twenty-first century, even though it has been waning steadily.

* * *

Solemn fast days were repeatedly appointed by the civil authorities at the time of public disasters. Thanksgiving services were offered in the aftermath of war, once the country seemed out of danger.[5] Some calamities were commemorated regularly. On these occasions, sermons were preached in all denominations, and often printed. Thanks to the computerized version of Sampson Letsome's *Preacher's Assistant*,[6] a

3 Alexandra Walsham has elaborately surveyed the concept in *Providence in Early Modern England* (Oxford, 1999).

4 'Still in the dark', *The Economist*, 30 August 2003, 53.

5 George W. Bush revived the tradition when he proclaimed 1 May 2003 as a 'national day of prayer' in the wake of Operation Iraqi Freedom: see http://www.whitehouse.gov/news/releases/2003/04/20030430-22.html (consulted on 29 May 2005).

6 Sampson Letsome, *The Preacher's Assistant, in two parts. Part I. A series of the texts of all the sermons and discourses preached upon, and published since the Restoration to the present time* (London,

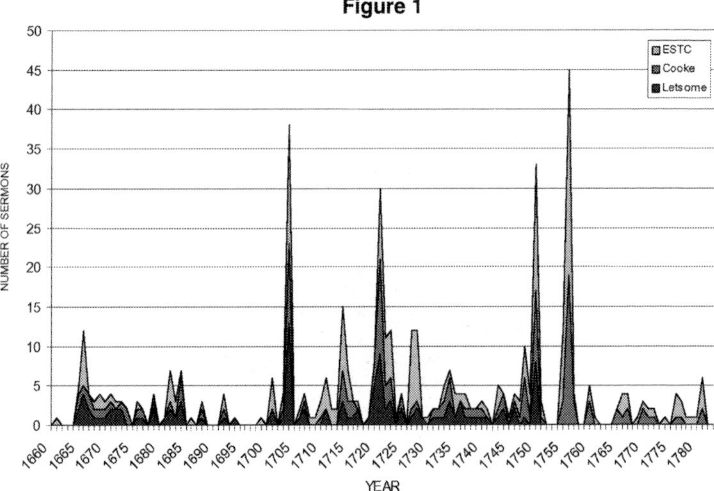

comparison with his successor, John Cooke (pr. 1783),[7] and above all with the *English Short-Title Catalogue, 1473–1800* (*ESTC*) online database, it is possible to draw up a list of these publications. Even though the 'large number'[8] of references especially at peak times of crisis may be impressive (fig. 1), these only represent a small proportion of contemporary pulpit literature. Many more sermons were preached than printed, even on official days of fast and prayer. Furthermore, calamities of all sorts[9] appear in only 113 out of 13,734 sermons catalogued by Letsome between the Restoration and the year of publication

1753). See my online article, 'The Preacher's Helper: a Computerised Version of Letsome's *Preacher's Assistant*', *Erfurt Electronic Studies in English*, 1999: http://webdoc.sub.gwdg.de/edoc/ia/ eese/eese.html (consulted on 29 May 2005).

[7] John Cooke, *The Preacher's Assistant, after the manner of Mr. Letsome. Containing a series of the texts of sermons and discourses published either singly, or in volumes, by divines of the Church of England and by the dissenting clergy since the Restoration to the present time. Specifying also the authors alphabetically arranged under each text – with the size, date, occasion, and subject-matter of each sermon or discourse* (Oxford, 1783). A hard copy of the computerized version of John Cook's catalogue by the late Professor Spaulding is on deposit with the Huntington Library, San Marino, California.

[8] T. D. Kendrick, *The Lisbon Earthquake* (London, 1955), 155; see also, for instance, Louis A. Landa's allusion to 'numberless sermons' at the time of the great London plague of 1665, in 'Religion, Science, and Medicine in *A Journal of the Plague Year*', reprinted in Daniel Defoe, *A Journal of the Plague Year*, ed. Paula R. Backscheider (London, 1722; New York, 1992), 284.

[9] Plague, fire, distemper of the cattle, pestilence, storm, wind, conflagration, frost, inundation, earthquake, and calamities in general.

Figure 2 -- LETSOME -- CALAMITIES

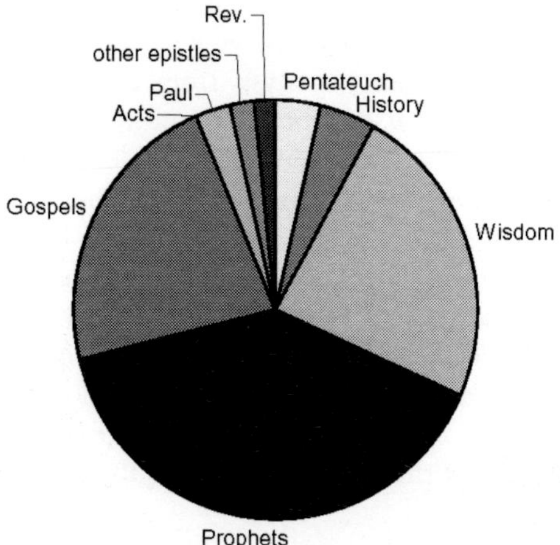

(1753), that is to say in less than one per cent of the overall homiletic production of the period under review. Even within this sub-genre, it is worth noticing another subdivision: earthquakes, plagues and fires tended to be discussed in 'fast-day' sermons, whereas war, rebellion, massacres and invasion were almost exclusively dealt with in 'thanksgiving' sermons.

The distribution of biblical texts is noteworthy (fig. 2). The fact that Old Testament quotations are much more frequent than verses from the New Testament should not lead one to jump to the conclusion that fear of a vengeful God was emphasized in these terrible circumstances. A closer look at the detail of biblical references shows, for instance, that the most recurrent idea in earthquake sermons preached in 1755–6 after the Lisbon disaster was repentance. Only once do the quotations that the twentieth-century French novelist Albert Camus had written down in his notebooks in preparation for *The Plague*[10] appear as introductory verses to these discourses on natural calamities. Besides, one also notices a kind of specialization: fast-day and thanksgiving sermons obviously referred to different excerpts from Scripture.

10 Deut. 28, 21; 32, 23, Lev. 26, 25: see Albert Camus, *Théâtre Récits Nouvelles*, ed. Jean Grenier and Roger Quilliot (Paris, 1962), 1947. Not unsurprisingly, the first quotation was used as an introductory quotation to a fast-day sermon against the plague by William Lupton, recorded in Letsome with a publication date of 1729.

Biblical quotations were carefully chosen to suggest that the cause of public disasters was the wrath of God. The hand of the Lord was clearly visible behind these terrible events, which were regarded as 'providences'. As a brief frequency analysis from a corpus of eighteenth-century sermons will show, the vocabulary of signs, wonders and miracles had given way to the terminology of providence,[11] with or without a capital 'P'. Similarly, the sermons on Providence far outnumbered those published on signs, wonder and fear, or the credibility of miracles.[12] A 'providence', in its grammatically 'countable' sense,[13] was to be interpreted as a particular instance of direct divine intervention. In other words, a disastrous accident or fatality was a sign of the workings and designs of Providence, in its grammatically 'uncountable' meaning. Interestingly enough, according to the *Oxford English Dictionary* this obsolete acceptation of the word dates back to the period between 1740 and 1814.[14]

Although 'a providence' was more frequently associated with what was 'awful' or 'distressing' and had to be submitted to as the act of God, the phrase could also be used in a positive, almost miraculous sense, as in the incident recorded in the *Gentleman's Magazine* of May 1755 when 'the cries' of a young man who had accidentally fallen into a deep well at night were heard two hours later by a passer-by who organized his rescue.[15] The same periodical later commented on the 'Signal Providence in the Escape of the Protestants'[16] in the Lisbon earthquake, when only the English and Dutch chapels had remained standing. The phenomenon was interpreted as 'supernatural' evidence of a '*particular* providence' whereby God had 'purposely' drawn out a line between two religious communities. Such cases of miraculous providences embedded within awful providences in a kind of Chinese box effect were the nearest instances that could be found of miracles within catastrophes similar to the examples in early modern Germany discussed by

11 In a sermon corpus of approximately one million words assembled for the purposes of private research, I have found 341 occurrences of providence(s), as against only 113 miracle(s), 105 sign(s), and 130 wonder(s).

12 For instance, Letsome listed only one sermon dealing with 'signs', two on 'wonder and fear', eight on 'miracles', and twenty-four on 'providence'.

13 Linguists now generally agree on the distinction between countable nouns that may be used with an indefinite article or a number and have a plural, and uncountable nouns that cannot be used with an indefinite article or a number and have no plural: see the inside front cover of *Macmillan English Dictionary for Advaned Learners* (London, 2002).

14 OED online, *s.v.* 'Providence', 5b (consulted on 20 December 2003).

15 *Gentleman's Magazine* 25 (1755), 225.

16 *Gentleman's Magazine* 26 (1756), 69.

Hartmut Lehmann.[17] Furthermore, there is evidence that 'particular providences' were almost synonymous with miracles.

Natural disasters were generally assumed to be a method by which God punished a sinful people, in the hope that they would repent and amend their ways. Thus, ultimately, human misbehaviour was seen to be the cause of public calamities. Strictly speaking, it was impossible to define an 'act of God' as free from human agency. Catholic and Protestant preachers alike were convinced that natural disasters were the just retribution for sin. In this respect, the discourse of the Catholic hierarchy at the time of the 1720 plague epidemic in the South of France did not differ from that of their British Protestant counterparts. Bishop Henri François-Xavier de Belsunce de Castelmoron, later praised by Pope in the *Essay on Man*[18] and by Voltaire in his *Ode on Fanaticism* (1736),[19] agreed with the idea that these evils were sent by Providence as a punishment for sin.

The idea was emphatically summarized, and satirized, by Albert Camus in his great novel *The Plague* (1947).[20] When the Algerian town of Oran in which the story is set suffers from an outbreak of the deadly disease, the Jesuit priest Father Paneloux is made to begin his first sermon with a striking statement: 'My brethren, a calamity has befallen you; my brethren, you have deserved it'.[21] There is evidence that the novelist had carefully collected historical information about the 1720 epidemic. Except for the change in personal pronouns, Father Paneloux may be heard to echo bishop Belsunce's pastoral instructions: 'Let us not doubt, my dear brethren, that it is through the excess of our crimes that we have deserved this outpouring from the vessels of the wrath of God'.[22] However, the disease in the novel is also partly an allegory of the Nazi occupation of France. The author criticized the French Catholic hierarchy for its defeatist attitude. Apparently, many a sermon had been preached all over the country in June and July 1940 explaining the

17 See in this volume Hartmut Lehmann, 'Miracles within Catastrophes: Some Examples from Early Modern Germany', 323–34.

18 Alexander Pope, *Essay on Man,* Epistle IV: 'Why drew Marseilles' good bishop purer breath,/ When nature sicken'd, and each gale was death?'

19 'Belsunce, pasteur vénérable,/Sauvait son peuple périssant', ll. 101–2 in *Ode sur le fanatisme* (1736): see *Voltaire électronique. Full-Text Database* (1998), P 16417.

20 *Théâtre Récits Nouvelles*, 1215–1350. A new, definitive edition is forthcoming.

21 Translation by Robin Buss (London, 2001; repr. 2002), 73; *Théâtre Récits Nouvelles*, 1294: 'Mes frères, vous êtes dans le malheur, mes frères, vous l'avez mérité'.

22 *Mandement de Monseigneur L'illustrissime et reverendissime Evêque de Marseille* (22 October 1720), 4: 'N'en doutons pas, Mes très-chers Freres, c'est par le debordement de nos crimes que nous avons merités cette effusion des Vases de la colere & de la fureur de Dieu'.

'disaster' of military defeat and foreign occupation by the fact that the nation had to make amends for many offences.[23] Strangely enough, the list of sins that would have to be paid for, according to the Abbot Thellier de Poncheville preaching in Oran cathedral in 1940,[24] did not differ all that much from the list provided almost two centuries earlier by the bishop of London responding to the London earthquakes. Here, there was 'too much' 'secularization' (*déchristianisation*), 'religious indifference' (*beaucoup d'indifférence religieuse*), 'blasphemy' (*trop de blasphèmes*) and 'immorality' (*trop d'immoralité*).[25] There, Thomas Sherlock lamented the increase in 'Infidelity and Immorality', 'Blasphemy and horrid Imprecations', 'Lewdness and Debauchery'.[26] As for eighteenth-century Marseilles, Belsunce and his opponents accused each other of bringing about divine wrath. The bishop criticized the Jansenists for denying the authority of the pontifical *Unigenitus* bull and for what he saw as their sacrilegious contempt of censorship and excommunication. The Jansenists, on the contrary, especially the Fathers of the Oratory, claimed that the disease provided evidence that God was on their side and chastised Belsunce's persecution policy.[27]

Historians now know that emphasis on private moral and sexual issues evaded, more or less consciously, the problem of collective human responsibility. The ship-owners of the *Grand Saint-Antoine,* one of whom was the first alderman of Marseilles, were 'much comforted' when they heard that 'pestilential fever' rather than bubonic plague had been diagnosed.[28] The ship, carrying a rich cargo of cotton, silk, wool and leather,[29] was therefore allowed to enter the port of Marseilles in

23 Jean Sarocchi, 'Paneloux, pour et contre, contre et pour', *Cahiers de Malagar XIII automne 1999: Il y a 50 ans La Peste de Camus* (Saint-Maixant, 2000), 101–3.

24 Sarocchi quotes Thellier de Poncheville's sermon, preached in Oran on 27 June 1940: 'Paneloux, pour et contre', 122–3.

25 Ibid.

26 Thomas Sherlock, *A Letter from the Lord Bishop of London To the Clergy and People of London and Westminster; On Occasion of the Late Earthquakes* (London, 1750), 7–8.

27 'Les P.P. de Loratoire de La Ciotat profitent de ce malheur pour debiter publiquement que cest moy qui ay atiré la peste a Marseille par mes persecutions aleur egard', in 'Copie [ms] d'une lettre de M. L'Evêque de Marseille le 4 ybre [oct?] 1720 a M. Larcheveque D'arles'. The champion of orthodoxy had recently had three thousand copies of a book written by the jansenist father Quesnel burnt: see Ch. Carrière, M. Courdurié and F. Rebuffat, *Marseille ville morte: la peste de 1720* (Marseilles, [1968]), 35 and 201–2, and Marcel Bernos, 'Face à la «peste janséniste»: Monseigneur de Belsunce et le Sacré-Cœur', *Marseille* 120 (1980), 33–5.

28 Charles Carrière and Marcel Courdurié, 'Un Document nouveau sur la peste de Marseille', *Provence historique* 33.131 (1983), 103–8.

29 Michel Goury, 'L'Épave présumée du *Grand Saint Antoine*', *Provence historique* 47.189 (1997), 449–67, 452.

May 1720. Private commercial interests had obviously prevailed over medical suspicion of malignancy and the common good, and the precautionary measures that had been taken to prevent the introduction of the disease had been bypassed. The civil authorities waited until the end of July to decide that the ship had to be burned down on account of the plague epidemic that it had brought to the town. It may therefore be argued that the divine scourge had actually been induced by irresponsible human decisions. Similarly, Camus may have criticized the Catholic hierarchy under the Vichy regime for targeting the wrong sins and advocating resignation instead of fighting compliance, cowardice and inertia. Typically, Father Paneloux is found to be 'better than his sermon'[30] when he joins the health teams. Far from being a mere allegory of 'the brown plague' of fascism, the disease in the novel may therefore represent all forms of ethical irresponsibility in general. The scourges that humankind brings down on itself are not unavoidable. 'Acts of God' need not always happen, if men behave properly.

Since 'national wickedness' was 'the cause of national misery', as one sermon title stated in 1756,[31] and man the second cause of disaster, the remedy was simple. 'National repentance' and reformation of manners were 'urged'[32] as the best way of trying to avert future calamities. For the paradox of natural disasters was that they were interpreted as the handiwork of a merciful and loving God, according to the principle that he who loves well castigates well. Theodicy was on the agenda. God's goodness and compassion could be vindicated in spite of his severe visitations on his people. Survivors and distant witnesses would learn 'at the Expence of others Experience'[33] to read the signs of God's patience in the admonitions that he sent them. Indeed, chastisement was only used by Providence as a last resort. Many other dispensations had been misread or ignored:

30 *The Plague*, 115; *Théâtre Récits Nouvelles*, 1340: 'Je suis content de le savoir meilleur que son prêche'.

31 Thomas Hunter, *National Wickedness the Cause of National Misery: A Sermon Preach'd at the Parish Church of Weverham in Cheshire on Friday, the Sixth of February. Being the Day Appointed, by Proclamation, to be Kept as a General Fast and Humiliation, on Account of the Late Dreadful Earthquakes, in Portugal, etc.* (Liverpool, 1756).

32 T. Richards, *National Repentance Urged from the Prospect of National Judgments: a Sermon, Preached at the Parish Churches of All Saints, in Northampton, On Friday the 6th of February, 1756 . . .* (S.p., 1756).

33 William Nowell, *A Sermon Preached at the Parish Church of Wolsingham, in the Bishoprick of Durham, On the 6th of February, 1756, Being the Day Appointed by his Majesty for a General Fast, on Account of the Dreadful Earthquake at Lisbon, Nov. 1. 1755* (Newcastle, 1756), 6.

> He has visited us with *Cold* and *Hunger*, with *Storm* and *Tempest*, with *Signs* in *Heaven*, and *Signs upon the Earth*, *War* abroad, and *Rebellion* at home; and, at this Time, with a grievous *Pestilence* among the Cattle.... Has it awakened any? Has it reclaimed any?[34]

Such providential warnings were meant to frighten men to a sense of guilt, contrition and amendment.

Prayer, fasting and repentance could appease God's wrath and avert his hand. In France, propitiatory ceremonies included a number of specifically Catholic features, such as processions, pilgrimages, exorcisms, auricular confessions, indulgences, veneration of relics, and devotion to saints as a matter of course. Many chapels were built to the patron saint of plague-sufferers, Saint Roch, who is usually represented with a jar of celestial ointment and accompanied by a dog holding providential food.[35] In a spectacular ceremony, the bishop of Marseilles consecrated the city to the worship of the Sacred Heart of Jesus. The high wind suddenly though temporarily abated, which was interpreted as a sign of God's approval.[36]

In spite of denominational differences, the idea was the same, for there was nothing new about it. The belief that impending doom could be averted by penitence and conversion may be traced back at least to Gregory of Tours' record of the speech delivered by the future Pope Gregory the Great to the Romans at the time of the plague epidemic in 590.[37] Bishop Belsunce was likely to have been familiar with Gregory of Tours' works. Patristic literature was also well known to Anglican clergy. The bishop of London trusted that divine anger could be placated:

34 [Morgan Powell], *The Hand of the Lord upon the Cattle. A Sermon Occasioned by the Distemper among the Cattle. Very Proper to be Read and Considered by all Persons, who have been, or may be Sufferers thereby* (London, 1747), 25.

35 A popular representation of Saint Roch is to be found in Sylvain Gagnière, 'Les Saints invoqués en temps de peste et de choléra dans le Comtat et ses abords', *Cahiers de pratique médico-chirurgicale* 11.6 (1937), 259–74, fig. 4 opposite p. 263. A moving prayer to Saint Roch was drawn by the notary Jean-François Bouyon when he and his fellow-aldermen spent some time in voluntary confinement in the town-hall of La Valette at the time of the plague epidemic: see Gilbert Buti, 'La Peste à La Valette en 1721: Livre jaune et grand témoin', *Provence historique* 47 (1997), 513–34, 527.

36 *Correspondance de Mgr de Belsunce Evêque de Marseille Composée de Lettres et Documents en partie inédits*, ed. Louis-Antoine de Porrentruy (Marseilles, 1911), 178.

37 'Oratio Gregorii ad plebem', *PL Database* online, vol. 071 [consulted on 2 March 2004]; a French translation is available in Grégoire de Tours, *Histoire des Francs*, transl. Robert Latouche, 2 vols (Paris, 1995), 2: 256–9. I owe this reference to Kate Cooper.

> let us not despair; . . . whatever Reason we have to condemn ourselves, yet of this we may be sure, that God has not *forgotten to be gracious*. To him then let us turn, with hearty Repentance for our Sins; and with a Resolution to do, each of us in his proper Station, what lies in our Power to stem the Torrent of Iniquity which threatens our Ruin.[38]

Similarly, the vicar general in Arles hoped that the intercession of Saint Roch, whose relics were located in the city, would ensure that prayers would be answered, and the plague avoided.[39]

History was to prove otherwise. It was not very long before the epidemic reached the city, as if the inhabitants' vow, reminding the Almighty of his mercy for Nineveh,[40] had remained unanswered. Likewise, bishop Belsunce confessed in a very moving private letter that courage failed him when he was surrounded by the dead and the dying even among members of the clergy who had assisted him in the epidemic. He was afraid that God had been 'deaf to his prayers, and little affected by his tears', which 'afflicted' him 'beyond what [he] could say'.[41] Indeed, one of the major metaphysical stumbling-blocks of retribution results from the affliction of good men who seem to be forsaken by God. Except when Providence draws a miraculously visible line between its friends and its enemies, as in the case of the Protestant chapels standing amid the ruins of Catholic Lisbon, the just and the unjust perish together in a natural disaster. One possible explanation is that, although they seemingly suffer the same fate, their retribution will come in the afterlife: 'it is a *Mercy* to the one and a *Punishment* to the other'.[42] Eschatological justice makes up for temporal injustice.

This interpretation was in keeping with the traditional religious discourse on the vanity of human pursuits and the need to prepare for one's death. The sudden blow of an earthquake and the outbreak of an epidemic underlined the natural frailty of civilization. Marseilles in

38 Sherlock, *A Letter from the Lord Bishop of London*, 12.

39 *Ordonnance de Monsieur le Grand-Vicaire,* 6 August 1720 [n.p.]: 'Le bonheur que nous avons de posseder dans nôtre Ville ses Saintes Reliques doit exciter nôtre confiance, & doit nous faire esperer, que nos prieres presentées à Dieu par un si bon Patron seront exaucées'.

40 François Peilhe, *La Misere du tems representée par un vœu que la Ville d'Arles fit à Dieu au sujet de la Contagion l'an 1721* (s.p., s.d.). Cf. Jonah 3.

41 'Copie d'une lettre de M. L'Evêque de Marseille': 'Dieu qui me punit a été sourd a mes prieres, et peu touché de mes larmes ce St homme [P. Melley] est mort hier a midi, je suis persuadé de son bonheur mais ce coup mafflige et me deconcerte audelà deceque je puis vous le dire'.

42 [Powell], *The Hand of the Lord upon the Cattle*, 19.

1720 and Lisbon in 1755, like Nineveh, Tyre, and Babylon in ancient times, had been thriving communities and large trading centres which were suddenly brought to ruins. Indeed, many 'acts of God' were urban phenomena, striking at the heart of large cities. Disaster had a levelling effect: 'without Distinction of Age or Sex, of Rank or Fortune, . . . Persons of every Condition and Circumstance fall undistinguished, and mix together in one and the same confused Mass of Misery and Desolation'.[43] 'Acts of God' thus turned human society upside down. They taught the moral lesson of human vainglory and sinfulness: 'We then learn . . . how vain are mortal Attainments, – the Empire of Arts or Arms, – how frail is earthly Happiness, and how great is human Wickedness'.[44]

If all human beings were equally sinners, however, why were some nations spared and others destroyed? Most preachers agreed that it would be unchristian to think that the earthquake of 1756 had been more disastrous than the mild tremors of 1750 because the Portuguese were greater sinners than the Londoners. The true end and design of the worst 'acts of God' might be to contribute to the general good by inflicting a punishment on some countries as a warning to other nations. Bishop Belsunce, for instance, publicly declared that in 1720 Marseilles was unfortunate enough to be 'an example to its neighbours and to all nations'.[45] The quasi consensus in Britain against the tyranny and superstition of Popery might have prompted interpretations of the earthquake as God's 'visible' judgements on the 'Bigotry'[46] of Catholic countries, especially on the eve of war.[47] However, it may have been a case of seeing the mote in Portugal's eye and not the beam in Britain's own. Perhaps the long catalogue of sins that were supposedly wide-

43 Nowell, *A Sermon Preached at the Parish Church of Wolsingham*, 3.

44 Hunter, *National Wickedness*, 12.

45 *Mandement de Monseigneur L'illustrissime et reverendissime Evêque de Marseille*, 5: 'nous avons le malheur de servir d'exemple à nos voisins & à toutes les Nations'.

46 John Milner, *Ruin Prevented by Repentance, Applied to Civil Societies: In Two Discourses Delivered at Peckham in Surrey. On the General Fast, February 6, 1756. Occasioned by the Late Dreadful Earthquake at Lisbon, and the Apprehension of Nearer Threatning Calamities* (London, 1756), 22.

47 The idea was satirized in an engraving published on 29 November 1755, 'An Attempt to assign the Cause of the late most Dreadful Earthquake & Fiery Irruption at Lisbon Or Suppression of Superstition & Idolatry & Persecution for Conscience sake the most probable means of averting National Calamities': *Catalogue of Political and Personal Satires Preserved in the Department of Prints and Drawings in the British Museum*, ed. Frederick George Stephens and M. Dorothy George, 11 vols (London, 1978), 3.2: no. 3329, 966–7; illustration in Kendrick, *The Lisbon Earthquake*, fig. VIII opposite p. 150.

spread in the nation, especially 'Libertinism and Infidelity', deserved as much 'the Chastisement of an offended God' as Catholic superstition.[48] The privilege of being spared was not to be read as a sign of lesser guilt or greater virtue, or as assurance of God's future presence on the side of the British army, for it was impossible for any human being to know how people would be judged on Doomsday. The oversimplified doctrine of retribution that is sometimes associated with the spirit of pre-capitalism, whereby earthly rewards and punishments bear a proportion to virtue and vice,[49] was obviously not applicable to public calamities. Disaster victims were only part of a grand providential design that called for submission, resignation, contrition and amendment. Optimism prevailed, in the Leibnitzian sense that everything is for the best. As Pope had stated in the *Essay on Man,* 'all partial Evil' was 'universal Good'.[50]

* * *

The most famous challenge to this interpretation came from Voltaire in his poem on the Lisbon earthquake. The philosopher's initial response to the earthquake was expressed in a letter written on 24 November to the banker Tronchin in Lyons, in which he refused to accept the optimistic interpretation of natural calamities: 'My dear sir, nature is very cruel. One would find it hard to imagine how the laws of movement cause such frightful disasters in the *best of possible worlds*'.[51] By the end of the month, he had completed the poem that conveyed his rejection of 'the illusion' that 'all is well' in a world in which evil and suffering strike indiscriminately: 'Leibniz does not tell me . . . why the innocent and the guilty suffer alike this inevitable evil'.[52] It was impossible to interpret the disaster as a punishment for sin: 'Was Lisbon, which no longer exists, more vicious than London, than Paris, plunged

48 Thomas Seward, *The Late Dreadful Earthquakes no Proof of God's Particular Wrath against the Portuguese: A Sermon Preached at Litchfield, on Sunday, December 7, 1755* (London, 1756), 18–19.

49 Ronald J. VanderMolen explains that such an 'ethic of success', a substantial modification of the Calvinistic doctrine of providence, which has become 'the basis of one very important element on the Weber-Tawney thesis', was 'inserted into Puritan thought' by Thomas Beard's 'uncritical' work *The Theatre of God's Judgments* (1597): 'Providence as Mystery, Providence as Revelation: Puritan and Anglican Modifications of John Calvin's Doctrine of Providence', *ChH* 47 (1978), 27–47, 45–6.

50 Epistle I, l. 284.

51 Theodore Besterman, *Voltaire* (Oxford, 1969; 3rd edn, 1976), 366.

52 Ibid., 369.

in delights? Lisbon is shattered, and Paris dances'.[53] The metaphysical problem of the existence of evil in a world ruled by a benevolent God is crystallized in a lapidary question: 'Has evil come from the author of all good?'[54] The poet surveys four unsatisfactory explanations, three of which are borrowed from traditional religious discourse. Either God exerts his vengeance on sinful man, or an indifferent creator ruthlessly follows the rules of nature, or our earthly life is but a trial and a straight gate to an eternal world. Alternatively, matter carries its own necessary forces of destruction. 'In vain', however, does man search for clues to the correct interpretation, for 'nature is silent' and God 'forsakes' humankind.[55] In this context of the absence of Providence, where it is impossible to read any signs even in the book of nature, Voltaire's agnosticism equally dismissed the misguided assumptions of providentialism, eschatological justice, and materialism.

The poem was circulated in the winter of 1755–6 but was only published in March 1756, and ran through many editions, at least in France.[56] It has been argued that it exerted considerable influence on his contemporaries, so much so that, in retrospect, the Lisbon earthquake may be seen as a turning-point in the history of ideas, that 'brought an age to an end'.[57] In England, the earthquake of 1750 had already seriously undermined providentialism when the predicted third tremor did not take place four weeks after the second one. The traffic jams due to the Londoners' attempt to flee from the hand of God had been in vain:

> Incredible numbers of people, being under strong apprehensions that *London* and *Westminster* would be visited with another and more fatal earthquake, on this night, according to the predictions of a crazy lifeguardman, and because it would be just 4 weeks from the last shock, as that was from the first, left their houses . . . so that the roads were never more throng'd, and lodgings were hardly to

53 Voltaire, 'Poème sur le désastre de Lisbonne: ou examen de cet axiome: «tout est bien»', in *Mélanges*, Jacques van den Heuvel and Emmanuel Berl, eds (Paris, 1961), 304–9, 304: 'Lisbonne, qui n'est plus, eut-elle plus de vices / Que Londres, que Paris, plongés dans les délices? / Lisbonne est abîmée, et l'on danse à Paris'.

54 Ibid., 307: 'De l'auteur de tout bien le mal est-il venu?'.

55 Ibid., 308: 'La nature est muette, on l'interroge en vain'.

56 It is difficult to know whether it was read in contemporary English translations. André Michel Rousseau, 'L'Angleterre et Voltaire (1718–1789). III', *Studies in Voltaire and the Eighteenth Century* 147 (1976), 599–1085, quotes a translation of Voltaire's poetical works in 1764 (pp. 980–1), and a French edition of the poem with a London imprint in 1756 (p. 1021).

57 See Kendrick, *The Lisbon Earthquake*, 139 and Besterman, *Voltaire*, 365.

> be procured at *Windsor*; so far . . . had their superstitious fears, or their guilty conscience, driven them'[58]

Soon, the horrors of what was to be called the Seven Years' War confirmed many people's pessimism. War was no longer seen as a providential disaster. In a private letter written in August 1756, Voltaire observed that men 'do themselves more harm on their little mole-hill than does nature. More men are slaughtered in our wars than are swallowed up by earthquakes'.[59] In 1761, a young French poet echoed Voltaire's statement: in his 'Ode to the Sun', on the calamities that had happened since the Lisbon earthquake, Ponce-Denis Écouchard Le Brun lamented the violent disasters that man had added to the horrors of natural disasters.[60] Acts of men now combined with acts of God in the attack on optimism. Even the sermonizers dissociated warfare from national judgments. Robert Gilbert, for instance, seemed to have partly lost his forefathers' confidence that God would fight for Britain:

> But who considers as he ought, how precarious this our Situation; how uncertain the issues of War; and the importance of the divine Presence with *Great Britain* . . . in this Crisis? . . . And what if he, in justice, should have put a Sword into the hands of our Enemies?'[61]

Similarly, John Milner blended doubt with the ethic of success:

> War has its desolations and terrors; . . . But then who can tell the issue of war? . . . The battle is not always to the strong. Yet if we humble ourselves, and put away every abomination, we do what is pleasing to God, and may hope for his presence and blessing on our enterprises.[62]

58 *Gentleman's Magazine* 20 (1750), 184. The anecdote was satirized in an engraving published on 4 April 1750, 'The Military Prophet: or a Flight from Providence. Address'd to the Foolish and Guilty, who Timidly Withdrew themselves on the Alarm of another Earthquake, April 1750', *Catalogue of Political Satires* 3.1: no. 3076, 772–4, which also quotes Horace Walpole's account of the panic; illustration in Kendrick, *The Lisbon Earthquake*, fig. I facing p. 22.

59 See Kendrick, *The Lisbon Earthquake*, 139, and Besterman, *Voltaire*, 372.

60 Kendrick, *The Lisbon Earthquake*, 140–1, mentions 'Ode XIV. Au soleil, sur les malheurs de la terre, depuis le désastre de Lisbonne, en 1755' (1761), *Œuvres de Ponce Denis (Écouchard) Le Brun*, ed. Pierre-Louis Ginguené, 4 vols (Paris, 1811), 1: 185: 'Fallait-il, Astre du Monde,/ Qu'à ces fatales horreurs,/ A ces Révoltes de l'Onde,/ L'Homme joignît ses Fureurs?'.

61 Robert Gilbert, *The Terms of National Happiness Stated and Recommended. A Sermon Delivered at Northampton, Feb. the 6th M.DCC.LVI. Appointed to be Observed, As a Day of General and Publick Fasting, Humiliation, and Prayer* (London, 1756), 20.

62 Milner, *Ruin Prevented by Repentance*, 42.

However, conventional discourse on public calamities continued to be preached and printed. Admittedly, the general fast appointed in England in the wake of the earthquake and on the eve of what came to be known as the Seven Years' War was observed on 6 February 1756, so that it is impossible to assess the effect – if any – of Voltaire's poem on contemporary pulpit literature. In his letter to Tronchin, Voltaire had asked: 'What will the preachers say?',[63] incidentally adding, in a kind of reverse miracle within the disaster: 'especially if the palace of the Inquisition is still standing'.[64] The odds are that religious discourse did not change overnight. Indeed, it survived at least well into the nineteenth century, was re-used at the time of the cholera epidemic of 1834,[65] and also, as we have already seen, as late as 1940 in France. It has also been occasionally applied to the AIDS epidemic. The HIV virus has been construed as divine punishment for people's sexual misbehaviour.[66] However, it can also be argued that the providential interpretation of disease has waned steadily. Increasingly, the religious discourse has had to coexist with more human explanations. One barrister from Aix writing to one of his colleagues at the time of the 1720 plague epidemic already suggested privately that starvation and poverty had contributed to the spread of the disease as much as God's wrath.[67] A century later, a writer in the *New York Times* declared in 1866 that 'Cholera is especially the punishment of neglect of sanitary laws; it is the curse of the dirty, the intemperate, and the degraded'.[68]

63 Besterman, *Voltaire*, 366.

64 Ibid.

65 Sylvain Gagnière, for instance, reproduces a lithograph showing how the town of Nîmes was protected from the cholera epidemic in 1834 by the intercession of the Virgin Mary and the souls of the Purgatory: 'Les Saints invoqués en temps de peste et de choléra', fig. 5 facing p. 268.

66 See for instance Paula R. Backscheider's preface to Defoe, *A Journal of the Plague Year*, x: 'In 1988 Cardinal Siri of Genoa called AIDS "a holy plague to punish sinners" '.

67 A letter from François Decormis to Pierre Saurin (who had left the city at the time of the epidemic), 29 January 1721: 'Je suis bien d'avis que la misère et la mauvaise nourriture ont beaucoup contribué au fléau, et que le proverbe: *après la famine la peste*, est bien véritable. Il l'est aussi que c'est une guerre divine où Dieu appesantit sa main sur nous', quoted in Charles de Ribbe, *Deux Chrétiennes pendant la peste de 1720 d'après des documents originaux* (Paris, 1874), 36 n. 2. An anthology of the correspondence was published by the same editor, *L'ancien Barreau du Parlement de Provence ou Extraits d'une correspondance inédite échangée pendant la peste de 1720 entre François Decormis et Pierre Saurin, Avocats au même Parlement* (Marseilles, 1861).

68 Quoted by Susan Sontag, 'AIDS and its Metaphors', in Defoe, *A Journal of the Plague Year*, ed. Backscheider, 250–8, 256. A search on the internet suggests that responses to the earthquake that devastated the ancient city of Bam, Iran, in December 2003 never hinted at a providential interpretation of the disaster, in spite of the geopolitical context.

* * *

By the mid-eighteenth century, the debate had been going on for many decades. Although there is often little evidence of popular response to discourse, it seems reasonable to assume that a trend of religious indifference and secularization was noticeable, on both sides of the Channel, from at least the early eighteenth century. The inhabitants of Marseilles, for instance, had not lost their sense of humour and derision when the plague raged in their city. A prayer to Saint Roch, ostensibly asking for the saint's support in the people's effort to placate divine wrath, ended with a distich asking him not to bring his dog to the city, for there was no bread left.[69] Similarly, historical work on ex-votos produced among all social classes at the time of the epidemic has shown that they did not follow the rules of the genre, in that they did not depict the horrors of the lethal disease, as if hell were on earth and God had forsaken humankind. Such untypical lack of representation of the disaster has been interpreted as meaning the absence of an aloof God, rather than his interposition in human history, hence as a sign of secularization.[70]

What was at stake was not only the issue of the presence or absence of God, but also his very existence. The debate focused on the interpretation of miracles. As Alexandra Walsham has shown,[71] it was generally agreed among English Protestants that miracles had ceased long ago, and that therefore contemporary Catholic or Jansenist[72] miracles were deceptive or superstitious. Nevertheless, the idea that miracles recorded in the Bible, especially in the New Testament, provided indispensable evidence of Christian revelation, was also commonplace. Hence the major emphasis placed by freethinkers and deists against miracles, in the 'crucial years' from the late 1690s to the early 1730s.[73] As Isabel

69 *Journal du Maître d'hôtel de Mgr de Belsunce Durant la peste de Marseille 1720–1722*, ed. D. Théophile Bérengier (Paris, 1878), 11–12, n. 3: 'Accablés de malheurs, entourés de la peste, /Grand saint Roch, nous ne craignons rien, / Et rien ne nous sera funeste /Si vous estes notre soutien./ Secourez ce peuple chrétien /Et venez apaiser la colère céleste./ Mais n'amenez pas votre chien,/ Nous n'avons pas de pain de reste'.

70 Gérard Fabre, *Epidémies et contagions: l'imaginaire du mal en Occident* (Paris, 1998), 137–43, and 'La Peste en l'absence de Dieu?', *Archives de Sciences sociales des Religions* 73 (1991), 141–58. However, Fabre's weak point is that his corpus is very small indeed, with only 14 items.

71 See in this volume, Walsham, 'Miracles in Post-Reformation England', 273–306.

72 On Jansenist miracles, see B. Robert Kreiser, *Miracles, Convulsions, and Ecclesiastical Politics in Eighteenth-Century Paris* (Princeton, NJ, 1978), *passim.*

73 Isabel Rivers, *Reason, Grace, and Sentiment: a Study of the Language of Religion and Ethics in England, 1660–1780. Volume I: Whichcote to Wesley; Volume II: Shaftesbury to Hume* (Cambridge, 1991, 2000), 2: 13.

Rivers has emphasized, these thinkers were not a cohesive group, but they shared a number of identifiable values.[74] William Wollaston, for one, argued against the idea that God should wish to suspend or alter the general laws of nature that he had established in his foresight:

> It is not *impossible,* that such *laws* of nature, and such a *series* of causes and effects may be *originally* designd [*sic*], that not only general provisions may be made for the several species of beings, but even in *particular cases*, at least many of them, may also be provided for without *innovations* or *alterations* in the course of nature. It is true, this amounts to a prodigious scheme, in which all things to come are as it were comprehended under one view, estimated, and laid together.[75]

Particular miracles and accidents thus simply fell within the general scheme of things designed by a prescient deity.

In this context, destructive calamities could not be read as awesome providences, but only as natural events due to natural causes. Thus, the city of Lisbon had been destroyed by a concurrence of the four elements, 'the Earth, the Air, Fire and Water':[76] the high wind fanned the fires that broke out as a result of the tremors which in turn produced a tidal wave. Whether the plague was contagious or miasmatic,[77] it could be spread by the air or by human contact rather than divine intervention, and fires were due to human negligence. The disaster was thus an act of man rather than God.

Preachers were well aware of the fact that freethinking was their enemy. In a dialectical argument, they borrowed their opponents' terminology in order to expose what they considered as the fallacies of natural philosophy. To them, the enlightened, rational explanation of collective calamities was short-sighted. Natural events were only secondary causes manipulated by God, who was consistently compared to a clock-maker or an architect: 'Who will you say makes the Clock strike at Twelve, but the Artist who composed it?'[78] In their attempts to maintain that disasters were acts of God, and to complete 'natural reli-

[74] The point had already been made by R. M. Burns, among others: *The Great Debate on Miracles: From Joseph Glanville to David Hume* (Lewisburg, PA, 1981).

[75] [William] Wollaston, *The Religion of Nature Delineated* (London, 1722; 8th edn, 1759), 178–9 and 187–9.

[76] Nowell, *A Sermon Preached at the Parish Church of Wolsingham*, 7.

[77] There was much debate over the cause of the disease, until the bacillus responsible for the plague was identified in 1894.

[78] Nowell, *A Sermon Preached at the Parish Church of Wolsingham*, 7.

gion' with revealed religion, their reference to an omnipotent creator and 'Governour of the world'[79] was in fact, with few exceptions,[80] distant from the Christian theology of incarnation, crucifixion and resurrection.

Such was the background to Hume's essay 'Of miracles'.[81] On this point, I would therefore slightly part company with Alexandra Walsham's statement that the Scottish philosopher was 'by no means representative of contemporary learned opinion'.[82] Admittedly, Hume was so unorthodox that, like Voltaire and many freethinkers, he had to exercise caution and disguise his views.[83] But it can also be argued that Hume dialectically borrowed arguments from the latitudinarians. In his claim that no Christian mystery or miracle is based on reasonable evidence, Hume used Archbishop Tillotson's contention that transubstantiation contradicts the 'testimony' of our senses.[84] Not unsurprisingly, Hume appreciated Voltaire's anti-providential stance. In a letter dated 12 April 1759 to Adam Smith, he wrote:

> Voltaire has lately published a small work called *Candide ou l'optimisme.*[85] It is full of sprightliness and Impiety, and is indeed a Satyre upon Providence, under Pretext of criticizing the Leibnitian System.[86]

* * *

Anglicans and Dissenters promptly responded to Hume's scepticism. Among the most sympathetic responses was an essay by William

79 Milner, *Ruin Prevented by Repentance*, 10.

80 Thomas Seward, canon of Lichfield, maintained that the crucifixion argued against the idea of temporal retribution: 'If others *Sufferings* are greater than ours, shall we dare to tax them with greater *Wickedness*, when the only *Sinless*, the only *Perfect Man* that ever lived, suffered the most painful, the most afflictive, and the most ignominious death?' in *The Late Dreadful Earthquakes no Proof of God's Particular Wrath against the Portuguese*, 12.

81 *Enquiries Concerning Human Understanding and Concerning the Principles of Morals*, ed. L. A. Selby-Bigge (3rd edn, Oxford, 1975), Section X: 'Of Miracles', 109–31.

82 Walsham, 'Miracles in Post-Reformation England', 273–306.

83 Rivers, *Reason, Grace, and Sentiment*, 2: 31–50; see also her article on 'Responses to Hume on Religion by Anglicans and Dissenters', *JEH* 52 (2001), 675–95, 676.

84 Hume, *Enquiries*, 109; Tillotson's argument is quoted by Rivers, *Reason, Grace and Sentiment*, 1: 71. See also Fred Wilson, 'The Logic of Probabilities in Hume's Argument against Miracles', *Hume Studies* 15 (1989), 255–75, 261.

85 An English translation of *Candide* was published in 1759: see Hywel Berwyn Evans, 'A Provisional Bibliography of English Editions and Translations of Voltaire', *Studies on Voltaire and the Eighteenth Century* 8 (1959), 9–121, 51.

86 Kendrick, *The Lisbon Earthquake*, 135 at n. 1, quoting *New Letters of David Hume*, ed. Raymond Klibansky and Ernest C. Mossner (Oxford, 1954).

Adams, then master of Pembroke College, Cambridge, who insisted on inferring from providential interpositions in 'punishing exemplary wickedness'[87] that miracles are possible and credible. What was at stake was the credibility of the Christian gospel. It is therefore easy to understand that the clerical establishment should have wanted to refute Hume systematically. Thus, John Hey in his *Lectures on Divinity* advised his Cambridge undergraduates to exercise 'caution . . . in reading Mr Hume's reasonings'.[88] Similarly, the Independent minister Philip Doddridge[89] or his disciple Caleb Ashworth included Hume's *Philosophical Essays* among the errors that pupils at the Northampton Academy were encouraged to read and criticize.[90] Many generations of Anglican and nonconformist students were thus familiar, albeit critically, with Hume's writings.

Scepticism may not have been the only competitor that the Church of England had to fight. Some ministers were apparently afraid that 'enthusiasm' might be lurking behind Methodist preaching. In his book on the Lisbon earthquake, T. D. Kendrick quotes a private letter in which archbishop Herring criticized Wesley's writings on the earthquake.[91] Neither John nor Charles Wesley's sermons disagreed with the traditional Anglican doctrine of providence[92] or with the idea that a disaster was a call for repentance. John Wesley had read Hume's essay on miracles and disliked it as intensely as his Anglican counterparts. However, Charles's sermon 'On the cause and cure of earthquakes'[93] is written in a passionate style full of exclamations and rhetorical questions, with some passages in the second person singular:

87 William Adams, *An Essay on Mr Hume's Essay on Miracles* (Shrewsbury, 1752), 21. Subsequent editions were published with the title *An Essay in Answer to Mr Hume's Essay on Miracles* (e.g. 2nd edn, London, 1754).

88 John Hey, *Heads of Lectures in Divinity, Delivered in the University of Cambridge* (3rd edn, Cambridge, 1794), ch. XV, § 18, p. 8.

89 The best biography of Doddridge is by Malcolm Deacon, *Philip Doddridge of Northampton, 1702–51* (Northampton, 1980).

90 Rivers, *Reason, Grace and Sentiment*, 1: 182, and 'Responses to Hume', 691, n. 91; eadem, *The Defence of Truth through the Knowledge of Error: Philip Doddridge's Academy Lectures* (London, 2003), 19–20.

91 See Kendrick, *The Lisbon Earthquake*, 159–62.

92 See John Wesley's sermon 67 'On Divine Providence', in *The Works of John Wesley, Sermons II: 34–70*, ed. Albert C. Outler (Nashville, TN, 1985), 535–50.

93 No. 9 in *The Sermons of Charles Wesley: a Critical Edition, with Introduction and Notes*, ed. Kenneth G. C. Newport (Oxford, 2001), 237–40; this sermon has sometimes been attributed to his brother John.

> The Lord was in the earthquake, and put a solemn question to thy conscience: Art thou ready to die? Is thy peace made with God? Was the earth just now to open its mouth, and swallow thee up, what would become of thee? Where wouldst thou be? In Abraham's bosom, or lifting up thine eyes in torment? . . . Who prevented thy damnation? It was the Son of God! O fall down, and worship him![94]

The style, rather than the ideas, of such exhortations resorting to fear was probably the kind of eloquence that the archbishop of Canterbury disapproved of. Other Anglican preachers were wary of appealing to their congregations' legitimate fear, for awe should not be confounded with contrition: 'But let us not deceive ourselves, and mistake this natural Fear for a religious Humiliation'.[95] Fear does not bring salvation. The frightening effect of the disaster might be more ephemeral than genuine repentance and amendment. On the whole, fast-day sermons did not preach fire and brimstone, but self-examination and moral improvement. Individual conversion would contribute to the common good and restore pre-established harmony: 'so much as each Person contributeth to the general Complaint, so much let it be his Portion to correct and remove, and all will then become perfectly well'.[96]

* * *

One may conclude that from the end of the seventeenth century onwards, and above all after 1750, the providential interpretation of 'natural disasters' as 'acts of God' was literally reactionary, in so far as it tried to respond to rational scepticism. Nevertherless it survived, however marginally, long after it had been questioned by 'enlightened' approaches. Language usage often betrays cultural patterns. That public calamities should still be referred to with two phrases, 'acts of God' and 'natural disasters' may mean that the traces of two different mentalities still somehow coexist in our world today, even after the man-made disaster of 11 September 2001.

Université de Paris X

94 Ibid., 236.

95 Hunter, *National Wickedness*, 20.

96 John Parnther, *A Sermon, Preached in the Parish Churches of Wath and Pickhill* (York, 1756), 14.

SEEING SALVATION: THE PLACE OF DREAMS AND VISIONS IN JOHN WESLEY'S *ARMINIAN MAGAZINE*

by ROBERT WEBSTER

> ON Whitsunday, I went to bed weak in body, but happy in mind. In my sleep, I dreamed that I heard a band of Angels singing around me in a most delightful manner. On this I awoke with my heart full of love, and quite transported. O if a blind world did but feel what I then did, how would They also love and adore the God of their salvation! How would they run in the way of Wisdom, and partake of the felicities of thy chosen![1]

> Does it follow that visions and dreams in general are bad branches of a bad root? God forbid! This would prove more than you desire. . . .[2]

John Wesley's *Arminian Magazine* has been severely neglected by contemporary scholarship. Apart from casual references that survey the history of religious magazines and their readers in modern British literature, little has been written about this extremely influential publication.[3] Such disregard, though regrettable, may be understandable once the history, scope, and impact of the magazine is perceived. The first issue appeared in 1778 with monthly instalments being released throughout Wesley's life and up until his death in 1791. For fourteen

1 *Arminian Magazine* x (1787), 192 [hereafter: *AM*].

2 John Wesley to Samuel Wesley, Jun./November 30, 1738, in *The Works of John Wesley*, ed. Frank Baker and Richard Heitzenrater, The Bicentennial Edition of the Works of John Wesley [hereafter: *BEW*], 16 vols ongoing (Oxford and Nashville, TN, 1980–[2003]), 25: 594.

3 As far as I am aware there are only four published articles dealing with the *AM*: Tom Albin, 'An Empirical Study of Early Methodist Spirituality', in Theodore Runyon, ed., *Wesleyan Theology Today: a Bicentennial Theological Construction* (Nashville, TN, 1985), 275–90; Samuel Rogel, 'John Wesley's *Arminian Magazine*', *Andrews University Seminary Studies* 22 (1984), 231–47; Margaret Jones, 'From "The State of My Soul" to "Exalted Piety": Women's Voices in the *Arminian/Methodist Magazine*, 1778–1821', in R. N. Swanson, ed., *Gender and Christian Religion*, SCH 34 (Woodbridge, 1998), 273–86; eadem, 'Some Eighteenth-Century Methodist Theology: the *Arminian/Methodist Magazine*', *Epworth Review* 27 (2000), 8–19. See also George Williams, '"The Word came with power": Print, Oratory, and Methodism in Eighteenth-Century Britain', unpublished Ph.D. thesis, University of Maryland, MD, 2002, 142–86.

years John Wesley edited and wrote for the magazine which comprised theological tracts, sermons, letters, poetry, various types of spiritual narratives, autobiographies, and portraits of leading lights in the Methodist movement. After his death, the editorial supervision was taken up by George Story, the Yorkshire Methodist preacher. In 1797 with the assistance of Joseph Benson its name was changed to the *Methodist Magazine* whereby it was circulated until 1821. Then for over a century from 1821 to 1932 the Methodist periodical was known as the *Wesleyan Methodist Magazine*; returning to its former title of the *Methodist Magazine* in 1933. It is then, arguably, one of the longest running religious periodicals in modern publishing history.

Certainly Wesley was both pleased and surprised by its success. At the beginning of its seventh year in 1784, Wesley wrote in his preface: 'I could not very easily have believed, had one told it me long ago, that this Work would grown under my hands, so as to extend to the beginning of a seventh Year!'[4] But grow it certainly did and with every year its influence increased throughout England. At the time of Wesley's death, over 13,000 copies were ready for distribution, twice the circulation of the popular middle-class *Gentleman's Magazine*. A cursory examination of John Wesley's Book Inventory manuscript held at the John Rylands Library in Manchester unlocks the scope of its readership and impressive growth:

> The number of *Arminian Magazine* printed at the press of Mr. Wesley's Decree were 7000 they continued to increase to the number of 24,000 & have succeeded to the . . . Number 135,000 . . . constantly been on sale at the Book Room from 1749 to his [John Wesley's] Death when the Stock on Hand was 7300 – the sale being constantly large.[5]

Wesley was adamant that the Methodists become known as a reading people and the materials which they studied should inculcate the richness and multi-dimensional aspects of piety that would aid and guide them in the pursuit of justifying and sanctifying grace.[6] In November

4 John Wesley, *AM* vii (1784), n.p.

5 John Rylands University Library of Manchester, Methodist Archives and Research Centre [hereafter: *MARC*], 'Book Inventory', n.p.

6 See the following articles by Randy Maddox: 'Kingswood School Library Holdings (*ca.* 1775)', *Methodist History* 40 (2002), 342–70; 'John Wesley's Reading: Evidence in the Book Collection at Wesley's House London', *Methodist History* 41 (2003), 118–33; 'John Wesley's

1790, the mature leader of the Methodist movement answered George Holder in correspondence:

> It cannot be that the people should grow in grace unless they give themselves in reading. A reading people will always be a knowing people. . . . Press this upon them with all your might; and you will soon see the fruit of your labours.[7]

In the following essay, we will examine the existence of dream narratives which John Wesley included in the *Arminian Magazine* with a view to understand how he believed visionary experiences substantiated both his own belief in an invisible world and also, which may be more important, in what manner he envisioned the belief in supernatural identities portrayed in dreams to be normative for the self-awareness in the wider movement of Methodist renewal.

Dreams and Visions have played a provocative role in Christian literature throughout its history.[8] A fascinating contribution offered by Methodist subculture emerged in the eighteenth century with the belief in dreams and visions and their power to evince particular models that promoted a specific Christian self-understanding. Throughout his published *Journals*, for example, John Wesley inserted various accounts which designated the ability of dreams to impress and influence the lives of human beings. Uncharacteristically, in an entry for November 19, 1738, Wesley recorded an autobiographical account of a dream that awakened him in the night. The dream, though not itself described in the *Journal*, was interpreted clairvoyantly:

> About that time (as I found in the morning) one who had been designed to be my pupil, but was not, came into the porter's lodge (where several persons were sitting) with a pistol in his hand. He then attempted twice or thrice to shoot himself, but it would not go off. Upon his laying it down, one took it up and blew out the

Reading: Evidence in the Kingswood School Archives', *Methodist History* 41 (2003), 49–67, and 'Remnants of John Wesley's Personal Library', *Methodist History* 42 (2004), 122–8.

[7] *The Letters of the Rev. John Wesley*, ed. John Telford, 8 vols (London, 1931), 8: 247.

[8] Lynn Thordike, 'Ancient and Medieval Dream-Books', in eadem, *A History of Magic and Experimental Science*, 8 vols (New York, 1923–58), 7: 290–302; Lisa M. Bitel, 'In *Visu Noctis*: Dreams in European Hagiography and Histories, 450–900', *History of Religions* 31 (1991), 39–59; Nancy Armstrong and Leonard Tennenhouse, 'The Interior Difference: a Brief Genealogy of Dreams, 1650–1717', *Eighteenth-Century Studies* 23 (1990), 458–78; Merle Curti, 'The American Exploration of Dreams and Dreamers', *Journal of the History of Ideas* 27 (1966), 391–416; and Mechal Sobel, *Teach Me Dreams: the Search for Self in the Revolutionary Era* (Princeton, NJ, 2000).

> priming. He was very angry, went and got fresh prime, came in again, sat down, beat the flint with his key; and about twelve, pulling off his hat and wig, said he would die like a gentleman, and shot himself through the head.[9]

In his sermon, 'Human Life A Dream', which was written on the eve of Wesley's death and later added to the *Arminian Magazine* by his editorial assistant, Wesley defined a dream as 'a kind of parenthesis inserted in life'.[10] Scattered throughout Methodist letters from the eighteenth century is the idea that dreams are a means of receiving knowledge, sometimes even communicating with those who have been transferred to the invisible world. Mary Fletcher, to cite one instance, received a letter from Miles Martindale, who was translating her deceased husband's essay, *Nature and Grace*. Martindale wrote to Fletcher in order to confirm a story that had circulated concerning a dream wherein the deceased John Fletcher appeared to his wife and communicated his pleasure of the translation:

> You saw either in a dream or vision the venerable Fletcher, with whom you conversed, and that it was from him you received the first news of the Translation, and there he even named me, to whome I had never the honourers of being known, as the Translator, and at the same time pronounced it either *well* or *very well done*'.[11]

In a significant but often overlooked article, 'Early Methodist Visions of the Trinity', noted Methodist historian Henry Rack has located three predominant visions in eighteenth-century Methodism: (1) Visions of Jesus Crucified, (2) Visions of Judgment, and (3) Visions of the Trinity.[12] In this essay, I note another type of visualization that

9 John Wesley, 'Journals and Diaries II (1738–43)', ed. W. R. Ward and Richard Heitzenrater, *BEW* 19: 21. See also the first edition of John Wesley's *Works* (1774), where this passage is prefaced by an asterisk to highlight the importance of this incident in his young life.

10 John Wesley, 'Human Life A Dream', *BEW* 4: 111.

11 *MARC*, MAM F1, 5/1/9, 'Miles Martindale to Mary Fletcher', Manuscript Letter/ 14 January, 1811.

12 Henry Rack, 'Early Methodist Visions of the Trinity', *Proceedings of the Wesley Historical Society* 46 (1987), 38–44, 57–69. Representations of visions of the Crucified may be found in: John Cennick, *The Beatific Vision; or, Beholding Jesus Crucified. Being the Substance of a Discourse Preached in Ballymenagh, in Ireland, in the Year 1755* (3rd edn, London, 1786), 1–19; visions of Judgement can be found in: 'Sarah Brough via Barnabas Brough', *AM* iii (1780), 593–601; and visions of the Trinity in: 'Letter LXVIII', an incomplete letter sent to John Wesley by Charles Perronet in May 1772, *AM* ii (1779), 199–212.

may be called dreams of perfection. All four categories find a place in the *Arminian Magazine* and corroborate other materials found elsewhere. Dreams of perfection fostered both the Methodists' pursuit of sanctification and also allowed the believer an important place in the Wesleyan theatre of the supernatural. Furthermore, the dream narratives found in the *Arminian Magazine* became a storehouse of religious information which the Methodists repeatedly cited both for their personal inspiration and in confirmation of their belief in otherworldly phenomena.

* * *

One of the first visionary experiences included in the *Arminian Magazine* came from the spiritual biography of Sarah Ryan. Her account is valuable for our analysis because it demonstrates the vital link which existed between the experience of dreams and the presence of sanctifying grace in the believer's life. Additionally, Sarah Ryan's autobiographical account, dated in the mid 1750s, offered an accessible model for understanding a type of Enlightenment psychology which held faith and reason together. As a number of contemporary Methodist autobiographies did, Ryan's account opened with an emphasis on the sinful condition of her soul along with the struggles for inward peace. 'The Spirit drove me one way', Ryan declared, 'my passions another; so that I was all a troubled sea'.[13] This condition persisted for seven years and when her husband left on a journey, she went to stay with a Jewish family. At this juncture of her story, Ryan became ill but neither family nor friends could provide the comfort she needed until one night she had a dream where she found herself in Mr Wesley's society room, confronted by an angel. Suddenly, Ryan awoke; then, just as quickly, she fell asleep again, and saw the beauty of heavenly tranquillity:

> I saw a beautiful garden, and the angel walking up to me, till he laid his hand upon my arm, and said three times, 'Come out from these Jews, or you will be damned'. I turned and said, 'If I live, I will amend my life'. He disappeared, and I awoke.[14]

Typical of messages that warned of impending disaster, there is in Ryan's account an indication not only of present sin but also looming danger, and therefore urgency. The instruction from the angel to flee

13 *AM* ii (1779), 299.
14 Ibid.

the Jewish family only accentuated, for Ryan, the necessity to discover an environment which will avail her the opportunity to experience salvation.

The next part of her narrative finds Ryan attending, albeit unwillingly, a service at Spitalfields church where John Wesley was preaching a sermon on the parable of the sower (Matt. 13, 18–23). When Wesley spoke of the verses which mentioned 'stoney ground', Ryan evaluated the landscape of her own heart. 'I knew all he said belonged to *me*'.[15] However, when he came to expound the portion of the passage which highlighted the 'good ground', Ryan realized that she had no personal experience of such terrain. After the completion of Wesley's sermon, Ryan – being physically faint – became conscious that she would be sustained only with a knowledge of Jesus Christ. Amazingly, words of promise entered her heart, 'thou shalt have a blessing', and she realized, though inadequately, 'the promise is for *me*!'[16] Much like John Wesley's own experience, many of the Methodist conversion narratives follow the Aldersgate model where reluctance to attend a society meeting was followed by the experience of being overcome by the realization that Christ died for one's personal sins. Stephen Prickett recently has noted the social importance of the Aldersgate trope, when he writes: 'The "strange warming" of John Wesley's heart in a little chapel in Aldersgate Street, in London, was to affect the religious lives of millions over the next two and a half centuries'.[17]

The next stage of Ryan's experience detailed, however, her desire for spiritual solitude and perfection, as she approached the altar:

> When I came up, my strength was quite gone, I threw my body across the rails, and, being overwhelmed with the power of God, was utterly regardless of outward things. Mr Wesley offered me the bread, but I was not able to take it; so he passed by me, and gave it me when he came back. When he spoke those words, 'The blood of the Lord Jesus Christ' they pierced my heart, and filled my soul with love to him. Immediately I said, 'This is the Faith by which the martyrs went to the flames'. I felt a change through my whole soul, and longed to be alone. As soon as I got home, I fell on my knees, and cried, 'Lord, are my sins forgiven?' I was answered,

15 *AM* ii (1779), 301; See also, John Wesley, 'Journals', *BEW* 18: 240–2.

16 *AM* ii (1779), 302.

17 Stephen Prickett, *Narrative, Religion and Science: Fundamentalism versus Irony, 1700–1999* (Cambridge, 2002), 136.

> There is no condemnation for them that are in Christ Jesus. But this did not satisfy. I wanted a clear witness, that my sins were forgiven; and ardently did I wish for the next Sunday, hoping I should receive it at the table'.[18]

Three weeks later Sarah Ryan attended a class meeting with her sister who was experiencing intense spiritual distress too. Upon exhorting her sister to believe in Christ, Ryan was overcome by divine power which caused her to collapse into her chair. As she fell, however, she lost her physical sight and instantaneously Christ appeared to her 'inward sight'. Ryan gave evidence of supernatural sight: 'O the beauty of the lovely Jesus, Behold him in his vesture dipt in blood!'[19] Her sister, then, inquired if she did now believe, wherein Ryan hesitantly affirmed that she did but '. . . felt something of a doubt still, and wanted a stronger witness'.[20]

The following night, while in solitary prayer, Ryan received divine confirmation of her experience; however, it is a week later in the Spitalfields church again that her yearning for peace culminated in a vision of Jesus and a little girl. In the vision, Ryan is shown that Christ has made her as the little child, with the implication that she should go on to Christian perfection '. . . and grow up to the measure of his stature'.[21] With this experience, Ryan was content to know that her destiny was to mature into the likeness of Christ.

* * *

Other narratives show what was, for John Wesley, a recurrent concern about the reality of the dark side of the invisible world. In a journal account that Wesley also included in the *Arminian Magazine* for 1783, Mr J. V. (John Valton) had a dream where he entered a house and saw the devil sleeping in a bed. Approaching the bed, he found the devil, and he '. . . got hold of his clothes and stript him naked'.[22] This act so angered the devil that he chased J. V. out of the house and down the street. Suddenly, he was charged by an audible voice which warned that the devil possesses all he touches. In desperation for escape and security, J. V. saw Christ, and surmised that he had invited him to touch the hem

18 Ibid.
19 Ibid.
20 Ibid.
21 *AM* ii (1779), 309.
22 *AM* v (1783), 459–60.

of his garment (Matt. 9, 20–22; Mark 5, 25–34; Luke 8, 43–48) and thus was instantly saved from his troubles.

Sometimes dreams can be signs of God's displeasure of the human heart which has embraced the cunning devices of evil. Daniel Defoe, at the beginning the Enlightenment, suggested that Satan had surreptitiously impressed his wicked scheme on Eve while she slept in the garden of Eden.[23] Furthermore, Defoe maintained, cunning men still adhered to the opinion that human behaviour might be influenced with a whisper into the ear of a sleeping individual.[24] Nothing hindered the pursuit of perfection for eighteenth-century Methodists, however, as did inbred sin. Christopher Hooper confessed that he had developed such a diabolical disregard for life that he and his friends were prone to cruelty, especially to animals, taking great pleasure in mangling and cutting to pieces dogs, cats, birds, and insects. One particular occasion, Hooper and the company he associated with found a great number of frogs which they mutilated and killed. 'That night', wrote Hooper,

> I dreamt I fell into a deep place full of frogs, and they seized on me from head to foot, and begun to eat the flesh off my bones. I was in great terror, and found exquisite pain until I awoke, sweating, and trembling, and half dead with fear.[25]

Evil, for the Methodists, had a real presence in the world and its existence, left unchecked, casts the votary into spiritual ruin. John Wesley and the early Methodists performed exorcisms throughout the eighteenth century, as I have shown elsewhere, as an attempt to rid people of possession by unclean spirits and allow the spirit of love and faith to be perfected in the life of the soul.[26]

23 Daniel Defoe, *The History of the Devil, as Well Ancient and Modern: in Two Parts* . . . (2nd edn, London, 1727), 105.

24 For a recent treatment of cunning folk, see Owen Davies, *Cunning-Folk: Popular Magic in English History* (London and New York, 2003).

25 *AM* iv (1781), 26.

26 See my forthcoming article, 'Those Distracting Terrors of the Enemy: Demonic Possession and Exorcism in the Thought of John Wesley', in Jeremy Gregory, ed., *John Wesley. Tercentenary Essays, Bulletin of the John Rylands Library* 86–7 (2004), 373–86. See also John Wesley, Journal, *BEW* 19: 110–11. Wesley also included numerous stories of demonic possession and exorcism in *AM*. The case of the Yatton demoniac, George Lukins the Bristol tailor, was told in great detail over five different issues in 1789; *AM* xii (1789), 155–9, 205–10, 264–9, 324–7, and 373–5. John Valton's account of the exorcism may be found in his manuscript Journal, *MARC*, 'The Christian Experience of the Late Rev. John Valton A Clerk in the Ordinance Office Afterwards a Most Zealous Minister in the Late Mr. Wesley's Connection', 24.

* * *

Dreams were also fertile ground for experiencing justification and sanctification and were repeatedly cited in early Methodist literature. Recorded in John Bennett's manuscript minutes for the conference of 1745, in Bristol, was a question concerning the Methodists and their view of dreams. The answer that Wesley gave was positive:

> We do not intend to do that. We learn from Acts 2.19 &c. to expect something of this kind in the last Days. And we cannot deny that saving Faith is of often given in Dreams and Visions in the Night, which Faith we account neither better nor worse, than if it comes by any other means.[27]

Repeatedly, the *Arminian Magazine* was a forum that provided Wesley with an avenue to corroborate his view of dreams and visions, often finding a connection between dreams and the essential doctrines of scriptural Christianity. Of course, Wesley and the Methodists were not alone in this technique. William Law, in his influential *Practical Treatise upon Christian Perfection*, had opened his discussion and claimed that the world men and women live in was '. . . a mere Wilderness, a State of Darkness, a Vale of Misery, where Vice and Madness, Dreams and Shadows, variously please, agitate, and torment the short, miserable Lives of Men'.[28] Additionally, Augustus Montague Toplady, the Calvinist and polemical opponent of Wesley's Arminianism, included dream stories in his *Gospel Magazine* where he observed the supremacy of the knowledge of the crucified Jesus over other forms of natural knowledge.[29] However, few outlined the shortcomings of sinful humanity and the necessity of achieving spiritual perfection more consistently than did John Wesley. On 8 March 1778, a Mr Roe recorded in his journal that a violent earth trimmer alarmed him into thinking a potential earthquake was impending. The possible destruction of his life caused him to reflect on the condition of his soul. 'I plainly saw,' wrote Roe,

> that I had been a sinner who deserved hell; but that God had forgiven me, and enabled me to forsake all . . . I had also some true

27 *MARC*, John Bennett, 'Manuscript Notes from the Methodist Conference in Bristol, August 1–2, 1745', Question 2.16, 30–1.

28 William Law, *A Practical Treatise upon Christian Perfection* (London, 1726), 16.

29 'The Sciences Hallowed at the Foot of the Cross, A Dream', in Augustus Montague Toplady, ed., *The Gospel Magazine or Treasury of Divine Knowledge: Designed to Promote Experimental Religion*, 10 vols (London, 1774–83), 1: 146–52, 185–8.

> sense of what a sanctified person must experience. They feel a clear sense of the remission of past sins: they are sensible, sin did *reign* in a carnal state; that it *remains* in a justified state; but that now *Christ reigneth alone.* They see they are sanctified in, but not of themselves. Glory be to God! These views bring power and peace to my soul.[30]

As was mentioned above, an early conference had affirmed that Methodists espoused the idea that justifying grace could be experienced either in the midst of awakened consciousness or in the margins of sleep and dreams too. Often the dream narratives were revelatory; making a visible and conscious expression of divine grace known by the believer. In a letter to John Wesley from Richard Rodda, the occurrence of an out of body experience was published for the readers of the *Arminian Magazine.* 'I thought myself,' wrote Rodda,

> that my soul had actually left the body, and was mounting upwards, like a bird in the air. I saw with the eyes of my mind, such glory as cannot be exprest. I saw the Eternal Sun of Righteousness shining more glorious than the Sun in its meridian lustre. Indeed I had such views of God and glory, as I never had before or since. My mother, on hearing that I was dead, ran to the bed, and raised me up in her arms. After sometime I again began to breathe; but the impression it left, will never be obliterated. It was much against my wish, that I was again restored to life; for it was the longing desire of my soul to depart and to be with Christ, of which I had full assurance'.[31]

Of course, matters could and did get out of hand. Throughout his life, the charge of enthusiasm was constantly attached to Wesley's emphasis on justifying and sanctifying grace. In the 1760s, controversy arose over the teaching of perfection and the unruly nature of some Methodists in regard to their experiences. Initially, Wesley was pleased with and encouraged by the Methodists' visions of sanctification, though, on occasion, episodes were accompanied by intense forms of ecstasy. In his extended correspondence with his older brother Samuel, for example, Wesley drew attention to John Haydon, a sceptic of the teaching of justifying grace, who was violently overcome with convulsions and rapture upon reading the last page of John Wesley's sermon

30 *AM* vii (1784), 189.
31 Ibid., 354.

on Justification by Faith.[32] However, within time, some society meetings became increasingly unsettled and were prone to wild and uncontrolled hysteria. John Walsh, the converted Irish Deist, wrote to Charles Wesley about his own observations of life in a society.[33] Especially disappointing, for John Wesley, was George Bell who had initially been seen as a man who was able to heal the sick through his prayers but was drawn into excessive fantasies; claiming to heal the blind, raise the dead, and even asserted that the world would come to a cataclysmic end on a particular day in 1762.[34]

* * *

The history of the *Arminian Magazine* and its appeal among the British lower class confirms that reading was not merely a pensive exercise but an activity which elicited features that were important for the political and social stability of a movement which endeavoured to contextualize a specific self-identity. Dream narratives provided the Methodists not only with material for inspiration, but were also a means of conceptualizing their own religious self-awareness in a world and time when the predominant trend was to view the universe under the paradigm of mechanical philosophy. Admittedly, Wesley and the Methodists were not alone in this pursuit. Following the genre of moral weeklies, British serials like the *Spectator*, *Tatler*, and *Guardian* encouraged people toward a specific understanding of virtue and cultural ideals. These standards, however, were not always openly received by the lower classes who often felt excluded or marginalized from the discourse.[35] Often, like the lower classes, Wesley faced opposition from the Enlightenment too. His affirmation of an invisible world and its viability for a modern self-understanding brought ridicule and polemical opposition throughout his life, which spanned the eighteenth century. Convinced, however, of supernatural identities, John Wesley vigorously argued for the viability of a belief in otherworldly realities and their importance in the natural world. Contrary to the *philosophes* of the period who ridiculed the plebeian belief in miracles and portents as irrational and

32 John Wesley, Letters I (1721–39), *BEW* 25: 645–7.

33 *MARC*, John Walsh, 'Ms Letter to Charles Wesley/August 11, 1762', EMV, 134.

34 Cf. *AM* iii (1780), 674–6, where John Wesley approvingly quotes a letter from George Bell who described his experience of sanctification; but then Wesley inserted his editorial comment at the end of the letter: 'Such *was* George Bell! What is he now?'.

35 Brian Young, 'Theological Books from *The Naked Gospel* to *Nemesis of Faith*', in Isabel Rivers, ed., *Books and their Readers in Eighteenth-Century England: New Essays* (London, 2001), 79–104. See also Don Herzog, *Poisoning the Minds of the Lower Orders* (Princeton, NJ, 1998).

superstitious, Wesley maintained that human experience evidenced the reality of an invisible world.[36] Additionally, Wesley buttressed his argument with the affirmation that the experiences of the lower classes were corroborated by a conceptual understanding that asserted a central place for miracles in the faith and work of Christianity.[37] With this two-pronged agenda before him, the *Arminian Magazine* provided a tool of instruction and inspiration. Often, though not solely, these stories originated from journal accounts of Methodists who were writing both for their own self-awareness and for Wesley himself who, as an indefatigable editor, was ever looking for materials that would demonstrate his notion that the experience of the supernatural was empirically observable in human nature. Wesley's dream narratives became an avid tool for bridging the natural and the supernatural.

However, Wesley's attention to dreams often came under attack. On the one hand, some of the societies, as we have noted, descended into superstition and disrepute. At the end of the long eighteenth century, for example, the Eclectic Society considered what type of endorsement should be given to dreams and visions. The positive quality of dreams was affirmed but with one caveat: 'Yet we must not lean too much towards the superstitious side. Mr. Wesley's people do this'.[38] It was an affront that nineteenth-century Methodism worked long and hard against during the following century. It also revealed, at one level, how reluctant Wesley was to abandon his beliefs against all odds. On the other hand, his determined persistence of including dream narratives in the *Arminian Magazine* revealed the importance of dreams for understanding the supernatural and its priority in the self-identity of the Methodist people. Though, in the end, John Wesley distanced himself and the Methodist movement from people like George Bell and Thomas Maxfield, he never abandoned the idea that dreams and visions provided a connection between the invisible world and the matrix of

[36] For a detailed examination of the *philosophes* and their attack on the idea of miracles in the Enlightenment, see Jonathan I. Israel, *Radical Enlightenment: Philosophy and the Making of Modernity, 1650–1750* (Oxford, 2001), 218–29.

[37] Henry D. Rack, *Reasonable Enthusiast: John Wesley and the Rise of Methodism* (3rd edn, London, 2003), 350: 'It is a mistake to dismiss this [the supernatural] as peripheral to Wesley's teaching and mission. It is fully in line with his general outlook, and could indeed be justified as an aspect of the same design as his histories and science: to show God's presence and action in the world to sceptics'.

[38] *Eclectic Notes: or, Notes of Discussions on Religious Topics at the Meetings of The Eclectic Society, London, during the Years 1798–1814*, ed. Josiah Pratt (2nd edn, London, 1865), 84–5.

human history; those who had been bound to the oppression and evil of sin were consistently and constantly giving evidence and testimony to a powerful presence with supernatural qualifications. 'There was nothing particularly unusual in this', writes Henry Rack, 'for a Methodist'.[39]

University of Oxford

39 Rack, Reasonable Enthusiast, 338.

THE MAGIC METHODISTS AND THEIR INFLUENCE ON THE EARLY PRIMITIVE METHODIST MOVEMENT

by JOHN W. B. TOMLINSON

THE role of the Magic Methodists and their leader James Crawford at the beginning of Primitive Methodism has been widely debated.[1] As a group noted for signs, wonders and miracles, they helped to provide the necessary experience and enthusiasm for a new revivalist movement. In the image of a poor agricultural labourer, Crawfoot represented a rustic and earthy beginning for a denomination that prided itself on its success amongst the poor. However, as a man 'unpolished by learning and refinement . . . strangely odd and uncouth in argument', he was a controversial figure.[2] To successive generations of Primitive Methodists Crawfoot with his associated supernaturalism was an embarrassment.[3]

The short relationship between the Magic Methodists and the Primitive Methodists raises two important issues. First, the role of signs, wonders and miracles in the emergence of a revivalist Church is crucial, but such phenomena need to be controlled if the sect is to develop into a denomination. Second, there is a link, however tenuous, between those with radical spiritual ideas that question the Church establishment and those whose political views challenge the *status quo* of society.

* * *

Hugh Bourne, one of the founders of Primitive Methodism, first met Crawfoot in the Forest of Delamere in Cheshire in June 1807. Bourne walked thirty miles from the Potteries to see the 'Forest Mystic' preside over a meeting of the Magic Methodists. He recalled how he saw:

1 For the most recent account see Henry D. Rack, *James Crawfoot and the Magic Methodists*, Anniversary Lecture at Englesea Brook Chapel and Museum (Englesea Brook, 2003).

2 John Walford, *Memoirs of the Life and Labours of the Late Venerable Hugh Bourne*, 2 vols (London, 1856, repr. Totton, 1999), 1: 204.

3 John Petty in *The History of the Primitive Methodist Connexion from its Origin to the Conference of 1859* (2nd edn, London, 1864), and Walford, *Memoirs*, are critical of Crawfoot and his group, while William Antliff in *The Life of Hugh Bourne, founder of the Primitive Methodist Connexion* (2nd edn, London, 1892), and George Herod, *Biographical Sketches of some of those preachers whose labours contributed to the origination and early extension of the Primitive Methodism Connexion . . .* (London, 1855), are more sympathetic.

> a woman struggling, as if in distress, and wondered why they did not pray for her. But two women placed her in a chair, and she appeared to have fainted away. I then thought, this is their trance work . . . at length the woman clasped her hands, and praised the Lord, and went on speaking occasionally without opening her eyes. She spoke of a fine green meadow, and said, 'Let me lie down'. She then spoke of a fine river . . . she spoke of trumpets, and called out 'Blow! blow! blow!'. She after a time called on a young woman by name, and said, 'Leave it'. And shortly after that she awoke up and came out of her visionary state. I then went up to the woman to enquire, but all in vain; only one of the women said, 'These things strengthen our faith!'.[4]

The meeting ended at midnight, but Bourne stayed on to talk with Crawfoot until two o'clock in the morning. He needed to satisfy himself that these strange happenings in the forest were of God and not the devil, as he had 'heard an evil report'.[5] After this encounter he was more than convinced of Crawfoot's soundness and his ability to call down the 'power', a display of supernatural gifts that was both a confirmation and an instrument of God's grace.[6] For the next six years Bourne and his co-worker William Clowes returned many times to Crawfoot's forest home and travelled with him on evangelistic journeys around Cheshire and Staffordshire and beyond. As such the leader of the Magic Methodists had a significant influence on the emergence of Primitive Methodism.

At this time there were many small groups of revivalist Christians, often restricted to a locality and associated with supernatural phenomena. Bourne and Clowes were leaders of their own small bands of Methodists, drawn into conflict with the Wesleyan authorities and into collaboration with other fringe groups. They were expelled from the Wesleyans not because of a difference of doctrine, but rather because of unacceptable practices, chiefly their involvement in camp meetings. At the first of these at Mow Cop on 31 May 1807 several hundred people gathered on the rocky outcrop of north Staffordshire for a day of 'singing, praying, preaching, exhorting, speaking experiences, giving historical statements, relating anecdotes and other striking

4 As described some years later and recorded in Walford, *Memoirs*, 1: 154–5.

5 John Rylands University Library of Manchester, Methodist Archives and Research Centre [hereafter: *MARC*], MS Bourne Autobiography, DDHB 2/1 (A) 39.

6 Antliff, *Life of Hugh Bourne*, 64, and Petty, *History*, 36–7.

occurrences'.[7] The controversial American evangelist Lorenzo Dow was the main preacher, although any man or woman was allowed to address the crowds. The message was one of personal salvation but it had a political and social context too. Dow was known for his Republican views.[8] Within sight of Mow Cop there was the landscape of the Potteries despoiled and polluted by industrialization and many of those present would have been affected by economic recession and the war in Europe. Such contemporary events were often regarded as 'signs', indications that the world was in need of conversion. The recent troubles in Ireland were used to illustrate the potency of the current age, and the very fact that they were at the beginning of a century encouraged a degree of millenarianism.[9]

The Wesleyan authorities saw the danger of such gatherings. A large crowd freely addressed by uneducated men and women and by foreigners was an unsettling occurrence. At the next Methodist Conference they displayed their loyalty to the status quo by issuing a strong condemnation:

> It is our judgement, that even supposing such meetings to be allowable in America, they are highly improper in England, and likely to be productive of considerable mischief.[10]

There were rumours that camp meetings were opportunities for licentious behaviour, particularly when they lasted into the night. Undoubtedly they could be lively events. On one occasion strange demonic figures dressed up with wings, horns and tails suddenly appeared and caused pandemonium in the crowd, but the preachers stood their ground, and the creatures, who had been sent by the local publican, slunk away.[11] The camp meetings were deliberately arranged 'to counteract the evil effects of the wake' even to the extent of pitching tents amidst the debauchery.[12]

Camp meetings were a show of strength, an expression of collective faith, and an opportunity to display the 'power'. Many of those who attended saw themselves engaged in a spiritual war between God and

7 Autobiography, DDHB, 2/1 (A) 29.

8 John Kent, *Holding the Fort: Studies in Victorian Revivalism* (London, 1978), 59.

9 Julia Stewart Werner, *The Primitive Methodist Connexion: its Background and Early History* (Madison, WI, 1984), 32; Kenneth Lysons, *A Little Primitive* (Buxton, 2001), 44.

10 *Methodist Magazine* (1807), 452.

11 H. B. Kendall, *History of the Primitive Methodist Connexion* (London, *c.*1890), 35.

12 Autobiography, DDHB 2/1 (A) 30; H. B. Kendall, *The Origin and History of the Primitive Methodist Church*, 2 vols (London, 1906), 2: 83–4.

the devil, often expressed in visions and signs, as recorded in the journals of Bourne and Clowes.[13] The camp meetings were pivotal both in a spiritual and a social sense. Years later Bourne reflected on how the meetings almost brought him to social and financial ruin through the threats of a local manufacturer acting as a magistrate.[14]

* * *

Hugh Bourne was a moorland carpenter who was converted at the age of twenty-seven chiefly through the reading of Fletcher's *Letters on the Supernatural Manifestation of the Son of God*.[15] He built and ran a revivalist Methodist chapel in a collier's garden at Harriseahead, north Staffordshire, from 1802. The Wesleyans were very reluctant to accept his converts, perhaps because of their social inferiority, and so Bourne became the leader of a group called the Camp Meeting Methodists, which in due course merged with others to form the Primitive Methodists. His discipline, organizational and literary skills, and modest financial means, made him an important leader of the new sect. However, it was through his influence that the sect became a denomination.

In the early years Bourne was greatly dependent on the charisma of others. Clowes was a popular preacher who boasted of his conversion from 'champion dancer, fighter, swearer'.[16] When he was a sinner he could draw a crowd to join him in drink, and when a preacher to join him in prayer. However, as a potter struggling to find work during economic recession, Clowes came to rely on the Primitive Methodist itinerant preachers' allowance of 14 shillings a week.[17] His refusal to give up alcohol remained a life-long contention with Bourne.

Crawfoot had an even greater influence on Bourne in the early years, and their relationship could even be described as intense, sometimes causing him almost to faint.[18] Crawfoot convinced Bourne to avoid marriage so as to stay holy. At this time Bourne recorded Crawfoot's effect upon him:

13 Kendall, *Origin and History*, 1: 147; *MARC*, MS Bourne Journal, DDHB 3; *The Journals of William Clowes* (London, 1844).

14 Journal, DDHB 2/1 (A) 33, 41.

15 Kendall, *History of the Primitive Methodist Connexion*, 9.

16 Ibid., 23.

17 Werner, *Primitive Methodist Connexion*, 75.

18 Journal, DDHB 3/4, 3 November 1808.

> My heart was opened, and the word seemed to soak into me like rain . . . he has seen many miracles. He also instructed me in the ministry, and in the Holy Spirit. O God make me faithful.[19]

Crawfoot became Bourne's spiritual guide, and extended Bourne's contact with the revivalist fringe. For a year Bourne became fully embroiled in the visions of the Magic Methodists, recording them graphically in his Journal.[20] The visions of the young women, and occasionally men and children, consisted of divine revelations of the spiritual standing of the leaders. The men and women, sometimes together, but more often separately, would appear in hierarchies, not unlike that of a preaching plan, holding the emblems of their office, the trumpet of evangelism and the cup of spiritual gifts. If one had discarded his trumpet or held his cup at a crooked angle this was seen as sign of divine disapproval. Crawfoot nearly always appeared at the top, closely followed by Dow and Clowes. However, Bourne tended to appear nearer the middle, a comment upon his less spiritual qualities as administrator. Although these visions were almost wholly expressed through young women, they were accepted as divine revelations. Bourne described them as 'a great benefit'.[21] It was through one of the visionaries that Bourne received his call to preach, a crucial step in his development as a religious leader.[22] The visions reached their peak in the spring and summer of 1811 but then came to an abrupt end, and it is not clear precisely why.

* * *

Visions, and other supernatural phenomena, had been part of Methodist spirituality from the beginning because of the emphasis on religious experience.[23] Bourne had 'read of visions or trance work in Mr. Wesley's journals'.[24] However, the visions of the Magic Methodists in the way that they comment on the leadership of the Church are unique in Methodist history.[25]

Crawfoot was active in other supernatural expressions of the 'power', such as faith healing and exorcisms. He miraculously cured a

19 Ibid., 14 November 1808.

20 Journal, DDHB 3/6, March and May 1810, DDHB 3/7, April, June and July 1811.

21 Journal, DDHB 3/6, 28 March 1810.

22 Ibid., 24 March 1809.

23 Henry D. Rack, *Reasonable Enthusiast: John Wesley and the Rise of Methodism* (London, 1989), 195–7, 432–5.

24 Autobiography, DDHB 2/1 (A) 39.

25 Henry D. Rack, *How Primitive was Primitive Methodism? An Examination of Some Characters and Characteristics* (Englesea Brook, 1996).

woman run over by a horse and cart, as Bourne enthusiastically recorded: 'We called to see Mrs Chapman. She is now able to walk abroad. This is an astonishing miracle'.[26] Mrs Chapman went on to have visions. Crawfoot convinced Bourne of the existence of witchcraft.[27] Bourne had a dream about being trapped in a pit with a black dog and interpreted this as a sign to exorcize a witch at Ramsor.[28] Bourne was taught by Crawfoot to make 'war against the enemy of souls' and expect him to 'make war in return' and to 'conquer or die'.[29] The supernatural conflict between good and evil, as experienced through visions, dreams, faith healings and exorcisms had become, at least for a short time, an article of faith for the early Primitive Methodists.

Through Crawfoot, Bourne's contact with the Christian fringe was extended, particularly with the less orthodox. In 1810 they met Joanna Southcott, the elderly prophetess who three years later claimed to be supernaturally pregnant with the Christ. Bourne had his doubts about her and said that as 'her writings frequently contradict scripture, it appears to me that she is really in witchcraft'.[30] In January 1811 they went to Tutbury to see Anne Moore, the woman who miraculously lived without food or water.[31]

As an agricultural labourer Crawfoot was poor, and it was for this reason, as well as his spiritual qualities, that the Bourne family supported him financially and hired him as the first itinerant preacher of Primitive Methodism. He was paid ten shillings a week from November 1809 to see him through the winter months in return for preaching at various places each side of the Cheshire-Staffordshire border.[32] For the next few years Crawfoot was pre-eminent in Primitive Methodism, opening the first new chapel at Tunstall in 1811, and taking the senior position as number one on the first preaching plans.

Of particular interest are the politics which accompanied Crawfoot's spiritual leadership. Bourne commented on their first meeting that Crawfoot 'dabbled a little in politics' and Herod has a cryptic reference to Crawfoot's sympathies for the disadvantaged.[33] In suggesting the

26 Journal, DDHB 3/6, 5 October 1810.

27 Ibid., 9 June 1810.

28 Walford, *Memoirs*, 1: 300; Journal, DDHB 3/7, 23 October 1810.

29 Autobiography, DDBH 2/1 (A) 67; Antliff, *Life of Hugh Bourne*, 80.

30 Journal, DDHB 3/6, 3 October 1810.

31 Walford, *Memoirs*, 1: 309.

32 Journal, DDHB 3/6, 17 November 1809; Autobiography, DDHB 2/1 (A) 75.

33 Autobiography, DDHB 2/1 (A) 40; Herod, *Biographical Sketches*, 249; Rack, *James Crawfoot*, 3.

name for the new sect he recalled his own memory of Wesley's desire for a more radical Methodism.[34] According to Crawfoot the context of Wesley's phrase 'the primitive methodists' was one of Jesus's most millenarian parables where the poor have a place at the banquet and the rich are excluded (Luke 14, 23). For a while Bourne was taken up with millenarian concerns.[35] From his Journal it appears that Crawfoot encouraged him to break away from the Wesleyans.[36] When Clowes was agonizing over whether to take part in one of the camp meetings knowing that it would lead to his expulsion Crawfoot said, ''Tis better to obey God than man'.[37] The 'power' cultivated in others by Crawfoot gave them the confidence to become a new sect, whose members would be on the margins of society. The visionaries were mostly young, female, poor and associated with a remote forest setting. It was a sect that pitted itself against the world as revealed in the choice of Acts 28, 22 as the verse for the class tickets: 'But we desire to hear of thee what thou thinkest: for as concerning this sect, we know that every where it is spoken against'. Revivalism had a link with a type of political radicalism.[38]

Under the influence of Crawfoot Bourne's spirituality was given a different focus. He taught Bourne the need for 'exercising the burthen of others',[39] that is to look beyond individual salvation to the saving of a whole community. This was confirmed for Bourne on a visit to Lichfield Cathedral:

> After the service began, it ran through my mind, 'Get thee out of this place, and beware of the woman that has the golden cup in her hand . . .'. I saw much lightness and sin amongst the parsons. It seemed like gross idolatry in them to spend their time in such a manner.[40]

Unable to stay any longer he grabbed his hat and rushed outside:

> I stopped all afternoon in Lichfield, and such a travail of soul came upon me as I never before experienced – it was for the city . . . I

[34] Crawfoot recalled Wesley's use of the phrase in 1790 – although Crawfoot's memory is disputed: see *Proceedings of the Wesley Historical Society* xxxvi (1967), 64.

[35] Journal, DDHB 3/2, 13 April 1808.

[36] Journal, DDHB 3/3, 28 June 1808; Antliff, *Life of Hugh Bourne*, 81.

[37] Walford, *Memoirs*, 1:283.

[38] Lysons, *A Little Primitive*, 47–8.

[39] Kendall, *Origin and History*, 150.

[40] Ibid.

> asked James Crawfoot at the Forest about this. He said it was the sign of the times. It was Jesus Christ travailing in me . . . I had found myself willing to die for them.[41]

However Bourne and Crawfoot parted company some time before the spring of 1813. Unfortunately Bourne's Journal for this period has been lost, or maybe it was never written because he was in a depression.[42] He admitted that he had 'been under uncommon sorrow and trouble of mind for several days'.[43] Bourne moved from an attitude of intense admiration of Crawfoot to one of disapproval. In the later autobiography, Crawfoot is described as 'illiterate', a 'strong drink preacher' and subject to 'improprieties' and an 'unbridledness of tongue'.[44] Crawfoot was expelled from the Primitive Methodists in 1813 for failing to keep his preaching appointments.[45] His removal may also be related to his 'predilection for counselling young women'.[46] Having extolled the spiritual virtue of celibacy he proposed to marry Hannah Mountford, who was not only one of the main young visionaries but also a servant in the Bourne household. However, because the marriage did not take place until 1816, this reason seems less likely.[47] Also, there may have been financial irregularities. Crawfoot claimed to have been burgled of £40 and Bourne later regretted that, having paid him ten shillings a week, some of it went on strong drink.[48]

Certainly there was a rivalry between Crawfoot and Bourne, and in this the visions were influential.[49] How much the visions were a cause for the split is uncertain, although some of the other visionaries were expelled around the same time.[50] The most notorious was Mrs Dunnel who had contracted a bigamous marriage.[51] In March 1813 Bourne

41 Kendall, *Origin and History*, 1:151; Walford, *Memoirs*, 1: 157.

42 This is suggested by J. T. Wilkinson, the most revered twentieth-century biographer of Bourne, in a letter dated 17 March 1958: the document was found in a book at the JRULM and is not catalogued.

43 Journal, DDHB 3/7, 26 November 1811.

44 Autobiography, DDHB 2/1 (A), 45, 59–60, 71–2, 74, 77.

45 Journal, DDHB 3/7, February to April 1813; Herod, *Biographical Sketches*, 267–8.

46 Michael Sheard, 'The Origins and Early Development of Primitive Methodism in Cheshire and South Lancashire, 1800–1860', unpublished Ph.D. thesis, University of Manchester, 1980, 65.

47 Rack, *James Crawfoot*, 13, n. 45.

48 Journal, DDHB 3/7, 22 December 1811; Journal, DDHB 2/1 (A), 75.

49 Herod, *Biographical Sketches*, 268.

50 Sheard, 'Origins and Early Development of Primitive Methodism', 74, states that the visions were a major part of the dispute.

51 Journal, DDHB 3/7, 29 December 1811.

emerges from his silent period soon to declare that supernatural gifts are not necessary for faith.[52] He gave up his belief in witchcraft and became much less involved with those on the supernatural fringe.[53] Bourne comments only a little on the reasons for the split. He wrote that Crawfoot betrayed his trust through what 'Mr. Wesley calls a miserable bigotry' and that Crawfoot had become 'a heathen and a publican' and his 'conduct has been horrid and shocking'.[54] Bourne was even critical of Crawfoot's Quaker garb, which had been adopted by other preachers, and famously described it as a 'hat whim'.[55] If Crawfoot had questioned the social *status quo*, this would have disturbed the conservative members of the emerging denomination. The Magic Methodists continued as a small group in the forest until 1831 and Crawfoot died in 1839.[56]

* * *

Bourne and Clowes went on to develop a rapidly expanding Church as Primitive Methodism moved from sect to denomination in the space of a few years. This was due in part to a good organizational structure provided by Methodist ecclesiology. Class meetings, local societies, stewards, local preachers, the quarterly meeting and connexional conference were all used very efficiently by the Primitive Methodists. In contrast to the Wesleyans the laity had greater power and were charged less for the privilege. Rapid growth itself was an inducement to become a denomination, for as they claimed, 'we have beaten the bushes and others have netted the game'.[57] To various urban and rural areas Primitive Methodism spread out from the Potteries and became one of the fastest growing denominations of the nineteenth century. Bourne wrote the rules and regulations for the societies in 1814 and published a denominational magazine from 1819. In the following year the first connexional conference was called. By 1824 the membership was over 33,000 and within five years they were sending missionaries to the USA. According to the Religious Census of 1851 the Primitive Methodist Connexion numbered over 106,000 members, more than one third of the Wesleyan total.

52 Journal, DDHB 3/7, 9 April 1813.
53 Rack, *How Primitive*, 17.
54 Journal, DDHB 3/7, 7 March, 12 April and 15 April 1813.
55 Herod, *Biographical Sketches*, 271.
56 Kendall, *Origin and History*, 1: 149.
57 Kendall, *History of the Primitive Methodist Connexion*, 114.

Because Primitive Methodism so quickly developed into a denomination the initial phase of signs, wonders and miracles was short. Supernatural phenomena did remain a feature of the connexion, but in a more controlled way. Such happenings were reported in the Primitive Methodist Magazine regularly until the middle of the century, but the visionaries were legislated against by the late 1820s. On a visit to the society at Prees Green in Shropshire in October 1828 Bourne passed comment on two young women who had gone into a trance. He stated the connexional policy: '1. None to go in vision if they can avoid it. 2. Not to lay too much stress upon it. 3. That faith, plain faith, which worketh by love, is greater than these things'.[58]

In the same way that spiritual experiences were regulated Primitive Methodism as a denomination adopted a neutralized political stance. Bourne was naturally conservative and suppressed political radicalism. For example, he curtailed the preaching at camp meetings so as to limit their disruptive potential.[59] In 1819 he criticized a preacher who spoke against a fox-hunting parson, and at the annual meeting at Tunstall in 1821 he tried to eject an anti-government speaker.[60] However, Primitive Methodism remained a body of 'instinctive radicals' and was the most political of all non-conformist denominations because of its working-class membership, democratic structure and theological views.[61] In the connexion there were political radicals, some of whom went on to help establish the trade union movement, and until the mid-nineteenth century Primitive Methodist preachers still experienced harassment from magistrates.[62] Because the connexion remained a revivalist denomination with a focus on radical change there was always scope for some political radicalism.[63]

Signs, wonders and miracles were essential elements in the birth of Primitive Methodism. Crawfoot and the Magic Methodists in the display of the 'power' helped to give the sect confidence to become established. However, the unpredictable and unsettling visions, and the association with a political radicalism, were an impediment to a

58 Kendall, *Origin and History*, 1: 288.

59 John T. Wilkinson, *Hugh Bourne, 1772–1852* (London, 1952), 118.

60 Sheard, 'Origins and Early Development of Primitive Methodism', 805–7; Lysons, *A Little Primitive*, 45.

61 E. J. Hobsbawm, *Primitive Rebels: Studies in Archaic Norms of Social Movement in the 19th and 20th Centuries* (Manchester, 1959), 129, 135–9.

62 Rupert Davies and Gordon Rupp, eds, *A History of the Methodist Church in Great Britain*, 4 vols (London, 1965–88), 2: 163.

63 Kent, *Holding the Fort*, 40, 42.

growing institution. In constructing an efficient denomination Bourne and the other conservative members had to limit the significance of the supernatural phenomena. The divine power so crucial in the early years was now to be expressed in the organizational and institutional life of the Church.

University of Birmingham

TRYING THE SPIRITS: IRVINGITE SIGNS AND THE TEST OF DOCTRINE

by TIMOTHY C. F. STUNT

WHEN Samuel Taylor Coleridge read Edward Irving's sermon in 1825 on the apostolic missionary ideal, he was disappointed that Irving had not met at the outset what would be the main objection of his more cautious antagonists. The absence in modern times of the *miraculous* gifts of the apostolic missionaries was a problem that, Coleridge felt, hung

> like a dead weight around the neck of his [Irving's] Reasoning. They say to themselves To whom Christ commended a supernatural independence of human means and aids, to them in the same commission he delegated superhuman powers . . . conferred for their performances. This argument Mr Irving should have met at the outset: for the Removal of this obstacle is as the foundation of all he would build up; inasmuch as not being removed it prevents the foundation from being laid.[1]

It seemed fair criticism and for five years, Irving waited for the miraculous seal of divine approbation. When it appeared to have been granted, it was ironic that the world scorned the miracles as well as Irving's missionary ideal.

* * *

The origins of the Catholic Apostolic Church emerging from Irving's congregation in the 1830s were from the start associated in the popular mind with 'miraculous' signs. These manifestations began in Fernicarry, Clydeside, on 30 March 1830, when the consumptive Mary Campbell spoke in an unknown tongue. During the previous year, south of the river, in Port Glasgow, another invalid, Margaret

[1] Edward Irving, *For Missionaries after the Apostolical School: a Series of Orations* (London, 1825), presented 'To his dear friend and kind instructor', BL, MS C.61. c.8. Manuscript comments are on pp. 131–2. For background details see Sheridan Gilley, 'Edward Irving: Prophet of the Millennium', in Jane Garnett and Colin Matthew, eds, *Revival and Religion since 1700: Essays for John Walsh* (London and Rio Grande, OH, 1993), 95–110, 98; Timothy C. F. Stunt, *From Awakening to Secession: Radical Evangelicals in Switzerland and Britain, 1815–35* (Edinburgh, 2000), 98–101 and *passim*.

Macdonald, had experienced spiritual ecstasies though apparently without *glossolalia*. Two weeks after Mary Campbell's experience, Margaret was bidden by her brother James to 'arise and stand upright' and on doing so was restored to bodily health. That day, James Macdonald wrote a similar command in a letter to Mary Campbell, who, on receiving the letter, rose from her bed and declared herself healed. In the following months Mary Campbell, Margaret Macdonald and her brothers frequently spoke in tongues and prophesied, attracting great interest and many visitors. Inevitably there was debate over their previous medical condition and whether the healings and utterances were of divine origin. The circle around Irving in London felt that these events were an answer to the criticisms described earlier by Coleridge. In August 1830 they sent a deputation, led by J. B. Cardale, whose favourable report was the earliest written account of the events.[2] Other contemporary descriptions by sympathizers were also written with access to precise details. Irving, whose assistant, A. J. Scott, came from Greenock, had visited Row in 1828 and knew the persons concerned. Robert Norton visited Clydeside and later married Margaret Macdonald. His first two accounts were written after her death but *before* his involvement with the Catholic Apostolic Church.[3]

Satisfied that the manifestations were genuine, several members of Irving's congregation gathered in Cardale's home to pray for a similar outpouring. On 17th October 1830, the rector of Albury, Hugh McNeile, proclaimed from a London pulpit that such gifts could be expected and within a week Eliza, the crippled daughter of the Revd Thomas Fancourt, was reported to have been miraculously cured.[4]

2 John Bate Cardale, 'On the Extraordinary Manifestations in Port-Glasgow', *Morning Watch* [hereafter: *MW*] 2 (Dec. 1830), 869–72.

3 Edward Irving, 'Facts Connected with Recent Manifestations of Spiritual Gifts', a series of articles in *Fraser's Magazine* 4 (1832), and Robert Norton, *Neglected and controverted Scripture Truths; with an Historical Review of Miraculous Manifestations in the Church of Christ; and an Account of their late Revival in the West of Scotland* (London, 1839); idem, *Memoirs of James and George Macdonald, of Port-Glasgow* (London, 1840); and idem, *The Restoration of Apostles and Prophets, in the Catholic Apostolic Church* (London, 1861). The more critical Robert Herbert Story, author of *Memoir of the Life of the Rev. Robert Story*... (Cambridge, 1862), was the son of a close associate of the participants. See also Andrew Landale Drummond, *Edward Irving and his Circle: Including some Consideration of the 'Tongues' Movement in the Light of Modern Psychology* (London, n. d. [1937]), 136–51; C. Gordon Strachan, *The Pentecostal Theology of Edward Irving* (London, 1973), 62–75; Stunt, *Awakening*, 228–36. Other primary sources relating to subsequent developments in Port Glasgow have been used in Tim Grass, '"The Taming of the Prophets": Bringing prophecy under control in the Catholic Apostolic Church', *Journal of the European Pentecostal Theological Association* 16 (1996), 58–70.

4 Henry Drummond, later an Apostle in the Irvingite Church, urged Thomas Chalmers

Christian journals discussed the cure, but there were no further manifestations until the following April when Cardale's wife, who had *not* accompanied him to Port Glasgow, spoke in an unknown tongue. Shortly before this, Mary Campbell (now Mrs William Caird) had arrived in London from Clydeside and she too prophesied in the Cardale household.[5]

With this gathering charismatic momentum, further healings were reported – most notably in July 1831, that of Maria Hughes a member of the congregation of Park Chapel, Chelsea. This incident followed a sermon in which the Revd Henry Owen had expressed his delight that his parishioners were willing to pray for divine healing. So far none of these events was *formally* associated with Edward Irving's congregation, though some members had been holding prayer meetings since May in his church in Regent Square – albeit unofficially. When, in August 1831, Edward Oliver Taplin, a schoolmaster, spoke in an unknown tongue at one of these meetings, the identification was stronger – the more so in mid-October when there were similar occurrences during the church's formal services. In the week prior to these public utterances the enthusiastic Henry Bulteel, a recent seceder from the established Church at Oxford, returned from London fully satisfied that the manifestations were genuine. During the next ten days he was responsible for two healings, including that of his sister-in-law, in Oxford.

The debate following these rather sensational episodes was predictable. Although some commentators reserved judgement, scoffers often mocked the credulous while sceptics were rebuked by believers. The *Morning Watch* described the scornful *Edinburgh Review* as 'the leader of the infidel party in Great Britain' and warned evangelicals that to reject the miracles as spurious was to ally themselves with Socinians, Neologists and blasphemers.[6] When the *Christian Observer* maintained that it was 'dangerous and unscriptural' to think that the age of miracles was revived, Eliza Fancourt's father trounced the magazine for not rescuing his daughter's healing 'from the sneer of the profane scoffer'.[7] Similar recriminations characterized the pamphlet controversy

to read Eliza Fancourt's account as Chalmers had recently opined that 'there was too much of seriousness about the accounts from Port Glasgow [for them] to be treated in the loose offhand manner that they had been by some', Stunt, *Awakening*, 249, n. 40.

5 For fuller details of this and the following paragraph, see Stunt, *Awakening*, 260–2, 268–9.

6 Ibid., 250, n. 41.

7 *MW* 3 (March 1831), 156–7.

between Bulteel and his critics in early 1832.[8] Meanwhile a correspondent of the *Evangelical Magazine* protested that 'the pretended gifts, and prophecyings [*sic*], and solemn babblings' of the 'unhappy visionaries' are 'among the most profane symptoms of the age in which we live', and enjoined readers 'never to give the extravagancies now going forward' their occasional sanction by setting foot in Irving's church even out of mere curiosity.[9]

Lurking behind these polemics, however, there was a theological dimension to the debate. The manifestations in both Scotland and London had occurred in the context of pastoral ministries that had provoked charges of heterodoxy. McLeod Campbell of Row had won the hearts of his parishioners but had earned the disfavour of the ecclesiastical authorities by stepping away from the Westminster Confession, rejecting a limited atonement, and insisting that Christ had died for all mankind. This issue was taken up by the Revd Baptist Noel, minister of St John's Chapel, Bedford Row, who had numbered among his parishioners John Cardale. Aware that, since his visit to Clydeside, Cardale was now attending Irving's services, Noel refrained from scorning those claiming the gifts, but unhesitatingly he advanced the theological issue as a cause for apprehension:

> God has never yet set the seal of miracles to error: else, where is the value of them as the seal of truth? But, unless I am misin<f>ormed, and misunderstand their writings, these pious persons have embraced the unscriptural notion that all men, even though they believe not in Christ, are so pardoned that sin is *no more imputed to them than to the believer;* that their guilt is done away through Christ, *just in the same sense that his [the believer's] is*; and that the only difference between them and him is that he [the believer] has become through faith really righteous, while they remain through unbelief essentially depraved.[10]

In his emphasis on Christ's compassion for mankind, McLeod Campbell had stressed the identification of Jesus with those whom he came to save. Irving in London had gone further and was already under

8 Grayson Carter, *Anglican Evangelicals: Protestant Secessions from the Via Media, c.1800–1850* (Oxford, 2001), 276–8; Tim Grass, '"The Restoration of a Congregation of Baptists": Baptists and Irvingism in Oxfordshire', *Baptist Quarterly* 37 (1998), 286–7.

9 *Evangelical Magazine* NS 9 (Dec. 1831), 522.

10 Baptist W. Noel, *Remarks on the Revival of Miraculous Powers in the Church* (London, 1831), 28–9.

investigation in 1830 for his insistence that although Christ had been completely without sin, he had shared 'the fallen nature' of mankind. Such had been the Lord's humanity, Irving argued, that he had been *capable* of sinning (peccable). This Christological aspect was more crucial than even the extent of the atonement and had a direct bearing on the issue of the miraculous. Both Irving and his assistant Alexander Scott had claimed that if Christ with a fallen human nature could perform miracles, then a redeemed humanity could expect to do likewise. Indeed their reasoning had prepared Mary Campbell and the Macdonald brothers for the possibility of the miraculous.[11]

Late in 1831, the editor of *The Record* who had no time for the manifestations took up the theological issue being convinced

> that the appearances [*sc.* manifestations] which have their centre and home in Mr. Irving's church in Regent Square, are delusive and visionary. Breaking out in Scotland in support of the evil figment of *universal pardon* they now exert themselves in Regent-square church as an adornment of that far deeper heresy which has issued from that sanctuary, which declares the *sinfulness* of the flesh of Christ.[12]

The *Morning Watch* retaliated that Irving had always emphasized Christ's sinlessness,[13] but such was the anxiety felt by many about Irving's Christology that writers otherwise sympathetic to the manifestations nevertheless often felt obliged to dissociate themselves from Irving's heterodoxy. Thomas Boys, the editor of the *Jewish Expositor,* was a rigorist, with no time for the apocrypha or continental neology, and had argued in a series of articles that miracles were a part of the Christian dispensation. Republishing the articles with a sympathetic account of Miss Fancourt's case, Boys maintained that 'where the doctrine of a Church or religious community is unsound, it does not follow that the community can have no miraculous manifestations'.[14]

Significantly, Boys nevertheless felt the need to reject Irving's teaching on Christ's humanity though he found extenuating circumstances. Claiming that the controversy had unmasked docetic tendencies among Irving's critics, he suggested that Irving's errors were only

11 Stunt, *Awakening*, 233–4.

12 *Record*, 21 November 1831.

13 *MW* 5 (Dec. 1831), 182–3.

14 Thomas Boys, *The Christian Dispensation Miraculous (republished from the Jewish Expositor)* (2nd edn, London, 1832), 104.

the product of circumstance and that, given time, the great preacher might abandon the language of peccability. In the meanwhile he felt that the religious world could be thankful that covert forms of Arian and Sabellian heresy had come to the surface and been recognized for the errors that they were. Clinging to straws of this sort, he was evidently troubled by the accusation that 'those who exercise [the gifts] testify expressly to that view [Irving's] of Christ's humanity', but he was not sufficiently troubled to question their validity or to conclude that 'the gifts and the heresy must stand or fall together'. Nevertheless, these anxieties were further exacerbated by critics who said that the manifestations could be the work of an evil spirit.

In the days of primitive Christianity, faced with rival pagan oracles such as the utterances of the Pythoness at Delphi, the apostle John had made clear that ecstatic utterances could be demonic and had instructed believers to 'try the spirits whether they be of God' (1 John 4, 1). While St Paul insisted that the speaker must be able to confess that 'Jesus is the Lord' (1 Cor 12, 3), the Johannine seal of divine authenticity was that the inspired speaker would be able to confess that 'Jesus Christ is come in the flesh' (1 John 4, 2). The second of these confessions had an understandable appeal to those emphasizing Christ's humanity. Norton, in his earliest account of the Clydeside utterances, tells us that because of such apostolic injunctions 'a meeting was held for this purpose, when, after prayer that utterance might be given, a confession of Christ was made by each one of the gifted persons present.' Norton's transcription of the Macdonald brothers' confession includes repeated, explicit allusions to Christ's human nature: 'Jesus, son of the Virgin's womb . . . Jesus in our nature . . . Glory to the word made flesh! Glory to the incarnate God . . . Glory to the Unity with our flesh . . . Glory to the risen Man! To God in our nature . . .'.[15]

* * *

The question of confessional authentication was an issue that evidently troubled Irving, particularly when he learnt of the case of the Gloucestershire clergyman, Edmund Probyn, in whose household several prophetic manifestations had occurred with the active participation of his young twin children.[16] Irving had been somewhat reassured to learn that Probyn and his curate had 'tried the spirits'. The

15 Norton, *Neglected Truths*, 396–7.

16 For a fuller discussion of this episode, see T. C. F. Stunt, ' "Trying the Spirits": the Case of the Gloucestershire Clergyman (1831)', *JEH* 39 (1988), 95–105.

curate had called upon the spirit in one of the twins to 'confess that Jesus Christ is come in the flesh' but was met with a loud refusal and shortly afterwards the boy was delivered and the spirit left him.[17]

However, it is clear from his letter, written to Probyn on 10 November 1831, that Irving had doubts about such a simple confessional test[18] and wanted further authentication of the prophets in his own church. Gathering the 'gifted' and some of the 'most judicious' brethren,[19] he read them Probyn's letters. The sequel as he described it to Probyn is instructive, and as it is not easily available for consultation, worth quoting at length:

> Before the second letter was half read, one of them [Miss E. Cardale] was made to speak in great power calling to try the Spirits, whereupon I rose in the middle of her utterance and put the question, 'Oh Spirit, believest thou that Christ is come in the flesh?' She continued to prophesy in the most glorious and powerful manner, confessing and adoring and lauding the humiliation of Christ and his glory. One joined and another, but they all, as it were in a divine chorus, went on testifying to the whole truth. Then singly one and another took up the burden of their Redeemer's work, and did so magnify and celebrate the Lord as that I never heard the like. So that we were all lost in admiration of the unity of the Spirit, and the superabundant evidence which he gave us of his being the Holy Ghost . . . [They then sang a psalm.] The Spirit having thus entirely satisfied us of his oneness with Jesus Christ, we proceeded after a second prayer to deliberate concerning you and your dear children. I had just opened my mouth intending to shew my mind, which was that you must not be content with categorical answers but observe whether it be the habit and delight of the Spirit to testify unto the personal work of Jesus in the flesh and his present work and glory in the spirit, when Mr Taplin was made to speak with great power these words first in a tongue and then in our own

17 *MW* 5 (March 1832), 152–4.

18 E. Irving to E. Probyn, 10 Nov. 1831 (Terling, Essex; Strutt Archives). H. Drummond's letter to J. J. Strutt of the same date is in the same collection. In places it provides specific details, which I have sometimes added in square brackets, but in general Irving's account is slightly more dispassionate.

19 Drummond's letter indicates that those present (other than Irving and himself) were Cardale, his wife and sister, William and Mary [née Campbell] Caird, Miss Hall, Taplin, Tudor and Armstrong [future apostles], Dr J. Thompson, D. Brown [Irving's assistant minister], and a Mr Barclay.

> language, 'Tell him to hear no Spirit that testifies of *himself*, but that testifies of *Jesus*, that he was crucified in the flesh, in our flesh, in our fallen flesh, and that he reigneth in the heavens, and that he will be glorified in his members who shall reign with him on the earth for ever and ever![20]

Further 'prophesyings' by Miss E. Cardale and others proclaimed 'that there was no safety or protection against the evil spirits but by abiding in Jesus and watching our most secret thoughts'.[21] The narrative then continues:

> We then proceeded to deliberate and were all of one mind, that the spirit [in the Probyn twins] was an evil spirit, and that it answering yes or no to the test was no proof, and that this is not the thing intended by *confessing* but a thorough impenetration of their utterances with the spirit of that truth, and that you *must seek to be filled with the spirit in order to discern this*. It was observed by one [Cardale] that Hermas in his Shepherd gives it as a test of the evil spirits that they desired to be consulted like the oracles, but the Holy Ghost speaks full of his own will.[22]

We have quoted from this letter at some length partly because it is not easily available for consultation, but also because it provides several useful pointers to Irving's thinking on the authentication of prophecy. One striking aspect of his response is that although at first he sought to comply with the Johannine test, he soon fell back on very much more temperamental and subjective modes of reassurance. 'Abiding in Jesus and watching our most secret thoughts' is probably the least precise mechanism for validation as it is entirely concerned with the condition of the observer as opposed to the conduct of the prophet. It is thus on a par with Irving's later advice to Probyn that he 'must seek to be filled with the [Holy S]pirit' if he is to discern the mind of the spirit speaking in his children. On the other hand, when he seeks objectively to consider the spirit's utterances, Irving adopts the suggestion that a true 'confession' on the part of the spirit should be found in the overall

20 E. Irving to E. Probyn, 10 Nov. 1831 (Terling, Essex; Strutt Archives), n.p.

21 Ibid.

22 *The Shepherd of Hermas*, Book II (Mandates) 11, 1–3, see *The Apostolic Fathers*, ed. Kirsopp Lake, Loeb Classical Library, 2 vols (London, 1917–19), 2: 111; but Cardale would only have been familiar with the text in William Wake, *The Genuine Epistles of the Apostolic Fathers* (1693), based on Latin manuscripts. For this passage, see J. Reiling, *Hermas and Christian Prophecy: a Study of the Eleventh Mandate* (Leiden, 1973).

'impenetration' of the utterances rather than in a single 'categorical' answer of 'yes' or 'no'. Recalling that Irving had long been an opponent of any use of the apocrypha, we should note that he was ready to base this position on a non-canonical scripture. It is also significant that when Taplin, the leading prophet in Irving's congregation, testified to the humanity of Christ, he adopted the specific language for which Irving had been accused of heresy, referring to Christ 'crucified . . . in our fallen flesh'.[23] In this respect he was far from being alone, as is apparent from Drummond's account of the same occasion where we learn that Miss Cardale

> and all the gifted persons present broke out in one simultaneous crash like the voice of many waters, & continued crying vehemently for about the space of half an hour[:] 'The Lord of glory was the virgin's Child, the babe in the manger was Jehovah's fellow, The King on the throne of Heaven was compassed with sinful flesh, He who died on the Cross shall come to reign over this earth for ever,' &c &c with a great deal more to the same effect.[24]

Doubtless the prophetic adoption of his Christology was reassuring for Irving, but for others it could be a stumbling block. However sympathetic they may have been to the piety and spirituality of those involved, both Noel and Boys found the doctrinal issue a cause for incredulity or at least anxiety. In some cases believers were so impressed by the signs of divine intervention that they were able temporarily to shelve these doctrinal concerns. When Henry Bulteel, an uncompromising Calvinist, became 'satisfied of the genuineness of the miracles of healing and tongues', his friend John Hill was pained to find that he was 'convinced moreover of their doctrine of general redemption'. Significantly, he reverted to his former Calvinism when he later concluded that the signs were of demonic origin, details of which he confided to another disillusioned prophet, Robert Baxter.[25]

In 1832 Robert Baxter published an extended critique of the early Irvingite 'prophesyings' which he now considered to have been spurious and (by implication) demonic. The exposure was all the more devastating because he had been a participant in the manifestations for

23 E. Irving to E. Probyn, 10 Nov. 1831 (Terling, Essex; Strutt Archives), n.p.

24 Partly quoted in Stunt, 'Gloucestershire Clergyman', 103, but the recipient of Drummond's letter [Strutt] is wrongly given as Probyn.

25 For an extract of Bulteel's disillusioned letter to Baxter, see Carter, *Anglican Evangelicals*, 279–80; cf. Stunt, *From Awakening*, 269, 271.

several months. He now agreed with Irving that the 'categorical' confession had been insufficient, but he also argued that, in November 1831, Irving had been disqualified from trying the spirits because of his 'own erroneous views concerning Christ's flesh'.[26] It seems that eventually Baxter's doctrinal orthodoxy had caught up with him, leading him to abandon a stance, which he had adopted for emotional or 'temperamental' reasons. Another who lost his earlier enthusiasm for the phenomena was Hugh McNeile. By December 1831 he was maintaining that the prophets did not comply with St Paul's instructions to the Corinthians about interpretation, but he also had more pragmatic objections. Those exercising the gifts tended to be self-complacent and to set themselves apart as superior to other Christians. 'A feeling is inculcated and cherished amongst them of their being martyrs . . . making a cross of this, glorying in suffering for conscience sake . . .'.[27] In short, the gifts seemed to minister to pride.

* * *

Whether Irving's Christology was heterodox or not is a question with which we are not concerned. Although doctrinal factors were adduced in opposition to (and sometimes in support of) the validity of the phenomena, they appear usually to have been of secondary significance. With the exception of Noel who avowed that he felt 'more sympathy with an honest though hurtful enthusiasm, than I can with a sour and supercilious orthodoxy',[28] more often than not, critics only used the doctrinal issue to confirm positions, which they had previously adopted for other reasons. Although Coleridge had correctly identified the criticism that Irving's readers might raise, perhaps he had not realized fully the emotional reservations that fuelled them.

Wooster School, Danbury, CT

26 Robert Baxter, *Narrative of the Facts characterizing the spiritual manifestations in Mr Irving's congregation. . .* (2nd edn, London, 1833), 131–2. Drummond claimed that Baxter's information 'was imperfect as to the facts', but did not take up the question of Irving's 'erroneous' Christology: [H. Drummond], *The Spirit in Mr Baxter tried by Scripture* (London, 1833), 38.

27 H. McNeile, 'The Nature and Design of Miracles', *The Preacher* 3 (Dec. 1831), 237, 244–5.

28 Noel, *Remarks*, 29.

'SIGNS AND WONDERS THAT LIE': UNLIKELY POLEMICAL OUTBURSTS AGAINST THE EARLY PENTECOSTAL MOVEMENT IN BRITAIN

by TIM WALSH

THE phenomenon of speaking in tongues was manifested at All Saints' Parish Church, Monkwearmouth, Sunderland, during the autumn of 1907. This outbreak rapidly became the object of criticism and opposition from a variety of sources, but one of the most vehement, if unexpected, emanated from an organization known as the Pentecostal League of Prayer. This non-denominational body had been established by Reader Harris Q. C. in 1891, and integral to its aims was the promotion of 'Holiness' teaching which advocated an experience of sanctification distinct from, and subsequent to, conversion. A network of branches had been established across England, and the Revd Alexander A. Boddy, vicar of All Saints', had been actively involved in its Sunderland branch prior to 1907. Harris, who was in Sunderland at the time of this new departure in All Saints', objected to the identification of the 'gift of tongues' with what he perceived to be genuine Pentecostal experience. One of the principal ironies of the situation is that his opposition was promulgated in the Pentecostal League's periodical *Tongues of Fire*. It is contested that this local controversy represents not only a curious chapter in the history of Protestant polemics against the miraculous, but that it embodied broader ramifications than might first appear, not least in the impetus generated toward the establishment of distinctive Pentecostal identity and orthodoxy.

* * *

On 5 October 1907, the London *Daily Chronicle* reported:

> Sunderland is in the grip of religious revival. It is not an ordinary revival, though it is accompanied by some of the more commonplace phases of – dare I say? – hysteria, which made such a strange figure of Evan Roberts in Wales. . . . According to the Revd Alexander A. Boddy, the vicar of All Saints, Monkwearmouth, Sunderland, 'More than 20,000 people throughout the world are now so filled with the Holy Ghost that they are speaking in

> tongues'. Of these, Mr. Boddy informs me, about twenty are to be found in his parish.[1]

The writer noted that this 'strange landscape' boasted its own Evan Roberts, 'Pastor Barratt, Cornishman, naturalised Norwegian, a dreamer if you will: a madman if you like', but nothing less than the 'heart and soul of a religious movement before which others pale'.[2] Thomas Ball Barratt (1862–1940) had undergone a Pentecostal experience while on a visit to New York during the latter half of 1906 that radically altered his subsequent life and ministry. What transpired after his return to Norway would earn him the posthumous designations 'spiritual father'[3] and 'apostle'[4] of the Pentecostal movement in Europe.

Alexander Boddy (1854–1930),[5] who displayed a keen interest in the phenomenon of the Welsh Revival of 1904–06, and had for some time held 'waiting meetings' for the purpose of attaining an anticipated spiritual outpouring, succeeded in convincing Barratt to visit Sunderland. It was during the course of an extended mission held at All Saints' during the autumn of 1907 that claims were made that not only had individuals been 'baptised in the Spirit', but that this had been accompanied by the spiritual gift of 'speaking in tongues'.[6]

1 'Revival Scenes: Alleged Healing', *Daily Chronicle*, 5 October 1907, 6; a more reverential account of 'the strange figure' at the centre of the Welsh Revival of 1904–6 is to be found in D. M. Phillips, *Evan Roberts: the Great Welsh Revivalist and his Work* (7th edn, London, 1923).

2 'Revival Scenes', 6. In the memoir which he later compiled, Barratt commented on the 'sweet epithets' to which he had been subjected, see T. B. Barratt, *When the Fire Fell and An Outline of My Life* (Oslo, 1927), 155.

3 Donald Gee, *The Pentecostal Movement: a Short History and an Interpretation for British Readers* (London, 1941), 180. This was for many years the sole significant work which dealt with British Pentecostalism's expansion during its early decades. A denominational leader and chronicler, Gee has been described as 'Pentecostalism's most penetrating thinker and most prodigious writer', see Ian M. Randall, *Evangelical Experiences: a Study in the Spirituality of English Evangelicalism, 1918–1939* (Carlisle, 1999), 210.

4 Nils Bloch-Hoell, *The Pentecostal Movement: its Origins, Development and Distinctive Character* (Oslo and London, 1964), 75.

5 Alexander Boddy is the best documented leader of early British Pentecostalism, a movement whose genesis has attracted scant scholarly attention. See Edith Blumhofer, 'Alexander Boddy and the Rise of Pentecostalism in Great Britain', *Pneuma: The Journal of the Society for Pentecostal Studies* 8:1 (Spring 1986), 31–40; Peter Lavin, *Alexander Boddy: Pastor and Prophet* (Sunderland, 1986); Martin Robinson, 'The Charismatic Anglican – Historical and Contemporary: a Comparison of the Life and Work of Alexander Boddy (1854–1930) and Michael C. Harper', unpublished M. Litt. thesis, University of Birmingham, 1976.

6 See Boddy's 'Tongues in Sunderland: the Beginnings of a Pentecost for England', unpublished pamphlet from the Donald Gee Centre for Charismatic and Pentecostal Research, Mattersey Hall, Doncaster [hereafter: DGC].

It must be observed, perhaps surprisingly, that opposition and criticism was not limited to what could be dismissed as a predictably hostile secular press. Grant Wacker's extensive explorations of early Pentecostalism in North America have informed his observation that 'the most dangerous enemies were ostensible colleagues in other parts of the Holy Ghost camp'.[7] In similar vein, some of the most vociferous and vehement critics of what was occurring during Barratt's endeavours in Sunderland were those who themselves shared the language of 'Pentecost' and the 'baptism of the Holy Spirit'.

* * *

Land's identification of Wesleyan-holiness as the 'spiritual fundament', which predated and influenced its emergence, has become something of a truism in studies of Pentecostalism.[8] What has been deemed Methodism's 'grand *depositum* of spiritual truth'[9] regained further impetus from nineteenth-century Holiness advocates.[10] Of the nuances which emerged, one of the most significant, and certainly the most pertinent to developments in Sunderland, was the association of this subsequent phase or experience with a 'filling' or 'Baptism of the Holy Spirit'.[11] For instance, Andrew Murray, one of the most prolific exponents of Holiness teaching, publicized this position in works such as *The Full Blessing of Pentecost: the One Thing Needful*.[12] According to Gee, the term 'Baptism of the Holy Spirit' was employed by Holiness advocates to convey a 'sense of a real spiritual crisis for the Christian subsequent to regener-

7 Grant Wacker, *Heaven Below: Early Pentecostals and American Culture* (Cambridge, MA, and London, 2001), 179.

8 Steven J. Land, *Pentecostal Spirituality: a Passion for the Kingdom* (Sheffield, 2001), 207; this aspect has been explored in Melvin E. Dieter, 'Wesleyan-Holiness Aspects of Pentecostal Origins', in Vinson Synan, ed., *Aspects of Pentecostal-Charismatic Origins* (Plainfield, NJ, 1975), 55–80, and in Donald W. Dayton, *Theological Roots of Pentecostalism*, Studies in Evangelicalism 5 (Metuchen, NJ, and London, 1987), 65–84.

9 Dieter, 'Wesleyan-Holiness Aspects', 60.

10 For a comprehensive treatment of the British situation see David Bebbington, *Holiness in Nineteenth-Century England: the 1998 Didsbury Lectures* (Carlisle, 2000).

11 This development has been documented in Donald W. Dayton, 'From Christian Perfection to the "Baptism in the Holy Spirit"', in *Aspects of Pentecostal-Charismatic Origins*, 39–54; for a British perspective on this 'pneumatological shift', see Randall, *Evangelical Experiences*, 30–3.

12 Andrew Murray, *The Full Blessing of Pentecost: the One thing Needful* (London, 1908; repr. 1944); for bibliographical details relating to the Holiness Movement in America and Britain, see Charles Edwin Jones, *A Guide to the Study of the Holiness Movement* (Metuchen, NJ, 1974).

ation'.[13] The emphasis was firmly upon 'cleansing from sin', attendant upon the agencies of a 'purifying baptism' and a 'refining fire'.[14]

Such conceptions are evident in the name chosen by the lawyer Richard Reader Harris (1847–1909) for the organization which he founded in 1891. The Pentecostal League of Prayer promoted itself as 'an inter-denominational union of Christian people', who employed prayer as the chief instrument in the attainment of their three-fold aims: 'the filling of the Holy Spirit for all believers', 'revival in the Churches', and 'the spread of Scriptural holiness'.[15] Harris's daughter and biographer recorded that by 1898 the Pentecostal League of Prayer had thirty 'Centres' in London, and more than a hundred beyond the metropolis. She stated that 'among the provincial centres, Plymouth and Sunderland were particularly flourishing'.[16] Boddy had been publicized as one of the leading clergymen in the Sunderland 'Centre',[17] and was afforded the distinction of addressing the League's annual conference held at Speke Hall, Battersea, on 3 May 1905.[18] It was while at a Pentecostal League Convention in Sunderland that Harris would hear, disapprove of, and ultimately condemn in the strongest terms, the 'Pentecostal' phenomena then occurring in the Parish Hall of one of the hitherto most loyal and respected members of the local branch of his organization.

It is interesting to observe that Harris had previously exhibited an aptitude for controversy and polemic when he ably and dramatically 'took up the cudgels' in defence of his version of Holiness orthodoxy.[19] It would appear that this was characteristic of the man who had simultaneously decried the 'energy of the Church for worldly matters', while lamenting the 'apathy of the Church in spiritual matters'.[20] He had gone so far as to publicize his recommendation that some churches be boarded up and marked with a warning: 'Condemned as a spiritual

13 Gee, *The Pentecostal Movement*, 4.

14 Ibid.

15 Mary Reader Hooker, *Adventures of an Agnostic: Life and Letters of Reader Harris Q.C.* (London, 1959), 111.

16 Hooker, *Adventures of an Agnostic*, 116.

17 'Pentecostal League Centre Meetings', *Tongues of Fire*, February 1905, 11.

18 'The Annual Meetings', *Tongues of Fire*, June 1905, 3.

19 Jack Ford, *What the Holiness People Believe: a Mid-Century Review of Holiness Teaching among the Holiness Groups of Britain*, J. D. Drysdale Memorial Lecture (Birkenhead, 1954), 51.

20 'The Pentecostal Baptism', *Tongues of Fire*, June 1905, 7.

insanitary area'.[21] This stridency would be redeployed as a local controversy with significantly broader ramifications ensued.

* * *

The irony of the situation was captured by a headline in the *Sunderland Echo* which read 'Speaking in Tongues: Rival Pentecostals'.[22] The report noted, with at least a modicum of bewilderment, that there was 'evidently something of a split –at any rate a divergence of opinion– in the Pentecostal agencies', as Pastor Barratt, then engaged in a series of services at All Saints' Parish Hall, had criticised 'some recent utterances' made by the founder of the Pentecostal League of Prayer. On the night in question, the hall was full, owing 'doubtless', in the estimation of the reporter, to the unusual nature of both the spiritual manifestations that had been occurring, and the controversy they had generated. It was no surprise that the evening was devoted to the central issue that had precipitated the contention, the subject of 'speaking in tongues'.[23]

The proceedings were opened by Revd A. A. Boddy who furnished the explanation for the phenomenon that 'they became so filled with the Holy Ghost, that joy flowed through their being and out of their mouths. They had wondrous joy when they felt the Holy Ghost speaking through them'.[24] The experience was described as 'a rapture', and Boddy expressed the opinion that 'for some centuries, owing to unbelief and indifference in the Church, this gift had been neglected'.[25] But he did think it possible that 'all the time there had been secretly those who had been speaking in tongues'.[26] He claimed to have received letters from elderly people who said that in the past they had received this divine endowment, but that they had been 'turned out' of their churches and derided as 'mad'.[27]

Boddy then went on to speak, somewhat curiously, 'in high terms of the purity of mind of Pastor Barratt'.[28] This assertion is more comprehensible when considered in the light of criticisms that were at that

21 Ibid. It is interesting to note that in his survey Charles Booth presented an unflattering assessment of Harris and his *modus operandi*: see Charles Booth, *Life and Labour of the People of London*, 3rd ser., Religious Influences, 7 vols (London, 1902), 5: 222–5.

22 'Speaking in Tongues: Rival Pentecostals', *Sunderland Echo*, 2 October 1907, 4.

23 Ibid.

24 Ibid.

25 Ibid.

26 Ibid.

27 Ibid.

28 Ibid.

time being advanced by Jessie Penn-Lewis, a teacher of some prominence within Holiness circles.[29] Mrs Penn-Lewis, as she was known, wrote to Boddy to inform him that on the authority of 'balanced, deeply taught souls in Sweden', she had become persuaded that Barratt 'had working through him a strong force of animal magnetism, making him almost like a galvanic battery'.[30] She expressed her conviction that 'there is being transmitted into the bodies of some of the most devoted children of God a power which for years will make them open to terrible onslaughts of the devil and cause them untold suffering'. She predicted that 'their awakening will be bitter, their nervous system wrecked, and the shock to their faith terrible'.[31]

An inescapable feature of the criticism and condemnations issued against the 'baptism of the Spirit', as it was then being propounded in All Saints', was the forthrightness and vehemence with which they were issued. Wacker observes that, on the other side of the Atlantic, what he designates 'radical evangelicals' did not engage early Pentecostals in detached or disinterested discussions, but hurled themselves into a 'brawl fought without rules, in the mud, with every rhetorical weapon at their disposal'.[32] While it would appear that North American opponents were slow in perceiving the threat and instigating their polemical onslaught, their British counterparts swiftly 'took up the cudgels' with conspicuous alacrity.

Mrs Penn-Lewis embarked on an extensive dissection and condemnation of this new phenomenon within weeks of the close of Barratt's mission in Sunderland. This appeared in the form of eight serializations in *The Christian* between January and March 1908, and attributed susceptibility to the recently perpetrated errors to the fact that the 'professing Church of God' had been for so long 'sunk in carnal ease and worldliness'. It was in her estimation consequent upon 'ignorance of the forces in the supernatural realm' that 'the Adversary, as an angel of light' had been able to 'lead astray some of the very elect'. Her prognosis

[29] Mary N. Garrard, *Mrs. Penn-Lewis: a Memoir* (London, 1930; repr. Bournemouth, 1947), 178, 181, 194; Mrs Penn-Lewis co-wrote a book with the central figure of the Welsh Revival in which they advocated a 'Holiness' conception of the 'Baptism of the Holy Spirit': Jessie Penn-Lewis and Evan Roberts, *War on the Saints* (3rd edn, Leicester, 1922), 282–5.

[30] DGC, Jessie Penn-Lewis, Letter to Alexander A. Boddy, 9 November 1907.

[31] DGC, Jessie Penn-Lewis, Letter to Alexander A. Boddy, 28 October 1907.

[32] Wacker uses the term 'radical evangelicals' to incorporate both principal American Holiness groupings, 'Holiness Wesleyans' and 'Higher Life fundamentalists': see his 'Travail of a Broken Family: Evangelical Responses to Pentecostalism in America, 1906–1916', *JEH* 47 (1996), 505–28, 506–8, 510.

was bleak: 'The marks will be left on the Church of Christ in sad shipwreck of faith and usefulness, in many who have been deceived'.[33]

An equally notable feature of this period of ideological divergence was the depth of conviction displayed by those who had but recently acquired this nuanced view of the 'baptism of the Spirit'. While Mrs Boddy had received her 'baptism' on 11 September, Alexander would not achieve his spiritual apotheosis until December 2, after Barratt's departure. What is remarkable is that this earnest Anglican vicar had so manifestly risked his reputation in the defence of an experience he had not yet attained during the autumn of 1907. He would host an informal event twelve months later to mark the anniversary of his reception of the 'sign and gift of 'Tongues'.' With the forty or fifty individuals who then gathered in the parish hall, Boddy offered thanksgiving for having been kept 'steadfast' through what he described as 'times of awful fiery testing'.[34]

Principal among such 'tests' was the address which Boddy had listened to with pain in Sunderland's Victoria Hall. This was the venue in which Reader Harris hosted meetings of the local branch of his organization. Boddy's former fellow advocate in the 'Pentecostal' cause had summarily denounced what he held to be a deviant aberration as 'tainted with uncleanness, immorality and wickedness'. In its defence Boddy expressed the conviction that the people who had embraced this conception of the Baptism of the Spirit were 'among the purest in the world'.[35]

The *Sunderland Echo* reported that on the night of 1 October 1907, Barratt had frankly informed those assembled at All Saints' that Mr Reader Harris had belittled 'speaking in tongues' by his assertions that it was the least of all spiritual gifts, and that 'the whole thing was full of danger and fanaticism'. Barratt advanced certain 'reasonings' which aimed to demonstrate that Mr Harris had 'fallen into a gross mistake'. No gift of the Holy Ghost could be deemed insignificant, and it was 'speaking in tongues' which had marked the birth of the Christian Church at Pentecost, which latterly had been the cause of much spiritual awakening across the world, and the ultimate purpose of which was to bring the Church 'nearer to Heaven'. In response to the charge of

33 Jessie Penn-Lewis, 'An Hour of Peril', *The Christian*, 9 January 1908, 12.
34 'Sunderland: A Joyful Gathering', *Confidence*, December 1908, 7–8.
35 'Speaking in Tongues: Rival Pentecostals', 4.

fanaticism, Barratt remarked that he had 'never seen more fanaticism anywhere than was shown by opponents of that movement'.[36]

He went on to refute at length Harris's insinuation of 'a weakening of the marriage tie'. The charge that 'a carnal life seemed to haunt movements of that kind' was deemed so false and unfair that it 'could not but grieve upright Christians that anything so abominable should have been intimated'. He remarked that the Pentecostal League had also 'suffered in that respect', but that it could not be dismissed as 'haunted by carnality' on that account. Furthermore, the fact that Harris had 'flung the taint of carnality against them all' was again deemed an insult to the thousands of devout souls who had earnestly and sincerely sought and attained this spiritual experience.[37]

Barratt found a point of agreement with Harris, whom he mischievously referred to as 'a King Charles head in the way of cropping up': a mutual denunciation of Spiritualism, 'the great remedy for which was Pentecostal experience'.[38] Yet beyond a shared parlance, they would have found little common ground in their diverging conceptions of the Pentecostal 'Baptism' which both, in varying ways, held to be nothing less than the spiritual panacea to all such ills, and the goal of the authentic Christian spiritual life.

* * *

The supreme irony of this divergence in Pentecostal taxonomy was the fact that a primary instrument employed in the denunciation of the gift of tongues was *Tongues of Fire*, the official organ of the Pentecostal League of Prayer. It was here that Pentecostal phenomena, as propounded by Barratt, were denounced as 'signs and wonders that lie'.[39] Harris informed his readership in the immediate aftermath of developments in Sunderland that what had occurred there bore 'those marks of counterfeit given to us in Scripture: confusion, errors of conduct, and the loosening of the marriage tie'. This phenomenon was something 'from which all true believers and indeed all decent people should hold aloof'. His final fateful conclusion would exclude compromise or accommodation in the future. He stated: 'Far be it from me to

36 Ibid.
37 Ibid.
38 Ibid.
39 Oswald Chambers, 'Tongues and Testing', *Tongues of Fire*, January 1908, 3.

discount any real work of God; but I desire to avoid – and to warn others to avoid – Satanic counterfeit'.[40]

Objections, many of which were similar to those made by Harris, were also advanced by the Revd Oswald Chambers (1874–1917), who would become leader of the re-designated 'League of Prayer' after the death of its founder in 1909. Indeed some of his trenchantly stated denunciations bordered on the apocalyptic: 'Supernatural signs and wonders, literally happening, are permitted by God to prove His people, and are allowed to mislead those who have not obeyed the Truth'.[41]

The identification of 'tongues' with the 'baptism of the Spirit' was equated with the pursuit of an additional sign or idol, a practice denounced in Deuteronomy 13, 2: 'And the sign or the wonder come to pass, whereof He spake unto thee, saying, *Let us go after other gods, which thou hast not known, and let us serve them*'. His prognosis was direct and damning: 'the children of God are ignorant where they ought to know'. Hosea 4, 6, was cited as a pithy indictment: 'My people are destroyed for lack of knowledge'. The outcome for the misguided, particularly those in positions of leadership, was nothing short of fearsome:

> This present 'Tongues Movement' is by permission of God to test His people . . . Let a teacher once get the *set* of the people off our Lord Jesus Christ to any sign or manifestations or power, and he is deserving in this day of as severe and drastic a rebuke as Peter gave Simon Magus: 'For I see that thou wilt become a gall root of bitterness and a bond of iniquity'. Acts viii, 23.[42]

Yet the remedy of the Book of Acts was itself deemed inadequate to the immediate exigency and Chambers pointed toward a 'more drastic measure than rebuke' as advocated in Deuteronomy 13, 5. In this passage, the errant 'Prophet' or 'dreamer of dreams' was to be put to death. What precisely was being advocated for the reader of *Tongues of Fire* in the early years of the twentieth century remains in the realms of conjecture. However it can be stated without equivocation that the 'League of Prayer', the designation 'Pentecostal' having been very deliberately elided from its nomenclature, was engaging in a very definite dissociation from a conception of 'Pentecostal' teaching which could not be countenanced.

40 Reader Harris, 'The Gift of Tongues', *Tongues of Fire*, November 1907, 1.
41 Chambers, 'Tongues and Testing', 3.
42 Ibid.

* * *

It is demonstrably the case that Pentecostalism was at a tentative stage of its evolution in Britain. Robinson surmises that Boddy must have entertained ambivalent feelings toward the end of 1907: a sense of fulfilment can only have been tempered by frustration and unease at the hurtful and damaging controversy that had also taken place. It was precisely in such a situation that the qualities of this resourceful Anglican vicar would come to the fore: 'The movement had not found a ready acceptance. Sunderland was now both famous and notorious. Much would now depend on the leadership of Alexander Alfred Boddy'.[43]

It has been observed that, although spurned, Pentecostalism brought 'vigorous reinforcement' to the conservative wing of Evangelicalism. The fissiparous nature of the American Holiness movement, which was mirrored in its British counterpart, rendered what Bebbington has termed the Holiness 'sectarian fringe', to be, in objective terms, 'remarkably small-scale'.[44] While both Holiness and emerging Pentecostal 'fringes' were diminutive in numerical terms in the first decade of the twentieth century, the contribution, witting and unwitting, of the former must be recorded as the histories of the latter, which has experienced exponential growth across a global platform,[45] come to be written.

Perhaps the most immediate and significant result of the climate of criticism was the fact that it precipitated and undeniably hastened the formulation of an emerging Pentecostal orthodoxy. A notable instance of this was the 'London Declaration', published before the end of 1909 in Boddy's uniquely influential *Confidence* magazine.[46] This had been formulated for the benefit of the many who were acknowledged to

43 Robinson, 'The Charismatic Anglican', 63.

44 David Bebbington, *Evangelicalism in Modern Britain: a History from the 1730s to the 1980s* (Grand Rapids, MI, 1992), 198, 178–9.

45 On the growth of Pentecostalism, see David Martin, *Tongues of Fire: the Explosion of Protestantism in Latin America* (Oxford, 1993) and idem, *Pentecostalism: the World their Parish* (Oxford, 2002); Harvey Cox, *Fire from Heaven: the Rise of Pentecostal Spirituality and the Reshaping of Religion in the Twenty-First Century* (London, 1996).

46 *Confidence*, edited by Boddy between 1908 and 1926, has been described as 'the official organ' and for a number of years 'the authoritative voice of British Pentecostal leadership': see Gee, *The Pentecostal Movement*, 45–6. It has more recently been the subject of doctoral research by Malcolm John Taylor, 'Publish and Be Blessed: a Case Study in Early Pentecostal Publishing History, 1908–1926', unpublished Ph.D. thesis, University of Birmingham, 1994.

have been 'stumbled' by criticism,[47] and served as both *credo* and *apologia* for the consolidating movement. The conviction of both the leaders who drafted this statement, and its signatories, was distinctly in support of a Baptism of the Spirit accompanied by *charismata*:

> It is clear from Holy Scripture that God bears witness both with signs and wonders, and with divers miracles, and distributions of the Holy Ghost, according to His own will. There is no hint in Holy Scripture that signs and miracles were to cease, or that gifts were to be withdrawn from the Body of Christ. It is more than possible that the weakness and unbelief of the Christian Church is the reason for these not being more generally manifested in these latter days.[48]

Perhaps the most striking feature of nascent Pentecostal orthodoxy was its deliberate faithfulness to Holiness teaching. While their American counterparts tended to reject their previously held Holiness ideals as not merely incomplete, but utterly misguided,[49] the first British Pentecostals, to a significant degree, retained and incorporated previously held schemas into emerging understandings. For the Holiness movement, a 'baptism of the Spirit' continued to be advocated, occurring without *charismata*, as the means of attaining purity and sanctification. The 'baptism' as postulated by Pentecostals constituted, in effect, a third blessing, the economy of salvation having been effectively expanded from two to three stages.[50] In contrast, Pentecostal sermons and articles promoted the notion that sanctification was the 'pre-requisite'[51] and precursor to a genuine baptism in the Spirit: many testified to having been 'saved', 'sanctified' and only subsequently 'baptised in the Holy Ghost'.[52]

The assertion that 'the Pentecostal Baptism with the Sign of Tongues is the most practical way of holiness that ever could be

47 'A London Declaration. The Baptism in the Holy Ghost: What we teach concerning the Evidence and the Results', *Confidence*, December 1909, 287–8.

48 Ibid.

49 Wacker, 'Travail of a Broken Family', 524.

50 See T. Rennie Warburton, 'Organisation and Change in a British Holiness Movement', in Bryan R. Wilson, ed., *Patterns of Sectarianism: Organisation and Ideology in Social and Religious Movements* (London, 1967), 106–37, 109.

51 R. T. Hackett, 'Heart Purity as a Necessary Preparation for Pentecost', *Confidence*, July 1912, 156.

52 'Croydon: Times of Blessing', *Confidence*, March 1912, 67.

known'[53] would not have gained the assent of Britain's principal Holiness advocates. Boddy had attended the Keswick Convention of 1907, where he disseminated the Pentecostal message by means of his pamphlet 'Pentecost for England (and other lands)'. Although 'thousands' of copies were distributed,[54] his overtures were not received by this, or any other, significant Holiness constituency. Instead, Holiness teachers such as Oswald Chambers continued to assert that the 'power from on high', which was to be expected after the resurrection,[55] was in no sense to be understood as 'magical' or associated with miracles of any kind. Rather it was held to be a power that would transform character and sanctify the faculties.[56] While nuanced understandings undeniably existed in relation to the precise nature of sanctification among various Holiness groups, a general consensus persisted that 'entire sanctification' and the 'baptism with the Holy Spirit' were two aspects of the same experience.[57]

* * *

Polemical 'outbursts', such as were precipitated by T. B. Barratt's mission in Sunderland during the autumn of 1907, served both to hasten the divergence and to steel the resolve of protagonists on both sides of this ideological divide. To the external observer it remains astonishing that so much combative energy could have been poured into such a tiny patch of theological space, but to those involved such rival apprehensions of the purpose for, and dynamics of, the 'baptism of the Spirit' were ultimate questions that probed not just their *modus operandi*, but their very reason for existence. This single issue became nothing less than 'the dynamite in the crevice'[58] that parted both long-standing colleagues and spiritual hemispheres. While Holiness advocates marshalled impressive resources to crush the menace in their

53 'Pentecostal Items', *Confidence*, March 1913, 61.

54 A. A. Boddy, 'The Pentecostal Movement: the Story of its Beginnings at Sunderland and its Present Position in Great Britain', *Confidence*, August 1910, 194. Although Boddy retrospectively refers to this pamphlet, no copies appear to have survived. The present writer has no reason to contradict Robinson's observation that 'unfortunately, to date, none are extant'. See 'The Charismatic Anglican', 42.

55 Luke 24, 49 and Acts 1, 8.

56 Oswald Chambers, *He Shall Glorify Me: Talks on the Holy Spirit and Other Themes* (London, 1941), 22, and idem, *If Thou Wilt Be Perfect: Talks on Spiritual Philosophy* (London, 1939), 16–18.

57 Ford, *What the Holiness People Believe*, 27, 42–51.

58 Wacker, 'Travail of a Broken Family', 509.

midst, what has been termed 'the enemy inside the gate'[59] proved all the more insidious because of its proximity. Individuals such as Reader Harris and Mrs Penn-Lewis, and the causes they represented, had urged an ongoing search for an uncompromising spiritual perfectionism, yet it was this very imperative which had spawned the offspring that appeared to threaten its progenitor's existence. Thus the new movement attracted its most vehement and venomous denunciations from its most unlikely critics.

For their part Barratt, Boddy and others endured the effusions of the 'heated brains and minds of those condemning the work'[60] and went on to consolidate the British manifestation of a phenomenon that would become global in its scope. Barratt's address to the annual Conference of the General Presbytery of the Pentecostal Assemblies of God in 1935[61] represented a return, not merely to the locality, but also to the very platform in Sunderland's Victoria Hall from which the movement, over whose birth he had presided, had been vilified and denounced. This homecoming embodied the concluding irony of this chapter in the history of signs, wonders and miracles, and the opposition that they have generated from unlikely sources within the Christian family.

University of Manchester

59 Ibid., 505–6, 526–7.

60 T. B. Barratt, 'The Truth about the Pentecostal Revival: Lecture given by Pastor T. B. Barratt in Zurich, London, and elsewhere', unpublished pamphlet now at the Pentecostal Archive, Regents Theological College, Nantwich, Cheshire [1908], 15.

61 Gee, *The Pentecostal Movement*, 180–1. Boddy never promoted or envisaged the establishment of a Pentecostal denomination or ecclesiastical structure; see his article 'Unity, not Uniformity', *Confidence*, March 1911, 60. This transition would only occur when his influence had considerably waned in the 1920s. On the origins and development of the Assemblies of God, see William K. Kay, *Inside Story: a History of the British Assemblies of God* (Mattersey, 1990) and idem, *Pentecostals in Britain* (Carlisle, 2000).

LIVING WITH SIGNS AND WONDERS: PARENTS AND CHILDREN IN EARLY PENTECOSTAL CULTURE

by GRANT WACKER*

'When I make a word do a lot of work like that', said Humpty Dumpty, 'I always pay it extra'.[1]

SINCE in this essay I make the word *Pentecostal* do a lot of work, I too think it is only fair to pay it extra. I use the term to refer to a religious movement that emerged from the vast and amorphous radical evangelical subculture in the United States in the sunset years of the nineteenth century. Like other radical evangelicals, Pentecostals fervently anticipated the Lord's imminent return, affirmed the miraculous healing of the body, and believed that the conversion experience should lead to another life-transforming event known as the baptism of the Holy Ghost. Unlike other radical evangelicals, however, Pentecostals also insisted that the baptism experience always manifested itself by speaking in 'unknown tongues'.[2]

Historians disagree about the exact sequence of events that initiated the Pentecostal movement, but most concur that an obscure revival that took place in the winter of 1901 in Topeka, Kansas, marked its primary point of origin. In the next ten years the full gospel (as partisans liked to call it) spread to most parts of the United States and many areas of the world. After World War II, Pentecostal or Pentecostal-like teachings and practices overflowed their historic boundaries in the radical evangelical tradition. They spilled into the Roman Catholic

* I wish to thank Pat Argue, Laurie Maffly-Kipp, Gary McGee, Brendan Pietsch, Cecil M. Robeck, Leigh Eric Schmidt, Russell Spittler, Angela Tarango, Mark Valerie, Wayne E. Warner and, especially, Andrew Stern, for critiquing an early draft of this essay. Cecil M. Robeck generously shared rare newspaper clippings.

1 Lewis Carroll, *Alice's Adventures in Wonderland and Through the Looking-Glass*, ed. Roger Lancelyn Green (New York, 1998), 191, also available at www.sundials.org/about/humpty.htm (consulted on 7 December 2003).

2 For the rich – and richly controverted – historiography of early Pentecostalism, see Augustus Cerillo Jr. and Grant Wacker, 'Bibliography and Historiography', in Stanley M. Burgess and Eduard M. Van der Maas, eds, *The New International Dictionary of Pentecostal and Charismatic Movements* (Grand Rapids, MI, 2002), 382–405. I do not know of any sustained scholarly treatment of children in early Pentecostal culture.

Church and into some of the mainline Protestant denominations. Converts in the latter two groups commonly called themselves Charismatics rather than Pentecostals but the family resemblance was unmistakable. In the latter half of the twentieth century, the Pentecostal message also spread across the Third World, sometimes through the work of American missionaries, sometimes in alliance with established Christian traditions, and sometimes amalgamated with indigenous faiths of less distinct orthodoxy. Today there may be ten million core adherents in the United States, another twenty million American sympathizers, and five-hundred million followers worldwide, making the Pentecostal-Charismatic movement the largest aggregation of Christians outside the Roman Catholic Church.[3]

This essay focuses on the Pentecostal movement's first generation, the men and women who largely defined its agenda for the rest of the century. The heart of their agenda was less to pray down the power than to figure out how to live with it – how to get from Sunday to Saturday. Their problem was, in short, the problem of prayers answered. Signs and wonders saturated early Pentecostal culture. Saints eagerly sought and regularly experienced diverse manifestations of miracles. Inexplicable healings, resurrections from the dead, utterances in unknown tongues, messages in unstudied foreign languages, levitations and portents in nature, angelic visitors and demonic invasions, apocalyptic journeys into the future – all formed the stuff of daily life. That being the case, the question was: how did routine life go on? When miracles took place constantly and everywhere, when the 'sky hung low' and the air crackled with the supernatural, how did one make a living, plan for the morrow and, sooner or later, face the hard realities of illness, old age, and death?

The answer was as simple as it was profound. The founders' genius lay in their ability to negotiate those two realms, the extraordinary and the ordinary, without compromising either one. They did it by holding fast to two convictions. First, the Holy Spirit literally took up residence in believers' physical bodies. That meant that the Holy Spirit governed every aspect of their lives. But it also meant something else. And the 'something else' takes us to the second conviction. Simply put, the Holy Spirit, thus incarnated, empowered believers to work miracles of

[3] Scattered passages in this essay draw from Grant Wacker, *Heaven Below: Early Pentecostals and American Culture* (Cambridge, MA, 2001), esp. 5–8, 128–9, 133, 271–2.

witness, healing, and material well being. Pray as if everything depended on God; work as if nothing did.

That dynamic – that seamless mixing of the extraordinary and the ordinary – expressed itself everywhere in early Pentecostal culture, including the relation between parents and children. That is the story I seek briefly to sketch in the following pages.

A word about method may be helpful. I conceive this essay as an exploration in 'lived religion'. As the American historian David D. Hall describes it, this approach deems practice – what people actually did – as the organizing centre of religion. It highlights the daily thinking and actions of the laity, focusing on the liminal space sandwiched between the sacred and the secular. Rather than trying to smooth out or explain away the ambiguous, overlapping, or contradictory meanings that ordinary people ascribed to their experience, lived religion looks for lay creativity in the face of prevailing notions about what was and was not respectable belief and behaviour. Recognizing the 'time-bound shape of practice', it assumes the likelihood of change over fixity and of contingency over inevitability. And holding suspect unexamined assumptions about the necessity of opposition between elite and popular, imposed and indigenous, and core and periphery, it looks instead for signs of complicity, exchange, and cross-fertilization. The goal, in short, is to accept rather than abridge or censure the 'messiness that leak[ed] into everyday life'.[4]

I also need to acknowledge what this paper does not do – what we might call its sins of omission. First, I largely describe the world parents saw, not the one children experienced. Second, my questions are not theirs. The original data are voluminous in quantity but they rarely provide direct answers to inquiries about children. We are left to tease responses from reluctant sources.

Finally, labels and boundaries. First-generation converts used *Holy Ghost* and *Holy Spirit* interchangeably, and they called themselves *Pentecostals*, *saints*, and *apostolics*, also interchangeably. I follow their practice. And since the boundaries between Pentecostals and other holiness folk remained porous until after World War I, I occasionally draw examples from the wider radical evangelical subculture when they aptly illustrate the point at hand.

4 David D. Hall, ed., *Lived Religion in America: toward a History of Practice* (Princeton, NJ, 1997), vii–xiii (editor's introduction).

* * *

At first glance, this essay's subject might have puzzled early Pentecostals. When it came to children, what was there to write about? After all, contrary to stereotype, the Holy Ghost movement was not conspicuously youthful. Indeed, scattered evidence, both statistical and anecdotal, suggests that the typical convert was more than a decade older than the average American (forty versus twenty-five), and measurably older than the average Protestant church member.[5] Moreover the casual reader of the early periodicals gains the impression that parents did not think very often or very deeply about the theological significance of children. Though adult saints frequently used endearing diminutives like 'O my little ones' when interpreting messages in tongues, those references were to themselves, not to actual children. One searches in vain for a sustained discussion of the meaning of covenant among generations, or of the family as a means of grace, or of the home as a site of Christian formation. Children, it seems, constituted a brute fact of life, some of them earnestly desired, some of them earnestly not desired, most of them just there.

Yet first appearances are deceiving. In fact, children paraded through the early literature frequently and prominently. They probably appeared most often in descriptions of public worship, especially at the revival's outset. Most sources failed to specify the children's exact age, but those that did normally spoke of boys and girls eight to fourteen. The phenomenon was perennial and to some extent transcultural, for the reports turned up year after year and on both sides of the Atlantic.[6] In short, far from overlooking children, Holy Ghost chroniclers went out of their way to note their presence.

But to say that saints often spoke about children in public worship is to tell only half the story. The other and more significant half is that they recurrently tried to depict children not as children at all but as miniature adults. With great admiration they told tales of children holding prayer meetings in the woods instead of playing among themselves. Like adults, they not only spoke in tongues but also spoke intelligible languages such as Spanish and Latin. Sometimes adults asked children to deliver the principal address of the meeting. The records never suggest that children prepared their talks as they might have

5 Wacker, *Heaven Below*, 206.

6 Sunderland *Daily Chronicle*, 8 October 1907; *South Wales Press*, 15 July 1914; *Apostolic Faith*, September 1906, 1.

done for a designated 'children's Sunday' in a mainline church. Rather, in the course of an otherwise routine worship service, a youngster would unexpectedly receive Holy Ghost baptism, speak in tongues, and then assume leadership of the meeting. Children displayed their newfound powers in various ways, by admonishing strangers of their evil ways, by singing in ecstatic speech, by visiting hospitals where they exercised gifts of healing, and by leading revival services.[7]

Admittedly, the relation between actual events and the narration of actual events remains elusive. Perhaps the children were, in their own minds, performing adult-like activities; or perhaps they were mimicking adults in some form of role-playing; or perhaps they were to some extent figments of adults' imaginations, allowing adults to see what they earnestly desired to see. Or all three at once. At this distance – maybe at any distance – it is hard to know for sure, and probably it does not matter a great deal even if we could.

However the primary texts are construed, the main point remains clear. In the eyes of the faithful, youthfulness posed no bar to spiritual maturity. A few youngsters such as Uldine Utley became professional child evangelists.[8] More common was adults' readiness to treat children and adolescents as if they possessed the wisdom of the ages. When the weekly *Pentecostal Holiness Advocate* was founded in 1917, young Walter Brack, all of eighteen, breathlessly wrote in to declare that after 'enjoying salvation' nearly three years, he still possessed the 'old time Holy Ghost religion' – and expected to 'stand true till Jesus comes'.[9] More telling than Brack's callow age was the editor's willingness to treat Brack's testimony as if it were the witness of a seasoned warrior in the Lord's army. In more routine ways too children enjoyed equality in the worshipping community. 'If you had knees', remembered Ida

[7] See, for example, according to theme, PRAYER MEETINGS: *Apostolic Faith*, January 1907, 2 [as several early Pentecostal periodicals bore the title *Apostolic Faith*, unless otherwise noted, all references in this essay denote the one edited in Los Angeles, 1906–8]; Max Wood Moorhead, in *Apostolic Faith*, September 1907, 4; *Apostolic Faith* [Oregon], September 1908, 1; *Glad Tidings*, January 1927, 13; HEALINGS: Max Wood Moorhead, in *Apostolic Faith*, September 1907, 4; XENOLALIA AND ADMONISHING STRANGERS: R. J. Scott, in *Apostolic Faith*, February–March 1907, 7; SINGING IN TONGUES: *Apostolic Faith*, June 1907, 1; preaching: *Apostolic Faith*, April 1907, 4; LEADING REVIVALS: *Apostolic Faith*, October 1906, 3; PROPHECY: L. Adams, in *Present Truth*, December 1909, 3; HORTATORY ROLE: Houston *Daily Post*, August 27, 1906.

[8] *Glad Tidings*, 1924, 1(?), lead article; Uldine Utley, *Why I Am a Preacher* (New York, 1931); Wacker, *Heaven Below*, 105, 305 and n. 48.

[9] Walter Brack, in *Pentecostal Holiness Advocate*, 10 January 1918, 3.

Robinson, bishop of the African American Greater Mount Zion Pentecostal Church of America, 'you were old enough to pray'.[10]

To be sure, the miniature adult theme was not unique to Pentecostals. Though historians have debated its pervasiveness in Christian history, there can be little doubt that rudiments of the idea have turned up in many times and places.[11] The family historian Margaret Bendroth reminds us that in the middle decades of the nineteenth century the miniature adult image gained special ascendancy among American mainline Protestants, and even in the early twentieth century it found expression in the concept of the child as a relatively complete 'seedling'.[12]

Thus the point here is not that early Pentecostals were unique but that they exaggerated tendencies found elsewhere, making them as stark as possible. The reason is easy to see. Spiritually gifted youngsters represented, in a radical and seemingly indisputable way, the Holy Ghost's operations in their midst. Such children could expatiate on the deep things of the Lord only because they, like the youthful Jesus engaging the teachers in the temple (Luke 2, 46), served as mouthpieces for the divine. Saints' accounts of child preachers rarely identified the minor by name, and almost never elaborated on the substantive content of their sermons. The child preachers themselves were really beside the point. When young women prophesied and old men listened it was because the Holy Spirit – not any ordinary mortal, and certainly not any ordinary mortal child – was actually doing the talking.

Nonetheless, in the end even the all-powerful Holy Spirit found himself subject to biology. When that happened – when children persisted in being children rather than robotic mouthpieces for the Divine Voice – they had to be controlled in two ways. The first was emotional: not loved too much. The second was physical: not indulged too much. Both efforts welled up from the same source: saints' resolve to achieve a purity so complete that the Holy Spirit's power would not be compromised by human limitations of any sort.

10 Robinson quoted in Harold Dean Trulear, 'The Mother as Symbolic Presence: Ida B. Robinson and the Mt. Sinai Holy Church', in James R. Goff Jr. and Grant Wacker, eds, *Portraits of a Generation: Early Pentecostal Leaders* (Fayetteville, AR, 2001), 309–24, 319.

11 See editor's introduction and various essays in Marcia J. Bunge, ed., *The Child in Christian Thought* (Grand Rapids, MI, 2001), esp. 12, 110, 162 and 302.

12 Margaret Lamberts Bendroth, *Growing up Protestant: Parents, Children, and Mainline Churches* (New Brunswick, NJ, 2002), 5.

* * *

Holy Ghost parents determined not to let natural affections compromise their love for the Work. If God's Spirit told them to abandon their offspring for the kingdom's sake, so be it. To be sure, leaving young ones at home in order to go out preaching the gospel was not unusual within the evangelical and especially the radical evangelical traditions. One thinks, for example, of Pearl S. Buck's *Fighting Angel*, which detailed her missionary father's ceaseless peregrinations in China, regardless of the personal cost to wife and children back home in the missionary compound.[13] But in the eyes of many contemporaries, Pentecostals appeared to go further than most, for they seemed almost oblivious to the pain of separation.[14]

The evidence for this claim is scattered yet convincing. Typical perhaps was the sojourn of Sister Anna Kelley, a member of Los Angeles's Upper Room Mission. In the spring of 1910 Kelley headed for China, leaving her husband and two young sons. The Pentecostal news account emphasized that she left without financial resources, trusting God to provide for all of her needs. We can reasonably infer that few of Kelley's friends found anything amiss in her action. The published story framed her decision as neither imprudent nor heroic but simply and matter-of-factly as the only acceptable response to the Holy Spirit's bidding.[15]

Pentecostals displayed their disregard for the conventions of family life in additional ways. For some, Christmas holidays came and went without a hint of recognition. Though in the early twentieth century Christmas had not yet turned into the marketing circus it soon became, to forego it, even in 1910, represented a self-conscious decision to subordinate the holiday to higher concerns.[16] For others, home life itself lurked as a distraction from the more pressing work at hand. The Quaker Pentecostal Levi Lupton complained that believers spent too much time and energy making 'comfortable homes and giving their

13 Pearl S. Buck, *Fighting Angel: the Portrait of a Soul* (New York, 1936); Bendroth, *Growing up Protestant*, 3, 21, 57–8.

14 Grant Wacker, 'Travail of a Broken Family: Radical Evangelical Responses to the Emergence of Pentecostalism in America, 1906–1916', in Edith L. Blumhofer *et al.*, eds, *Pentecostal Currents in American Protestantism* (Urbana, IL, 1999), 23–49, esp. 33–5.

15 *Upper Room*, March 1910, 4.

16 See for example D. C. O. Opperman, manuscript diary, Flower Pentecostal Heritage Center, Springfield, MO, Christmas Eve, 1905; Levi Lupton, in *New Acts*, 30 November 1905, 4.

children so much education'.[17] Instead, they should be out on the stump, serving as 'preachers and missionaries with strong cryings and tears to God'.[18] The diary of the pioneer educator D. C. O. Opperman, which ran from 1905 to 1912, revealed a man so preoccupied with the Work that he gave only perfunctory notice to his marriage and the birth of his first two children. He failed to mention the name of his third child.[19]

Parents struggled to make the Holy Spirit's priorities their own. William H. Piper, a successful Chicago pastor in the radical evangelical tradition, fretted that if he cast his lot with the Pentecostals he might lose his job. What then? 'It was in the midst of winter', Piper remembered, 'I had a wife and six children to support, but no income and no bank account'.[20] But convert he did, and, as far as we know, he never looked back. If some Pentecostals discountenanced the routine securities of life, others worried about the bonds that tethered them to earth. That outlook helps explain why a parent's desire to see a child saved could be interpreted as an 'interest in the world.' If parents were *truly* heaven-bound, the reasoning evidently ran, they would not be compromised by any earthly concern, including anxiety for their children's souls.[21]

Occasionally the Holy Spirit's stern demands pointed in the reverse direction, telling children to abandon parents. The China missionary E. May Law wrote of the grief that her aged mother felt when she left for a second term abroad. But then in classic Pentecostal fashion Law warned that parents' feelings should be subordinated to the missionary call. 'Don't count it loss to send one to the foreign fields!', she urged.[22] Remembering how her father had risen to the challenge, she continued, '[G]ive them a Godspeed, though your own heart breaks'.[23] When the youthful Howard Goss entered Pentecostal ministry, his father,

17 Levi Lupton, in *New Acts*, 20 September 1906, 5.

18 Ibid.

19 Opperman manuscript diary, Flower Pentecostal Heritage Center.

20 W. H. Piper, in *Latter Rain Evangel*, January 1910, 2.

21 *Pentecostal Evangel*, 1 November 1919, 5. The unnamed questioner in this 'Question and Answer' column asked about the souls of 'loved ones', but E. N. Bell's consoling answer – 'turn the burden' over to God – focused on parents and children. He distinguished acceptable desire from unacceptable anxiety.

22 E. May Law, *Pentecostal Mission Work in South China: an Appeal for Missions* (Falcon, NC, [1916]), 16–17.

23 Ibid.

apparently unchurched, told Goss 'never to darken his doors again'.[24] Goss remained undeterred, and eventually became a prominent official in one of the smaller Pentecostal denominations. In that case the rupture proved reparable, for the senior Goss later converted in a Methodist revival. But just as often, one suspects, the real-life narrative did not come to rest in the 'smooth waters of a happy ending'. At the Holy Ghost and US compound in Durham, Maine, some parents who found themselves troubled about the perils of religious fanaticism defected while their adult children stayed – and berated their parents for their apostasy.[25]

In actual life things could grow very complicated. The record contains instances of individuals who feared that their spouses and children would abandon them if they persisted in obeying the Holy Spirit. Arthur Watson, a foot soldier in the Canadian Salvation Army, told of the rejection he endured when he elected to leave the Salvation Army and cast his lot with Toronto's fire-baptized Hebden mission. His wife, he wrote, threatened to leave him. Watson wavered, went back to the Salvation Army, but knew it was not right. As soon as he did, his 'heart was like a stone', his 'health broke down', and he nearly died. Watson returned to the Pentecostal fold, but paid a price. 'It has meant many tears and sorrow to have my own dear ones turn their backs on me'.[26] We do not know the end of the story. Like most of the figures that walk across the historical stage in the early periodicals, Watson makes one brief appearance and then disappears from view.

If Pentecostals proved willing to distance themselves from their own children, they proved equally willing to drive a wedge between outsiders and *their* children when the full gospel cause seemed to require it. Though the evidence is often vague, there are good reasons to believe that Holy Ghost meetings, campsites, and schools attracted youthful visitors against their parents' wishes. Sometimes such scenes could turn truly nasty. Levi Lupton apparently made the mistake of concealing one Arthur Smith at his Alliance, Ohio, camp meeting. The

24 Howard Goss excerpted in Ethel E. Goss, *The Winds of God: the Story of the Early Pentecostal Days (1901–1914) in the Life of Howard A. Goss as Told by Ethel E. Goss* (New York, 1958), 10, 81.

25 Shirley Nelson, *Fair, Clear and Terrible: the Story of Shiloh, Maine* (Latham, NY, 1989), 218, 225. In the first instance the child was nineteen; in the second the context implies that the children were adults. The quotation is from Anne Blue Wills, 'Imagination beyond Belief: the Cultural Sources of Hannah Whitall Smith's Devotional Writing', Ph.D. thesis, Duke University, 2001, 154.

26 Arthur Watson, in *Promise*, March 1910, 7–8, 8.

record suggests that Smith's mother encouraged local toughs to invade the meeting, squirt Lupton and various worshippers with diluted sulphuric acid, and retrieve her child.[27] In Rohnerville, California, a Roman Catholic young woman – 'of age' – adopted M. L. Ryan's radical holiness teachings. When she proposed to leave the area with Ryan and three other converts to attend Pacific Holiness College, an angry crowd, possibly including the young woman's kinfolk, surrounded Ryan, horsewhipped him, and then drove him out of town. 'It became noised abroad', said one editor, 'that the preacher was trying to break up the family'.[28]

On occasion, parents' protective instincts ran so deep they sought to shield even adult children from the full gospel threat. When an Illinois barber named Walter J. Higgins started preaching on the Holy Ghost circuit, his father came to Walter's first revival meeting to 'break it up'. The father thought Walter had been 'hypnotized'. Later the father asked Walter in a 'sharp tone of voice' if he had joined the 'holy-rollers'. Predictably, however, Walter's example prevailed and the father himself was soon 'gloriously converted'.[29]

* * *

If the Holy Spirit ordered believers to leave their loved ones at home at a moment's notice, the same Voice also directed them to keep their children strictly disciplined. The aim was twofold: first to build youngsters' character, and second to give back to God a clean vessel willing to do his work.

Examples abound. At the quasi-Pentecostal community in Shiloh, Maine, for example, Frank W. Sandford encouraged whipping and forced fasting until it became clear to the child and, one suspects, to by-standers as well that the child's will had been wholly conquered.[30] Sandford represented an extreme position, but his views and practices stemmed from assumptions broadly shared in Pentecostal culture. 'No failure in life is so great as failing to control your children', Oregon's *Apostolic Faith* warned. And if anyone supposed that it was sufficient for children to obey in large matters, they were wrong. God expected

27 *Free Methodist*, 2 July 1907, 417. The article implies that Smith's mother instigated the incident in order to retrieve her child.

28 Levi Lupton, describing the incident, in *New Acts*, 11 January 1906, 7.

29 Walter J. Higgins, *Pioneering in Pentecost: my Experiences of 46 Years in the Ministry* (Bostonia, CA, 1958), 9, 16.

30 Nelson, *Fair, Clear, and Terrible*, 206.

offspring to 'obey in everything'.[31] For the unmarried Susan C. Easton, who had directed the broadly evangelical Women's Missions Board in India before converting to the revival, 'submission to parental authority' needed to be instilled no later than the second or third year of the child's life.[32] The noted Bible teacher Frank M. Boyd attributed much of the crime sweeping the country to rebellious, undisciplined children. Though Boyd himself had no children, he harboured few doubts about whom to blame: distracted and indulgent parents too weak to discipline their offspring. None should be surprised, he grumbled, for the 'widespread spirit of disobedience to parental authority' had been predicted long ago in Scripture as a 'sign of the times'.[33]

Given those rigorist assumptions, it is not surprising that Pentecostal schools went out of their way to highlight the recreational activities they prohibited. The promotional literature of the Holiness School in Falcon, North Carolina, was typical. In the entire town, one magazine boasted, one could not buy tobacco or 'dope drinks' or find 'Theaters, Circuses, Moving Picture Shows, Base Ball Games, Social Parties and Dances' – all 'agencies of evil' sending young people to their 'eternal destruction'.[34] The China missionary E. May Law recalled that she had transported two Chinese 'little fellows' to the Falcon institution where, among other benefits, no tobacco products or 'deadly picture shows' could be found in the community. The cultural disruption those children surely experienced, if recognized at all, apparently seemed acceptable when measured against the evils they were spared.[35]

Pentecostals' real or perceived treatment of their children, including their expectation that children would conform to the rigorous behavioural protocols of Holy Ghost worship services, provoked outsiders' hostile scrutiny. The prominent Plymouth Brethren evangelist Harry A. Ironside thought that one adolescent woman in Portland, Oregon, had 'contracted brain-fever through the unnatural excitement' of saints' meetings. As a result she had lost all of her hair.[36] In 1906 the Los Angeles *Express* reported a rumour that 'Holy Rollers' were contem-

31 *Apostolic Faith* [Oregon], no. 21 [about 1913], 2.

32 S. E. Easton, in *The Ram's Horn*, repr. without citation in *Triumphs of Faith*, April 1908, 96.

33 Frank M. Boyd, in *Full Gospel Missionary Herald*, January 1922, 3.

34 *Apostolic Evangel*, 23 August 1916, 4.

35 Law, *Pentecostal Mission Work*, 19–20.

36 Harry A. Ironside, *Apostolic Faith Missions and the So-Called Second Pentecost* (New York, [*c*.1910]), 11.

plating child sacrifices to 'appease the wrath of God . . . and timid women are keeping close watch over their little ones'.[37] Probably few believed the story, yet the fact that such a claim would be published at all in a secular newspaper intimated the degree of apprehension the new movement engendered.

Sometimes the issue seemed to be simple solicitude by the state for the welfare of minors caught up in the follies of a new and irregular sect. In 1907 a Birmingham, Alabama, newspaper noted that in that town two probation officers and a Presbyterian pastor had teamed up to investigate 'rumors of neglect of children and inhuman practices' by Holy Ghost devotees.[38] At different times and places municipalities passed laws or directives to bar children from meetings or even to remove them from Pentecostal homes.[39] Occasionally the law cracked down on apostolics when they refused medical attention for ailing children (or adults). In 1915, for example, Walter Barney, a member of the Church of God in Foster Falls, Virginia, served four months at hard labour for the manslaughter death of his child after Barney refused to call a physician or administer medicine.[40]

We need to be cautious here. Pentecostals' severity undoubtedly stemmed from multiple motives. In late Victorian America many people, especially among the working class, disciplined their children firmly. Moreover, saints may have gone out of their way to draw a distinction between child*like*ness and child*ish*ness since outsiders so often accused them of behaving like juveniles themselves. A Massachusetts editor crabbed that they acted like a 'company of religious children', preoccupied with 'noise', 'outward parade', and 'fantastic performances'.[41]

Nonetheless, the evidence, considered whole, leaves little doubt that religion, more than any other motive, fired Pentecostals' steely determination to keep their children strictly disciplined. The child's will had to be displaced so that the Holy Spirit's will could reign in its place. Florence Crawford, the indomitable head of Portland's Apostolic Faith Mission and the mother of three, made the point forcefully when she insisted: 'God wants His people to . . . be very careful to keep their chil-

37 Los Angeles *Express*, 20 July 1906, 1.

38 Birmingham *Age-Herald*, 23 June 1907, 27.

39 Maria B. Woodworth-Etter, *Signs and Wonders: God Wrought in the Ministry for Forty Years* (Indianapolis, IN, 1916), 429; *Apostolic Faith* [Oregon], December 1908, 4.

40 Mickey Crews, *The Church of God: a Social History* (Knoxville, TN, 1990), 74–5.

41 A. Adams, in *Spirit of the Word*, June–July 1907, 36.

dren in subjection to them'.[42] That much was standard evangelical fare. But a following line revealed that the word subjection held special meaning in radical evangelical and especially Pentecostal culture: 'Oh it is such a comfort and rest to know that your family is in subjection and you can go anywhere for Jesus, and all the time you are absent know the instructions you left at home will be carried out to the letter'.[43] The goal was clear: the child's will, no less than the parent's, had to be freed from all taint of human self-interest so that the Lord's instructions could be heard clearly and obeyed precisely.

Saints sought to arrange all earthly affairs, down to the smallest details of the home life, so as to minimize human invention. The willingness of the unmarried and the childless to expatiate on those matters was telling, for they supposed that daily experience had nothing to do with the issue. To establish an arena where the Holy Spirit alone reigned supreme served as the ever present, all-consuming goal.

Even so, the dictates of the parental heart, re-enforced by the ideals of secular progressivism, also influenced those jut-jawed warriors. They found themselves more awash in the currents of modern life than they imagined. That part of the story now merits our attention.

* * *

We begin with the obvious: most turn-of-the-century Americans loved their children and, despite ideological directives to the contrary, so did Pentecostals. In 1920 Halcy Tomlinson, the twenty-nine-year-old daughter of the Church of God's general overseer, A. J. Tomlinson, died in childbirth. Her father's otherwise humdrum diary revealed a grief almost inexpressible.[44] For that matter, Halcy's own diary, kept for a few months as a young teenager, brimmed with tender, awe-filled admiration for her redoubtable father.[45] If A. J. Tomlinson typified family bonds in times of sorrow, the Assemblies of God leader Alice Reynolds Flower typified them in times of joy. A prolific essayist, mother of six and, in time, centenarian matriarch, Flower offered sage advice. The open display of 'affection and appreciation', she wrote, should stand as the mark of any well run Christian home. Life was hard

42 *Apostolic Faith* [Oregon], no. 21 [about 1913], 2. For biographical details, see Cecil M. Robeck Jr., 'Florence Crawford: Apostolic Faith Pioneer', in *Portraits of a Generation*, 219–36.

43 *Apostolic Faith* [Oregon], no. 21 [about 1913], 2.

44 *Diary of A. J. Tomlinson*, ed. Homer J. Tomlinson (Jamaica, NY, 1955), 144.

45 Halcy Olive Tomlinson, *Our Sister Halcy: This Is Her Own Personal Journal Written When She Was Fifteen 1906–1907* (Cleveland, TN, 1974).

enough. It needed to be softened by a 'goodby[e] kiss' and a 'welcoming kiss'.[46]

Sometimes Pentecostal parents, like most mothers and fathers, revealed their deepest feelings by what they left unsaid. The public prayer of a nameless soul in Sunderland, England, spoke for mothers and fathers from the beginning of time. 'Guide my bairns', one pleaded, 'for Thou hast the power. Guide them aright'.[47] And if little children felt heavy in the hand, grown ones lay heavy on the heart. 'Please pray for my son who is in France that he may come home safely', wrote one parent. Away in the army, the son had not written for some time. '[Pray] that he will give his heart to God, and that I may soon hear from him'.[48] There are good reasons to believe that such comments, coming from men and women in a wide variety of social locations, represented Holy-Spirit-filled parents' deepest natural instincts. Blood ran thick.

These scenarios suggest that the ideology of child indifference was more polyphonic than first meets the ear. For one thing, early Pentecostals, like the partisans of most religious movements, were a mixed lot. If a large majority held that the Work came first, whatever the cost, a small but vocal minority demurred. For example, William J. Seymour, a founder of the Azusa Mission, worried that sometimes things had gone too far. He scolded saints who failed to honour their domestic obligations. 'God does not tell you to forsake your family', Seymour warned. 'Under false teaching, children have been left to go half naked, women have left their husbands, and husbands leave their wives to wash and scrub, and the Bible says that is worse than infidelity'.[49] Similarly, in 1920 the general assembly of the Pentecostal Assemblies of the World resolved not to endorse 'any mother leaving her children and going out into the work of the Lord . . . without leaving her children in the hands of reliable persons'.[50] Looking back on these texts, we are left to wonder. What should we focus on? The social practice? Or the admonition that aimed to curb it?

46 Alice Reynolds Flower, *Grace for Grace* (Springfield, MO, [1961]), 23. Flower wrote autobiographically, but clearly she meant the comment prescriptively.

47 *Daily Echo and Times*, 4 October 1907, 2. On Pentecostals in Sunderland, see in this volume Tim Walsh, '"Signs and Wonders that Lie": Unlikely Polemical Outbursts Against Early Pentecostals in England', 410–22.

48 E. M. T. and R. B., in *Christian Evangel*, 8 February 1919, 15.

49 W. J. Seymour, in *Apostolic Faith*, November 1906, 3. Seymour was referring both to those who gave away all of their money and to those who abandoned their families in order to 'go out and teach'.

50 *Voice in the Wilderness*, vol. 2 [1920], 15.

Then too in real life walking away from one's family was easier to assert than to do. Contrary to the stereotype of the religious fanatic shorn of human feelings, ample evidence suggests that for many stalwarts the ideology did little to dull the heartache of separation. The endlessly peripatetic Frank Bartleman illustrates the complex dynamics that could come into play. When the Holy Spirit directed Bartleman to spend nearly a year travelling around the world visiting Pentecostal mission stations, he promptly obeyed, leaving his wife and three small children at home in Los Angeles virtually 'without means'.[51] Yet – and this is the key point – Bartleman also said that when he left his children, grief so overwhelmed him he struggled not to faint. 'There are very few men that hate separation from their families more than I do', but the call – the Call – left no choice. When Bartleman encountered a friend on a street in Los Angeles, the friend, apparently trying to be sympathetic, asked, '[D]on't you want to go up [in the Rapture] with your family?'. Bartleman's response revealed worlds within worlds of meaning: 'I looked him in the eyes and said, "Dear brother, I would just as soon meet my family in the air as in Los Angeles" '.[52]

And then there was F. M. Britton. His pattern may not have been typical, but neither was it rare. Born in 1870, Britton, like many of the founding figures, seemed blessed with a steel spinal column. Britton criss-crossed Georgia and northern Florida preaching the full gospel. He supported his first wife when she 'stood true to God and died without drugs'. Two of his fourteen children also died without drugs or, apparently, doctors.[53] On one occasion, which seemed to typify many, Britton found himself sixty miles from home and without train fare. With the matter-of-factness of a weather forecast, he reported that he hoofed the distance in two days, slept on a church bench, used his Bible and songbook as a pillow, and somehow squeezed by on ten cents worth of crackers. 'When I got in sight of home', the footsore pilgrim intoned, 'I saw my good patient sweet wife look and see me, and she and the children came running to meet me. Oh, how glad I was no mortal tongue can tell'.[54]

Clearly, Pentecostals were perfectly capable of sacrificing *and* loving their families at the same time. If the spectacular signs and wonders that

51 Frank Bartleman, *Azusa Street*, ed. Vinson Synan (Plainfield, NJ, 1980), 146 [originally published in 1925 as *How 'Pentecost' Came to Los Angeles – How It Was in the Beginning*].

52 Frank Bartleman, in *Latter Rain Evangel*, July 1910, 7.

53 F. M. Britton, *Pentecostal Truth* (Royston, GA, [1919]), 243–6, 243.

54 Ibid., 226.

marked their worship services distinguished them from most Christians, the conflicting emotions that they manifestly felt just as surely identified them with most Christians. They bled like anyone else.

* * *

There was more to the story, though. Saints' inclination to critique or even disregard the otherworldly ideology of child-indifference reflected a growing sense that children embodied a priceless resource for the culture. Pentecostals were not alone here. At the turn of the century American society, like much of the Western world, experienced a new interest in young people's welfare. Americans increasingly saw children less as miniature adults than as children with age-specific needs and attributes. Differently stated, in the newer outlook youngsters occupied their own unique place in the life cycle. Toys, board games, and children's literature betokened the advent of the fully realized child. The causes of that reorientation of attitudes in the broader culture are complex and need not detain us. The main point is that by 1900 millions of thoughtful Americans had come to see childhood as a time of spontaneity, innocence, and free-floating imagination. Progressive reformers such as John Dewey at Columbia and George Coe at Union Theological Seminary, as well as progressive institutions like the Religious Education Association, encouraged those ideals in the public schools and in Christian education programmes.[55]

Pentecostals imbibed progressive, child-centred notions more than they realized. For one thing, they instinctively grasped the benefits of functional specialization, creating programmes and materials geared to meet juveniles' unique needs. Almost from the outset, leaders set aside times for special children's meetings, which typically took place on Friday afternoons or Saturday mornings.[56] Influenced perhaps by the old Wesleyan notion of the band (which organized members by age, sex, and marital status), enthusiasts soon established meetings for other age- or status-specific groups, such as empty nesters[57] and mothers-only.[58] They also targeted adolescents. One leader astutely recognized that the 'slow, dragging and listless' music offered in other churches

55 Bendroth, *Growing up Protestant*, 53–5, 62–7 and 70; T. J. Jackson Lears, *No Place of Grace: Antimodernism and the Transformation of American Culture, 1880–1920* (New York, 1981), 145–6.

56 Levi Lupton, in *New Acts*, 12 July 1906, 5; *Midnight Cry* [New York], March–April 1911, 4.

57 San Jose *Mercury*, 17 and 20 August 1921.

58 *Apostolic Faith*, May 1907, 1.

repelled young people who were seeking wholesome 'amusement' along with true religion. But saints, he happily reported, attracted younger worshippers precisely because they had discarded threadbare conventions and replaced them with lots of singing at 'break-neck speed'.[59]

A prudent regard for the future took another, more lasting form. For brevity we might call it, simply, education. For Pentecostals, education meant training for today and preparation for tomorrow, generation after generation, until Jesus returned. Though a few saints disparaged formal training, most of them rushed to defend it, at least training of the right kind. A. C. Holland, editor of the Pentecostal Holiness Church's *Apostolic Evangel*, spoke for most when he argued that the twin evils of the day were education for its own sake (what a later generation would call secular humanism) and no education at all. The solution lay in education conducted under Christian auspices with Christian purposes.[60]

So it was that Pentecostals immediately set out to establish schools of all sorts and grade levels.[61] They rarely tried to erect alternatives to the rapidly growing public school system, but short- and long-term Bible training institutes soon dotted the map from coast to coast. In 1917 the Assemblies of God urged all Holy-Spirit-filled young people to enrol in 'some properly and scripturally accredited Bible Training School'.[62] Scanning the standard denominational histories, one is struck by the sheer number of educational enterprises that every one of the major bodies launched within months or years of their founding.[63]

Weekly Sunday schools, even more than daily academic schools, revealed the shrewdness of saints' practical, plan-ahead instincts. Though some leaders initially resisted Sunday schools and Sunday school literature (because they looked too much like the humanly fabricated programmes of the established denominations), others just as vigorously supported efforts to 'teach the children to reverence God's Word'.[64] At their first general meeting, held in the mountain hamlet of

59 Goss, *Winds of God*, 129.

60 A. C. Holland, in *Apostolic Evangel*, 23 August 1916, 2.

61 *Apostolic Faith*, December 1906, 3, which refers to 'our Bible school up at Azusa St. Mission'.

62 *Minutes of the General Council of the Assemblies of God* . . ., 1917, 19.

63 Lewis Wilson, 'Bible Institutes', in *The Dictionary of Pentecostal and Charismatic Movements*, 57–65.

64 [Church of God] *Book of Minutes* (1906), 16, quoted in Charles W. Conn, *Like a Mighty Army: a History of the Church of God, 1886–1976* (2nd edn, Cleveland, TN, 1977), 67.

Camp Creek, North Carolina, Church of God elders urged every local assembly to establish a children's programme and to operate it every week of the year. They advised workers to identify locales where no Sunday schools existed and then to set one up even if there was no Pentecostal church in the area. A strong Sunday school, they surmised, might 'pav[e] the way for more permanent work in the future'.[65]

A Successful Sunday School, first issued in 1934 by Ralph M. Riggs, reflected the irresistible power of modern efficiency ideals, smooth organization, and tight record keeping, all in the interest of children's proper nurture. Though this influential work saw publication slightly after the period of our main concern, Riggs was around from the beginning. As a teenager in 1914 he attended the organizing meeting of the Assemblies of God. Later he served as a missionary, pastor, Bible school teacher, district superintendent and, finally, general superintendent.[66] He spoke for many.

Riggs sounded as if he had been reading F. W. Taylor, the prophet of timed-work procedures who revolutionized production and business practices across the country.[67] Though Riggs stressed that successful Sunday schools required earnest prayer and systematic Bible study by teachers and students alike, the bulk of his book resembled a manual for setting up a smooth-running Boy Scout troop or girls' softball league. The volume brimmed with aphorisms worthy of Ben Franklin: 'A busy church is a happy church';[68] '[B]egin at the bottom and organize up';[69] 'Good organization is indeed the body of spirituality';[70] if you want effective teachers, look for 'first-rate common sense or a good grade of intelligence'.[71] First-generation Pentecostals cared nothing for organizational flow charts when they stood behind the pulpit, but when they got down to the hard work of setting up Sunday schools – the institutions that would replicate their culture among the next generation – they readily shifted gears.

Models evidently drawn from contemporary business practices marked every page. Why not? 'Business is business if it is the Lord's

65 [Church of God] *General Assembly Minutes 1906–1914: Photographic Reproductions of the First Ten General Assembly Minutes* (Cleveland, TN, 1992), 17.

66 Biographical data in Wayne Warner, ed., *Touched by the Fire* (Plainfield, NJ, 1978), 139, 142, and 'Riggs, Ralph Meredith', by Lewis Wilson, in *New International Dictionary*, 1022–3.

67 Frederick Winslow Taylor, *The Principles of Scientific Management* (New York, 1911).

68 Ralph M. Riggs, *A Successful Sunday School* (Springfield, MO, 1934), 15.

69 Ibid., 47.

70 Ibid., 92.

71 Ibid., 73.

business', Riggs averred, 'and successful business requires industry'.[72] He began, almost predictably, with a few statistics. Lest anyone doubt the importance of Sunday schools, he wrote, '[c]arefully compiled statistics' revealed that seventy-five per cent of all conversions occurred among Sunday school children between the ages of twelve and twenty and most of the remaining twenty-five per cent took place among adults with solid Sunday school training.[73] Even so, those conversions did not happen automatically. Careful organization stood behind them all.

A successful Sunday school should resemble a well-oiled machine, run by an experienced, efficient superintendent, staffed with punctual, well-informed teachers, and organized around a systematically prepared curriculum. Teachers should tailor all lessons to the students' age and imaginative capacity. The school should feature a comprehensive promotion and reward system. The faculty should meet regularly. The resulting advantages would be (among others) 'unity, zeal, education, and' – listen closely – 'a saving of time'.[74] Those goals could be achieved, however, only if each meeting ran according to a 'definite order of business', informed by 'carefully prepared reports from the various administrative and departmental superintendents'.[75] Success required continual vigilance against sloppiness.[76] Riggs's standing admonition for his readers proved as forceful as it was simple: '[E]ven the Spirit of God . . . will be able to operate far more smoothly and effectually if a well organized and efficient body is provided Him'.[77] So it was that in Riggs's hand a miracle-based denial of the usefulness of human wisdom turned into a clear-eyed affirmation of its necessity.

* * *

There it was then, the juxtaposition that had complicated and energized Pentecostal culture from the beginning: the ever present mingling of the supernatural and the natural; the miraculous and the mundane; the 'lightning in the bottle'. Where should an otherworldly disregard for one's earthly offspring leave off? Where should a this-worldly regard for passing along a godly – or was it a goodly? –

72 Ibid.
73 Ibid., 12.
74 Ibid., 88.
75 Ibid., 88–9.
76 Ibid., 91.
77 Ibid., 30.

heritage begin? Those impulses were hard to balance but balance them they did. And by any reasonable measure of such things they did it remarkably effectively.[78]

If otherworldly idealists distanced themselves from their children because the Holy Spirit told them to do so, this-worldly realists took pains to make sure that Pentecostal schools passed their annual efficiency check. Representatives of the two impulses spoke with different accents but they used a common language of religious aspiration. From a distance we can almost hear their voices blending, the two as one. Together they taught three generations of Pentecostal children that it really was possible to live with signs and wonders, day in, day out. The secret was to make every day Sunday.

Duke University

[78] The quotation comes from Professor James A. Mathisen of Wheaton College (IL), personal conversation, March 1992. By 2001 the attorney general of the United States – arguably the third most powerful person in the nation – would be a Pentecostal. See Glenn Gohr, 'J. Robert Ashcroft: a Man of Prayer and Faith', *Assemblies of God Heritage*, Summer-Fall 1996, 18–19, 23, 49; Gary B. McGee, *People of the Spirit: the Assemblies of God* (Springfield, MO, 2004), 537–9.

ANGELS IN THE TRENCHES: BRITISH SOLDIERS AND MIRACLES IN THE FIRST WORLD WAR

by KATHERINE FINLAY

IN their interactions with the soldiers during the First World War the British military chaplains were afforded the opportunity to see the Christian body in microcosm.[1] The chaplains' frontline experiences shaped their positions on popular religion and the sincerity of Christian belief and practice amongst Britain's youth.[2] A comparative assessment of clerical responses to soldiers' claims of the miraculous not only demonstrates a critical divide in clerical understanding of the supernatural – a divide which is more appropriately separated along theological rather than denominational lines. It also indicates that many of the differences between Catholic and Protestant evaluations of popular religion were, fundamentally, differences of clerical perception rather than popular practice and belief.[3]

To a greater extent than Protestants, Catholics maintained not only that miracles and wonders had occurred previously but that they still had relevance in the modern world.[4] Both Anglo- and Roman Catholic teaching emphasized the importance of accepting 'miraculous' occurrences which took place in the routine life of Catholics, namely in the sacraments and through the assistance offered by saints and angels.[5] For Roman Catholics this position was affirmed even more firmly when, in response to challenges created by modern science and philosophy, the

1 See especially D. S. Cairns, *The Army and Religion* (London, 1919); Charles Plater, ed., *Catholic Soldiers* (London, 1919); Anon., *Catholics of the British Empire and the War* (London, 1916); Arthur Herbert Gray, *As Tommy Sees Us: a Book for Church Folk* (London, 1917) and Stephen H. Louden, *Chaplains in Conflict: the Role of Army Chaplains since 1914* (London, 1996).

2 See Alan Wilkinson, *The Church of England and the First World War* (1st edn, London, 1978; 2nd edn, 1998), 169–96; Albert Marrin, *The Last Crusade: the Church of England in the First World* (Durham, NC, 1974), 135–42; Alan Wilkinson, *Dissent or Conform?: War, Peace and the English Churches 1900–1945* (London, 1986), 33–6; Stuart Mews, 'Religion and English Society in the First World War', unpublished Ph.D. thesis, University of Cambridge, 1973, 173–87; Thomas Johnstone and James Hagerty, *Cross on the Sword: Catholic Chaplains in the Forces* (London, 1996), 100–90; Adrian Hastings, *History of English Christianity 1920–1990* (London, 1991), 30–140.

3 Michael Snape, 'British Catholicism and the British Army in the First World War', *Recusant History* 26 (2002), 354–52, and Wilkinson, *Church of England*, 153–68.

4 See Mary Heimann, *Catholic Devotion in Victorian England* (Oxford, 1995), 33.

5 Ibid., 115.

Vatican rejected Modernism in the *Syllabus of Errors* (1856), preferring instead a more conservative approach to scientific advances and also a more literal interpretation of supernatural events recorded in the Bible.[6] Because Catholic teaching maintained these clear lines regarding supernatural phenomena, Catholic clergy had an established means by which to test the validity of claims to the miraculous.[7] Therefore, when confronted with claims about miracles, even while Catholic priests questioned the legitimacy of individual cases, they also had a system by which to assess, and thus the capacity more willingly to accept, the possibility of supernatural assistance.

Protestants varied widely in their views of the miraculous but most non-Catholics did not maintain a strong devotion to saints or guardian angels and they tended to recognize the symbolic value rather than the actual efficacy of sacramental and religious assistance.[8] While accepting that heaven and earth were in some ways related, most Protestants did not tend to make this link as easily as Catholics did, and the Protestant Churches did not have a coherent system by which they could establish this link definitively. Amongst some Protestants there also existed a growing scepticism with regard to supernatural events recorded in the Bible; the bodily resurrection of Christ and the Virgin Birth were both called into question by some theologians.[9] Most Protestants did not adopt this more extreme theological stance but they nevertheless had fewer points than Catholics by which they could legitimately connect the natural with the supernatural.[10] The supernatural was, therefore, not only considered inexplicable but was recognized as extraordinary, and most Protestant clergy did not believe that supernatural intervention occurred on a regular basis.

Although their Churches' positions on supernatural intervention differed from one another, both Catholic and Protestant soldiers made claims of supernatural experiences during the war. These typically took one of three forms: (1) miraculous intervention by an angel or saint;

[6] See Sheridan Gilley and W. J. Shiels, *A History of Religion in Britain: Practice and Belief from Pre-Roman Times to the Present* (Oxford, 1994), 278.

[7] J. Derek Holmes, *More Roman than Rome: English Catholicism in the Nineteenth Century* (London, 1978), 13–47.

[8] Terence Thomas, *The British: their Religious Beliefs and Practices* (London, 1988), 64.

[9] Ibid., 63–4. William Sanday and Hensley Henson were two of the more controversial proponents of these ideas. See *The Church Times*, 21 December 1917, 538 for the debate surrounding Henson's beliefs.

[10] A. E. J. Rawlinson, *Authority and Freedom: the Bishop Paddock Lectures for 1923* (London, 1924), 97, and H. Horne, ed., *Chaplains in Council* (London, 1917).

(2) miraculous protection by an object of piety or religious significance; and (3) miraculous protection given to a religious image. In their interactions with the soldiers, both Catholic and Protestant clergy were required to consider the legitimacy of the miraculous claims which were made. Their responses to these claims were affected not only by the subjective credibility of the claim made and the person who made the claim, but also by the cleric's own understanding and level of acceptance of supernatural workings in the Christian life.

Although chaplains tended to view miraculous claims with at least some degree of scepticism, both Protestants and Catholics could in theory accept the possibility of the individual miracles which soldiers at the front claimed to have experienced or witnessed. The Anglican chaplain, E. E. Hayward noted that the trenches seemed to contain 'an inexhaustible amount of mystery and revelation' which came in 'dribblets by way of communicative patients' to the chaplains who were serving at the front.[11] Careful scrutiny had to be applied, but some claims of miraculous assistance were accepted as legitimate by some Protestants. In 1917, Reverend Montague Bere wrote of a soldier whom he met in hospital, whose miraculous claims appeared to Bere to be quite convincing. This man claimed that he had been accompanied in battle by what Bere labelled a 'Friend in White'. According to the soldier, when he and two other soldiers had been lying in a shell-hole in an attempt to escape machinegun fire, 'a fourth came and lay with them' and this Friend put his hand on the head of the one who had come to the hospital'.[12] After further inquiry, Bere said of the man:

> I find him a sergeant with DCM – a very fine specimen indeed. He held a position for twenty-four hours single-handed at the end, all his 21 men being laid out. In the night he had to sit on a dead officer and he so managed his bombs and machinegun and rifle that the enemy thought the position strongly held. So he is not the sort to see hallucinations, and he says his 'Companion' has never left him when he has been under fire.[13]

Although Bere did not claim to understand the man's story nor did he have a specific framework in which to fit such an idea, it is notable that he did acknowledge the legitimacy of the man's claim and the possi-

[11] Imperial War Museum, First World War Collection, 'Religion', E. E. Hayward file, Hayward to his aunt, 14 October, 1916.

[12] Ibid., Montague Bere file, Bere to his sister, 29 March 1917.

[13] Ibid., 30 March 1917.

bility of supernatural assistance. It is equally significant that Bere based his assessment on his belief that the man seemed capable of discerning reality from imagination rather than on criteria set by his Church.

The difficulty of assessing miraculous claims was particularly obvious in 1914, when Protestants and Catholics debated whether or not they should accept the popular claim that angels came to the aid of the British soldiers during the first battle of Mons. The most challenging aspect in this matter was that Arthur Machen, an occultist and novelist known for his tales of supernatural horror, claimed that he had written the story of such miraculous intervention in his fictional work, *The Bowman*, even before the story of Mons became popular. Although there was widespread scepticism amongst both Catholics and Protestants, a number of chaplains were willing to accept the possibility that a miracle had occurred in Mons. The Evangelical chaplain Reverend Bulstrode asserted that he believed that Angels were in Mons whether the angels had been seen or not.[14] A correspondent for the Anglo-Catholic organ, *The Church Times*, asserted:

> So many people have given their accounts that it happened, it must be true. If God is ever going to help out a people, it will be now when the English are so obviously in the right. It has happened before when the archangel Uriel destroyed the hosts of Sennacharib.[15]

After asserting this, however, this correspondent also acknowledged that while there was much to be said in support of such possibilities there was also, 'a good deal to be said on the other side'. He noted that although many people claimed to have seen the angels, their experiences did not validate the event. However, he also asserted that the simple fact that the angels were not seen by all of the men did not discount the possibility that they had been present.

Such a dilemma brought to the fore the basic questions which were being asked at the time, namely, whether or not specific miracles took place, whether or not the miraculous or supernatural forces were real and active factors in modern experience and if so, by what means miracles could be validated and distinguished from fanciful stories.[16] The heart of these questions as well as the difference between Catholic and

14 Ibid., Bulstrode file, Bulstrode diary, p. 47.

15 *The Church Times*, 9 July 1915, 47.

16 See Wilkinson, *Church of England*, 194–5.

non-Catholic belief were considered by a correspondent in *The Church Times* who asserted that to a Catholic who prayed 'at Michaelmas that the angels may "Succour and defend us on earth"', the primary concern was not whether or not angels were at the battle or even whether people had seen the angels; Catholics accepted that angels were certainly present at the battle since they were always present and watching over their charges. Thus, the question was really whether or not the angels had intervened in any particular way during this battle.[17] This particular topic was dealt with by a Roman Catholic homilist at St Dominic's Priory, Haverstock Hill, who asserted:

> It is not the question whether anyone caught a glimpse of them with his eyes, or a sound with his ears. It is above sense, greater than sense. Sense may fail, but faith remains. . . . Our traditions are greater than our past, and today our facts are greater than our traditions. But because we believe, independently of the words and visions of men, and know the angels are there, and because we can commit everyone that falls to God knowing that for each there is an angel that is guarding, for us there must be never a failure, never a triumph, but the will of God alone.[18]

In part because Catholics recognized the presence of the supernatural in normal, everyday settings, they also distinguished general acceptance of the supernatural from instances of specific miraculous intervention. Thus, when considering the possibility of angels appearing at Mons, Stephen Rawlinson, the Senior Catholic Chaplain in France, wrote to General French saying:

> The direct question is – was there supernatural intervention at Mons? A man writes to the *Daily Mail* and says it is a fiction invented by himself; on the other hand we had a man in Birkenhead (Private Cleaver) who was himself at Mons and saw the Angels.[19]

Given the ambiguous nature of the matter, Rawlinson suggested that the army should find 'six men of good character' who had all claimed to have seen the angels to sign an affidavit in which they attested to the experience they had at the front. Although sceptical, he concluded by

17 *The Church Times*, 13 August 1915, 148.

18 *The Tablet*, 28 August 1915, 286.

19 Downside Abbey, Rawlinson Collection, Letters 1915–1917, Rawlinson to General French, 15 August 1915.

saying: 'If this manifestation has actually occurred, it is the most glorious and sublime event since the day of Pentecost; what a grand uplift would the firm assurance of it give to the religious life of England!'[20]

This broader acceptance of, as well as the more systematic way of testing the validity of claims about the supernatural was particularly critical in distinguishing Catholic from Protestant approaches. The difference was based largely on the fact that Catholics so thoroughly accepted the relationship between the natural and the supernatural that they had a coherent system of assessing claims of supernatural intervention and miracles.[21] Protestants, by contrast, were willing to accept the idea that miracles could occur, but they did not have such a clearly established framework by which to assess the miraculous. In his wartime diary the Anglican chaplain, E. C. Crosse, articulated the difficulty of this discernment in practical terms, saying that, at the front: 'Mere hatefulness of the place caused men to fall back on God as 'some sort of guardian angel'.[22] However, he also indicated the superstitious and ineffectual nature of this belief, saying that after having spent some time at the front, most men exchanged their idea of providence for more fatalistic positions.[23] It is understandable, then, that Protestants could not approach the particular questions of Mons in a united or coherent way; they would have had to agree first more generally about what constituted a miracle, how to validate supernatural experience and how to separate the supernatural from the superstitious.

The difference between the Catholic and non-Catholic position can be seen even more obviously when examining the approaches of British Christians to miraculous claims involving individual guardian angels. Although some Protestants were willing to accept the extraordinary claims surrounding the angels of Mons, Wilfred Monod presented the uniquely Catholic understanding of protecting angels at the Oratory in Paris in 1914. He claimed that the soldiers in France were:

> . . . Surrounded by a great cloud of witnesses – an invisible legion of Guardian Angels. . . . The Chevaliers of Fire commune with our own, they espouse their cause, they identify themselves with them

20 Ibid.

21 See H. Atteridge, *Army Chaplains in the Great War* (London, 1916).

22 Imperial War Museum, First World War Collection, 'Religion', E. C. Crosse file, E. C. Crosse, unpublished war diary, n.p.

23 Ibid.

> in the kingdom of the Spirit, so that they become mystically inseparable. Lord, open Thou our eyes that we may see them.[24]

Such ideas were generally accepted within Catholicism and were the basis by which both Roman and Anglo-Catholics understood and practised their faith. Indeed, the Belgian primate, Cardinal Mercier even maintained that in Catholicism the Church was not divided in two with part of the Church on earth and the other part in heaven. Rather, he claimed that there was only one Church which passed through two distinct phases: 'What the elect see, we believe, what they possess we hope for, those whom they love, God, Christ and His Mother the Angels and saints we also love; humbly no doubt but with a love like theirs'.[25]

This difference was further demonstrated in the positions maintained by Catholics and Protestants with regard to whether or not divine aid was available to specific individuals who prayed for the intercessions of angels or saints. For instance, one Catholic soldier credited his miraculous escape to the Sacred Heart and Mary saying that they had brought him safely home: 'I am as sure of that as I am of this morning's daylight. My little son offered his first Communion to bring his daddy back, and his little prayer was answered'.[26] The presence of Christ in the Eucharist was also recognized by Catholics as a means of miraculous assistance. Father Willie Doyle told of one occasion when he knew that his regiment was waiting in a village for him to say Mass and that many of them would be going to the trenches in the afternoon. If he did not turn up, they would lose the chance of Confession and Holy Communion, but the only way to reach them was by means of a 'shell swept road'. Given the sacramental needs of the men, he decided to go. He said of the experience:

> Call it a miracle if you will, but the moment I turned the corner, the guns ceased firing, and not a shell fell until I was safely in the village church. My confidence in God's protection was not misplaced.[27]

Many Protestants would not have chosen to call this a miracle. This was in part because of their understandable scepticism regarding specific miracles. However, it was also in part because they had no established

24 George Bedborough, *Arms and the Clergy, 1914–1918* (London, 1934), 77.
25 Cardinal D. J. Mercier, *The Voice of Belgium* (London, 1917), 55.
26 *The Tablet*, 26 August 1916, 268.
27 E. M. G., *A Brave Soldier* (Melbourne, 1942), 20.

means by which to assess the nature of divine assistance nor did they have a position regarding the nature of God's presence in the sacraments and objects of religious devotion which was accepted across the range of Protestant Christianity.

This difference was also evident in the ways in which Catholics and Protestants regarded devotional aids. Because of their belief in the miraculous benefits of the saints and the sacraments, Catholics were encouraged to carry rosaries, devotional badges, scapulars and medals. Although the men believed that these could offer protection and this at times crossed over into superstition, Catholics accepted that this was not entirely problematic. A respondent to *Catholic Soldiers* justified this saying:

> It is probable that many Catholic soldiers are content to carry their rosaries about with them, seldom or never 'saying' them. And no doubt the 'souvenir' or 'keepsake' idea often comes in. Yet seldom, if ever, is the rosary regarded, even by an ill-instructed Catholic, merely as a charm or mascot. It is certainly looked upon as 'protective' but this through the intercession of the Mother of God in whose honour the rosary is carried.[28]

When viewed in such a way, medallions and amulets were seen as aids to Christian devotion rather than objects of worship. This idea did not extend to the Protestant Churches. Although Protestant chaplains were willing to accept the possibility of miracles, miraculous badges and images which were specifically intended for the protection and assistance of their possessors were regarded as items of superstition even when they carried some religious significance.[29] In some instances, non-Catholics even questioned the orthodox use of pious aids by Catholics. In response to this scepticism, the Catholic chaplain Henry Day defended the orthodox use of devotional aids, saying that his men were not merely 'fond of decorations' but that they were 'Soldiers of Christ and Our Lord as well as soldiers of the King'.[30]

Just as Catholics claimed that God provided protection for people who carried devotional aids, they also claimed that God offered specific protection to religious statues and crucifixes. In one area of the front, a statue of Mary had not only escaped a bombardment but stood with an

28 Plater, *Catholic Soldiers*, 25.
29 *The Tablet*, 6 October 1917, 427.
30 Atteridge, *Army Chaplains*, 18.

unexploded shell lying next to it. This statue was regarded with such awe that some men in that region erected a shrine overlooking the battlefield in honour of the statue.[31] After seeing a crucifix at Loos which had been preserved in a similarly extraordinary fashion, Father William Doyle noted in his war diaries: 'Surely if the Almighty can protect the image of His Son, it will be no great difficulty to guard His priest also, as indeed He has done in a wonderful way'.[32]

Non-Catholics also took notice of such images. For instance, the soldier-turned-author, Talbot Kelly, was impressed by a crucifix in Montauban, of which he noted: 'By a great heap of rubble that must have been the Church stood an almost untouched crucifix'.[33] Non-Catholics were as taken as Catholics by the famous leaning Virgin of Albert; this was a statue of Mary which had crowned the church in the village of Albert, but which had been shelled so that it stood at an angle over the town, with the Baby Jesus suspended precariously above the village. The Protestant soldier, G. V. Dennis, spoke of a time when he went to Albert, noting how the myths surrounding the statue were inconsistent. Upon arrival in the town he discovered that the French believed that the war would end in a German victory if the leaning Madonna fell from her position and that, because of this, she had been secured with steel cables. He lamented this action since, as he recorded, the English soldiers had always heard that the war would end with an allied victory if the statue were to fall.[34] Because of such interest in these religious images, *Army and Religion*, the wartime poll about religious beliefs in the army, noted with some optimism:

> Men have noticed the crucifixes they have passed in France. It is a symbol which they like. It bears possibilities. Not much is yet attached to it, but it is the Crucified Christ rather than the Risen Christ which appeals.[35]

Questions about the significance which should be attached to these figures and whether miracles could be assigned to them was, however, still a basic matter of debate for Protestants. While it was clear that

31 *Stonyhurst Magazine* (February 1917), 1834.

32 Alfred O'Rahilly, *Martyr Priest: the Life and Death of Father William Doyle S.J., Who Died in the 'Great War'*, ed. John Harney (Limerick, 1998), 27.

33 R. B. Talbot Kelly, *A Subaltern's Odyssey: Memoirs of the Great War, 1915–1917*, ed. R. G. Loosmore (London, 1980), 93.

34 Imperial War Museum, First World War Collection, 'Religion', D. V. Dennis, File, 'A Kitchener Man's Bit', unpublished war memoir, 1928.

35 Cairns, *Army and Religion*, 42.

people were affected by the Christian images and crucifixes which survived, there was no consensus amongst Protestants about what this meant for Christian faith more broadly. Because Protestant teaching had no established place where supernatural assistance could be evaluated, Protestants were left to assess miraculous claims by means of their private judgement. This ambiguity resulted in the very careful approach and general wariness of Protestant clergy to claims to miracles which were made by the men.

The place of Christian symbols and the relationship between the natural and supernatural was much more clearly defined for Catholics as can be seen in the Catholic responses to the leaning Virgin in Albert. In a letter which was written to *The Tablet* one correspondent claimed:

> Thousands have read of the wonder of the great statue of the Virgin and Child that once crowned the tower of the basilica at Albert, and that still hangs out horizontally from its base over the town. Albert, its church and hospital were shelled by the Germans in the autumn of 1914, and a religious of the hospital visiting the place in February of last year thus describes what she saw: 'It is Jerusalem in ruins, but dominated by Mary, who seems to show these ruins to her Divine Son'.[36]

This sense of reality was a distinguishing characteristic of the Catholic approach to objects of religious piety and the closeness with the supernatural made Catholics more accepting of the possibility of miracles.

As seen in these several examples, both the different ways in which Catholics and non-Catholics understood the supernatural in terms of their theological positions, as well as the ways in which the Churches dealt with the inexplicable, played into the different responses which Catholics and non-Catholics had towards claims about miracles at the front. Although beliefs were important on a personal level, the frameworks in which the Churches had to deal with those beliefs proved to be equally influential in shaping the British clerical understanding of miracles during the First World War.

Wolfson College, Oxford

36 *The Tablet*, 19 August 1916, 229.

MIRACLES, MESSIAHS AND THE MEDIA: THE MINISTRY OF A. H. DALLIMORE IN AUCKLAND IN THE 1930S

by LAURIE GUY

DALLIMORE'S healing-evangelism ministry was in its heyday in 1932. Originally from Britain, Dallimore had spent periods of time in relative obscurity in New Zealand, Alaska and Canada, prior to returning to New Zealand in 1927. His life journey included involvement in Baptist, Anglican and Methodist churches, but by the time he returned to New Zealand Dallimore had embraced a Pentecostal-style healing ministry.

From a handful of people in 1927, his meetings overflowed the Auckland Town Hall in 1932, with well over two thousand attendees. What drew the crowds? Miracles? Hope? Lively, dramatic and colourful meetings? Media publicity? All these answers may have some validity. Crucial also, however, are the times in which this ministry took place. Although Dallimore's own preaching largely ignored his social context, that context was a major factor in the mass following that emerged in 1932. This paper will therefore explore that context as well as media publicity in seeking to understand the Dallimore phenomenon.

* * *

Interwar New Zealand was a nation in search of a messiah. Messianic figures flourish most readily in hard times. New Zealand, just emerging from the distress and suffering of World War I and the 1918 influenza epidemic, underwent prolonged periods of recession and hardship in the 1920s. New Zealand historian Keith Sinclair saw that decade as a time of 'loss of confidence, hesitancy, disillusionment'.[1] There followed, in his view, 'a period of hysteria', a grasping at straws.[2] For example, credulous voters elected 'a very decrepit financial wizard', Sir Joseph Ward, as prime minister in 1928 because he promised a new economic boom based on a £70,000,000 overseas loan. His party later explained that Ward had meant to say £7,000,000 a year for ten years

1 Keith Sinclair, *A History of New Zealand* (4th edn, Auckland, 1991), 245.
2 Ibid.

(which was no more than the then incumbent government was borrowing). The confused and muddled promise never came to fruition. At his resignation and death in 1930, Ward was a failed messiah, with New Zealand in the grip of a deepening depression.[3]

Despair and anger during the worst of the depression in 1932–3 led to major rioting, smashing shop windows and looting goods in three of New Zealand's four largest cities. The climate of desperation fostered the flourishing of Social Credit 'funny money' ideas – a straw of hope for a drowning society. Social Credit's chief international exponent, Major Douglas, argued that Western economic woes were largely caused by insufficient purchasing power. The solution was to replace expensive bank credit with government initiative to create an almost unlimited supply of cheap or free public credit.

The atmosphere of despair and searching for hope led to Michael Joseph Savage's Labour Party sweeping to power in 1935. While not embracing Social Credit, Savage and Labour were clearly influenced by its ideas, if only to the extent of recognizing the need to increase the amount of money-purchasing power in the hands of the people.[4] Savage, as Prime Minister, soon held near-messianic status in the eyes of many poorer people. 'They think I am God', he reportedly boasted to others in his inner circle.[5] At his death in 1940, the depth of the nation's grief for its economic saviour was immense. When Savage's body arrived in Auckland, 200,000 Aucklanders (more than two-thirds of Auckland's total population) either met the train or lined the streets as his body made its way to Mission Bay.[6] The Savage Memorial, his burial site, acts as a continuing reminder of his near-messianic status. Savage's portrait long graced the walls of many a living room after his death, alongside that of the British reigning monarch.[7]

* * *

Religious as well as socio-economic messianism was prominent in New Zealand's inter-war period. T. W. Ratana's healing ministry, begun in 1918, soon led to twenty to one hundred visits to his residence daily. By

3 Ibid., 254.

4 Savage was markedly reserved about Social Credit ideas but others of his party were much more accepting: Barry Gustafson, *From the Cradle to the Grave: a Biography of Michael Joseph Savage* (Auckland, 1986), 148–9, 171–2.

5 John Alexander Lee, *Simple on a Soap-Box: a Political Testament* (Auckland and London, 1963), 50, 62.

6 Gustafson, *From the Cradle*, 271.

7 Ibid., 1.

1921, over three thousand people had professed to be cured through his ministry. In 1921–2 Ratana's meetings often drew thousands throughout New Zealand. The Ratana Church, in which Ratana had an apostolic role, was formed in 1925. That church soon became the second largest church for Maori Christianity in New Zealand. Ratana's messianic stature through his healing ministry was enhanced by his position as *Mangai* (Mouthpiece) of the Holy Spirit and in some eyes at least he was *kaiwhakaora* (saviour) for his people.[8]

Healing-evangelist Smith Wigglesworth brought Pentecostal fervour to New Zealand in 1922. Crowds of three thousand packed his meetings in the Wellington Town Hall, with hundreds more unable to gain admission.[9] When prayed for, some would fall to the floor in a cataleptic state.[10] Indirect healing through blessed handkerchiefs was another feature, with one thousand anointed-and-prayed-over handkerchiefs remaining to be claimed after the Wellington meetings.[11] Dramatic and packed-out meetings occurred in other main cities of New Zealand in 1922 and again in 1923. Thus was New Zealand Pentecostalism born. Dallimore's theology and style of ministry were also Pentecostal, although he denied he was Pentecostal, because to him Pentecostalism was marked by '"wild fire" and noise and extravagance'.[12]

Very different religious hope came in the depression era through Colin Scrimgeour, known widely through his radio ministry as 'Uncle Scrim'. Scrim was an abbattoir worker union delegate by the age of fifteen. At this time he had no attachment to Christianity and had not read the Bible.[13] However, his mother on her death-bed gave Scrim a New Testament and urged him to make something of his life. Two years later, with minimal theological understanding, the twenty-one-year-old Scrim began training as a Methodist minister.[14] A misfit in training, he left after four months to become a Home Missioner. At the

8 A. Ballara, 'Ratana, Tahupotike Wiremu', in *The Dictionary of New Zealand Biography, Volume 3: 1901–1920* (Auckland, 1996), 414–18, 417.

9 J. E. Worsfold, *A History of the Charismatic Movements in New Zealand* (Bradford, 1974), 113.

10 J. Kemp, 'Faith Healing: a Sympathetic Warning', *NZ Baptist* [hereafter *NZB*], December 1923, 247–8, 248; idem, 'Pentecostalism or the Tongues Movement', *NZB*, February 1926, 49–52, 52; editorial note by J. J. North, *NZB*, October 1927, 290.

11 Worsfold, *A History*, 125–6.

12 *Revival Fire Monthly* [hereafter *RFM*] I, 5 (September 1934), 5 (copy in NZ Baptist Archives, Carey Baptist College, Auckland).

13 'The Scrimgeour Story', Spectrum tape series 378, 1981, tape 1, side 1.

14 Letter of application for the Methodist ministry: C. G. Scrimgeour to Revd T. G.

onset of the great depression he was City Missioner in Auckland. His entrepreneurial style led to packed-out services for 1,500 people in the Strand Theatre in 1929–30.[15] However, his church's sabbatarian scruples clashed with Scrim's showing movies on Sunday evenings to draw the crowds. The clash led to the discontinuance of the movies and a collapse of attendance.[16] Scrim soon resigned as City Missioner. By then he had regular radio programs providing him with a mass following. Through this, Scrim developed a kind of radio church, 'The Fellowship of the Friendly Road'. It claimed to have no dogmas and its vision seemed to amount to little more than being nice and friendly towards others and having optimism for the future.[17] In Scrim's words: 'Friendship is the keystone of the whole structure'.[18] In depression's dark days, Scrim's cheery message engendered hope for thousands of followers. When Scrim faced the risk of being put off air by the government, he called a public meeting in the Auckland Town Hall. The meeting was packed out with a further seven thousand people outside.[19] Large-scale indignation over government jamming of Scrim's radio programme a few days prior to the 1935 election is likely to have enhanced the massive swing to Labour in the polls a few days later.[20]

* * *

Dallimore was similarly a bearer of hope in tough times. It is this that fostered major public response to his ministry. Dallimore himself exhibited the certainty that commonly accompanies the self-taught person:

> It is fifteen years ago that I began a study of the Bible and that was rather an intense reading of it than a systematic study. Fortunately, I had not had a Bible for twenty-five years prior to that time. That sounds queer, doesn't it? But I mean that my receptive mind was not clogged up with rubbish and error. I was a fallow field as it were, and that is the best for cultivation and planting. I had been lying fallow for twenty-five years. When I did begin to read, I read

Brooke, 17 May 1923: Methodist Church of New Zealand Archives (Auckland), T. G. Brooke correspondence, inward box D214, Brooke Book 27, p. 312.

15 *Methodist Church of New Zealand: Minutes of the Annual Conference, 1930*, 118–19.

16 Ibid., 134–6.

17 C. G. Scrimgeour, *Hello Everybody: the Friendly Road* (Auckland, 1933), 1.

18 Ibid., 3.

19 L. Edwards, *Scrim: Radio Rebel in Retrospect* (Auckland, 1971), 59.

20 A. K. Davidson, 'Scrimgeour, Colin Graham', in *The Dictionary of New Zealand Biography, Volume 4: 1921–1940* (Auckland, 1998), 465–6, 465.

> clear of earlier impressions. I had no text books to help me to understand thank goodness.[21]

His pride in his self-learning, his strongly opinionated nature and his adventurous spirit meant marked deviance from conventional orthodoxy. Dallimore was anti-trinitarian, apparently holding an adoptionist understanding of Jesus,[22] and a belief that the Holy Spirit is the power or 'Breath' of God rather than a 'person'.[23] His eschatology involved soul sleep at death, with an awakening after the millennium.[24] He espoused British-Israel teachings accompanied by a major focus on the Great Pyramid of Giza. In Dallimore's perspective, this monument had been built according to divine plan, such that its measurements provided markers for the unfolding of subsequent events. This interpretation led to his prediction in 1932 that the heir to the British throne would be a second Davidic messiah, never marrying, but ushering in the reign of Jesus Christ in 1936.[25] Unfortunately, the future Edward VIII failed to live up to expectations.

Along with idiosyncratic teachings went idiosyncratic practices. It was these that gave Dallimore much of his drawing power, even if many of the attendees simply came for the fun and excitement of his sensational meetings.[26] When Dallimore prayed for people, most went 'under the power', falling to the floor and staying in a cataleptic-type state for some time afterwards. The phenomenon was so common that Auckland magistrate and supporter, E. C. Cutten, claimed in 1932 that 'going under the power' had occurred between twenty and forty thousand times in Dallimore's ministry over the previous five years without any mishap.[27]

Blessed handkerchiefs were also a feature. In his 1932 *Healing by Faith* book, Dallimore reproduced 127 letters by people claiming healing through his ministry. Of these, nearly half (52) involved the use of handkerchiefs, some of which were posted to sick friends and relatives. Two individuals in Britain were apparently healed in this manner,

21 *RFM* II, 2 (June 1935), 5.

22 *RFM* III, 4 (August 1936), 3.

23 *RFM* I, 7 (October 1934), 4.

24 *RFM* III, 3 (July 1936), 2.

25 A. H. Dallimore, *Britain-Israel* (2nd edn, Auckland, s.d. [1932]), 80–1, 84–5. For later comment on this by Dallimore, see *RFM* III, 9 (January 1937), 3.

26 *NZ Observer*, 7 September 1933, 4.

27 *NZ Herald* [hereafter *NZH*], 16 December 1932, 13.

one from goitre and the other from cancer.[28] The healing of animals – cows, horses, sheep and roosters – received newspaper prominence.[29] The rooster's healing had particular appeal:

> A poultry fancier living at the North Shore had telephoned him to say that a special cockerel which he owned was ill, continued Mr Dallimore. The man's wife said, 'You had better wring its neck.' The man replied, 'No, if Mr Dallimore can cure a cow he can cure a rooster.' 'He got a handkerchief', said Mr Dallimore, 'and the rooster was cured – again by the wonderful healing power of Jesus.' Laughter and applause greeted the announcement.[30]

A blessed handkerchief healed a motorbike battery in 1934, providing the owner with lights to attend Dallimore's Sunday night meeting.[31] Broken-down clocks were restarted[32] and broken-down irons could become 'hotter than usual' when a handkerchief was applied.[33]

Attendees at Dallimore's early meetings in Auckland in December 1927 were so few that he later gloried in once having an audience of one, a fourteen-year girl, in a building that seated 1,200.[34] Rapid growth followed, however, with Dallimore baptizing one hundred adults in the Auckland Tepid Baths in November 1931.[35] The following August, his now two thousand-plus attendees began packing the Town Hall for his Sunday night meetings. Major controversy erupted; Free-Methodist minister, Kenneth Melvin, was also filling the Town Hall with 'indignation' meetings to denounce Dallimore's teachings and practices.[36] The interdenominational Auckland Council of Christian Congregations and the local branch of the British Medical Association together set up a committee of inquiry to investigate Dallimore's alleged results. On the committee were nine medical representatives (mainly specialists), eight clergy and three university

28 *Auckland Star*, 5 December 1932, 9.

29 *Auckland Star*, 24 October 1932, 3; 21 November 1932, 3; 28 November 1932, 9; *NZH*, 28 November 1932, 11.

30 *NZH*, 24 October 1932, 10.

31 *RFM* I, 7 (November 1934), 8.

32 *RFM* II, 12 (April 1936), 7.

33 *RFM* IV, 3 (July 1937), 4; IV, 5 (September 1937), 8.

34 *RFM* XI, 6 [actually X, 6] (October 1943), 3.

35 *Dominion*, 3 November 1931, 10. For one of the earliest media reports on his meetings, see *NZH*, 14 July 1930, 10.

36 *NZH*, 22 October 1932, 6; 31 October 1932, 10; 7 November 1932, 10.

representatives.[37] Dallimore refused to co-operate with the committee. The committee's report identified four types of outcomes:

1. Cases claimed as cured but not substantiated;
2. Cases where serious breakdown followed;
3. Cases where no improvements were noted;
4. Cases where death followed.[38]

In the committee's view Dallimore's faith-healing results in no way differed from those of '"non-religious" mental healing or suggestion'. Any positive effects stemmed from 'the cruder arts of suggestion' that Dallimore employed. Features such as 'the incomprehensible gibberish called "speaking with tongues"' and the 'degrading spectacle known as "going under the power"' meant that the whole 'exhibition' could best be described as 'a vaudeville show under the cloak of religion'.[39]

* * *

The committee's report led quickly to the revoking of Dallimore's licence to use the Town Hall.[40] The mayor acknowledged that his negative view of Dallimore's use of the Town Hall was coloured by representations made to him by 'people in very high positions indeed'.[41] A key Dallimore supporter, stipendiary magistrate, E. C. Cutten, who attended Dallimore's meetings from early times until Cutten's final years in the 1940s,[42] headed a delegation that presented a seven-thousand-signature petition to the city councillors. The outcome was the overturning of the ban by twelve votes to ten. Dallimore was back in the Town Hall. However, the full tide of attendance rapidly ebbed. After only two more meetings in the Town Hall, Dallimore's meetings returned to the smaller though sizeable Covenant Hall, where he had begun in 1927.[43] Though Dallimore's star waned, he still drew crowds of six hundred in 1939 and maintained substantial meetings into the

37 *The Dallimore Campaign Exposed: the Full Report of the Joint Clerical, Medical, and Professorial Committee of Inquiry into the Faith Healing Mission Conducted by Mr. A. H. Dallimore, 1932* (Auckland, 1932), 1.

38 Ibid., 2–5.

39 Ibid., 6–7.

40 Auckland City Council Finance Committee Meeting Minutes dated 31 October 1932 (Auckland City Archives).

41 *NZH*, 4 November 1932, 12.

42 *N.Z. Referee and Social Tattler*, 1 February 1934, 31; *RFM* II, 11 (March 1936), 2; *RFM* XI, 6 [actually X, 6] (October 1943), 7. In the 1930s New Zealand judicial system, Cutten's status as stipendiary magistrate was equivalent to that of a district court judge today.

43 *RFM* I, 12 (April 1935), 3.

1940s.[44] At his retirement in 1957, aged eighty-four, however, his meetings were reduced to only thirty or forty attendees.[45]

Much of Dallimore's success in 1932 was media-fed. He had the good fortune to experience outspoken opposition to his ministry. Indignation meetings, floods of letters for and against his ministry in the two main Auckland newspapers, the committee of inquiry, and the revoking and reinstatement of usage of the Auckland Town Hall, all fed the controversy, making him a household name. Cutten claimed eleven years later: '[The] period of persecution and attack . . . gave such publicity to Mr Dallimore's work that he could fill the Town Hall to overflowing.'[46] Dallimore throve on the publicity, confessing later that he 'enjoyed himself' in the spotlight of opposition.[47] The swirl of controversy meant that for a couple of months his Sunday meetings had major Auckland newspaper focus. However, sensationalism concerning healed roosters and Dallimore's claim to having personally been raised from the dead[48] eventually ceased to be newsworthy. Six months after ceasing to fill the Town Hall, Dallimore pined for fresh controversy:

> We are informed that our friends in opposition having failed to end our work for suffering humanity by a noisy attack by word and pen, are now trying a stony silent offensive. It is not altering the fulfilment of Christ's promises in our midst at all. Miracles are still being wrought through our prayers and belief in our Lord's veracity.[49]

Dallimore had a magnetic personality. His *New Zealand Truth* obituary in 1970 spoke of his 'mesmeric hold over the general public and his devoted followers'. *Truth*'s question, 'Was he a Saviour – or was he a

[44] For comment on his waning influence, see description of his 1933 New Plymouth mission as a 'flop': *NZ Observer*, 7 September 1933, 4–5. On six hundred attendees in 1939, see non-sourced newspaper clipping (probably from *Pix* in the first part of 1939) in the Dallimore papers currently being classified at NZ Baptist Archives. For reference to continuing 'splendid attendances' at Dallimore's meetings in 1943, when Dallimore was seventy, see letter of retired magistrate, E. C. Cutten: *RFM* XI, 6 [actually X, 6] (October 1943), 7.

[45] *NZH*, 21 December 1957, 1.

[46] Letter in *RFM* XI, 6 [actually X, 6] (October 1943), 7.

[47] *RFM* XI, 6 [actually X, 6] (October 1943), 3.

[48] *Auckland Star*, 21 November 1932, 3; *NZH*, 21 November 1932, 10. Dallimore made a later similar assertion, that he had been returned from the dead, through the prayers of his mother, in *RFM* X, 5 (September 1943), 3; also *RFM* XIX, 3 (July 1952), 1.

[49] Advertisement in *NZH*, 3 June 1933, 5.

fraud?',[50] is suggestive of Dallimore's near-messianic status. Dallimore built his ministry very much around himself. His *Revival Fire Monthly*, which he published for twenty years, carried the sub-title 'Dallimore's magazine'. He received marked adulation, especially from women who were much to the fore in seeking healing.[51] Of the approximately one hundred and twenty-seven letters Dallimore quoted in *Healing by Faith*, seventy-six are identifiable as written by women and only sixteen by men.[52] In one mission a number of women, though not receiving physical healing, stated that they had experienced a wonderful spiritual exaltation after the laying on of hands.[53] Adulation of Dallimore is patent in a letter written by a 'sister in Christ' and happily published by Dallimore in his magazine, reflecting on the twenty-fifth wedding anniversary celebration of the Dallimores:

> When you and Mrs Dallimore stood up a moment before you spoke, I looked around at all the faces, which were eagerly and silently looking up to you, when a mist or a white light seemed to rise out of the ground around us, well over our heads, making the trees above us appear as if we were entering nightfall, but where the people sat and stood. It was lit up with a soft white light, especially around you and Mrs Dallimore. I could feel the power coming upon me and around the others near by. . . . A soft breath, with vibration as of electricity, went over the whole gathering, just as you both turned and looked at each other with a smile on your faces. Then you spoke.[54]

Doctors and clergy typically saw Dallimore's dominating and charismatic personality as being the explanation of his ministry. This led to 'miracles', which were essentially the result of suggestion.[55] Adulation, eccentricities and heresies associated with Dallimore could suggest that his miracles were essentially pseudo-miracles. That was the near-consensus of doctors and clergy. No doubt their antagonism was strengthened by Dallimore's aggressive attacks on medical practice, and on the churches for providing support for orthodox medicine.

50 *NZ Truth*, 11 August 1970.

51 Comment on high percentages of women filing onto the stage for healing prayer can be seen in *Auckland Star*, 7 November 1932, 9.

52 Identification of women was made through their names, their titles (Mrs, Miss etc.), references to their husbands, the nature of their medical problems etc.

53 *NZ Observer*, 7 September 1933, 4.

54 *RFM* II, 11 (March 1936), 2.

55 For example, Bishop Cherrington, *NZH*, 29 October, 1932, 11.

Dallimore's hostility to orthodox medicine meant that his claimed cures were seldom submitted to orthodox medicine for verification. It is therefore hard to give any objective answer to the question whether Dallimore brought physical healing to people.

Margaret Macpherson was a well-known writer and journalist. Her article, 'Magic – Black and White: Some Wizards I Have Known in England and New Zealand', placed Dallimore in her 'white magic' category.[56] Her narrative of her healing three years earlier indicates the ambiguity and complexity of the healing phenomenon. Macpherson had been incapacitated for weeks at a time each winter by lumbago (a complaint of imprecise medical definition). While in this state in 1931, she ended up at a Dallimore meeting. She was impressed:

> He was no showman. He wore an ordinary lounge suit, no robes. The lights blazed full upon him. No dim religious tones, no stage effects. Only one thing was striking and interesting. As the service proceeded his aura increased in brightness. I am not one of those psychic people who naturally see the aura. No, this was a real brightness which all my party could see distinctly. It even blotted out the white glare of the electric lamp above him.[57]

Dallimore recognized her – he had already met her in the street – and called her to the front. 'Before I could say "Knife!" he had made his cross on my brow and I was flat on my back with the rest.' Later, after getting up and leaving the hall she was quizzed by one of her party as to why she fell over. Her reply was, 'I went over just out of love and courtesy for the man. I couldn't shake their faith by standing up; I just couldn't.' Her questioner then said she had overlooked one thing in telling her story:

> 'Margaret, you're CURED! You ran down the street! Where's your stick? You left it in the meeting!' It was true. A.H. Dallimore (or rather the power that he has contracted) had cured me of lumbago of over twenty years' standing.[58]

Were there miracles? Or was it simply suggestion mediated through a hypnotic personality? Certainly, hundreds, probably even thousands of people testified to renewed health through Dallimore's ministry.

56 M. Macpherson, 'Magic – Black and White: Some Wizards I Have Known in England and New Zealand', *NZ Referee and Social Tattler*, 1 February 1934, 30–1.

57 Ibid.

58 Ibid., 31. Emphasis original.

The question of miracle or suggestion in relation to each one cannot be totally resolved by an historian's judgement.[59] One thing, however, can be stated with confidence: much of what happened stemmed from media spotlight on a figure of messianic hope in the dark days of the depression.

Carey Baptist College and University of Auckland, Auckland

[59] See the photo of voluminous bundles of letters to Dallimore testifying of healing in *Pix*, 8 July 1939, 23.

MIRACLES IN THE MAKING OF TWENTIETH-CENTURY SPANISHNESS: RAMÓN MENÉNDEZ PIDAL, BUÑUEL'S *VIRIDIANA* AND *ISIDRO EL LABRADOR*

by ANTHONY LAPPIN

THIS paper will suggest how the recounting of miracles (the first textual, the other filmic) was designed to support a particular ideology of Spanishness during the twentieth century. Both miracles here analysed were presented as having taken place during the late eleventh or early twelfth century, a key moment in the history of Spain, a point at which its Christian kingdoms began successfully to challenge the dominance of the Muslim states of Al-Andalus.

* * *

The first miracle is narrated by one of the most important of Spanish early twentieth-century medievalists, Ramón Menéndez Pidal (1869–1968), in his account of the late eleventh century that focuses upon a most characteristic and intriguing individual: Rodrigo Díaz de Vivar, 'el Cid' (d. 1099). Rodrigo Díaz was champion of the king of León, Sancho II, who was assassinated whilst besieging his sister Urraca's Zamora; he was subsequently banished twice by Sancho's successor, Alfonso VI, and went on to conquer the glittering prize of Valencia before his death.

Menéndez Pidal took advantage of a miracle recounted in the late eleventh-century hagiography of Saint Dominic of Silos (*c.*1010–73) to close a chapter that narrated the experiences of his hero as a mercenary in the employ of the Muslim emir of Saragossa. The tale that attracted Pidal's attention was one of a number concerning an escape from captivity, a particular specialization within Saint Dominic's thaumaturgy.

A man, Bellitus, had been captured whilst fighting against the Christian emperor of Spain, Alfonso VI; he was sitting on the doorstep of his master's house when a Christian knight passed by, took pity on him, and encouraged him to pray to Saint Dominic of Silos since the saint had freed many, including the knight himself. So Bellitus did, and that night his guards got drunk and he escaped.[1] Pidal's version – first published in 1926 – is given below:

> And here we may interpose an incident, which, though slight in itself, is not without significance. One of the Cid's knights was passing along a street in Saragossa, when he came across a Christian captive lying in a doorway, worn out and emaciated, his feet in chains. Deeply moved, the knight spoke to the man, who with much lamentation explained that he was Vellido of Palencia and had been captured when serving in King Alphonso's army, since when he had endured two years of slavery in Saragossa. The knight sought to comfort him by telling of how he also suffered captivity but had been freed through the intercession of Santo Domingo of Silos. Whereupon the captive gave himself tearfully to prayer; and that same night his guards got drunk, his chains were miraculously removed, and the holy Abbot of Silos led him out of the city a free man. This edifying scene helps us understand how the fortunes and the dangers of war fomented religious feeling, and not licence [*leg.* moral laxity], amongst the knights who fought in Islamic lands.[2]

The story has remained recognizable: Vellido (the romance form of Bellitus) is at the door of his master's house, and is encouraged by the knight to seek help from Dominic; Vellido also escapes when his guards get drunk. Yet two elements are taken from other, later accounts of escape miracles at the shrine: Bellitus's shackles falling off and the highly ambiguous description of the saint's leading him out of the city – a detail which implies that Dominic appeared to Vellido without, however, spelling it out, thereby preventing the miracle from being read as merely the result of either Muslim incompetence or the man's undeserved good fortune.[3] Two further elements are highly significant, however; one is a mistranslation, and the other is an unwarranted assumption.

Menéndez Pidal dates this miracle to 1091, and thus places it as occurring during the period when the Cid was employed as a merce-

1 Grimaldus, *Vita Dominici Exiliensis*, III.10, ed. Vitalino Valcárcel, *La 'Vita Dominici Silensis' de Grimaldo. Estudio, edición crítica y traducción*, Centro de Estudios 'Gonzalo de Berceo' 9 (Logroño, 1982), 478.

2 Ramón Menéndez Pidal, *The Cid and his Spain*, tr. Harold Sunderland (London, 1934), 291–2; Spanish text in idem, *La España del Cid*, 2 vols (1st edn, 1926; rev. edn, Madrid, 1947; repr. Madrid, 1969), 1: 424–5.

3 See Anthony Lappin, *The Medieval Cult of Saint Dominic of Silos*, MHRA Texts and Dissertations 56 (Leeds, 2002), 354–61.

nary by the Muslim emir of Saragossa. There is no reason to associate this miracle either with that date or with the Cid.[4] The mistranslation regards what Vellido was doing when he was captured. The Latin text is quite clear that the man was seized by Muslim soldiers who fought for Alfonso VI ('Bellitus . . . a Sarracenis in exercitu regis Aldefonsi fuit captus')[5] – and would imply that the benificiary of the miracle was in fact fighting for the hated Almoravids against the Christians when he was taken. This was too messy a picture for Menéndez Pidal to contemplate, since it would not have provided him with a moral message and would, moreover, have presented a distinctly unflattering view of Christians motivated not by faith but by filthy lucre.

The moral that Menéndez Pidal appends to the tale is significant (as indeed he claimed it was), because this story is placed as the concluding element in his chapter detailing the Cid's employment as a mercenary by the emir of Saragossa. His retelling of the story presents both a captive and a knight as devout Christians, untouched by the possibility of moral decadence offered by the sensual Oriental culture that surrounded them. During the time that Rodrigo Díaz was forced by circumstance into the employ of a Muslim ruler, his men (and by extension he himself) were saved from any stain of corruption. The miracle could show divine favour upon the fighting men who retained a true faith and unblemished character, and could be used as a redoubt to allay any suspicion of the Cid's behaviour in taking money from the ruler of a faith antagonistic to his own.

Now, if this 'moral' had been written a few years later, its resonance with Franco's use of Moroccan troops in the Civil War would be obvious. But it was written several years before. Rather too much has been made of Pidal's supposed support for the Falangists, and whilst it is true that his book on the Cid became a set text in Spanish military academies under Franco, Menéndez Pidal's loyalty was to, before any political creed, Spain; or, more specifically, to a concept of Spanishness which was most surely characterized by the ultra-Castilian Cid.[6]

Menéndez Pidal's desire to show the firm moral fibre of the Cid's

4 Discussed in Lappin, *The Medieval Cult*, 9. Menéndez Pidal did not think that the miracles were arranged in chronological order, yet was prepared to date this miracle on the basis of an extrapolated chronology: *La España del Cid*, 1: 268.

5 Grimaldus, *Vita Dominici*, III.10, ll. 1–2, ed. Valcárcel, 478.

6 Peter Linehan, 'The Court Historiographer of Francoism? *La Leyenda Oscura* of Ramón Menéndez Pidal', *Bulletin of Hispanic Studies* (Glasgow) 73 (1996), 437–50; M. E. Lacarra, 'La utilización del Cid de Menéndez Pidal en la ideología militar franquista', *Ideologies and Literature* 3 (1980), 95–127.

men (and, by analogy, of the Cid himself), was in part motivated by the attack on this national hero written sixty years earlier by Reinhardt Dozy (1820–83), who had published his translations from Arabic chroniclers' descriptions of Rodrigo Díaz's eventful career, accompanied by his devastating deductions.

For Dozy, following the Arabic sources, the Cid was a ruthless adventurer, a man with few morals, cynical and brutal, motivated only by worldly success and a thirst for bloodshed. He was mercenary, seeking profit wherever it was to be found, with little concern for loyalty or the suffering of others, and given to horrific executions.[7] Such a testimonial would have warmed the heart of many an eleventh-century baron, but a culture of politeness separated Dozy's lifetime from the eleventh century; and so the Cid's sterling qualities looked medieval and barbaric from the vantage-point of the post-Enlightenment world. Dozy, not a man to be satisfied with little, extended his attack from the Cid to the Christian peoples of the peninsula:

> Yet these two nations [Christian and Muslim], so different in appearance, had some things fundamentally in common: they were both corrupt, treacherous and cruel; and if the Moors were generally rather indifferent regarding their faith, if they consulted astrologers in preference to the learned men of their religion, if they held it not shameful to serve a Christian king, there were also Castilian knights who had no scruple in '*vivre à augure*' (living according to auguries) as it was said in those times, to take Muslims into their pay, to go into battle against their own religion and their fatherland under the flag of an Arab kinglet, or to pillage and burn monasteries and churches.[8]

Unsurprisingly, Dozy's attack rankled. The Cid's character had been sanitized in Spain, a process that had already begun when the cause for his canonization was started by Philip II.[9] The Aragonese Joaquín Costa

[7] Reinhart Pieter Anne Dozy, *Le Cid, d'après de nouveaux documents* (Leiden, 1860), 33 (cruelty), 51 (cruelty again), 107 (perfidy and cruelty), 113 (treachery), 122 (giving captive Christians to a Muslim ruler), 134 (lying), 152 (devastation of Christian lands), 202–3 (blood-lust), 210 (greed).

[8] Dozy, *Le Cid*, 109 (my translation). He also included (p. 117) the treachery of a Navarrese knight who was involved in a fratricidal attempt to assassinate the emir of Saragossa; the attempt failed, and the emir had the knight decapitated.

[9] Dozy's musings upon Philip II's pious hope to have the Cid sainted are a good example of his abrasive style: 'but it is quite remarkable that it was the dour and standoffish Philip II who asked for the Cid to be placed on the list of saints; the Cid who was more Muslim than Catholic, who, even in his tomb, wore Arab dress; the Cid whom Philip would

(1846–1911), probably the most gifted of the late nineteenth-century Spanish progressive politicians, argued that the Cid was both a symbol of the nation and an example to all, indeed the incarnation of the individual's civic conscience.[10] Julio Puyol y Alonso (1865–1937) complained in 1910 that Dozy had been motivated by a 'systematic hatred' of all things Spanish, and had attacked, with the 'fanatic's mad complacency' the symbol which the Spanish people had, for eight hundred years, considered the 'incarnation of their chivalric sentiments'. The implication that the Spanish people of the Middle Ages were 'corrupt, treacherous, and cruel' was not missed, either, and did not fail to attract Puyol's ranting scorn.[11]

Menéndez Pidal's defence of the Cid's men was, in effect, backward looking, to debates from the previous century and to an idea of Spanishness which was forged after the expulsion of Muslims and given definitive expression by Pidal's teacher, the great Marcelino Menéndez y Pelayo (1856–1912), particularly in his monumental *Historia de los heterodoxos españoles*, 3 vols (Madrid, 1880–2). Such an ideal was given new currency by military involvement in Africa, and in particular the cataclysmic defeat of the retreating Spanish forces at Annual in July 1921 by Abd al-Kirim (1882–1963) when some 14,000 Spanish soldiers were either killed or taken prisoner.[12] The eventual effect of the defeat was to pave the way for Primo de Rivera's dictatorship, and the air was thick with disputes over the nature and purpose of the army, and no little concern for captives held by Abd al-Kirim.[13]

A miracle occurring, as Pidal put it, 'en tierras de moros' (in lands of the Moors – which must call to mind *Mauritania*), was used to reassert the Spaniard's God-given and historic virtue, emphasise a model of devout behaviour even for soldiers, and underline Menéndez Pidal's

have had burnt as a heretic, and as a blasphemer by his Inquisitors, had he lived under his reign; the Cid whom the nation had idolized because it looked on him as the champion of liberty, of that liberty that Philip knew well how to stifle in Spain', *Le Cid*, 253 (my translation). Dozy's views were adopted by Anglo-American scholarship: see, for example, H. E. W., 'El Cid', in *Encyclopedia Britannica: a Dictionary of Arts, Sciences, Literature and General Information*, 29 vols (11th edn, Cambridge, 1910–11), at http://52.1911encyclopedia.org/C/CI/CID.htm (consulted on 23 January 2004).

10 Joaquín Costa, 'El programa político del Cid Campeador' and 'El Cid en Santa Gadea', in idem, *Oligarquía y caciquismo, Colectivismo agrario, y otros escritos (antología)*, ed. Rafael Pérez de la Dehesa, Libros del Bolsillo 51 (Madrid, 1969), 172–4, 174–9, esp. 172–3, 179.

11 Julio Puyol y Alonso, 'El Cid de Dozy', *Revue hispanique* 23 (1910), 1–53, 2–3 (my translation).

12 Simon Barton, *A History of Spain* (London, 2004), 207; Sebastian Balfour, *Deadly Embrace: Morocco and the Road to the Spanish Civil War* (Oxford, 2002), 52–120.

13 Carolyn P. Boyd, *Praetorian Politics in Liberal Spain* (Chapel Hill, NC, 1979), 183–208.

own wish to present true Spanishness as reflected in the Castilian Cid and his men, distancing it from the present sad and shameful reality. This view chimed with reformist elements in the army who wished to emphasise manly virtue in the face of the Muslim irregulars and their numerous atrocities. The later adoption of *La España del Cid* as a set text in military acadamies was the result of its author's encapsulation of the virtues admired by military men of his own generation who had served 'en tierras de moros'.

It can only be wondered at that, in his description of the miracle, Pidal chose to ignore the new historical methods that were being applied to biblical and hagiographic narratives and which had aroused such fervent support and opposition in the early years of the century.[14] Although Menéndez Pidal was willing to offer a partial analysis of the source of the miracle,[15] he not only offered an a-critical description of the tale itself, but also added some miraculous elements for good measure. It is a strange sight to see a historian so totally disarmed when faced with religious discourse, but in Menéndez Pidal's ideology, religion existed to serve Spain rather than the other way around. This inherently conservative view, both in terms of historical method and in its search for a moral meaning to history, was later appropriated by Fascist machismo and right-wing Catholicism, although its roots go much further back into a distant past, but not quite as distant as Rodrigo Díaz de Vivar himself. Indeed, this instance of the narration of a miracle should be seen as characteristic of Menéndez Pidal's much wider project, that of rehabilitating the historical accuracy of the *Poema de Mio Cid*, which Dozy had dismissed as a poetic fiction dating from the early thirteenth century, thereby allowing himself to distinguish the honourable Cid of literature from the repugnant, vicious and cruel Cid of history.[16] Menéndez Pidal spent almost all of his academic life defending the thesis that the *Poema* was, in whole or in part, written in the first half of the eleventh century, within a generation of the Cid's death.[17] With this dating, of course, Dozy's incrimination of Rodrigo

14 David G. Schultenover, SJ, 'Luis Martín García, the Jesuit General of the Modernist Crisis (1892–1906): on Historical Criticism', *The Catholic Historical Review* 89 (2003), 434–63, 444–61.

15 See above, n. 4.

16 Dozy, *Le Cid*, 2, 85.

17 *Cantar de Mio Cid. Texto, gramática y vocabulario*, ed. Ramón Menéndez Pidal, 3 vols (Madrid, 1910–11), 1: 19–28, 32–3, 73–6; *Obras completas de R. Menéndez Pidal*, III: *Cantar de Mio Cid. Texto, gramática y vocabulario*, 3 vols (2nd edn, Madrid, 1944–46), 1167–70; he later suggested that two authors (one of *c.*1110, one of *c.*1140) were responsible: Ramón Menéndez

Díaz de Vivar was unwarranted, since the Cid of literature and the Cid of history, so firmly separated by Dozy, could be made to cleave together again, with the emphasis falling upon Rodrigo's nobility of heart and soul rather than allowing any weight to the *damnatio memoriae* carried out by contemporary Muslim historians.[18] In Pidal's view, 'some biographers have committed a complete absurdity of scholarly method by presenting the Cid solely in the lurid light which his Muslim enemies cast over him, concealing much in the deep shadows it threw'.[19]

* * *

In 1961, Buñuel's satirical masterpiece, *Viridiana*, took the Cannes *Palme d'Or* jointly with a the French film.[20] According to Buñuel's biographer, John Baxter, the celebration of the awards ceremony was followed by an attack on the sacrilegious aspects of the film by a Spanish Dominican, Fr Fierro, in the *Osservatore romano*, sparked by the parody of Leonardo da Vinci's representation of the Last Supper at the end of the film. This article resulted in the film's being banned in Spain and Italy, although Catalan entrepreneurs offered daytrips over the border from Barcelona to take in a morning's shopping and an afternoon of the now-scandalous *Viridiana*.[21] Franco's régime seized all copies remaining in Spain and furthermore refused the film the right to

Pidal, *En torno al 'Poema del Cid'* (Barcelona, 1963), 117–64. The early dating has been all but abandoned in recent years in favour of a date *c.*1200: see, for example, Juan Carlos Bayo, 'La datación del *Cantar de Mio Cid* y el problema de su tradición manuscrita', in Alan Deyermond, David G. Pattison and Eric Southworth, eds, *Mio Cid Studies: 'Some Problems of Diplomatic' Fifty Years on*, Papers of the Medieval Hispanic Research Seminar 42 (London, 2002), 15–35; *Cantar de Mio Cid*, ed. Alberto Montaner, Biblioteca Clásica 1 (Barcelona, 1993), 8.

18 Dozy, *Le Cid*, 2; Richard Fletcher, *The Quest for the Cid* (London, 1989), 202.

19 Ramón Menéndez Pidal, *El Cid Campeador*, Collección Austral 1000 [*sic*] (Madrid, 1950), 14 (my translation); there is, perhaps, an allusion in Pidal's use of a word I have translated as 'lurid', *rojizo* (i.e., reddish), to the secondary, Cold-War meaning of *rojo*, namely radical or revolutionary [Real Academia Española, *Diccionario manual e ilustrado de la lengua española* (Madrid, 1950), 1343], and which suggests a political slant to the criticism of the unnamed Dozy for his reliance upon infidel historians.

20 *Viridiana*. Dir. Luis Buñuel. Producciones Alatriste (Mexico), Films 59 (Spain), UNINCI S.A. (Spain). 1961. *Buñuel: 100 Years. It's Dangerous to Look Inside/Buñuel: 100 años. Es peligroso asomarse al interior* (New York, 2001; 1st publ. (with French translation) Madrid, 2000), 102. A translation of the script is available in Luis Buñuel, *Viridiana*, ed. Inga Karetnikova, trans. Piergiuseppe Bozzetti, Script and Director (Portsmouth, NH, 1996). The French film was *Une aussi longue absence*. Dir. Henri Colpi. Procinex-Lyre, Galatea (France/Italy). 1961.

21 John Baxter, *Buñuel* (London, 1994), 254–5. Now, however, the DVD of the film is being distributed in Italy by Multimedia San Paolo (the Catholic religious order most con-

be distributed as a Spanish film, although fifty percent of the funding had been provided by government agencies.[22] A negative had been smuggled out of the country before the Cannes showing (hidden in a van under a bullfighter's cape), and this ensured its distribution.[23]

Viridiana tells the story of a young novice who abandons her convent to take up residence in the house of her uncle, bringing with her a crown of thorns and other ascetic paraphernalia that become an object of fetishistic masochism. Her uncle, who sees her as the image of his dead wife (who died the night of their wedding, leaving the marriage unconsummated), eventually hangs himself due to his perverted passion for Viridiana – which she was at some (unconscious) pains to provoke. After his death, Viridiana opens the house and puts her share of the inherited wealth to use in feeding and clothing a group of beggars, whose misbehaviour ends in the sacrilegious banquet that caused such scandal, and the rape of Viridiana herself. She subsequently abandons her religious enthusiasms and becomes the mistress of her amoral cousin and co-heir. As Franco said, when he eventually saw the film, 'I can't understand the fuss',[24] but Buñuel's film was produced at a highly sensitive moment before Vatican II, when, moreover, Franco's regime was attempting to shift its ideological presentation from Fascist state to responsible member of the UN (which Spain joined in 1955) – a shift which led them to invite the exiled Buñuel to make a film there in the first place.

A hagiographical film appeared two years after *Viridiana*: *Isidro el labrador* (Isidore the ploughman).[25] This filmic hagiography tells the tale of the patron saint of Madrid, a twelfth-century ploughman, who was canonized, however, only in the seventeenth century.[26] It is a

cerned with evangelization through the media) in the series 'L'occhio della libertà': DV 16, 236647DS.

22 Baxter, *Buñuel*, 3, 255.

23 Baxter, *Buñuel*, 255.

24 Ibid.

25 *Isidro el labrador*. Dir. Rafael J. Salvia. Cifesa (Spain). 1963.

26 The original thirteenth-century life is by one Ioannes Diaconus (perhaps the Franciscan, Juan Gil de Zamora), *Vita Isidori agricole* (BHL 4494), *ActaSS*, 3 May, 514–16, or F. Fita, 'Leyenda de San Isidro por Juan Diácono', *Boletín de la Real Academia de Historia* 9 (1886), 97–157; further discussion in Javier Pérez-Embid Wamba, *Hagiología y sociedad en la España medieval: Castilla y León (siglos XI–XIII)* (Huelva, 2002), 331–7. Lope de Vega consecrated one epic poem [*San Isidro Labrador* (1599)] and three plays [*San Isidro Labrador de Madrid* (published 1617), *La niñez de San Isidro, La juventud de San Isidro* (both 1622, to celebrate his canonization)]; Lope also presided over a poetic contest in the saint's honour [published as the *Justa poética en honor de San Isidro* (1620)] and published *Fiestas en la canonización de San Isidro* (1622). Philip III had sought Isidro's beatification after being cured by his intercession; this was

socially-inspired piece, in that it reflects an ideal, beneficent feudalism in which peasants and nobles live happily thanks to the excellent example of Isidro as a model of labour relations, the complete opposite of Buñuel's Marxist-Surrealist vision. Yet the theme chimed with the ideals of the then director general of cinema in Franco's government, García Escudero, who espoused a neo-Realist 'social cinema' that could serve as a vehicle for a propagandistic return to traditional and sacred values centred upon family, church and a semi-feudal conception of the world. These views were popularized from 1961 (the year of *Viridiana*) in the film magazine *Nuestro cine*.[27] García Escudero had been sacked ten years earlier for his relative radicalism, but was reappointed in 1962 because his successor as director general was in turn sacked for his lax supervision of *Viridiana* itself.[28]

* * *

Isidro el labrador is a good example of what Raymond Carr defined as 'films embodying the puritanical, "heroic" ethos of the regime'.[29] It begins with Isidro's birth in a walled town, the threat of Moorish attack explicitly never far away. As a grown man, the saint has constantly to face down challenges to his faith, his sense of justice or his manliness. The scenes I shall comment on are variations to the legend as commonly known until then. The more canonical form of the first miracle retells how Isidro was accused because his own field produced more than his master's. Isidro handed over his own grain, contenting himself with the straw. 'And miraculously, the straw became grain'.[30]

In the film, however, Isidro collects a group of beggars around himself. Unlike *Viridiana*, he forces them to work for their living, threshing corn so they all might eat – rather than relying on generous and undeserved handouts. Even when they are oppressed by the over-mighty steward, who confiscates their grain on the grounds that

decreed by Paul IV on 24 June 1619; Gregory XV canonized him on 13 May 1622. The saint's relics were translated during the second half of the eighteenth century from the church of San Andrés to the Colegiata de San Isidro in Madrid, where they still remain.

27 Marsha Kinder, *Blood Cinema: the Reconstruction of National Identity in Spain* (Berkeley, CA, 1993), 31, 35, 332.

28 *Buñuel: 100*, 102.

29 Raymond Carr, *Modern Spain, 1875–1980* (Oxford, 1980), 164.

30 Rafael María López Malús, *Vida de San Isidro Labrador* (Seville, 1998), 13. Another variant is that Isidro is accused before his master of working less than others, because of his frequent attendance at Mass, but then his parcel of land produces more grain than anyone else's; see, for example, 'San Isidro labrador', *ETWN: Red Global Católica*, at http://www.ewtn.com/spanish/Saints/Isidro_labrador5_15.htm (consulted 7 December 2004).

there is so much they must have stolen it, Isidro's humility produces a miracle so that they might be fed. He turns back to work, threshing the already threshed straw, proclaiming that, although the straw is nothing, 'In nothing, there God is'. The phrase, which draws its inspiration from the writings of Teresa of Ávila and John of the Cross, is followed by the miraculous multiplication of grain, to the astonished eyes of the beggars, who kneel devoutly before the marvel. Even the beggar who is an embittered cynic and acts as antagonist throughout the film, although not ready to kneel himself, comically forces a blind beggar (who, unable to see the prodigy, had remained standing) to his knees in the proper attitude of respectful, devout and silent wonderment.

The miracle indicates Isidro's *castizo* Spanishness. The multiplication of food at once recalls the miracles of Jesus, but Isidro's explanation of the miracle, that it has come about through the 'nothingness' of God, places him in the great tradition of the Spanish mystics, whilst at the same time suggesting that submission to corrupt (or plain mistaken) authority and hard work will be rewarded by God more than an overt struggle for simpler forms of justice. The conflict between traditional demands for *machismo* and religious expectations of humble submission is evident through the film.

* * *

Buñuel's vision, corrosive of any belief in social or divine harmony, is refocused, in insisting on the value of honest toil and its reward even in an oppressive and corrupt environment. The poor, under Isidro's tutelage, survive and prosper. Isidro is himself married to a saint (Santa María de la Cabeza),[31] and they have a child. The publicity for *Isidro* shows the handsomely bearded Javier Escrivá holding a child on one knee whilst smiling at another young girl (his son and his lord's daughter respectively).[32] Religious devotion is depicted in a family setting and as a means of social bonding rather than, as in *Viridiana*, an expression of repressed sexual desire in a society of unattached, repugnant and perverted individuals.

It was fitting that a response to *Viridiana* should be found within a

31 María's relics were not venerated until the late sixteenth century; she was canonized by Benedict XIV in 1752 (Manuel González López-Corps, 'Santa María de la Cabeza Viuda, 9 Septiembre', http://www.congregacionsanisidro.org/santa.htm, consulted on 7 December 2004).

32 A reproduction is provided at 'Bibliografía: San Isidro de Madrid', by the Congregación de San Isidro de Madrid: http://www.geocities.com/congregacionsanisidro/libro.htm (consulted on 7 December 2004).

hagiography. Buñuel's film itself is a form of anti-hagiography, a genre well known to Spain and whose finest example is to be found in Miguel de Unamuno's *San Manuel Bueno, mártir.*[33] The name 'Viridiana' was taken from a little-known saint whose painting Buñuel had seen in Mexico, depicted 'in ecstasy contemplating the instruments of the passion: the cross, the crown of thorns, the nails, the sponge, *etc.*'.[34] Her rejection of the convent to live 'in the world' is a reflexion of the growing impatience with established forms of religious life and a privatized judgement regarding spiritual progress that was characteristic of the period immediately before and after Vatican II in Catholic countries. Viridiana chooses to ignore her abbess's protests; the latter, in her strictly disciplinarian manners and the repeated observation that Viridiana's schemes would all end in tears, may be seen as a Buñuelian self-incarnation in imitation of Cervantes's learned canon in the *Quixote*. But Viridiana continues her asceticism and love of the poor, until, that is, Buñuel allows undoing of the basic hagiographic rule that the virginal saint, no matter what threats to her physical integrity are offered, should retain her status as a *virgo intacta*, even (or especially) if that did require deliverance by miraculous forces.[35]

Viridiana is delivered, but by her cousin, and only after the rape has occurred. After the rape, Viridiana 'converts' from a repressive piety to mini-skirts, modern music and a *ménage à trois*. Thus the Spanish tradition of devout piety is surrendered to the modern world; or the pleasures of masochistic repression are exchanged for those of active sexual competition. In this, Buñuel is being resolutely Freudian, emphasising that female sexuality is in essence masochistic, and Viridiana, by unconsciously desiring rape, is liberated by it.[36] The modern insistence

33 Two filmic hagiographies were released in Spain during the same year as *Viridiana*: *Teresa de Ávila* [Dir. Juan de Orduña. Agrupa Films Cooperativa Cinematográfica (Spain). 1961] and *Rosa de Lima* [Dir. José María Elorrieta. Esp. Coop. Cinemat. Unión (Spain). 1961] – the latter starring (as Rosa herself) María Mahor, who also played as the saint's wife in *Isidro el labrador*. *Rosa de Lima* had an unavoidable emphasis upon self-mortification, and its production was spurred by the resounding success of *Fray Escoba* [Dir. Ramón Turrado. Copercines (Spain). 1961. See Rafael Escoba, 'España y América: 500 años a través del cine', *Film Historia* 2 (1992), 181–219]. Knowledge that *Rosa* was underway may perhaps have been important in the direction that Buñuel took with *Viridiana*, particularly as Rosa has a much more conscious struggle to resist the sexual attractions of an aged roué.

34 Buñuel's own words, cited by Agustín Sánchez Vidal, *Luis Buñuel: obra cinematográfica* (Madrid, 1984), 249 (my translation).

35 Kathryn Gravdal, *Ravishing Maidens: Writing Rape in Medieval French Literature and Law*, New Cultural Studies 4 (Philadelphia, PA, 1991), 24.

36 On the Freudian model of female sexuality, see John Forrester, 'Rape, Seduction and Psychoanalysis', in Sylvana Tomaselli and Roy Porter, eds, *Rape: an Historical and Social*

that God does not manifest himself in the world echoes through the unpunished blasphemy of the beggars' Last Supper and the deflowering of the holy virgin. *Viridiana*, from this point of view, is about miracles that do not happen.

Sexual tension is represented in *Isidro el labrador*, but certainly not in the same way. Isidro's wife stays over-long at a pilgrimage; evil tongues begin to mock Isidro that she has found another man. Unable to bear the insult, Isidro sets out to the Marian shrine with those who had accused his wife. They are all reduced to stunned silence as María levitates in mystical prayer over the river towards them. The family unit can function through traditional religious devotions, which should not necessarily be abandoned in a search for a deeper spirituality; and familial bonds can be maintained through religion even when the spouses were separated – a point of importance when the economic emigration of the country's menfolk was becoming a more visible element of the nation's experience.

The miracles presented by Menéndez Pidal and *Isidro el labrador* reassert that the medieval past of Spain could be characterized by men and women uncorrupted by moral laxity. They look back to the past in order to find an ideal image of the country, that they see as representing true Spanishness. This evocation of traditional concepts of nationality necessarily recalled a feudalism which Buñuel found easy to attack and the makers of *Isidro* were at some pains to defend.

Part of the essential Spanishness that was evoked is a Catholicism that found its major expression in religious devotions and was given divine approval by miracles; indeed, these devotions functioned mainly through recounting, expecting, and experiencing miracles. The Cid and Isidro were deployed as symbols through which such a sense of identity would be articulated. The Cid, the successful soldier par excellence, could be held up as the true image of a nation whose self-esteem had been battered in Cuba in 1898 and subsequently in Africa against their old and infidel enemy. Isidro could be put forward as an ideal to an increasingly godless capital, and, through his patronage of agricultural labour, to the countryside as well.

University of Manchester

Enquiry (Oxford, 1986), 57–83; John M. Macdonald, *Rape: Offenders and their Victims* (Springfield, IL, 1971), 91–2.